Contents

18 Fernando de Noronha   462

19 Florianópolis   473

Appendix: Brazil in Depth   484

Index   490

List of Maps

An Invitation to the Reader

In researching this book, we discovered many wonderful places—hotels, restaurants, shops, and more. We're sure you'll find others. Please tell us about them, so we can share the information with your fellow travelers in upcoming editions. If you were disappointed with a recommendation, we'd love to know that, too. Please write to:

Frommer's Brazil, 4th Edition
Wiley Publishing, Inc. • 111 River St. • Hoboken, NJ 07030-5774

An Additional Note

Please be advised that travel information is subject to change at any time—and this is especially true of prices. We therefore suggest that you write or call ahead for confirmation when making your travel plans. The authors, editors, and publisher cannot be held responsible for the experiences of readers while traveling. Your safety is important to us, however, so we encourage you to stay alert and be aware of your surroundings. Keep a close eye on cameras, purses, and wallets, all favorite targets of thieves and pickpockets.

About the Authors

A native of California, **Shawn Blore** has lived and worked in a half dozen countries and traveled in at least 50 more (but who's counting?). Long a resident of Vancouver, Shawn has for the past few years made his home in Rio de Janeiro. He is an award-winning magazine writer and the author of *Vancouver: Secrets of the City* and co-author of *Frommer's Brazil,* and *Frommer's Portable Rio de Janeiro.*

Alexandra de Vries made her first journey to Brazil at the ripe old age of 1 month (alas, few of her food reviews from that trip survive). In recent years, Alexandra has returned many times to travel, explore, and live in this amazing country. Alexandra co-writes *Frommer's Portable Rio de Janeiro,* about her favorite place to live, and *Frommer's South America,* about her favorite places to visit.

Other Great Guides for Your Trip:

Frommer's South America
Frommer's Portable Rio de Janeiro

Frommer's Star Ratings, Icons & Abbreviations

Every hotel, restaurant, and attraction listing in this guide has been ranked for quality, value, service, amenities, and special features using a **star-rating system.** In country, state, and regional guides, we also rate towns and regions to help you narrow down your choices and budget your time accordingly. Hotels and restaurants are rated on a scale of zero (recommended) to three stars (exceptional). Attractions, shopping, nightlife, towns, and regions are rated according to the following scale: zero stars (recommended), one star (highly recommended), two stars (very highly recommended), and three stars (must-see).

In addition to the star-rating system, we also use **seven feature icons** that point you to the great deals, in-the-know advice, and unique experiences that separate travelers from tourists. Throughout the book, look for:

Finds	Special finds—those places only insiders know about
Fun Fact	Fun facts—details that make travelers more informed and their trips more fun
Kids	Best bets for kids and advice for the whole family
Moments	Special moments—those experiences that memories are made of
Overrated	Places or experiences not worth your time or money
Tips	Insider tips—great ways to save time and money
Value	Great values—where to get the best deals

The following **abbreviations** are used for credit cards:

AE	American Express	DISC	Discover	V	Visa
DC	Diners Club	MC	MasterCard		

Frommers.com

Now that you have this guidebook to help you plan a great trip, visit our website at **www.frommers.com** for additional travel information on more than 3,600 destinations. We update features regularly to give you instant access to the most current trip-planning information available. At Frommers.com, you'll find scoops on the best airfares, lodging rates, and car rental bargains. You can even book your travel online through our reliable travel booking partners. Other popular features include:

- Online updates of our most popular guidebooks
- Vacation sweepstakes and contest giveaways
- Newsletters highlighting the hottest travel trends
- Online travel message boards with featured travel discussions

What's New in Brazil

New lodges in the Pantanal, new beaches in Bahia, new restaurants and samba clubs in Rio de Janeiro. And of course we are always on the lookout for wonderful places to eat or shop or drink or sleep in and highlight what's worth your time.

RIO DE JANEIRO ACCOMMODATIONS

On everyone's lips for nearly 2 years, the new **Fasano** hotel (✆ 021/3202-4000) has finally opened in Ipanema, the only hotel in the world designed top to bottom by renowned *enfant terrible* of the design world Phillippe Starck. Rooms, lobby, everything lives up to expectations. The rooftop pool deck is a thing of beauty.

Equally distinct, and quite a change from most of Rio de Janeiro's high-rise accommodations, the **Santa Teresa Cama e Café B&B Network** (✆ 021/2224-5689) offers spectacular rooms in one of the city's most charming neighborhoods. The participating homes range from mock German castles to colonial homes to Art Deco mansions from the 1930s.

If you want to stay on the quaint hilltop with a higher standard of luxury, try **Mama Ruisa** (✆ 021/2242-1281), opened recently in a century-old hillside mansion. Beautifully decorated, and named after cultural icons, each of the seven suites also features all the modern trimmings such as wireless Internet, cable TV, and air-conditioning. On the very tiptop peak of Santa Teresa, **Solar de Santa** (✆ 021/2221-2117) offers wonderfully comfortably accommodations in a beautiful mansion on a shaded hilltop.

Finally, one of the most venerable of Copacabana's hotels, the **Olinda Classic Othon** (✆ 021/2545-9091) has gotten a much-needed makeover. The lobby has been transformed into an elegant salon with a restaurant and piano bar. All the common spaces have Wi-Fi Internet access. And in the rooms, the dark colonial furniture has been tossed, replaced by lighter woods, soothing pale colors, and stylish furniture.

RIO DE JANEIRO DINING

On the second floor of the Modern Art Museum, the clean and modern interior of the **Laguiole** (✆ 021/2517-3129) matches the classic modern design of this Rio landmark building. The food is modern Brazilian, with a subtle touch of French. The wine list is encyclopedic: over 600 labels and 8,000 bottles!

Up in the newly bustling hilltop 'hood of Santa Teresa, the new star on the block is **Espirito Santa** (✆ 021/2508-7095), which features a great patio looking over the Santa Teresa hillsides and excellent Brazilian food, with a strong flavoring from the Amazon. One popular starter features a rack of ribs from the Tambaqui fish, served with a pesto made from the jambu herb.

Though spectacular by nature, funky is hard to find in Rio de Janeiro, so **Miam Miam** (✆ 021/2244-0125) has found the perfect niche. This hip eatery/lounge/

bar is whimsically decorated with fabulous kitsch touches, making for a cozy room divided into a lounge area with couches and love seats and a somewhat more staid dining room. The lounge is perfect to enjoy a cocktail and share some appetizers.

Steak lovers can take comfort in the advent of **Giuseppe Grill** (© 021/2249-3055), a worthwhile addition to the dining scene in Leblon. We came here on a rare cold Rio night looking only for a good steak and a bottle of red, and left thoroughly impressed with the outstanding steak (you can choose from grilled beef or slowly roasted beef on a charcoal grill), the affordable wine list, the pleasant, modern room, and the attentive professional service.

What do you do if you're the son of a famous French chef? If you're Thomas Troisgros you open a restaurant, **Bistrô 66** (© 021/2266-0838), offering a traditional take on French bistro food, at a fraction of what dad charges at his high-end affair. The younger Troisgros's cozy eatery offers outstanding dishes including Moules Mariniere, a big steaming pot of mussels in a fragrant white-wine sauce, perfect for dipping with some crusty bread; or risotto with Parma ham, brie, and rucula; or excellent roasted lamb with a tomato and lemon *farofa* confit and a delicious grilled duck in orange sauce. All at an affordable price.

RIO DE JANEIRO NIGHTLIFE

For lovers of live music the Lapa neighborhood is still strong, and now there's a "new Lapa" arriving on the scene. Just beyond the Praça Mauá, close to the port area, one of Rio's older neighborhoods, Gamboa, features lovely 19th-century buildings, pretty squares, and a fascinating history (this is where slaves were brought upon arrival and according to many, the birthplace of samba). It is also on the cusp of an urban revival similar to that seen in Lapa 10 to 15 years ago. A few visionary musical entrepreneurs have set up shop, including **Trapiche Gamboa** (© 021/2516-0868), a gorgeous three-story building from 1856 that has been transformed into a fabulous live venue playing, what else, samba. More recent newcomers include Rio's hottest new gay dance club **The Week** (© 021/2253-1020) and **Sacadura** (© 021/2233-0378), a more upscale live-music venue. Keep on eye on Gamboa, as more new places are opening up every couple of months.

With **Botafogo's** revived nightlife scene it was only a matter of time before it would produce a decent live-music venue, and the **Cinemathèque Jamclub** (© 021/2359-0216) is all that. With only 150 places, it remains small enough to feel intimate but large enough to draw some big names on the local music scene, including both Preta Gil (Gilberto Gil's daughter) and Martinalia (daughter of Martinho da Vila). The outside area has a lovely patio and bar, perfect for a pre- or post-concert bite or drink.

One of Rio's newest concert venues, the **Vivo Rio** (© 021/2272-2900) is located right next to the Museu de Arte Moderno on Rio's downtown waterfront. Since opening it's been drawing all the big-name concerts, both Brazilians and foreign acts like BB King.

SÃO PAULO ACCOMMODATIONS

Although not a Philippe Starck hotel like the one in Rio, the São Paulo **Fasano** (© 011/3896-4000) was the first hotel opened under the name of the successful São Paulo restaurateur family. Using their many years of hospitality experience, the São Paulo Fasano has quickly become one of the top hotels in the city. The hotel is decorated with elegant 1930s period furniture, combined with clean modern design elements. And the location is outstanding, smack in the middle of São Paulo's most elegant and visitor-friendly Jardins neighborhood. If you prefer luxury over location, then the **Sofitel São Paulo** (© 0800/703-7003) should be your first choice. The combination of French sophistication and Brazilian hospitality results in one fine luxury hotel. Just across from Ibirapuera Park, the hotel is ideal for those who like to start the day with a walk or a vigorous game of tennis; this is one of the few hotels in the city with its own courts. Those traveling on a weekend can often book a room online for rates as low as R$250 to R$300 (US$125–US$150/£68–£81)!

SÃO PAULO DINING

One of São Paulo's hottest (or should we say coolest) dining lounges is **Skye** (© 011/3055-4702) at the Unique Hotel. People come not only to experience this fantastic hotel, nicknamed *"melancia"* (watermelon) for its interesting shape, but also to enjoy the rooftop restaurant. The views of the São Paulo skyline are spectacular and the kitchen serves up innovative Brazilian cuisine.

SÃO PAULO ATTRACTIONS

The hottest new cultural attraction in Latin America's biggest city is, wait for it, the **Museum of the Portuguese Language** (© 011/3326-0775). Okay, I know what you're thinking, but it genuinely is very cool, even if your command of Portuguese is only limited. Set in a vast former train station, the museum takes full advantage of the space to offer displays that are creative, interesting, interactive, visually fabulous, and fun.

SALVADOR ACCOMMODATIONS

Finally Pelourinho has the boutique hotel it deserves. At the top of a steep cobblestone street leading up from largo Pelourinho itself, the **Convento do Carmo** (© 071/3327-8400) has the perfect

location on the outside, and luxurious accommodations inside. Indeed, considering the original 17th-century convent was designed to shield its residents from the pleasures of the flesh, the conversion carried out by the Portuguese Pestana group did a remarkable job leading the old girl into the lap of luxury. The hotel's common areas—the round tiled pool and restaurant in the cloister, the lounge tucked into one of the arcades, the large library—are a delight.

Truly in the heart of Pelourinho, the new **Solar dos Deuses** (© 071/3320-3251) overlooks the square in front of the São Francisco church. This lovely pousada has seven rooms, each one decorated in honor of an orixá, the African deities of the candomblé. All rooms are elegantly furnished with period furniture and feature lovely high ceilings, hardwood floors, and large windows looking out over the square or side street just off the square.

SALVADOR DINING

The trend in fine dining in Salvador continues out toward the harborfront, where the new **Amado** (© 071/3322-3520) offers ultimately cool waterfront dining—the room is vast and gorgeous, mixing wood and stone and glass with open views over the waterside deck and the harbor and bay beyond. The cuisine takes traditional Bahian ingredients—manioc and seafood principally—and puts them to use in innovative ways, always with lovely presentation. For those not into fish, the menu boasts an equally intriguing array of chicken and beef creations.

The other hot new area in Salvador is Rio Vermelho, home of the tiny hidden gem called **Dona Mariquita** (© 071/3334-6947). Tucked away in a little laneway opposite the main square, this small restaurant is full of surprises, including a decor featuring high-quality Northeastern crafts and artwork, and some truly excellent caipiroscas. The food takes traditional Northeastern dishes and adds a twist or bit of spice. Even better, on Fridays there's live music.

Also in Rio Vermelho, but hidden at the top of a steep street, one finds the **Lambreta Grill** (© 071/3335-0107). Here Japanese chef Fukino runs one of the most popular yet laid-back seafood restaurants in town. The restaurant decor is ultra-basic, but wait until you taste the food! Try the seafood symphony—*sinfonia de frutos do mar;* a piping hot steel griddle brought to your table piled high with juicy morsels of squid, prawns, mussels, and octopus, served with a side of potatoes and palm heart.

NATAL

Little more than a year old, the **Serhs Natal Grand** (© 084/4005-2000) is the newest and most luxurious of the top-end resorts strung along the ocean-side Via Costeira. Rooms are fresh, bright, and modern, all with tile floors, clean bright bathrooms and balconies facing out over the sea. Recreational facilities at this Spanish-run hotel are top-notch. The entire front deck of the hotel is one sprawling wavy pool, dotted here and there with little Jacuzzi islands. The sports center offers volleyball, soccer, and basketball, whereas the Japanese spa offers a full range of massage and beauty treatments. The Kid's Club features a kids' pool and indoor children's recreation area. On the beach, the hotel offers volleyball and soccer, plus beach chairs and a lifeguard service.

While in Natal, the ideal place to get a look and taste of Nordestino food, the cuisine of Brazil's dry, cattle-raising Northeast is at **Mangai** (© 084/3206-3344). Mangai offers a self-serve buffet— or better, a smorgasbord—featuring over 40 different Nordestino dishes, some of them traditional favorites, other wonderful inventions made using traditional local ingredients such as *carne-de-sol* (sun-dried beef), *macaxeira* (sweet manioc root), and *farofa* (ground, roasted manioc root). The *carne-de-sol na nata* (butter-sautéed sun-dried beef) is a house specialty.

THE PANTANAL

Wildlife viewing is always a matter of luck and patience, even in a place as rich as the Pantanal. Large predators like jaguars are a particular challenge. But one of the best ways of improving your odds is to visit the **Jagaur Ecological Reserve (JER)** where an astonishing one in four guests sees one of these huge South American cats. It's a very long way (110km/ 68 miles) down the bumpy Transpantaneira, and the accommodations are expensive and only basic, but for a view of that big cat it may be worth it. For the 75% of guests who do not see jaguars, there is still the usual vast array of caiman and colorful birds, so rare in the rest of the world, so common in the Pantanal. Note that it's probably best to book your stay here through **Open Door Tours** (© 067/3321-8303). The JER has been in operation for a number of years, and while operations in the field run smoothly, their booking operations have been a little on the amateur side. Better to deal with professionals.

1

The Best of Brazil

There's a joke Brazilians like to tell: When the world was created, one of the archangels peered over God's shoulder at the work in progress and couldn't help noticing that one country had been especially favored. "You've given everything to Brazil," the archangel said. "It has the longest beaches, the largest river, the biggest forest, the best soil. The weather's always warm and sunny, with no floods, hurricanes, or natural disasters at all. Don't you think that's a little unfair?" "Ah," God replied, "just wait until you see the people I'm putting there."

Accuracy rarely comes with a punch line, but there's a significant grain of truth in that tale. Brazil as a nation *is* unusually blessed. Five thousand miles of coastline— some of it packed with cafes and partygoers, but long stretches blissfully empty. Rainforests and wetlands teem with exotic critters. Some of the oldest cities and civic architecture in the New World (and one of the newest cities in the entire world) are here. Restaurants match the snobbiest standards, with regional cuisines that have yet to be discovered in culinary capitals like New York or L.A. Music lovers could make Brazil a lifetime study. And let's not forget a little thing called Carnaval.

And about those Brazilians: They work as hard as anyone in the First World, and many a good deal harder. In recent years Brazil has devoted time and resources to improving its tourism infrastructure, reflected in the new airports, hotels, and inns that have sprung up around the country. Yet no one could accuse Brazilians of worshiping efficiency. They'd much rather get along than get things done; the goal is, above all, harmony. Harmony can mean an entire Sunday spent watching soccer or afternoons off for quality time with your buddies at the beach. It can mean countless hours of effort for a single night's party. But above all, harmony mandates never taking anything all that seriously. And at this, Brazilians excel. Read on to discover some of the best this country has to offer.

1 The Most Unforgettable Travel Experiences

- **Attend Carnaval in Rio:** The biggest party in the world. Whether you dance in the streets, watch thousands participate with their elaborate costumes in the samba parade, or attend the fairy-tale Copacabana Palace ball, it's the one event not to miss! See chapters 2 and 5.
- **Watch a Soccer Game at Maracanã Stadium:** Nothing can prepare you for a game at the largest stadium in the

world. Up to 100,000 fans sing, dance, and drum for hours in one of the biggest parties in town. See chapter 5.
- **Get to Know Pelourinho:** The historic center of Salvador is a treasure of baroque churches, colorful colonial architecture, steep cobblestone streets, and large squares. See chapter 9.
- **Hear the Drummers in Pelô:** At night the historic heart of Salvador comes alive with music. Most impressive are

Brazil

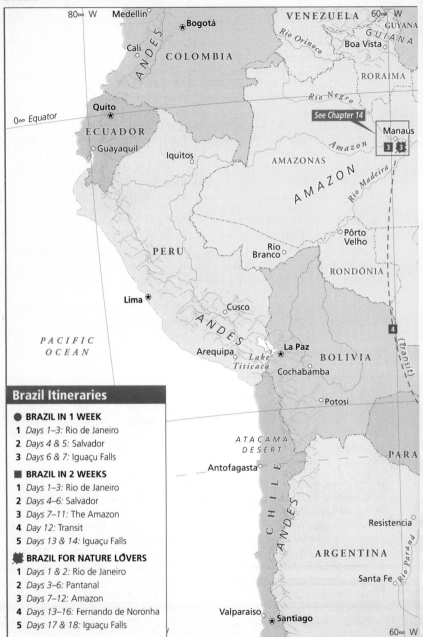

80∞ W   Medellín
Bogotá
Cali
COLOMBIA
VENEZUELA   60∞ W
GUYANA
Rio Orinoco
Boa Vista
GUIANA
RORAIMA
Rio Negro
0∞ Equator
Quito
ECUADOR
Guayaquil
Iquitos
AMAZONAS
Amazon
AMAZON
See Chapter 14
Manaus
3 3
Rio Madeira
Pôrto
Velho
PERU
Rio
Branco
RONDÔNIA
Lima
Cusco
ANDES
PACIFIC
OCEAN
Arequipa
Lake
Titicaca
La Paz
Cochabamba
BOLIVIA
4
(Transit)
Potosí
ATACAMA
DESERT
Antofagasta
CHILE
ANDES
PARA
Resistencia
Rio Paraná
ARGENTINA
Santa Fe
Valparaíso
Santiago
60∞ W

Brazil Itineraries

● **BRAZIL IN 1 WEEK**
1 *Days 1–3:* Rio de Janeiro
2 *Days 4 & 5:* Salvador
3 *Days 6 & 7:* Iguaçu Falls

■ **BRAZIL IN 2 WEEKS**
1 *Days 1–3:* Rio de Janeiro
2 *Days 4–6:* Salvador
3 *Days 7–11:* The Amazon
4 *Day 12:* Transit
5 *Days 13 & 14:* Iguaçu Falls

❧ **BRAZIL FOR NATURE LOVERS**
1 *Days 1 & 2:* Rio de Janeiro
2 *Days 3–6:* Pantanal
3 *Days 7–12:* Amazon
4 *Days 13–16:* Fernando de Noronha
5 *Days 17 & 18:* Iguaçu Falls

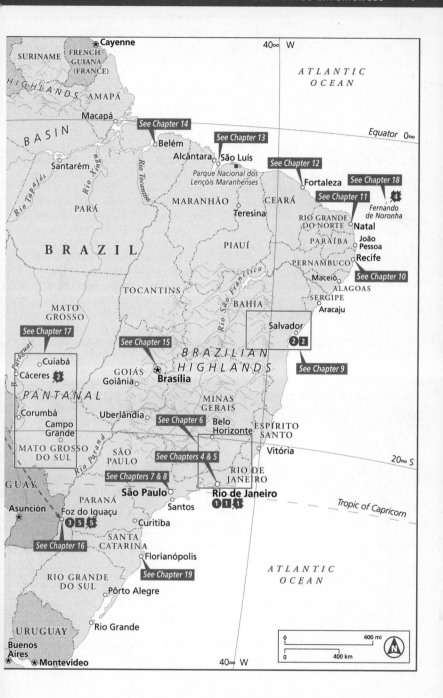

the Blocos Afro, the all-percussion bands that create a rhythm and beat with their drums so intense it sends shivers down your spine. See chapter 9.

- **Herd Water Buffalo in Marajó:** The buffalo ranches on this island in the mouth of the Amazon offer city slickers a unique cowboy experience. Riding out on horseback, visitors to Fazenda Sanjo help round up the water buffalo herd and bring it back to the ranch. See chapter 14.

- **Watch the Sunset Over the Lençóis Maranhenses:** The magical snow-white dunes interlaced with strings of turquoise, blue, and green lagoons make one of the most spectacular sights in all of Brazil. See chapter 13.

- **Kayak in the Amazon:** To explore the rainforest in depth, nothing beats a slow descent of an Amazon tributary; the kayak provides the freedom to view the rainforest at leisure, guides explain the workings of this ecosystem, and cooks prepare meals of delicious Amazon fish. See chapter 14.

- **Wildlife Viewing on Horseback in the Pantanal:** Richer in birdlife by far than the Amazon, but far too soggy to hike, the wet fields of the Pantanal are best explored on horseback. And if you like it fast, there's nothing like galloping through the fields, as a flurry of colorful birds scatter and caiman scurry off underfoot. See chapter 17.

- **Admire the Modernist Architecture of Brasilia:** Built from scratch in a matter of years on the red soil of the dry *cerrado,* Brasilia is an oasis of modernism in Brazil's interior. Marvel at the clean lines and functional forms and admire some of the best public art in the country. See chapter 15.

- **Get Drenched at Amazing Iguaçu Falls:** These falls consist of 275 cataracts along a 2.5km (1½-mile) stretch of the Iguaçu River. The water's power mesmerizes as you stare into the roiling cauldrons. See chapter 16.

2 The Best Beaches

- **Ipanema, Rio de Janeiro:** Yes, this is one of the most urban beaches in the world, but it's still one of the country's prime tanning spots. The long stretch of white sand is perfect for observing the tan and lovely (male and female alike). Or watch a game of volleyball while having a beer and some fresh seafood; if you feel like it, go for a swim or a stroll. See chapter 5.

- **Boipeba, Bahia:** The perfect island getaway, Boipeba makes Morro de São Paulo seem busy and hectic. Just south of Morro, Boipeba offers glorious empty beaches framed by rows and rows of palm trees. At Boca da Barra, where the river *Inferno* meets the ocean, huge sand banks appear at low tide. You can choose whether to

swim on the freshwater side or play in salty ocean. See chapter 9.

- **Porto de Galinhas, Pernambuco:** Development in Porto de Galinhas has been kept resolutely small-scale. No high-rises mar the unpretentious town of Porto de Galinhas, which boasts perhaps four streets—enough for a dozen restaurants, a bank, some surf shops, and a beachside bar or two. See chapter 10.

- **Ponta Negra, Manaus:** Not an ocean beach but a river beach, Ponta Negra, on the shores of Rio Negro, is the most popular tanning spot in the dry season. All the standard beach accouterments are present, including vendors plying food, drinks, and souvenirs. Beach kiosks serve up snacks until the wee hours. See chapter 14.

- **Fernando do Noronha:** The island archipelago of Fernando do Noronha has so many spectacular beaches, it's hard to single out just one. Praia do Leão offers wild crashing surf and sea turtle hatchings in season. The most gorgeously secluded is Praia da Baía do Sancho, a crescent of red sand on shimmering clear blue water that can only be reached by clambering down a rickety iron ladder through a chasm in the cliff side. See chapter 18.

- **Praia Mole, Florianópolis:** Praia Mole is one of the most popular beaches on the beautiful southern island of Santa Catarina (aka Florianópolis). Perfectly white fluffy sand, lush green vegetation, and rocky outcrops give the beach an isolated, paradisiacal feel. Yet, the strand is anything but quiet, packed with a bohemian crowd of locals from Floripa, yuppie tourists, surfers, gay and gay-friendly sunbathers, and families. See chapter 19.

3 The Best Outdoor Adventures

- **Hang Gliding in Rio:** Running off the edge of a platform with nothing between you and the ground 800m (2,624 ft.) below requires a leap of faith, so to speak, but once you do, the views of the rainforest and beaches are so enthralling that you almost forget about the ground until your toes touch the sand at São Conrado beach. See chapter 5.

- **Hike or Bike the Chapada Diamantina:** These highlands inland from Salvador have rock formations similar to the buttes and mesas of the American Southwest. They also have waterfalls and natural waterslides of smooth red marble, plus lots of great hiking and biking trails. See chapter 9.

- **Canoeing the Amazon:** Just you and a canoe in the jungle. Your senses heighten as you listen to the sounds of the forest, watch for splashes in the water, and peer into the trees to find birds, sloths, and monkeys. See chapter 14.

- **Tree Climbing in the Amazon Forest:** Get off the river and delve into the forest. Most visitors only see the trees from the bottom up. Actually climbing into the tree will give you a whole new perspective on the forest and its ecosystem. See chapter 14.

- **Swimming in the Lençóis Maranhenses:** The end of the rainy season signals the best time of year to visit the dunes at Lençóis National Park. June to October, the dunes are full of crystal-clear freshwater lagoons. A swim is the best reward for hiking through the desert of dunes. See chapter 13.

- **Swimming in the Waterfalls of Chapada dos Guimarães:** The red-rock formations of this minicanyon hide some spectacular waterfalls nestled in small stands of lush tropical forest. With dozens and dozens of falls and trails, it's not hard to find one all for yourself. See chapter 17.

- **Riding a beach buggy from Natal to Fortaleza:** The long coast from Natal to Fortaleza is one of the last places on earth with hundreds of kilometers of unobstructed sand. Make the 4-day journey by dune buggy and never once leave the beach, exploring vast towering dunes along the way. See chapter 11.

- **Diving in Fernando de Noronha:** Brazil's best diving is found on this small archipelago off the coast of

Pernambuco. See dolphins, turtles, manta rays, and lots of underwater caves. Crowds are limited, because only 420 visitors are allowed on the island at a time. See chapter 18.

4 The Best Encounters with Wildlife

- **Go, Turtles, Go!** (Bahia): From mid-February to April you have a good chance to watch turtle hatchings at Praia do Forte Tamar's turtle project. See how these tiny sea turtles crawl out of the egg, and cheer them on as they waddle to the ocean for their first swim. See chapter 9.

* **Bird Spotting in the Pantanal:** Even if you're not a birder, the Pantanal has hundreds of species to spot, some as big as your little brother, others as colorful as Carnaval. Plus hungry caiman and giant river otters, and sometimes even jaguar, all of it best viewed from horseback. See chapter 17.

- **Caiman Spotting** (the Amazon): Spotting caiman (alligators native to South America) involves setting out in a canoe after the sun has set. Boating through the dark Amazon forest is quite an experience, but nothing quite prepares you for the sight of those caiman eyes that light up in the beam of the spotlight. See chapter 14.

- **Butterflies in Iguaçu:** Everyone talks about the falls; few mention the butterflies. The lush rainforest provides the perfect environment for many colorful species, and everywhere you go lovely butterflies are aflutter. Hard to miss is the metallic-blue Morpho butterfly; it's about the size of your hand. See chapter 16.

- **Sea Horses in Porto de Galinhas:** The roots of the mangroves in Porto de Galinhas are home to one of the most magical sea creatures, the sea horse. Guides dive in the water to look for these delicate animals and are usually successful in scooping one up (literally, in a glass jar). Once you have had a chance to learn a little bit more about the animal it goes back into its natural habitat. See chapter 10.

- **Red Araras** (the Pantanal): The sunset over the red-rock formations in the Chapada dos Guimarães, north of Cuiabá, is a magical experience in itself. Even more special is the view of scarlet macaws working the thermals off the sheer cliffs in the warm glow of the setting sun. See chapter 17.

5 The Best Museums

- **Museu Internacional de Arte Naïf do Brasil** (Rio de Janeiro; ✆ 021/ 2205-8612; www.museunaif.com. br): Don't miss this little museum, just a few hundred yards from the Corcovado tram station. The practitioners of naive art (also called primitive or ingénue art) paint from the heart, creating colorful and expressive drawings. Visitors will recognize many popular scenes from Cariocas' daily life—a soccer game at the Maracanã stadium, the samba parade, the beaches, and neighborhood cafes. See p. 102.

- **Museu de Arte Sacra** (Mariana; ✆ 031/3557-3259: One of the best collections of sacred art in Brazil can be found in the small town of Mariana, just outside of Ouro Prêto. The vast collection of impressive gold and silver works is displayed in a gorgeous old colonial mansion. See p. 175.

- **Monument to Latin America** (São Paulo; ✆ 011/3823-4600; www. memorial.org.br): Designed by famed

Brazilian architect Oscar Niemeyer, the monument is, well, *so* Niemeyer—shy of a visit to Brasilia, it's the best place to see Brazilian modernism in all its concrete austerity. See p. 210.

- **Museum of the Portuguese Language** (São Paulo; © 011/3326-0775; www.museudalinguaportuguesa.org.br). Who would have thought you could make a whole museum about so esoteric a topic? Who would have thought you could make it so engaging? Among other displays, the museum features a 100m-long (328-ft.) wall-size screen showing images and clips that illustrate words unique to Portuguese. Unique and unforgettable. See p. 210.

- **Pinacoteca do Estado** (São Paulo; © 011/3229-9844): The Pinacoteca

in São Paulo is the place to come for anyone who wants to see Brazilian art. The museum has an excellent collection of Brazilian art from the 19th and 20th centuries, including works by Alfredo Ceschiatti, the artist who designed many of the sculptures in Brasilia. See p. 215.

- **Museu de Arte Sacra** (Salvador; © 071/3243-6310): One of the finest museums in Salvador, the Arte Sacra displays one of Brazil's best collections of Catholic art. The artifacts are shown in the monastery adjoining the Igreja de Santa Teresa, a simple, beautiful building that is itself a work of art. The collection includes oil paintings, *oratorios* (small cabinets containing a crucifix or saint image), and amazing silver work. See p. 255.

6 The Best Festivals & Celebrations

Well, Carnaval—*that's* an obvious choice (and already covered under "The Most Unforgettable Travel Experiences," above). Here are some other favorites:

- *Reveillon*/New Year's Celebration (Rio de Janeiro): Close to two million people gather for one of the most spectacular New Year's celebrations in the world. It starts on the evening of December 31 and continues well into the morning of January 1. The main event takes place on Copacabana Beach—live music, fireworks, and the muted Candomblé religious ceremonies. For details contact Riotur (© 021/2217-7575; www.rio.rj.gov.br/riotur) or Alô Rio (© 021/2542-8080). See chapter 5.

- **Washing of the Steps of Bonfim Church** (Salvador): One of the most important religious ceremonies in Salvador takes place on the third Thursday of January when hundreds of women in traditional Bahian dress form a procession and carry perfumed water to wash the church

steps; 800,000 onlookers and revelers accompany them. For details contact Bahiatursa (© 071/3321-2463; www.bahiatursa.ba.gov.br). See chapter 9.

- **Celebration of Yemanjá, the Goddess of the Sea** (Salvador): On February 2, watch the devotees throughout Brazil offer flowers, perfumes, and jewelry to the sea. It's celebrated on the beach with music and food. The largest celebration takes place in Salvador on Praia Vermelha. For details contact Bahiatursa (© 071/3321-2463; www.bahiatursa.ba.gov.br). See chapter 9.

- **Bumba-meu-boi** (São Luis): A party that gets the whole city involved, the Bumba-meu-boi is a fascinating folk festival centered around the story of a bull that gets killed and resurrected. The festivities take place over several months as there are several stages to each part of the story. Contact the São Luis Tourist Office for details on what happens when (© 081/3462-4960). See chapter 13.

- **The Passion Play** (Nova Jerusalem, near Recife): South America's largest passion play takes place at Nova Jerusalem, just outside of Recife in the Northeast of Brazil. Performances are daily in the 10 days leading up to Easter. For details contact Recife Tourist Information (② **081/3462-4960** or 081/3341-6090). See p. 309.

7 The Best Hotels

- **Hotel Sofitel** (Rio de Janeiro; ② **0800/241-232** or 021/2525-1232): Considered Rio's best hotel, the Sofitel combines old-world elegance and style with one of the city's best locations, across from the Copacabana Fort and steps from Ipanema. See p. 68.
- **Fasano** (Rio de Janeiro; ② **021/3202-4000;** www.fasano.com.br) The first-ever complete hotel—top to bottom, inside and out—designed by the famous *enfant terrible* of the design world Phillippe Starck. Rooms and lobby are lovely. The rooftop pool deck is a masterpiece. See p. 64.
- **Convento do Carmo** (Salvador; ② **071/3327-8400;** www.pousadas.pt). A 17th-century convent in the very heart of a 17th-century city, restored to 21st-century luxury. Unforgettable. See p. 240.
- **Marina All Suites Hotel** (Rio de Janeiro; ② **021/2172-1100**): The Marina All Suites is Rio's first design hotel; all suites are luxuriously furnished. The two-bedroom oceanview Diamante suite is surely the city's most beautiful suite. See p. 65.
- **Portinari** (Rio de Janeiro; ② **021/3222-8800**): Designed by eight different Brazilian designers and architects, the hotel offers a wonderful showcase of Brazilian style and inventiveness; everything from the furniture to the lighting and accessories is unique. Best of all, this style doesn't get in the way of comfort. See p. 69.
- **Colonna Park Hotel** (Búzios; ② **022/2623-2245**): On a hillside overlooking two beaches in Búzios, Colonna Park has one of the best views in town. The elegantly furnished rooms are done in cool blue and white, and the best room in the house has a deck with views of both beaches. See p. 157.
- **Unique** (São Paulo; ② **011/3055-4700**): Extraordinary high-design rooms and suites feature the cleanest-of-clean white-on-white decor, luscious bedding, sparkling bathrooms with Jacuzzi tubs, a plethora of room gadgets, plus a rooftop view of the Avenida Paulista's power skyscrapers and lush green Ibirapuera park. See p. 200.
- **Tropical Manaus** (Manaus; ② **0800/701-2670** or 092/3659-5000): The Tropical Manaus is without a doubt *the* hotel in town. Set in its own piece of rainforest on the banks of the Rio Negro, the hotel is built in an elegant colonial style. Rooms are spacious, and the amenities are top-notch; archery lessons, a zoo, wakeboard lessons, a wave pool, salon, and more await you in the middle of the Amazon. See p. 373.
- **Bourbon Cataratas** (Foz do Iguaçu; ② **0800/451-010** or 045/3521-3900: Make sure you don't forget to see the falls! The Bourbon Hotel has plenty to keep you busy. Over 3km (2 miles) of trails through orchards and tree nurseries are the perfect place to watch for toucans, butterflies, and parrots. The pool deck has three large pools to soak up those rays or an indoor wave pool and spa for a dreary day. Active types can play a game of tennis, try the climbing wall, and play volleyball or soccer. See p. 433.

8 The Best Pousadas

- **Pousada do Mondego** (Ouro Prêto; ✆ 031/3551-2040): Wake up to the unforgettable view of Ouro Prêto's most famous church, São Francisco de Assis, just outside your window. Early in the morning the surrounding hills are often shrouded in mist. See p. 172.
- **Solar da Ponte** (Tiradentes; ✆ 032/3355-1255): In the heart of Tiradentes, one the most charming colonial villages, Pousada Solar da Ponte is a real retreat. The spacious antique furnished rooms look out over the cobblestone streets. The lovely garden, library, and sitting rooms are perfect for a relaxing day. A yummy breakfast is served in the dining room overlooking the garden. See p. 178.
- **Pousada Santa Clara** (Boipeba; ✆ 075/3653-6085): For a romantic getaway or just a few days of blissful relaxation, there's no place better than this lovely pousada, on the small island of Boipeba south of Morro de São Paulo. Each room is uniquely decorated, and many feature a veranda and large windows looking out over the lush tropical garden. The nearly deserted beach is only 5 minutes away, if you walk slowly. See p. 286.
- **Pousada do Amparo** (Olinda; ✆ 081/3439-1749): In the heart of Olinda's old town, Pousada do Amparo is a perfectly restored 18th-century house.

Set on a hillside, the views from the rooms and back deck of Olinda, the ocean below, and Recife in the background are amazing. Elegantly furnished in period style, the pousada is a real labor of love of the owners. See p. 303.
- **Tabapitanga** (Porto de Galinhas; ✆ 081/3552-1037): The oceanfront rooms of Tabapitanga are so close to the beach that light sleepers may want to close their veranda doors to keep the sound of the waves out. All rooms feature bright and cheerful artwork, king-size beds, and a veranda with hammock and lazy chair. See p. 320.
- **Manary Praia Hotel** (Natal; ✆ 084/3204-2900): On the beach of Ponta Negra in Natal, the Manary Praia offers luxurious and comfortable accommodations. The hacienda-style mansion is an excellent home base for exploring some of the best beaches in the Northeast. See p. 326.
- **Araras Eco Lodge** (Pantanal; ✆ 065/3682-2800): This lodge is the best in the Pantanal for wildlife viewing and experiencing the lifestyle of the *pantaneiro* cowboy. Accommodations are rustic but the quality of guides, the amazing food, and unparalleled wildlife are worth it. The owner has a history of environmental work in the region and runs an excellent program. See p. 445.

9 The Best Dining Experiences

- **Experiencing *Feijoada*, the National Dish:** It's impossible to single out one restaurant in all of Brazil for its *feijoada*. Just try it and try it right. Start with a *caipirinha* (that potent, delicious lime and sugar-cane drink) and some *caldo* (soup), followed by steaming hot black beans with all the

various meats. Side dishes include *farofa*, cabbage, orange slices, and white rice. Dab some *malagueta* peppers on the beans for an extra kick.
- **Street Food:** Whether you want prawns, chicken, tapioca pancakes, coconut sweets, or corn on the cob, it can all be purchased on the street for

next to nothing. Don't be afraid to try some of the best snacks that Brazil has to offer.

- **All Beef, All the Time:** Rodízio *churrascarias* are all-you-can-eat meat orgies. The best cuts of beef are served up one after another; try one or two, or try them all. As long as you can take it they dish it out. Our favorite is surely *picanha,* the lean, tender rump steak—it will melt in your mouth. One of the country's most popular restaurants is **Porção,** a nationwide chain. Their flagship location is in Rio's Flamengo neighborhood (© **021/2554-8535**), with views of the bay and Sugarloaf Mountain. See p. 81.

- **Colonial Coffee in Rio:** For the most elegant coffee experience, visit **Confeitaria Colombo** (© **021/2221-0107**). This 19th-century Belle Epoque establishment is one of the most beautiful salons in all of Brazil. See p. 77.

- **Italian Cuisine in São Paulo:** For some of the best Italian food in the world (well, outside of Italy), head to São Paulo's **Fasano** (© **011/3062-4000**) (©). The city's immigrants have created delicious new-world interpretations of some old-world classics. See p. 204.

- *Moquecas* **in Salvador:** You can't say you've been to Salvador without trying *moqueca,* the tasty stew of fresh seafood with coconut milk, lime juice, cilantro, and red dendê palm oil. Try **Jardim das Delicias** (© **071/3321-1449**) See p. 245.

- **Fine Dining in Porto de Galinhas: Beijupirá** (© **081/3552-2354**), in a small resort town in Brazil's Northeast, is perhaps one of the most pleasant little restaurants in the country. The decorations are whimsical and rustic, the food an inspired Brazilian cuisine that makes use of fresh seafood, tropical fruits, and spices. See p. 321.

- **The Regional Cuisine of Belém:** Located in the Tropics, on the Amazon River but at the mouth of the ocean, Belém has access to a richer assortment of ingredients than almost anywhere else in Brazil. Local chefs make the most of the variety. For regional cuisine, try **Lá em Casa** (© **091/3424-4222**). See p. 402.

- **Eating Fish in the Pantanal:** Anywhere in the Pantanal you can try the phenomenal bounty of the world's largest flood plain. *Paçu, dourado,* and *pintado* are just a few of the best catches. In Cuiabá, visit **Peixaria Popular** (© **065/3322-5471**). See p. 444.

10 The Best Markets

- **Feirarte** (Rio de Janeiro): This crafts market on Rio's most historic square features a range of artists showcasing their handiwork. There are leatherwork, ceramics, glass, and silver, not to mention food and drink stands and less-talented vendors with more touristy souvenirs. See p. 130.

- **Antiques Fair** (São Paulo): Every Sunday from 10am to 5pm there's an **antiques fair** in the open space beneath the **MASP** building on Avenida Paulista. Dealers are registered, and the quality of the wares is often good. See p. 211.

- **Japanese Market** (São Paulo): One of the largest Asian street markets takes place every **Sunday** on the **Praça da Liberdade** (next to the Liberdade Metrô stop) in São Paulo's Liberdade neighborhood. The city's Japanese residents celebrate their heritage with an excellent and inexpensive selection of Japanese cuisine and arts and crafts. See p. 211.

- **Mercado Modelo** (Salvador; ✆ 071/3243-6543): Souvenir junkies will think they've died and gone to heaven. In the former Customs building, this market has around 300 merchants selling a large variety of souvenirs: leather goods, hammocks, instruments, masks, carvings, paintings, lace, terra-cotta figurines, and jewelry. See p. 256.
- **Mercado Adolpho Lisboa** (Manaus; ✆ 092/3233-0469): This beautiful

iron-and-glass market hall is a great place to see exotic Amazonian fish, fruits, and vegetables. A number of stalls have indigenous handicrafts at reasonable prices. See p. 378.

- **The Ver-o-Peso Market** (Belém; no phone): The Ver-o-Peso is a vast waterside cornucopia of outrageously strange Amazon fish, hundreds of species of Amazon fruits found nowhere else, traditional medicine love potions, and just about anything else produced in the Amazon, all of it cheap, cheap, cheap. See p. 405.

11 The Best Nightlife

- **Arco do Teles** (Rio de Janeiro): Tucked away in an alley just off the Praça XV, the Arco de Teles reveals perfectly preserved colonial buildings set on narrow cobblestone streets, lined with restaurants and cafes. With over 15 bars and botequins it doesn't matter which one you pick; walk around and see what's doing. If you get there after 10pm you'll be lucky to find a seat at all. See p. 139.
- **Centro Cultural Carioca** (Rio de Janeiro; ✆ 021/2242-9642; www.centroculturalcarioca.com.br): This beautifully restored building from the 1920s hosts local musicians and big names who specialize in samba, MPB, choro, and gafieira. The room is cozy and intimate, and guests sit at small tables to watch the shows. See p. 136.
- **Carioca da Gema** (Rio de Janeiro; ✆ 021/2221-0043): One of the hottest nightspots in the samba-rich sector of Lapa, Carioca da Gema offers some of the finest pagode and samba. Just steps from the Lapa aqueduct, Carioca da Gema is one of the many small music venues in this funky bohemian neighborhood. The

best night to come is Thursday. See p. 136.

- **Rua das Pedras** (Búzios): The hottest beach resort close to Rio, Búzios is the place to go if you're on a mission to party. Nightlife central is on the Rua das Pedras where the pubs, bars, discos, and restaurants stay open on weekends until 3 or 4am. One of the most popular spots is the Mexican bar and disco **Zapata,** very busy during vacations and weekends. See p. 159.
- **Skye** (São Paulo; ✆ 011/3055-4702): One of the city's trendiest bars, Skye also comes with one of the best views in the city. On the Unique Hotel's top floor, the bar's large glass windows and pool deck offer spectacular skyline views of South America's largest city. See p. 208.
- **Rabo do Peixe** (São Paulo; ✆ 011/3845-2296): If there is such a thing as a typical Brazilian pub, this is it. On a street corner, the patio fans out on all sides, and tables are packed every day. A great spot to kick off your evening with a cold beer and the best *picanha* in town. See p. 232.

- **Pelourinho** (Salvador): Many nights of the week Pelourinho transforms itself into one big music venue. Two of the most popular venues are the Praça Quincas Berro D'Agua and the Largo Pedro Archanjo. At the Praça do Reggae, there's always reggae playing. See chapter 9.
- The **Reviver** (São Luis): Now that it's been brought back to life, the historic downtown of São Luis has a new name—Reviver. It's packed with bars and restaurants that center around the Rua da Estrela. One of prettiest is **Antigamente** (© 098/3232-3964). Most tables spread out on the sidewalk and there's live music every evening. See p. 356.

2

Planning Your Trip to Brazil

Brazil is a vast, sprawling country, with much to see and do—from the Amazon rainforests to the civilized beaches of Rio to the restored colonial buildings of Salvador and the hundreds of frolicking dolphins of Fernando de Noronha. This chapter helps you figure out where to begin: where and when to go; how to get there; what precautions to take; and best of all, how to save money on your trip.

1 The Regions in Brief

Brazil's 170 million citizens inhabit the fifth-largest country in the world, a nation about 10% larger than the continental United States. The **Amazon** dominates the northern third of the country—a vast tropical rainforest with the river at its heart. The country's central interior is dominated by the *planalto,* a high dry plateau covered in *cerrado,* a type of dry savanna reminiscent of that of Southern Africa. The chief city in this region is the planned federal capital Brasilia. West of the *planalto* but south of the Amazon rainforest you find the **Pantanal,** a wetland the size of France that is one of best places to see wildlife in the whole of South America. Brazil's **Northeast** is a land apart. Running roughly from São Luis to Salvador, the coast is dominated by midsize cities and sugar cane, the culture strongly Afro-Brazilian, while on the dry interior plateau those Nordestinos who haven't yet fled to the cities eke out a bare living on the land. Brazil's two chief cities, **Rio de Janeiro** and **São Paulo,** stand within a few hundred miles of each other close to the country's south coast. São Paulo is the larger and more important of the two, but Rio, the former capital and *cidade maravilhosa* (marvelous city), is by far the

more interesting. The small southern tip of the country is inhabited largely by descendants of European immigrants. It's the most densely settled and best-organized part of Brazil. The area boasts the astonishing natural wonder of **Iguaçu Falls,** for many visitors a must-see. The island of Santa Catarina, also known as **Florianópolis,** boasts over 40 beaches and is the favorite summer destination in the south.

RIO DE JANEIRO Few cities are as striking. The city folds itself into the narrow bits of land between tropical beaches and mountains that leap to 750m (2,500-ft.) heights (one of these is crowned by the city's landmark statue of Christ). The city offers much in the way of sightseeing, from nature to sunbathing to museums and historic neighborhoods. The culture, perhaps best expressed in music and nightlife, is just as appealing. Samba is alive and well, augmented by many vibrant newer forms of distinctly Brazilian music. The event of the year is Carnaval, the biggest party of the world. And believe me when I say that Cariocas—as Rio residents are known—know how to throw a party.

SÃO PAULO   Some 25 million people live in and around São Paulo, the largest city not only in Brazil but in all of South America. São Paulo is Brazil's New York. It's the melting pot that attracts the best and brightest to make their fortune. The city overflows with restaurants, including the best fine dining in Brazil. São Paulo has emerged as the cultural capital of Brazil, rich with art galleries and strong in new theater. And it's the best place in Brazil to shop.

THE NORTHEAST   Even in a country with such strong regional distinctions, Brazil's Northeast (Nordeste) stands apart. Roughly speaking, the Nordeste encompasses the area from Salvador to São Luis, including cities such as Recife, Natal, and Fortaleza. Everything Nordeste is different: the food richer, the cities more historic, the beaches longer and whiter, the music more vibrant, the politics more Byzantine, and traditionally more corrupt. This was the first part of Brazil to be settled, the area where sugar cane and slavery dominated economy and society for more than 3 centuries. The downturn in the sugar economy left the area a backwater, and only with the recent advent of tourism have Nordeste fortunes really begun to pick up. For visitors the Northeast offers a year-round tropical climate with long white sandy beaches, historic cities, and a vibrant Afro-Brazilian culture, which is reflected in the cuisine, the festivals and, especially, the music and dance. Olinda is a quiet colonial gem of a city, while Salvador's 16th-century colonial core has been transformed into a stroller's dream.

THE AMAZON   The largest rainforest in the world is so vast it defies easy description: All of western Europe would fit comfortably with room to spare beneath its leafy canopy. Thanks in large part to media coverage of the many threats to this region, interest in eco-tourism and visits to the Amazon have skyrocketed. The main staging ground for trips to the Brazilian Amazon is the city of Manaus, located where the Rio Negro joins the Rio Solimões to form the Amazon. Manaus itself is surprisingly modern. Moderately interesting in itself, its real interest is as the starting point for expeditions into the rainforest. Options include everything from day trips on the Amazon to multiday trips to virgin rainforest where one can catch sight of countless unique plants and animals. In contrast to Manaus, the city of Belém, located at the mouth of the Amazon, is an old and settled city, with numerous churches and a historic downtown, and the incredible Ver-o-Peso market, where the entire produce of the Amazon is bought and sold. Close to Belém in the mouth of the Amazon river is Marajó, an island larger than Switzerland, dotted with buffalo ranches and rich with birdlife. Halfway between Manaus and Belém there is Santarem, and the astonishing white sand beaches of Alter do Chão.

THE CENTER WEST   Brazil's center west is a broad flat plain, dotted here and there with craggy highlands, and populated chiefly by ranchers, cowhands, and increasingly by large commercial farms. It was in the midst of this vast and not especially intriguing region that nearly 50 years ago Brazil erected its striking modernist capital, Brasilia. While the capital may be the region's man-made wonder, the natural wonder is the Pantanal. A wetland the size of France, the Pantanal has traditionally been overlooked in favor of the Amazon, but that's changing as people become increasingly aware of the incredible wildlife-viewing opportunities the area offers. More than 600 bird species, anacondas, jaguars, caiman, giant otters, and anteaters are just some of the animals found in the wetlands. As this area lacks the dense foliage of the Amazon, the animals are much easier to spot.

THE SOUTH The southern part of Brazil, made up of the states of Paraná, Santa Catarina, and Rio Grande do Sul, boasts a temperate climate and good soil, attributes that long attracted large numbers of European immigrants. It's a settled, well-organized region. The prime beach destination in the south is Florianópolis, a large island that boasts over 40 beaches, clean waters, and excellent restaurants and nightlife. The Iguaçu Falls, a UNESCO World Heritage Site, are located on the border of Brazil, Argentina, and Paraguay. These spectacular falls are made up of 275 falls that cascade from 72m (240 ft.) down a 2.5km-wide (1½-mile) precipice in a fabulous jungle setting.

2 Visitor Information, Entry Requirements & Customs

ENTRY REQUIREMENTS

For an up-to-date, country-by-country listing of passport requirements around the world, go to the "Foreign Entry Requirement" Web page of the U.S. State Department at **http://travel.state.gov**.

VISITOR INFORMATION

The Brazilian national tourism agency, **Embratur,** has a good site at www.embratur.gov.br. The agency also has representatives overseas:

- **In the U.S.:** New York (© **646/378-2126;** fax 646/378-2034; e-mail: ebt.us@embratur.gov.br/assistant.ebt.us@embratur.gov.br. Los Angeles (© **310/341-8394;** e-mail: ebt.us2@embratur.gov.br/assistant.ebt.us2@embratur.gov.br.
- **In the U.K.:** 18 Greyhound Rd., London, W6.8NX (© **20 7396 5551;** Fax: 20/7396-5599; e-mail: ebt.uk@embratur.gov.br/assistant.ebt.uk@embratur.gov.br).

The Brazilian Embassy in the U.K. has an outstanding website including links to all the state and many city tourism websites: **www.brazil.org.uk**.

Other Brazilian embassies abroad also provide good tourist information:

- **In the U.S.:** 3006 Massachusetts Ave. NW, Washington, DC 20008 (© **202/238-2700;** fax 202/238-2827; www.brasilemb.org).
- **In Canada:** 450 Wilbrod St., Ottawa, ON K1N 6M8 (© **613/237-1090;** fax 613/237-6144; www.brasembottawa.org).
- **In the United Kingdom:** 32 Green St., London W1K 7AT (© **020/7399-9000;** fax 020/7399-9100; www.brazil.org.uk).
- **In Australia:** 19 Forster Crescent, Yarralumla, Canberra ACT 2600 (© **02/6273-2372;** fax 02/6273-2375; www.brazil.org.au).
- **In New Zealand:** 10 Brandon St., Level 9, PO Box 5432, Wellington 6001 (© **04/473-3516;** fax 04/473-3517; www.brazil.org.nz).

ENTRY REQUIREMENTS

VISAS Nationals of the United States, Canada, and Australia require a visa to visit Brazil. British nationals (and holders of an E.U. passport) and New Zealand passport holders do not require a visa, but do need a passport valid for at least 6 months and a return ticket. A number of visa types are available; cost, processing time, and documentation requirements vary. American citizens pay US$100 for a standard single-entry tourist visa that is valid for 90 days (add another US$10 for handling fees, passport photos, and courier costs if you don't live near a consulate). Count on at least 2 weeks of processing time. For Canadians a similar visa costs C$72 and takes about the same processing time. Visas for Australians cost A$90, plus local handling fees, and again take about 2 weeks to process.

Tips   Don't Leave Home without a Picture ID

Bring an alternative picture ID, like a driver's license or student ID. You are required to carry ID in Brazil, and it's sometimes requested when entering office buildings or even tourist sites. Your passport is safer in the hotel safe and not required except for official transactions.

Upon arrival in Brazil, visitors will receive a 90-day entry stamp in their passport and a stamped entry card. Hang on to the card for dear life, as losing it will result in a possible fine and a certain major hassle when you leave. If necessary, the visa can be renewed once for another 90 days. Visa renewals are obtained through the local Policia Federal. This is best done in large cities where the staff has experience with tourists.

Shortly after the United States began fingerprinting Brazilian visitors, Brazil in a tit-for-tat bit of retaliation implemented its own fingerprint program for U.S. visitors. In its first few months the system caused numerous long delays; nowadays the fingerprint requirement is fulfilled with a quick and efficient digital reading of a single thumb digit.

For more information regarding visas and to obtain application details, contact the Brazilian consulate in New York (© **917/777-7777**; www.brazilny.org); Los Angeles (© **323/651-2664**; www. brazilian-consulate.org); or Miami (© **305/ 285-6200**; www.brazilmiami.org). Links will connect you to the consulate closest

to you. Canadians can apply through Toronto's Brazilian consulate (© **416/ 922-2503**; www.consbrastoronto.org). In the U.K., more information is available at www.brazil.org.uk. Australians can log on to www.brazil.org.au, and in New Zealand inquiries can be made in Wellington at **04/473-3516** or check www.brazil. org.nz.

CUSTOMS

WHAT YOU CAN BRING IN   As a visitor you are unlikely to be scrutinized very closely by Brazilian Customs; however, there are random checks, and your luggage may be thoroughly inspected. Visitors are allowed to bring in whatever they need for personal use on their trip, including electronics such as a camera and laptop. If you are bringing in new electronic items you may be asked to register the item to ensure that you will take it with you when you leave. Gifts purchased abroad worth more than US$500 must be declared and are subject to duties for the value over US$500. Merchandise for sale or samples should also be declared upon arrival.

3 Money

The official unit of currency in Brazil is the Real (pronounced ray-*all;* the plural is Reais, pronounced ray-*eyes*), which the Brazilian government introduced in 1994 in an attempt to control inflation. International money speculations around the 2002 presidential elections sent the Real into a tailspin, arriving at a record low of nearly R$4 to the U.S. dollar. When it

became clear the new leftist president Lula da Silva was actually planning to follow a quite conservative monetary policy, the Real settled back around R$3 to the U.S. dollar. Since then, the U.S. dollar has been on a steady decline to its current level around R$2 to the dollar. For travelers this means that Brazil is still affordable, though not the bargain it was in years past. We give the prices in Reais (R$), U.S. dollars (US$), and British pounds (£), accurate as of press time and calculated at the rate of R$1 = US50¢ or R$2 = US$1. Other currency equivalents are UK£1 = R$3.75; 1€ = R$2.60; C$1 = R$1.85; A$1 = R$1.60; NZ$1 = R$1.40. The U.S. dollar is likely to continue its current decline, which might tempt you to convert those dollars into Reais, but remember that the Real is also subject to a substantial yearly devaluation because of inflation. For safety reasons, the best bet is to keep your dollars in your bank account and use ATMs to withdraw cash as needed. *Tip:* When exchanging money, be it cash or traveler's checks, always keep the receipt. You will need it in case you want to change back any unused Reais at the end of your trip. See **www.xe.com** online for an easy currency converter.

THE U.S. DOLLAR The ongoing fall of the U.S. dollar has in some cases made it difficult to get accurate rates. Up until 2004, many businesses based their rates on the U.S. dollar. With the dollar's fall, some businesses have lowered their Real prices to keep a steady dollar price, others have increased the Real rate, and still others have switched over to accounting in euros. For U.S. travelers, it means that Brazil has gotten a little bit more expensive. When prices are listed in U.S. dollars only, it's because these companies quote their prices directly in dollars. If in doubt, ask. And though it's a bad idea to carry large wads of cash, it can be helpful to bring a small amount of U.S. cash ($10s or $20s only, no $100s) as an emergency supply in case that ATM is broken or your credit card isn't working. Even in the smallest towns people will know the exchange rate, and someone will be happy to take the U.S. dollars off your hands.

TRAVELER'S CHECKS Traveler's checks aren't a very good idea in Brazil.

Most shops won't accept them, hotels give a miserable exchange rate (if they cash them), and many banks have a strange policy that they will not cash your traveler's checks unless you have an account at that branch of that bank. The Banco do Brasil is the only bank that will cash them with a minimum of hassle but will charge a US$20 service fee.

ATM NETWORKS The best way to get cash at a reasonable exchange rate is by withdrawing money from an ATM. Brazil's financial infrastructure is very sophisticated, and ATMs were common here even before they were used in western Europe. You will find them everywhere in Brazil, even in the smallest towns. The only trick is finding one that works with your card. ATMs are linked to a network that most likely includes your bank at home. **Cirrus** (© 800/424-7787; www.mastercard.com) and **PLUS** (© 800/843-7587; www.visa.com) are the two most popular networks in the U.S.; call or check online for ATM locations at your destination. You need to have a four-digit PIN to be able to access ATMs in Brazil. For most ATMs the limit is R$1,000 (US$500/£267) but depending on the machine these amounts may be lower.

The vast majority of travelers find they are able to use the HSBC and Banco do Brasil ATMs bearing a PLUS/Visa and Cirrus/MasterCard logo. Almost all Brazilian airports have HSBC and Banco do Brasil ATMs. However, it's not a bad idea to bring two different cards to increase your access options with other banks. (Small towns normally only have one ATM. It will be PLUS/Visa or Cirrus/MasterCard, but not always both.) Bradesco, Banco 24 Horas, and Citibank ATMs are often compatible with PLUS/Visa. If in doubt, check with your bank to find out which Brazilian bank networks are compatible with your card.

Also, plan ahead to ensure that you have enough cash; for safety reasons many ATMs do not operate 24 hours. Often they will close after 10pm or only allow a small amount of cash to be withdrawn during the off-hours. Your best bets for late-night withdrawals are airports, malls, or gas stations.

Finally, make sure that during New Year's and Carnaval you get enough cash ahead of time, as machines often run out of money by the end of the holidays.

Tip: Before you leave home write down all your card numbers, expiration dates, and contact phone numbers. Leave a copy with someone you can easily reach, and e-mail a copy to yourself and save it in an account that can be accessed anywhere, like Hotmail or Yahoo!, so you have the information at your fingertips in case of loss or theft.

CREDIT CARDS The best exchange rates can be obtained through credit cards, which are accepted at most Brazilian shops and hotels and restaurants. Just keep in mind that you are sometimes able to negotiate a better discount on a room or in a store if you pay cash. The most commonly accepted cards are Visa and MasterCard. American Express and Diners Club are also often accepted. It's a good idea to have at least two cards as some stores and restaurants may only accept one card (usually Visa or MasterCard; Diners and Amex are less common, especially in small towns). Keep in mind that many banks now assess a 1%-to-3% "transaction fee" on **all** charges you incur abroad (whether you're using the local currency or U.S. dollars). But credit cards still may be the smart way to go when you factor in things like exorbitant ATM fees and the higher exchange rates and service fees you'll pay with traveler's checks.

4 When to Go

High season in Brazil lasts from the week before Christmas until Carnaval (which falls sometime in Feb or early Mar, depending on the year). Flights and accommodations are more expensive and more likely to be full during this period. Book well ahead of time for accommodations during New Year's and Carnaval. This is the most fun time to travel—towns and resorts are bustling as many Brazilians take their summer vacations, the weather's warm, and New Year's and Carnaval are fabulously entertaining. If you want to spend New Year's in Brazil, it's best to arrive after Christmas. The 25th is really a family affair, and most restaurants and shops will be closed.

Other busy times of the year include Easter week and the months of July, when Brazilian schools and universities take their winter break, and August, when most Europeans and North Americans visit during the summer vacation. This is probably the worst time of year to travel; prices go up significantly, and except for in the north and parts of the Northeast, the weather can be iffy and downright chilly anywhere south of Rio de Janeiro. One year in Rio, I suffered through 4 straight weeks of rain, and temperatures as low as the 40s and 50s (5–10 Celsius) are not unheard of in the south. If you want to take advantage of the best deals and still have good weather, consider visiting Brazil in September or October. The spring weather means warm days in São Paulo, Iguaçu, and Rio, and tropical heat everywhere else; in the Amazon and the Pantanal you'll be there just before the wet season starts. As an added bonus, in Rio you'll be able to attend some of the samba school rehearsals as they get ready for Carnaval (yes, they start 4 months early). Another good period for a visit is after Carnaval (early to mid-Mar, depending on the dates) through May, when you can take advantage of low-season prices, particularly in hotels, while still enjoying good weather.

WEATHER

As Brazil lies in the Southern Hemisphere, its seasons are the exact opposite of what Northern Hemisphere residents are used to: **summer is December through March and winter June through September.** Within the country the climate varies considerably from region to region. In most of Brazil the summers are very hot. Temperatures can rise to 110°F (43°C) with high humidity. The **Northeast** (from Salvador north) is warm year-round, often with a pleasant breeze coming off the ocean. Temperatures hover between the low 80s and mid-90s (upper 20s to mid-30s Celsius). The winter months (June–July) are slightly wetter, but even then the amount of rain is limited—a quick shower that cools things down briefly before giving way to more sunshine. As befits a rainforest, the **Amazon** is also hot and humid year-round, with temperatures hovering around the mid-90s to low 100s (mid-to high 30s Celsius). The dry season lasts from June to December and is often called "summer" by the locals as it is hot and sunny. As the rivers recede, beaches and islands reappear. The wet season typically runs from December to May and is referred to as "winter." The humidity is higher in the rainy season, building up over the course of the day to produce a heavy downfall almost every afternoon. Even then, however, mornings and early afternoons can be clear and sunny. The **Pantanal** is very hot in the rainy season, with temperatures climbing over the 100°F mark (low 40s Celsius). Most of the rain falls December through March. The driest time of the year is May through October. In these winter months things cool down

considerably, though nighttime temperatures will seldom drop below 68°F (20°C). **Rio** has very hot and humid summers—100°F (38°C) and 98% humidity are not uncommon. Rio winters are quite mild, with nighttime temperatures dropping as low as 66°F (19°C), and daytime temperatures climbing to the pleasant and sunny mid-80s (30°C). Cariocas themselves find this lack of heat appalling, and will often throw on a coat or heavy sweater when the temperature drops below 70°F (21°C). In their defense I should note that most houses and apartments are completely without heat, and many restaurants and stores lack windows or doors, so it can feel quite cool. **São Paulo** has a similar climate to Rio's, hot in the summer and mild in winter. As São Paulo sits atop a plateau at approximately 700m (2,300 ft.) of elevation it can sometimes get downright chilly, with daytime lows June through September sometimes reaching 54°F (12°C). **South of São Paulo,** things get even colder in the winter. In Florianópolis, many restaurants and even some hotels and pousadas shut down for the winter season. Also, in the mountain resort of **Petrópolis** and the historic towns of **Ouro Prêto** and **Tiradentes,** it often gets cold enough to see your breath (41°F/5°C) in the fall and winter, and Brazilians will travel here to experience winter.

HOLIDAYS

The following holidays are observed in Brazil: New Year's Day (Jan 1); Carnaval (Feb 2–5, 2008, Feb 21–24, 2009, Feb 13–16, 2010); Easter (Mar 21, 2008, and Apr 10, 2009); Tiradentes Day (Apr 21); Labor Day (May 1); Corpus Christi (May 22, 2008, and June 7, 2009); Independence Day (Sept 7); Our Lady of Apparition (Oct 12); All Souls' Day (Nov 2); Proclamation of the Republic (Nov 15); and Christmas Day (Dec 25). On these days banks, schools, and government institutions will be closed, and some stores may be closed as well.

Brazil's biggest holidays are New Year's and Carnaval (see "Everything You Need to Know about Carnaval" and "Reveillon: New Year's Eve in Rio," both in chapter 5). Easter is also a big celebration in a number of towns around the country, particularly in the historic towns of Minas Gerais and Novo Jerusalem outside Recife. Reservations are recommended for those planning to attend these events.

BRAZIL CALENDAR OF EVENTS

January

New Year's Celebration. In Rio de Janeiro close to two million people gather for one of the most spectacular New Year's celebrations in the world. Starting on the evening of December 31 and continuing well into the morning of January 1, the main event takes place on Copacabana beach with live music and fireworks, as well as Candomblé religious ceremonies. For details contact Riotur (© 021/2541-7522; www.riodejaneiro-turismo.com.br) or Alô Rio (© 021/2542-8080). January 1.

Three Kings Festival in Salvador. Salvador celebrates the Three Kings Festival with a procession and events around the Praça da Sé in the old town. Contact Bahiatursa (© 071/3321-2463; www.bahiatursa.ba.gov.br) for details. January 6.

Washing of the Steps of Bonfim Church. This is one of the most important religious ceremonies in Salvador when hundreds of women in traditional Bahian dress form a procession and carry perfumed water to wash the church steps, accompanied by 800,000 onlookers and revelers. Contact Bahiatursa

(© 071/3321-2463; www.bahiatursa.ba.gov.br) for details. Third Thursday of January.

Saint Sebastian Day. The patron saint of Rio de Janeiro is honored in this regional holiday. The highlight is a procession to the city's modern cathedral. For details contact Riotur (© 021/2541-7522; www.riodejaneiro-turismo.com.br) or Alô Rio (© 021/2542-8080). January 20.

February

Celebration of Yemanjá, the Goddess of the Sea. Devotees throughout Brazil offer flowers, perfumes, and jewelry to the sea. Celebrations take place on the beach with music and food. The largest celebration takes place in Salvador on Praia Vermelha. Contact Bahiatursa (© 071/3321-2463; www.bahiatursa.ba.gov.br) for details. February 2.

Carnaval. This event can take place anywhere from early February to mid-March. Carnaval begins the weekend before Ash Wednesday and ends on the morning of Ash Wednesday. For the next 3 years, the dates are as follows: Feb 2–5, 2008; Feb 21–24, 2009; Feb 13–16, 2010. The largest celebrations take place in Rio, Salvador, and Recife/Olinda. For details contact Riotur (© 021/2541-7522; www.riodejaneiro-turismo.com.br) or Alô Rio at © 021/2542-8080. In Salvador contact Bahiatursa (© 071/3321-2463; www.bahiatursa.ba.gov.br) for details. Contact the Recife tourist office Empetur at (© 081/3232-8409, and for information on Olinda call © 081/3305-1048. Book ahead if you plan on attending this event.

March

Easter Weekend (Semana Santa). This important Catholic holiday is celebrated with processions and concerts. Ouro Prêto, with its 13 baroque churches, is a popular destination during Easter. Contact Ouro Prêto Tourist Information (© **031/3551-2655**) for details. (Upcoming Easter dates: Mar 21, 2008; and Apr 10, 2009.)

Passion Play, Nova Jerusalem. South America's largest Passion Play takes place in Nova Jerusalem, just outside of Recife in Brazil's Northeast. Daily performances. For more information contact Recife Tourist Information (© **081/3232-8409** or 081/3341-6090). Ten days preceding Easter.

Grand Prix, São Paulo. Brazilians are car-racing fanatics; watching a big race in the company of Brazilian fans is an event in itself. The Grand Prix at Interlagos (a suburb of São Paulo) is the prime event in the country. Contact www.gpbrasil.com.br for more information, or call the tourist office in São Paulo (© **011/3231-2922** or 011/3251-0970). Third week of October. Check website for exact dates.

April

Week of the Inconfidencia. Tiradentes Day on April 21 is a national holiday, but only Ouro Prêto has made it into a large event with celebrations, plays, and cultural events taking place. Contact Ouro Prêto Tourist Information (© **031/3551-2655**) for details. Week of April 16 to April 21.

June

Bumba-meu-boi. In São Luis in Maranhão, the peasant folklore festival Bumba-meu-boi begins June 1 with the baptizing of the bull, and continues throughout the month, culminating with a large street party on June 30, the feast day of São Marçal. In São Luis, contact the State Tourism Agency (© **098/3231-2000;** www.turismo. ma.gov.br).

Festas Juninas. Folklore event in honor of saints Anthony, John, and Peter. Celebrated throughout Brazil, this harvest festival offers country music, bonfires, hot-air balloons, and fun fairs. In Rio contact **Riotur** (© **021/2541-7522;** www.riodejaneiro-turismo. com.br) or **Alô Rio** (© **021/2542-8080**). June 13 to June 14.

Bauernfest, Petrópolis. Petrópolis celebrates the German heritage of its many settlers with a week of German food, folklore, and music. Contact **Petrotur** (© **0800/241-516** or 024/2243-9300; www.petropolis.rj.gov.br) for details. Last weekend of June and first week of July.

July

Sailing Festival, Ilhabela. Yachties don't want to miss Brazil's largest sailing event, which takes place on Ilhabela, off of São Paulo. For details call © **012/3472-2300** in Ilhabela, or **011/3151-3616** (www.ilhabela.com. br) in São Paulo. Third week of July.

September

Independence Day. This is Brazil's national holiday. Most cities hold military parades. In Rio de Janeiro this impressive event takes place around Avenida Rio Branco.

Film Festival Rio BR, Rio de Janeiro. Rio's film festival showcases Brazilian and international films (www.festival dorio.com.br). Subtitles are in Portuguese, but there is usually a good selection of international movies. In Rio contact Riotur at © **021/2541-7522;** www.riodejaneiro-turismo.com. br or Alô Rio at © **021/2542-8080.** Late September to the first week of October.

October

Free Jazz Festival, Rio de Janeiro and São Paulo. A 3-day jazz festival with national and international acts. In Rio contact Riotur (© **021/2541-7522;** www.riodejaneiro-turismo.com.br) or Alô Rio (© **021/2542-8080**). In São

Paulo contact the **CIT** (Central de Informações Turisticas) at ℭ **011/3231-2922** or 011/251-0970. Mid- to late October.

Cirio of Nazaré, Belém. Hundreds of thousands of the faithful parade an icon of the Virgin of Nazaré through the streets and harbor of Belém. Second Sunday of October (upcoming dates are Oct 11, 2008; and Oct 12, 2009). Contact **Belémtur** (ℭ **091/3242-0900**).

International Film Festival, São Paulo. The festival presents the best films of Brazil, Latin America, and the world. Most venues concentrate around the Avenida Paulista. Contact ℭ **011/3141-0413,** or check www.mostra.org. Last 2 weeks of October.

São Paulo Bienal. Art, theater, music, and architecture—the biggest arts event in Latin America takes place every even year in Ibirapuera Park. For schedules and information contact the Fundação Bienal de São Paulo (ℭ **011/5574-5922;** www.bienalsaopaulo.org.br).

November

Aleijadinho Week, Ouro Prêto. Special exhibits and presentations about the beloved sculptor. Contact Ouro Prêto Tourist Information at ℭ **031/3551-2655** for details. November 14 to November 21.

December

Santa Barbara, Salvador. This festival is celebrated with processions, music, and dance. Santa Barbara is the Candomblé equivalent of Iansã, the goddess of wind. Contact Bahiatursa (ℭ **071/3321-2463;** www.bahiatursa.ba.gov.br) for details. December 4.

Christmas Eve. Brazilians go to midnight Mass to celebrate Christmas. Mass is usually followed by a late-night supper with family. December 24.

Reveillon **(New Year's Eve),** Rio de Janeiro. See "*Reveillon:* New Year's Eve in Rio" p. 151. December 31.

5 Health & Safety

HEALTH

Standards for hygiene and public health in Brazil are generally high. Before leaving, however, check with your doctor or with the Centers for Disease Control (www.cdc.gov) for specific advisories. Use common sense when eating on the street or in restaurants.

VACCINATIONS Before going, check your vaccinations and get booster shots for tetanus and polio if required. Children ages 3 months to 6 years may be required to show proof of polio vaccination. One vaccination that is definitely recommended for Brazil is **yellow fever.** Outbreaks are sometimes reported in the Amazon, the Pantanal, Brasilia, or even Minas Gerais. Make sure you get an international certificate of vaccination as Brazilian authorities sometimes require proof of vaccination for people going to or coming from an affected area. Travelers who have been to Colombia, Bolivia, Ecuador, French Guyana, Peru, or Venezuela within 90 days prior to their arrival in Brazil **must** show proof of yellow fever vaccination. Keep in mind that the vaccine takes 10 days to take effect.

DENGUE FEVER Dengue fever is a viral infection transmitted by mosquitoes. It's unfortunately common in Rio de Janeiro. It's characterized by sudden onset high fever, severe headaches, joint and muscle pain, nausea/vomiting, and rash. (The rash may not appear until 3–4 days after the fever.) Proper diagnosis requires a blood test. The illness may last up to 10 days, but complete recovery can take 2 to 4 weeks. Dengue is rarely fatal.

The risk for dengue fever is highest during periods of heat and rain, where stagnant pools of water allow mosquitoes to breed. Though it strikes most often in poorer communities, the disease has infiltrated Rio's more affluent neighborhoods. There is no vaccine for dengue fever. Symptoms can be treated with bed rest, fluids, and medications to reduce fever, such as acetaminophen (Tylenol); aspirin should be avoided. The most important precaution a traveler can take is to avoid mosquito bites in dengue-prone areas. Try to remain in well-screened or air-conditioned areas, use mosquito repellents (preferably those containing DEET) on skin and clothing, and sleep with bed nets. For up-to-date information on the status of dengue fever in Brazil, consult the Centers for Disease Control website (www.cdc.gov) before departing.

OTHER HEALTH CONSIDERATIONS   If traveling to the Amazon or the Pantanal, a malaria prophylaxis (usually pills that you take daily) may be recommended.

BRAZILIAN PHARMACIES   If you do wind up with traveler's tummy or some other ailment (upset stomach, diarrhea, sunburn, or rash), Brazilian pharmacies are a wonder. Each has a licensed pharmacist who is trained to deal with small medical emergencies and can make recommendations for treatment. The service is free and medication is fairly inexpensive. If you take medication that may need replacement while in Brazil, ask your doctor to write out the active ingredients of the prescription, as many drugs are sold under different trade names in Brazil. Many drugs available by prescription only in the U.S. and Canada are available over-the-counter in Brazil. While this is incredibly convenient, the downside is that Brazilians are the world's biggest pill-poppers who will happily "prescribe" drugs for themselves or their relatives or friends at the slightest whiff of sickness.

AIDS & STDS   According to recent UN statistics, Brazil has the dubious honor of ranking third in the world for total number of people with HIV infections. Though condom usage is becoming more accepted—thanks in part to the examples shown in popular nighttime soaps on TV—the reality is that some people still won't use them, and AIDS and other STDs are still being spread. So be careful and be safe—always insist on using a condom. Though condoms are readily available in Brazilian pharmacies, it's best to bring your own; brands are more reliable in North America and Europe. To purchase condoms in Brazil ask for a *preservativo* or a *camisinha* (kah-mee-*zeen*-ya), literally a small shirt; the latter word is the commonly used term for condom.

OTHER HEALTH CONSIDERATIONS   The Brazilian sun is very strong, particularly in summer (the North American winter, when most travelers from above the Equator are quite pale). Sunscreen of at least SPF 15 should be applied frequently. Tourists rarely encounter snakes and are even more rarely bitten. You'll find ticks most everywhere in Brazil, but the only place I considered them a nuisance was hiking in highland areas like the Chapada Diamantina inland from Salvador (see chapter 9) or the Chapada Guimarães near Cuiabá.

WHAT TO DO IF YOU GET SICK AWAY FROM HOME

If you worry about getting sick away from home, consider purchasing **medical travel insurance.** In most cases, however, your existing health plan will provide all the coverage you need. However it is wise to check any conditions and/or limitations on your coverage. Be sure to carry your identification card in your wallet.

Pack **prescription medications** in your carry-on luggage. Carry written prescriptions in generic, not brand-name, form, and dispense all prescription medications from their original labeled vials. Also bring along copies of your prescriptions in case you lose your pills or run out.

Contact the **International Association for Medical Assistance to Travelers (IAMAT)** (© **716/754-4883** or 416/652-0137). This organization offers tips on travel and health concerns in the countries you'll be visiting, and lists many local English-speaking doctors. When you're abroad, any local consulate can provide a list of area doctors who speak English (though it may be hard to find one with more than a basic knowledge of English, even in larger cities). If you do get sick, you may want to ask the concierge at your hotel to recommend a local doctor—even his or her own. This will probably yield a better recommendation than any 800 number would. If you can't find a doctor who can help you right away, try the emergency room at the local hospital.

SAFETY

Sometime in the 1980s Brazil began developing a world reputation for violence and crime. Rio especially was seen as the sort of place where walking down the street was openly asking for a mugging. Some of this was pure sensationalism, but there was a good measure of truth as well. Brazil at the time was massively in debt to First World banks, and the combination of crippling interest payments and International Monetary Fund austerity measures left governments at all levels with no money for basics, such as street lighting and police, much less schools and hospitals.

Fortunately, in the early '90s things began to turn around. The debt crisis eased, leaving governments with some discretionary spending, and with the advent of the 1992 World Environment Conference in Rio, Brazilians realized they had a serious image problem on their hands. Governments began putting money back into basic services, starting with policing. Cops were stationed on city streets, on public beaches, and anywhere else there seemed to be a problem. At the same time governments began working on extending water and sanitation to some of the city's poorer residents in the *favelas* (shantytowns).

The decade-long expansion that followed made massive new investments in tourism infrastructure feasible. Many cities got brand-new airports. A domestic tourism boom ensued, making the protection of tourists even more of a political imperative. Nowadays, though still not perfect by any means, Rio, São Paulo, and Brazil's other big cities have bounced back to the point where they're as safe as some large international cities.

Statistically, of course, Rio and other big Brazilian cities still have very high crime rates, including high rates of violent crime. Most of that crime, however, takes place in the favelas and shantytowns of the far-off industrial outskirts. Brazil is a highly unequal society and the burden of crime and violence falls disproportionately (and unfairly) on the country's poor. But unless you go wandering unaccompanied into a hillside favela (not recommended), you're unlikely to be affected.

That said, in large centers such as São Paulo, Rio, Salvador, and Recife, common-sense rules still apply. Don't flash your valuables. Diamond rings and Rolex wristwatches are a no-no. Always have a few small bills ready in your pocket or bag to avoid pulling out your wallet in public places. Plan your sightseeing trips to the city's central core during office hours when there are lots of people about. By all means bring your camera or video-recorder, but keep it inside a backpack or purse, and only take it out when you want to use it. Don't stroll Copacabana beach at 3am with R$1,000 in your pocket and a video camera pressed to your eyeball (a true story, alas). And though public transit is safe during the day and evening, watch for pickpockets when it gets really packed, and come nightfall, use taxis instead. Be careful at night; stick to the main streets where there is traffic and other pedestrians, and avoid dark alleys or deserted streets.

Perhaps even more importantly, *keep your wits about you in traffic!* Brazilian drivers (with a few exceptions) show no respect for pedestrians and there's no such thing as pedestrian right of way. So be very careful when crossing the street, particularly at night when drivers will often run red lights. Also pay special attention when crossing one-way streets; many drivers, especially those who drive motorcycles or delivery bicycles, think that the one-way rule does not apply to them and will happily go the wrong way.

DEALING WITH DISCRIMINATION

Outside of the big cities such as São Paulo, Rio de Janeiro, and Salvador, openly gay men or women will certainly draw attention and perhaps be subjected to comments or jokes. Brazil is still a macho culture and any open sign of affection between people of the same sex will meet with disapproval.

African Americans shouldn't encounter much in the way of discrimination. However, mixed couples (particularly where the woman is black and the man is not) may encounter discrimination in hotels or bars because people may assume that the woman is a Brazilian prostitute who has hooked up with a gringo guy. Particularly in Rio and the Northeast such "temporary couples" are a common sight, and people will make assumptions based on appearances.

ECO-TOURISM

The International Ecotourism Society (TIES) defines eco-tourism as "responsible travel to natural areas that conserves the environment and improves the well-being of local people." You can find eco-friendly travel tips, statistics, and touring companies and associations—listed by destination under "Travel Choice"—at the TIES website, www.ecotourism.org. **Ecotravel.com** is part online magazine and part eco-directory that lets you search for touring companies in several categories (water-based, land-based, spiritually oriented, and so on). Also check out **Conservation International** (www.conservation.org)—which, with *National Geographic Traveler*, annually presents **World Legacy Awards** (www.wlaward.org) to those travel tour operators, businesses, organizations, and places that have made a significant contribution to sustainable tourism.

At the moment, eco-tourism is very trendy in Brazil. Unfortunately, many of Brazil's "eco-tourism" operators offer nothing that even comes close to the ideals of eco-tourism. Often, Brazilians will label any tourism that takes place in nature as "eco-tourism," without any concern for preservation, sustainable local development, and so forth. Whenever possible, we have tried to highlight companies that practice real eco-tourism. This often means that they cost more than some of the other operators but we believe that your experience will be better and that the payoff for the environment and the community will be worth it as well.

VEGETARIAN TRAVEL

At first glance, Brazil is not a very vegetarian-friendly country. Indeed, the all-you-can-eat grilled *churrasco* meat orgy that Brazilians love so much is likely a vegetarian's worst nightmare. Don't expect much sympathy from Brazilians either. They will not understand why anybody would even want to be a vegetarian. That said, Brazil is also a country with a lot of fruit and vegetables, and many of the restaurants that serve meat will also have fabulous salads, vegetable dishes, and pastas. If you eat fish and seafood you will be able to eat almost anywhere. If you don't eat meat but are okay with eating in restaurants that serve meat, you'll be fine.

6 Tips for Travelers with Special Needs

TRAVELERS WITH DISABILITIES

Travelers with disabilities will find Brazil challenging. Those who use a wheelchair to get around will find that very few places are accessible. In the large cities, increasing numbers of hotels, restaurants, and attractions are making themselves accessible. The trick lies in getting to them. Sidewalks are often uneven, ramps are usually absent, and buses and taxis are not adapted to handle a wheelchair. For some additional resources on traveling with a disability, contact **Access-able,** P.O. Box 1796, Wheat Ridge, CO 80034 (© **303/232-2979;** www.access-able. com). Its website has links to country-specific resources such as accessible hotels, tour operators, and other useful information. **Flying Wheels Travel** (© **800/ 535-6790;** www.flyingwheelstravel.com) offers escorted tours and cruises that emphasize sports and private tours in minivans with lifts.

Organizations that offer information to disabled travelers include **MossRehab** (www.mossresourcenet.org), which provides a library of accessible-travel resources online; the **American Foundation for the Blind (AFB)** (© **800/232-5463;** www.afb.org), a referral resource for the blind or visually impaired that includes information on traveling with Seeing Eye dogs; and **SATH** (Society for Accessible Travel & Hospitality) (© **212/447-7284;** www.sath.org; annual membership fees: $49 adults, $29 seniors and students), which offers a wealth of travel resources for all types of disabilities and informed recommendations on destinations, access guides, travel agents, tour operators, vehicle rentals, and companion services. **AirAmbulanceCard.com** is now partnered with SATH and allows you to preselect top-notch hospitals in case of an emergency for $195 a year ($295 per family), among other benefits.

For more information specifically targeted to travelers with disabilities, the community website **iCan** (www.ican online.net/channels/travel) has destination guides and several regular columns on accessible travel. Also check out the quarterly magazine *Emerging Horizons* (www.emerginghorizons.com; $17 per year, $22 outside the U.S.); and *Open World* magazine, published by SATH (see above; subscription: $13 per year, $21 outside the U.S.).

FOR GAY & LESBIAN TRAVELERS

Gay and lesbian travelers will find small but vibrant gay communities in São Paulo, Rio de Janeiro, Salvador, and some of the other big cities, more often geared toward men than women. However, public displays of affection are not common among gays and lesbians even in the cities, and in small towns and communities the level of acceptance is significantly lower—rude remarks and jokes are almost guaranteed, though physical violence is thankfully rare.

One Brazilian travel agency in Rio that specializes in tours for gay and lesbian travelers is Rio G Travel, Rua Teixeira de Melo 31, Ipanema (© **021/3813-0003;** www.riogtravel.com.br).

FOR SENIORS

Senior travelers can try and ask for discounts, though these are reserved for those over 60 or 65 years of age who can show Brazilian ID. Still, it's worth asking at tourist attractions if there's a discount.

The phrase to use is "*Tem disconto para idosos?*"

Elderhostel (© **877/426-8056;** www. elderhostel.org) arranges study programs for those age 55 and over (and a spouse or companion of any age) in the U.S. and in more than 80 countries around the world. Most courses last 5 to 7 days in the U.S. (2–4 weeks abroad), and many include airfare, accommodations in university dormitories or modest inns, meals, and tuition. Many reliable agencies and organizations target the 50-plus market. **ElderTreks** (© **800/741-7956;** www. eldertreks.com) offers small-group tours to off-the-beaten-path or adventure-travel locations, restricted to travelers 50 and older.

Recommended travel publications for seniors include: the quarterly magazine *Travel 50 & Beyond* (www.travel50and beyond.com); *Travel Unlimited: Uncommon Adventures for the Mature Traveler* (Avalon); *101 Tips for Mature Travelers,* available from Grand Circle Travel (© **800/221-2610** or 617/350-7500; www.gct.com); and *Unbelievably Good Deals and Great Adventures That You Absolutely Can't Get Unless You're Over 50* (McGraw-Hill), by Joann Rattner Heilman.

FOR FAMILIES

Brazilians love kids. They will go out of their way to please children, yours and everyone else's. In fact you will see children out and about a lot more than in the U.S. or Canada, even at restaurants, bars, or late-night events. Perhaps because Brazilian children are used to going out a lot more, they seem to always behave very well in public, playing with other kids or amusing themselves, with few of the hissy fits that sometimes accompany evenings out with North American youngsters. Traveling with children is a wonderful way to meet Brazilians, as people will be receptive, friendly, and inquisitive. Hotels

are very accommodating but do usually charge 10% to 25% extra for children over the age of 6 or 12 who stay in the same room as a parent or guardian. In most hotels, the age limit and the amount of extra percentage charged can be flexible and is certainly worth bargaining over. **Family Travel Network** (www. familytravelnetwork.com) offers travel tips and reviews of family-friendly destinations, vacation deals, and thoughtful features such as "What to Do When Your Kids Are Afraid to Travel" and "Kid-Style Camping."

If a child is traveling with people other than his or her parents, or even if the child is only traveling with one of his or her parents, it is a good idea to have a notarized letter from the parents confirming permission for the child to travel. Buses and airlines sometimes demand such a letter before allowing a child to board. For even greater safety, have the notarized letter stamped by the Brazilian consulate or embassy. (Please contact the Brazilian consulate or embassy for further information.)

Brazilians can be incredibly picky (in moments of frustration in dealing with Brazilian bureaucrats we have used words other than "picky") when it comes to paperwork; showing an embassy stamp makes a difference because that means that somebody in authority has already approved it.

For details on entry requirements for children traveling abroad, go to the U.S. State Department website (travel.state. gov).

To locate accommodations, restaurants, and attractions that are particularly kid-friendly, refer to the "Kids" icon throughout this guide.

Recommended family-travel Internet sites include **Family Travel Forum** (www. familytravelforum.com), a comprehensive site that offers customized trip planning; **Family Travel Network** (www.familytravelnetwork.com), an award-winning site that offers travel features, deals, and tips; **Traveling Internationally with Your Kids** (www.travelwithyourkids.com), a comprehensive site offering sound advice for long-distance and international travel with children; and **Family Travel Files** (www.thefamilytravelfiles.com), which offers an online magazine and a directory of off-the-beaten-path tours and tour operators for families.

FOR WOMEN

Machismo is alive and well in Brazil, but it's a kinder, gentler machismo than in other parts of Latin America. Single women and a few women traveling together will undoubtedly attract masculine attention. There are upsides to this. It's usually fairly harmless and can sometimes lead to some fun conversations. Brazilian men, it seems, have an insurmountable urge to flirt. Perhaps because flirting is such a way of life, they take rejection well. Indeed, the object of the exercise lies mostly in the act of flirtation itself—actually making a conquest appears to be not terribly important. Wearing a wedding ring (fake or real) will throw up only the flimsiest of barriers; it will be either completely ignored, seen as a challenge, or solicit questions such as "How married are you?" or "What kind of husband would let you out of his sight?" However, if you are not interested, just say so or walk away if necessary and that is usually enough. The downside is that it's difficult for a woman to go out for a drink by herself and not receive attention. If you're not comfortable with this, you may want to form up a mixed group with other travelers or else stick to higher-end restaurants or hotel bars. Brazilian women in groups of two or three often link arms or hold hands as a sign that they are not interested in male attention. Use common sense to avoid situations where you may find yourself alone with someone giving you unwanted attention. At night, taking taxis is safer than walking by yourself.

TRAVELERS WITH FOOD ALLERGIES

If you are allergic to nuts you should be extra careful around certain dishes. Especially those with a seafood or shrimp allergy may want to check before ordering stews from the Northeast such as *moqueca, vatapá,* and *bobó.* These dishes often have ground-up shrimp or sometimes nuts in the sauce. Also, many fish dishes come with shrimp sauce which may not be listed on the menu. Desserts often have nuts in them so always ask before digging in. Peanuts are *amendoim* (ah-man-doo-*een*), cashews in Portuguese are *castanha de caju* or *caju* (ka-*stan*-ya de *ka*-zhoo) for short, and Brazil nuts are known as *castanha do Pará* (ka-*stan*-ya doh pa-*rah*). The general word for nuts is *nozes* (no-*zhes*) and you can let people know that you have an allergy by saying *"Tenho alergia de amendoim"* (*ten*-yo ah-lehr-*gee*-ah de ah-man-doo-*een*).

AFRICAN-AMERICAN TRAVELERS

Brazil is experiencing an increase in the number of African-American visitors interested in learning about the African roots of Brazilian culture. Most of these travelers visit Salvador, the Brazilian city with the highest percentage of residents of African descent, as well as Rio, which is more of a melting pot but where Afro Brazilian culture is also strong. Brazil Nuts (www.brazilnuts.com) offers several packages that focus on African religions, festivals, and culture. They can also customize a trip according to your requirements. The Internet offers a number of helpful travel sites for African-American travelers.

Agencies and organizations that provide resources for black travelers include **Rodgers Travel** (© 800/825-1775;

www.rodgerstravel.com), a Philadelphia-based travel agency with an extensive menu of tours in destinations worldwide, including heritage and private-group tours.

7 Getting to Brazil

BY PLANE

Rio de Janeiro and São Paulo are the two major gateways to Brazil and are served by most international airlines. The two big Brazilian airlines—Varig and TAM—also operate a number of international flights. Contact numbers given are for the United States and Canada unless otherwise stated. Please check the websites or contact your travel agency for details. Up until 2006, **Varig** (© **800/Go-VARIG;** www.varig.com) was the Brazilian airline with the most international connections to North America, Europe, Asia, and the rest of South America. However, after going through a major crisis and hovering on the edge of bankruptcy, Varig—though it survived—had to give up most of its international routes. **TAM** (© **888/ 2FLY-TAM;** www.tam.com.br) has picked up some of Varig's slack and has added more international flights to Europe and in the U.S. to Miami and New York. Relative newcomer, low-budget carrier **Gol** (www.voegol.com.br) has also done well in the Varig shake-up and now offers a number of South American destinations (Argentina, Chile, Peru and Bolivia), a good alternative for those traveling within South America.

If you plan to visit a few countries in South America, the **Mercosur pass** is worth considering. Participating countries include Brazil, Paraguay, Uruguay, Argentina, and Chile. The pass is valid for a maximum of 30 days and allows you to visit all countries, with a minimum of two stops and a maximum of eight stops, and a restriction of two stops per country. To be eligible to purchase the pass you need to buy your international ticket with United, American, Delta, Continental, or any of the national airlines of the participating countries (for example, LanChile in Chile, Varig or TAM in Brazil, or Aerolinas Argentinas in Argentina). The cost of a Mercosur pass depends on flying mileage. Typical fares are US$295 for 1,200 to 1,900 miles, US$585 for 3,200 to 4,200 miles, and US$1,075 for 7,200 miles or more. (For reference, a flight from Rio to Buenos Aires requires 1,232 miles, while Rio to Santiago de Chile uses up 1,825 miles.) The best way to get more information is to check with your travel agent.

BY PACKAGE TOUR

Many travel agencies offer package tours to Brazil, but few have the knowledge to effectively customize your trip or make interesting recommendations. To book a package with Brazil travel experts, contact **Brazil Nuts,** 1854 Trade Center Way, Suite 101A, Naples, FL 34109 (© **800/ 553-9959** or 914/593-0266; www.brazil nuts.com). The owners and staff are indeed nuts about Brazil and possess a vast amount of knowledge about the country and its attractions. Depending on your needs you can book just a flight and hotels, or you can add one or more group excursions in more inaccessible places such as the Amazon. Their website is a font of information, and staff can answer any questions you may have about Brazil.

Note: Brazilian travel agents still have a firm grip on the hotel market, and Brazilian hotels will usually offer their lowest rates to travel agents instead of posting them on their websites. Once you have narrowed down your hotel options, it can pay to contact an agency like Brazil Nuts to compare rates.

Another excellent resource on Brazil and South America travel in general is **South America Travel** (formerly 4Star-Brazil; PO Box 11552, Washington, DC 20008; © **800/747-4540;** www.south americatravel.com). Similar to Brazil Nuts, South America Travel offers packages customizable to whatever level you're comfortable with. A number of interesting add-ons are available—outdoors lovers will be pleased to see some great hiking and camping options. The company has local offices in Rio, Lima, and Buenos Aires.

A good travel agency to book your ticket through is **Santini Tours,** 6575 Shattuck Ave., Oakland, CA 94609 (© **800/769-9669** or 510/652-8600; www.santours.com). The owner as well as many of the travel agents are Brazilian and can give you many useful suggestions on air-pass routings and answer any questions you have about your itinerary. In addition to selling tickets and air passes, Santini can also arrange customized tours, including everything from airport transfers to sightseeing and guided tours.

8 Getting Around Brazil

BY PLANE

Though there are highways and buses, the sheer vastness of Brazil (and the absence of rail travel) makes air travel the only viable option for those who want to visit a variety of cities and regions. However, the Brazilian airline industry has been experiencing turbulent times of late. The last 6 years has seen the bankruptcy of two Brazilian carriers, Transbrasil and Vasp, followed by the near demise of the country's flagship carrier Varig. A new, smaller Varig flew out of bankruptcy protection, minus most of its international and domestic routes. On top of that there has been ongoing labor unrest among air-traffic controllers, set off by a mid-air collision over the Amazon, the blame for which controllers felt was unfairly placed on them. And as if that wasn't enough, a still-unexplained crash (investigators are leaning toward pilot error) at São Paulo's busiest domestic hub led to a complete reshuffling of Brazil's domestic air routes. All of which has meant delays, delays, cancellations, and more delays. The president sacked the head of the civilian air agency in mid-2007, and the new chief seems to be bringing order back to the skies. However, travelers should stock up on patience before entering a Brazilian airport. (It may

well not be required, but you never know). During peak travel times (holidays, high season) long delays are a not unlikely occurrence.

The big winner from all this uproar has been domestic no-frills carrier Gol, which now even offers international flights within South America. Tam has also increased the number of destinations, internationally and domestically.

For those traveling larger distances in Brazil there is also the option of purchasing an air pass with Tam (much to the envy of Brazilians this pass is available to foreigners only). The pass offers travelers four flights within a 21-day period. Air passes need to be purchased and booked outside of Brazil. Only limited changes are allowed once you arrive in the country. Also, it's a good idea to read the small print before choosing your pass. Often flights between Rio and São Paulo's downtown airports are excluded (meaning you have to use the international airports) and the pass does not allow returns on the same stretch.

TAM (© **0800/123-100** in Brazil; www.tam.com.br) offers four segments for US$479 if you arrive on an international Tam flight (otherwise the pass costs US$560), with the option of a fifth leg

⟨Tips⟩ Domestic Travel Do's and Don'ts

There are a few tricks to avoiding delays and cancellations when flying domestically in Brazil. First up, if at all possible, avoid flights stopping or connecting through São Paulo. That may be hard to do; the city serves as Brazil's major hub, and its airports as a result have a tendency to get clogged and backed up. Second, travel early in the day: Delays tend to accumulate throughout the day and lead to bigger and bigger backlogs. Third, don't book tight connections, especially if you have to transfer from the domestic airport in Rio or São Paulo to the international airport. For a simple connection within the same airport, give yourself an hour. For a transfer from domestic to international airports, allow for at least 2 hours in Rio and 3 hours in São Paulo.

for another US$120. The pass is valid for 21 days. Check TAM's special English-language site for more details on the air pass (www.tamairlines.com). If you're traveling to only one or two destinations within Brazil, it can be cheaper to skip the air pass and buy a separate ticket. You can check the prices with TAM or **Gol** (© **0300/789-2121** in Brazil; www.voegol.com.br). This airline has modeled itself after American discount carriers like Southwest Airlines—quick bookings online and no-frills flights between popular destinations such as Rio, São Paulo, Salvador, Recife, Fortaleza, Manaus, Belém, Campo Grande, and Brasilia. Tickets can be purchased at the airport or on the Internet. The company flies brand-new Boeing 737s and provides friendly and efficient service.

BY BUS

Bus travel in Brazil is comfortable, efficient, and affordable. The only problem is, it's a long way from anywhere to anywhere else. Tickets can be purchased ahead of time with reserved seats. All buses are nonsmoking, and in most cases people adhere to the regulations. On many popular routes travelers can opt for a deluxe coach with air-conditioning and *leito* (seats that recline almost flat).

BY CAR

Car rentals are expensive, and the distances are huge. From Recife to Brasilia is 2,121km (1,315 miles); Salvador to Rio is a 1,800km (1,116-mile) drive. Within Brazilian cities, renting a car is only for the bold and foolish: Drivers are aggressive, rules sporadically applied, and parking a competitive sport. That said, there are occasions—a side trip to the mountain resorts of Rio, a visit to the historic towns of Minas Gerais, or a drive to the Chapada dos Guimarães outside of Cuiabá—where a car makes sense. Contact numbers for rental companies are given in each chapter.

Each company normally has a national rate, and only rarely are there local discounts or special offers. For a tiny car (a Fiat Palio or Gol) with air-conditioning, you can typically expect to pay around R$70 (US$35/£19) per day plus R$.55 (US27¢/£.15) per kilometer or R$110 (US$55/£30) per day with unlimited mileage. Add to that another R$30 (US$15/£8) per day for comprehensive insurance. Gasoline costs R$2.60 (US$1.30/£.70) per liter, about US$4.50/gallon. Officially you need an international driver's license but we have never encountered any problems having a U.S., Canadian, or European license. To obtain an international license,

> ### *Tips* **What to Bring to Brazil**
>
> A few items are so expensive or of such poor quality in Brazil that you should stock up before coming—film and other camera supplies, for one. Brazilian batteries are not only expensive, but they also seem to last only half as long as American varieties. Most toiletries can be purchased at reasonable prices at *farmacias* (drugstores). Contact lens wearers should bring enough solution to last their trips, as lens fluid is insanely expensive (US$15 for a travel-size bottle).
>
> What *shouldn't* you pack? Clothes and shoes in Brazil are inexpensive and of good quality; pack light and pick up some local fashions after you arrive. Bring a swimsuit for the first day, but then buy a Brazilian one. Generally speaking, summer (Nov–Mar) is hot *everywhere*. Jeans and heavy cotton T-shirts are too thick. Bring a light rain jacket and one light long-sleeved shirt to guard against overeager air-conditioning.

contact your local automobile association. While expensive, the comprehensive insurance is probably a good idea as Brazilian drivers are not as gentle with their cars as folks in North America. Bumpers are meant to be used, Brazilians believe, and if a bit of nudging is required to get into that parking spot, so be it. Note that Embratur warns travelers to avoid the cheaper local car-rental companies, which sometimes skip on the requisite insurance and maintenance.

9 Tips on Shopping

Brazil offers excellent shopping opportunities, particularly for leather goods such as shoes, belts, purses, and wallets. Clothing is also very affordable and often of good quality. Styles follow the opposite seasonal calendar so those visiting Brazil in the Northern Hemisphere winter can stock up on an excellent summer wardrobe. Sizes follow the European numbering (36, 38, 40, and so on) or are marked P (*pequeno* = small), M (*medio* = medium), and G (*grande* = large); U stands for *tamanho único* (one size).

Everywhere in Brazil there are H. Stern and Amsterdam Sauer stores selling gemstones and jewelry. Brazil has a phenomenal variety of stones, and these stores are worth a visit as they offer the largest selection of top-quality stones and jewelry. Both have their flagship stores in Rio de Janeiro. CDs of Brazilian artists are best purchased in the large cities where prices are more competitive, ranging from R$12 (US$6/£3.25) for certain promotional series to R$35 (US$18/£9.50) for a full-priced CD. Illegal bootleg recordings of the same artists are widely sold at markets and street fairs. Regional crafts vary from woodcarvings to textiles to jewelry and leather products. Buying locally will guarantee the best selection and prices. Though it's not like Egypt or Southeast Asia, a little bit of haggling is acceptable, particularly with street vendors. Even in stores one can ask for a discount when buying more than one item or when paying cash. Shops will often advertise prices *"a vista"*—this means cash purchases only, which can be 10% to 20% cheaper than when paying by credit card.

10 Tips on Accommodations

Brazil offers a wide range of accommodations. In the large cities there are modern high-rise hotels as well as apartment hotels (or rental flats for you Brits) known in Brazil as apart-hotels. The apart-hotels are often a better deal than regular hotel rooms, offering both cheaper rates and more space: a separate living room, bedroom, and kitchen. The drawback is that you sometimes don't get the pool and restaurants and other amenities of a hotel. Some of the better hotel chains that you will find in Brazil are the Accor Group (www.accorhotels.com.br). This French company operates a number of brands such as the Sofitel luxury hotels, the excellent Parthenon apart-hotels, and the Mercure and Ibis. The last two are fairly new and most hotels are only a few years old. The Mercure offers more comfortable accommodations; the Ibis is the Motel 6 version, clean and reliable but no frills.

A more high-end chain with numerous new properties is the Meliá (www.sol melia.com). The Blue Tree (www.blue tree.com.br) is also represented in many Brazilian cities. The older properties in the chain are not the best but the modern ones are excellent. A relative newcomer is the Atlantica Hotels (www.atlanticahotels. com.br) chain. Some of its best-known brands are the Comfort Suites and Quality. Both are good affordable hotels with modern amenities and standards.

Outside of the large cities you will often find pousadas, essentially our equivalent of a bed-and-breakfast or small inn. Accommodations prices fluctuate widely. The rates posted at the front desk—the rack rate or *tarifa balcão*—are just a guideline. Outside of high season and on weekends you can almost always negotiate significant (20%–30%) discounts. High season is from mid-December to Carnaval (mid- to late Feb), Easter week, long weekends (see "Holidays," earlier in this chapter, for Brazilian holidays), and July (winter vacation). Notable exceptions are Brasília and São Paulo, where business just dies during high season and weekends and rooms are heavily discounted.

Tip: Always check the quotes you have obtained from a hotel with a travel agency such as Brazil Nuts or South America Travel as many hotels will give their best rates to travel agents and stick it to individual travelers or those who book via the Internet. The Copacabana Palace quoted us a price of US$220/£110 to US$450/£225 for a room, whereas Brazil Nuts can sell you that same room for US$150/£75!

Hotel charges for children are all over the map. Most hotels will allow children under 6 years of age to stay for free in their parent's room, but over 6, the rates can vary from a 10% surcharge to a full adult supplement rate. Please note that these rates and policies are always negotiable.

Unlike North American hotels, Brazilian hotel rooms do not feature coffeemakers, irons, or ironing boards, although the latter can sometimes be delivered to your room upon request. Even in luxury hotels, the complimentary toiletries are usually very basic, so pack your own. On the other hand, a generous breakfast is almost always included free of charge, the exception being five-star hotels, which charge for breakfast.

Accommodations taxes range from nothing to 15%, varying from city to city and hotel to hotel. Always check in advance.

FAST FACTS: Brazil

Addresses When writing addresses in Brazil, the street number follows the name of the street ("Av. Atlântica 2000" would roughly translate as "2000 Atlantic Ave."). Often in smaller towns a street name will be followed by the abbreviation "s/n." This stands for *sem numero* (without number), and is used when a building sits on a street but has no identifying number. Other words you might come across are: *loja* (shop or unit), *bloco* (building or block), and *sala* (room or suite, often abbreviated "sl."). In mailing addresses, the postal code usually follows the two-letter state abbreviation.

Business Hours Stores are usually open from 9am to 7pm weekdays, 9am to 2pm on Saturdays. Most places close on Sundays. Small stores may close for lunch. Shopping centers are open Monday through Saturday from 10am to 8pm most places, though in Rio de Janeiro and São Paulo they often stay open until 10pm. On Sundays many malls open the food court and movie theaters all day, but mall shops will only open from 2 to 8pm. Banks are open Monday through Friday either from 10am to 4pm or from 9am to 3pm.

Credit Cards If you need to report a lost or stolen credit card or have any questions, you can contact the agencies anywhere in Brazil with the following numbers: American Express (© **0800/785-050**), MasterCard (© **0800/891-3294**), Visa (© **0800/891-3680**), and Diners Club (© **0800/784-444**).

Electricity Brazil's electric current varies from 100 to 240 volts, and from 50 to 60Hz; even within one city there can be variations, and power surges are not uncommon. For laptops or battery chargers, bring an adaptor that can handle the full range of voltage. Most hotels do a good job of labeling their outlets, but when in doubt check before plugging in! Brazilian plugs usually have three prongs: two round and one flat. Adapters for converting North American plugs are cheap (R$3/US$1.50/£.75) and widely available.

Embassies & Consulates All embassies are located in Brasilia, the capital. Australia, Canada, the United States, and Great Britain have consulates in both Rio and São Paulo. New Zealand has a consulate in São Paulo.

In Brasilia: *Australia,* SES, Quadra 801, Conjunto K, lote 7 (© 061/3226-3111). *Canada,* SES Av. das Nações Quadra 803, lote 16 (© 061/3424-5400). *United States,* SES Av. das Nações Quadra 801, lote 03 (© 061/3312-7000). *Great Britain,* SES Av. das Nações Quadra 801, lote 8 (© 061/3329-2300). *New Zealand,* SHIS QI 09, conj. 16, casa 01 (© 061/3248-9900).

In Rio de Janeiro: *Australia,* Av. Presidente Wilson 231, Suite 23, Centro (© 021/3824-4624). *Canada,* Av. Atlântica 1130, 5th floor, Copacabana (© 021/2543-3004). *United States,* Av. Presidente Wilson 147, Centro (© 021/3823-2000). *Great Britain,* Praia do Flamengo 284, Flamengo (© 021/2555-9600).

In São Paulo: *Australia,* Alameda Ministro Rocha Azevedo 456, Jardim Paulista (© 011/3085 6247). *Canada,* Av. das Nações Unidas 12901, 16th floor (© 011/5509-4321). *United States,* Rua Henri Dunant 500, Chácara Santo Antonio (© 011/5186-7000). *Great Britain,* Rua Ferreira de Araujo 741 (© 011/3094-2700). *New Zealand,* Al. Campinas 579, 15th floor, Cerqueira Cesar (© 011/3148-0616).

Emergency Numbers For police dial ℂ **190**; for ambulance or fire department dial ℂ **193**; for fire dial ℂ **193**.

Internet Access Web access is widespread in Brazil; Internet cafes are inexpensive and ubiquitous. Even in the smallest of towns we found at least one Internet cafe. Prices range from US$1 to US$4 per hour; luxury hotels usually charge the most, anywhere up to US$15 per hour.

Language The language of Brazil is Portuguese. If you speak Spanish you will certainly have an easier time picking up words and phrases. In the large cities you will find people in the tourism industry who speak good English, but in smaller towns and resorts English is very limited. If you are picking up language books or tapes, make sure they are Brazilian Portuguese and not Portuguese from Portugal: big difference! A good pocket-size phrase book is *Say It in Portuguese* (Brazilian usage) by Prista, Mickle, and Costa; or try *Conversational Brazilian Portuguese* by Cortina.

Liquor Laws Officially Brazil's drinking laws only allow those over 18 years to drink, but this is rarely enforced. Beer, wine, and liquor can be bought any day of the week from grocery stores and delis. Beer is widely sold through street vendors, bakeries, and refreshment stands.

Mail Mail from Brazil is quick and efficient. Post offices *(correios)* are found everywhere, readily identifiable by the blue-and-yellow sign. A postcard or letter to Europe or North America costs R$1.60 (US80¢/£.43). Parcels can be sent through FedEx or regular mail (express or common; a small parcel—up to 2.5kg/5½ lb.—costs about R$45/US$23/£12 by common mail and takes about a week or two).

Maps Good maps aren't Brazil's strong suit. Your best bet for city maps is the *Guia Quatro Rodas—mapas das capitais;* this pocket book for sale at all newsstands (R$12/US$6/£3) has indexed maps of all state capitals, including São Paulo, Rio, Salvador, Manaus, Brasilia, and Recife. Unfortunately it does not include any highways. The best highway map is sold with the *Guia Quatro Rodas Brasil* (for sale on newsstands for R$35/US$18/£9.30), a Brazilian guidebook.

Newspapers & Magazines There are no English-language newspapers or magazines in Brazil. Foreign papers and magazines are only easily found in Rio and São Paulo. The most popular Brazilian newspapers are *O Globo* and *Jornal do Brasil,* published out of Rio, and *Folha de São Paulo,* the leading business paper published in São Paulo. The most popular current affairs magazine (the equivalent of *Newsweek*) is *Veja,* published weekly. In Rio and São Paulo, *Veja* magazine always includes an entertainment insert that provides a detailed listing of nightlife, restaurants, and events.

Restrooms Restrooms in Brazil can be marked in a few different ways. Usually you will see *mulher* or an M for women and *homem* or an H for men. Sometimes it will read *damas* or D for ladies and *cavalheiros* or C for gentlemen. It's not a bad idea to carry some toilet paper with you as in many public restrooms, the toilet attendant doles out sheets only grudgingly.

Safety Sometime in the 1980s Brazil began developing a world reputation for violence and crime. Some of this was pure sensationalism, but there was a good measure of truth as well. Fortunately in the early '90s things began to turn around. Governments began putting money back into basic services, starting with policing. Though still not perfect by any means, Rio, São Paulo, and Brazil's other big cities have bounced back to the point where they're as safe as most large international cities. Statistically, of course, Rio and other big Brazilian cities still have very high crime rates. Most of that crime, however, takes place in the favelas and shantytowns of the far-off industrial outskirts. Avoid wandering in or near the hillside favelas. At night use taxis instead of public transportation, and stick to well-lit and well-traveled streets. Don't flash jewelry or wads of cash. And beware of pickpockets. Outside of the main cities, Brazil remains quite safe.

Smoking The bad news for nonsmokers is that Brazilians tend to smoke more than in the U.S. and Canada. The good news is that in recent years smoking regulations have begun to be enforced and even Brazilians are starting to cut back. Most public buildings are now nonsmoking, as are all long-distance buses and planes. Though most malls, bars, clubs, and many hotels and restaurants do not have nonsmoking areas, you can always try. Ask for *area para não-fumantes,* the nonsmoking area.

Taxes There are no taxes added to goods purchased in Brazil. Restaurants and hotels normally add a 10% service tax. In Rio, the city also levies a 5% tax on hotels. All airports in Brazil charge departure taxes; this is usually included in the ticket price but it's wise to check. Domestic departures cost around R$21 (US$10/£5) at most airports, and international departures are a hefty R$108 (US$54/£27). Payment can only be made in cash with U.S. dollars or Brazilian currency but *not* in a combination of both.

Time Zones Brazil has three time zones. The coast, including Rio de Janeiro, Salvador, and as far inland as São Paulo and Brasilia, is in one time zone. The ranching states of Mato Grosso and Mato Grosso do Sul, the Pantanal, and the Amazon around Manaus are in the second time zone, 1 hour behind Rio. The third time zone includes the state of Acre and the western part of the Amazon, 2 hours behind Rio. The time difference between cities in Brazil and North America varies by up to 2 hours over the course of the year as clocks spring forward and fall back for daylight saving time. From approximately March to September Rio de Janeiro is in the same time zone as New York City. From October to February, Rio is at least 1 and often 2 hours ahead of New York (for example, noon in New York City is 2pm in Rio).

Telephones International GSM cellphones usually work in Brazil. Charges can be high—usually US$1 to US$1.50 (£.50–£.75)per minute. A better option is to buy a local SIM card, which gives you a local Brazilian number and allows you to pay local Brazilian rates (about R$1/US50¢/£.25 per minute for local calls, R$1.40/US70¢/£.40 for long distance). There is no charge to receive calls if you are in your home area. Outside your area code, roaming charges of about R$1/US50¢/£.25 per minute apply. There are a number of cellphone providers that sell SIM chips in Brazil, but the only one that provides service throughout the country is TIM (www.tim.com.br). There are TIM kiosks in all major malls and airports and department stores. Note that after you buy a TIM SIM chip, you will have to call and register your account (as part of its anti-crime laws Brazil does not allow anonymous cellphone accounts). You will need to give your name and passport number. Cards that allow you to add credit to your account are available at newsstands throughout Brazil. Public phones in Brazil can be found everywhere and are called *orelhões*. To use these phones you need a phone card, for sale at all newsstands. Ask for a *cartão telefonico*. Dialing a local number is straightforward; just dial the number without the area code. However, for long-distance dialing, telephone numbers are normally listed with a three-digit prefix, followed by the area code, followed by the seven- or eight-digit number (for example, 0XX-21-5555-5555). Since phones were deregulated, a number of very competitive companies have sprung up. The two digits that fill in the XX are the number of the appropriate service provider (in Portuguese this is called the *prestadora*). Any phone can be used to access any service provider. In some cities there may be a choice of two or three providers. The only code that works in all of Brazil (and the only *prestadora* code you need to remember) is the one for *Embratel*—21 (which also happens to be the area code of Rio). So, if you were dialing long distance to a number in Rio, you would dial 0-21 (selecting Embratel as your provider), 21 (Rio's area code), and 5555-5555 (the number). Dialing long distance to a number in São Paulo, you'd dial 0-21-11-5555-5555.

To phone internationally, you dial 00 + 21 + the country code + area code + phone number. International collect calls can be requested by dialing **000-111,** or automatically by dialing 90 + 21 + country code + area code + phone number. Major long distance company access codes are as follows: AT&T ✆ 0800/890-0288; MCI ✆ 0800/890-0012; Sprint ✆ 0800/888-8000; and Canada Direct ✆ 0800/890-0014.

To dial from the U.S. or Canada to Brazil, dial 011 + 55 (the country code) and then the area code without the 0 (for example, 21 for Rio, 11 for São Paulo).

Tipping A 10% service charge is automatically included on most restaurant and hotel bills and you are not expected to tip on top of this amount. If service has been particularly bad you can request to have the 10% removed from your bill. Taxi drivers do not get tipped; just round up the amount to facilitate change. Hairdressers and beauticians usually receive a 10% tip. Bellboys get tipped R$1 to R$2 (US50¢–US$1/£.25–£.50) per bag. Room service usually includes the 10% service charge on the bill.

Water The tap water in Brazil is increasingly safe to drink. However, as a result of the treatment process it still doesn't taste great. To be on the safe side, drink bottled or filtered water (most Brazilians do). All brands are reliable; ask for *agua sem gas* for still water and *agua com gas* for carbonated water. However, you can certainly shower, brush your teeth, or rinse an apple with tap water.

3

Suggested Brazil Itineraries

A vast, beautiful, sprawling country, Brazil covers nearly as much land area as the United States, and has regions as geographically different from each other as Arizona is from Vermont, and as culturally diverse as Boston and Salt Lake City. Getting even a taste of such an ocean of experiences requires time and air travel. Most of the itineraries below cover just over 2 weeks. If you have more time, by all means add destinations from other routes, or better yet, slow down and take things easy. It is a vacation, after all.

Obviously, possibilities are endless. Itineraries below try to combine what is best in Brazil—its people and culture and music, its history, and its natural wonders, be they beaches, islands, or vast tropical forest.

1 Brazil in 1 Week

You've got a week, and you want to see Brazil? Your first step should be to talk your boss into giving you another week, preferably two. Failing that, the route below gives a quick taste of three of Brazil's highlights: Rio de Janeiro, the historic city of Salvador, and the natural wonder of Iguaçu Falls. It'll be a busy week, though. Those who like a more laid-back pace should skip either Salvador or Iguaçu.

Days ❶–❸: Rio de Janeiro ✮✮✮
To get into the Brazilian spirit, start off your trip in **Rio de Janeiro.** After getting settled in your hotel, head for the beach. Enjoy the scene, tan a bit (but don't overdo it). Watch the sunset from **Arpoador.** You'll be tired from the flight, so take it easy with a good dinner in one of the top restaurants of **Ipanema** or **Leblon.** On day 2 get out and see the mountains. Take a tram up to the **Corcovado,** or take a jeep tour up through **Tijuca Forest.** Stop by Cinelândia in Rio's Centro in the afternoon. That night, discover the late-night Carioca lifestyle. Have dinner around 11pm, then catch some samba, played live in **Lapa.** You'll be sleeping late the next day, so spend some more time at the beach, or

take a trolley up to explore the hillside neighborhood of **Santa Teresa.** All this should acclimatize you to the Brazilian way before you set off to explore the rest of the country.

Days ❹ & ❺: Salvador ✮✮✮
Early on day 4, catch a flight for **Salvador.** This is the city where the country's African roots are strongest. Stay in one of the lovely pousadas in **Pelourinho** like the **Redfish** (p. 241), or pamper yourself with a stay in the restored 17th-century **Convento do Carmo** (p. 240). Wander through Pelourinho's 17th-century streets. In the evening, try some Bahian cuisine, then go out and enjoy the music in Pelourinho after dark. Next day, take the boat tour of the **Bay of All**

Saints, or head out to the church of **Bonfim,** or tour the lovely **Museu de Arte Sacra.** Or if you're the Energizer Bunny, do all three.

Days ❻ & ❼: Iguaçu Falls ✿✿✿

A final must-see—one of the most awe-inspiring natural wonders of the world—**Iguaçu Falls.** The early flight from Salvador should get you to Iguaçu before 2pm. Store your stuff and go see the falls. Today stick to the Brazilian side. Don't forget to take the **Macuco boat safari** (p. 437). Unforgettable.

Your next step the next day depends on flights. There are afternoon flights from Iguaçu that will get you to São Paulo in time to connect with your evening flight back to North America. Theoretically, you could get up early (again) and make the trip to the Argentine side and make it back in time for that 4pm flight. Or you could do the sensible thing and stay another night in Iguaçu. Get up a little later, and go explore the Argentine side at a leisurely pace. That night, have dinner somewhere in downtown Foz do Iguaçu.

Next morning, you can catch an early flight to São Paulo and spend the day exploring, or you can dawdle by the hotel pool in Iguaçu (or go see the **Bird Park,** p. 437), before catching a later flight to São Paulo and connecting to your evening flight home.

2 Brazil in 2 Weeks

In 2 weeks, you can get a good taste of Brazil at a pace that won't leave you with post-holiday stress disorder. The route below takes you to Rio de Janeiro and the historic city of Salvador. You then have the option of spending time in the Amazon or on a beautiful Bahian beach. The Amazon is fascinating, but it requires both money and travel time. This route includes Iguaçu Falls and a brief taste of the urban sophistication that is São Paulo.

Days ❶–❺: Same as Above

Day ❻: Salvador ✿✿✿

With your extra day in Salvador, dig deeper into this city's treasures at a leisurely pace; head out to the church of **Bonfim,** or tour the lovely **Museu de Arte Sacra.** See the lighthouse and beaches of **Barra.**

Days ❼–⓫: The Amazon ✿✿✿

Catch an early flight to **Manaus.** It's time to experience a bit of the largest standing rainforest on earth, the Amazon. On your first day you should have time to see the highlights of Manaus, including the famous **Opera House.** The next morning, set off early for a jungle lodge (or better yet, if you have more time, go kayaking through the forest with **Amazon Mystery Tours,** p. 395). Choose a smaller lodge farther from the city. Don't go to the Ariaú. Although the area around Manaus is hardly unexplored, a few days will allow you to experience the fauna and flora of a tropical rainforest. Enjoy the trees, the monkeys, the caiman, and the bright pink dolphins.

Day ⓬: Transit

It's going to take a day of taxis, boats, and airplanes to get you to your next destination, Iguaçu.

Days ⓭ & ⓮: Iguaçu Falls ✿✿✿

A final must-see—one of the most awe-inspiring natural wonders of the world—**Iguaçu Falls.** The early flight from Salvador should get you to Iguaçu before 2pm. Store your stuff and go see the falls. Stick to the Brazilian side today. Don't forget to take the **Macuco boat safari**

(p. 437). Unforgettable. The next day, go explore the falls from the Argentine side. You can catch an early flight to São Paulo and spend the next day exploring, or you can dawdle by the hotel pool in Iguaçu (or go see the **Bird Park,** p. 437), before catching later flight to São Paulo and connecting to your evening flight home.

3 Brazil for Families

Brazilians love children nearly as much as they love beaches, beer, and music. Maybe more. This route combines Brazil's top destinations in ways that will allow both you and your kids to have fun.

Days ❶ & ❷: Rio de Janeiro 🎿🎿🎿

To get into the Brazilian spirit, start off your trip in **Rio de Janeiro.** See the must-sees such as the **Corcovado, Sugar Loaf,** and **Copacabana beach,** while discovering the typically Brazilian *joie de vivre* and the late-night Carioca lifestyle—spend an afternoon at the beach, watch the sunset at **Arpoador,** drink beers in an old-fashioned bar in the hillside neighborhood of **Santa Teresa,** dance to samba in **Lapa,** start dinner after midnight. More than seeing the sights, it will acclimatize you to the Brazilian way before you set off to explore the rest of the country.

Days ❸–❻: Olinda and Porto de Galinhas 🎿🎿🎿

From Rio, it's only a short flight to Recife and Olinda. As historic as **Salvador,** Olinda is more lived in, full of artists, among them the famous puppet makers who show works in the **Puppet Museum** (p. 311). Spend a day here, then head south to the beachside village of Porto de Galinhas. Snorkel the shallow reef pools full of fish. Look for sea horses in the tidal mangroves.

Days ❼–⓫: Amazon 🎿🎿🎿

Catch an early flight to Manaus. It's time to experience a bit of the largest standing rainforest on earth, the Amazon. On your first day you should have time to see the highlights of Manaus, including the famous Manaus Opera House. Set off early the next morning for a jungle lodge. Choose a smaller lodge farther from the city. Don't go to the Ariaú. Although the area around Manaus is hardly unexplored, a few days will allow you to experience the fauna and flora of a tropical rainforest. Enjoy the trees, the monkeys, the caiman, and the bright pink dolphins.

Days ⓬–⓯: Belém and the Island of Marajó 🎿🎿

From Manaus, fly to Belém, and hop on a ferry for the big river island of **Marajó.** Spend a few days on a buffalo ranch—we recommend the Fazenda Sanjo—with a Marajó family, riding horses, herding buffalo, and seeing caiman and flocks of bright red roseate spoonbills (p. 410).

Days ⓰ & ⓱: Iguaçu Falls 🎿🎿🎿

A final must-see on a first-time visit—one of the most awe-inspiring natural wonders of the world—is **Iguaçu Falls.** You can easily spend 2 days exploring the falls from various angles and in various ways: on foot, by boat, by train, and by helicopter.

4 Brazil for Nature Lovers

Buildings, history, beautiful bodies—none of that interests the nature lover. What they want to see are trees, birds, butterflies, and animals lurking and playing in their native habitats.

Days ❶ & ❷: Rio de Janeiro ✦✦✦

Yes, it's a city of 12 million. But it's one of those rare cities with an intimate relationship with nature. Instead of the busy beach neighborhoods, stay in one of the small B&Bs in hilltop **Santa Teresa.** Take a guided hike through the **Tijuca** rainforest with **Rio Hiking** (p. 182). Take a walk below the Sugarloaf by **Praia Vermelha,** and admire the birdlife and rainforest and with luck, the troupe of marmosets that make their home on the hillside. Go up to the **Corcovado,** look down at Rio, and see how ocean, beach, city, and forest merge into one.

Days ❸–❻: The Pantanal ✦✦✦

Then catch a flight to **Cuiabá** and head down the **Transpantaneira** into the **Pantanal.** This flooded landscape is a birdwatcher's dream, so bring your binoculars and several pencils to keep track of all new species you'll be seeing.

Days ❼–❿: Amazon ✦✦✦

From the Pantanal, fly north to the **Amazon.** The species diversity is greater here, but the very richness of the foliage makes the animals and birds much harder to see. So enjoy the trees. And the monkeys, and dolphins, and parrots. Go out on a kayak trip on the upper Amazon with **Amazon Mystery Tours** (p. 395). Or head for one of the lodges far from **Manaus,** preferably the **Mamiraua Reserve** (p. 392).

Days ⓭–⓰: Fernando de Noronha ✦✦

From Manaus, catch a flight all the way out to **Fernando de Noronha.** A vastly different ecosystem, this semi-desert tropical island is home to large schools of spinner dolphins, not to mention the sea turtles that lay their eggs on the islands' long beaches. If you scuba dive, bring your gear. If you don't, there's still plenty to see above the surface of the water.

Days ⓱ & ⓲: Iguaçu Falls ✦✦✦

Take the long flight all the way south to **Foz do Iguaçu,** one of the natural wonders of the world, Iguaçu Falls. Astonishing enough in themselves, the falls create a misty microclimate perfect for toucans, dusky swifts (which actually nest on the cliff behinds the waterfalls), and bright colorful butterflies. In the rainy season thousands of the colorful insects float and flutter at the edge of the roaring falls.

5 Brazil for the Active Traveler

This is the itinerary for those who want to be out doing—hiking, climbing, swimming, diving. Brazil is rich in outdoor sports, be they on mountain peaks, on the beach, in the ocean or underneath it. This route starts in Rio, then has three different options for hiking—in the mountains near the city, on an island covered in Atlantic rainforest, or farther north in the dry highlands of Bahia. The route then includes time in Fernando de Noronha and the Lençóis Maranhenses, two magical landscapes found nowhere outside Brazil.

Days ❶ & ❷: Rio de Janeiro ✦✦✦

Arrive in **Rio de Janeiro.** Spend a half-day rock climbing up the **Sugarloaf,** or else hike the **Floresta de Tijuca,** a vast rainforest that wraps itself around the city. Or rent a board and catch the surf bus out to **Barra** for the city's best waves.

Days ❸–❻: Teresopolis to Petrópolis ✦

The 2-to-3-day hike between the royal cities of **Teresopolis** and **Petrópolis** takes in the high mountain terrain (approximately 1,500m/4,900 ft.) in Serra dos Órgãos mountains close to Rio de

Janeiro. Hiking specialists **Rio Hiking** can arrange transfer to and from the city, and make your trek more comfortable.

OR

Days ❸–❻: Chapada Diamantina ⭑⭑

Fly to **Salvador** and get a bus or plane up to the **Chapada Diamantina.** This magic highland area is full of bluffs and buttes and waterfalls, and laced with stunning crystal caverns. Do day hikes from the city of **Lençóis,** or contract a guide to take you on a multiday trek past the Falls of Smoke (Cachoeira de Fumaça).

Day ❼: Transit Day

Whether you start from Rio, Ilhabela, or the Chapada Diamantina, it's going to take you most of a day to get to the island of Fernando de Noronha.

Days ❽–⓫: Fernando de Noronha ⭑⭑

Grab your scuba gear and go diving. This isolated archipelago has the best underwater sea life in Brazil. **Atlantis Divers** (p. 469) is the company to go with. Don't forget to rent a buggy and explore the island. While you're there, try to see the baby sea turtles hatch.

Days ⓬–⓯: Lençóis Maranhenses ⭑⭑

From Fernando, fly to **São Luis** and catch a plane or bus for **Barreirinhas,** gateway to the **Lençóis Maranhenses.** An ecosystem unlike anything else on earth, the Lençóis is a vast desert of shifting white-sand dunes, chock-full of rainwater. In the wet season the rainwater collects to form countless crystal pools and lakes in the depressions between dunes. Best of all, the sand is so fine-grained that it's cool on your feet, even in the height of summer.

6 Brazil for Architecture & History Buffs

This is for those who like to stroll and observe and learn, understanding a country's culture by researching its history, and by close observation of that most enduring of the visual arts, architecture. The route takes in both of Brazil's former capitals (Rio de Janeiro and Salvador), the rich baroque cities of Minas Gerais, and the modern new city of Brasilia.

Days ❶–❸: Rio de Janeiro ⭑⭑⭑

Start in **Rio de Janeiro.** Brazil's former capital is rich in history. Tour the **Museu Histórico Nacional** and the **Quinta da Boa Vista** where the Emperor Pedro II lived in baroque splendor, collecting scientific specimens all the while. Wander the **Paço Imperial** where the emperor once ruled, and the nearby **Praça XV** where rebellious army officers brought his reign to an end. Don't forget to have a look at the **Palácio Gustavo Capenema** in Rio's downtown. Designed by LeCorbusier and Oscar Niemeyer, this building

is where the Brazilian love affair with modernism began, where the seeds of what became Brasilia were laid.

Days ❹–❼: Historic Cities of Minas Gerais ⭑⭑⭑

Rent a car (or hop on a bus) and take a road trip through the **historic cities of Minas Gerais, Ouro Prêto, Mariana,** and **Tiradentes.** These cities were awash in gold when the colonial baroque was at its height. Admire the churches and fine buildings, and the phenomenal sculpture works of crippled sculptor **Aleijadinho.**

Days ❽–❿: Salvador ✸✸✸

Back in Rio, catch a flight to **Salvador.** Stay in one of the lovely pousadas in **Pelourinho** like the **Redfish.** Wander through the 17th-century streets of Pelourinho, and marvel at the wealth brought by sugar. Tour the **Museu de Arte Sacra** to see the fine artwork wrought from Brazilian silver.

Days ⓫–⓭: Recife and Olinda ✸✸

From Salvador fly north to **Recife,** a city founded not by the Portuguese but by the Dutch, who conquered northern Brazil for a time. For more on this period, tour the city's fine **history museum,** housed in the **Fort of Five Points.** To compare Dutch and Portuguese styles of city-building, travel but a few miles north to **Olinda,** the former capital of the region, and a city built by the Portuguese. Olinda rivals Salvador for the quality of its churches and historic buildings.

Days ⓮ & ⓯: Brasilia ✸✸

Leave the 17th century behind and make a bold leap into the modern world. Fly to **Brasilia.** Admire the fluid and futuristic architecture of **Oscar Niemeyer.** Judge for yourself whether the world's first fully planned national capital has succeeded or failed in making Brazil the country of the future.

Day ⓰: São Paulo ✸

From Brasilia, fly to **São Paulo.** See Niemeyer's later (and to my mind, inferior) works such as the **Monument to Latin America.** Then see what Brazilian architects are doing now. Walk the Avenida Paulista. If you can afford it, stay at the Hotel Unique. If you can't, have a drink on its rooftop bar. Admire the run of skyscrapers on the Avenida Paulista in the distance.

7 Brazil Beaches, Beaches & Beaches

This is the trip for those who think white grains of silicon assembled together by the seaside is the sole and perfect definition of paradise. Brazil is especially blessed with beaches: urban beaches, party beaches, surfing beaches, and wild, desolate, and lonely beaches. This tour takes a short splash on all of them.

Days ❶–❸: Rio de Janeiro ✸✸✸

Start in **Rio de Janeiro,** and spend a couple or a few days experiencing the beach culture of the cidade maravilhosa. There are dozens of kilometers of beach, all of them within the city limits. Key beaches to explore include **Copacabana, Ipanema, Leblon, São Conrado, Barra,** and the **Grumari.**

Days ❹ & ❺: Salvador ✸✸✸

From Rio, take the plane to **Salvador.** Enjoy the colonial architecture and the music scene for a day, but don't forget to test out the music and dining on Salvador's best urban beach, **Stella Maris.**

Days ❻–❿: Morro de Sao Paulo and Boipeba

From the Bahian capital take the catamaran south 2 hours and party for a day or two in **Morro de São Paulo.** In this little beach resort even the streets are made of sand. Then take a short boat trip one island south to relax for a day or two on **Boipeba,** one of the most relaxed and isolated beaches on the Bahian coastline.

Days ⓫–⓰: Natal to Fortaleza by Dune Buggy

From Boipeba, take the boat back to Morro and catch a plane back to Salvador airport in time to make a connecting flight to **Natal,** a city surrounded by sand. Rent a dune buggy and explore the sand, sea, and massive sand dunes that stretch from the city's edge hundreds of kilometers north. Better yet, make a **4-day journey by beach buggy** with **Buggy & Cia** to **Fortaleza** (p. 335).

OR

Days ⑪–⑯: São Luis and Lençóis Maranhenses

Either way, your next leg should be by plane to **São Luis.** It's worth spending a day wandering this historic city, before catching a plane or bus for the town of **Barreirinhas,** gateway to the **Lençóis Maranhenses.** The Lençóis are not so much beach as a vast Sahara-like desert of perfect white-sand dunes, laced with countless rainwater lakes. You can hike the dunes, swim in the lagoons, and visit the wild, untouched coast nearby.

Days ⑰–⑳: Florianópolis

Returning to São Luis, catch a long flight down to **Santa Catarina,** and spend some days on the southern, surf-crazy island of **Florianópolis.** Rent a car and drive to the southern tip of the island and feast on fresh oysters.

Settling into Rio de Janeiro

Say "Rio" and mental images explode: the glittering skimpy costumes of Carnaval; the statue of Christ, arms outspread on the mountaintop; the beach at Ipanema or Copacabana, crowded with women in minuscule bikinis; the rocky height of the Sugarloaf; or the persistent rhythm of the samba.

Fortunately in Rio there's much more beyond and behind the glitter: historic neighborhoods, compelling architecture, wildlife and nature, dining (fine and not so fine), nightspots, bookshops, cafes, museums, and enclaves of rich and poor. In Rio, the more you explore, the more there is.

Stunning as the physical setting is— mountains tumbling down to sandy beaches, then the sea—Rio was not always the *cidade maravilhosa* (marvelous city) it would become. The town grew up as a shipping center for gold and supplies during Brazil's 18th-century gold rush. In recognition of the city's growing commercial importance, the capital was transferred from Salvador to Rio in 1762, though the city remained a dusty colonial backwater.

In 1808, Portuguese Prince Regent Dom João (later King João VI) fled Lisbon ahead of Napoleon's armies and moved his court and the capital to Rio. Accustomed to the style of European capitals, the prince and the 12,000 nobles who accompanied him began to transform Rio into a city of ornate palaces and landscaped parks. High culture in this new imperial city arrived in the form of a new library, an academy of arts and sciences, and the many glittering balls held by the imported elite. King João's son, Pedro, liked Rio so much that when the king returned to Lisbon, Pedro stayed on and declared Brazil independent.

Now the capital of a country larger and richer than many in Europe, Rio grew at a phenomenal pace; by the late 1800s it was one of the largest cities in the world. Many of the newcomers came from Europe, but a sizable portion were Brazilians of African descent who brought with them the musical traditions of Africa and the Brazilian Northeast.

A new "low culture" of distinctly Brazilian music began to develop in the city's poorer neighborhoods. The high point of the year for both high and low cultures was the celebration of Carnaval. In palace ballrooms the elite held elaborate costume balls. In the streets, poorer residents would stage their own all-night parades. Not until the 1920s did the two celebrations begin to merge. It became, if not respectable, at least possible for elite and middle-class Brazilians to be seen at on-street Carnaval parades. Low culture likewise influenced composer Heitor Villa-Lobos, who incorporated Brazilian rhythms and sounds into his classical compositions. Gowns and costumes at the elite balls got more elaborate, not to mention more risqué. At about the same time, the first road was punched through to Copacabana, and Cariocas (as Rio residents are called) flocked to the new community by the beach.

All of these elements came together in the 1930s with the opening of The Copacabana Palace hotel—a luxury hotel on Copacabana beach with a nightclub that featured exclusively Brazilian music. The 1933 Fred Astaire–Ginger Rogers musical *Flying Down to Rio* portrayed Rio as a city of beach, song, and beautiful, passionate people. The image held enough truth that the iconography has stuck through the end of the 20th century and beyond.

In the years following World War II, São Paulo took over as Brazil's industrial leader; the federal capital was moved inland to Brasília in the early 1960s. By the 1980s, violence and crime plagued the country, and Rio was perceived as the sort of place where walking down the street was openly asking for a mugging. For a time Cariocas feared for the future of their city—needlessly, it turned out. In the early 1990s, governments began pouring money back into basic services; cops were stationed on city streets, on public beaches, and anywhere else there seemed to be a problem. Public and private owners began renovating the many heritage buildings of the city's colonial core. Rio's youth rediscovered samba, returning to renovated clubs in the old bohemian enclave of Lapa. Now a city of some seven million and growing, Rio remains the country's media capital, an important business center, and Brazil's key tourist destination.

1 Rio de Janeiro Essentials

ARRIVING

BY PLANE

Most major airlines fly to Rio de Janeiro, sometimes with a stop or connection in São Paulo.

Rio de Janeiro's **Antônio Carlos Jobim Airport** (✆ **021/3398-4527**), more commonly known as **Galeão Airport,** is 20km (12 miles) from downtown. The second terminal, Terminal 2, is used by Varig and its Star Alliance partners. All other airlines use Terminal 1, which is connected to Terminal 2 by a walkway.

On the third floor of Terminal 1 is a Banco do Brasil office (open daily 8am–10pm), as well as ATMs of HSBC and Banco 24 Horas, both of which use the Visa/PLUS system. The American Express office (open daily 6:30am–10pm) is located in the arrivals hall of Terminal 2.

Taxis at Galeão are a challenge. Drivers will start to hassle you the minute you step through the sliding doors. The safe bet is to buy a prepaid fare at the **Transcoopass** desk in the arrivals hall (✆ **021/2560-4888;** all major credit cards accepted). Rates range from R$58 (US$29/£16) to Flamengo, and R$60 to R$70 (US$30–US$35/£16–£19) to the beach hotels of Copacabana and Ipanema. Prepaid taxis are about 40% more expensive, but give you peace of mind; it doesn't matter if you get stuck in traffic or the driver takes the long route. On the other hand, if you know what you're doing (or can bluff), you can cut those prices significantly just by hailing a regular taxi out in front of the terminal. A ride to Copacabana should cost about R$40 (US$20/£11) in average traffic conditions. Note that if you don't know what you're doing, your friendly Rio taxi man may well take you on a detour long enough to double that price, or even claim the meter reads in dollars.

Realtur/Reitur Turismo (✆ **0800/240-850**) runs an airport bus service to the tourist areas along the beaches of Flamengo, Botafogo, Copacabana, Ipanema, Leblon, and Barra da Tijuca. From 5:30am to 11pm a bus departs every 30 minutes and takes approximately 1 hour to make the full trip from the airport to Barra. R$6 (US$3/£1.60) per person. Note that it only stops on the beach avenue. Check with your hotel to see if it's within walking distance of the bus stop.

SANTOS DUMONT AIRPORT   Rio's second airport, **Santos Dumont,** Praça Senador Salgado Filho (© 021/3814-7070), is located downtown. Surrounded by the Baia de Guanabara and a hop and a skip from the Sugarloaf, this scenic airport is used by **TAM, Gol,** and **Varig** for the Rio–São Paulo shuttles. The Realtur bus stops at Santos Dumont on its way to and from the international airport. The bus trip from Santos Dumont to Copacabana takes about 20 minutes. Taxis are available in front of the airport; a ride to Ipanema costs about R$30 (US$15/£8). Prepaid vouchers can also be purchased at the taxi counter in the arrivals hall. A variety of bank machines, including a Banco do Brasil and HSBC ATM, are located at the center entrance of the airport.

BY BUS

All long-distance buses arrive at the **Novo Rio Rodoviaria,** Av. Francisco Bicalho 1, Santo Cristo (© 021/3213-1800; www.novorio.com.br), located close to downtown in the old port section of the city. Going to or from the bus station it's best to use a taxi. It's not a great area to walk around with all of your belongings. Prepaid taxi vouchers are available at the booth next to the taxi stand. A ride from the bus station to Ipanema will cost about R$35 (US$18/£9.50) prepaid.

BY CRUISE SHIP

Cruise ships dock in the terminal almost opposite Praça Mauá. Downtown is an easy walk, and public transit is close by. If returning to the ship after dark, it's best to take a taxi. Praça Mauá becomes a somewhat seedy red-light district in the evening.

VISITOR INFORMATION

Riotur (© 021/2217-7575; www.riodejaneiro-turismo.com.br) provides excellent information on the city of Rio de Janeiro and operates a number of offices and kiosks around town. At **Rio's international airport** (© 021/3398-4077), booths in the international arrivals halls of both Terminal 1 and Terminal 2 (© 021/3398-2245 for both) are open daily from 6am to midnight. A third booth in the domestic arrivals hall is open from 6am to 6pm. At Rio's main bus station, **Rodoviaria Novo Rio,** there's a counter in the arrivals area, open 8am to 8pm (© 021/2263-4857). The main **Riotur Information Center** (© 021/2541-7522) is on Av. Princesa Isabel 183, Copacabana. Open Monday to Friday 9am to 6pm, this office has the largest selection of brochures and information. Riotur also operates an information line, **Alô Rio** (© 021/2542-8080), with English-speaking staff, Monday to Friday from 9am to 6pm.

A must-have is Riotur's *Guia do Rio–Rio Guide* booklet, published every 3 months. Written in both English and Portuguese, it lists all tourist attractions, events, and festivals, and has many other useful phone numbers. Riotur also publishes a number of brochures specifically on outdoor sports, museums, and Carnaval. The office in Copacabana is most likely to stock all these publications.

The Rio de Janeiro state tourism agency **TurisRio** (© 021/2215-0011; www.turisrio.rj.gov.br) offers information on destinations outside the city. Their office, on Rua da Ajuda 5, 6th floor, Centro, is open Monday to Friday from 9am to 6pm.

Rio de Janeiro at a Glance

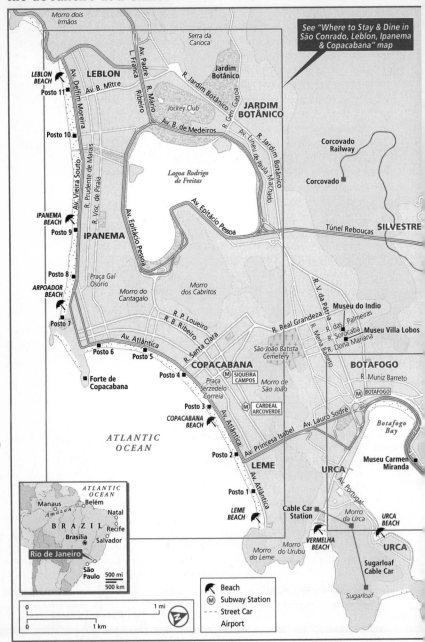

See "Where to Stay & Dine in São Conrado, Leblon, Ipanema & Copacabana" map

Morro dois Irmãos

Serra da Carioca

LEBLON

Jardim Botânico

JARDIM BOTÂNICO

LEBLON BEACH
Posto 11

Av. Delfim Moreira

Av. B. Mitre

Av. Padre L. França

R. Mário Ribeiro

R. Jardim Botânico

R. Gen. Garzon

Jockey Club

Av. B. de Medeiros

Posto 10

Av. Vieira Souto

R. Prudente de Marais

R. Visc. de Piraja

Lagoa Rodrigo de Freitas

Av. Lineu de Paula Machado

R. Jardim Botânico

Corcovado Railway

Corcovado

IPANEMA BEACH
Posto 9

IPANEMA

Av. Epitácio Pessoa

Av. Epitácio Pessoa

Túnel Rebouças

SILVESTRE

Posto 8

Praça Gal Osório

Morro do Cantagalo

Morro dos Cabritos

R. V. da Patria

Museu do Indio

ARPOADOR BEACH

R. P. Loueiro

R. B. Ribeiro

R. Real Grandeza

R. das Palmeiras

R. Sorocaba

Museu Villa Lobos

Posto 7

Av. Atlântica

R. Santa Clara

R. Mena Barreto

R. Dona Mariana

Posto 6

Posto 5

São João Batista Cemetery

BOTAFOGO

COPACABANA

Posto 4

SIQUEIRA CAMPOS

Morro de São João

R. Muniz Barreto

Forte de Copacabana

Praça Serzedelo Correia

CARDEAL ARCOVERDE

BOTAFOGO

ATLANTIC OCEAN

Posto 3

COPACABANA BEACH

Av. Atlântica

Av. Lauro Sodré

Botafogo Bay

Posto 2

Av. Princesa Isabel

LEME

URCA

Museu Carmen Miranda

Posto 1

Av. Atlântica

Cable Car Station

Morro da Urca

URCA BEACH

LEME BEACH

VERMELHA BEACH

URCA

Morro do Leme

Morro do Urubu

Av. Portugal

Sugarloaf Cable Car

Sugarloaf

Brazil inset map

ATLANTIC OCEAN

Manaus   Belém

Amazon

Natal

BRAZIL

Recife

Brasília

Salvador

Rio de Janeiro

São Paulo

500 mi

500 km

Beach
(M) Subway Station
- - - Street Car
Airport

0 — 1 mi
0 — 1 km

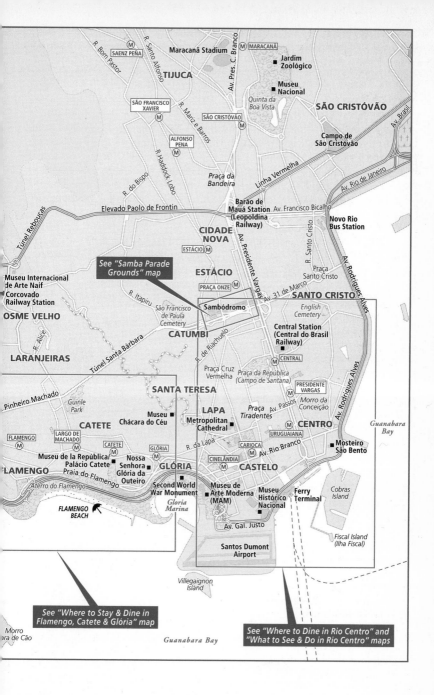

SAENZ PEÑA Ⓜ

R. Bom Pastor
R. Santo Afonso

Maracanã Stadium

Ⓜ MARACANÃ

Jardim
Zoológico

Museu
Nacional

Av. Pres. C. Branco

TIJUCA

R. do Bispo

SÃO FRANCISCO
XAVIER Ⓜ

R. Mariz e Barros

SÃO CRISTÓVÃO Ⓜ

ALFONSO
PENA Ⓜ

Quinta da
Boa Vista

SÃO CRISTÓVÃO

Campo de
São Cristóvão

Av. Brasil

Linha Vermelha

R. Haddock Lobo

Praça da
Bandeira

Av. Rio de Janeiro

Elevado Paolo de Frontin

Barão de
Maúa Station
(Leopoldina
Railway)

Av. Francisco Bicalho

Novo Rio
Bus Station

Túnel Rebouças

CIDADE
NOVA

ESTÁCIO Ⓜ

Av. Presidente Vargas

R. Santo Cristo

See "Samba Parade
Grounds" map

Museu Internacional
de Arte Naïf
Corcovado
Railway Station

R. Itapiru

ESTÁCIO

PRAÇA ONZE Ⓜ

Av. 31 de Março

Praça
Santo Cristo

SANTO CRISTO

OSME VELHO

São Francisco
de Paula
Cemetery

Sambódromo

English
Cemetery

Av. Rodrigues Alves

R. Alice

CATUMBI

R. de Riachuelo

Central Station
(Central do Brasil
Railway)

LARANJEIRAS

Túnel Santa Barbara

R. Santa Barbara

Praça Cruz
Vermelha

Praça da República
(Campo de Santana)

Ⓜ CENTRAL

PRESIDENTE
VARGAS

Pinheiro Machado

Guinle
Park

SANTA TERESA

Praça
Tiradentes

Av. Passos

Morro da
Conceição

Guanabara
Bay

CATETE

Museu
Chácara do Céu

LAPA

Metropolitan
Cathedral

R. da Lapa

Av. Rio Branco

CENTRO

Mosteiro
São Bento

FLAMENGO Ⓜ

LARGO DE
MACHADO Ⓜ

CATETE Ⓜ

GLÓRIA Ⓜ

URUGUAIANA Ⓜ

CARIOCA Ⓜ

Museu de la República/
Palácio Catete

FLAMENGO

Nossa
Senhora
Glória da
Outeiro

Praia do Flamengo

GLÓRIA

CINELÂNDIA Ⓜ

CASTELO

Aterro do Flamengo

Second World
War Monument

Museu de
Arte Moderna
(MAM)

Museu
Histórico
Nacional

Ferry
Terminal

Cobras
Island

FLAMENGO
BEACH

Gloria
Marina

Av. Gal. Justo

Fiscal Island
(Ilha Fiscal)

Santos Dumont
Airport

Morro
ara de Cão

See "Where to Stay & Dine in
Flamengo, Catete & Glória" map

Villegaignon
Island

Guanabara Bay

See "Where to Dine in Rio Centro" and
"What to See & Do in Rio Centro" maps

RIO'S NEIGHBORHOODS IN BRIEF

Geography has played a huge part in Rio's development; the city has squeezed into any available space between mountain and ocean. Rio is traditionally divided into four zones: North (Zona Norte), Center (Centro), West (Zona Oeste) and South (Zona Sul). A much more detailed description of Rio's neighborhoods can be found in "Neighborhoods to Explore" in chapter 5.

ZONA NORTE   Large and least interesting from a visitor's perspective, the **Zona Norte** stretches from a few blocks north of Avenida Presidente Vargas all the way to the city limits. With only a few bright exceptions—the **Maracanã** stadium, the **Quinta da Boa Vista** gardens, and **Galeão Airport**—the region is a dull swath of port, residential high-rise, industrial suburb, and favela. It's not the sort of place one should wander unaccompanied.

ZONA OESTE   The Zona Oeste houses some of the poorest and some of the richest neighborhoods of the city. On one side there's Cidade de Deus—featured in the movie *City of God*—a huge low-income housing project built in the 1960s to relocate people from downtown slums out to what was then the far edge of the city. Nowadays, those with money are voluntarily relocating to the seaside condominium enclaves in **Barra da Tijuca** and **Recreio.** Most visitors will only ever visit the restaurants and malls in Barra or drive through Recreio to reach **Grumari,** a pristine beach on the city's outskirts.

CENTRO   Rio's **Centro** neighborhood, the oldest part of the city, is where you'll find most of the city's notable churches, squares, monuments, and museums, as well as the modern office towers where Rio's white-collar elite earn their daily bread. Roughly speaking, Centro stretches from the **São Bento Monastery** in the north to the seaside **Monument to the Dead of World War II** in the south, and from **Praça XV** on the waterfront east to the **Sambódromo** (near Praça XI). On weekends, particularly Sundays, this area becomes very deserted, and a little too spooky to warrant a visit.

ZONA SUL–THE BAY   Just to the south of Centro lies the fun and slightly bohemian hilltop neighborhood of **Santa Teresa,** and then one after the other the neighborhoods of **Glória, Catete,** and **Flamengo.** These last three were the fashionable sections of the city around the start of the 20th century, located as they were on flat ground by the edge of Guanabara Bay. Other neighborhoods in this section of the city include **Botafogo** and **Urca** (nestled beneath the Sugarloaf), and in the narrow valley behind Flamengo the two residential neighborhoods of **Laranjeiras** and **Cosme Velho.** Today they're all still pleasant and walkable—Botafogo was more commercial, but has been undergoing a residential boom over the past few years; Catete and Flamengo contain a number of historic buildings—but their bloom faded in the 1920s when engineers cut a tunnel through the mountainside to Copacabana.

ZONA SUL–THE BEACHES   Then, as now, the big attraction was the ocean. Where Centro and Flamengo sit on Guanabara Bay, **Copacabana, Ipanema, São Conrado,** and **Barra de Tijuca** face the open Atlantic. The waves are bigger, the water cleaner, and the beaches more inviting. First to be developed, **Copacabana** officially covers only the lower two-thirds of the beach. The northern third (the bit closest to Urca, farthest from Ipanema) is known as **Leme.** That said, it's impossible to tell where Leme ends and Copa begins. Taking a 90-degree turn around a low headland, one comes to **Ipanema.** Like Copacabana, Ipanema is a modern neighborhood, consisting almost exclusively of high-rise apartments from the '60s and '70s. Here, too, the same stretch of beach is considered to be two neighborhoods:

Ipanema sits next to Copacabana, while the area at the far end of the beach is known as **Leblon.** Again, the two ends of the beach are nearly indistinguishable, though Leblon has a few more restaurants. Behind Ipanema there's a lagoon, the **Lagoa Rodrigo de Freitas,** which is circled by a pleasant 8.5km (5.25-mile) walking/cycling trail. At its north end, farthest from the beach, stand the two quiet residential neighborhoods of **Lagoa** and **Jardim Botânico,** the latter named for the extensive botanical gardens around which the area grew.

At the far end of Ipanema stands a tall sheer double-pointed rock called the **Pedra Dois Irmãos (Two Brothers Rock).** The road carries on, winding around the cliff face to reach the tiny enclave of **São Conrado.** One of the better surfing beaches, this is also where the hang gliders like to land after swooping down from the 830m (2,700-ft.) **Pedra de Gâvea.**

At night, the wide beaches are dark and mostly deserted; if you're in the mood for a moonlit stroll, stick to the brightly lit and police-patrolled pedestrian walkway that parallels the beach.

BEYOND THE BEACHES   Beyond São Conrado the road goes up on stilts to sneak beneath the cliffs until reaching **Barra da Tijuca.** More like Miami Beach than Rio, Barra—as it's usually called—is a land of big streets, big malls, big cars, and big condominium towers (see "Zona Oeste," above).

GETTING AROUND
BY PUBLIC TRANSPORTATION

Rio may seem like a large and sprawling city, but the neighborhoods in which visitors spend most of their time are very easy to get around in. From Centro south to São Conrado, the neighborhoods hang like beads on a string on the narrow strip of land between the ocean and the mountains. Most neighborhoods are thin and narrow; Copacabana in some sections is only 5 blocks deep. You can almost always see the mountains or the ocean, or both; with landmarks like that it's pretty hard to stray too far from where you want to go.

BY SUBWAY   By far the easiest way to get around is by subway; in Centro and the Zona Sul it covers almost every major area of interest. (The exception is Ipanema/Leblon, which isn't slated to get subway service for another 4 or 5 years but now has a bus/subway service.) There are only two lines: Line 1 goes north from downtown—it's useful for going to the Maracanã and the Quinta da Boa Vista—while Line 2 begins at the Central Station and goes south, covering most of Centro, then swinging thorough Glória, Catete, Flamengo, and Botafogo before ducking through the mountain to its final destination in Copacabana. Extremely quick, the trip takes about 20 minutes to move you from Centro to Copacabana (as compared to a 40–60-min. bus ride in rush hour). The system is very safe and efficient. You purchase tickets at the entrance of the stations, either from a machine or from a ticket booth. The subway system is gradually expanding its integrated Metrô/bus service, with new air-conditioned buses feeding into the Metrô system from a number of popular destinations. Some of the more popular routes include: Metrô/Ipanema (to Ipanema; transfer at Siqueira Campos); Metrô/Gavea or Barra (to Leblon and Gavea or Barra; transfer at Siqueira Campos); Metrô/Rodoviaria (to the main bus terminal; transfer at Largo do Machado); Metrô-Paula Matos (to the hillside neighborhood of Santa Teresa; transfer at Cinelândia); Metrô-Urca (to the Sugarloaf; transfer at Botafogo); and Metrô-Cosme Velho (to the Corcovado; transfer at Largo do Machado). The price is the same as a

---

Tips   **Know the Subway Hours**

The subway operates Monday through Saturday from 5am to midnight. On Sundays and statutory holidays the Metrô runs from 7am to 11pm. Special schedules apply during New Year's and Carnaval when trains will run all night.

---

regular Metrô ticket, but you have to request your specific destination at the ticket booth; the *Metrô na superfície* tickets are different from regular subway tickets. After you use the electronic ticket to enter the subway turnstile it's returned so that you can present it on the bus at the transfer station.

A single Metrô or Metrô-na superficie ticket costs R$2.30 (US$1.65/£.60). Multiple tickets are available, but there's no volume discount whatsoever.

BY BUS   Rio's buses follow direct, logical pathways, sticking to the main streets along much the same route you'd take if you were driving. What's more, they're fast. Once inside it's a good idea to wedge yourself in your seat; Rio drivers like to lean into the turns.

Some of the more important routes are listed with hotel or attraction listings, but you'll likely find many more that suit your needs. From Centro to Copacabana alone there are more than 30 different buses. Figuring out which to take is straightforward. The route number and final destination are displayed in big letters on the front of the bus. Smaller signs displayed inside the front window (usually below and to the left of the driver) and posted on the side of the bus list the intermediate stops. Armed with that information and a map, it's fairly straightforward to figure out which route the bus will take and how close you will get to your destination. A bus going from Praça XV in Centro out to Copacabana, for example, would show COPACABANA as the final destination, and on the smaller sign list intermediate destinations such as CINELÂNDIA, GLÓRIA, LARGO DO MACHADO (in Flamengo), and RIO SUL (the big mall in Botafogo). *Tip:* If you're going from Ipanema or Copacabana all the way to Centro (or vice versa), look for a bus that says VIA ATERRO in its smaller window sign. These buses get on the waterfront boulevard in Botafogo and don't stop until they reach downtown.

Buses only stop if someone wants to board. If you see your bus coming, wave your hand at the driver. Most buses are boarded from the front and exited from the rear. Have your bus money ready—R$2 to R$3.50 (US$1–US$1.75/£.55–£.95)—as you will go through a turnstile right away. You pay for each ride; there are no transfers. Buses are safe during the day; just watch for pickpockets when it gets busy. In the evening, when fewer passengers ride, it is better to take a taxi.

BY TAXI

Taxis are plentiful and relatively inexpensive. They're the perfect way to reach those out-of-the-way places and the best way to get around in the evening. Regular taxis can be hailed anywhere on the street. You will also find taxi stands throughout the city. A ride from Copacabana to Praça XV in Centro costs about R$22 (US$11/£6), a ride from the main bus station to Leblon, R$35 (US$18/£9.50) in traffic. Radio taxis are about 20% more expensive, often work with a set fee per destination, and can be contacted by phone; try **Coopertramo** (© **021/2560-2022**) or **Transcoopass** (© **021/ 2560-4888**). Most hotels work with radio taxis so if you don't want to pay extra just walk to the corner and hail your own regular taxi. Radio taxis are said to be more reliable (and they have air-conditioning as well), but we've never had a problem with any regular taxi.

BY VAN

When you see the chaotic bus-ridden streets of Rio de Janeiro, it's hard to believe that there could be a shortage of buses. However, in the last few years the city has seen an explosion of additional bus services provided by Volkswagen vans and micro-buses. Although vans were at first illegal, the city eventually legalized them. Fares range from R$2 to R$4.50 (US$1–US$2.25/£.55–£1.20) and quality ranges from downright scary to clean, modern vehicles. Those that circulate along the Zona Sul waterfront and farther out to Barra da Tijuca are generally quick and efficient. Vans can be hailed anywhere and will let you off anywhere on their route.

BY FERRY

Rio has a number of ferries operated by **Barcas SA** (© **021/2533-7524**), departing from Praça XV downtown. The busiest ferry route is the one connecting downtown Rio with the city of Niterói across the bay—also reached by car and bus by crossing the 14km (8½-mile) bridge. The service to Niterói runs 24 hours a day, with hourly service between midnight and 5am. The cheapest ferry (R$2/US$1/£.55) is the regular one, taking about 25 minutes to cross. The catamaran and *aerobarco,* a hydrofoil, cross the same route in less than 10 minutes and cost R$4 (US$2/£1.05). A popular ferry for tourists as well as Cariocas on the weekend is the route to Paquetá, a large car-free island in the Baia da Guanabara. The ferries to Paquetá depart Rio at 5:15am, 7:10am, 10:30am, 1:30pm, 3:30pm, 4:35pm, and 7pm; the fare is R$4.50 (US$2.25/£1.20).

BY CAR

A car is not required for exploring Rio; a combination of public transit (in the daytime and evening) and taxis (late at night) gets you pretty much anywhere in the city for very little money. But for information about renting a car, see the entry for "Car Rentals" under "Fast Facts: Rio de Janeiro," below.

The truth is, driving in Rio is not for the weak of heart. Traffic is hectic, street patterns confusing, drivers just a few shades shy of courteous, and parking next to nonexistent. Better to get used to the city traffic as a pedestrian first and rent a car only if you're going out to destinations such as Petrópolis and the historic towns of the Minas Gerais region (for more, see chapter 6).

SPECIAL DRIVING RULES   The rule is, *there are no rules.* Okay, maybe we're exaggerating. Traffic has improved immensely in recent years since police began using photo-radars. People now wear seat belts and stop at red lights during the day. However, Cariocas still drive aggressively. Lane dividers are either absent or ignored. Any space larger than 4 inches between your car and the one in front will be instantly occupied by another driver. Later at night red lights become optional. Be careful when approaching intersections.

FAST FACTS: Rio de Janeiro

American Express In The Copacabana Palace Hotel at Av. Atlântica 1702, loja 1, Copacabana (© **021/2548-2148**); open Monday to Friday 9am to 3pm. At the international airport, in the arrivals hall of Terminal 2 (© **0800/7020-777**); open daily from 6:30am to 10:30pm.

Area Code The area code for Rio de Janeiro is **021.**

Banks & Currency Exchange Banco do Brasil has branches at Rua Joana Angelica, Ipanema (© 021/2522-1442), Av. N.S. de Copacabana 594, Copacabana (© 021/2548-8992), and international airport, Terminal 1, third floor (© 021/3398-3652); all have 24-hour ATMs. For currency exchange try Bank Boston, Av. Rio Branco 110, Centro (© 021/2508-2700); Citibank, Rua da Assambleia 100, Centro (© 021/2291-1232); and Imatur, Rua Visconde de Pirajá 281, loja A, Ipanema (© 021/2219-4205).

Business Hours See "Fast Facts: Brazil," in chapter 2.

Camera Repair **Foto Cantarino,** Largo de São Francisco de Paulo 23, 1st floor (© **021/2221-4918;** Metrô: Uruguaiana), is one of the best repair shops in town. It's open Monday to Friday 9am to 4:30pm.

Car Rentals At Antônio Carlos Jobim International Airport there are **Hertz** (© 021/3398-4421), **Interlocadora** (© 021/3398-3181), and **Unidas** (© 021/3398-3452). At Santos Dumont Airport there are **Hertz** (© 021/2262-0612), **Interlocadora** (© 021/2240-0754), and **Unidas** (© 021/2240-6715). In Copacabana there are **Hertz,** Av. Princesa Isabel 500 (© 021/2275-7440), and **Localiza Rent a Car,** Av. Princesa Isabel 150 (© 021/2275-3340). Rates start at R$100 (US$50/£27) per day for a compact car with air-conditioning. Insurance adds R$30 (US$15/£8) per day.

Consulates Australia, Av. Presidente Wilson 231, Suite 23, Centro (© **021/3824-4624**). *Canada,* Av. Atlântica 1130, 5th floor, Copacabana (© **21/2543-3004**). *U.S.,* Av. Presidente Wilson 147, Centro (© **021/3823-2000**). *Great Britain,* Praia do Flamengo 284, 2nd floor, Flamengo (© **021/2555-9600**).

Dentist: **Sorriclin,** Rua Visconde de Pirajá 207/209, Ipanema (© **021/2522-1220**).

Doctor **Medtur,** Av. N.S. de Copacabana 647, Suite 85, Copacabana (© **021/2235-3339**). Ask your hotel for further recommendations, as they may have an arrangement with a doctor nearby.

Electricity 110V. Some hotels have plugs for both 110 and 220 volts.

Emergencies Police © **190;** fire and ambulance © **193;** tourist police, Av. Afrânio de Melo Franco 159, Leblon (contact line © **021/3399-7170**).

Hospitals Public hospital emergency rooms can be found at Miguel Couto, Rua Bartolemeu Mitre 1108, Leblon (© **021/3111-3800**) or at Souza Aguiar, Praça da Republica 111, Centro (© **021/3111-2629**). Private emergency rooms can be found at the Cardio Trauma Ipanema, Rua Farme de Amoedo 86, Ipanema (© **021/2525-1900**) and at the city's best hospital, Copa D'or, Rua Figueiredo de Magalhães 875, Copacabana (© **021/2545-3600**).

Internet Access Internet cafes or Lan Houses can be found everywhere.

Laundry & Dry Cleaning **Lavanderia Ipanema**, Rua Farme de Amoedo 55, Ipanema (© 021/2267-2377), is open Monday to Saturday 8am to 8pm. A medium load, washing and drying, costs R$20 (US$10/£5.40). For an extra R$6 (US$3/£1.60) the attendants wash, fold, and pack your laundry. **Lavakilo**, Rua Almirante Gonçalves 50, loja A, Copacabana (© 021/2521-5089), is open Monday to Friday 7:30am to 7:30pm and Saturday from 8am to 5pm. Charged by the kilo, a 1-kilogram load costs R$8 (US$4/£2.15) for washing and drying. Dry cleaning starts at R$6.50 (US$3.25/£1.75) per item.

Mail Look for the yellow-and-blue sign saying CORREIOS. **Downtown:** Rua Primeira de Março 64, Centro (© 021/2503-8331); **Copacabana:** Av. N.S. de Copacabana 540, Copacabana (© 021/2503-8398); **Ipanema:** Rua Visconde de Pirajá 452, Ipanema (© 021/2563-8568). The international airport also has a post office, open 24 hours.

Maps **Riotur** (Av. Princesa Isabel 183, Copacabana) has helpful small maps of the main tourist areas.

Newspapers Your best bet for international papers is the newsstands along Visconde de Pirajá in Ipanema, and the bookstore Letras e Expressões, Visconde de Pirajá 276, Ipanema (© 021/2521-6110).

Pharmacies In Ipanema, **City Farma**, Rua Gomes Carneiro 144 A (© 021/2247-3000 or 021/2523-2020), is open 24 hours. They also deliver. All credit cards accepted. Also open 24 hours is **Drogaria Pacheco**, Av. N.S. de Copacabana 115, Copacabana (© 021/2295-7555).

Safety Though Rio once had an unsavory reputation for street violence, in the early 1990s governments began to pour money back into policing and there have since been significant improvements. That said, there are still several things to keep in mind. It's a bad idea to wander unaccompanied into any of the favelas (shantytowns) found in and around the city; this is where most of the crime in Rio takes place. In the ritzy areas like the Zona Sul, favelas cling to steep hillsides and ridge tops. It's also best to avoid the city center (Centro) on weekends, particularly Sundays. Centro on the weekends remains mostly empty, and more than a little eerie. Avoid the beaches at night, which are dark and mostly deserted (stick to the brightly lit and police-patrolled pedestrian walkway that borders the beach). At night, traveling by taxi is recommended—don't rely on public transportation. Finally, as in any large metropolitan area, it's wise to observe common-sense precautions: Don't flash jewelry and large amounts of cash, and stick to well-lit and well-traveled thoroughfares.

Taxes The city of Rio charges a 5% accommodations tax, collected by the hotel operators. This amount will be added to your bill. Hotels may also add a 10% service charge to your bill. There are no taxes on retail items.

Telephone See "Fast Facts: Brazil," chapter 2.

Time Zones Rio de Janeiro is 3 hours behind GMT. During daylight saving Rio's time difference changes to 2 hours behind GMT.

Tipping See "Fast Facts: Brazil," chapter 2.

Visa Renewal If you need to extend your visa, go to the **Policia Federal**, Av. Venezuela 2, Centro (just behind the Praça Mauá), © 021/3213-1400, open

Monday to Friday 10am to 5pm. The fee is R$69 (US$35/£19), and you may need to show evidence of sufficient funds for your stay and a return ticket.

Weather Rio's summers, from December to March, are hot and humid. Temperatures rise routinely above 105°F (40°C). In the spring and fall, the temperatures stay between the high 70s and low 90s (high 20s to low 30s Celsius). In the winter, June to Aug, it can cool off at night to as low as 59°F (15°C), but during the day temperatures range from the 70s to the mid-80s (20s Celsius). Most rain tends to fall in the summer in short intense tropical showers, or in the winter in longer drizzly showers.

2 Where to Stay

Though Rio boasts a number of hotels, there's surprisingly little variety: there are few pousadas, boutique hotels, or fancy bed-and-breakfasts, at least not in the beach neighborhoods. (The exception is the hilltop neighborhood of Santa Teresa, which has pousadas in heritage buildings and quaint historic B&Bs galore.) In Copacabana and Ipanema, the vast majority of hotels are in modern high-rises, many built in the '60s and '70s, most with a similar layout and design. The difference between hotels thus lies in the location, the room size, the amenities, and, of course, the view. The best rooms always face the ocean and are priced accordingly. Note that if you choose not to stay in a prime oceanview room, you often get much better value by staying at the best room in a less expensive hotel away from the beach than by paying for a cheaper room in an expensive beachfront hotel.

The best-known hotel area is **Copacabana,** with easy access via Metrô back to the city core, and a good selection of inexpensive hotels close to the beach. One beach over from Copacabana, **Ipanema** and **Leblon** have become increasingly popular over the past decade and now boast better nightlife and trendier shopping than Copa. The only real disadvantage to staying here is the lack of a subway line, but there are lots and lots of buses.

Farther out in **Barra da Tijuca** is where you will find the city's newest and most modern hotels. Hotels out here are close to the convention center and the big new malls and office complexes, but it's a 30-to-60-minute cab ride from Ipanema and Copacabana and the people and street life that make Rio so fascinating.

Back toward downtown you find the lively and more historic neighborhoods **Glória, Catete,** and **Flamengo.** Located a 15-minute subway ride from both downtown and Copacabana, they offer excellent budget options as well as luxury accommodations rivaling The Copacabana Palace but at a much better price.

The hilltop neighborhood of **Santa Teresa** now boasts a few wonderful pousadas, B&Bs, and boutique hotels, most of them in the gorgeous converted mansions of Rio's 19th-century elite. Santa Teresa offers curving cobblestone streets and terrific views in all directions, and a bohemian artistic feel. The only drawback is access; getting up to or down from Santa Teresa is a matter of a bus or taxi ride.

In the lobby, hotels always list the rack rates on a sign behind the desk, but you can expect to pay 50% to 80% of this amount, depending on the season, the staff person, and your bargaining skills. Prices are quite flexible; always negotiate. Sometimes just paying with cash can result in a 10% to 15% discount.

Where to Stay & Dine in São Conrado, Leblon, Ipanema & Copacabana

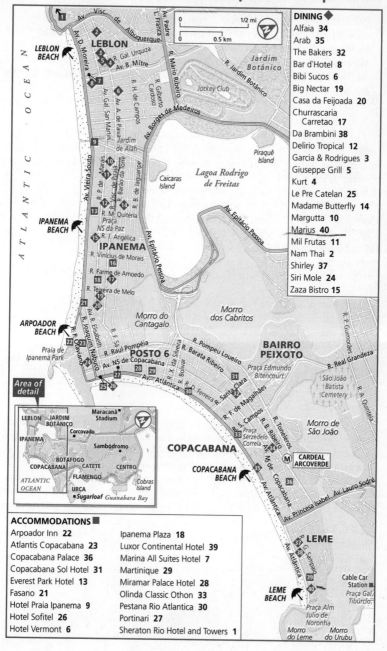

DINING ◆

Alfaia **34**
Arab **35**
The Bakers **32**
Bar d'Hotel **8**
Bibi Sucos **6**
Big Nectar **19**
Casa da Feijoada **20**
Churrascaria
  Carretao **17**
Da Brambini **38**
Delirio Tropical **12**
Garcia & Rodrigues **3**
Giuseppe Grill **5**
Kurt **4**
Le Pre Catelan **25**
Madame Butterfly **14**
Margutta **10**
Marius **40**
Mil Frutas **11**
Nam Thai **2**
Shirley **37**
Siri Mole **24**
Zaza Bistro **15**

ACCOMMODATIONS ■

Arpoador Inn **22**
Atlantis Copacabana **23**
Copacabana Palace **36**
Copacabana Sol Hotel **31**
Everest Park Hotel **13**
Fasano **21**
Hotel Praia Ipanema **9**
Hotel Sofitel **26**
Hotel Vermont **6**

Ipanema Plaza **18**
Luxor Continental Hotel **39**
Marina All Suites Hotel **7**
Martinique **29**
Miramar Palace Hotel **28**
Olinda Classic Othon **33**
Pestana Rio Atlantica **30**
Portinari **27**
Sheraton Rio Hotel and Towers **1**

> **Tips** **Beware Dengue Fever in Brazil**
>
> Occasionally Brazil experiences outbreaks of dengue fever, a malaria-like illness transmitted by mosquitoes. Most of the cases were reported in the state of Rio de Janeiro, with additional outbreaks in São Paulo as well. See the section on "Health" in chapter 2 for more on dengue fever, and for the latest information on the situation in Rio, check the Centers for Disease Control website (www. cdc.gov) before you leave.

The only time of year when it's difficult to get a deal is during **high season,** from the week before Christmas through the end of Carnaval. The city overflows with visitors from all over the world, not to mention Argentines and Brazilians taking their summer holidays. New Year's and Carnaval are the tourism industry's cash cows, and during this time most hotels will only accept reservations for set package deals—usually a 2- or 3-night minimum stay for New Year's and a 5-night minimum stay for Carnaval—at highly inflated prices. Shop around in advance if you're going to be in Rio during these times; packages (*especially* the less expensive ones) sell out by October or November. Most hotels now have websites and will provide quick information upon request.

Make sure to ask about taxes that will be added to your bill. Most hotels charge a 10% service tax, a 5% city tax, and, if they are a member of the Rio Convention and Visitor's Bureau, a tourist tax of R$3 to R$9 (US$1.50–US$4.50/£.80–£2.45) per day. This can add up to a total of 18% extra on your bill.

Breakfast *(café de manha)* at Brazilian hotels is almost always included in the room price and at most places includes a nice buffet-style spread including bread, meats, cheeses, fruits, eggs (sometimes), and *café com leite,* strong coffee served with hot milk. In recent years a few of the more expensive hotels have taken to charging for *café de manha;* if this is the case it's noted in the review.

SÃO CONRADO/BARRA DA TIJUCA

The only reason to stay beyond Leblon is if you prefer your hotel with a large leisure area such as tennis courts and large swimming pools. Close to the convention center and the new business centers, hotels in Barra usually have huge recreational areas. The drawback is that you're anywhere from 30 minutes to an hour or more from Ipanema and Copacabana (depending on traffic) and thus quite isolated from the people and street life that make Rio so fascinating. If you do choose Barra, resign yourself to long cab or bus rides.

VERY EXPENSIVE

Sheraton Barra Hotel & Suites ✦✦✦ *Kids*   Located on Barra's premier stretch of waterfront, the Sheraton offers the most modern and luxurious accommodations in Rio. All 292 rooms face the ocean and all have balconies. Classic rooms are located on floors 1 to 5. Preferred rooms take up floors 6 to 15. All rooms come with a large desk, a sitting area with a 29-inch TV, and a wet bar. Beds are indulgent, with a firm king-size mattress, cozy fleece blanket, plump duvet, and five cushy pillows. What really sets this hotel apart is the leisure area. There are two swimming pools and Jacuzzi tubs set in a beautifully landscaped garden, a state-of-the-art fitness center, squash courts, a fully equipped business center, and a trendy lounge. Guests also have access to the 27-hole Itangá golf course. There's a free shuttle to the Barra Shopping.

Av. Lúcio Costa 3150 (aka Av. Sernambetiba), Barra da Tijuca, 22630-011. ℰ 021/3139-8000. Fax 021/3139-8085. www.sheraton-barra.com.br. 292 units. R$460 (US$230/£124) classic room double; R$635 (US$318/£171) preferred room double; R$675 (US$337/£182) junior suite double. Extra person R$145 (US$72/£39). Children 12 and under stay free in parent's room. AE, DC, MC, V. Bus: 2113. **Amenities:** Restaurant; 2 bars; 1 outdoor heated adult pool and 1 outdoor heated children's pool; health club; sauna; children's playground; concierge; tour desk; courtesy shuttle to Barra Shopping; business center; salon; room service; massage; laundry service; dry cleaning; nonsmoking rooms. *In room:* A/C, TV, dataport, kitchenette, minibar, fridge, coffeemaker, hair dryer, safe.

Sheraton Rio Hotel & Towers ★★★ (Kids   The Sheraton is the only large luxury hotel with a fabulous leisure area that is still relatively close to the Zona Sul. You are only a 30-minute walk from Leblon or a 10-minute taxi ride from Ipanema. It is also the place where Rio's societal divisions will stare you right in the face, or rather, into your room. Located directly on its own beautiful pocket beach, the Sheraton sits in the shadow of a hillside favela. Guests in the north-facing rooms awake to the calls of roosters roaming round the small brick shacks across the road. As sharp as the contrast may seem, there is a friendly mingling of tourists and locals on the beach (which is kept very safe by hotel security). The hotel itself is the ultimate in luxury, featuring three large swimming pools in a beautiful parklike setting, beachfront access, and sweeping ocean views. The rooms are spacious and very bright. All have verandas with a partial or full ocean view, and the interiors have recently been upgraded with new light fixtures, large desks, and dual phone lines. The location is suitable for children, and the hotel staff offer lots of activities to keep little ones busy.

Av. Niemeyer 121, São Conrado, Rio de Janeiro, 22450-220 RJ. ℰ 0800/210-750 or 021/2274-1122. Fax 021/2239-5643. www.sheraton-rio.com. 559 units. R$330–R$450 (US$165–US$225/£89–£121) standard double; R$400–R$560 (US$200–US$280/£108–£151) oceanview double; R$550–R$760 (US$275–US$380/£149–£205) junior suite double. Check the Internet for specials. Extra person add 25%. Children 10 and under stay free in parent's room. Breakfast not included. AE, DC, MC, V. Free parking. No public transit. **Amenities:** 3 restaurants; bar; disco; 3 outdoor heated pools; tennis courts (extra charge); health club (extra charge); sauna; children's center; game room; concierge; tour desk; car rental; courtesy shuttle service; business center; shopping arcade; salon; room service; massage; babysitting; laundry; dry cleaning; nonsmoking floors; executive-level rooms. *In room:* A/C, TV, dataport, minibar, fridge, hair dryer, safe.

Windsor Barra ★★ (Kids   Open since September 2005, the Windsor Barra is all modern design on the outside. Inside, rooms feature classic, elegant furnishings and color schemes that are easy on the eye—lots of beiges and moss greens. The superior apartments are on lower floors and have side views of the ocean. The best rooms are the spacious deluxe corner rooms on the higher floors—these have both side and full ocean views, plus a Jacuzzi tub. The best view in the house is reserved for the leisure area; the swimming pools and bar boast a sweeping 360-degree view of Barra Beach and surroundings.

Av. Sernambetiba 2630 (aka Av. Lúcio Costa), Barra da Tijuca, 22620-170. ℰ 021/2195-5000. Fax 021/2195-5050. www.windsorhotels.com. 338 units. R$440 (US$220/£119) double superior; R$660 (US$330/£178) double deluxe.

(Tips **Where *Not* to Stay in Rio**

The only neighborhood to avoid hotel-wise is downtown Rio. The Praça Mauá hotels may look like a bargain, but this area transforms into a red-light district at night when the office workers have gone home.

⟨Tips⟩ Know About the Beach Entrance

Maybe it's to keep sand from tracking in the lobby, or maybe it's to avoid having the Speedo-clad squeezing into an elevator full of suits. For whatever reason, many beachfront hotels have a separate entrance and elevator for those going to the beach. Normally marked ENTRADA DE BANHISTAS or ENTRADA DE SERVIÇO, these elevators lead to the hotel service entrance where—as a bonus for following the local etiquette—you can pick up a beach towel, chair, and umbrella. Returning from the beach you enter the same side entrance and drop the stuff off again.

Extra person 25%. Children 6 and under stay free in parent's room. AE, DC, MC, V. **Amenities:** 2 restaurants; 2 bars; 1 outdoor heated adult pool and 1 outdoor heated children's pool; health club; sauna; concierge; tour desk; business center; salon; room service; massage; laundry service; dry cleaning; nonsmoking rooms. *In room:* A/C, TV, dataport, kitchenette, minibar, fridge, coffeemaker, hair dryer, safe.

IPANEMA/LEBLON

One beach over from Copacabana, **Ipanema** and **Leblon** have become increasingly popular over the past decade and now boast better nightlife and trendier shopping than Copa. Leblon, in particular, is fast becoming Rio's prime neighborhood for fine dining. There are both affordable hotel options and outstanding luxury accommodations. The only drawback? It's a bit far from downtown, and lacks a subway connection. The bus ride into Centro is normally about 40 minutes, but during weekday rush hours it can take up to an hour.

VERY EXPENSIVE

Fasano ✦✦✦ The famous *enfant terrible* of the design world Phillippe Starck is known for his chairs and hotel lobbies and other high-end hotel bits the world over; this was his first-ever opportunity to design a complete hotel. Top to bottom, inside and out, it's all Starck. The opportunity came courtesy of a noted São Paulo hotelier family (named Fasano) who asked Starck to bring his unique gifts to bear designing a boutique hotel on a small but privileged site on Ipanema beach. The result does not disappoint. From lobby lounge and restaurant to rooftop pool deck the hotel displays Starck's sense for space and materials. The rooftop pool, in particular, is a thing of beauty, a low square pond of chiseled white marble with an infinite edge that seems to flow out the parapet and join with sand and sea. Hallways are completely covered in wood paneling, which together with a big Dr. Seuss chair and floor-panel room numbers gives the hallways a James Bond/Austin Powers shaggalicious kind of feel. Inside, rooms feature the same design sense: The queen-size beds are set off at an oblique angle to the room's basic rectangle. There's a small desk area and kind of wavy kitschy wall mirrors, plus a bathroom with rainfall showers and wide, square white basin, a motif carried on in the rooftop pool. The high level of design may make up for the superior rooms' rather less than generous dimensions, and lack of balcony or ocean view. (Or it may not.) The deluxe oceanview rooms are a much more comfortable size, with the same bed design, plus a small sitting area and a balcony featuring a pair of lovely '50s modern chairs, made from tropical hardwood instead of teak. The difference in feeling is significant (as for the price, what's a few hundred dollars when you're splurging?). The oceanview suites are larger still, with a retractable silk curtain to separate off a comfortable little sitting area, which comes with its own separate bathroom facilities. The quality of everything in all rooms—bedding, bathroom products, bathrobes—is all top-notch. And if you can't afford the room rate, it's still worth coming in for a fancy cocktail in the lobby lounge or big white restaurant bar, to admire the high design and watch the beautiful people at play.

Av. Vieira Souto 88, Ipanema, Rio de Janeiro, 22420-000 RJ. ℂ 021/3202-4000. Fax 021/3202-4010. www.fasano. com.br. 91 units. R$945 (US$470/£255) superior double; R$1,440 (US$720/£389) deluxe oceanview; double R$2,500 (US$1,225/£675) oceanview suite. Extra bed R$150 (US$75/£40). Children 12 and under stay free in parent's room. Inquire about seasonal discounts. AE, DC, MC, V. Valet parking. Bus: 415. **Amenities:** Restaurant bar; rooftop pool; small spa; well-equipped fitness center; sauna; concierge; business center; room service; massage; babysitting; laundry; dry cleaning; nonsmoking floors. *In room:* A/C, TV, dataport, minibar, hair dryer, safe.

Marina All Suites Hotel ★★★ *Finds*   Design with a capital D. The Marina All Suites is the brainchild of a consortium of local architects and decorators who bought, gutted, and redecorated all the rooms, in the process reducing the original layout of six rooms per floor to a very spacious three. All are so precociously modern they positively squeak, with original pieces of art and a style unique to each unit. The two-bedroom Suite Diamante must be the most beautiful suite in Rio and is said to be Gisele Bündchen's favorite room when in town. The "basic" suites (basic being an understatement) are studio apartments. The design suites have a separate bedroom. All feature an American kitchen (microwave, fridge, and wet bar), ample desk space and sitting areas, spacious bathrooms, and luxurious furnishings, making this truly one of Rio's most outstanding hotels. On the top floor, there's a lounge with Internet terminals and a DVD movie theater. The restaurant Bar d'Hotel is one of the hipper nightspots in Rio (see entry under "Where to Dine," later in this chapter).

Av. Delfim Moreira 696, Leblon, Rio de Janeiro, 22441-000 RJ. ℂ 021/2172-1100. Fax 021/2294-1644. www.marina allsuites.com.br. 38 units (some with showers only). R$700–R$930 (US$350–US$465/£189–£251) basic suite; R$980–R$1,200 (US$490–US$600/£265–£324) design suite; R$1,900 (US$950/£513) Suite Diamante. AE, DC, MC, V. Free parking. Bus: 474. **Amenities:** Restaurant; pool; excellent gym; sauna; game room; concierge; business center; room service; massage; babysitting; laundry service. *In room:* A/C, TV, dataport, kitchen, minibar, fridge, microwave, toaster and coffeemaker, hair dryer, electronic safe.

EXPENSIVE

Everest Park Hotel ★★   Less luxurious than its sister hotel the Everest Rio, the Everest Park is also cheaper, making it a reasonable option for business travelers looking to economize. All 25 units have high-speed Internet access and a large workspace upon which to spread out papers. The rooms themselves are also spacious, with a small hallway area at the entrance opening up to two twin beds. (Reserve a double bed when booking and staff will join the twins together to make a comfortable double.) Recent renovations have added new carpets, and the bathrooms have also been redone and now feature bathtubs, large bright mirrors, and hair dryers. True, there's no business center, but guests can access the one at the Everest Rio Hotel just half a block away around the corner.

Rua Maria Quiteria 19, Ipanema, Rio de Janeiro, 22410-040 RJ. ℂ 0800/244-485 or 021/2525-2200. www.everest. com.br. 25 units. R$260 (US$130/£70) double. Up to 25% discount in low season and weekends. AE, MC, V. No parking. Bus: 474. **Amenities:** Room service; laundry. *In room:* A/C, TV, dataport, minibar, fridge, safe.

Hotel Praia Ipanema ★★★   Straddling the border between Ipanema and Leblon, the Praia Ipanema offers luxury beachfront accommodations at a less than luxury price. The hotel is within walking distance of Lagoa, the upscale shopping and restaurants of the Zona Sul, and the restaurants and bars of Leblon. All 105 units offer balconies and

ocean views, a full one in the case of the 55 deluxe rooms and a partial (from the side) view for the 46 superior rooms (which, it should be noted, are actually larger than the deluxe rooms). The best rooms begin at the 10th floor and carry upward, as the views of sand and sea get ever more spectacular. Three-day weekend specials (Fri–Sun) often include drinks, lunch or dinner, and a late checkout for the same price as two regular nights.

Av. Vieira Souto 706, Ipanema, Rio de Janeiro, 22420-000 RJ. © 021/2540-4949. Fax 021/2239-6889. www.praia ipanema.com. 105 units. R$500 (US$250/£135) superior double; R$595 (US$298/£161) deluxe-view double. AE, DC, MC, V. No parking. Bus: 474 or 404. **Amenities:** Restaurant; 2 bars; rooftop outdoor pool; small gym; tour desk; business center; room service; laundry service and dry cleaning; beach service. *In room:* A/C, TV/VCR, dataport, minibar, fridge, hair dryer, safe.

Ipanema Plaza ✪✪✪   A member of the Dutch Golden Tulip hotel chain, the Ipanema Plaza is located just 1 block from Ipanema beach. The hotel's modern and sleek design looks fabulous, and the attention to detail carries over into the rooms. Furnished in beige tones and cherrywood, the rooms are quite spacious, particularly the deluxe rooms. A number of them come with a large balcony, and all double beds are king-size; twin beds are much larger than the average Brazilian single bed. If you're splurging, the master suites are gorgeous and have a separate sitting room adjacent to the bedroom. The hotel recently inaugurated the Ipanema floor. All rooms on this floor have ocean views and come with high-end extras such as a 29-inch flatscreen TV. A delicious buffet breakfast is included in the rate. The hotel is close to Rio's upscale gay neighborhood and has a reputation for being very gay-friendly.

Rua Farme de Amoedo 34, Ipanema, Rio de Janeiro, 22420-020 RJ. © 021/3687-2000. Fax 021/3687-2001. www. ipanemaplazahotel.com. 135 units. R$400 (US$200/£108) superior double; R$490 (US$245/£132) deluxe double; R$610 (US$305/£165) Ipanema floor double. Extra person 25%. Children under 10 stay free in parent's room. AE, DC, MC, V. Bus: 474 or 404. **Amenities:** Restaurant; bar; rooftop outdoor pool; small gym; tour desk; business center; room service; laundry service and dry cleaning; beach service. *In room:* A/C, TV/VCR/DVD, dataport, minibar, hair dryer, safe.

MODERATE

Arpoador Inn ✪ *Value*   The only budget-priced oceanfront hotel in Ipanema, the Arpoador Inn enjoys a privileged location on a quiet stretch of beach popular with the surf crowd, and just around the corner from Copacabana. Even better, the beach in front of the hotel is closed to cars and is therefore pleasantly quiet. The deluxe rooms all face the ocean. The furniture is simple but the rooms are bright and spotless. Obtaining these does require booking ahead; if they're full, the superior rooms, which look out over the street behind the beach, make an acceptable alternative. The only rooms to avoid are the standard ones, which are very small, dark, and look into an interior wall.

Rua Francisco Otaviano 177, Ipanema, Rio de Janeiro, 22080-040 RJ. © 021/2523-0060. Fax 021/2511-5094. www. arpoadorinn.com.br. 50 units (showers only). R$170 (US$85/£46) standard double; R$220 (US$110/£59) street-view superior double; R$350 (US$175/£95) deluxe ocean view. Extra person R$90 (US$45/£24). Children 6 and under stay free in parent's room. AE, DC, MC, V. No parking. Bus: 474. **Amenities:** Restaurant; room service; laundry. *In room:* A/C, TV, fridge, safe.

Hotel Vermont ✪   The Vermont sits smack in the middle of Ipanema's swankiest shopping district, and thanks to the rates at this small budget hotel, you'll have plenty of cash left for conspicuous consumption. Thanks to a recent renovation, all rooms now have tile floors, new furniture, large mirrors, and clean, modern fixtures. Standard rooms face out the back and are simply furnished with two twins or a double bed, a closet, and a desk. Superior rooms are a little more spacious but they also get some street noise, although at night traffic slows down significantly. Most of the rooms have twin beds so if you want a double it's best to reserve in advance. Note that the hotel is a bad choice for those with limited mobility—access to the hotel elevators is up one flight of stairs.

Rua Visconde de Pirajá 254, Ipanema, Rio de Janeiro, 22410-000 RJ. © 021/2522-0057. Fax 021/2267-7046. hoteis vermont@uol.com.br. 85 units (most have showers only). R$190 (US$85/£51) standard or superior double. Extra person R$60 (US$30/£16). Children 2 and under stay free in parent's room. AE, DC, MC, V. No parking. Bus: 415. **Amenities:** Tour desk; laundry. *In room:* A/C, TV, wireless Internet, minibar, safe.

COPACABANA

Copacabana may not be the upscale neighborhood that was in the days when bossa nova was young, but there are still advantages to staying in this part of the city. Prices are lower than in Ipanema and you will find all the services a tourist is likely to need. Also, Copacabana is strategically located; it's only a 10- to 15-minute cab ride to Ipanema or to downtown, and there's excellent bus service and a Metrô line, which makes it easy and convenient to get downtown or to places farther out, such as the Sambodromo or the Maracanã soccer stadium.

The best hotels are on the Avenida Atlântica and some of its cross streets. Avoid the hectic Nossa Senhora de Copacabana Avenue and Rua Barata Ribeiro.

The drawback to Copacabana is that you share the hood with seniors, lots and lots of other tourists, vendors, hawkers, hustlers and, in certain sections, street hookers and (mostly foreign) johns (it's particularly bad around Av. Prado Junior and in front of the Help discothèque). With some common precautions the neighborhood is just as safe as Ipanema, but you do get that extra local flavor. We find it quite colorful and a part of what makes Copa unique. However, it may not be for everybody. Leme, at the far end of Copa, could be the perfect alternative for those who want to have all the benefits of being close to Copa without sinking in the midst of it.

VERY EXPENSIVE

The Copacabana Palace 🐱🐱   The spot where beachfront luxury in Rio all began, The Copacabana Palace is the place to splurge. True, things have gotten more crowded since this opulent vision first appeared on a lonely stretch of sand, but the 84-year-old Palace still maintains its Jazz Age charm. Taking full advantage, however, requires approaching things with Gatsbyesque confidence. Take, for example, the city-view rooms. Or rather, don't take them. Though cheaper, they offer not a drop of ocean view. Deluxe beach-view rooms give you that coveted ocean view but to get value for money at the Palace it's really a case of go big or go home, and there's nothing bigger than the penthouse suites. Elegant and tastefully decorated, these spacious one-bedroom suites have their own private veranda overlooking Copacabana beach. Just as stylish and almost as spacious are the poolside suites, which also feature a partial ocean view. Now that is the kind of life we were intended to live. The hotel recently added a high-end spa to its services. Note that the rates listed here are rack rates. Check the website or contact a travel agency for discounts and package deals.

Av. Atlântica 1702, Copacabana, Rio de Janeiro, 22021-001 RJ. © 0800/211-533 or 021/2548-7070. Fax 021/2235-7330. www.copacabanapalace.orient-express.com. 226 units. R$1,010 (US$510/£273) deluxe city-view double; R$1,380 (US$690/£373) deluxe oceanview double; R$1,830 (US$915/£494) junior suite double; 1-bedroom suite R$2,480 (US$1,240/£670). Seasonal discounts available, special weekend packages, 2 nights for the price of 1, including breakfast and Sat Feijoada lunch. Extra person about 25%. Children 12 and under stay free in parent's room. AE, DC, MC, V. Free parking. Metrô: Arcoverde. **Amenities:** 2 restaurants (under "Where to Dine," later in this chapter); bar; large outdoor pool; rooftop tennis courts; health club; Jacuzzi; sauna; concierge; tour desk; car rental; business center; salon; room service; massage; babysitting; laundry; dry cleaning; executive-level rooms. *In room:* A/C, TV, dataport, kitchen, minibar, hair dryer, safe.

Hotel Sofitel 𝕲𝕲𝕲   One of Rio's most elegant hotels, the Sofitel is also one of the most cleverly designed: the U-shaped structure guarantees a large number of the 388 rooms a full or partial view of the shimmering ocean. Located on the edge of Copacabana directly opposite the Copacabana Fort, this flagship of the French Sofitel chain also offers superb service and a clean modern look to match. All rooms have balconies, soundproof windows, and electronic safes big enough to hold a laptop. Superior rooms are elegantly decorated with brand-new furnishings and fixtures, and come with a partial ocean view. Deluxe rooms differ only in offering a guaranteed full ocean view. For sunbathing there's a complimentary beach service on Copacabana beach itself, or else a choice of two swimming pools, one to catch the morning sun and the other for the afternoon rays. The pool area, the hotel bar, and the outstanding Pré-Catelan restaurant (see Pré-Catelan review, later in this chapter) have all been renovated recently. Breakfast not included (R$50/US$25/£14).

Av. Atlântica 4240, Copacabana, Rio de Janeiro, 22070-002 RJ. ℂ **0800/241-232** or 021/2525-1232. Fax 021/2525-1200. www.accorhotels.com.br. 388 units. R$468 (US$234/£126) superior double; R$675 (US$338/£182) deluxe double; R$900 (US$450/£243) junior suite double. Children 12 and under stay free in parent's room. AE, DC, MC, V. Free parking. Bus: 474. **Amenities:** 2 restaurants (see Le Pré-Catelan under "Where to Dine," later in this chapter); bar; 2 pools; health club; sauna; concierge; tour desk; car rental; business center; shopping arcade; room service; massage; babysitting; laundry; dry cleaning; nonsmoking rooms and floors; executive-level rooms. *In room:* A/C, TV, dataport, minibar, fridge, hair dryer, safe.

EXPENSIVE

Miramar Palace Hotel 𝕲𝕲   The flagship of the excellent Windsor chain, the Miramar offers luxury beachfront accommodations at a reasonable rate. The hotel sits on a corner, offering rooms with both full and partial ocean views. The recently renovated rooms have modern blond-wood furniture and splashes of cheerful tropical colors. Standard rooms are spacious and located on the lower floors (4–13); you can still see the ocean albeit from the side. Superior rooms on the 14th and 15th floors have better views but give up some space in exchange for a veranda. The deluxe rooms all have gorgeous views of Copacabana. The best rooms in the house are the suites. All are corner units, where the light pours in through large windows on both sides. The spacious bedrooms have elegant marble bathrooms and a jetted tub with a view of Copacabana beach. The hotel restaurant hosts an excellent *feijoada* lunch on Saturdays.

Av. Atlântica 3668, Copacabana, Rio de Janeiro, 22070-001 RJ. ℂ **021/2195-6200.** Fax 021/2521-3294. www.windsor hoteis.com. 156 units (many with bathtubs). R$230 (US$115/£62) standard double; R$320 (US$160/£86) superior double; R$350 (US$175/£95) deluxe double. Children 10 and under stay free in parent's room. AE, DC, MC, V. Free parking. Bus: 128 or 474. **Amenities:** Restaurant; bar; rooftop pool; exercise room; Jacuzzi; sauna; concierge; tour desk; business center; room service; laundry; nonsmoking floors. *In room:* A/C, TV, dataport, minibar, hair dryer, safe.

Olinda Classic Othon 𝕲𝕲 𝒱alue   A lovely heritage building, the Olinda has finally gotten a much-needed makeover. The lobby has been transformed into an elegant salon with a restaurant and piano bar. All the common spaces have Wi-Fi Internet access. Elevators have been upgraded to the 21st century, and all the rooms have been renovated. The dark colonial furniture has been tossed, replaced by lighter woods, soothing pale colors, and stylish furniture. All rooms now feature a modern phone system, electronic keys, a flatscreen TV and broadband Internet service. The superior rooms, which face the back of the building, are a bit smaller and have twin beds or a queen-size bed. The much nicer deluxe oceanview rooms have a king-size bed. Some rooms also have a balcony. The spacious suites are worth the upgrade; these all face the ocean and have a veranda and a separate sitting room.

Av. Atlântica 2230, Copacabana, 22041-001 RJ. ℂ/fax **021/2545-9091**. www.hoteis-othon.com.br. 102 units (showers only). R$205 (US$102/£55) double standard; R$285 (US$142/£77) double deluxe; R$330 (US$165/£89) double suite. Extra person add 40%. Children 10 and under stay free in parent's room. AE, DC, MC, V. No parking. Metrô: Arcoverde. **Amenities:** Restaurant; bar; room service; laundry. *In room:* A/C, TV, minibar, safe.

Pestana Rio Atlântica ★★★   Always one of the nicest hotels on the Avenida Atlântica, the Pestana looks brand-new thanks to a recent overhaul. The best rooms in the house, without doubt, are the *Oceanica* suites. These large rooms offer ocean views and large balconies, and come elegantly furnished with dark wooden furniture and splashes of yellow and beige. They are among the best in Copa, if you can afford the splurge. The standard and superior rooms are more plainly furnished and have a side view. Standard rooms look out over the buildings adjacent to the hotel. Superior rooms (on the 10th floor and higher) have a partial ocean view. There's a good fitness center and the rooftop pool area offers a massage room, sauna, and Jacuzzi. Breakfast costs R$36 (US$18/£10).

Av. Atlântica 2964, Copacabana, Rio de Janeiro, 22070-000 RJ. ℂ **021/2548-6332**. Fax 021/2255-6410. www. pestana.com. 216 units. Standard double R$432 (US$216/£117); superior R$478 (US$239/£129); suite oceanica R$730–R$1,070 (US$365–US$535/£197–£289). Children 10 and under stay free in parent's room. AE, DC, MC, V. Valet parking. Metrô: Arcoverde. **Amenities:** Restaurant; bar; outdoor pool; health club; Jacuzzi; sauna; concierge; tour desk; business center; room service; massage; babysitting; laundry; dry cleaning; nonsmoking rooms; rooms for people w/limited mobility. *In room:* A/C, TV, dataport, minibar, hair dryer, safe.

Portinari ★★   The only thing that keeps Rio's premier design hotel from getting three stars is its location just off the busy Avenida N.S de Copacabana; it lacks the sex appeal of a beach address. Inside, the hotel is fabulous. A team of 10 well-known Brazilian designers gave each floor a unique look. Styles range from classic-romantic with elegant furniture and pale colors to the environmentally friendly rooms, furnished using only recycled wood and natural fabrics. Our favorite rooms are the ones designed by Marcia Muller. Perfect for couples, the design is sensuous with gorgeous indirect lighting and luxurious white linens. The shower is separated by a glass wall from the bedroom and allows you to see silhouettes in the bathroom. All rooms come with queen-size or twin beds with 200-thread linen and goose down pillows, 21-inch flatscreen TVs, and high-speed Internet. The spacious suites feature large bathrooms (some with sauna or tub) and DVD players. Check the website for excellent specials.

Rua Francisco de Sá 17, Copacabana, 22080-010 RJ. ℂ **021/3222-8800**. Fax 021/3222-8803. www.hotelportinari. com.br. 66 units. R$270 (US$135/£73) double; R$325–R$380 (US$163–US$180/£88–£103) suite. Extra person add 25%. Children 10 and under stay free in parent's room. AE, DC, MC, V. Valet parking R$30 (US$15/£7.50) per day. Bus: 415. **Amenities:** Restaurant; coffee shop; bar; rooftop pool; small workout room; sauna; concierge; room service; laundry; dry cleaning; 2 nonsmoking floors; rooms for those w/limited mobility. *In room:* A/C, TV, dataport, minibar, hair dryer, safe.

MODERATE
Atlantis Copacabana Hotel ★   Located between Ipanema and Copacabana on a quiet residential street, the Atlantis Copacabana Hotel is perfect for those who like to keep their options open. Either beach is within minutes from your hotel, and shopping and restaurants are easily accessible as well. The hotel offers basic accommodations; all 87 rooms are standard with only a small variation in size and layout; rooms ending in 07 and 08 (for example, nos. 107 and 108) are slightly larger. Rooms above the eighth floor that look out the back offer a view of Arpoador and Ipanema beach.

Rua Bulhões de Carvalho 61, Copacabana, Rio de Janeiro, RJ 22081-000. ℂ **021/2521-1142**. Fax 021/2287-8896. www.atlantishotel.com.br. 87 units (showers only). R$180–R$240 (US$90–US$120/£49–£65) double. Extra person R$50 (US$25/£14). Children 5 and under stay free in parent's room. AE, DC, MC, V. Limited street parking. Bus: 128 or 474. **Amenities:** Rooftop pool; sauna; tour desk; concierge; room service; laundry. *In room:* A/C, TV, minibar, fridge, safe.

Copacabana Sol Hotel ✮✮ *Finds*   If you don't mind being off the waterfront, the Copacabana Sol offers good value and pleasant accommodations only 4 blocks from Copacabana beach. Much of the money obviously went into the lobby; with its colorful furniture and modern art, it borders on funky. Rooms were not neglected, however, nor were the suites. The latter, in particular, are a great deal. Spacious and cool with granite floors, the suites have a comfortable sitting room and gorgeous bathrooms with Jacuzzi tubs and separate showers. The superior and standard rooms have very small bathrooms with showers only. Superior rooms overlook the street and have balconies and a small sitting area. As the Rua Santa Clara is not too noisy (especially at night), these rooms are preferable to the alley-facing standard rooms (which also lack balconies).

Rua Santa Clara 141, Copacabana, Rio de Janeiro, 22041-010 RJ. ℂ **0800/254-477** or 021/2549-4577. Fax 021/2255-0744. www.copacabanasolhotel.com.br. 70 units. R$165–R$190 (US$83–US$95/£45–£51) standard and superior double; R$250 (US$125/£68) suite double. Extra person R$40 (US$20/£11). Children 5 and under stay free in parent's room. AE, DC, MC, V. Free parking. Bus: 128 or 474. **Amenities:** Restaurant; tour desk; concierge; business center; room service; laundry. *In room:* A/C, TV, dataport, minibar, fridge, safe.

Luxor Continental Hotel ✮✮✮ *Finds*   Located in a quiet residential neighborhood just off Copacabana, the Luxor offers outstanding value. Rates seldom top R$250 (US$125/£67) and online bookings can even be less than that. For that you get services that are worthy of a deluxe hotel: room service and business center, high-speed wireless Internet, a large fitness room, and rooftop pool. The rooms themselves are comfortable albeit a tad on the plain side with a double bed or twins (make sure you state your preference when booking), a small table and chairs, and counter. Bathrooms have showers only but come with hair dryers. The Luxor is set 1 block from Leme Beach, which is really the continuation of Copacabana beach. However, Leme is a cul-de-sac so traffic is much lighter than in Copa and with fewer hotels it is also not as touristy. Leme's big advantage is its strategic location; both downtown and Ipanema are only a 15-minute cab ride away and Copacabana is a 10-minute stroll. To make the most of the view, reserve a room on the 16th floor or higher that faces the ocean. Nonsmokers will be happy to know that the entire hotel is nonsmoking.

Rua Gustavo Sampaio 320, Leme, Rio de Janeiro, 22010-010 RJ. ℂ **021/2546-1070**. Fax 021/2541-1946. www.luxor hoteis.com.br. 275 units (showers only). R$218 (US$109/£59) standard double; R$240 (US$120/£65) superior double; R$272 (US$136/£73) deluxe double. Extra person 25%. Children 12 and under stay free in parent's room. AE, DC, MC, V. No parking. Bus: 472. **Amenities:** Restaurant; bar; outdoor pool; health club; sauna; concierge; 24-hr. business center; room service; laundry; nonsmoking hotel; rooms for those w/limited mobility. *In room:* A/C, TV, dataport, minibar, hair dryer, safe.

INEXPENSIVE

Martinique ✮ *Value*   The Martinique is the newest budget option of the Windsor chain. Located just around the corner from the Miramar, the hotel is only half a block off the Avenida Atlântica and offers excellent value. The hotel consists of two buildings side-by-side that were gutted and then joined together. This makes for some mazelike hallways and some small rooms, but on the plus side, the hotel is brand-new and the rates are affordable. The best rooms are the superior ones that look out over the street. The ones closest to the corner (rooms that end in 13 such as nos. 413 and

513) even have a partial ocean view. The standard rooms look out over the back lots of the adjacent buildings. However, all are pleasantly furnished in bright colors and have comfortable beds. Nice details at this price level include the hair dryer, makeup mirror, electronic safe, and high-speed Internet in each room. Most rooms are a tad on the small side and accommodate two people only. If you require a room for three, reserve ahead of time. The hotel even has a rooftop pool and sun deck but with the beach only 300 feet away you'd have to be pretty lazy not to make it out the door.

Rua Sá Ferreira 30, Copacabana, Rio de Janeiro, 22071-100 RJ. © 021/2195-5200. Fax 021/2195-5222. www.windsor hoteis.com. 117 units. R$190–R$220 (US$95–US$110/£51–£59) double. Extra person 25%. Children 10 and under stay free in parent's room. AE, DC, MC, V. Bus: 415. **Amenities:** Restaurant; rooftop pool; cardio equipment; concierge; room service; nonsmoking floors; laundry. *In room:* A/C, TV, minibar, hair dryer, safe.

FLAMENGO, CATETE & GLÓRIA

These older neighborhoods just south of downtown offer a range of excellent accommodations. Staying here will allow you to experience the real Rio, where tourists are a minority. These neighborhoods are also architecturally interesting and offer many glimpses into Rio's fascinating history. The chief drawback to the area is its distance from the ocean beaches.

VERY EXPENSIVE

Mama Ruisa ★★ *Finds*   For a very different hotel experience, consider spending a few nights in the quaint hilltop neighborhood of Santa Teresa. French owner Jean Michel Ruis opened up a lovely bed-and-breakfast in an almost 100-year-old mansion. Beautifully decorated, each of the seven suites is differently furnished and styled with elegant furniture and all the modern trimmings such as wireless Internet, cable TV, and air-conditioning. The Josephine Baker room, Jean Cocteau room, and Carmen Miranda room are junior suites and in addition to being a little bit bigger they also feature a private balcony with a view of the Glória Outeiro church and Guanabara bay. Breakfast is served on your balcony out on the sun deck. The small inn also has a lovely pool and garden with a gazebo perfect for spending a lazy afternoon reading a book. The Largo dos Guimarães, Santa Teresa's main square and "restaurant row," is only a 5-minute walk away.

Rua Santa Cristina 132, Santa Teresa, Rio de Janeiro, 20241-250 RJ. © 021/2242-1281. Fax 021/2210-0631. www. mamaruisa.com. 7 units. R$500 (US$250/£135) double; R$700 (US$350/£189) junior suite double. Children 10 and under stay free in parent's room. AE, DC, MC, V. Free parking. Bus/Metro: Integrated bus/metro from Carioca metro stop. **Amenities:** Outdoor pool; tour desk; limited room service; laundry; dry cleaning. *In room:* A/C, TV, dataport, minibar, fridge, hair dryer.

EXPENSIVE

Hotel Florida ★★ *Finds*   A gem of a hotel, the Florida is popular with business travelers from São Paulo who know a good deal when they see it: On top of a reasonable room rate the Florida offers free parking, free local calls, and free Internet access. Built in the 1940s, the hotel doesn't suffer from the modern "small room" syndrome, and the spacious and pleasant rooms offer either granite floors or new carpeting. The standard rooms overlook the rear or the side of the building and come with showers only. Both the superior and deluxe rooms offer views and have bathrooms with whirlpool tubs. The nicest rooms are those overlooking the lush gardens of the Palácio do Catete, Brazil's former presidential palace. The deluxe rooms are the most spacious, with a large entrance hall, king-size bed, sitting area, and desk. The hotel offers excellent discounts on weekends when its regular business travelers stay home.

Santa Teresa Bed & Breakfast Network 𝒦𝒦

Quite a change from most of Rio de Janeiro's high-rise accommodations, the **Santa Teresa Cama e Café B&B Network** (℗ **021/2224-5689** or 021/2221-7635; www.camaecafe.com.br) offers beautiful rooms in one of the city's most charming neighborhoods. The participating homes are often quite spectacular and situated in some of Santa Teresa's finest locations. The staff does a great job matching you according to your price preference, language skills, and interests. Hosts include a variety of resident artists and chefs, as well as people who have an interest in Brazilian music, art, and history. Houses range from century-old mansions to Art Deco villas to spacious apartments with fab views. Prices range from R$90 to R$180 (US$45–US$90/£24–£49), depending on the luxuriousness of your digs. But for as little as R$120 (US$60/£32) you can book yourself into a fabulous house with great views, swimming pool, and garden. The drawback to Santa Teresa is its isolation. In the evening you need to rely on taxis to get around. However, in the daytime you can grab a bus and be at the Metrô or downtown in 20 minutes. Santa Teresa in itself is worth a day or two of exploration. It's a perfect retreat, away from the beach.

Rua Ferreira Viana 81, Flamengo, Rio de Janeiro, 22210-040 RJ. ℗ **021/2195-6800**. Fax 021/2285-5777. www.windsor hoteis.com. 312 units. R$250 (US$125/£67) standard double; R$275 (US$137/£74) superior double; R$320 (US$160/£86) deluxe double. Extra person add 25%. Children 10 and under stay free in parent's room. AE, DC, MC, V. Free parking. Metrô: Catete. **Amenities:** Restaurant; bar; outdoor rooftop pool; weight room; sauna; concierge; tour desk; business center; room service; laundry; dry cleaning; nonsmoking floors. *In room:* A/C, TV, dataport, minibar, fridge, hair dryer, safe.

Hotel Glória 𝒦𝒦   The grande dame of Rio hotels, the Glória was built in 1922 (a year before The Copacabana Palace) to provide luxury accommodations for dignitaries attending Brazil's centennial celebrations. An annex was added in the '70s in the same style, making the 630-room Glória one of Rio's largest hotels. Yet somehow it doesn't feel huge and impersonal. If you can, reserve a deluxe room—the views of the bay and the Sugarloaf are well worth it. Those rolling in cash can consider the junior suites—located on the corners—each of which features a large living room furnished with lovely antiques, and a spacious master bedroom with big windows overlooking some of Rio's finest scenery. A little bit smaller than the deluxe rooms, the pleasant superior and standard rooms offer garden views. All the rooms in the annex have been completely renovated and look great, though they are not overly large. But no matter which room you get, you can indulge in the outstanding amenities: lovely gardens, the best sun deck in the city with views of the bay, marina, and Sugarloaf, two large heated swimming pools, and an outstanding fitness center.

Rua do Russel 632, Glória, Rio de Janeiro, 22210 RJ. ℗ **0800/213-077** or 021/2555-7272. Fax 021/2555-7283. www. hotelgloriario.com.br. 630 units (standard rooms in annex have showers only). Standard rooms R$285–R$360 (US$142–US$180/£77–£97) double; superior and deluxe rooms R$320–R$460 (US$160–US$234/£86–£124) double. Extra person R$80 (US$40/£22). Children 10 and under stay free in parent's room. AE, DC, MC, V. Metrô: Glória. **Amenities:** 4 restaurants; bar; 2 outdoor heated pools; health club; sauna; concierge; tour desk; car rental; business center; salon; room service; massage; babysitting; laundry; dry cleaning; nonsmoking floors. *In room:* A/C, TV, dataport, minibar, fridge, hair dryer, safe.

Solar de Santa 𝒦𝒦   Solar de Santa offers a wonderful home away from home. This beautiful mansion in Santa Teresa offers comfortable accommodations in a lovely setting.

Where to Stay & Dine in Flamengo, Catete, Glória & Santa Teresa

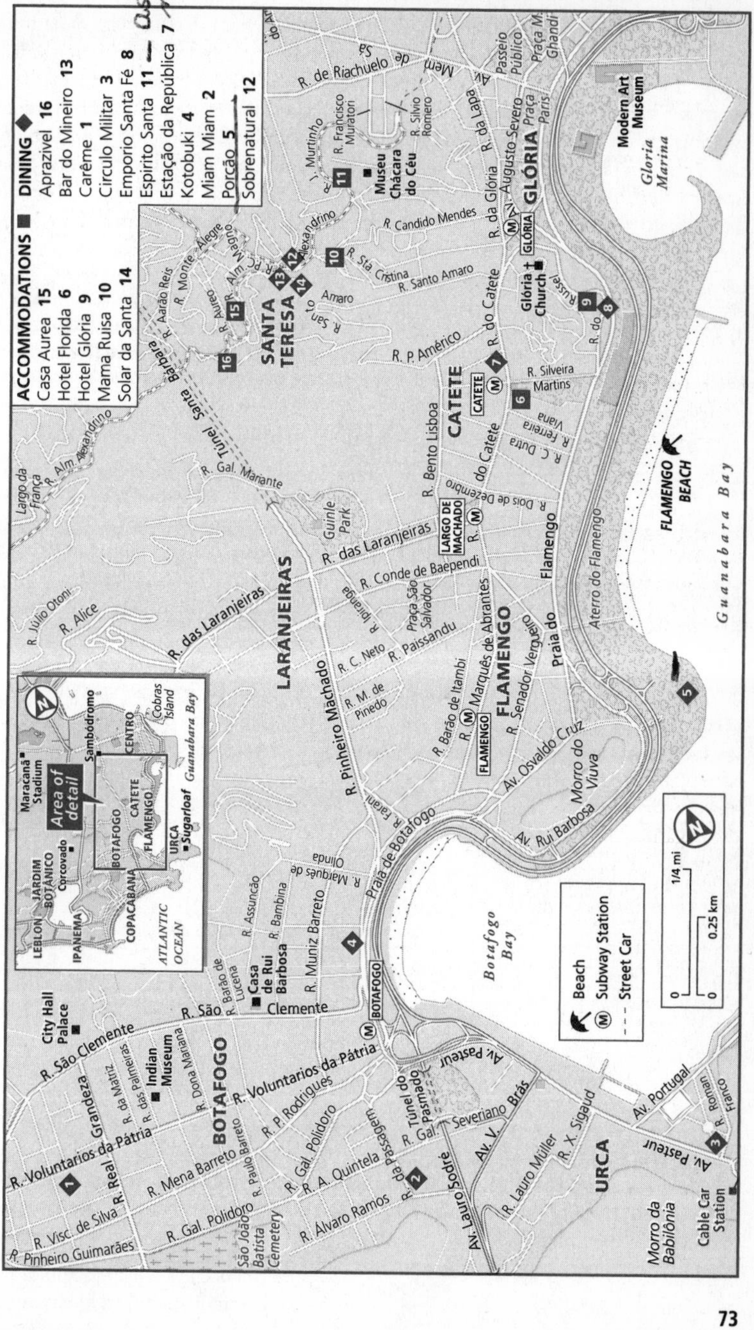

asa - next door

ACCOMMODATIONS ■

Casa Aurea **15**
Hotel Florida **6**
Hotel Glória **9**
Mama Ruisa **10**
Solar da Santa **14**

DINING ◆

Aprazivel **16**
Bar do Mineiro **13**
Carême **1**
Circulo Militar **3**
Emporio Santa Fé **8**
Espirito Santa **11**
Estação da República **7**
Kotobuki **4**
Miam Miam **2**
Porção **5**
Sobrenatural **12**

73

The main house features two apartments with a private bathroom and veranda overlooking the garden and Santa Teresa. The two other rooms don't have a private bathroom and are therefore only rented out to people traveling together who don't mind sharing a bathroom, for example a group of friends or a couple with children. There is also a bungalow with a very private deluxe room, a king-size bed, and large bathroom set back from the house. The large common dining room and living room, which open up to a large veranda and deck, are beautifully decorated with high-end crafts made by local artists. Because of the limited number of rooms, the Solar offers a very affordable option of renting the entire house, accommodating up to 12 people! This means that in addition to having the run of the house, you can also use the kitchen. Perfect for a few families traveling together.

Ladeira do Meireles 32, Santa Teresa, Rio de Janeiro, 22210 RJ. (C) 021/2221-2117. Fax 021/2221-6679. www.solar desanta.com. 5 units (3 suites and 2 rooms without bathroom; these latter ones are only rented with the suites). Suite R$400 (US$200/£108) double; room without private bathroom R$165–R$220 (US$82–US$110/£45–£59) double; bungalow R$560 (US$280/£151). Entire house (up to 13 people) R$1,600 (US$800/£432). Children 10 and under stay free in parent's room. AE, V. **Amenities:** Tiny outdoor pool; massage; babysitting; TV lounge; laundry. *In room:* A/C, fan, Wi-Fi.

MODERATE

Casa Aurea   The Casa Aurea is only a short walk up the road from the main square in Santa Teresa and offers very affordable accommodations. Popular with younger travelers and backpackers, the pousada offers rooms with shared bathrooms or private rooms with an en suite bathroom. The rooms are simply furnished but very clean and pleasant with high ceilings and large windows with wooden shutters. The large house has a gorgeous garden and patio, outdoor reading lounge, sitting room, and barbecue area, and is decorated with lovely artwork by some of the well-known artists from Santa Teresa.

Rua Áurea 80, Santa Teresa, Rio de Janeiro, 20240-210 RJ. (C) 021/2242-5830. www.casaaurea.com.br. 60 units. R$150 (US$75/£40) private bathroom double; R$120 (US$60/£32) shared bathroom double. Children 7 and under stay free in parent's room. No parking. **Amenities:** Laundry; Internet. *In room:* Fan.

3 Where to Dine

Cariocas love to eat out. Better yet, they love to linger over their meals. Waiters in Rio would never dream of coming by to ask you to "settle up" so they can go off shift. So take your time. Dawdle. Savor. Enjoy.

Rio offers an endless variety of places to eat. There are the *chopperias,* the place for cold beer and casual munchies. Slightly more upscale are the botequins, many of which are open to the early hours. There are hundreds of food kiosks, each with its own specialty, be it barbecued prawns, Bahian finger food, or vegetarian sandwiches. And on top of all that, there's a wide variety of restaurants in all neighborhoods, ranging from inexpensive to very expensive, from simple sandwiches to delicious steaks,

Where to Find Dining Maps

For maps of restaurants in the neighborhoods of Leblon, Ipanema, Copacabana, Botafogo, Flamengo, and Catete, see the "Where to Stay & Dine" maps, earlier in this chapter.

Where to Dine in Rio Centro

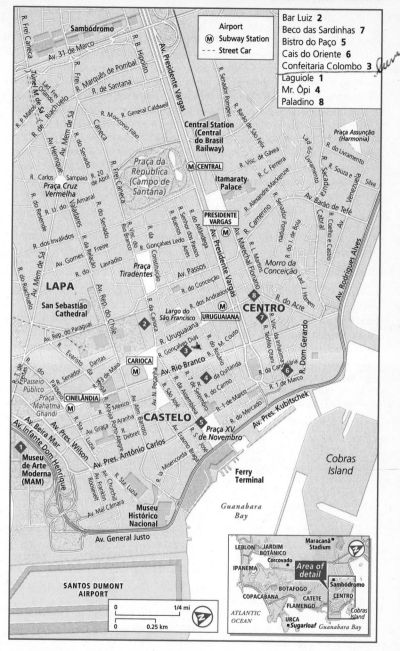

Airport	Bar Luiz **2**
M Subway Station	Beco das Sardinhas **7**
- - - Street Car	Bistro do Paço **5**
	Cais do Oriente **6**
	Confeitaria Colombo **3**
	Laguiole **1**
	Mr. Ôpi **4**
	Paladino **8**

Moments   Don't Shy Away from Street Food

When it comes to street vendors and food, you read a lot of strange things in travel guides. Never eat meat. Don't touch fruit. Don't eat anything at all. Only drinks. In cans. Insist on ice cubes made from bottled water. Sheesh!

Rio is *not* Rangoon, nor the fetid fever swamps of 19th-century Benin. Yes, tap water is best avoided. It won't kill you; it's just so chlorine-saturated that it tastes like *eau de* swimming pool. Some of the best meals I've had in Brazil have been purchased from a street vendor. One night in Rio, on the Rua Ouvidor, we came across a man and his charcoal brazier, selling skewers of fresh-grilled prawns, lightly salted and doused with lemon. We bought two skewers, which lasted about 40 seconds . . . so we went back for four more . . . and then another four. The moral? Eating from street vendors is fine, as long as you take precautions. Does the vendor look clean and healthy? Is the food stored in a cooler? Are Brazilians queuing up? If so, odds are the food's good, and whatever supplies he has in his cooler haven't been hanging around long enough to go bad. So eat, enjoy, and don't have a cow. Or rather, *do,* if that's what they're selling.

from fresh sushi to the complicated stews and sauces of Brazil's Northeast. There's no excuse for going hungry in Rio.

Portions often serve two people, especially in more casual restaurants. Always ask or you may well end up with an extraordinary amount of food. In Portuguese ask, *"Serve para dois?"* (pronounced *sir*-vay p'ra doysh—"does it serve two?").

The standard Brazilian menu comes close to what some restaurants label as international cuisine: pasta, seafood, beef, and chicken. Except in Brazil, these are served with a local or regional twist. The pasta may be stuffed with *catupiry* cheese and *abóbora* (a kind of pumpkin); the chicken could have *maracujá* (passion fruit) sauce. Brazilian beef comes from cows just like in the rest of the world, but in Brazil the cows are open-range and grass-fed, making for a very lean beef which comes in uniquely Brazilian cuts such as *picanha* (tender rump steak), *fraldinha* (bottom sirloin), or *alcatra* (top sirloin). And of course, for side dishes no Brazilian meal is complete without *farofa* and rice or black beans.

Most restaurants are open from around 11am until 4pm and then again from 7pm until midnight or later. There are also quite a few establishments that will stay open all day, especially on the weekends when people leave the beach at 4pm to go eat lunch. Sunday is often the busiest day for lunch as extended families get together for a meal. Many restaurants close Sunday evening. The exception to the these hours is in Rio's downtown, where restaurants cater to the office crowd; only a few of them remain open evenings and weekends.

These days you will find more and more **kilo** (*quilo* in Portuguese) restaurants. The food is laid out in a large buffet, and at the better ones there's a grill at the back serving freshly cooked steaks, chicken, and sausage. Kilos aren't all-you-can-eat. Rather, you pay by weight (but the quality is *much* better than at American lunch buffets). If you're not familiar with Brazilian food, it's a great way to see all the dishes laid out in front of you; you can try as little or as much as you like. Even better, there are often a variety of salads and vegetables that are often hard to come by elsewhere in Brazil. The system works as follows: When you enter the restaurant, you're given a piece of paper on which all your orders are recorded. Don't lose this slip or you'll have to pay a ridiculously high penalty. You grab a plate, wander by the buffet and grill, filling up on whatever catches your eye (all items have the same per-kilogram cost, which is usually advertised both outside and inside the restaurant), and then take the plate to the scale to be weighed. The weigher records the charges on your bill, after which you find a table. Normally a waiter will then come by and take your drink order, adding these charges to your tally. On your way out the cashier sums it all up.

Tip: Small cups of strong dark coffee (called *cafezinhos*) are usually served free by the cashier or exit. Look for a thermos and a stack of little plastic cups.

CENTRO
EXPENSIVE
Cais do Oriente ★★★ ASIAN/MEDITERRANEAN   The area behind the Arco de Teles is better known for the bustling outdoor bars that pack the alleyways behind the Rua Primeiro de Março, but Cais do Oriente is anything but casual. This former 19th-century warehouse has undergone major renovations and emerged as a stunning venue for a restaurant and bar, complete with opulent antique furniture, large mirrors, and elegant furnishings. The menu is all over the map, literally, covering the Orient as well as the Mediterranean. You'll find Asian dishes such as sweet-and-sour duck with fried rice tossed with cashews and pistachio nuts or a Thai squid dish with oyster sauce and a green papaya salad. The Mediterranean dishes include prawn risotto with basil and grilled salmon served with a Gorgonzola-and-ricotta-stuffed pancake and the beautiful fresh figs with goat cheese and Parma ham. The bar upstairs is a great venue for live music on Fridays or Saturdays (cover R$20–R$35/US$10–US$18/£5.50–£9.50).

Rua Visconde de Itaboraí 8, Centro. © 021/2233-2531. www.caisdooriente.com.br. Main courses R$28–R$50 (US$14–US$25/£7.50–£14). AE, DC, MC, V. Tues–Sat noon–midnight; Sun–Mon noon–4pm. In the evenings taxi recommended. Bus: 119. Get off 1 stop past the Praça XV.

Confeitaria Colombo ★★★ BRAZILIAN/DESSERT   Tucked away in a narrow side street off the busy Avenida Rio Branco, this stunning Victorian tearoom hasn't changed much since it opened in 1894. The spacious room is divided into three sections. Two large counters flanking either side of the entrance serve up sweets and savory snacks with coffee or other refreshments for those in too much of a hurry to sit down. The remainder of the ground floor is taken up by an elegant tearoom, where a variety of teas, sandwiches, salads, and sweets are served on fine china underneath a '20s stained-glass window. The upstairs room is reserved for full lunches—on Saturdays the *feijoada* (black beans and pork stew) is worth a trip downtown.

Rua Gonçalves Dias 32, Centro. © 021/2232-2300. www.confeitariacolombo.com.br. Tearoom snacks and lunches R$10–R$25 (US$5–US$13/£2.70–£6.75); buffet lunch or Sat Feijoada buffet R$45 (US$23/£12) including dessert. Tea service R$8–R$20 (US$4–US$10/£2–£5.40). AE, DC, MC, V. Mon–Fri 8:30am–7pm; Sat 9am–5pm. Metrô: Carioca.

Laguiole ★★★ BRAZILIAN   On the second floor of the Modern Art Museum, the Laguiole restaurant fits in with its surroundings. The long, rectangular dining lounge is clean and modern, with clean metallic finishings. The food is modern and Brazilian, with a subtle touch of French. Some of our favorites include the large grilled prawns with mango chutney, or duck breast with wild cherries. Fish lovers will enjoy the sole filet, served on a bed of spinach with a carrot soufflé. As for choosing some

wine to go with lunch, you may want to ask for help from sommelier—the wine list is one of the largest in the country, over 600 labels and 8,000 bottles!

Inside the MAM, Av. Infante D. Henrique 80, Aterro do Flamengo. ⓒ 021/2517-3129. Main courses R$36–R$50 (US$18–US$25/£10–£14). DC, MC, V. Mon–Fri noon–5pm. Taxi recommended.

MODERATE

Bar Luiz *Finds* GERMAN   One of Rio's most beloved little restaurants, Bar Luiz has been around since 1887. Originally called Bar Adolf (after the owner), it moved to its current location on the Rua da Carioca in 1927. Then, as now, the bar was a popular hangout for intellectuals and politicians, which may have been why the owner was so quick to change the name in 1942. Name aside, the bar hasn't changed much over the years. The long room is simply furnished with wooden tables, chairs, and a lovely tile floor. The walls are plainly adorned with old photographs of Rio, while overhead big Casablanca fans whirl to keep the heat down. Even the menu has stayed much the same, in honor of the first German owner. Cariocas flock here to gorge themselves on generous portions of sausage and sauerkraut, Wiener schnitzel, Kassler ham, and potato salad. (Health craze, what health craze?) The draft beer—lager and dark—is pumped through a 2,400-foot-long refrigerated hose before finding its way into your glass. *Prosit!*

Rua da Carioca 39, Centro. ⓒ 021/2262-6900. Main courses R$12–R$25 (US$6–US$13/£3.25–£6.75). AE, DC, V. Mon–Sat 11am–11pm. Metrô: Carioca.

Bistro do Paço *Finds* BRAZILIAN   The perfect spot to escape the heat and noise in downtown Rio. Inside this little oasis inside the historic Paço Imperial, the thick whitewashed walls keep out the bustle while you recharge your batteries in the cool shade of the inner courtyard. The restaurant serves mostly bistro fare as well as a daily lunch special that will set you back R$15 to R$26 (US$7.50–US$13/£4–£7) for a plate of roast beef with a side order of pasta, spinach crepes with a ricotta-and-mushroom stuffing, or a chicken filet with applesauce and sautéed vegetables. For a light snack try a quiche, a freshly made sandwich with grilled vegetables, or a cold-cut plate. Desserts are strictly European: Austrian *linzertortes,* German fruit strudels, and Black Forest chocolate cakes, all of which go so well with a Brazilian *cafezinho.*

Praça XV 48 (inside the Paço Imperial), Centro. ⓒ 021/2262-3613. Main courses R$15–R$26 (US$7.50–US$13/£4–£7); sandwiches and quiches R$8–R$16 (US$4–US$8/£2–£4.25). AE, DC, MC, V. Mon–Fri 10am–8pm; Sat–Sun noon–7pm. Bus: 119 or 415.

Mr Ôpi ✶✶ KILO   One of the better kilo restaurants, Mr Ôpi can get pretty busy during prime lunch hours. If you can, time your visit for a little later in the afternoon; anytime after 2pm should be less hectic. However, you can't blame people for packing this restaurant because the food is delicious, with plenty of options for both the calorie-conscious and the gluttonous. The special light-cuisine dishes are marked and list ingredients and calories for the diet-conscious; the rest of us can feast on the excellent choices of pasta, cheeses, and antipasto, in addition to the meat and fish served fresh from the grill. On Fridays, the buffet always includes feijoada.

Rua da Quitanda 51, Centro. ⓒ 021/2507-3859. Per kilo R$34 (US$17/£9). DC, MC, V. Lunch Mon–Fri 11am–4:30pm. Bus: 119 or 415 to Praça XV.

INEXPENSIVE

Beco das Sardinhas (Rei dos Frangos Maritimos) ✶ *Finds* BRAZILIAN   Known as "the sardine triangle," this corner in Rio's historic downtown is the perfect place to spend a Friday afternoon as locals gather to unwind from the workweek. It started in the '60s when the Portuguese owners of three small restaurants began selling fried sardines. They would cut open the fish and fry them like a filet, dubbed *frango maritimo* (chicken of the sea) by a jesting customer, and the name stuck to one of the restaurants. These days the triangle has expanded to include six restaurants in a pedestrian area between Rua do Acre and Rua Mayrink Veiga. Every Friday after 6pm it transforms into a giant TGIF party. The patio tables and counters fill up almost as quickly as the fried sardines, salted and breaded in manioc flour, come piping hot off the grill. Accompanied by a *loira gelada* ("icy blond," the local nickname for draft), it's the perfect way to start a weekend. Once the crowd reaches critical mass, someone will inevitably strike up some samba and the party will ignite.

Rua Miguel Couto 139, Centro. Ⓒ 021/2233-6119. Everything under R$15 (US$7.50/£4). No credit cards. Mon–Fri 11am–10pm. Metrô: Uruguaiana.

Paladino ★★ BRAZILIAN   Is Paladino a deli, with racks of spices and jars of capers and artichoke hearts? Is it a liquor store, as the hundreds of glass bottles lined up in gleaming wooden cases seem to suggest? Or is it, as the crowds seem to indicate, a bustling lunch bar with some of the best draft beer in town? Is an exact definition really important? Probably not. What matters is that the beer is clear and cold and comes at the wave of a finger, the atmosphere is that of Rio in the Belle Epoque, and the sandwiches and snack plates are delicious. *Pratinhos,* as the latter are known in Portuguese, cost next to nothing—R$4 to R$8 (US$2–US$4/£1.10–£2.15)—and come loaded with sardines (whatever you do, order the sardines!) or olives, cheese, or great heaping stacks of smoked sausage. For about the same price there are also sandwiches, packed thick with cold cuts or cheese. All of this delectable nosh is served up by old-fashioned waiters in black pants and white shirts. Since 1907 an eclectic mix of lawyers, shopkeepers, workers, and executives has come here, and though none have ever succeeded in defining exactly what it is, they've never stopped coming.

Rua Uruguaiana 226, Centro. Ⓒ 021/2263-2094. Reservations not accepted. Sandwiches and side dishes R$4–R$15 (US$2–US$7.50/£1.10–£4). No credit cards. Mon–Fri 7am–8:30pm; Sat 8am–noon. Metrô: Uruguaiana.

SANTA TERESA
EXPENSIVE

Aprazível ★★★ *(Finds* BRAZILIAN   When owner and chef Ana Castilho opened her house for a community event in 1996, she thought it would be a one-time happening. Now, 10 years later, she still runs her restaurant out of her home 4 days a week and things show no sign of slowing down. Part of the charm is the house itself. The restaurant takes up several rooms and spills over into the garden. And then there is the view of downtown Rio and Guanabara Bay. The kitchen serves up an intriguing variation on Brazilian cuisine, with an emphasis on tropical flavors. Interesting starters include fresh grilled palm hearts, and pumpkin cream soup with prawns, tart apple, and cream. A popular main course is the *peixe tropical,* grilled fish in an orange sauce, served with coconut rice and baked bananas. A more hearty dish is the grilled lamb chop au jus and couscous. Desserts are best savored slowly. Our favorites were the *Morango do amor* (strawberries flambéed in orange juice and Cointreau) and the *Folia de Ouro Prêto* (grilled pineapple served with lime zest and coconut ice cream and a dash of *Limoncello* lemon liquor). Live *Chorinho* music on Thursdays.

Rua Aprazível 62, Santa Teresa. Ⓒ 021/3852-4935. www.aprazivel.com.br. Reservations recommended. Main courses R$38–R$55 (US$19–US$28/£10–£15). AE, MC, V. Thurs 8pm–midnight; Fri–Sat noon–midnight; Sun 1–6pm. Taxi recommended.

Espirito Santa ★★ BRAZILIAN One of the newcomers in Santa Teresa, Espirito Santa seems to have found the perfect formula for success: a cute restaurant, a great patio looking out over Santa Teresa, and excellent Brazilian food. Chef Natacha Fink, who hails from the Amazon, has developed a menu around a number of Brazilian dishes with the emphasis on Amazonian cuisine. A very popular starter is the Tambaqui "ribs," breaded pieces of *tambaqui* (a popular Amazonian fish) served with a pesto made from the jambu herb. Alternatively, try the crabmeat served in a crunchy farofa. The salads also combine some interesting ingredients; try the green salad with toasted Brazil nuts and a passion-fruit vinaigrette. Main courses include a variety of fish and seafood dishes as well as meat dishes. The seafood *bobó,* a stew with coconut milk and spices, is excellent and great for sharing. For a lighter meal opt for the grilled fish with a cashew crust, served on a bed of grilled fresh palm heart. Meat lovers should try the *bacuri* steak, grilled filet mignon served with a bacuri (Amazonian fruit) sauce and mashed sweet potatoes. Equally exotic is the grilled duck filet, served with an *açai* sauce. For dessert, there's warm gâteau filled with guava cream and cheese.

Rua Almirante Alexandrino 264, Santa Teresa. (✆ 021/2508-7095. Main courses R$28–R$44 (US$14–US$22/£7.50–£12). AE, DC, MC, V. Mon, Wed, and Sun noon–7pm; Thurs–Sat noon–midnight. Closed on Tues. Bus: 214, or take the tram, getting off just before the Largo dos Guimarães.

MODERATE

Sobrenatural ★★ SEAFOOD/BRAZILIAN One of the most popular restaurants in Santa Teresa, the open and spacious Sobrenatural is still often packed for lunch and dinner. The menu consists of seafood in a variety of shapes and sizes. Order a caipirinha and some shrimp dumplings *(pasteis de camarão)* to start with—each portion comes with 10 dumplings so it's great for sharing. The menu offers several grilled fish options, but the house specialty is really the *moqueca.* Just pick what kind of fish you want and it will come served in a piping hot stew with coconut milk, palm oil, shrimp sauce (optional), rice, and *pirão* (manioc purée). Portions are generous; mosquecas serve two people, the seafood spaghetti feeds up to three. *Note:* this open, breezy restaurant is great in summer but best avoided on rainy days.

Rua Almirante Alexandrino 432, Santa Teresa. (✆ 021/2224-1003. Main courses R$46–R$58 (US$23–US$29/£13–£16) for 2. AE, DC, MC, V. Daily noon–midnight. Bus: 214, or take the tram, getting off at the Largo dos Guimarães.

INEXPENSIVE

Bar do Mineiro ★ *Finds* BRAZILIAN The inland state of Minas Gerais is looked on as a culinary capital of sorts in Brazil, the source of down-home hearty comfort food. Bar do Mineiro is a little piece of Minas in Santa Teresa. Not limited to food, this combo restaurant, art gallery, and antiques shop also serves up an amazing variety of cachaça (the potent sugar-cane liquor found in *caipirinhas*). Also on offer are cachaça infusions: fruit and spices are soaked in the fiery cane alcohol, adding flavor and color to the booze. Supposedly this too is typically Mineiro, though to tell the truth the owner is such a homeboy, he'd likely claim beer was a Minas invention. About the food, however, there can be no doubt: Meals are hearty and portions generous. Appetizers include sausages and *pasteis*—savory pastries with a variety of stuffings, including sausage, cheese, or cabbage. The *frango com quiabo* (stewed chicken with okra) is popular, as is the *Feijão tropeiro*—much thicker than the *feijoada,* this bean dish is made with brown instead of black beans.

Rua Pascoal Carlos Magno 99, Santa Teresa. (✆ 021/2221-9227. Main courses R$14–R$24 (US$7–US$12/£4–£6.50). AE, V. Tues–Thurs 11am–2am; Fri–Sat 11am–3am; Sun 11am–midnight. Bus: 214, or take the tram, getting off at the Largo dos Guimarães.

> (*Moments*) **You Say *Farofa*, I Say . . . Blech**
>
> **Shawn says:** I never got *farofa*. What I mean is, I got it with *every* meal. Really, what is the point? *Farofa* (flour taken from ground manioc root, then baked with oil) has the dry, crumbly consistency of sawdust—and not coincidentally, that's what it tastes like. Brazilians painstakingly disguise the flavor, sometimes with raisins and dried fruit, but the end result tastes like . . . sawdust with raisins or dried fruit. Eating it made sense in the days when Brazilians lived in peasant huts; *farofa* was the sole source of carbohydrates. Like potatoes for the Irish, *farofa* kept them going. But Brazilian cooking now incorporates lots of carbs—like rice. Potatoes. French fries. Sometimes all three at once. But no matter how many starches are piled on your plate, *farofa* will be there to top it off.
>
> **Alexandra says:** *Farofa*—what's not to like? The coarsely roasted flour of the manioc root is the perfect companion to a Brazilian meal. Served plain, *farofa*'s nutty flavor stands up, while allowing it to soak up the juices on your plate only enhances its flavor. Every Brazilian has his or her favorite *farofa* recipe. My mother makes the best sweet *farofa* with bananas and raisins; it tastes as delightful as some of the best stuffings I've had. Other cooks prefer a savory version, adding spicy chorizo sausage, olives, or bacon. A *feijoada* is just not the same without *farofa*. Next time skip those greasy french fries and add some *farofa* to your plate. *Bon appétit!*

URCA
MODERATE

Circulo Militar ★★ *Finds* BRAZILIAN Whenever we hanker for dinner and a view (one of the best views in the city, in fact) we head to the Circulo Militar. This fabulous view of the Sugarloaf and Bay comes courtesy of the Brazilian armed forces (hey, if you're gonna run the country, you may as well take the best views). From the tree-shaded patio of a military club in Urca called the Circulo Militar, you look out across a tiny bay full of fishing boats to the sheer solid sides of the Sugarloaf. Come in the evening and you also get the lights of Niterói twinkling far off across the waters of Guanabara Bay. Civilians are completely welcome at the club (though some of the prime tables are sometimes reserved for officers). The menu serves up standard Brazilian fare (the two stars are for the view, not for the food) such as the *churrasco* for two with beef, sausage, chicken, and pork served with fries and rice (R$32/US$16/£9). In the evenings the kitchen fires up the wood-burning oven and turns out some decent pizzas. There's live music from 8pm onward, Tuesday through Sunday.

Praça General Tiburcio s/n, Praia Vermelha (on the far right, inside the military complex). ℂ 021/2275-7245. Main courses R$20–R$36 (US$10–US$18/£5.50–£10). No credit cards. Daily noon–midnight. Bus: 107 from downtown, 512 from Ipanema and Copacabana.

FLAMENGO/GLÓRIA/CATETE
VERY EXPENSIVE

Porcão ★★ BRAZILIAN/STEAK A mass carnivorous orgy, Porcão is where you go not to sample or taste or nibble, but to munch and stuff and gorge yourself on some of the best beef the world has to offer—in this case served up with some of the best views in the world. Porcão is a *churrascaria* (a chain, in fact; there are several in Rio, but this one has the best view) operating on the rodízio system. It's one price for all you can eat (dessert and drinks are extra), and once you sit down, an onslaught of waiters comes bearing all manner and variety of meat (steak cuts, roast cuts, filet mignon, chicken breast, chicken hearts, sausage of diverse kinds, and much more) which they slice to perfection on your plate. The "stop sign" card you receive is supposed to regulate this serving army—green means go ahead, and red says no more— but considering how little respect Cariocas have for red lights in general, it's hardly surprising that waiters keep coming no matter how abjectly you wave your little red surrender sign. Oh, and don't forget the nonmeat dishes: Included in your meal is a buffet with dozens of antipasto items, hot and cold seafood dishes, and at least 15 different kinds of salads and cheeses. Alas, no doggy bags allowed.

Av. Infante Dom Henrique s/n, Parque do Flamengo. ✆ 021/2554-8535. Reservations accepted. R$68 (US$34/£18) per person all-you-can-eat meat and buffet. 50% discount for children 6–9, free for children under 6. AE, DC, MC, V. Daily 11:30am–1am. Taxi recommended.

EXPENSIVE

Emporio Santa Fé ✿✿ BRAZILIAN/PASTA   This lovely two-story restaurant overlooking the Aterro do Flamengo is one of the best restaurants in Flamengo. The ground floor has a small wine bar and a few tables but you really want to head upstairs and, if possible, grab one of the window tables in the elegant L-shaped dining room. The chef's forte is pasta; all dishes are made fresh and combine some creative flavors. We loved the ravioli with prawns in a leek sauce with mushrooms as well as the *Tortele Tricolor*, pasta rounds stuffed with smoked ricotta, figs, and Parma ham. Steak lovers have plenty to choose from, including filet mignon medallions with grilled brie and potatoes, or grilled tournedos in a balsamic jus, served with rice and mushrooms. The wine list has over 400 options covering most of the world's regions, many reasonably priced (under R$70/US$35/£19).

Praia do Flamengo 2, Flamengo. ✆ 021/2245-6274. Reservations accepted. R$32–R$58 (US$16–US$29/£9–£16) main courses. AE, DC, MC, V. Sun–Thurs noon–midnight; Fri–Sat noon–2am. Bus: Any bus to Praia do Flamengo.

MODERATE

Estação da República ✿✿ *Kids* KILO   The Estação is top of the heap in that unique Brazilian category, the kilo restaurant. It offers a daily selection of at least 20 salads, a range of pastas, and many Brazilian favorites such as *feijoada* (bean stew), *vatapá* (seafood stew), and *bóbó* (shrimp stew). Fancier dishes include carpaccio and sushi. The *pièce de résistance* is the grill in the back of the restaurant where skilled chefs serve you a choice of beef, chicken, and a wide assortment of fish. It's a great place for children; they can see the food and try as much or as little as they like. Make your selection, weigh your plate, and find yourself a seat; drinks are served at your table. If the ground floor looks packed, take the escalator up to the second floor.

Rua do Catete 104, Catete. ✆ 021/2225-2650. Reservations not accepted. R$32 (US$16/£9) per kilo. AE, DC, MC, V. Daily 11am–midnight. Metrô: Catete.

BOTAFOGO
VERY EXPENSIVE

Carême ✿✿✿ *Finds* BRAZILIAN   These days you are more likely to see chef Flavia Quaresma on TV than at her own restaurant. Ever since she opened her cozy Botafogo bistro, Flavia has turned into a food sensation. What's behind the fuss? It may just be that macho Brazilian culture still finds a top female chef something of a novelty. But her food does genuinely impress. The menu is deliberately kept small in order to give dishes the attention they deserve. On our most recent visit we started off with a brie soup with pear and nuts and some oysters in a sauce of sparkling wine. The pastas and risottos can be ordered in a small version as an appetizer or in a larger version as an entree. The menu usually offers a fish of the day as well, and several meat options such as the rack of lamb with star anise and basmati rice, the ostrich steak with pasta stuffed with Gorgonzola and dried plums, or roasted duck served with Japanese pumpkin purée and lychee sweet-and-sour sauce. For dessert try the passion-fruit mousse with ginger, berries, and a raspberry coulis. The wine list is conservative with a small selection of well-chosen merlots, cabernet sauvignons, and chardonnays.

Rua Visconde de Caravelas 113, Botafogo. ⓒ 021/2537-2274. Reservations required. R$48–R$58 (US$24–US$29/ £12–£14). AE, DC, MC, V. Tues–Sat 8pm–close (usually around 1am). Bus: 176 or 178.

EXPENSIVE
Miam Miam ★★ CONTEMPORARY   Funky is hard to find in Rio de Janeiro, so Miam Miam has found the perfect niche to fill. This funky and hip eatery/lounge/bar is whimsically decorated with fabulous kitsch touches, without trying too hard. The result is a cozy room divided into a lounge area with comfortable couches and love seats and a somewhat more staid dining room. The lounge area is really the place to be, perfect for enjoying a cocktail and sharing some appetizers. The menu offers a range of high-end pub food: salads, sandwiches, pastas, risotto, and a few main courses such as a grilled tuna in a peppercorn crust or a steak with baked potato. If you are planning to eat a full meal you may want to opt for one of the Formica tables but make sure you grab that spot on the couch for dessert and an after-dinner drink.

Rua General Góes Monteiro 34, Botafogo. ⓒ 021/2244-0125. Main courses R$21–R$37 (US$8.75–US$16/£4.50– £8). Tues–Fri noon–3pm and 7:30pm–midnight; Sat 8pm–1:30am. Bus: 472.

Kotobuki ★ JAPANESE   The food at Kotobuki is good, very good even, but it's not really better than a number of other Japanese restaurants around Rio. What is outstanding is what you're watching while you eat. Kotobuki offers a sweeping view of Botafogo Beach and Botafogo Bay with the pretty boats at anchor in the marina, and, backstopping it all, the soaring Pão de Açúcar. Located in the seventh-floor food court of the Botafogo Praia Shopping (I know, but food-court food is *different* in Brazil), Kotobuki offers lunchtime specials including the *prato executivo:* 15 pieces of sushi and sashimi with a miso soup (called *misoshuri* in Brazil), or beef stir-fry with rice and miso and a sunomuno salad for R$22 (US$11/£6). The *teppanyaki* for two is skillfully prepared at your table, as the chef cooks up thin slices of beef, tofu, and vegetables. A favorite lunch special, particularly on the weekends, is the all-you-can-eat Japanese buffet. It offers a variety of sushi, sashimi, appetizers, tempura, and *yakisoba* for R$38 (US$19/£10) on Sunday to Thursday and R$42 (US$21/£11) from Friday to Sunday and holidays.

Praia de Botafogo 400, 7th floor, Botafogo. ⓒ 021/3141-9595. Reservations accepted, but window tables are on a first-come, first-served basis. R$19–R$48 (US$9.50–US$24/£5–£13). AE, DC, MC, V. Daily 11:30am–midnight. Metrô: Botafogo.

COPACABANA/LEME
VERY EXPENSIVE
Le Pré-Catelan ★★★ FRENCH   Although the Pré-Catelan has been one of Rio's best restaurants for ages, now it finally looks the part. Gone are the posh, glitzy 1980s *Dynasty*-style opulence and glamour. The dining room has been completely redone in

black and white and now has a modern, contemporary bistro-feel; a much more fitting decor for one of the most interesting menus in the city. After years of serving up one of the best tasting menus in town, ultra talented Chef Roland Villard has finally succumbed to pleas of customers to keep the best dishes around for more than a few weeks. Back to a regular menu, the dishes are anything but ordinary. The chef himself comes to each table to review the menu and explain the evening's dishes. Some of the best we've tried so far include the langoustine carpaccio served on a bed of crab salad with avocado mousse, a trio of grilled, raw, and marinated tuna and the beautifully presented *namorado* fish. Other outstanding dishes include the grilled rack of lamb or veal *ossobucco*. Sommelier Jean Pierre is on hand to assist in choosing an appropriate wine from the 250 choices on offer. The after-dinner cheese cart has some interesting choices, such as a fresh goat cheese made in Teresopolis. Desserts—yes, there is more food—are made from scratch. If you can't choose, order the *symphonie* of desserts for a taste of four or five mini-desserts. Enjoy, indulge, and walk off the calories along Copacabana's beach boulevard with a smile on your face.

Hotel Sofitel, Av. Atlântica 4240, Copacabana. ℰ **021/2525-1232**. Reservations required. Dress: business casual. Main courses R$44–R$68 (US$22–US$34/£12-18). AE, DC, MC, V. Mon–Wed 7:30–11:30pm; Thurs–Sat 7:30pm–midnight. Bus: 415.

Marius STEAK   One of the better all-you-can-eat rodízio systems, Marius serves up prime cuts of beef. In addition to this carnivore's dream, the buffet also includes excellent seafood such as fresh oysters, shrimp, langoustines, smoked salmon, and paella, in addition to salads and other side dishes. But back to what we came for. Here at Marius, waiters will come out over and over with your favorite cuts of steak, whether it is juicy tender rib-eye, T-bone, rack of lamb or any of the other kinds of typical Brazilian beef cuts such as maminha, alcatra, picanha, and fraldinha.

Av. Atlântica 290A, Leme. ℰ **021/2543-6363**. Reservations accepted. R$79 (US$40/£21) per person, all-you-can-eat buffet. AE, DC, MC, V. Mon–Fri noon–4pm and 6pm–midnight; Sat–Sun noon–midnight. Bus: 472.

EXPENSIVE

Da Brambini 🏆 *Finds* ITALIAN   For traditional Italian food in a cozy little bistro, look no further than Da Brambini. Decorated with family photos of the Brambinis, who hail from northern Italy, the restaurant has the welcoming and friendly atmosphere of an Italian trattoria. To start with, indulge in the *couvert*—a tasty antipasto platter with olives, salami, tuna paste, grilled eggplant, and freshly baked breads. Other worthwhile appetizers include the polenta with fresh funghi or with Gorgonzola. The main courses include veal with mushrooms, traditional *osso buco* (veal shanks stewed in wine), as well as a number of outstanding pasta dishes. Da Brambini certainly doesn't skimp on ingredients; the handmade ravioli with shrimp is just swimming with the little critters, all smothered in a creamy seafood sauce. The linguine with mussels, *sururu* (a tiny clam), and *vongole* are equally tasty. An Italian restaurant is bound to have a half-decent wine list, and Da Brambini doesn't disappoint with a good selection of Italian reds, starting at R$39 (US$20/£11) a bottle. The service is unhurried, and the staff is happy to let you linger over your dinner.

Av. Atlântica 514, Leme. ℰ **021/2275-4346**. Reservations recommended. Main courses R$28–R$46 (US$14–US$23/£7.50–£13). AE, DC, MC, V. Daily noon–1am. Bus: 472.

Siri Mole ★★ BAHIAN   Siri Mole is one of the best Bahian restaurants in town. Although the location on the corner of the busy Rua Francisco Otaviano is less than inspired, the food is worth the trip. The *moquecas* are outstanding, perfectly balancing the coconut milk, red dendê palm oil, and fresh cilantro that give the rich flavor to this signature dish. Try a moqueca with prawns, octopus, fish, or lagoustine. The grilled seafood or fish are also excellent, but make sure your table tries at least one moqueca. Portions are a reasonable size and can often be shared. A great way to sample some of Siri Mole's best is during Saturday's lunch buffet (noon–5pm) when the restaurant serves up a variety of delicacies (R$42/US$21/£11 per person, all you can eat). Whatever you try, make sure to save a bit of room for dessert. A cool and smooth favorite is the *quindim,* a creamy coconut pudding. For a bigger sugar hit try the *cocada*—pure coconut mixed with pure cane sugar—then wash it down with a hot and black *cafezinho.*

Rua Francisco Otaviano 50, Copacabana. ✆ 021/2267-0894. Reservations accepted. Main courses R$60–R$95 (US$30–US$47/£16–£26). AE, DC, MC, V. Mon 7pm–midnight; Tues–Sun noon–midnight. Bus: 415.

MODERATE

Alfaia ★★ *Finds* PORTUGUESE   This lovely neighborhood restaurant, tucked away off Avenida N.S. de Copacabana, has been serving up great Portuguese food for 15 years. The house specialties are the dishes made with *bacalhau* (salted codfish). Start off with the perfectly deep-fried *bolinhos de bacalhau* (codfish dumplings). The most popular main course is the *bacalhau à Bras,* oven-baked codfish served with potatoes, scrambled egg, onion, and olives. The cod dishes also come in half portions. We found that with appetizers and dessert the half dish was plenty for two people. Other dishes include the classic sole *á belle meuniére* sauce, with butter, garlic, and mushrooms and side of potatoes and vegetables. The grilled octopus with red peppers, onions, and roasted potatoes is also a good choice. The wine list includes some excellent Portuguese whites and reds. For dessert there are delicious Portuguese pastries. The bestseller is the pastel de nata, a flaky pastry stuffed with creamy custard.

Rua Inhangá 30, Copacabana. ✆ 021/2236-1222. Main courses R$46–R$85 (US$23–US$43/£12–£23) for 2. AE, DC, MC, V. Mon–Sat noon–midnight; Sun noon–11pm. Metrô: Cardeal Arcoverde.

Arab ★★★ MIDDLE EASTERN   Arab not only has one terrific waterfront patio (on Copa beach), but it also serves delicious Middle Eastern cuisine. For lunch the kitchen puts on an excellent kilo buffet, great for trying a variety of dishes. Offerings include tasty salads with chickpeas, lentils, grilled vegetables, and outstanding main dishes such as the roasted chicken with apricots, couscous with cod, grilled lamb kabobs, and piping hot, fresh pita breads. In the evenings, dishes are a la carte. Our favorites include the tray of *mezzes* (appetizer plates). Perfect for sharing, these plates come with enough munchies for three or four people and include hummus, baba ghanouj, savory pastries with ground beef or lamb, and other finger food. For a main course try the lamb dishes such as the *fakhas kharouf,* a lamb stew in red wine served with saffron rice and toasted almonds. The couscous dishes with chicken or lamb are also delicious and great for sharing. Desserts are dangerously rich and include sweet pastries made with sugar, rosewater, and almonds or pistachios.

Av. Atlântica 1936, Copacabana. ✆ 021/2235-6698. Main courses R$25–R$42 (US$13–US$21/£6.75–£11). AE, DC, MC, V. Mon 5pm–1am; Tues–Sun 8am–1am. Metrô: Cardeal Arcoverde.

Finds Where to Find the Finest *Feijoada*

For the best *feijoada* in town, try one of the following restaurants (on a Sat, of course—lunch only). **Confeitaria Colombo** serves an outstanding *feijoada* in the loveliest dining room in town, Rua Gonçalves Dias 32, Centro (② **021/2221-0107**). **Galani**, on the 23rd floor of the plush Caesar Park Hotel, Av. Vieira Souto 460, Ipanema (② **021/2525-2525**), is famous for its Saturday buffet. Even fancier is the spread at the Sheraton's **Mirador**, Avenida Niemeyer, São Conrado (② **021/2274-1122**). After lunch you'll welcome the 30-minute walk back to Leblon.

INEXPENSIVE

The Bakers QUICK BITE/DESSERT   The Bakers offers the perfect combination of American-style sandwiches and Brazilian sweets and desserts. The sandwich menu includes a variety of breads not often seen on Carioca menus, including ciabatta, eight-grain, whole wheat, and challah. The Al Pacino sandwich comes with Parma ham, mozzarella, sun-dried tomatoes, and a Mediterranean dressing. The Romeo and Juliette is a delicious combination of chicken breast, herb-flavored *catupiru* cheese, greens, and an apricot dressing. Once you've chewed through one of those, you can move on to the dessert. Choose from a mouthwatering selection of cakes and pies, such as Ecstasy, a chocolate cake with fresh strawberries, whipped cream, and chocolate sauce, or for something more nutty, the chocolate mousse cake with cashews. The bakery also serves up a mean brew of cappuccino with a rich and luscious layer of foam.

Rua Santa Clara 86, Copacabana. ② 021/3209-1212. www.thebakers.com.br. Everything under R$15 (US$7.50/£4). No credit cards. Daily 9am–8pm. Bus: 415.

Shirley ★★ Finds SPANISH   This hole-in-the-wall Spanish seafood restaurant has been packing them in for years and still has locals and visitors lining up on the weekends. The restaurant is small, the tables close together, and the older waiters not exactly perky, but the food is worth the trip. When you finally nab a spot, order the *couvert* while perusing the menu; you get a plate of chunky sardines in tomato sauce, olives, and lots of pickled veggies. It's better than many of the appetizers, and goes quite nicely with the house sangria. The menu offers a range of fish and seafood dishes, including typically Spanish items such as paella and zarzuela, a soup-like stew. The prawn dishes are made with the fresh, monster-size prawns you see in the display window. Fish lovers have the option of sole, sea bass, and snapper, which can be grilled, sautéed, broiled, or breaded. Plates come with generous side dishes of vegetables, potatoes, or rice and will easily feed two people.

Rua Gustavo Sampaio 620, Leme. ② 021/2275-1398. Main courses R$26–R$56 (US$13–US$28/£7–£15); most are for 2 people. Daily 11am–midnight. No credit cards. Metrô: Integração. Bus from Metrô: Cardeal Arcoverde to Leme or bus 472.

IPANEMA
VERY EXPENSIVE

Madame Butterfly ★★ JAPANESE   Rio's favorite Japanese restaurant, Madame Butterfly continues to offer creative and interesting cuisine. The two sisters Marina and Teresa who run the restaurant are always on the look out for new ideas and of some uniquely Japanese dishes (not adapted to Western taste buds) such as *umewan* soup, a rich broth made with Japanese plums, algae, and horseradish as well as delicious Brazilian-Japanese hybrids such as *gyoza* with Brazilian *abóbora* pumpkin, ginger-flavored lobster served on a cheese risotto, or a caramelized lamb chop with ginger and sesame seeds. Another interesting twist is the *casquinha de siri*, a Japanese-inflected version of the traditional Bahian appetizer. As done in the Butterfly, the dish features crabmeat and spices on a half shell sprinkled with fresh fish eggs. Madame Butterfly also serves exquisite Kobe beef. Try a grilled skewer or carpaccio. To sample a variety of dishes, diners can also opt for a tasting menu for two (R$115/US$57/£31).

Rua Barão de Torre 472, Ipanema. © 021/2267-4347. Reservations recommended on weekends. R$36–R$88 (US$18–US$44/£10–£24). AE, DC, MC. Daily noon–1am. Bus: 415.

Margutta ✷✷✷ ITALIAN Restaurants often have a limited life span so those that have been around for 10 years or more must be doing something right. Remember to reserve a table—even on a Tuesday night the place was packed. Owner and chef Paolo Neroni greeted us at the door. He is there on most nights to personally oversee the finishing touches on all dishes before they are served. We started off with deliciously sautéed mushrooms, followed by the *farfalle al gamberi e zafferano*, bowtie pasta with prawns in creamy saffron. For our entree we tried the signature dish, the *Pesce alla Neroni* (oven-roasted fish with fine herbs and a side of roasted potatoes and tomatoes). What really impressed us was the simplicity of the dishes. No convoluted sauces, long lists of ingredients, or fancy fusion. Most dishes seem to consist of three or four ingredients and just the right amount of herbs to balance out the flavors. The result is a simple and elegant cuisine that brings out the best of all ingredients. The restaurant itself is lovely: cozy and intimately lit and pleasantly decorated with nice linen and fresh flowers. All in all it's easy to see why Margutta is still at the top of its class.

Av. Henrique Dumont 62, Ipanema. © 021/2259-3718. Reservations recommended. R$28–R$68 (US$14–US$34/ £7.50–£18). AE, DC, MC. Mon–Fri 6pm–1am; Sat and holidays noon–1am; Sun noon–midnight. Bus: 415.

EXPENSIVE

Zazá Bistrô Tropical ✷✷ BRAZILIAN/FUSION Zazá is Rio's funkiest eatery, serving up a creative and interesting menu of South American cuisine fused with Oriental flavors. Everything about Zazá is fun, from the playful and eclectic decorations to the unique and excellent dishes. Diners can choose from a table on the terrace or in the dining room. The more adventurous can ask for a spot upstairs where everyone sits on the floor, leaning back on masses of silk-covered pillows. Surrounded by candlelight and lanterns, the room feels like a palace from the *Arabian Nights*. The menu offers plenty of choices. Appetizers include a deliciously grilled squid salad served on a bed of greens with an orange vinaigrette and mango chutney, or an order of mini-*acarajés* (deep-fried dumplings made of mashed beans and stuffed with spicy shrimp) served with tomato chutney instead of the usual hot-pepper sauce. Main courses also mix up the flavors. Try the *namorado* fish filet served with a purée of banana and palm heart, or a prawn ravioli served with grilled salmon in a saffron sauce. For vegetarians there is always a daily special, made with seasonal produce and interesting spices.

Rua Joana Angelica 40, Ipanema. © 021/2247-9101. R$28–R$42 (US$14–US$21/£7.50–£11). AE, DC, MC, V. Sun–Thurs 7:30pm–1am; Fri–Sat 7:30pm–1:30am. Bus: 415.

MODERATE

Casa da Feijoada ✷ BRAZILIAN Brazilian tradition dictates that the full-on *feijoada* meal is only served on Saturdays, leaving you high and dry bean-wise the other 6 days of the week. That's where the Casa da Feijoada comes to the rescue. There may be restaurants with better *feijoada* in town—there are certainly better-decorated ones—but what they can't offer you is *feijoada* when you want it. At the Casa any old day of the week you can experience Brazil's national dish with all the trimmings. To get off to a good start try the *caldo de feijão* (bean soup), washed down with a *batida de limão* (lime cocktail) to line your stomach, as the Brazilians would say. Now you are ready to bring on the actual bean stew, served in a clay pot with whatever meat you've a hankering for, be it sausage, bacon, *carne seca* (dried meat, highly recommended), pork loin, and other more obscure cuts. Side dishes include white rice, stir-fried cabbage, *farofa* (roasted manioc flour), and orange slices. If you like it spicy, ask for some *pimenta,* and they will bring you oil-soaked *malagueta* peppers to drizzle on the beans. Have another lime cocktail standing by in case you underestimate the heat.

Rua Prudente de Moraes 10, Ipanema. ℂ 021/2523-4994. R$21–R$38 (US$8.75–US$16/£4.50–£8) main course; *feijoada* meal R$49 (US$25/£13) per person, including appetizers, dessert, and drinks. AE, DC, MC, V. Daily noon–11pm. Bus: 415.

Churrascaria Carretão *(Kids)* *(Value)* BRAZILIAN/STEAK   For a *churrascaria* meal without breaking the bank, try Carretão. The system is similar to many rodízio restaurants: Meats are delivered to your table by a constant parade of waiters carrying a variety of cuts, and you can help yourself to a large buffet with a selection of 20 salads, various types of sushi, and even some grilled fish such as salmon or trout. In addition to beef, Carretão also serves up a variety of pork, sausage, chicken, and turkey cuts. Children under 5 eat free, those ages 5 to 9 pay only half price. Just keep them away from the fancy fruit smoothies and desserts that the waiters eagerly push on you; these jack up the bill pretty quickly.

Rua Visconde de Pirajá 112, Ipanema. ℂ 021/2267-3965. Reservations accepted. R$28 (US$14/£7.50) all-you-can-eat, drinks and desserts extra. AE, DC, MC, V. Daily 11am–midnight. Bus: 404 or 474 (corner Teixeira de Melo). Also in Copacabana: Rua Ronald de Carvalho 55, ℂ 021/2543-2666, and Rua Siqueira Campos 23, ℂ 021/2236-3435.

Delirio Tropical *(G)* BRAZILIAN   For a lighter and healthier meal or snack, stop in at the Delirio Tropical. The menu includes delicious fresh salads such as the caprese (a layered tower of sliced tomatoes, basil, and mozzarella), salpição (shredded chicken with carrots and corn), pasta salads, and at least six other salads. You have the option of putting together a meal with a selection of salads alone or you can add some grilled meat or make a choice from the daily specials of hot dishes, such as stuffed cannelloni or roast beef. The sandwich bar also makes excellent sandwiches, with your choice of bread, filling, and salad. The service is cafeteria-style, so you choose your dishes, load up your tray, and find a spot. The advantage is that it is fast and the buffet always offers a delicious selection of fresh salads, vegetables, and light meals. Perfect brunch spot!

Rua Garcia d'Avila 48, Ipanema. ℂ 021/3201-29774. Main courses R$14–R$32 (US$7–US$16/£4–£8.50). AE, MC, V. Daily 9am–9pm. Bus: 415.

INEXPENSIVE

Big Nectar *(Value)* QUICK BITE   One of Rio's best *lanchonetes* (dinner or lunch counter), Big Nectar is a bit like a magician's top hat. You glance into this hole-in-the-wall diner and think there's nothing there, then the guy behind the counter conjures up any kind of fruit juice you care to name, all of it made fresh and to order. Actually, the menu in this standing-room-only spot lists just over 25 different kinds of fruit juice. In addition to the standards such as passion fruit *(maracujá),* pineapple *(abacaxi),* or cashew fruit *(caju),* there's *carambola* (star fruit), *goiaba* (guava), *jaca* (jack fruit), and *açerola* (red juice from the tiny *açerola* fruit). This is where things get fun. You can mix anything with anything else. Try *laranja com açerola* (orange juice with *açerola*, a very popular combination); *maracujá* with mango; or pineapple and guava, cashew, and açerola. Some of these work, some don't. The magicians behind the counter are full of suggestions if you have any doubts. Or just throw caution to the wind and see what comes out of the hat. For a quick lunch or snack, Big Nectar also serves a selection of sandwiches and individual-size pizzas.

Teixeira de Melo 34A, Ipanema. No phone. Everything under R$12 (US$6/£3.25). No credit cards. Daily 7am–midnight. Bus: 404 or 474.

LEBLON
VERY EXPENSIVE
Bar d'Hotel ★★ *Finds* ITALIAN   On the first floor of the Marina Hotel in Ipanema, this hip eatery overlooks the most famous beach in the world yet doesn't even try to cash in on the view. Instead, what attracts the trendy crowd to eat, drink, and be merry is each other. Artists, actors, soccer players, designers, and others too cool to look at the ocean compete for each other's attention, all the while trying not to look like they're looking. Fortunately, above and beyond the posing the food is also great, so we mere mortals can remain happily oblivious to the star-spying and just have fun. If you have to wait at the bar for a table (very likely if you don't make reservations), try a lemon kir royal (champagne with lemon sorbet) or a sake *caipirinha*. Once seated, the waiter will come over with a blackboard listing the daily specials. The cuisine leans toward Italian with tropical accents. Appetizers include four types of bruschetta; the sampler plate comes with one of each. Main courses range from a delicious goat cheese ravioli in tomato sauce to a curried prawn risotto with banana-chutney grilled salmon served with a rich and creamy artichoke risotto. The restaurant is also open for breakfast and lunch, but the cool people don't show up until after 11pm. The restaurant is also a great place to just have a drink.

Av. Delfim Moreira 696, 2nd floor (inside the Marina All Suites Hotel), Leblon. ✆ 021/2540-4990. Reservations recommended. Main courses R$24–R$48 (US$12–US$24/£6.50–£13). MC, V. Thurs–Sat 7am–2am; Sun–Wed 8am–midnight. Bus: 415.

Garcia & Rodrigues ★★ BISTRO   Garcia & Rodrigues was once a veritable food megacomplex, with a deli, bakery, cafe, patisserie, ice-cream parlor, fine dining, and wine bar, but things have since been restructured and simplified. There is no longer a Garcia nor a Rodrigues in the enterprise, and what remains is an excellent bistro with a simple menu and an outstanding bakery and cafe. Open daily from 8am, the cafe serves up an excellent breakfast, a great selection of sandwiches, cheese plates, and some of the finest baked goods in town. The bistro opens at noon and offers risottos, pasta, grilled steak, and seafood, including a wonderful grilled salmon in orange-saffron sauce. You can also put a great spread together by ordering various appetizers such as the carpaccio, the bruschetta with brie, honey, and chutney, and a cold-cut or pâté plate, served with a basket of freshly baked bread. Luckily the wine cellar (or rather attic) remains; the maitre d' will happily help you choose an appropriate bottle.

Av. Ataulfo de Paiva 1251, Leblon. ✆ 021/2512-8188. Main courses R$24–R$52 (US$12–US$26/£6.50–£14). AE, DC, MC, V. Cafe and bakery daily 8am–midnight; bistro Mon–Thurs noon–12:30am. Bus: 415.

EXPENSIVE
Giuseppe Grill ★★ STEAK   We came here on a rare cold Rio night looking only for a good steak and a bottle of red wine. We left thoroughly impressed with this

Rio's Avenida Gourmet

We could probably fill half the Rio section with reviews of restaurants on the **Rua Dias Ferreira**. This windy street on the far edge of Leblon has become a one-stop shop for gourmands. For vegetarians, there's not one but two restaurants: the excellent kilo-restaurant **O Celeiro** (Rua Dias Ferreira 199; ℂ 021/2274-7843). You pay by the weight so help yourself to the delicious offerings and grab a spot on the large patio. And then there's the new kid on the block, **Quitanda Vegetal** (Rua Dias Ferreira 135; ℂ 021/2249-2301), which offers a lunch service that includes a variety of vegetarian and light cuisine dishes. To enjoy a stylish afternoon tea with all the trimmings, head over to **Eliane Carvalho** (Rua Dias Ferreira 242; ℂ 021/2540-5438). Closed on Mondays. Those who prefer to linger over their food can try **Doce Delicia** (Rua Dias Ferreira 48; ℂ 021/2249-2970), which serves grilled chicken, steak, or fish and your choice of two side dishes. For pasta there's **Quadrucci** (Rua Dias Ferreira 233; ℂ 021/2512-4551), which is open for lunch and dinner and has a great patio. For fine dining there are a number of options, mostly only open in the evenings. **Zuka** (Rua Dias Ferreira 233; ℂ 021/3205-7154) offers creative seafood dishes such as crab in filo pastry or grilled tuna in a cashew-nut crust. Across the street you'll find **Carlota** (Rua Dias Ferreira 64; ℂ 021/2540-6821), chosen by *Condé Nast Traveler* as one of the 50 most exciting restaurants in the world. Chef Carlota opened this Rio restaurant after her original São Paulo digs became the toast of the town. As in the original, her Rio dishes are fresh and creative, although people have complained that the portions are small. Farther down on the corner of Rua Rainha Guilhermina is the sushi hot spot of the city, **Sushi Leblon** (Rua Dias Ferreira 256; ℂ 021/2512-7830). On Thursday through Saturday evenings the lines can be long, but most people don't seem to mind the wait. If you're up on who's who in the Brazilian entertainment world, you can pass the time spotting artists and actresses. If a smaller and intimate sushi venue is more your style, check out **Mirai** (Rua Dias Ferreira 116; ℂ 021/2511-1476). This very stylish hole in the wall seats no more than 30, making it the perfect place for a romantic evening. The menu is quite varied—try the deep-fried tuna roll with a honey-sweetened soy sauce for dipping or the tempura prawn roll with smoked salmon.

restaurant; not only was the steak outstanding and the wine list affordably priced, the dining lounge itself is a pleasant, modern room, service was excellent and attentive—and oddly enough, we had some of the best grilled octopus ever! The house specialty is beef, no doubt about it. You can choose from grilled beef or slowly roasted beef on a charcoal grill. Both options include excellent cuts such as prime rib, Argentine chorizo steak, filet mignon, and rump steak as well as beef ribs, pork, and chicken. Each main course comes with a side dish; you can choose from a variety of salads, rice, and potatoes served fried, roasted, baked, or sautéed. And then oddly enough, the restaurant also serves up a selection of outstanding fresh seafood. Have a look at the catch of the day and ask for the waiter's recommendation. We went with the octopus, grilled to perfection and served tossed with arugula as a warm salad and were thoroughly impressed. Best of all, a steak dinner for two with appetizers, a bottle of Argentine Malbec, and coffee barely cracked the US$100 (£54) mark.

Av. Bartolomeu Mitre 370, Leblon. ✆ **021/2249-3055**. Main courses R$36–R$58 (US$18–US$29/£10–£16). AE, DC, MC, V. Mon–Thurs noon–4pm and 7pm–midnight; Fri–Sat noon–1am; Sun noon–11pm. Bus: 415

Nam Thai ⭐⭐ THAI   The best Thai restaurant in Rio is also the only Thai restaurant in Rio. Fortunately, the food is quite good! The restaurant is small and cozy and has an extensive menu with all the classic Thai dishes and a few selections from other Asian countries, including dim sum appetizers, Vietnamese pho soup, and a Malaysian mild curry. That said, we recommend starting off with one of the Thai soups, either the Tom Kha Kai, a rich coconut broth with chicken and lemon grass, or the clear and spicy shrimp soup, Tom Yum Kung. Main courses include a variety of Thai curries, either green or red, and your choice of beef, prawn, chicken, or duck. The duck curry is excellent. The rich meat can hold its own against the spicy red curry, and pieces of pineapple add a perfect sweet-tangy flavor. Other dishes worth trying include the pad Thai rice noodle or the fried rice noodle with squid, broccoli, and fresh basil. Fish lovers will enjoy one of the steamed fish dishes, delicately flavored with lemon grass or ginger and garlic. If you still have room for dessert, try the flambéed fruit with clove and cinnamon ice cream to finish your meal with a hint of spice.

Rua Rainha Guilhermina 95, Leblon. ✆ **021/2259-2962**. www.namthai.com.br. Main courses R$22–R$48 (US$11–US$24/£6–£13). AE, DC, MC, V. Mon 7pm–1am; Tues–Fri noon–5pm and 7pm–1am; Sat noon–1am; Sun noon–11pm. Bus: 415.

INEXPENSIVE

Bibi Sucos ⭐ *Value* QUICK BITE   The overhead menu at this popular neighborhood juice bar is refreshingly straightforward: juice, juice, and juice. You pick a fruit combination, and into the blender the ingredients go. It's trendy in newly health-conscious Rio to add on a scoop of protein powder for strength, *guaraná* for energy, or pollen for general health. Bibi also sells hamburgers, grilled-cheese sandwiches, and a variety of Brazilian savory pastries.

Av. Ataulfo de Paiva 591, Leblon. ✆ **021/2259-4298**. Everything under R$10 (US$5/£2.75). No credit cards. Daily 8am–2am; later on weekends if busy. Bus: 415.

KURT *Value* DESSERT   So what if Leblon has a higher than average number of dessert shops? This is one we couldn't leave out. Long a mainstay of Leblon, German pastry maker Kurt passed away a few years ago but his legacy (and treats) live on. Now in the hands of Kurt's grandsons (who obviously inherited the sweet gene; they run the pastry shop The Bakers; see review in "Copacabana/Leme," earlier in this chapter), this tiny shop in Leblon remains one of the best places in town to go for an *apfel strude,* pecan pie, or apricot cake. A famous Kurt creation is the "bee sting" (picada de abelha), a chocolate cake, the recipe of which is a closely guarded family secret.

Rua General Urquiza 117 (corner of Rua Ataulfo de Paiva), Leblon. ✆ **021/2294-0599**. Everything under R$15 (US$7.50/£4). No credit cards. Mon–Fri 8am–7pm; Sat 8am–5pm. Bus: 415.

Mil Frutas ⭐ DESSERT   One of the best ice-cream parlors in town, Mil Frutas offers a whole gamut of chocolate and fruit flavors, including some exotic ones from northern Brazil such as *açai, cupuaçu,* and *caja.* The staff is happy to give you a taste of several flavors before you decide on one, or two, or three.

Rua Garcia d'Avila 134, Ipanema. ✆ 021/2521-1584. Everything under R$12 (US$6/£3.25). No credit cards. Daily 10:30am–1am. Bus: 415.

JARDIM BOTANICO
VERY EXPENSIVE

Quadrifoglio ✦✦✦ ITALIAN   Another Rio favorite, Quadrifoglio proves that you don't need trendy gimmicks to run a successful restaurant. Chef and owner Silvia Bianchi shows off her skills in the kitchen, making some of the family favorites she learned from her grandmother in Italy. No frilly, prissy cuisine; Silvia's food is rich and hearty. Maitre d' (or should that be maîtresse?) Marlene is a wealth of knowledge at the front end. She knows the menu inside out and can offer excellent suggestions for wine. The list includes—surprise—a good variety of Italian. Most bottles will set you back R$60 to R$120 (US$30–US$60/£16–£32). Memorable dishes include the *mignonette al gorgonzola* (steak in a creamy Gorgonzola sauce, served with fresh pasta) and the *agnello al rosmarino* (a succulently grilled filet of lamb with fresh rosemary and a side of pumpkin gnocchi). Those who like veal will love the tender veal on a bed of orange risotto. True, this is not exactly light cuisine, but the dishes are worth a calorie splurge. And speaking of splurging, one of the best desserts we have come across recently was the *profumi mediterranei*—roasted fresh fig served with a scoop of lavender ice cream and topped with toasted almonds and some crème anglaise. I wish my grandmother had taught me to cook like that!

Rua J.J. Seabra 19, Jardim Botânico. ✆ 021/2294-1433. Reservations recommended. Main courses R$34–R$58 (US$17–US$29/£9–£16). AE, DC, MC, V. Mon–Fri noon–4pm and 7:30pm–1am; Sat 7:30–1am; Sun noon–5pm. Bus: 572 (from Leblon or Copacabana) or 170 (from downtown).

EXPENSIVE

Capricciosa ✦ PIZZA   One of the trendiest pizza restaurants in town, Capricciosa is where the hip and beautiful people eat. A large wood-burning oven dominates the back of the room and turns out great-tasting pizzas and calzones, from the plain Pizza Margarita with mozzarella, Parmesan, and fresh basil and tomato to the signature Capricciosa with tomato, ham, artichoke, mushrooms, bacon, and egg. The restaurant also has a delicious cold-cut and antipasto buffet, served with slices of homemade crusty bread, and offers a selection of pasta dishes. Those who prefer a more low-key and intimate setting can opt for the wine bar, to the left of the busy and bustling main dining room; the menus are the same. This ain't cheap pizza . . . in fact at these prices you could be digging into a juicy steak or a tasty seafood dish elsewhere, but that is the price you pay to hobnob with Rio's rich and famous.

Rua Maria Angelica 37, Jardim Botânico. ✆ 021/2527-2656. Main courses R$28–R$42 (US$14–US$21/£7.50–£11). AE, DC, MC, V. Daily 6pm–1am (later if it's busy). Bus: 572 (from Leblon or Copacabana) or 170 (from downtown).

MODERATE

Couve Flor ✦ KILO   The mother of all kilo restaurants, Couve Flor is where it all started in the mid-'80s. Even now that the system has been widely adopted, Couve Flor still goes the extra mile. The menu offers an astonishing range of dishes, including elaborate and interesting options such as rabbit stew, fish *moqueca*, fresh pasta, at least 20 different kinds of salads, and grilled meats. The buffet even offers vegetarian choices such as stroganoff made with soybean *meat*. In the evenings Couve Flor also serves a selection of pizzas from a wood-burning oven, and the weekend lunch buffet is legendary with even more dishes and a choice of 15 desserts. The beauty of the kilo system is that you can have a bite of as many dishes as strike your fancy.

Rua Pacheco Leão 724, Jardim Botânico. ✆ **021/2239-2191.** www.couveflor.com.br. Price per kilo: R$34–R$39 (US$18–U$20/£9–£11). AE, DC, MC, V. Mon–Fri noon–5pm and 7–11pm; Sat noon–11pm; Sun 11:30am–9pm. Bus: 572 (from Leblon or Copacabana) or 170 (from downtown).

Da Graça ✿ CAFE   Half the fun of going to Da Graça is in seeing the decor. It's wonderfully kitsch, decorated top to bottom in colorful hippie junk. The menu consists of numerous small dishes that you can mix and match according to your appetite. The main dishes change daily, but can include a *namorado* fish with capers or salmon with herb crust. Remember, these are just small portions. You can add a side of rice, salad, a baked potato with curry, or a penne with lemon sauce. In the evenings there are a few more snack options such as sardines, samosas, or falafel. This is a great place to go for a drink or a snack, rather than a full meal.

Rua Pacheco Leão 780, Jardim Botânico. ✆ **021/2249-5484.** R$8–R$24 (US$4–US$12/£2–£6.50). AE, DC, MC, V. No credit cards. Tues–Sun noon–2am. Bus: 572 (from Leblon or Copacabana) or 170 (from downtown), get off at corner Rua Jardim Botânico with Pacheco Leão, 10-min. walk or take bus 406 from Flamengo.

LAGOA
EXPENSIVE

Bistrô 66 ✿✿✿ FRENCH   Bistrô 66 chef Thomas Troisgros may not be the best French chef in town (that honor belongs still to Tom's *papa,* Claude), but the younger Troisgras has certainly inherited his father's culinary skills. This cozy eatery offers outstanding, authentic French cuisine at still-affordable prices. If you're a seafood fan don't miss the Moules Mariniere, a big steaming pot of mussels in a fragrant white-wine sauce, perfect for dipping with some crusty bread. Another great appetizer is the fresh shiitake mushroom carpaccio with generous shavings of fresh Parmesan cheese. Main courses include pastas and risottos, including the house specialty, a risotto with Parma ham, brie, and rucula or a fettucini with fresh mushrooms and white truffle olive oil. Meat dishes include an excellent roasted lamb with a tomato and lemon *farofa* confit and a delicious grilled duck in orange sauce. You can also order a more simple steak dish—filet mignon or tender picanha and your choice of sauce (pepper, red onion, or wine). All dishes are served with either crispy thin potato slivers or basmati rice. And then there are the desserts: scrumptious apple pie, mango strudel, and a variety of delicious pastries. The only catch at this restaurant? The wine list. The very, very expensive wine list. Bottles start at R$120 (US$60/£32) and quickly go stratospheric. However, choose one of the (very few) affordable options and you can still enjoy a top-notch French meal without blowing your credit limit.

Av. Alexandre Ferreira 66, Lagoa. ✆ **021/2266-0838.** www.66bistro.com.br. R$38–R$52 (US$19–US$26/£10–£14) or R$72 (US$36/£19) for an appetizer, main course and dessert (any item from the a la carte menu). MC, V. Tues–Sat noon–midnight; Sun noon–4pm. Taxi recommended.

Olympe - close to
Botanical Gardens -

5

Exploring Rio de Janeiro

Most visitors to Brazil start or end their visit in Rio de Janeiro. A wise choice. There may be wider beaches in the north, higher mountains in the south, and larger jungles in the Amazon, but nowhere else on earth is there that wonderful combination of white-hot sand and tall green peaks, with a blaze of urban humanity filling all the spaces in between. Most people stay in the beachfront neighborhoods of Copacabana and Ipanema. They're great places to soak up the sun and to people-watch. But even if your time is limited, it's worth making the effort to explore further. In the historic downtown neighborhoods of Centro, Lapa, and Santa Teresa you'll find narrow cobblestone streets, grand plazas, gold-covered churches, and buildings of the baroque, Beaux Arts, and Art Deco styles.

Shoppers will be in heaven; browse the crafts markets for souvenirs or check out the small shops in downtown's pedestrian streets. Upscale shoppers will love the Rio Sul mall and the fancy boutiques in Rio's tony Ipanema. If you have the energy, Rio's stunning setting offers numerous recreational activities: hiking, hang gliding, surfing, rock climbing, and kayaking are just a few options. Taking in a game of soccer is an adventure in itself. Nowhere are the crowds larger or livelier than at Rio's Maracanã stadium. The city's vibrant cultural scene comes to life in the evening and never disappoints: See some of the local samba bands in Lapa, or emerging talents at the city's many live music venues, or splurge to see a big national star such as Caetano Veloso.

SUGGESTED RIO DE JANEIRO ITINERARIES

If You Have ❶ Day

For most of us pale-skinned gringos, it's an act of utter insanity on the first day to set foot on the beach during the peak afternoon sunshine. On your first day **hit the beach early.** Enjoy the clear air and an hour or so of tanning in the softer morning rays. Then head up to the **Corcovado** and see Rio laid out below you in all its glory. Stop in for a quick lunch at any of Rio's countless kilo restaurants, then in the afternoon head to **Centro** to explore what you've seen from on high. Wander **old Rio,** making sure to check out the Uruguaiana shopping district,

and to poke your head into any one of countless baroque churches. Finish your walk with a nice cold *chopp* (beer) at a sidewalk cafe in **Cinelândia,** or in the countless patios in the **Arcos do Teles.** Have dinner back in the Zona Sul, at one of the top-notch restaurants in **Leblon.** If it's a Saturday in pre-**Carnaval** season, go see a **samba school rehearsal.** Or find a **botequim** or restaurant that plays music and enjoy Rio until the wee hours.

If You Have ❷ Days

On your second day get some culture. Go see the **Museu de Arte Moderna (MAM),** or if painting's not your thing see the **Museu Histórico Nacional,** the **Forte de Copacabana,** or **Ilha Fiscal.** Have lunch overlooking **Sugarloaf (Pão de Açúcar)** at the **Circulo Militar** in **Urca** (see dining review in chapter 4). Afterward, work off those calories by climbing up to the Pão de Açúcar's peak. Reward yourself for your efforts by having dinner at the **Porcão** on **Flamengo** beach—all-you-can-eat Brazilian barbecue, with a view of the bay and the Sugarloaf thrown in (see dining review in chapter 4). In the evening, go for a drink, some dancing, and some live Brazilian music at any of a number of spots in **Lapa.**

If You Have ❸ Days

In the morning take the old streetcar across the **Arcos da Lapa** to the quirky hilltop neighborhood of **Santa Teresa.** See the **Museu Chácara do Céu.** Enjoy the view at the **Ruin Park,** or have lunch in an outdoor café. In the afternoon, go **hang gliding.** Soar above the beach, feeling the wind, admiring the mountains and the waves below. Or if that's a bit too much, take a hike in the rainforest in **Tijuca National Park,** or stroll amid the stately palm trees in the **Jardim Botânico.** In the evening, stroll the walkway round the edge of the **Lagoa.** Have a snack, a beer, or dinner at one of the many kiosks. Find a kiosk with a band and enjoy the music and the prime people-watching.

If You Have ❹ Days Or More

Take Marcelo Armstrong's **Favela Tour** through the huge and hidden neighborhood of **Rocinha.** Or check out the sights in **Niterói** across the bay. Try some extreme sports, like **rappelling** or **rafting.** Or take a gentle tour down the coast to the **Museu Casa do Pontal** and **Grumari beach.** If you've got several days to spare, go inland to the summer capital of **Petrópolis,** or the pretty historical cities of **Paraty** or **Ouro Prêto** and **Mariana.** Or else head up the coast to **Búzios** and do some **scuba diving** or just hang out on the long white **ocean beaches.** Lord knows, you could even spend more time on the beach in Rio.

1 The Top Attractions

CENTRO

Ilha Fiscal ★★   This little blue-green ceramic castle afloat on its own island in the bay off Praça XV looks like the dwelling place of a fair elfin princess, but in fact was built as the headquarters for the Brazilian Customs Service. Initially a rather prosaic building was planned, but Emperor Pedro II intervened, demanding that the gem of a site be given a jewel box of a building. Designer Adolpho Del-Vecchio complied, making charming use of the Gothic Revival then sweeping Europe. Much of the interior of this gorgeous building is taken up by a small museum on the Brazilian navy (it *is* their island). The tour lasts about 2½ hours. On weekdays, tour goers travel to the island by boat, whereas on weekends the trip is by bus along a causeway.

The navy also offers a separate 90-minute boat tour of four small islands bristling with destroyers, aircraft carriers, and lots more military hardware. The voyage to Ilha Fiscal, Ilha das Cobras, Ilha dos Enxadas, and Ilha Villagagnon takes place aboard a World War I–era tugboat.

Av. Alfredo Agache s/n, Centro (behind Praça XV). ⓒ **021/2104-6992.** Admission R$8 (US$4/£2) adults, R$4 (US$2/£1) children 12 and under. Guided tours only. Departures Thurs–Sun. Boat tours depart at 1:15pm and 3:15pm; visits to the Ilha Fiscal depart at 1pm, 2:30pm, and 4pm. Closed statutory holidays. Call to confirm hours at ⓒ 021/2233-9165. Bus: 119 or 415 (Praça XV).

Museu de Arte Moderna (MAM) ✨✨   Located in the waterfront Flamengo park, the MAM is a long, large, rectangular building lofted off the ground by an arcade of concrete struts, giving the structure the appearance of an airplane wing. Inside, like the arches of a Gothic cathedral, the concrete struts do all the load-bearing work, allowing for walls of solid plate glass that welcome views of both city and sea. The structure also provides a vast interior display area free of pillars and other obstructions. Displays change constantly—check the website to see what's on—but at all times the MAM presents the best of what's happening in Brazil and Latin America, as well as providing a temporary home to big traveling international exhibits. Signage—a rare bonus—is in both English and Portuguese. The MAM also has a cafe, a bookstore, and a film archive containing over 20,000 Brazilian titles. Allow an hour to 90 minutes.

Tip: Have a look at the garden from the second-floor patio: The lawn, wavy shapes included, is the work of Brazil's great landscape architect Roberto Burle Marx.

Av. Infante Dom Henrique 85, Parque do Flamengo (Aterro), Centro. © 021/2240-4944. www.mamrio.com.br. Admission R$5 (US$2.50/£1.35) adults, R$2 (US$1/£.50) students and seniors, free for children 12 and under. Tues–Fri noon–6pm; Sat–Sun noon–7pm. Metrô: Cinelândia. Bus: 472 or 125 (get off at Av. Beira Mar by the museum's footbridge).

Museu Histórico Nacional ✨✨   The place for anyone looking for a good overview of Brazilian history from Cabral's arrival in 1500 to the present. Housed in the former national armory, the National History Museum features seven permanent exhibits on themes such as early exploration, coffee plantations, and modernism, each of which is illustrated with abundant maps and artifacts. Even better, much of the Portuguese signage comes with often very opinionated English translation. Keep in mind that Brazilian museums haven't bought into the "interactive learning" idea. Instead, displays consist of glass cases and explanatory text. They're carefully curated—one case shows a mattock used in an 18th-century peasant rebellion juxtaposed with a bright red banner of the modern Sem-Terra movement, a telling evocation of the land distribution problem that has plagued the Brazilian countryside for 400 years and counting. Allow 2 hours (longer if you're a serious history buff).

Praça Marechal Âncora s/n. © 021/2550-9224. www.museuhistoriconacional.com.br. Admission R$6 (US$3/£1.50) adults, R$3 (US$1.50/£1) seniors and children 12 and under. Tues–Fri 10am–5:30pm; Sat–Sun 2–6pm. Bus: 119 or 415 (10-min. walk from the Praça XV).

Museu Nacional de Belas Artes ✨   A classic museum in the European tradition, the Museu Nacional de Belas Artes houses a vast collection of European and Brazilian art, with an emphasis on 18th- and 19th-century European work. The building, built in 1908, is worth a visit by itself. Though the layout is confusing, the art itself is beautifully displayed. The museum has two galleries of Brazilian art. The highlight is the collection by Frans Post, Brazil's first landscape painter, which is displayed with other works from the 17th, 18th, and 19th centuries. The gallery is undergoing extensive renovations and parts of the museum may not be open for viewing. Also worthwhile is the beautiful collection of Italian baroque paintings, some brought to Brazil in 1808 by the fleeing Portuguese King João VI. The center rooms are used for temporary exhibits of Brazilian artists. Allow an hour.

Av. Rio Branco 199, Centro. © 021/2240-0068. www.mnba.gov.br. Free admission. Tues–Fri 10am–6pm; Sat–Sun 2–6pm. Metrô: Cinelândia.

Paço Imperial ✨   For 155 years this was the administrative nerve center of Brazil, serving as the governor's palace and then as the home and office of Brazil's emperors from 1808 until the fall of the monarchy in 1888. It's a pleasingly simple structure,

What to See & Do in Rio Centro

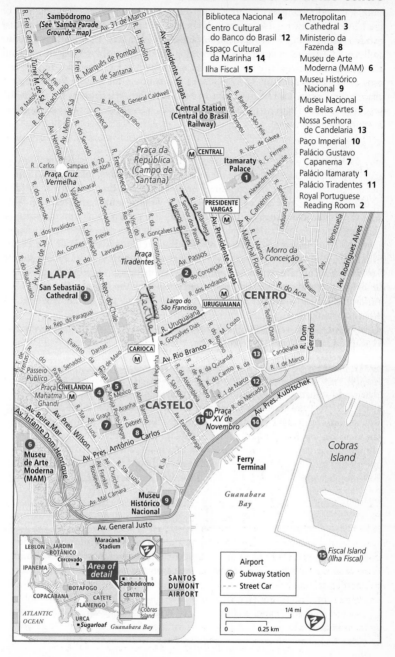

Sambódromo
(See "Samba Parade Grounds" map)

Biblioteca Nacional **4**
Centro Cultural
  do Banco do Brasil **12**
Espaço Cultural
  da Marinha **14**
Ilha Fiscal **15**

Metropolitan
  Cathedral **3**
Ministerio da
  Fazenda **8**
Museu de Arte
  Moderna (MAM) **6**
Museu Histórico
  Nacional **9**
Museu Nacional
  de Belas Artes **5**
Nossa Senhora
  de Candelaria **13**
Paço Imperial **10**
Palácio Gustavo
  Capanema **7**
Palácio Itamaraty **1**
Palácio Tiradentes **11**
Royal Portuguese
  Reading Room **2**

Central Station
(Central do Brasil
Railway)

Praça da
República
(Campo de
Santana)

Praça Cruz
Vermelha

Itamaraty
Palace ❶

PRESIDENTE
VARGAS

LAPA
San Sebastião
Cathedral ❸

Praça
Tiradentes

Morro da
Conceição

CENTRO

Largo do
São Francisco

URUGUAIANA

CARIOCA

Praça CINELÂNDIA
Mahatma
Ghandi

CASTELO

Praça
XV de
Novembro

Museu
de Arte
Moderna
(MAM) ❻

Museu
Histórico
Nacional ❾

Cobras
Island

Ferry
Terminal

Guanabara
Bay

Av. General Justo

Fiscal Island
(Ilha Fiscal) ❶❺

LEBLON JARDIM
        BOTÂNICO
        Corcovado ■
IPANEMA

Maracanã ■
Stadium

Area of
detail

Sambódromo

SANTOS
DUMONT
AIRPORT

BOTAFOGO
COPACABANA CATETE
            FLAMENGO CENTRO

ATLANTIC
OCEAN

URCA
■ Sugarloaf

Cobras
Island

Guanabara Bay

Airport
Ⓜ Subway Station
--- Street Car

0   1/4 mi
0   0.25 km

97

long, low, and rectangular, its many high-ceilinged rooms arranged around a pair of cool interior courtyards. Nowadays it serves as an exhibition hall for traveling cultural exhibits, some of which are excellent, but most of which, alas, are in Portuguese only. Still, it's an extremely pleasant and interesting building to walk through. A room on the ground floor charts the history of the palace, with maps, paintings, and engravings. Allow about an hour. The cafe in the courtyard on the ground floor is a great place to take refuge on hot afternoons in Rio (open the same hours as the museum).

Praça XV 48, Centro. ℰ 021/2533-4407. www.pacoimperial.com.br. Free admission. Tues–Sun noon–6pm. Bus: 119 or 415 (and many others).

SANTA TERESA
Museu Chácara do Céu ✪✪   A wealthy man with eclectic tastes, Raymundo Castro Maya had this mansion built in the hills of Santa Teresa, then filled it with all manner of paintings, pottery, and sculpture. The house itself is a charmer, a stylish melding of hillside and structure that evokes Frank Lloyd Wright's work in the American West. The views from the garden are fabulous. Inside, you get a glimpse into the eccentric mind of the collector. Castro Mayo seems to have had three chief interests—European painters (Impressionists like Monet and Matisse, and more daring stuff like Picasso and Dalí); Brazilian art, particularly 19th-century landscapes; and Chinese pottery. He also seems to have felt some kinship between the three. Thus on an upper floor landing do we find a cubist painting by Dutchman Kees Van Dongen next to an 18th-century Brazilian landscape, both of them hung over an antique Chinese vase. See what you think.

Rua Murtinho Nobre 93, Santa Teresa. ℰ 021/2507-1932. www.museuscastromaya.com.br. Admission R$3 (US$1.50/£1) adults, free for children under 12. Free admission Wed. Wed–Mon noon–5pm. Tram: Curvelo.

CATETE, GLÓRIA & FLAMENGO
Museu da República—Palácio do Catete ✪✪   It's gratifying to find a museum that works so hard to grab your interest. Located in a gorgeous baroque palace that from 1897 to 1960 served as the official residence of Brazilian presidents, the three floors of exhibits in this museum try to engage visitors on the history and politics of the Brazilian republic. More traditional displays preserve the air of the palace in its administrative days—a formal ballroom with a long leather-covered table was where the cabinet used to meet (ho-hum). The best—and most biased—exhibit is the three-room hagiography of President Getulio Vargas. It's a curious treatment for this museum,

---

Tips Getting to know Santa Teresa

Visitors to Santa Teresa should stop by the **Santa Teresa Visitor Information Center** (ℰ 021/2509-6875 or 021/9858-6875; www.santateresatour.com), located next to the movie theater in the Largo dos Guimarães, the neighborhood's main square.

The center offers a variety of information on Santa Teresa, including sights, accommodations, dining, and local artists. A daily 3-hour walking tour departs from here—R$75 (US$38/£20) per person, including pickup/drop-off at your hotel. Call ahead to arrange a specialized tour of the many artists' studios in the neighborhood.

> **(Tips) Take a break**
>
> The perfect spot for a break in Santa Teresa is the **Jasmim Manga Café,** Largo
> dos Guimarães 143, Santa Teresa (© **021/2242-2605**). This cute courtyard cafe
> serves outstanding coffees and desserts.

given that Vargas brought the First Republic to an end with a coup in 1930. Still, they
do a great job, creating a multimedia sensory experience of Getulio's life and times
with audio clips, newsreels, photos, and personal effects. Behind that, in a softly back-
lit glass case, is the pearl-handled .32-caliber Colt that Getulio used on the night of
August 24, 1954, to blast a fatal hole in his heart. Allow an hour to 90 minutes.

The formal gardens surrounding the palace are well worth a walk. There's a cafe in
an artificial grotto and a small branch of the wonderful Folklore Museum containing
puppets and folk art from around Brazil. Admission is free.

Rua do Catete 153, Catete. © **021/2558-6350**. www.museudarepublica.org.br. Admission R$6 (US$3/£1.50) adults,
free for seniors and children 11 and under. Free on Wed and Sun. Tues–Fri noon–5pm; Sat–Sun 2–6pm. Metrô: Catete.

BOTAFOGO & URCA

Museu do Indio ⭐⭐ *Kids*   Housed in an elegant 19th-century mansion in a quiet
part of Botafogo, the Indian Museum's collection is one of the most important in
Latin America, with over 14,000 artifacts, 16,000 papers and books on indigenous
topics, and over half a million historical documents on Brazilian Indian tribes. All that
sounds a little dry, but the museum is anything but. Instead, its exhibits are some of
the most innovative and artistic I have come across in a Brazilian museum, including
striking wall-size black-and-white photos adorned with colored feathers and a display
on kids' toys where the objects dangle from the ceiling at various heights. The sym-
bolism of the hunt is portrayed in a dark room with just a ray of light illuminating the
floor, casting an eerie glow on spears and animal skulls. There are no signs in English,
but the exhibits are so vivid they speak for themselves. For kids there is a gallery with
(washable) body paint and a large selection of stamps so they can practice adorning
themselves as warriors, hunters, chiefs, or shamans. It's a great spot for children and
an easy place to spend 2 hours. As a good portion of the displays are outside, avoid
going on a rainy day.

Rua das Palmeiras 55, Botafogo. © **021/2286-8899**. www.museudoindio.org.br. R$3 (US$1.50/£1) all ages (free for
children in strollers), free on Sun. Tues–Fri 9am–5:30pm; Sat–Sun 1–5pm. Metrô: Botafogo.

Sugarloaf (Pão de Açúcar) ⭐⭐⭐   Along with samba, beaches, and beautiful
women, the Sugarloaf remains one of the original and enduring Rio attractions.
Deservedly so. Standing on its peak, the entire cidade maravilhosa lays at your feet:
the beaches of Ipanema and Copacabana, the favelas of Babylonia, the Tijuca Forest,
Christ the Redeemer on his mountain, the Bay of Guanabara, and the fortresses at the
edge of far-off Niterói. It's a truly beautiful sight. The cable car leaves every half-hour
from 8am to 10pm daily, more frequently if there are enough people waiting. The
ascent is in two parts: The first from the ground station in Urca to the 220m (721-ft.)
Morro de Urca, the second up to the 396m (1,299-ft.) Sugarloaf itself. Trams are
timed so it's next to impossible to make both trips without spending transition time
on the Morro, so better to relax and enjoy life. The Morro offers excellent views, as
well as a cafe, snack bar, restaurant, souvenir stands, and children's play area.

Tip: If you're feeling active, hike up. The trail is challenging, but oh, the rewards! You start just above the crashing waves, and the views just keep getting better as you go. See "Hiking" under "Outdoor Activities" later in the chapter for details.

Av. Pasteur 520, Urca. © 021/2546-8400. www.bondinho.com.br. Admission R$35 (US$18/£9.50) adults, R$18 (US$9/£5) children 6–12, free for children under 6. Daily 8am–9pm. Last ride up at 8pm. Metrô: Botofogo, then catch the integração bus marked Urca.

LAGOA
Jardim Botânico ★★   A photograph of the main avenue of the Botanical Gardens—a procession of stately imperial palms punctuated by a splashing classical fountain—graces nearly every tour brochure of Rio. Fortunately, the reality lives up to the photos. In the nearly 2 centuries since Emperor Dom João VI founded the original, the botanical garden has grown to 348 acres and added 6,000 species of tropical plants and trees to its collection. It's now one of the few places near Rio to see standing Brazilwood (Pau Brasil) and other species from the Atlantic rainforest. Many trees and shrubs are labeled with common and Latin names, but there's not much in the way of explanation (be sure to ask the cashier for a map). Botanical buffs can call the visitor center (see number below) to book a guided tour; English- and Spanish-speaking guides are available. There is no extra cost for the guided tour, it just depends on availability. Most visitors, however, just enjoy the peace and beauty of a meander along the many little paths, garden trails, and greenhouses. The bromeliad and orchid greenhouses are especially nice. My personal favorite was a greenhouse full of tropical carnivores—pitcher plants and Venus flytraps. A cafe and a small bookshop are on-site.

Rua Jardim Botânico 1008. © 021/3874-1808. www.jbrj.gov.br. Admission R$4 (US$2/£1.10) adults, free for children 7 and under. Daily 8am–5pm. Bus: 170 (from Centro), 571 (from Glória-Botafogo), or 572 (from Zona Sul).

ZONA SUL
Forte de Copacabana ★★   Simply massive. Built on the eve of World War I by the German arms-maker Krupp, Copacabana Fort boasts walls of reinforced concrete 12m (39 ft.) thick. They protect a whacking great cannon (305mm) that could fire a deadly shell 23km (14 miles) out to sea. The army has done an excellent job presenting the interior as it was when it was a working bastion. Rooms contain then-state-of-the-art instruments (lots of brass wheels and finely scaled calipers) for targeting and aiming the great guns. And down in the very bowels of the fort the cannons are still in place. Best of all, the bored soldiers guarding the place never leave the gate, so you're free to touch, fiddle, and play as much as you want. Twirl the knobs on the great cannon until its muzzle points toward your hotel, trundle a shell over from the magazine via the overhead conveyer belt, stuff it in, and let fly. (Actually the gun probably doesn't fire, but you can certainly have fun pretending.) Allow about an hour.

A nuanced evaluation of the army's role in Brazilian history would be a fascinating thing, but you won't find it at the laughable **Army History Museum.** Army history

Tips Take a Break
Inside the Jardim Botânico, the Café Botânica serves above-average pastries and coffees. For children there are hot dogs and minipizzas and an array of sweets. Open daily from 8am to 5:30pm (© 021/2512-1848).

Tips **Take a Break**

The **Café do Forte,** located on the seaside ramparts of the Forte de Copacabana, offers some of the best views in town and then some. To further sweeten
those views, enjoy a coffee or a snack from the Café do Forte menu. Operated
by the Confeitaria Colombo (see "Where to Dine: Centro," p. 77), the cafe
offers outstanding pastries, cakes, and sandwiches. Open Tuesday to Sunday
10am to 8pm (© **021/2247-8994**). To enter you must pay the R$3 (US$1.50/£1)
visitor fee at the fort entrance.

---

as told here seems to end around 1960, just 4 years before the army (once again) put
an end to democracy.

Praça Coronel Eugênio Franco 1, Copacabana. © **021/2521-1032**. Admission R$3 (US$1.50/£1) adults, free for seniors and children 8 and under. Price includes admission to the Army History Museum (see above). Tues–Sun
10am–5pm. Bus: 415 to far end of Copacabana Beach.

Forte do Leme ✦✦✦ *Finds*   One of Rio's best-kept secrets (even most Cariocas
haven't been up here). On the top of the 600-foot granite rock you get a 360-degree
view of Copacabana and Guanabara Bay; you can see why the military wants to keep
the fort to itself. The main gate is toward the back of the square at the end of Leme
beach. Once inside, you make your way up a cobblestone road that winds around the
back of the hill. Even on a hot day the trail stays cool thanks to the surrounding lush
forest. Often you can spot squirrel-size sagui monkeys running up and down the
power lines. It's only a 20-minute walk to the top and you'll be rewarded with a most
splendid view of Copacabana beach and beyond. High-powered spotting scopes
improve the view even more.

Tip: Grab some snacks and drinks from the Zona Sul supermarket in Leme (Av.
Atlântica 866) and have a picnic at the top.

Praça Almirante Julio de Noronha s/n, Copacabana. © **021/2275-7696**. Admission R$3 (US$1.50/£1). Sat–Sun
8am–4pm. Metrô: Cardeal Arcoverde/integração bus to Leme or bus 472.

COSME VELHO

Corcovado ✦✦✦ *Kids*   The price is a bit steep but then so is the rail line, its narrow gauge winding upward past hillside shacks, through trees and tangled rainforest
creepers, up and ever up, yea unto to the very feet of Christ. A stylish Art Deco Christ,
30m (98 ft.) high on a mountaintop 710m (2,329 ft.) above sea level. Recently, the
Corcovado was chosen as one of the new Seven Wonders of the World. The view from
his toes is definitely worth the money. The mountains, the bay, and the city all lay
revealed beneath your feet. It's enough to give you a feeling of omniscience. The statue
was originally intended to mark the 100th anniversary of Brazilian independence in
1922, but due to a funding shortfall, it didn't open until 1931. At the peak station
there's a small refreshment and souvenir stand, but not much else. A pair of escalators
whisks you up to the base of the statue. Allow about 2 hours round-trip, including
time spent gazing at the glory that is Rio. Note that touts at the ground station will
almost certainly approach you offering a bus trip to the Corcovado plus another viewpoint a little lower down for R$30 (US$15/£8) or whatever price you can bargain
with them. Though it's not a bad deal, you do miss out on the nifty train ride.

(Train Station) Rua Cosme Velho 512, Cosme Velho. ℭ 021/2558-1329. www.corcovado.com.br. Admission R$36 (US$18/£10) adults, R$18 (US$9/£5) children 6–12, free for children 5 and under. Trains going up depart every 30 min. from 8:30am–6:30pm daily. Last train down 7:30pm. Bus: 422, 583, or 584 to Cosme Velho.

Museu Internacional de Arte Naif do Brasil ⭐⭐   Don't miss the Museu de Arte Naif, located just a few hundred yards from the Corcovado tram station. Sometimes known as primitive or ingénue art, its practitioners paint from the heart, portraying the daily life of common folks. Whatever they may lack of technical skill they more than make up for by the cheerful and expressive drawing and the vibrant use of color. Two of the largest naive art paintings in the world are on display here: one a massive 4×7m (13×23 ft.) picture-postcard view of Rio, the other a mural that in portraying the history of Brazil since 1500 wraps itself around three of the mezzanine walls. The top floor is exclusively reserved for local artists. Visitors will recognize many popular scenes from Cariocas' daily life, such as a Flamengo-Fluminense soccer game at the Maracanã stadium, the samba parade, the beach, and the small neighborhood botequim cafes. A number of pieces are for sale, but be aware that "naive" doesn't mean cheap. Prices range from R$200 to R$6,000 (US$100–US$3,000/£54–£1,620). Expect to spend 45 minutes.

Rua do Cosme Velho 561, Cosme Velho. ℭ 021/2205-8612. www.museunaif.com.br. R$6 (US$3/£1.50) adults, R$3 (US$1.50/£1) children (your Corcovado train ticket gives you 50% discount at the museum). Tues–Fri 10am–6pm; Sat–Sun noon–6pm. Bus: 422, 583, or 584 to Cosme Velho.

FARTHER AFIELD

Jardim Zoológico—Rio City Zoo ⭐ *Kids*   If you haven't got time to get to the Amazon, this may be the place to come. Though not huge, the zoo is green, leafy, and pleasant, and has about 2,000 different species on display, most of them Brazilian. It's particularly good for birds. There are toucans (of Fruit Loops cereal fame), macaws, and other colorful tropical species, some in an open aviary so you can walk among them while they fly around. (That doesn't apply to the harpy eagle: The zoo's example of the world's largest raptor sits caged and alone, looking both ominous and forlorn.) The reptile house and primate displays are also quite good. Some displays are inevitably small and cramped, which may produce cries of pity from the environmental activist, but all in all the zoo does a creditable job reproducing habitats while providing access to the public.

Quinta da Boa Vista s/n, São Cristóvão. ℭ 021/3878-4200. Admission R$5 (US$2.50/£1.35). Free for children less than 1m (39 in.) tall. Tues–Sun 9am–4:30pm. Bus: 472 or 474.

Museu de Arte Contemporânea—Niterói ⭐⭐   Oscar Niemeyer's spaceship design for Niterói's new Contemporary Art Museum has done for this bedroom city

---

Fun Fact Welcome to Smile City

Residents of Rio often refer to the city of Niterói across the bay as "Smile City." It's not a compliment on the friendliness of Niterói's inhabitants (known as *Fluminenses*), but rather a dig at Niterói's reputation as an affordable but somewhat dull second best to the cidade maravilhosa itself. The name comes, say the oh-so-smug Cariocas, as a result of what happens when you ask a Fluminense where he lives: an embarrassed giggle is followed up with a sickly smile, and only then do they blurt out the awful truth: "Niterói."

> **Tips   Exploring What's Beyond the Saucer**
>
> From Niemeyer's saucer-shaped museum, it's only a short stroll to Niterói's main beach, Icaraí. The beach itself makes for a pleasant walk, and the views of Rio are fabulous. One of Niterói's main shopping streets, Rua Coronel Moreira Cesar, runs parallel to the beach, 1 block up. The stretch between Rua Miguel Frias and Rua Otavio Carneiro is lined with boutiques and *galerias* (small shopping centers). You can take a break at the bakery and restaurant **Confeitaria Beira Mar,** Rua Coronel Moreira Cesar 149, corner of Rua Pres. Backer (✆ 021/ 2711-1070). For an excellent kilo lunch try **Buzin,** Rua Pereira da Silva 169 (✆ 021/ 2711-5208), just 2 blocks past Rua Colonel Moreira Cesar. To return to the ferryboats, catch any bus on the waterfront that says *BARCAS*. You can also catch a van straight to Ipanema via downtown and Copacabana (R$4/US$2/£1).

what Gehry's Guggenheim did for Bilbao, Spain: put it on the map (at least in Brazil). Set atop a promontory with a stunning view of Rio, the all-white flying saucer says clearly yet elegantly that here is a landmark structure. The magic continues inside with an observation gallery following a band of picture windows around the outside circumference, inviting patrons to gaze on Rio, the Sugarloaf, Guanabara Bay, and the city of Niterói itself. As a gallery, however, the museum has drawbacks. Circular buildings are inherently difficult to make functional. Still, curators do their best, bringing in a constantly changing selection of the best of Brazilian contemporary art (think abstract sculpture, textiles, and painting). Even so, one can't help thinking the best piece of work on display is the building itself. Allow about an hour.

Mirante de Boa Viagem s/n, Niterói. ✆ 021/2620-2400. www.macniteroi.com.br. Admission R$4 (US$2/£1), free for children 7 and under. Tues–Sun 10am–6pm. From Praça XV take the ferry to Niterói, then take a short taxi ride along Niterói's waterfront and up the hill to the museum.

Museu Nacional (Quinta da Boa Vista) ⭐⭐   This pretty pink baroque palace that was once the home of Brazil's royal family is now home to vast and incredibly varied collection; many items were originally acquired by the Emperor Pedro II and Empress Teresa, who dabbled respectively in botany and archaeology. The grand entrance hall shows many of the more exotic items: mastodon trunks, a saber-tooth tiger skull, the full skeleton of a giant Pleistocene sloth (5m/16 ft. long!), and a monster meteorite cut in cross section so visitors can run their hands across its polished iron-nickel surface. Beyond the main hall the collection becomes more ordered. One vast wing is devoted to the works of man (mostly *homo brazilienses*). On display are dolls dressed in regional costumes, weapons and masks of aboriginal tribes, whips and saddles from interior cowboys, and much more. The other wing attempts to present all of life, beginning with the smallest protozoa. The displays here are old—many seem to date from the '50s—but what makes it worthwhile is the quality of the specimens: pretty corals, a giant crab that looks like a monster from a '50s horror movie, tarantulas in abundance, a vast collection of fish, and stuffed specimens of most of the mammals found in Brazil. A particular gross-out favorite was the protozoa room, chock-full of models and photographs of all the various parasites that feed on human flesh. Signage is in Portuguese, but is not essential to see and enjoy. I spent a good 2 hours here; others less keen on natural history could probably do it in an hour. The grounds are open daily and are a popular weekend destination for families with children.

Quinta da Boa Vista s/n, São Cristóvão. ℂ 021/2568-8262. Admission R$3 (US$1.50/£1) adults, free for seniors and children 10 and under. Tues–Sun 10am–4pm. The park is open daily from 5am–6pm. Metrô: São Cristóvão or bus 472 or 474.

2 Other Museums & Cultural Centers

CENTRO

Centro Cultural do Banco do Brasil ⭐   It's worth stepping inside this gorgeous neoclassical building just to gaze up at the soaring domed atrium. Once the HQ of Brazil's national bank, the building was converted in 1989 into one of the city's premier cultural spaces. Inside (in lovely, cool air-conditioning) there's a pleasant cafe on the mezzanine that serves a wonderful afternoon tea (Tues–Sun 3–8pm; R$30/US$15/£8), a small bookstore on the ground floor with an excellent selection of art and architecture books (many in English), several small galleries on higher floors that feature changing exhibits on art and culture, and three theaters. For coin freaks there's also a small permanent exhibit on Brazilian coinage through the centuries. Allow 30 minutes.

Rua Primiero de Março 66, Centro. ℂ 021/3808-2020. Free admission; theaters or events may charge a separate fee. Tues–Sun 10am–9pm. Bus: 136 or 415.

Espaço Cultural da Marinha (Kids   With a destroyer, a submarine, and some great ship models, the Navy Cultural Center is guaranteed to delight naval and maritime buffs. The display space is located on the old Customs dock on the waterfront. That means it's narrow and thin, the exhibits extending ever backward to the end of the pier. On display are countless ship models, including a full-size replica of the royal barge and countless small-scale models of everything from the *Golden Hind* to primitive Brazilian sailing rafts. More interesting for nonmodel freaks are the displays on underwater archaeology, including a wide variety of relics—coins, Delft blue china, jewelry—from the 1648 wreck of the *Nossa Senhora do Rosario*. Moored outside the museum are the ***Riachuelo,*** a 1970s-era submarine, and the ***Bauru,*** a small World War II destroyer. Self-guided tours of these ships (also free) run from noon until 5pm. This is also the place from which one departs for tours of **Ilha Fiscal** ⭐⭐.

Av. Alfredo Agache s/n, Centro. ℂ 021/2104-6025. Free admission. Tues–Sun noon–5pm. Bus: 119 or 415 (Praça XV). From Praça XV turn right (north) and walk underneath the elevated freeway for about 100m (328 ft.).

Real Gabinete Português (Royal Portuguese Reading Room) ⭐   A temple to books. The interior of Real Gabinete Português is four stories tall, capped with a stained-glass cupola and illuminated by an elaborate chandelier. It's worth stepping inside just to see the room. Created in 1837 by the culture-starved (so they said) Portuguese, the reading room contains over 350,000 volumes, many of them from the 17th and 18th centuries. Just by showing ID (and maybe filling out a form—it depends on who's working) visitors can request, obtain, and peruse these books, for as long as the room is open.

Rua Luís de Camões 30, Centro. ℂ 021/2221-3138. Free admission. Mon–Fri 9am–6pm. Metrô: Carioca or bus 125 to Praça Tiradentes.

BOTAFOGO

Museu Carmen Miranda ⭐   If Carmen Miranda could see her museum, she'd roll over in her grave (spilling pineapples and bananas everywhere). A concrete bunker in a postage stamp–size park surrounded by four lanes of traffic hardly seems a fitting tribute to the flamboyant '40s film star. Inside the banana bunker, however, the small collection does a fine job illustrating Carmen Miranda's star appeal. A large number of her publicity photos are on display blown up to near life-size, along with smaller photos showing the story of her life and career, including her 1939 American break-through in the Broadway musical *Streets of Paris*. Also on display is the outfit she wore to the 1941 Academy Awards ceremony, as well as jewelry and accessories, including the trademark tall fruit hats. The museum also has a large collection of video docu-mentaries, biographies, the movies she starred in, and a compilation of her songs. The receptionist is delighted to play these for visitors.

Av. Rui Barbosa s/n (across the street from no. 560), Flamengo. (*C*) 021/2299-5586. R$3 (US$1.50/£1) for adults and children over 5, free for seniors and children 5 and under. Tues–Fri 11am–5pm; Sat–Sun 1–5pm. Bus: 172 (from Ipanema or Copacabana) or 433 from Centro.

Museu Villa-Lobos   This small, slightly quirky museum is dedicated to the life of Heitor Villa-Lobos, Brazil's greatest composer, noted for including Brazilian instru-ments and sounds in his compositions and for using Brazilian folklore in his work. The collection includes musical instruments used by the composer, and some of his personal effects. The English signage is excellent, but even so, expect to spend no more than half an hour. For real fans, the museum library has musical scores, letters, mono-graphs, records, tapes, and movies. The museum website has sound bites of Villa-Lobos's most famous pieces and a comprehensive list of links with resources on Brazilian music.

Rua Sorocaba 200, Botafogo. (*C*) 021/2266-3845. www.museuvillalobos.org.br. Free admission. Mon–Fri 10am–5:30pm. Metrô: Botafogo.

FARTHER AFIELD
Island of Paquetá *Kids*   For an old-fashioned Carioca day trip, visit the island of Paquetá in Guanabara Bay. The destination has been a favorite since 1808, when Dom João VI began spending his summers on the island. In some ways not much has changed. On weekends, families hop on the ferry for the 1-hour crossing. Upon arrival, stop off at the Paquetur booth across from the ferry terminal to pick up a map of the island (Praça Pedro Bruno s/n; open Wed–Mon 11am–5:30pm). No cars are allowed on Paquetá. Instead, visitors can rent bicycles (starting at R$1.50/US75¢/£.40 an hour) or ride in a horse and buggy (R$35/US$18/£9.50 for an hour, including stops) to see the sights. Paquetá is fairly small, so it'll only take an hour to see most of the 11 beaches, historic sights, and small parks. However, you may want to take time to stop for a snack at one of the many beachside kiosks or grab lunch at the **Restau-rante Charretão** (Praça Bom Jesus 15; (*C*) 021/3397-0052; serves meat and seafood) or at the **Hotel Lido,** overlooking the Praia de José Bonifacio ((*C*) 021/3397-0377; kilo restaurant and ice-cream parlor). Also bring enough film (or memory cards) to take photos of the fabulous views of the bay and surrounding mountains. Although locals swim in most Paquetá beaches, the only ones given a green light by the City of Rio are Praia da Imbuca, Praia de José Bonifacio, and Praia da Moreninha. Including travel time, allow 4 to 6 hours for the trip, depending on whether you take the fast or slow ferry. Weekends are best for seeing the "bustle" on the island and sharing the beaches and parks with visiting Rio families and locals. Weekdays—especially between April and November—are very quiet.

> ## *Tips* Tour du Jour
>
> Rio Hiking (*©* 021/2552-9204; www.riohiking.com.br) offers an excellent day tour (R$150/US$75/£40 per person) that includes a visit to the Museu Casa do Pontal, Sitio Burle Marx, and time for a swim or a walk along Grumari, one of the city's loveliest beaches.

Ferry (*©* 021/2533-7524) departs from Praça XV, R$4–R$8.50 (US$2–£4.25/£1–£2.25) 7:10am, 10:30am, 1:30pm, 4pm, and 5:45pm. Ferry Paquetá-Rio departs daily at 9am, noon, 3pm, 5:30pm, and 7:30pm. Fast ferry Paquetá-Rio departs at 10:30am, 12:30pm, 2:30pm, and 4:30pm. It's a good idea to confirm return times upon arrival in Paquetá.

Maracanã Stadium   Once the largest soccer stadium in the world and the temple of Brazilian soccer, the Maracanã got off to an inauspicious start at the 1950 World Cup when close to 200,000 spectators in the brand-new stadium saw Brazil lose the cup final to arch-rival Uruguay. (The loss still hurts—if you want to taunt a Brazilian soccer fan, just mention the 1950 Cup. Fortunately this was only a temporary set-back—Brazil went on to win five World Cups.) The best way to experience the Maracanã stadium is with a couple hundred thousand other fans at one of the big games (see "The *Only* Spectator Sport in Rio," later in this chapter). For those who don't have that opportunity or want a behind-the-scenes look, there are guided tours. An English-speaking guide takes visitors through all floors of the stadium, including the dressing rooms, all the while delivering a seemingly endless stream of Brazilian soccer trivia.

Rua Profesor Eurico Rabelo s/n São Cristovão. *©* 021/2299-2941. Daily 9am–5pm. No tours during events or games. R$20 (US$10/£5.40), free for children under 12. Metrô: Maracanã. Enter through gate 16.

Museu Casa do Pontal *★★*   The museum's a long way from downtown Rio: an hour's drive from Copacabana along the coastal road past Barra de Tijuca. The good news is it's a really nice museum in a gorgeous location—ocean on one side and the mountains on the other. Inside, the more than 5,000 pieces collected by French designer Jacques van de Beuque present a beautiful overview of Brazilian culture. The collection's charm lies in the beauty of its naive portrayal of traditional rural Brazilian life. The thousands of small clay sculptures, combined with woodcarvings and cloth and metal tableaus, depict religious and music festivals and farm and family routines. Adults may enter the x-rated sculpture department to see the hilarious sculptures in very compromising positions. One of its most famous rooms houses a wonderful mechanical diorama that represents an *escola de samba* (samba school)—complete with cheering audience—marching in the Carnaval parade.

Estrada do Pontal 3295, Recreio dos Bandeirantes. *©* 021/2490-3271. Admission R$8 (US$4/£2) adults, R$6 (US$3/£1.50) students and seniors, free for children 7 and under. Daily 9:30am–5pm. No public transit.

3 Architectural Highlights

HISTORIC BUILDINGS & MONUMENTS

Rio's a great place for architecture buffs, and an even better place to watch what happens when overconfident urban designers set their hands to the task of urban renewal. For a city so blessed with mountains, ocean, and historical roots several centuries deep, Rio's movers and shakers have suffered from a striking sense of inferiority. As a result, various well-meaning Cariocas have since the early 1900s taken turns ripping out, blowing up, filling in, and generally reconfiguring huge swaths of their city in order to make Rio look more like Paris or Los Angeles or, lately, Miami Beach. The results of these various movements are—for better and worse—now and forever on permanent display.

AROUND CINELÂNDIA

"Rio Civilizes Itself!" Armed with this slogan and a deep envy of what Baron Haussman had done in Paris, engineer-mayor **Pereiro Passos** set to work in 1903, ripping a large swath through Rio's Centro district to create the first of the city's grand boulevards, the **Avenida Central.** So efficient was "Knock-it-down" Passos that the old colonial Rio he set out to demolish can now be found only in the few square blocks around the **Travessa do Comércio** to the north of **Praça XV.** Accessed via the **Arco do Teles**—an arch built in 1790 to allow passage through a commercial building facing the square—it's a charming area of narrow cobblestone streets and gaily painted colonial shops, now much missed by civilized Cariocas.

The boulevard Passos created in its stead, however, was also quite graceful. Now renamed the **Avenida Rio Branco,** it runs from **Praça Mauá** south past the grand neoclassical **Igreja de Nossa Senora da Candelária** to what was then the waterfront at the **Avenida Beira Mar.** The four-story Parisian structures that once lined the street are now found only in photographs, replaced by tall and modern office towers. (Rio Branco remains the heart of Rio's financial district.) The best place to witness the handiwork of these turn-of-the-20th-century Parisizers is on the **Praça Floriano,** referred to by most Cariocas by the name of its subway stop, **Cinelândia.** Anchored at the north end by the extravagant Beaux Arts **Teatro Municipal,** and flanked by the equally ornate **Museu de Belas Artes** and neoclassical **Biblioteca Nacional,** the praça beautifully emulates the proportions, the monumentality, and the glorious detail of a classic Parisian square. The Teatro Municipal was in fact explicitly modeled on the Paris Opera House and inaugurated on Bastille Day (July 14) 1909. (Visitors can poke their heads into all of these buildings, but the best place to appreciate the square may well be seated at an outdoor cafe enjoying a nice cold draft.)

AROUND CASTELO

The next stage in urban reform came in the early '20s, when a group encouraged by public health advocate **Oswaldo Cruz,** backed by a development consortium, decreed that the hilltop castle south of Praça XV had to go; the 400-year-old castle was a breeding ground, they said, for pox, plague, and other infectious diseases. In 1922, the castle was blown up, the hill leveled and—starting in the early '30s—construction begun on a series of government office towers inspired by the modernist movement then sweeping Europe. The first of these—then the Ministry of Education and Health but now known as the **Palácio Gustavo Capenema** (Rua da Imprensa 16; see "Palaces," below)—listed among its architects nearly all the later greats of Brazilian architecture, including **Lucio Costa, Oscar Niemeyer,** and **Roberto Burle Marx,** with painter **Candido Portinari** thrown in for good measure. International architects sat up and took note; other less avant-garde government departments commissioned architects with different ideologies, resulting in a **War of the Styles** that raged through the remainder of the 1930s. Perhaps the most bombastic counter-volley was the overblown neoclassical **Ministerio da Fazenda** building (Av. Presidente Antônio Carlos at Av. Almirante Barroso). The resulting enclave of office towers, known as Castelo, lies on the patch centered on the **Avenida Presidente Antônio Carlos.** Chiefly of interest to architectural buffs, it should be toured only during office hours.

AROUND CIDADE NOVA

Knock-it-down Passos had nothing on **Getulio Vargas.** On the national scene the Brazilian dictator was creating a new quasi-fascist political structure called the Estado Novo; in his capital city, he set about creating a **Cidade Nova** to match. In 1940, on Vargas's personal order, a monster 12-lane boulevard was cut through the city fabric from the beautiful **N.S. de Candelária Church** out through the **Campo de Santana** park to the northern edges of downtown. Anchoring this new megaboulevard was the **Central Station** (known officially as the Estação Dom Pedro II, it's worth popping in to see the Art Deco interior), a graceful Modern building with a 135m (443-ft.) clock tower that still stands overlooking the city, providing a much-needed reference point in the northern half of downtown. Vargas's plan called for the entire 4km (2½-mile) street to be lined with identical 22-story office blocks. Cariocas, however, seemed to have a limited appetite for Identi-cubes. Only a few were ever built; they can be seen on the block crossed by Rua Uruguaiana. Even 60 years later, much of the rest of this ultra-wide boulevard remains effectively vacant. As a silver lining, however, there was lots of space left for architect Oscar Niemeyer to build the **Sambodromo,** the used-once-a-year permanent Samba Parade Ground. Designed in typically Niemeyer all-concrete style, it stands in the shadow of an elevated freeway, about 1km (½ mile) along Presidente Vargas.

AROUND ATERRO

The next great reconfiguration of Rio came 2 years after the federal capital fled inland to Brasilia. City designers took the huge high hill—**Morro Santo Antônio**—that once dominated the Largo da Carioca, scooped away the earth and dumped it on the beach from Lapa to Flamengo, creating a vast new waterfront park. On the rather raw spot where the hill once stood there arose the innovative cone-shaped **Catedral Metropolitana,** and at the intersection of the new avenidas **República do Chile** and **República do Paraguai,** a trio of towering skyscrapers, the most interesting of which is the "hanging gardens" headquarters of Brazil's state oil company **Petrobras.** On the waterfront park—officially called Parque do Flamengo but most often referred to as Aterro, the Portuguese word for landfill—designers created new gardens and pathways, a new beach, and a pair of modernist monuments: the **MAM** (Modern Art Museum) and the impressive **Monument to the Dead of World War II.** Not incidentally, the park also bears two wide and fast roadways connecting Centro with the fashionable neighborhoods in the Zona Sul.

PALACES

There aren't a lot of true palaces in Rio, for the simple reason that the aristocracy wasn't around long enough to build many. But as if to make up for this lack of palaces, Brazilians have taken to granting any number of grand structures the appellation "palace." The **Palácio Tiradentes,** Av. Presidente Antônio Carlos s/n (© **021/2588-1411**), for example, was built in 1926, long after the aristocracy had departed. Located at the back edge of Praça XV, this rather overwrought neoclassical structure was built to serve as the Brazilian Federal Legislature, which up until then had been meeting in an old jailhouse. Four years after its inauguration, dictator Getulio Vargas overthrew the government and turned the palace into his ministry of propaganda. Nowadays the building serves as the legislature for the state of Rio de Janeiro. Visitors can tour the permanent display that runs down the outside corridor of the building, but since the text-heavy exhibit is exclusively in Portuguese, there's probably not much point.

Older and more graceful is the **Palácio Itamaraty** ✧, Rua Marachel Floriano 196, near the Central Station (ℭ **021/2253-7691**). Built in the 1850s for a coffee merchant with the rather grand title of Baron de Itamaraty, the charming neoclassical design—the front has pink walls pierced by granite arches—was sold to the new republican government in 1889 and long served as the ministry of foreign affairs. It has since been converted into the Museum of History and Diplomacy, but this is now closed indefinitely *(sem previsão)*. However, as one small museum display remains open (again in Portuguese only), you do have an excuse to get past the guard (you have to show ID) and wander back to the gorgeous interior courtyard where two ranks of imperial palms flank a long reflecting pond in which jet-black swans swim round.

The most impressive palace in Rio is actually the most modern. Or rather, capital-M Modern. Located in the city's office district, the **Palácio Gustavo Capenema** ✧, Rua da Imprensa 16 (no phone), was designed and built from 1932 to 1936 by a team of Brazil's top architects, then the best practitioners of modernism in the world. On the team were Oscar Niemeyer and Lucio Costa (the pair who would later design Brasilia), landscape architect Roberto Burle Marx, and artist Candido Portinari, who did much of the tile work that covers the buildings. Supervising as design consultant was Swiss über-modernist Le Corbusier. The result can be underwhelming at first, but that's because 70 years later we've seen a lot of things similar. But when this was built, no one had ever done anything like it. The entire structure has been raised on pilings 40 feet off the ground, creating an open, airy plaza beneath. And unlike later modernists, this team paid attention to the details: The support columns are covered in beautiful marble, the few ground-level walls in intriguing blue-and-white tile—many designed by Portinari. Ordinary people enjoy the open space thus created. Architectural fans can stand and admire this building for hours.

CHURCHES & TEMPLES

Rio is awash with churches, with some 20 in Centro alone. Likely the most impressive church in Rio is **Nossa Senhora de Candelária** ✧✧, set on a traffic island of its own at the head of Avenida Presidente Vargas (ℭ **021/2233-2324**). Although a church has stood on the spot since the 1680s, the current clean and simple neoclassical design dates from a renovation begun in 1775. Particularly worth noting are the huge and ornate cast-bronze doors, the ceiling panels telling the story of the church, and the two large Art Nouveau lamps on either side of the pulpit; they look like cast-iron Christmas trees. Open Monday through Friday from 8am to 4pm, and Saturday and Sunday from 9am to noon.

Overrated **The Church That's Not Worth the Hike**

Still impressive, if not quite worth the hype or the long trek, is the **Mosteiro São Bento,** located on a hill on the far-north corner of downtown. Access is via an elevator located in Rua Dom Gerardo 40; open daily from 8 to 11am and 2:30 to 6pm. The church itself is a shining example of the Golden Church, the high baroque practice of plastering every inch of a church's richly carved interior in gold leaf. We find it disappointing the way the church forecourt has been transformed into a car park. And the monastery's strategic hilltop has no view whatsoever. Sunday morning Mass features Gregorian chanting by the monks. Service begins at 10am, but arrive early if you want a seat.

Worth a visit and much more centrally located is the **Igreja da Ordem Terceira de São Francisco da Penitencia** ⭐, Largo da Carioca 5 (© **021/2262-0197**). Set on a hilltop overlooking Largo da Carioca, this and the Church of Santo Antônio next door form part of the large Franciscan complex in the city center. The São Francisco church is simply outstanding: Interior surfaces are filled with golden carvings and hung with censers of ornate silver. Open Tuesday through Friday 9am to noon and 1 to 4pm.

On a hilltop all its own is the **N.S. de Glória do Outeiro** ⭐, which can be accessed via the stairway located next to Rua da Russel 300 (© **021/2557-4600**). It's unique among churches in Rio, thanks to its octagonal ground plan and domed roof. The hill on which it stands was the strategic point taken from an invading French force by the city's founder, Estácio de Sá, paving the way for the settlement of Rio on March 1, 1565. Open Tuesday through Friday from 9am to noon and 1 to 5pm, and Saturday and Sunday from 9am to noon.

Last and most innovative of Rio's significant churches is the **Catedral Metropolitana** ⭐⭐, Av. República de Chile 245 (© **021/2240-2669**). Some dislike this building, finding its shape disconcerting and its interior dark. I love it. At each of the four cardinal compass points a rectilinear latticework of concrete and stained glass soars upward, tilting inward as it rises. Where they meet at the ceiling there's another stained-glass latticework—a cross—shining softly with light filtered in from the sky. The form is modern; the feeling is soaring High Gothic. Open daily from 7am to 6pm; Mass is held Monday through Friday at 11am and Sunday at 10am.

Note: The neighborhood around the cathedral is best visited on weekdays. The area can be unsafe on weekends when the streets are deserted.

4 Neighborhoods to Explore

Rio is normally divided into three zones: **North (Zona Norte), Center (Centro),** and **South (Zona Sul).** Largest and least interesting from a visitor's perspective, the **Zona Norte** stretches from a few blocks north of Avenida Presidente Vargas all the way to the city limits. With only a few bright exceptions—the Maracanã stadium, the Quinte de Boa Vista gardens, the neighborhoods of Vila Isabel and Tijuca, and Galeão (Tom Jobim) airport—the region is a dull swath of port, lower-middle-class housing, industrial suburb, and favelas. After dark, it is definitely not the sort of place one should wander unaccompanied. The **Zona Sul** is the name given to the beach neighborhoods of **Copacabana, Ipanema, Leme, Lagoa,** and **São Conrado. Centro** is a bit more difficult to nail down. Defined narrowly, it's the old downtown and business section (described below). Used in a broader sense, Centro also includes older residential neighborhoods like **Santa Teresa, Catete,** and **Glória.**

CENTRO ⭐⭐

The place where it all began, Rio's **Centro** neighborhood contains most of the city's notable churches, squares, monuments, and museums, as well as the modern office towers where Rio's white-collar elite earn their daily bread. Roughly speaking, Centro stretches from the **Morro de São Bento** in the north to the seaside **Monument to the Dead of World War II** in the south, and from **Praça XV** on the waterfront east more or less to the **Sambodromo.** It's a compact, pleasantly walkable area; crossing from one side of downtown to the other on foot takes no more than 45 minutes.

Rio (and Centro's) first and most important square is **Praça XV,** located in the center of the city's old waterfront. This is the place where governors and emperors resided, and the site where the Brazilian republic was proclaimed on November 15, 1889. Notable sights around the square include the **Paço Imperial,** the **Palácio Tiradentes,** and, on the north side of the square, the **Arco do Teles.** Walk through this unobtrusive old archway, and you come to a tiny remnant of old colonial Rio, complete with narrow shop fronts and cobblestone streets. The area's main street, the **Travessa do Comércio,** transforms into a lively outdoor patio/pub in the evenings.

Forming the back edge of Praça XV is **Rua Primeiro de Março,** a busy commercial street with a number of churches, including the **Ordem Terceiro do Carmo,** the **Santa Cruz dos Militares,** and near the far end of the street the massive yet lovely **Nossa Senhora de Candelária.** Continue along Primeiro de Março to the end, and you come to the foot of the hill upon which rests the **São Bento Monastery.** Southward, the Premeiro de Março transforms into **Avenida Presidente Antônio Carlos,** the main street of a not-very-interesting area of government office towers known as **Castelo.**

Continuing west from Praça XV along either the **Rua Ouvidor** or the **Rua Sete de Setembro** takes you to Centro's prime upscale shopping enclave. Its far border is marked (more or less) by the **Avenida Rio Branco.** Created in 1905 as an answer to Paris's Champs-Elysées, Rio Branco is still the city's most desirable commercial address. It runs from the cruise-ship terminal on the **Praça Mauá** southward to the pretty Parisian square known as **Cinelândia.** About halfway along, a block to the east of Rio Branco, lies the large irregular **Largo da Carioca.**

Though not very interesting in itself, the square is useful as a landmark. Above it on a hilltop stands the glorious golden **Igreja de Santo Antônio.** To the north of the square, from **Rua da Carioca** to the vast, traffic-choked wasteland known on maps as the **Avenida Presidente Vargas,** and from **Avenida Rio Branco** in the east to the **Campo de Santana** park in the west, lies one of Rio's prime walking, shopping, and sightseeing areas. It's an area of narrow, irregular streets, two-story shops, little squares, and charming small churches. Among the chief sights are the **Largo de São Francisco de Paula,** the **Real Gabinete Português (Royal Portuguese Reading Room),** and an old-style tearoom called the **Confeitaria Colombo.** Shopaholics will enjoy the **informal market** centered on the **Uruguaiana** Metrô stop and the bargains to be had elsewhere in the neighborhood.

Looking south, the Largo da Carioca marks the transition from old Rio to new, and from low-rise to high-rise. Toward the east, **Avenida República de Chile** boasts many of the city's most important commercial skyscrapers, including the landmark **Petrobras** building and the distinctive conical ziggurat that is the **Catedral Metropolitana.** Just south of the modern concrete cathedral, the past makes a token resurgence in the form of the **Arcos da Lapa,** a Roman-style aqueduct that now carries trams south from the city center up to the hilltop neighborhood of **Santa Teresa.**

South and west of Largo da Carioca lies **Cinelândia** (officially called **Praça Floriano**), a Parisian city square faithfully reproduced all the way down to the opera house (or **Teatro Municipal,** as its called) and the many sidewalk cafes. Many of the highrises surrounding the square show the Art Deco and modern touches of buildings from the '30s and '40s. Across from the Teatro stands the lovely neoclassical Biblioteca Nacional. It's worth poking your head in just to see the grand entrance hall with staircases extending up through a lofty atrium five floors high.

South again from Cinelândia, making use of a pedestrian overpass to cross a pair of wide and busy roads, you come to the man-made **Parque do Flamengo;** the chief sights in the park are the **Museu de Arte Moderna (MAM)** and the soaring concrete **Monument to the Dead of World War II.**

LAPA

A tiny, funky little neighborhood once known as the "Montmartre of the Tropics," Lapa is easy to find. It's centered at the **Largo da Lapa** at the foot an old picturesque aqueduct known as the **Arcos da Lapa.** In addition to those two sights, Lapa offers some lovely old colonial buildings and—in recent years—an active nightlife scene.

SANTA TERESA ★★

Most hilltop neighborhoods in Rio are favelas—unsanctioned shantytowns. Santa Teresa is anything but—it's a respectable, slightly bohemian neighborhood with a number of sights to lure visitors. Chief among these is the *bonde,* the old-fashioned streetcar that whisks passengers from downtown over the **Arcos da Lapa** into Santa Teresa. The attractions in the **Museu Chácara do Céu** (see "The Top Attractions," earlier in this chapter) are worth a visit, and when you're done, wander the neighborhood enjoying the fabulous views, and the mix of modern, colonial, and Art Deco architecture.

Note: The Santa Teresa tram station is not easy to find. It's behind the big "hanging gardens" Petrobras building, on Rua Prof. Lélio Gama, a little street that runs off Rua Senador Dantas. A less charming but certainly more efficient connection is the Metrô/bus integração; take the Santa Teresa bus from the Cinelândia Metrô station (make sure you purchase the Metrô-integração ticket and save the stub to present to the bus driver).

GLÓRIA/CATETE/FLAMENGO ★

Extending south from the Glória Metrô stop to the top end of Botafogo bay, these three neighborhoods once comprised Rio's toniest residential area—that is, until the tunnel to Copacabana opened in 1922. Recently, however, the area's made a comeback as Carioca yuppies and other urban pioneers have discovered the advantages (high ceilings, huge windows, and so on) of the old 19th-century houses, while residents and visitors alike have realized that thanks to the Metrô, the area is but minutes from both Centro and Copacabana. The main north-south street—known variously as the **Rua da Glória,** the **Rua do Catete,** and the **Rua Marques de Abrantes**—is well worth an afternoon or evening stroll. Particularly pretty is the **Largo do Machado,** located at the Metrô stop of the same name. For visitors, the chief attractions in this area include the lovely hilltop **Church of Our Lady of Glória** and the **Catete Park and Palace,** home to the **Museum of the Republic.**

BOTAFOGO

The neighborhood Botafogo reacted to the rise of Copacabana and Ipanema by reinventing itself as a secondary commercial center. Its broad streets contain a number of office high-rises and big retail shopping malls, including the **Shopping Rio Sul,** the first mall to open in the city. The neighborhood is experiencing quite the revival with many new apartments going up and the opening of a several new movie theaters and restaurants. Botafogo has a couple of worthwhile sights of its own, including the **Villa-Lobos** and **Indian museums** and the bustling food fair and nighttime music-jam in the **Cobal Public Market.**

URCA

Urca is the pretty little neighborhood nestled round the foot of the Pão de Açúcar. Partly residential, partly home to a naval training college, the area was built on a land-fill during the 1920s, thus accounting for the Art Deco and modern style of many of the neighborhood's buildings. Architecture aside, for nonresidents the only reason to visit Urca is for the views. The first is from the peak of **Sugarloaf (Pão de Açúcar),** reached by cable car from Urca's Avenida Pasteur. The second view can be enjoyed while strolling the seawall on **Avenida Portugal.** A jutting peninsula, Urca provides an excellent vantage point from which to gaze back at the Rio skyline; its relative iso-lation makes it safe to stroll blithely along even late at night. And for those who think views go best with something cold, the third and final view spot is from a table at the **Circulo Militar** (see restaurant review on p. 81), on the edge of **Praia Vermelha.** The view of the Sugarloaf is without a doubt the best in town.

COPACABANA 𝄞𝄞

Beach! The one word comprises everything there is to say about Copacabana, but then it's a word that contains within it an endless variety of human behavior. Four kilome-ters (2½ miles) long and bright white, Copacabana beach is the stage upon which peo-ple swim, surf, jog, preen, make sand castles, sunbathe, and play volleyball. The broad and beautifully landscaped **Avenida Atlântica** runs along the beach's entire length. Running parallel two streets inland, **Nossa Senhora de Copacabana** is the main shopping and commercial street. These two avenues and their many cross streets con-tain numerous hotels, restaurants, and bars. For more on Rio's beaches, see "Beaches, Parks & Plazas," below.

IPANEMA 𝄞𝄞

The famous stretch of beach immortalized in Tom Jobim's song "The Girl from Ipanema" nestles in between Copacabana, Leblon, and Lagoa. No more than 8 blocks wide in some areas, it is one of the most coveted residential neighborhoods in all of Rio. Built mostly after Rio's Art Deco boom, there are very few landmark buildings to speak of; most apartment buildings are nondescript, some downright ugly. What Ipanema does offer is great shopping on **Rua Visconde de Pirajá** and its side streets, an excellent nightlife scene, some terrific restaurants, and of course, the beach, the major recreation area for residents and visitors alike. Joggers and walkers cruise the black-and-white pat-terned sidewalk every day of the week, but Sunday is the day to see and be seen when the beachside **Avenida Vieira Souto** is closed for traffic and people cycle, inline skate, and scooter along, at all times showing tans and tight form to advantage.

LEBLON 𝄞𝄞

A smaller and, if anything, trendier version of Ipanema, Leblon sits directly to the east of Ipanema; the dividing line is the drainage canal for the Lagoa, now landscaped into a park called the **Jardim de Ala.** The most significant difference between the two neighborhoods is the street names. The beachside avenue in Leblon is known as **Avenida Delfim Moreira,** while the main shopping street is **Avenida General Mar-tin.** Most of the best restaurants cluster around the end of **Avenida Ataulfo de Paiva** where it meets **Rua Dias Ferreira.**

LAGOA

Lagoa is an odd neighborhood, as the focus is the big lagoon (**Lagoa Rodrigo de Freitas**) that drains into the ocean between Ipanema and Leblon. For the majority of

Cariocas, this is primarily a recreation area. They come to walk, cycle, inline skate, or run the 8.5km (5.25-mile) pathway that circles the lagoon. In the afternoon and evening, the neighborhood's pleasures become more hedonistic as people come to the many waterside kiosks to grab a drink, have some food, or listen to live music.

BARRA DE TIJUCA

The Brazilian envy of things American has finally expressed itself in architecture. Though ostensibly part of Rio de Janeiro, Barra (as it's usually called) looks and feels much like an American beach city, like L.A. or Miami Beach. Streets are wide and filled with 4×4s because in Barra—as in L.A.—only somebody who's a nobody walks. Instead, folks here drive—to the beach, to their penthouse apartment, or to the full-size replica of Studio 54 at the **American Center** mall.

TIJUCA NATIONAL PARK

Backstopping all of these Zona Sul neighborhoods is the massive **Tijuca National Park.** Mostly mountainous, the 3,300-hectare (8,151-acre) forest was begun in the 1800s as a personal project of the Emperor Dom Pedro II. It's invariably shown on maps as one big swatch of green, but in fact any number of shantytowns (favelas in Portuguese) have taken over parkland, usually in areas adjacent to official city neighborhoods. The park that's left—and there's lots of it—is cut through with excellent walking and hiking trails, many leading to peaks with fabulous views. Climb to the top of the Pico da Tijuca at 1,022m (3,352 ft.) on a sunny day, and beneath your feet you'll have a view of every neighborhood in Rio.

5 Beaches, Parks & Plazas

BEACHES

Beaches are to Rio what cafes are to Paris. And while each beach has its own particular traits, there are some general rules to help you take the waters like a true Carioca.

BE PREPARED   First and foremost: **Get a Brazilian bikini** (though perhaps not if you're male). No matter how funky or fashionably teeny your swimsuit looked up north, on a Rio beach it's guaranteed to scream *gringo*. And if you're thinking the figure's not quite bikini-ready, relax. In Brazil everybody and their grandma wears a two-piece. (Note, however, that no matter how small they may shrink that top, Brazilian women *never* go topless—that's for the heathen French.)

Second: **Don't be a pack rat.** If you carefully observe your fellow beachgoers you'll note that Brazilians bring neither picnic basket nor backpack full of stuff and gadgets. Why would you bring when everything you could possibly desire is for sale on the beach? Blankets, inflatable mattresses, and quilts are likewise no-nos. A foldable beach chair is acceptable for women; Brazilian men stand or sit on the sand. Parasols are for little kids. All you really need is a towel, sunscreen, and a little bit of cash for beer, food, and other incidentals. Third and most important: **Relax.** Go for a little swim, chat with the one that brung ya or the cutie on the towel next door, have a beer and some snacks, and soak up those rays.

For further discussion of the more subtle social beach-going dynamics, see "Know the Beach Rules," below.

WATER CONDITIONS   The beaches facing Guanabara Bay (primarily Flamengo and Botafogo) are nearly always too polluted for swimming. Thanks to a substantial current, the ocean beaches (Copacabana, Ipanema, and Barra) are much cleaner, but

Frommer's Moment: *Baywatch* Rio-Style

On hot summer days, Cariocas take to the ocean like fish to water, except of course, that many Cariocas can't swim. On days when wind and waves get rough, this can lead to some exciting beach theater. One day as we were sitting on Leme beach a helicopter zoomed down along the surf line from the direction of Copacabana, stopping to hover over a spot some 50 feet offshore. We could see a swimmer in the circle of water beat flat by the helicopter blades. The swimmer had obviously been struggling in the water for some time unnoticed. A rescue jumper appeared in the open door of the chopper, then plunged into the ocean. The helicopter then lowered a big net and scooped up swimmer and diver. It hovered over to the beach and plopped the swimmer unceremoniously on the sand. The rescuer was then raised on a line and the helicopter sped off; the swimmer skulked into crowd. Five minutes after it began the beach was back to normal again. On a busy weekend, helicopters can perform up to 200 such rescues.

even so, sometimes after a heavy rain the fecal coli form count rises beyond acceptable levels. The newspaper *Globo* prints a daily beach report listing all beach closings. Consult that or ask at your hotel.

SAFETY ISSUES   Another argument for traveling light to the beach is security. It's unlikely you will get mugged on a Rio beach in the daytime, but leaving that iPod, wallet, or pocket camera on the sand while you head off for a swim *is* an open invitation for someone to relieve you of your valuables. And I would advise against any moonlit beach strolls. At night the wide beach is dark and deserted; if you want waterfront views stick to the large sidewalk fronting the beach—it's well lit and patrolled often by the tourist police.

THE BEACHES   **Botafogo** and **Flamengo** are fine and picturesque for an afternoon stroll, but too polluted for swimming. Off by itself out in Urca, **Praia Vermelha** ✦ faces out toward the ocean and is often fine. In addition to a fabulous view of the Sugarloaf, this beach is relatively unfrequented, especially by tourists. On the other hand, it's almost completely lacking in waves.

The first of the ocean beaches to see development back in the '20s, **Copacabana** ✦✦ remains a favorite. The wide and beautifully landscaped Avenida Atlântica is a great place for a stroll. (The wavy landscaped sidewalk mosaic is the work of landscape designer Roberto Burle Marx.) When the feet start to tire, pull up a chair at any of the countless beachside kiosks, grab a chilled coconut or a *cerveja,* and spend some time admiring the picture-perfect view. The area at the far end of the beach near the Forte de Copacabana is where fishermen beach their small craft; it's a good place to wander if you want freshly grilled shrimp or other seafood. For those with other fish to fry, the area in front of the Copacabana Palace around the Rainbow kiosk is a well-known gay area.

The *postos* (lifeguard stations) along Copacabana and Ipanema beaches are open daily from 8am to 8pm. They offer first aid (free if needed) and changing and toilet facilities for a charge of R$1 (US50¢/£.25). Postos are numbered 1 through 11 starting

Fun Fact **Know the Beach Rules**

Certain unspoken, gender-specific rules govern the public behavior of men and women on the beach at Ipanema—and I believe, by extension, on all Brazilian beaches. What follows is a (mostly) tongue-in-cheek rundown of beach-going do's and don'ts.

Sunbathing 101: The most important rule is that *nothing* shall come between a man and the raw, hot sand. A man who uses a beach chair, a towel, or a *kanga* is not a man but a gringo, and must be shunned. A Brazilian man must plant his Lycra-covered butt down in hot white silicon, making sure his lower back and thighs are covered in sticky white grains.

There are certain exceptions. A man may sit on a sheet of folded newspaper. A man may sit on a *tiny* corner of a woman's *kanga,* provided the woman is beautiful and he occupies no more than 3% of the total *kanga* surface. A man may also stand, drinking a *cerveja* (beer), looking around manfully and sharing the company of other men.

A woman must sit on a *kanga*. Beach chairs are also acceptable. Women do not touch the sand, nor do women stand. Women do not join in beach sports such as soccer or foot volley, nor do they plod sweatily down the beach pretending to be joggers. The acceptable positions for women are lounging on their backs, lying dreamily on their bellies, or sitting cross-legged in a circle with at least three other women.

When rising from the sand—or newspaper, or corner of a woman's *kanga*—a man may not brush the sticky white sand from his butt. A man may not touch his butt. A man who touches his butt is not a man but a *bicha* (sissy) or a gringo.

A woman, when rising from the sand, must brush herself voluptuously, making sure both glutes are thoroughly massaged from waist down to lower thigh. Particular attention must be paid to readjusting the bikini bottom so that it rests comfortably between her butt cheeks.

from Leme and ending in Leblon. Cariocas will often use them as a reference point instead of the cross streets.

Ipanema Beach ★★★ was famous among Brazilians even before Tom Jobim wrote his famous song about the tall and tan and young and lovely girl he saw and sighed over. Stretching almost 3km (2 miles) from the foot of the Pedra Dois Irmãos to the Ponta Arpoador, the beach at Ipanema is a strand like nowhere else. Part of the attraction does involve observing the self-confident sensuality with which the Ipanema *garotas* (girls) stroll the sands. (Equal-opportunity purists should note that there's an equivalent amount of male beefcake on hand—it just doesn't inspire songs or poetry.) But more than anything, Ipanema is a carnival. Watch the games of volleyball or *footvollei* (like volleyball, but no hands allowed), beach soccer, surfing, and wakeboarding. Forgot your bikini? Wait a moment and a vendor will stop by with one for sale—along with towels, sarongs (called *kangas* in Brazil), hats, shades, peanuts, beer, cookies, Walkmans, suntan lotion, Styrofoam airplanes, Winnie-the-Pooh books, sticks

Water Frolicking 101: Men *must* swim or at least pretend to swim (many Cariocas actually don't know how to swim but will fake it). A man who dibbles his toes or contemplates the waves with a far-off look in his eye is not a man but a gringo, and must be shunned. Men approach the sea in a series of angry stomps, stopping at the waterline to regard the surf with a steely glare before sprinting forward and diving into a breaking wave. Once immersed, a man may swim farther out, or he may bodysurf. A man may *not* play in the waves.

Women may play in the waves, turning their backs to the surf and giggling as the water breaks over them. This, however, is rare. Generally, a woman dips her toes, advances as deep as mid-calf, and then waits for a breaker, at which time she squats and allows the surf to immerse her bikini bottom. If this is found to be too traumatizing, a woman may also bring a cup to the beach, dip it in the frothy foam and pour the water over various parts of her body, thoroughly massaging each part for *at least* 30 seconds afterward.

Beach Flirting 101: Men and women do not enter the water together. This is not to say they do not interact. For instance, a man may approach a group of no more than three pretty women sitting cross-legged on their *kangas* and ask them to watch his shorts and sandals while he manfully attacks the ocean. Their agreement obtained, the man will then place his stuff on the sand near their *kangas* and stomp angrily toward the surf, which he will regard with a glare all the more steely for the fact that he knows three pretty women are admiring the manful way he's attacking the elements. The women will ignore him, missing the determined plunge into the roiling surf and the angry stomp back up the beach. But at least they will never call him a gringo!

of grilled shrimp, shelled coconuts, even deep-muscle massages. Claim a piece of sand on Ipanema, and all of life's essentials will come to you.

The section just around the point from Copacabana—called **Praia do Arpoador**—is a prime surf spot and a great location for watching the local dudes take to the waves. One of the surf schools also runs lessons for kids from the local favelas. The area around Posto 8 (opposite Rua Farme Amoedo) is Ipanema's gay section.

Farther down into **Leblon** (still the same beach, just a different name once you cross the canal) you will find the **Baixo Baby.** This play area, equipped by corporate sponsors with lots of playground equipment and beach toys, is a popular gathering place for nannies and parents to watch their kids run around and do what kids do on a beach, play with sand.

Off on its own surrounded by mountains, **São Conrado Beach** offers some fine scenery and a (relative) sense of isolation. Its other main claim to fame is as a landing strip for all the hang gliders (*asa delta* in Portuguese) who leap from nearby peaks.

Farther from the city is the beach at **Barra de Tijuca.** The only reason to go out here is if you're a surf-head desperate for a wave. The surfing is said to be the best in Rio, particularly around the Barraca de Pepê (Pepê's Shack) where surfers like to gather. The only reason to go even farther beyond Barra is to get to Grumari, a lovely small beach set in a nature reserve. Grumari has no high-rises or beachside restaurants, just lush vegetation and a few kiosks by the side of the road. However, don't expect to get away from the crowds even this far out; especially on weekends the place is packed.

PARKS & GARDENS

In addition to numerous beaches, Rio is also blessed with a variety of parks. On the waterfront near Centro there's **Flamengo Park,** a good place to stroll in the late afternoon if you're looking for a nice view of the Sugarloaf.

Out in the other direction, just past the northern edge of downtown, lies the **Quinta da Boa Vista,** the royal family's former country residence, on Avenida Bartolomeu de Gusmã, just a short walk from the Sao Cristóvão Metrô stop. Though it's been a century or more since the exiled royals departed, their former country residence is as delightful now as it was when the royal princesses scampered round the villa gardens. Designed in the Romantic style by French landscape architect Auguste Glaziou, the Quinta da Boa Vista has all the tricks of the gardener's trade: tree-lined dells, small ponds and waterfalls, a grotto, a lookout, even a temple of Apollo. The park is also home to the city zoo and the national museum (see "The Top Attractions," earlier in this chapter). Open daily from 7am to 6pm.

Closer to the city core lies the **Campo de Santana,** opposite the Central Metrô stop on Avenida Presidente Vargas. A pretty, formal park, its fence and four iron gates protect 50 species of trees, four ponds, and a grotto. The fence also encloses numerous *agoutis* (a bizarre-looking mini-capybara), ducks, peacocks, and marmosets, as well as a large collection of stray cats. Open daily from 7am to 7pm.

Last and best, the **Parque Nacional da Tijuca (Tijuca National Park)** ★★ is a wonder. At more than 8,000 acres it's the biggest urban forest in the world and one of the last remnants of Atlantic rainforest on Brazil's southern coast. It's a great place to go for a hike (see "Outdoor Activities," below), splash in a waterfall, or admire the view (see "Where to Go for Spectacular—and Free—Views," below). Among its more special points are the Pico de Tijuca, the Corcovado, the Vista Chinesa, and the Pedra da Gávea.

SQUARES & PLAZAS

What's the difference between a *largo* and a *praça?* Simple, although not really. A *praça* is a city square, and a *largo* is, well, also a city square except a *largo* is always bigger than a *praça*, except—like with the Largo de Boticario—when it isn't.

Tucked away just a few hundred meters uphill along Rua Cosme Velho from the Corcovado Train Station is one of Rio's prettiest squares, the **Largo de Boticario** ★★, named for the druggist Luis da Silva Souto who settled there in 1831 (*boticario* is an old-fashioned Portuguese word for druggist). It's a gem of a spot, with five gaily painted colonial houses encircling a fountain in the middle of a flagstone square. Mature fig trees overhead make for abundant shade, while traffic noise seems completely drowned out by the soft gurgling of the Rio Carioca (from which residents of Rio derive their nickname) taking its last few breaths of air before disappearing forever beneath the city streets. Calm and picturesque, it's well worth the 5-minute detour if you're going to the Corcovado anyway.

CLOSED
due to
accidental demolition

WEGEN BISSIGEN
EICHHÖRNCHEN GESCHLOSSEN

CERRADO
CABRAS

Κλειστό
Μετεωρίτες

POOL CLOSED
プール も
ELECTRIC EELS
閉鎖中

Hotel
closed for
facelifting

FERMÉ POUR
RAISON
DE GRÈVE
DES BONNES

FECHADO!
POR CAUSA DE
ATAQUES DOS CROCODILOS

— I don't speak
sign language.

A hotel can close for all kinds of reasons.

Our Guarantee ensures that if your hotel's undergoing construction, we'll let you know in advance. In fact, we cover your entire travel experience. See www.travelocity.com/guarantee for details.

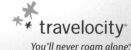
travelocity
You'll never roam alone.

Moments Where to Go for Spectacular—and Free—Views

Rio's best two views—from the Sugarloaf and the Corcovado—are both ticket-charging attractions. But in a city with so much geography it's impossible to fence off everything. What follows are views you get for free.

Smack in the middle of Botafogo is the **Mirante do Pasmado**. It is walkable (enter off Rua General Severino, close to the Shopping Rio Plaza), although it would probably take you at least 30 minutes. A lot easier is to take a taxi up and then walk back down. The views of Sugarloaf, the bay, and the Christ are quite spectacular. At night, there are a few *barracas* (kiosks) where Cariocas like to go after a night of clubbing. Another great viewpoint can be found in Leblon.

Just a short 3km (2-mile) drive uphill along Estrada da Canoa from the beach at Sao Conrado, the **Canoas Lookout (Mirante de Canoas)** provides a view of São Conrado, Rocinha, and the Pedra Dois Irmaos near Leblon, and looking back uphill, the 2,100-foot **Pedra Bonita** from whence the hang gliders launch. Carry on up the road for 2km (1¼ miles), then turn left on Caminho da Pedra Bonita, and you too can stand by the hang gliders as they launch.

The military fort in Leme (see **Forte do Leme**, p. 101) offers the most spectacular views of Copacabana, the Bay of Guanabara, and Sugarloaf. At R$3 (US$1.50/£1), it's effectively free.

The best way to arrive in **Praça XV de Novembro** is by sea—if not on a sailing ship from Portugal then a ferry from Niterói will do the trick. Rio's most important square, Praça XV is also its most abused. Earlier generations of city planners took this main ceremonial square, ran six lanes of traffic in front of it, a freeway over the top of it, then knocked down most of the old structures used to frame the space, and erected 20-story glass blocks. Still, some of the old charm shines through (and six lanes of traffic have been sunk in an underground tunnel, which helps). To your right as you arrive, beyond a statue of Dom João VI on a horse, is the **Chafariz do Mestre Valentim,** an ornate fountain that marks Rio's former coastline.

Perhaps the city's prettiest square (next to Cinelândia) is the **Largo do Machado** in the Catete neighborhood. Perfectly proportioned, the square is dominated by the **Igreja Matriz de Nossa Senhora da Glória,** a strange but rather elegant combination of traditional Greek temple and a three-story bell tower. As an added bonus, there are a number of Parisian-style sidewalk cafes on the square's northern flank.

Also well worth a visit is the **Largo de São Francisco de Paula** in Rio's old shopping district. There's an outdoor market on one side of the square, and on the other the huge baroque-style **Igreja de São Francisco de Paula.**

For a further discussion on the city's best squares and plazas, see "Neighborhoods to Explore," earlier in this chapter.

6 Especially for Kids

There are few things in Rio that *aren't* for kids. Brazilians take their children everywhere—restaurants, bars, even dances—and voice no objection when others do the

> **Tips** **DIY When It Comes to Tours**
>
> When booking a tour or outdoor adventure, it's best to make the call yourself. (Don't worry about a language barrier; most tour operators speak English.) The concierges and desk staff in most hotels are remarkably mercenary. If they make the booking it will cost you anything from 10% to 50% more. Nor will you necessarily get the tour you want. Rio concierges are notorious for informing guests that a tour they wanted is "full," then putting them on a tour with another company—one that offers the concierge a bigger cut.

same. Still, there are few places that stand out as being especially kid-friendly. First and most obvious is the **beach.** Sun, surf, and sand castles have kind of an enduring kid appeal. For younger children the beach at **Leblon** features the **Baixo Baby,** a free play area equipped with all manner of toys and play stuff geared for toddlers. On Sundays and holidays, the waterfront avenues that line the beaches of Flamengo, Copacabana, Ipanema, and Leblon are closed for cars. With no traffic, the miles and miles of waterfront become the world's best playground. Both adults and children will enjoy the pleasant bustle of Carioca families going for a stroll and there's plenty of entertainment to boot. You'll find an array of buskers such as jugglers, magicians, musicians, stilt-walkers, and fire-eaters as well bike rentals and small electric toy-car rentals. For slightly older kids, the **city zoo (Jardim Zoológico**—see "The Top Attractions," earlier in this chapter) is guaranteed to delight and just possibly to educate. One of the few museums of interest to kids is the **Museu do Indio** (see "The Top Attractions," earlier in this chapter) in Botafogo. The museum offers kids stamps and (washable) body paints so they can practice adorning themselves like natives; the re-creations of Indian houses on the grounds are fun places to crawl in and out of. In Catete, the beautiful (if slightly formal) **Parque do Catete** has a *brinquedoteca,* a kind of toy library from which you can loan out toys by the hour for a nominal fee (about R$7/US$3.50/£2 per hour). Few kids can resist the fun of a train—or tram ride. The Santa Teresa tram zooms over a high aqueduct, then snakes through the narrow streets of this old neighborhood.

7 Organized Tours

BUS TOURS   Gray Line (© 021/2512-9919; www.grayline.com) offers a number of tour itineraries: the R$65 (US$33/£18) tour of Rio's historic downtown and the R$65 (US$33/£18) boat tour of Guanabara Bay are reasonable value; the R$80 (US$40/£22) half-day tour (morning or afternoon) of the Corcovado or Pão de Açúcar is really a bit of a racket; all they're providing is transfer to and from the train station or gondola at a markup. If your time is limited you can combine several tours and see the Corcovado, Sugarloaf, and historic Rio in one full-day trip for R$190 (US$95/£51), lunch included.

BOAT TOURS   Saveiros Tour (© 021/2225-6064; www.saveiros.com.br) offers 2-hour tours of Guanabara Bay aboard an old wooden fishing schooner. Cost is R$35 (US$18/£10), children 5 to 10 R$15 (US$7.50/£4), children under 5 free, including snacks of fresh fruit. Departure is at 9:30 or 11am Tuesday through Sunday from the Glória Marina (Metrô: Glória). The tour takes in Ilha Fiscal and the navy yards, has a look at the Sugarloaf from the sea, then treks across the bay to Niterói to look at the huge Fortaleza Santa Cruz that once guarded the mouth of Guanabara Bay. If you prefer a sunset tour of the bay, contact **Marlin Yacht Charters** (© 021/2225-7434). They offer a daily tour (with a minimum of four people) from 3 to 5pm, taking in the main sights of the Bay such as the Rio-Niterói bridge, the Sugarloaf, and the beaches and fort on the Niterói side, across from Rio. Boats depart from the Glória Marina. Confirm reservations until 1pm for same-day departures. Adults and children 8 and over R$40 (US$20/£11). Children under 8 are half price or free (depending on your negotiation skills).

HELICOPTER TOURS   Rio is a town where taking the high ground is rewarded. **Helisight** (© 021/2511-2141, on weekends 021/2542-7895; www.helisight.com.br) offers sightseeing tours by helicopter. Prices range from R$150 (US$75/£41) per person for a 6-minute circuit around the statue of Christ to R$300 (US$150/£81) per person for a 12-minute flight over the Christ, Botanical Gardens, Rocinha, Lagoa, Leblon, Ipanema, Copacabana, and the Sugarloaf. There's a minimum of three people per flight. Tours depart from Urca Hill (halfway up to the Sugarloaf) and from the shore of Lagoa (opposite the rowing stadium in Leblon).

SPECIALTY TOURS   Rio's hillside favelas, or shantytowns, are huge, complex, and fascinating—a whole other world, in fact—but as an outsider it's difficult (and dangerous) to navigate your way through this world. Licensed guide Marcelo Armstrong of **Marcelo Armstrong's Favela Tour** ⚜ (© 021/9989-0074 mobile, or 021/3322-2727; www.favelatour.com.br) knows the territory; he's been doing tours since 1993, longer than any of his competitors. A 3-hour tour costs R$70 (US$35/£19) if booked directly, including pickup and drop-off. A portion of the fee goes to fund a school that tour-goers get to visit. To enjoy some of the city's best hiking trails, book one of the many city nature tours with **Rio Hiking** (© 021/2552-9204 or 021/9721-0594; www.riohiking.com.br). Many of the city's trails and viewpoints are hard to access without a car. Rio Hiking's knowledgeable English-speaking guides will take you on some of the best hikes and show you some interesting parts of the city not always explored by visitors. One of the most popular tours is the visit to the Tijuca Forest,

---

Finds **Puppet, Beach & Plant Tour**

Two of Rio's more interesting museums and its last semiwild beach are unfortunately so far south that most people never visit. **Rio Hiking** (© 021/9721-0594 or 021/2552-9204; www.riohiking.com.br) offers a 1-day tour, taking in all three of these sites: the **Burle Marx Estate, Grumari Beach,** and the **Casa do Pontal Museum.** Burle Marx was Brazil's most famous landscape designer (responsible for the wavy lines on the Copacabana sidewalk, among other things). At his 100-acre estate he assembled more than 3,500 species of plants, which he grouped according to their shape and texture. The tour spends 2 hours at the estate, then heads to the red sand of Grumari Beach for 3 hours of relaxing and a grilled fish lunch at a beachside restaurant, followed by a visit to the Museu Casa do Pontal, which houses an astounding variety of clay figures as part of its vast folk-art display (see "The Top Attractions," earlier in this chapter). Cost for a private excursion with English-speaking guide, not including lunch, is R$150 (US$75/£41).

which includes all the main sights of the park, a 2-hour hike to the highest peak in the park, and a visit to Santa Teresa for R$170 (US$85/£46) per person for a full day. For a very different tour, experience **Ikoporan's** community tours (✆ **021/3852-2916;** www.ikoporan.org). This local organization sets up volunteer projects for foreign visitors who would like to help a community organization. Those who don't have the time to dedicate to volunteering can spend a day visiting one or more community projects, getting to know some of the social projects that support some of Rio's most socially disadvantaged groups, learn more about social issues, and talk to staff, volunteers, and local residents. Tours start at R$140 (US$70/£38) and include transportation, an English-speaking guide, and lunch. Part of the proceeds are donated to the projects.

TRAM TOURS   Rio has far more tram track than gets used by the daily tram to and from Santa Teresa. Every Saturday, some of this track gets put to use for a special tram tour. The **tour** departs at 10am and 2pm and runs about 2 hours; tickets are R$4 (US$2/£1). The ride takes you up toward the Dois Irmãos and the forest above Santa Teresa. It's a unique opportunity to see some more of this charming neighborhood and the gorgeous Tijuca forest. For further information call the **Museu do Bonde** (✆ **021/2215-8581**). *Note:* The tram station is not at all easy to find. It's behind the big "hanging gardens" Petrobras building, on Rua Prof. Lélio Gama, a little street that runs off Rua Senador Dantas.

8 Outdoor Activities

ADVENTURE SPORTS   Rio Hiking ✮✮ (✆ **021/9721-0594;** www.riohiking. com.br) has evolved into Rio's adventure-sport specialist, offering a range of exciting outdoor sports that take full advantage of Rio's extraordinary geography. To date, Rio Hiking offers **rock climbing, rafting, ocean kayaking, cycling, scuba diving, surfing** (with lessons), and **rappelling.** Depending on the sport, half-day adventures cost from R$80 to R$150 (US$40–US$75/£22–£40), full-day adventures from R$150 to R$250 (US$75–US$125/£40–£67), guides and transfer to and from your hotel included. The **white water–rafting** trip takes you to a river about 2 hours north of Rio with Class III (and sometimes Class IV) rapids. The descent takes about 3 hours. Cost is R$190 (US$95/£51). The company also offers 3-day **trekking** trips (see "Trekking," below). **Rio Adventures** (✆ **021/2705-5747** or 021/8204-7559; www. rioadventures.com) offers a couple of 1-day adventure-sport options from Rio. On the **rappelling** trip, you drive past Barra de Tijuca to beautiful Guaratiba, hike for an hour to a cliff overlooking an undeveloped beach, then rappel down a 377m (115-ft.) rock face. Then you hang out, swim for bit, and head back. For a fun outing that's sure to bring out the inner-Tarzan or Jane, try the tree canopy ride in the Tijuca Forest. While safely secured in a harness, you climb 15 to 50 feet above the ground and make your way from tree to tree across swing-bridges, tunnels, and walkways. Minimum age is 12. Cost is R$190 (US$95/£51) per person for two people, including transportation and lunch. With a bigger group the price goes down significantly.

BICYCLING   Rio by Bike (✆ **021/2247-7269** or 021/9798-1804) offers guided tours of the city as well as bike rentals. The most popular tour goes along the beaches of the Zona Sul and then through the tunnel to Urca and the Flamengo waterfront as far as the Museum of Modern Art (MAM). A visit as far as downtown or Glória can also be arranged, or those who prefer to cycle around the Lagoa can discuss their preferences with the guide. Bicycles for the guided tour cost R$120 (US$60/£32) for up to four people. Those who prefer to explore Rio's waterfront on their own can just rent the bicycles, R$10 (US$5/£3) per hour or R$60 (US$30/£16) for a full day. A refundable deposit of R$50 (US$25/£14) is required to rent the bike.

GOLFING   Rio's only public golf course is out in Barra da Tijuca. Golden Green (Av. Conde de Marapendi 2905; © **021/2434-0696**) is a 3-par 6-hole course located inside a private condominium but open to the public without a membership. Golden Green is open Tuesday to Sunday from 7am to 6pm. Greens fees are R$50 (US$25/£14) Tuesday to Friday and R$60 (US$30/£16) on weekends and holidays. One of the city's best courses (18 holes) is the elegant **Gávea Golf Club,** Estrada da Gávea 800, São Conrado (© **021/3332-4141**). However, the club—like virtually every golf course in Brazil—is private. The Copacabana Palace Hotel and the Sheraton Rio Hotel are a few of the hotels that have an arrangement allowing their guests to tee off. If you are a golf fiend, check first with your hotel of choice for privileges.

JEEP TOURS   Although we always thought they looked kind of goofy, the open jeep tours are incredibly popular with visitors to Rio. The most popular tours are the ones through the Tijuca Forest combined with a visit to the Corcovado (R$95/US$48/£26 per person). For information and bookings call © **021/9298-3071** mobile, or 021/2484-2279; www.indianajungle.com.br.

HANG GLIDING   For a bird's-eye view of Rio's beaches and mountains, check out **Just Fly Rio** ☆☆ (© **021/9985-7540** mobile, or 021/2268-0565; www.justfly.com.br). Flight instructor Paulo Celani used to be an agricultural engineer, until he decided he'd much prefer to fly for a living. That was more than 20 years ago. Since then Paulo has soared in tandem with hundreds of people ages 5 to 85. There's no experience or special skills necessary, aside from a willingness to run off a ramp into the open sky. It's one of the most exciting things you can do in Rio, well worth the R$200 (US$100/£54) per flight, pickup and drop-off included. *Tip:* If you are keen on flying, contact Paulo on the day you arrive in Rio. As the activity is weather dependent (and what may be a great day for the beach may not be the best flying weather), you can let Paulo contact you when flying conditions are best.

HIKING   **Rio Hiking** ☆☆ (© **021/9721-0594;** www.riohiking.com.br) offers guided hiking trips to most of Rio's peaks. The 4-hour Sugarloaf trip, which includes a short stretch of rock climbing, costs R$120 (US$60/£32). The 6-hour Pedra da Gávea hike offers terrific views, a waterfall in the middle, and an ocean dip at the end. Cost is R$150 (US$75/£40). Less strenuous is the Tijuca Forest tour, which involves a tour of the forest, stops at a waterfall and a couple of lookouts, and a 2-hour hike to Pico de Tijuca. Cost is R$170 (US$85/£46), with the option of returning via the fascinating hilltop neighborhood of Santa Teresa. Guides Denise Werneck and Gabriel Barrouin know Rio well, speak excellent English, and are a delight to be with.

SEA KAYAKING   The Bay of Guanabara is perfect for kayaking. The guides at Rio Hiking (© **021/9721-0594;** www.riohiking.com.br) organize kayaking tours out of Praia Vermelha in Urca out and around some of the small islands. The fiberglass kayaks aren't quite up to North American quality, but it's nice to be on the water. Cost is R$160 (US$80/£49) for a half-day tour, including transfers, refreshments, and English-speaking guide.

SURFING   California's not the only hot surfing spot in the world. Rio has a number of good spots to catch the waves. And if the waves aren't as big as in Hawaii, the water's certainly warmer than Vancouver Island. The surfing beach closest to the main part of Rio is **Arpoador Beach** in Ipanema. Waves are between 1 and 3m (3–10 ft.). São Conrado Beach is off and on. Sometimes there are good 2m (6½-ft.) waves, sometimes it's dead. Out in Barra de Tijuca the main surf beach is **Barra-Meio,** a 1km-long (½-mile) stretch in the middle of the beach (around Av. Sernambetiba 3100). Waves average around 2m (6 ft.). Carry on down that same beach another 6.5 to 8km (4–5 miles), and you come to **Macumba-Pontal,** a 2.5km (1½-mile) beach with waves up to 3m (10 ft.). If you've brought your board and just need transport, there's a **surf bus** that departs the Largo do Machado at 7am, 10am, 1pm, and 4pm and goes along Copacabana, Arpoador, São Conrado, and Barra de Tijuca as far as Prainha, past Recreio. Call to confirm departure times (© **021/2539-7555** or 021/8702-2837; www.surfbus.com.br); tickets cost R$3 (US$1.50/£1) each way. If you need a board, **Hot Coast,** Galeria River, Rua Francisco Otaviano 67, loja 12, Ipanema (© **021/ 2287-9388**), rents short boards, fun boards, and long boards for R$40 (US$20/£11) a day. You need to book ahead if you want a board on the weekend. If you're looking for **lessons** there's a surf school conveniently located in Ipanema. The **Escolinha de Surf Paulo Dolabella** (© **021/2259-2320**) is in front of the Caesar Park Hotel. The regular lessons are Tuesday and Thursday from 8 to 10am and 3 to 5pm, but you can also arrange for a lesson on the weekends or other days. Drop-in rates are R$30 (US$15/£8) per hour, including the equipment. However, like true surf dudes, they will neither have nor answer phones; you have to go find them. **Riohiking (021/ 9721-0594;** www.riohiking.com.br) also offers a half-day surf lesson and includes transportation, gear, and a lesson, R$150 (US$75/£40).

TREKKING   Rio Hiking 🌟🌟 (© **021/9721-0594;** www.riohiking.com.br) offers a number of **guided 2- to 3-day treks** in the mountains or rugged coast around Rio. Particularly recommended is the 2-day trek in the **Serra dos Órgãos National Park** (R$440/US$220/£119), where the Atlantic rainforest is pristine and the views extraordinary. Avid hikers will certainly enjoy the spectacular hikes in Itatiaia National Park. Located about 3 hours from Rio, on the border of the states of Minas Gerais and São Paulo, the park is home to the highest peak in the state, the 2,787m (8,000-ft.) Agulhas Negras. This 3-day trip takes you to some of the most region's best scenery and includes a visit to the waterfalls in the lower part of the national park, a full-day hike to the highest peak in Rio state, and on the third day a 4-hour hike to the stunning rock formations of the Prateleiras (shelves), with an optional rappel. This 3-day package costs R$660 (US$330/£178) per person and includes accommodations, food, specialized guides, and transportation. All you have to bring are sunscreen, hiking boots, warm clothes, and a raincoat.

9 The *Only* Spectator Sport in Rio

FUTEBOL **AT THE MARACANÃ** 🌟🌟🌟   The best and only true way to experience the world's largest soccer stadium is to come during a big game. What an experience! Fans arrive at Maracanã, Rua Profesor Eurico Rabelo s/n (© **021/2569-4916;** Metrô: Maracanã), hours beforehand, literally—for a 4pm game they arrive at 1pm *at the latest*—and the world's biggest party begins. Outside folks drink ice-cold beer. Inside the *torcedores* (fan club members) bring out the samba drums and pound away for a good half-hour, psyching themselves up before parading in the banners—huge flags in team colors—to the wild applause of their fellow fans. Then the other team parades in their flags, and your team boos. Then your side sings a song insulting their team. Then their team sings a song insulting your team. Then they unveil a massive

---

Tips **Beware of Organized Soccer Fun**

Organized trips to the Maracanã are a scam. They often charge R$80 to R$100 (US$40–US$50/£22–£27) for a ticket and bus transport (to a stadium that's on the Metrô line). Even if you took a cab there and back, you'd still come out ahead.

---

banderão covering half the stadium. Then your side unveils your *banderão*. Samba drums beat all the while. Eventually after several hours of this silliness a soccer game breaks out. And the best thing about the Brazilian game is they have utter contempt for defense; it's attack, attack, attack for the full 90 minutes. The four best teams in Rio are Flamengo, Fluminense, Botafogo, and Vasco de Gama. Any game pitting one of these teams against another is worth seeing. Scheduling is incredibly complex, but it's guaranteed your hotel clerk (or bellhop) will know about the next big game. Tickets are quite affordable, ranging from R$10 to R$40 (US$5–US$20/£1.35–£11).

Tip: While you can sit in the neutral stands in the middle, it's more fun if you choose sides. Violence at Brazilian football never came anywhere close to the problems seen in Europe; since they prohibited beer inside and reduced the stadium seating capacity, it's vanished almost altogether.

10 Shopping in Rio
THE SHOPPING SCENE

If Cariocas had to list their primary joys in life, shopping certainly wouldn't come out on the very top—there are, after all, beaches, music, and sex to consider—but it'd certainly be in the top five. Even on the beach vendors will peddle an enormous range of products. Elsewhere clothing, shoes, arts and crafts, musical instruments, and other souvenirs can all be had at good prices.

The old downtown neighborhood of Centro offers great deals for clothes and shoes. Fun to explore are the pedestrian streets around **Rua da Alfândega, Rua Uruguaiana,** and **Rua Buenos Aires,** jampacked with hundreds of merchants in small shops side by side. Back in the '70s the area was slated to be demolished to make room for a viaduct, but over 1,200 shopkeepers formed a merchant's association and banded together to put a halt to the development. The best days for shopping are Monday through Friday when downtown is full of office workers. Throughout downtown you will also find street vendors hawking a variety of wares, everything from portable radios to pirated CDs and see-through bra-straps. The area around **Largo da Carioca** has a number of market stalls and street vendors. More upscale clothing can be found around the **Rua Gonçalves Dias,** with many stores selling Brazilian brand names and local designers.

Botafogo has two interesting shopping centers, the **Botafogo Praia Shopping** and the older **Rio Sul.** Rio Sul was one of the first malls of Rio and is still a very popular shopping destination. Many Brazilian stores can be found in this mall, and it makes a convenient place to browse and get a sense for brands and prices.

Copacabana, Ipanema, and Leblon don't have any large malls, just boutique malls known as *galerias* in Brazil. The prominent shopping areas are the main streets of the neighborhood. In Copacabana, **Nossa Senhora de Copacabana** is the main shopping street, with the best stores concentrated around the Rua Santa Clara and Rua Figueiredo de Magalhães. The beachfront area also houses a street market on Saturdays and Sundays, selling souvenirs and arts and crafts from various regions of Brazil. For upscale and exclusive shopping in Ipanema, try **Rua Visconde de Piraja,** especially between the **Rua Anibal de Medonça** and **Rua Vinicius de Moraes.** Another popular destination for Rio's well-heeled shoppers is the classy São Conrado Fashion Mall, located in São Conrado, a neighborhood wedged in between Leblon and Barra. Those who prefer mega-malls may want to head straight for Barra da Tijuca. This newly developed neighborhood is home to many malls, including the **Barra Shopping**—the largest mall in Latin America.

Hours for small stores and neighborhood shops are typically Monday through Friday from 10am to 7pm, and 9am to 1pm on Saturday. Malls are usually open from 10am to 10pm Monday through Saturday and limited hours on Sundays (2–8pm). In tourist areas shops will often be open on weekends.

While street vendors and markets take only cash, most shops accept one or more type of credit card. Often you can negotiate a discount for paying cash instead of with a credit card. Sometimes you will see two prices listed on items: *á vista* (always the lower price) refers to cash payments, *cheque ou cartão* is the price for payments made with a check or credit card. Please note that there is a difference between *Credicard* (a brand of credit card) and *cartão* or *cartão de credito* (the generic word for any kind of credit card).

SHOPPING FROM A TO Z
ANTIQUES
Shopping Cassino Atlantico   Attached to the Sofitel Hotel, this 180-store mall specializes in antiques and art galleries. Browsers enjoy the antiques fair that takes place every Saturday from 11am to 7pm throughout the mall. Av. Atlântica 4240, Copacabana. ✆ **021/2523-8709.** Bus: 474.

ARTS & CRAFTS
Brasil&Cia   This store in Ipanema specializes in Brazilian arts and crafts. The items are not cheap but the selection offers quality artwork made from wood, ceramics, paper, and fibers. Look for the collection of ballerina dolls made from gourds and painted in delicate colors and patterns. Rua Maria Quitéria 27, Ipanema. ✆ **021/2267-4603.** www.brasilecia.com.br. Bus: 472.

O Sol   O Sol is run by a nonprofit society dedicated to supporting and promoting the work of regional artists. The collection varies from beautiful but not very portable furniture pieces to portable miniature terra-cotta sculptures, chess sets, and textiles, including carpets and wall hangings. Rua Corcovado 213, Jardim Botânico. ✆ **021/2294-5099.** www.artesanato-sol.com.br. Bus: 572.

Pé de Boi   In Laranjeiras on your way to the Corcovado, Pé de Boi's collection goes beyond just Brazilian arts and crafts to include work from popular Peruvian, Ecuadorian, and Guatemalan artists. It's also a great spot to browse for arts and crafts from other Brazilian regions such the Amazon, Pernambuco, and Minas Gerais. Rua Ipiranga 55, Laranjeiras. ✆ **021/2285-4395.** www.pedeboi.com.br. Bus: 584.

Trilhos Urbanos   A great little store in Santa Teresa, Trilhos Urbanos sells a variety of Brazilian artwork, including paintings, photographs, and crafts made out of tile, paper, and other materials. Rua Almirante Alexandrino 402, Santa Teresa. ✆ **021/2242-3632.** Tram stop: Largo dos Guimarães.

BEACHWEAR

Blue Man   My favorite swimwear store, Blue Man is known for its original designs and prints. Bathing suits and bikinis can be found in various styles, often allowing you to mix and match tops and bottoms for your preferred look. It features some male swim trunks as well. Visconde de Pirajá 351, loja 108, Ipanema. © 021/2247-4905. Bus: 474. Also with outlets in the Rio Sul and Fashion Mall shopping centers.

Bum Bum   The best-known place to shop for the infamous Rio bikini. Collections vary constantly, but one thing never changes—the smaller the better. The styles and colors on display will give you a quick feel for the current beach fashions for both men and women. Rua Vinicius de Morais 130, Ipanema. © 021/2521-1229. Bus: 415.

Lenny Niemeyer   Lenny Niemeyer, or simply Lenny is quickly becoming one of Brazil's premier beachwear designers. Recently Nicole Kidman ordered several of her pieces after seeing Lenny's collection in *Vanity Fair*. Her collection includes both bikinis and bathing suits, and she recently added bags and accessories. Rua Garcia d'Avila 149, Ipanema. © 021/2227-5537 and several other stores, including in the São Conrado Fashion Mall. www.lenny.com.br. Bus: 415.

Rosa Chá   Another Brazilian beachwear label that is now available internationally is Rosa Chá. Designs here are intricate and the materials go far beyond plain lycra. The collection also includes a good variety of one-piece suits. Note that this is not the place to come looking for bargains. São Conrado Fashion Mall, Estrada da Gávea 899, shop 221 F, Gávea. © 021/3322-1849. www.rosacha.com.br. Bus: 593.

BOOKS

Letras e Expressoes   The Ipanema store offers an excellent selection of foreign magazines and newspapers. The travel section also offers a number of excellent books on Rio, including some beautiful coffee-table books. Internet terminals are available. The Leblon store also has a decent music collection and excellent coffee shop. Rua Visconde de Pirajá 276, Ipanema. © 021/2521-6110. Bus: 415. Also at Av. Ataúlfo de Paiva 1292 C, Leblon. © 021/2511-5085.

Livraria da Travessa   With floor-to-ceiling shelves stuffed with books, this store positively invites hours-long browsing sessions. They have a good collection of English-language books, plus children's books and guidebooks. On the mezzanine there's a cafe that serves coffees, sweets, sandwiches, and wines. Av. Rio Branco 44, Centro. © 021/2253-8949. Bus: 128. Also at Rua Visconde de Pirajá 462, Ipanema. © 021/2287-5157. Bus: 474 or 128.

CARNAVAL COSTUMES

Casa Turuna   For those creative types who want to make their own Carnaval costume, Casa Turuna is the supplier of choice. Established in 1920, this store in Rio's downtown sells everything you can imagine: beads, feathers, sequins, fabric, headdresses, and so much more. Rua Senhor dos Passos 122, Centro. © 021/2224-0908. Metrô: Central.

FASHION
For Men

Sandpiper   Trendy casual wear that is a bit more upscale than Taco (see below) but still fun and hip. A great spot for shirts or informal jackets. Like most men's stores in Brazil, they add a few more splashes of color than you may be used to. Rua Santa Clara 75, Copacabana. © 021/2236-7652. Metrô: Arcoverde.

Siberian For more dressy menswear check out Siberian. The store sells its own label as well as several other Brazilian labels and focuses on quality clothing at still an affordable price. Especially their fall and winter collection sales offer great bargains for those who live in colder climates and want to pick up some cords or long-sleeved shirts. Rua Lauro Muller 116, Shopping Rio Sul, Botafogo. © 021/2543-2881. Bus: 119 or 415.

Taco Inexpensive good-quality casual wear. A nice pair of jeans can be had for as little as R$40 (US$20/£11). It has good selections of casual dress shirts and T-shirts in lots of different colors. Most products are 100% Brazilian cotton. Rua Gonçalves Dias 56, Centro. © 021/2242-3315. Another branch at Av. Rio Branco 151, Centro. © 021/2221-2323. Metrô: Carioca.

Toulon An excellent spot to pick up some smart casual wear. Good-quality jeans, khakis, colorful long-sleeve cotton dress shirts, and T-shirts at reasonable prices. Rua Visconde de Piraja 135, Ipanema. © 021/2247-8716. www.toulon.com.br. Bus: 474. Also at Av. N.S. de Copacabana 978, lojas B/C, Copacabana. © 021/2247-1051. Bus: 474.

For Women

Folic Folic sells upscale clothing for women over 30. The clothes are sophisticated and elegant and fit beautifully. The collection ranges from casual, including jeans, to office wear and evening wear. The store will make any adjustments to your purchases for free to ensure the absolutely perfect fit. The March and August sales at Folic are legendary as prices drop up to 70%. N.S de Copacabana 690, Copacabana. © 021/2548-4021. www.folic.com.br. Bus: 415.

Gang Jeans If you have always wanted to have a curvier behind, then this is the store for you! Vogue magazine described Gang Jeans as "wonderbras for your buttocks." The jeans are incredibly tight but, thanks to a secret formula of fabrics, also very comfortable. Best of all, they are designed to enhance your best asset and boost your confidence. The collection always includes plain styles as well as some decorated with strass stones or embroidery. Shopping Rio Sul, Rua Lauro Muller 116, 2nd floor, shop 201, Botafogo. © 021/2543-9264. www.gang-rio.com.br. Bus: 474.

XPTO For young and colorful fashion at very affordable prices, check out XPTO. The collection includes lots of dresses made of excellent quality cotton. Many of the pretty skirts come with matching tops that can be bought separately or mixed and matched with other styles. The clothes at XPTO are playful and fun, but many of the pieces are wearable for all ages. Rua Gonçalves Dias 55, Centro. © 021/2252-3100. www.xpto online.com.br. Metrô: Carioca.

Galleries

Ateliê Selaron A local artist who works out of his atelier just behind the Sala Cecilia on Lapa Square, Selaron is well known for his paintings and the interesting frames he creates. He is also the artist who created the mosaics on the famous Lapa steps. Escadaria do Convento 24 (enter off the Rua Joaquim Silva), Lapa. © 021/2242-0922. Metrô: Cinelândia.

Ateliê Tetê Cappel and Eduardo Fallero Studio Smaller is better; this duo has made their fame creating tiny reproductions of well-known landmarks—famous tourist sites, but also small-scale versions of bars, houses, and heritage buildings. Rua Vinicius de Moraes 190, Ipanema. © 021/2522-1141. Bus: 415.

HB-195 This gallery in Santa Teresa exhibits work from a variety of local contemporary artists. The view you get from this lovely house is just a bonus. Follow the signs for the Chácara do Céu museum, and instead of turning a sharp left on Rua Murt-inho Nobre, continue straight ahead for another 20m (67 ft.) to Rua Hermenegildo Barros. Open Wednesday to Sunday 2 to 7pm. Rua Hermenegildo Barros 195, Santa Teresa. ℭ 021/2508-9148. Tram: Santa Teresa.

GIFTS & SOUVENIRS

Ely's Gems and Souvenirs   One of Rio's largest souvenir stores, Ely's offers the typical woodcarvings, Bahian dolls, T-shirts, and mugs, but the good stuff—beautiful creations in silver, gold, and stones—is on the right-hand side, in the jewelry section. Ely herself shows you around. Av. N.S. de Copacabana 249, loja D. ℭ 021/2541-2547. Metrô: Arcoverde.

Gilson Martins   For fun, colorful, and practical souvenirs, check Gilson Martins' collection of bags. That is, bags in the broad sense, which includes purses, backpacks, wallets, and toiletry bags. His "Brasil" collection is decorated in yellow and green, often with designs of the Brazilian flag. Visconde de Piraja 462, Ipanema. ℭ 021/2227-6178. www.gilsonmartins.com.br. Bus: 474.

JEWELRY

Amsterdam Sauer   The best-known name in Brazil for gems, jewelry, and souvenirs made with semiprecious and precious stones. The Ipanema location houses both the store and museum; it's worth a visit even if you're not looking to buy. The museum shows off many of Mr. Sauer's original finds when he first came to Brazil in 1940 and started working as a miner, gemologist, geologist, and finally as a jeweler. The store offers a wide range of jewelry and loose gemstones including emeralds, aquamarines, imperial topaz (mined only in Brazil), tourmalines, citrines, and Brazilian opals. The staff is friendly and low-pressure. Items can be delivered to your hotel. Rua Visconde de Piraja 484, Ipanema. ℭ 0800/266-092 or 021/2512-9878. www.amsterdamsauer.com. Bus: 474.

H. Stern   If you're anywhere near a hotel in Rio, it's only a matter of time before you receive an invitation to visit an H. Stern store, transportation complimentary. Or you can just phone a store and they'll be pleased to come pick you up. (I once read a story about a man who saved on cab fare by calling the H. Stern store nearest his destination whenever he went out. He paid nothing for taxis, but wound up buying his girlfriend a very expensive ring.) The store in Ipanema is the world headquarters. Specializing in precious and semiprecious stones, the company also owns mines and polishing shops, guaranteeing the quality of their products from start to finish. Rua Garcia D'Avila 113, Ipanema. ℭ 021/2259-7442. www.hstern.net. Bus: 474.

Silvia Blumberg   For truly unique designs in gold or silver visit Silvia Blumberg's store in Ipanema. This award-winning designer mostly uses Brazilian stones, but is now developing a collection that combines precious metals with Amazon seeds and nuts. Her creations range from the loud and flamboyant and fun to elegant and discreet. If Silvia's in, you'll get to hear the story behind each of her pieces. Visconde de Piraja 300, store 214, Ipanema. ℭ 021/2513-4181. www.silviablumberg.com.br. Bus: 474.

LEATHER GOODS

Mala Amada   Run out of space for all your souvenirs? Mala Amada has an excellent selection of handbags, purses, briefcases, and wallets. All are made with high-quality Brazilian leather and produced in the store's own factory. Rua Visconde de Piraja 550, Ipanema. ℭ 021/2239-8648. www.malaamada.com.br. Bus: 474. Also Rua da Carioca 13, Centro. ℭ 021/2262-0676. Metrô: Carioca.

MALLS & SHOPPING CENTERS

Botafogo Praia Shopping   The mall's spread out over seven floors, so you spend a lot of time on the escalators, but that's the only drawback. There's an excellent selection of clothing stores, and for your photo needs, the Kodak Rio photo shop on the ground floor. The seventh floor food court has three excellent restaurants (Kotobuki [p. 83], Emporium Pax, and Enseada), with gorgeous views of Botafogo beach and the Pão de Açúcar. Praia de Botafogo 400, Botafogo. ℭ 021/2559-9559. Bus: 512 (to Alfredo Gomes). Metrô: Botafogo.

Rio Sul   One of the most popular malls in the city, Rio Sul is very accessible, located in Botafogo just before the tunnel that goes to Copacabana. With over 450 stores, a movie theater, and an excellent food court, Rio Sul is always busy and a great place to get a feel for Brazilian fashion and prices. Rua Lauro Muller 116, Botafogo. ℭ 021/2545-7200. Bus: 119 or 474.

São Conrado Fashion Mall   The São Conrado Fashion Mall is the favorite haunt for Rio's well-heeled and fashion-conscious shoppers. If you are up on Brazilian movie stars and models this will be the place to spot them! Over 150 stores carry national and international designers. The mall's food court is the best in town with a number of high-end restaurants. Estrada da Gávea 899, São Conrado. ℭ 021/2322-2733. Bus: 178.

Shopping Leblon   Rio's newest mall sits right on the edge of Leblon and Ipanema and offers an elegant shopping experience. The mall offers a good selection of upscale stores and labels but certainly not as high-end as the São Conrado Fashion Mall. The excellent food court has views of the lagoon and the Corcovado. Rua Afrânio de Melo 290, Leblon. ℭ 021/3138-8000. Bus: 415.

MARKETS

Feira Hippie Ipanema   In the '60s this square was the hippie hangout in Rio, and it's still a fun place to browse for arts and crafts. Open every Sunday, rain or shine, 8am to 6pm. Praça General Osorio (intersection of Rua Teixeira de Melo and Rua Visconde de Pirajá). No phone. Bus: 474.

Feirarte   If you need to grab some last-minute souvenirs, the two Feirarte markets in Copacabana are ideal. The smaller market operates only on the weekends in front of the Lido park (cross street Rua Rodolfo Dantas). The larger market runs every night from 6pm to 1am on the median, opposite Rua Djalma Ulrich. On offer are the standard array of souvenirs such as T-shirts, jewelry, leatherwork, ceramics, precious stones, bikinis, and paintings. Bus: 119 or 415.

Feira do Rio Antigo (Lapa Antique Market)   Every first Saturday of the month, the Rua do Lavradio becomes a large bustling outdoor antique market. Although not quite garage-sale prices, good bargains can still be had. Of couse an event in Lapa wouldn't be complete without samba; live music performances in the afternoon. Arrive early if you are serious about bargain hunting. Rua do Lavradio, Lapa. Bus: 464.

MUSIC

Modern Sound   Music buffs will think they have died and gone to heaven. This store houses an amazing collection of music. The staff is very knowledgeable and happy to help, but half the fun is browsing through the large wooden CD bins. In the evenings, the store is often used as a small concert venue. To check the programming go to their website and look under *Allegro Bistrô Musical* for details. Rua Barata Ribeiro 502, Copacabana. ℭ 021/2548-5005. www.modernsound.com.br. Bus: 415.

Toca de Vinicius *(Finds)*   In the heart of Ipanema, this small temple is dedicated to the god of bossa nova, poet and composer Vinicius de Moraes. The second floor even houses a tiny shrine with original manuscripts, photos, and even a piece of hair from the great poet himself. Anything related to bossa nova can be found in this tiny store: an impressive collection of CDs and vinyl, songbooks, and (mostly Portuguese) books and magazines on the smooth and mellow sounds of Brazil. Rua Vinicius de Moraes 129, Ipanema. (℃) 021/2247-5227. www.tocadovinicius.com.br. Bus: 474.

MUSICAL INSTRUMENTS

The *berimbau*, that wooden string instrument from Bahia, is one of Brazil's most popular souvenirs, but for music lovers there are many more interesting instruments to choose from (most of which are far more portable). The Rua da Carioca has turned into Music Store Central with at least five shops grouped together on its short length. Look for rattles that fit in the palm of your hand, or else pick up a tambourine or small set of drums. The *agôgô* is an interesting-looking double bell used to keep a beat. Guitar players will love the *cavaquinho*, a Brazilian mandolin. It's what gives samba its distinctive twang. For these and more visit **Musical Carioca,** Rua da Carioca 89 ((℃) 021/2524-6029); **Casa Oliveira Musicais,** Rua da Carioca 70 ((℃) 021/2252-5636); or **Guitarra Prata,** Rua da Carioca 37 ((℃) 021/2262-9659). Metrô: Largo da Carioca.

PERFUME

O Boticario   A Brazilian success story, O Boticario is known for its fragrances made with flowers and herbs. In recent years the store has branched out (a la The Body Shop) to include skin-care products and makeup, but the most popular items remain the lightly scented perfumes and soaps for men, women, and children. Various locations including Av. Rio Branco 120, loja 48, Centro. (℃) 021/2509-6979. Metrô: Uruguaiana.

SHOES

Arezzo   If Carioca women had to choose a favorite shoe store, it would undoubtedly be Arezzo. This company always seems to stay just a step ahead of the trends without being too avant-garde, and the prices are reasonable. It also sells a great selection of high-quality leather purses. Various locations, including Rio Sul and Rua Visconde de Pirajá 295, Ipanema. (℃) 021/2521-4737. Bus: 415.

Constança Bastos   Consider yourself a real shoe *connaiseur* if you have already heard of 30-year-old Constança Bastos, the Manolo Blahnik of Brazil. This young designer's shoes are taking the fashion world by storm and are perfect for elegant evening wear. Stars like Charlie Theron and Cameron Diaz have recently worn her creations. Constança's latest project has been the creation of a more affordable, casual label called Peach. Various locations, including the São Conrado Fashion Mall, Estrada da Gávea 899, São Conrado. (℃) 021/2422-0355. www.constancabasto.com.br. Bus: 178. Shopping Leblon, Rua Afrânio de Melo 290, Leblon. (℃) 021/2511-8801. Bus: 415. The Peach label can be found at the Rio Sul, Av. Lauro Muller 116. (℃) 021/2295-5632. Bus: 119.

Mr. Cat   Mr. Cat goes for classic designs, business as well as evening wear, for men and women. All shoes are made of high-quality Brazilian leather. Prices are very reasonable, ranging from R$80 to R$150 (US$40–US$75/£22–£41) for a pair of top-quality leather men's dress shoes. Rua Visconde de Piraja 414, loja D, Ipanema. (℃) 021/2523-4645. Bus: 474. Another branch at Rua Gonçalves Dias 18, lojas D, E, Centro. (℃) 021/2509-1163. Metrô: Carioca.

SPORTING GOODS

Galeria River   Cool central; not just one shop but a minimall with at least a dozen sports and outdoor stores that sell skateboards, surf gear, inline skates, and climbing equipment as well as accessories such as clothing, sunglasses, and hiking boots. A great place to pick up tips on where to go, lessons, and local hangouts. Galeria River, Rua Francisco Otaviano, Ipanema. No phone. Bus: 128.

SURF SHOPS

Hot Coast   One of the few surf stores that stocks rentals, Hot Coast is conveniently close to the best surf spot in Ipanema, Arpoador beach. It's open Monday through Saturday only, so you'll need to book ahead if you want to surf over the weekend. Rentals range from R$20 to R$40 (US$8.40–US$17/£4.20–£8.50) for a short board, fun board, or long board. Galeria River, Rua Francisco Otaviano 67, loja 12, Ipanema. ✆ 021/2287-9388. Bus: 128.

11 Rio After Dark

It's an open question whether Cariocas possess some hidden nightlife gene or whether they've trained themselves for decadence through years and years of practice. Whatever the case, Rio has a lot to keep you busy at night. It starts early and continues very late. Cariocas themselves don't make a big deal about a night on the town: They're happy either heading out for beers or dancing to forró music or eating shrimp in some hole-in-the-wall botequim. However, if you as a visitor want to go for the quintessential Rio experience, you have to learn to pace yourself. Whether you spend the day seeking out sights or on the beach, head back to your hotel in the afternoon for a wee nap. Trust me, this will be the key to making it through the night. Once you're up again, head out in the cool early evening for a coconut juice on the beach. Sip it while watching the sunset (in summer around 8pm), then around 9pm stroll over to a patio for a predinner drink. **Jobi** in Leblon is a great spot. On weekends maybe walk along the pathway by the Lagoa and find a table at one of the kiosks. Plan to have dinner around 10pm, to be ready for your evening of dancing around midnight or 1am. (Most places don't even open until 11pm.) Your options at this point depend on the day and the time of year. If you're in Rio between September and Carnaval, attending one of the **samba school rehearsals** on Saturday night is a must. Otherwise, on a Thursday night see who's playing at some of the hip samba spots in Lapa like the **Rio Scenarium, Carioca da Gema,** or the **Centro Cultural Carioca.** Or just enjoy the scene by the Arcos de Lapa on a Friday night. Of course, there are a number of discos and bars to choose from, and then there are always the botequins, Rio's neighborhood bars. Wherever you wind up, after 3 or 4 hours dancing you may find yourself getting peckish. For a late-night or early-morning snack, stop in at the **Pizzeria Guanabara** or **Jobi,** both in Leblon and open until at least 5am on weekends. By the time they throw you out, it'll just be time to wander down to the beach and watch the sunrise, ready for a new morning—and another night—in Rio.

To find out more about listings for arts and entertainment, check the Friday editions of the *O Globo, O Dia* or *Jornal do Brasil* newspapers. Available at all newsstands (buy early in the day, as they sell out quickly), all three publish a detailed weekly calendar of events, including nightlife, performing arts, concerts, and other events in the city. The Rio tourism agency **Riotur** also publishes a detailed booklet of events in English and Portuguese called *Guia do Rio or Rio Guide,* available at its main information center at

(*Fun Fact* **Words to Help You Through the Night**

Here's some vocabulary to help you decipher the listings information from the newspapers.

Under *Música* or *Show* you will find the listings for live music. Lovers of Brazilian music should look for anything under *Forró, MPB* (*música popular brasileira*), *Bossa Nova, Choro, Pagode,* or *Samba.* Listings under *Pista* refer to events at nightclubs or discos. Most listings will include the price of admission: *Couvert* is the cover charge and *consumação* states the drink minimum. It is quite common to have two rates, one for women *(mulher)* and one for men *(homem),* the latter usually paying more.

Children's programs are listed under *Infantil* or *Parà Crianças.* Please note that many dance clubs offer a matinee program on Saturdays or Sundays for teenagers. The days of the week are given in abbreviations: *seg* or *2a* (Mon), *ter* or *3a* (Tues), *qua* or *4a* (Wed), *qui* or *5a* (Thurs), *sex* or *6a* (Fri), *sab* (Sat), and *dom* (Sun).

Av. Princesa Isabel 183 in Copacabana, or call **Alô Rio** at © **021/2542-8080** for information on events around town; they keep an updated list and their staff speak English.

THE PERFORMING ARTS

The performing-arts season in Brazil runs from early April until early December. April is a particularly good time—the equivalent of the Northern Hemisphere's September—as theaters and companies unveil their programs and kick off with their season premieres.

Centro Cultural do Banco do Brasil   The two theaters in the center host regular recitals, concerts, and dance performances as well as Portuguese-language theater. There are also regular photography and art exhibits in the center's small exhibition rooms. Check the website for more information. Rua Primeiro de Março 66, Centro. © 021/3808-2000. www.cultura-e.com.br. Admission varies from free to R$30 (US$13/£7.50). Exhibits are always free. Metrô: Uruguaina.

Sala Cecelia Meireles   This lovely heritage building on the Largo da Lapa is a very popular venue for classical music, offering concerts and recitals. You will often also find more modern Brazilian rhythms such as bossa nova, jazz, and choro. Check the newspaper to find out what is playing. Largo da Lapa 47, Centro. © 021/2224-3913. www.sala ceciliameireles.com.br. Ticket prices R$20–R$80 (US$10–US$40/£5.50–£22). Metrô: Cinelândia.

Teatro Municipal   Brazil's prime venue for the performing arts, the elegant Parisian-style Teatro Municipal stages everything from opera to ballet to symphony concerts. The theater's ballet corps and symphony orchestra perform regularly throughout the year, and the theater also hosts many visiting companies. Besides the formal programming, the theater also offers an inexpensive noon-hour opera series *(opera do meio-dia)* and Sunday morning concerts starting at 11am for R$1 (US40¢/ £.20)! Check the newspapers for updated programming. Praça Marechal Floriano s/n, Centro. © 021/2299-1633. www.theatromunicipal.rj.gov.br. Ticket prices range from R$15–R$70 (US$7.50–US$35/£4–£19) on most performances. Metrô: Cinelândia.

Teatro Rival   This small theater has just received a major overhaul and is a great venue for seeing local and popular national acts, mostly of MPB. Ticket prices are quite reasonable so give it a shot. You may be looking at the next Marisa Monte or one of Brazil's many talented performers who haven't made it big internationally. Rua Alvaro Alvim 33, Centro. ☏ 021/2240-4469. www.rivalbr.com.br. Ticket prices R$10–R$60 (US$5–US$30/£3–£16). Metrô: Cinelândia.

MUSIC & DANCE CLUBS

Throughout the summer, the city of Rio organizes concerts, outdoor movies, and other events in Copacabana. Check with Alô Rio (☏ 021/2542-8080) or pick up the event listing *Rio Incomparavel* from Riotur for a complete overview.

Check out the Rio Hiking website (www.riohiking.com.br) for excellent tips on where to catch live music or just grab a drink and meet people. (Click on "about us" and then "Rio hints.") Rio Hiking's owner Denise Werneck is as passionate about Rio's nightlife as she is about exploring her city's exuberant nature trails and keeps her ear to the ground to find out what the latest local trends are. She usually lists some suggestions on her website (www.riohiking.com.br, see under Rio hints) but if you don't like going out by yourself, you can also book a tour to some of the hippest places around for R$120 (US$60/£32) (☏ 021/2552-9204), a great way to meet other travelers as well.

In most clubs and discos you can expect to pay a cover charge. Women usually pay less than men; you'll see the two prices listed at the door. Often there is also a drink minimum which can go up as high as R$120 (US$60/£32) at upscale Ipanema clubs. In most venues you are handed a paper card or electronic swipe card upon entry that is to be used to record all your purchases. The bill is then settled when you leave. A 10% service charge will be included, and a tip on top of that is not required. Hang on to your card for dear life. If you lose it you'll be charged an astronomical fee.

Many clubs have a restricted VIP area overlooking the dance floor, usually with comfortable couches or tables. The definition of VIP varies from club to club: Sometimes it's for members only, sometimes you can get in if you call and reserve ahead of time, and sometimes all that's required is paying a higher drink minimum. The advantage of being in the VIP area is you get a guaranteed seat in an area off-limits to most of the rest of the crowd, allowing you to leave your drinks, jackets, or purses at your table while you're dancing.

TRADITIONAL BRAZILIAN MUSIC

Asa Branca   The upbeat rhythms and catchy accordion tunes of forró have taken such a strong hold in Rio that even a traditional samba citadel like the Asa Branca— located in the heart of the Lapa nightlife scene—now dedicates most of the week (Wed and Fri–Sun) to forró. Thursday is samba night. The crowd doesn't get going until midnight and dancing lasts until the early hours. Open Wednesday through Sunday after 10pm. Av. Mem de Sá 17, Lapa. ☏ 021/2232-5704. Cover R$5–R$15 (US$2.50–US$7.50/£1.35–£4). Bus: 464.

Elite   One popular *gafieira,* or traditional dance hall, is the Elite, tucked in behind an arcade of Romanesque arches on the second floor of a little pink-and-plaster gem of a colonial building in Centro. Even if you can't dance, it's worth having a drink and watching in awe and admiration as some of the older folks strut their stuff. Often these couples will dress the part: men in crisp linen suits and wing-tip dance shoes and women in rustling silk dresses with ballooning '50s-style skirts. Only open Friday

> ### (*Moments* The *Gafieira* of Days Gone By
>
> The traditional ballroom dance halls known as *gafieiras* once defined the Carioca nightlife scene. Still worth a visit even if you can't dance, *gafieiras* are a legacy of the elegant days of old, when couples would dress for the occasion and everyone knew the steps. Most folks don't show up in suits or ball gowns anymore, but couples still dance with elegance and the tunes are unmistakably Brazilian: samba, *pagode,* a bit of rumba or foxtrot, and nowadays lots of forró.

(after 7pm), Saturday (after 10pm), and Sunday (after 6pm). Rua Frei Caneca 4, Centro. (✆ 021/2232-3217. Drink minimum R$6 (US$3/£1.50). Taxi recommended.

Estudantina   Only open on Friday and Saturday, the *gafieira* Estudantina is another mainstay on the Carioca ballroom scene. Many students of the dance school come and show off, but newcomers and novices are made to feel equally welcome. A 10-piece band plays every weekend. Doors open at 11pm. Arrive early to grab a table. Praça Tiradentes 79, Centro. (✆ 021/2507-8067. Cover R$6–R$15 (US$3–US$7.50/£1.50–£4). Bus: 125 to Praça Tiradentes.

Plataforma 1 *(Overrated*   Ah, the tourist trap. Every city has one. Some are fun in a tacky kind of way. This one should be labeled with a radioactive sticker reading AVOID. What's offered is supposedly a song-and-dance showcase of Brazilian culture, but the reality is a mediocre supper served up with a glitzy Vegas-style show. The whole slick and packaged product has all the spontaneity and charm of a McDonald's Big Mac combo—and about as much connection to Brazilian culture. Rua Adalberto Ferreira 32, Leblon. (✆ 021/2274-4022. Admission price depends on whom you book through. Minimum price R$100 (US$50/£27). Bus: 415.

Samba School Rehearsals   If you are in Rio in the period from September up to Carnaval, you can attend a samba school rehearsal to get a feel for the event and the rhythms. Although located in the poorer neighborhoods away from the Zona Sul, a number of the *quadras* (where the rehearsals are held) are very accessible and just a short taxi ride away (for more information see p. 149). Mangueira, Salgueiro, Vila Isabel, Viradouro, and Rocinha are easy to get to by taxi from the Zona Sul and are used to receiving foreign visitors.

LIVE MUSIC

Aside from these listings, many small *chopperias* and botequins (see "Bars & Pubs," below, for longer descriptions of these two institutions) will often have a singer or small combo playing. Usually there's a small cover charge (*couvert* in Portuguese) for this entertainment. By sitting down and listening you're agreeing to foot the bill. The fee is automatically added to your tab. If you want to know what the couvert is before deciding to stay, simply ask the waiter. The key phrase is *"Quanto é o couvert?"* or "How much is the cover?"

Café Sacrilégio *(Finds*   Located next door to Carioca da Gema, the Café Sacrilégio could be its twin. The venues look similar—both are renovated heritage homes—and both house excellent samba bands. It's hard to say which one is better. We usually poke our heads in, listen to the music, and pick the one that we like best. Either way it's hard to go wrong. Best of all, Café Sacrilégio is open every night of the week. Rua Mem de Sá 81, Lapa. (✆ 021/3970-1461. Cover usually R$15–R$20 (US$7.50–US$10/£4–£5.50). Bus: 464.

Canecão   It's old and tattered but it's also got tradition. Everyone who's anyone in Brazilian music has played this aging 3,000-person auditorium, from Djavan to Milton Nascimento to Gal Costa. The best sections in the house are the tables in Section A and the **balcão nobre.** These give you great views of the stage and a chance to have a drink or a snack. Avoid the *poltronas* (numbered seats) as these have horrible side views of the stage. The box office and theater are just across the street from the Rio Sul shopping center. Av. Venceslau Brás 215, Botafogo. ⓒ 021/2543-1241. www.canecaopetrobras. com.br. Ticket price range from R$20 (US$10/£5) to R$140 (US$70/£38) for front-row seats at the big-ticket shows. Bus: 474 to Rio Sul.

Carioca da Gema *(Finds)*   One of the best little venues in town, Carioca da Gema offers all samba all the time. Even on weeknights when many other places are closed or slow, Carioca da Gema is often hopping (see "Nightlife Zones: Lapa," below). The busy nights are Friday and Saturday when latecomers will be left with standing room only. The show normally kicks off at 9pm so come early if you want to grab a spot close to the stage, and enjoy a bite to eat while waiting for things to heat up. Open Monday through Saturday. Rua Mem de Sá 79, Lapa. ⓒ 021/2221-0043. Cover varies but is rarely more than R$18 (US$9/£5). Bus: 464.

Centro Cultural Carioca ✦✦ *(Finds)*   This beautifully restored building from the 1920s (just off the Praça Tiradentes) makes a great live-music venue. Housed on the second floor, the Centro Cultural hosts local musicians and big names who specialize in samba, MPB, *choro,* and *gafieira.* The room is cozy and intimate, and guests sit at small tables to watch the shows. No shows on Sunday, usually. Rua do Teatro, Centro. ⓒ 021/2242-9642. www.centroculturalcarioca.com.br. Cover varies, usually R$15–R$20 (US$7.50–US$10/£4–£5). Bus: 125 to Praça Tiradentes.

Cinemathèque Jamclub   With Botafogo's revived nightlife scene it was only a matter of time before it would produce a decent live-music venue and the Jamclub is all that. With only a 150 places, it is intimate and small and still manages to draw big names on the local music scene. Both Preta Gil (Gilberto Gil's daughter) and Martinalia are regular performers here. The outside area has a lovely patio and bar, perfect for a pre- or postconcert bite or drink. Rua Voluntários da Pátria 53, Botafogo. ⓒ 021/2359-0216. www.jamclub.com.br. Cover depends on event but rarely exceeds R$30 (US$15/£8). Metrô: Botafogo.

(Finds) **The New Lapa—Gamboa**

Just beyond the Praça Mauá, close to the port area is one of Rio's older neighborhoods, Gamboa. It has many lovely 19th-century buildings, pretty squares and a fascinating history (this is where slaves were brought upon arrival and according to many, the birthplace of samba) and it just on the cusp of an urban revival similar to Lapa's 10 to 15 years ago. A few visionary entrepreneurs have set up shop here; the pioneer was **Trapiche Gamboa** (Rua Sacadura Cabral 155; ⓒ 021/2516-0868; closed Sun and Mon). Taking up a gorgeous three-story building from 1856, it has been transformed into a fabulous live-music venue playing, what else, samba. More recent newcomers are **The Week** (Rua Sacadura Cabral 154; ⓒ 021/2253-1020), Rio's hottest new gay dance club, and **Sacadura** (Rua Sacadura Cabral 147; ⓒ 021/2233-0378), a more upscale live-music venue. It's worth keeping on eye on this area because it seems like new places are opening up every couple of months.

(Tips) Nightlife Zones: Lapa

Bars and clubs have their moments, and so do neighborhoods over time. Lapa is definitely on the up again. In the roaring '20s Lapa's vibrant nightlife earned it the nickname "Montmartre of the Tropics." It fell on hard times in the '50s and '60s, but in the last few years Lapa has undergone a major revival as even Cariocas from trendy Ipanema and Leblon come here to party. City and state governments have sat up and taken notice, investing money renovating some of the neighborhood's gorgeous heritage buildings, encouraging the development of restaurants and bars, and pumping R$5 million (US$2.5 million/£1.35 million) into the revitalization of the **Rua do Lavradio.**

Things hop almost every night of the week, but the best days are Thursday, Friday, and Saturday. Lapa's nightlife consists of two different kinds of experiences. There are the carefully preserved heritage buildings turned music venues such as Carioca da Gema, Estrela da Lapa, Rio Scenarium, and Café Sacrilégio that offer some of the best samba in town. Then there is the much grittier street scene, centered around the Rua da Lapa and the parallel running Rua Joaquim Silva. These two streets are a major *point* (definition of *point* on p. 143) where mostly young people come to drink, chat, flirt, and dance. The small music venues on the Rua Joaquim Silva are anything but nicely renovated (some are big-time sleazy), but half the fun is walking around and poking your head in (cover rarely exceeds R$5/US$2.50/£1.35). In a 2-block range you will hear anything from reggae to samba to brega, hip-hop, funk, and salsa. The square in front of the arches is packed with food and drink stalls. As long as you stick to the main streets that have lots of people on them the area is quite safe at night.

Circo Voador   You can't miss this venue; it's a large tentlike structure (the name translates as *flying circus*) located right beneath the aquaduct in Lapa. Modeled after the original '80s *Circo* that was the venue for avant-garde, up-and-coming artists, the new Circo Voador is one of the most eclectic venues in town, offering everything from samba and pagode, to house, funk, and even the Village People (yes, the men from the YMCA). It's a great venue. The open structure is perfect for Rio's tropical climate and a large outdoor patio allows you plenty of space to take in the music under the stars, with the rambling of the streetcar on the arches overhead for company. Rua dos Arcos s/n, Lapa. (C) 021/2533-5873. www.circovoador.com.br. Cover depends on event but ranges from R$10–R$60 (US$5–US$30/£3–£16). Bus: 464.

Estrela da Lapa   Proof that Lapa's appeal extends beyond the young and bohemian. This elegant star in the neighborhood caters to the moneyed 35-and-older Zona Sul crowd. Music varies from jazz to salsa, samba, swing, and even instrumental. The venue—a restored Lapa mansion—is lovely, and though the stage is small, three levels of seating make for enough room even on busy nights. Rua Mem de Sá 69. (C) 021/2507-6686. www.estreladalapa.com.br. Cover ranges from R$10–R$30 (US$5–US$15/£3–£8). Bus: 464.

Rio Scenarium ★★★ *(Overrated)*   It may seem like a contradiction to give the Rio Scenarium both three stars and an overrated at the same time but let me explain. The Rio

Scenarium is probably the most beautiful bar in Rio. Located in a renovated warehouse on the edge of Lapa, this antiques-store-turned-bar is one of the places that played a big role in reviving Lapa's nightlife several years ago when there were few classy options available. Now, however, I'd say the Rio Scenarium is a victim of its own success. Recommended by every single guidebook and travel article about Rio, the place is often packed with more gringos (and women who like gringos) than locals. Although still worth seeing, don't make this your only stop when exploring Lapa's music scene. Rua do Lavradio 20, Centro. ℭ 021/2233-3239. Cover R$15–R$20 (US$6.25–US$8.40/ £4–£8). Taxi recommended.

Vivo Rio ✸✸✸   One of Rio's newest concert venues, the Vivo Rio is located right next to the Museu de Arte Moderno on Rio's downtown waterfront. Similar in size to the Canecão, it has been specializing in big-name concerts, with both Brazilian and foreign artists, with people like BB King, Maria Bethania, and Gilberto Gil. The only drawback here is the high ticket prices—R$180 (US$90/£48) or more for a decent seat is not unheard of in this venue. Rua Infante Dom Henrique, Centro, next to the Museu de Arte Moderna. ℭ 021/2272-2900. www.vivorio.com.br. Cover R$60–R$300 (US$30–US$150/£15–£75). Taxi recommended.

DANCE CLUBS

Baronneti   One of the most happening dance clubs in Rio, Baronneti attracts a well-to-do and attractive crowd in their 20s to 40s. Part of their secret is the minimum drink requirement; at a stiff R$70 (US$30/£15) minimum for guys on Saturdays, there's no rubbing elbows with the riffraff here. What you get is a fine-looking classy upscale club, two floors of fabulous dance music to dance the night away, plenty of couches, and a chill-out space. Rua Barão da Torre 354, Ipanema. ℭ 021/2522-1460. www.baronneti.com.br. Drink minimum women R$20–R$50 (US$10–US$25/£5–£14), men R$50–R$80 (US$25–US$40/£14–£22). Bus: 474.

Bunker   Not everyone swoons to bossa nova or the upbeat sounds of samba and forró. At Bunker 94, Rio's young and pierced move to the pounding sounds of techno,

---

Ladies of the Night . . . and Day

They've been an integral part of the neighborhood since the '40s, the working girls and their customers who occupy selected slices of the Copacabana waterfront. The good news is that these places are not dangerous or even overly sleazy. Indeed, it can be interesting observing the hustle and bustle and to and fro, though the atmosphere is not exactly family entertainment (unless you come from a very odd family). Regular hangouts for sex tourists and working women include the Balcony Bar and the Lido square, which is also home to a number of strip clubs. This area is between the Copacabana Palace and the Avenida Prado Junior, Copa's main drive-by thoroughfare for street prostitutes. Farther down the waterfront by the Help disco, the Terraço Atlantico is where johns and hookers hook up in the afternoon and early evening. For those who like people-watching it can make for a fascinating scene. The area around the Rio Othon Hotel is another popular meeting place. Daytime contacts are made at the Meia Petaca patio or else out on the beach while working on that tan line.

hip-hop, trance, and house as spun by three different DJs on three different dance floors. This is a gay-friendly club. Open Thursday through Saturday after 11pm. Rua Raul Pompeia 94, Copacabana. ℃ 021/2247-8724. Cover R$10–R$20 (US$5–US$10/£3–£5). Bus: 415.

Fosfobox Fosfobox is Copacabana's trendy *club du jour,* or rather *de nuit.* Located in a small basement off Rua Siqueira Campos, the club only has room for about 150, who hear discs spun by a variety of DJs. On Thursday it's rock, Friday and Saturday are house and techno. Open Wednesday through Sunday. Rua Siqueira Campos 143, 22A basement, Copacabana. ℃ 021/2548-7498. www.fosfobox.com.br. Cover R$20 (US$10/£5). Metrô: Siqueira Campos.

Help *(Overrated)* Often recommended by hotel concierges to (sometimes unsuspecting) male visitors, Help is where gringo travelers and Brazilian working girls meet. No self-respecting Carioca woman would be seen in the place, which means that beautiful dark-eyed lovely with whom you're getting on so well with is definitely expecting payment. Most negotiate their rates at the start of the evening, just to keep everything upfront. Av. Atlântica 3432, Copacabana. ℃ 021/2522-1296. Cover R$15–R$25 (US$7.50–US$13/£4–£7). Bus: 474.

Melt Melt is a great unpretentious club that has been making quite a name for itself with excellent live music by a variety of interesting artists. Open daily, the small club offers a range of music, varying from hip-hop to salsa, dance, or samba-rock, and in the summer months samba on Sunday. Rua Rita Ludolf 47, Leblon. ℃ 021/2249-9309. Cover R$15–R$40 (US$7.50–US$20/£4–£11). Bus: 415.

00 Pronounced *zero-zero,* this nightclub is located right next to the Planetarium in Gávea. The club has a large outdoor deck with wooden benches and comfortable recliners, perfect for those warm summer evenings. The inside space is divided into a restaurant area and a small bar and dance floor. The dance floor, alas, is not only small but also located in front of the bathroom doors. However, the fabulous outside space and beautiful people make up for that. Still, 00 is better as a bar than a club. Rua Padre Leonel France 240, Gávea. ℃ 021/2540-8041. www.00site.com.br. Cover R$20–R$30 (US$10–US$15/£5–£8). Taxi recommended.

BARS & PUBS

There are various ways that bar and restaurant owners can extract money from guests: One of them is the *couvert.* The *couvert* in restaurants used to refer to the small appetizer plate that is served when you first arrive—olives, bread and butter, pâté, and the like. Nowadays it's also the name given to a live-music fee. If the bar has a musician playing, chances are something between R$2 and R$10 (US$1–US$5/£.50–£3) per person or per table will be added to your bill. Always ask when going into a restaurant or bar with live music if there is a cover or *"couvert para a música,"* to avoid any surprises when your bill comes.

BOTEQUINS

Arco do Teles Tucked away in an alley just off Praça XV, the Arco do Teles looks like a movie set of old Rio. Perfectly preserved colonial two-stories are set on narrow cobblestone streets lined with restaurants and cafes. Though it's a good place for a quick lunch, prime time is after work hours, especially on Thursday and Friday. Office workers flock here to grab a few cold chopps and catch some music before heading home. Often they forget to go home. As the evening wears on, tables and chairs take over the alley, creating a large impromptu patio—it's one of the best people-watching spots in town. With over 15 bars and botequins it doesn't matter which one you pick. If you get there after 10pm you'll be lucky to find a seat at all. Travessa do Comércio, Arco

Moments The Culture of Botequins

Botequins are to Rio what pubs are to London and cafes are to Paris: the spot where locals gather, be it for end-of-day drinks or impassioned late-night philosophizing. Brazilians refer to botequins as *pé sujos*—literally "dirty feet"—meaning they're nothing fancy, often just plastic tables and fluorescent lights (though rich in character and local flavor). Some botequins have developed into popular nightlife attractions, offering live music and excellent food, and drawing crowds from all over the city. But most botequins remain small, not very fancy watering holes where one can kick back with a cold beer, have some snacks, and catch up with the latest gossip. See a description of the most popular ones below.

do Teles (from the Praça XV, facing toward the bay, you will see the arch that marks the entrance to the alley on your left). Bus: 110 or 415.

Belmonte   An old-fashioned botequim with the bright lights, dark-wood furniture and tile floors, the Belmonte serves up great beer, sandwiches, and snacks at almost any time of the day, but in the evenings and on weekend afternoons things get really hopping: Patrons spill out on the sidewalk, making do with improvised tables made out of barrels. Although now a local chain with brand-new old-fashioned Belmonte's in Lagoa, Ipanema, and Copacabana, the Flamengo Belmonte remains the best. Praia do Flamengo 300, Flamengo. (✆ 021/2552-3349. Bus: 464.

Bip Bip   Another internationally acclaimed botequim—the Parisian daily *Le Monde* featured this tiny bar on its front page—Bip Bip owes its fame to an outstanding musical program. Tuesday and Sunday nights are the best evenings to catch some great samba or *pagode* (a more mellow kind of samba); it's not unusual to see some Brazilian greats such as Beth Carvalho, Nelson Sargento, Walter Alfaiate, and others come out to sing and play. Owner Alfredo Melo—*Alfredinho* to most everyone—tries to keep his neighbors happy, so on Sunday the live music winds down early at 10pm. The bar stays open daily until 1am. Rua Almirante Gonçalves 50, Copacabana. (✆ 021/2267-9696. Bus: 432.

Bracarense   Once voted the best botequim in town—the *New York Times* even proclaimed it the best in Brazil—Bracarense may be suffering a bit from its own success. On Saturday when the botequim is packed, service often slows to a crawl. Still, Bracarense's beer remains top-shelf. Food quality is another key part of the botequim experience, particularly the little munchy appetizers that go so well with beer. At Bracarense these are in the expert hands of the Minas Gerais native Alaíde, who works miracles in the small kitchen. Rua José Linhares 85, Leblon (corner of Ataulfo de Paiva). (✆ 021/2294-3549. Bus: 464.

Jobi   Jobi is busy any day of the week, but on Friday and Saturday a line is guaranteed. You may as well make friends with others in the line, as chances are you'll be seated closely together in this intimate, cozy bar. Conversations frequently fly across the tables. Like many botequins, Jobi has excellent beer, tasty snacks, and a great atmosphere. On top of that, Jobi stays open until 4:30am, making it a favorite post-party haunt to wind down from an evening out. Av. Ataulfo de Paiva 1166, Leblon. (✆ 021/2274-0547. Bus: 434.

OTHER BARS & PUBS

Academia da Cachaça A field trip to the Academia da Cachaça puts the concept of advanced education in a whole new light. Here you can dispute and discuss the finer points of the fiery white cane liquor that is Brazil's national drink. For though all *cachaça* comes from cane juice, not all *cachaças* are created equal. The selection at the Academia is overwhelming. Ask the bartenders for advice, and begin that lifelong intellectual quest for the perfect "white one." Just don't down them on an empty stomach. The menu here offers a variety of Brazilian snacks to munch on while trying yet one more shot. Or two more shots. Or three. Or . . . Rua Conde de Bernadotte 26, loja G, Leblon. ✆ 021/2239-1542. www.academiadacachaca.com.br. Bus: 415.

Bar do Adão This lovely heritage house in Botafogo houses an excellent bar that serves up the best *pasteis* in town, or the second-best *pasteis,* as the original Bar do Adão in the Zona Norte neighborhood of Grajau first developed their recipe for success. Made out of light fluffy dough, the *pasteis* come in an amazing variety of fillings, are quickly deep-fried, and arrive piping hot at your table. The 60 different flavors include brie and apricot, Gorgonzola and sun-dried tomato, prawns and cream cheese, shiitake mushrooms and more. On Tuesday nights it is two for one. Rua Dona Mariana 81, Botafogo. ✆ 021/2535-4572. Metrô: Botafogo.

Devassa What started as a cute neighborhood bar in Leblon is slowly spreading around the city. The original location on the Rua General San Martin still packs them in on most nights but patrons now have the option of heading out to the Jardim Botânico location and enjoying the large patio. The Devassa microbrews can now be purchased at many other bars around the city. The most popular Devassa brews are the blond *(loura)*, redhead *(ruiva)*, and brunette *(morena)*. Rua General San Martin 1241, Leblon. ✆ 021/2540-6087. Bus: 415 or Metro/bus from Siqueira Campos stopAv. Lineu de Paula Machado 696, Jardim Botânico. ✆ 021/2294-2915. Bus: 572 (get off at Rua Jardim Botânico, corner Rua J.J. Seabra).

Finds The Kiosks of Lagoa

They began as lowly concession stands, but the kiosks around the Lagoa Rodrigo de Freitas have evolved into a fun, casual nightlife scene. Known in Portuguese as *quiosques da Lagoa,* they're the perfect place to stroll, munch, drink, and people-watch. Set at regular intervals along the pleasant green path that girdles the Lagoa, the kiosks range in size and quality from simple snack stands to full-fledged restaurants and entertainment centers. The cuisine ranges from Brazilian basic to Lebanese, Japanese, or Italian, while the entertainment ranges from a boom box on volume "11" to excellent live bands (some of which charge a small cover). The thickest concentration of kiosks begins opposite the Jockey Club. Another grouping clusters close to the Parque da Catacumba at the Ipanema and back end of Copacabana of the Lagoa. They're open year-round, but they're especially popular in summer; weekday hours are from 6pm onward—they get busy around 10pm—and on weekends from noon onward. A full loop around the Lagoa is 7.5km (4½ miles), making for a pleasant 2-hour walk.

Garota de Ipanema *(Overrated)*   The bossa nova tune "The Girl from Ipanema" (*Garota de Ipanema* in Portuguese) is indeed a thing of sublime beauty, composed in one afternoon by poet Vinicius de Moraes and singer Tom Jobim while the two sat drinking chopp and watching the Brazilian beach beauties go by in a little bar then called the Veloso. Though still there, the bar is now somewhat less than beautiful and anything but sublime. After the tune became a world hit the bar changed its name and plastered the song's lyrics and score on the wall in a blatant attempt to cash in. Jobim and Moraes themselves shunned the place in short order, driven out by the hordes and attendant crass commercialism. Nowadays, the beer is cold and the food okay (both come at a premium), and the people walking by are still tall, tan, young, and lovely, but the Garota itself is neither a musical nor cultural hot spot. Rua Vinicius de Moraes 49 A, Ipanema. ℂ 021/2523-3787. Bus: 434.

Mercado Cobal de Humaitá *(Finds)*   Is it a bar? Is it a restaurant? Or is it a great seething mass of people at plastic patio tables quaffing chopp, munching food, and listening to tunes from one or more live bands? That last is probably the best description of the nighttime scene at the Mercado Cobal. By day a mild-mannered fruit and vegetable market, at night the Mercado transforms itself into a huge outdoor bar scene. Seven or eight different restaurants and *chopperias* (a downscale botequim; *chopperias* sell draft beer and very basic snacks) all meld into one large bustling patio, with busy waiters racing up and down the aisles trying to keep their tables straight. **Galeto Mania** serves up a tasty grilled chicken, **Pizzapark** offers a full range of pizzas, and **Manekineko** whips up tray after tray of fresh sushi, while **Espirito Chopp** serves the best cold draft beer. The beauty of this place is that you don't have to commit to one specific restaurant. Once you've found a table, just order food from any of them. With superhero skill, the waiters somehow manage to keep track of it all. Cobal de Humaitá, Rua Voluntarios da Patria 446, Botafogo. Galeto Mania. ℂ 021/2527-0616. Manekineko ℂ 021/2537-1510. Bus: 178.

Espaço de Convivência Tumbao do Malevo *(Finds)*   Yes, you do have to climb up the steep stairs but you will be rewarded by a funky outdoor patio that serves great tapas and drinks. This lovely old house in Santa Teresa opens its door Friday through Sunday and makes for a great spot to grab a drink and a bite and maybe catch a band in the evening. Rua Paschoal Carlos Magno 121, Santa Teresa. ℂ 021/2242-9434. Bus: 464.

(Finds) Waterfront Upgrade

In 2006 the city of Rio began a major overhaul of the sidewalk kiosks along the waterfront, knocking down the old ones and rebuilding from scratch. 19 modern glass kiosks with spacious wooden decks, a state-of-the-art bar and kitchen, and underground washrooms and showers have been built. So far all the new kiosks have been inaugurated along Leme and Copacabana beach. Ipanema and Leblon are slated for upgrades in the next 2 years. Several of these are being run by popular bars or restaurants. Across from Rua Miguel Lemos is the Siri Mole kiosk, serving Bahian seafood dishes. To enjoy a glass of champagne, visit the Champanheria opposite Rua Constante Ramos. For a sample of cachaça try the Cachaçaria Mangueira kiosk toward Leme, in front of Rua Hilário de Gouveia.

Moments Making Your *Point*

Rio is full of *points*. Pronounced poin-*chee* in Portuguese, a point is a location on the street that attracts people who attract other people who attract people who provide food, drinks, sometimes music, and all the other ingredients of a party. Complicated? Here's an example: One night we were headed over to Galeria Café with some friends. Just as we got there we met up with some other friends, and when we saw there was a bit of a line we got to chatting outside and bought some beers from a street vendor. Some other friends came, and other people whom we didn't know but who were there to meet some of their friends. We ordered more beers, and later some munchies from another vendor; before we noticed it was time to go home. We never did set foot in the bar we intended to patronize. That evening was a classic *point*—a fun, impromptu street party. No one can say for sure when one will emerge, or why they show up where they do. Points just . . . *are*.

GAY & LESBIAN NIGHTLIFE

Rio's gay community is fairly small, certainly smaller than one would expect from a city of 10 million people. For all Rio's reputation for sexual hedonism, the macho culture still predominates. As lasciviously as heterosexual couples may behave in public, open displays of affection—even hand-holding—between same-sex couples are still not accepted in Brazil. The big exception, of course, is Carnaval, when many straight and gay men dress as women (Carmen Miranda is always a popular costume), and parades with drag queens are cheered by everyone. But this spirit of openness lasts only until the last samba drums fade away at the dawn of Ash Wednesday.

Currently, the most popular nightspot is in Ipanema around the Galeria Café on the Rua Teixeira de Melo. During the day the stretch of sand close to Posto 8 (opposite the Rua Farme de Amoedo) is also popular. Copacabana has a number of gay clubs and bars as well as a popular meeting place on the beach at Rainbow's, in front of the Copacabana Palace Hotel. In Rio's old downtown there are a few popular places around the Avenida Mem de Sá and Rua do Lavradio. A good resource to pick up is the latest edition of the *Gay Guide Brazil,* a small booklet available at some of the clubs and bookstores in Ipanema, or check http://riogayguide.com. The Brazilian term for gay friendly is GLS, which stands for gay, lesbian, and sympathizers. Often you will see this abbreviation used in listings or restaurant and bar reviews.

After you get tired of the beach, go to **Bar Bofetada,** Rua Farme de Amoeda 87 (© 021/2227-6992). Located just a few blocks from Ipanema's prime gay beach, this botequim is perfect for a beer, snack, and flirt with local guys.

Set in a lovely small gallery stunningly decorated with a changing display of work by local artists, the **Galeria Café,** Rua Teixeira de Melo 31E, Ipanema (© 021/2523-8250; www.galeriacafe.com.br.; Bus: 415), packs a gorgeous collection of men, shoulder to shoulder, bicep to bicep, into its combo art space, dance club, and bar. Those that can't fit—and there are many—just hang out in front. The Galeria really gets hopping, inside and out, after 1am. The cover charge is R$10 to R$25 (US$5–US$13/£3–£7), open from Wednesday through Sunday.

Also popular is **Dama de Ferro (the Iron Lady),** Rua Vinicius de Moraes 288, Ipanema (© 021/2247-2330; www.damadeferro.com.br). Decorated by artist Adriana

Lima, who also did the amazing decor at Galeria Café, Dama de Ferro is the it-spot at the moment, popular with gays and straights; high tolerance for electronic music is a must. Cover is R$10 to R$25 (US$5–US$13/£3–£7), open Wednesday through Sunday.

Le Boy, Rua Raul Pompeia 102, Copacabana (© **021/2513-4993;** www.leboy.com.br; Bus: 415), is the largest and best-known gay club in Rio. It's glamorous, funky, and extremely spacious with a soaring four-story ceiling hovering somewhere above the dance floor. A range of special events attracts national and international celebrities and assorted (beautiful) hangers-on. Go after midnight, when things really start to hop. The club is open Tuesday through Sunday; cover ranges from R$5 to R$15 (US$2.50–US$7.50/£1.35–£4) for men. This may be the only club in town where women pay more than men; any night of the week the cover for women is set at a hefty R$60 (US$30/£16). All for equal opportunity, Le Boy's owner recently inaugurated **La Girl** next door, Rua Raul Pompeia 102 (© **021/2247-8342**), Rio's first truly upscale nightclub for gay women with excellent DJs and Gogo girl shows. La Girl is open on Monday and Wednesday to Sunday (men allowed only on Mon and Sun). Cover ranges from R$5 to R$15 (US$2.50–US$7.50/£1.35–£4).

The Week, Rua Sacadura Cabral 154, Saude (© **021/2253-1020;** www.theweek.com.br), is the new hottest gay dance club in town. This huge mega-dance club can hold 2,000 people and is packed every Saturday night. Famous national and international guest DJs and Go Go boys keep the crowd going. Open Saturdays at midnight. Often open for events on Fridays and Wednesdays; check listings.

12 Everything You Need to Know About Carnaval

Ah, Carnaval. The name evokes explosive images of colorful costumes, lavish floats, swarming masses, and last-minute debauchery before the sober Lenten season begins. Though it may look like sheer entertainment, Carnaval means hard work and dedication for many Cariocas; to some, it's a full-time job.

WHAT'S IT ALL ABOUT?   The religious aspect of the celebration faded some time ago, but Carnaval's date is still determined by the ecclesiastical calendar, officially occupying only the 4 days immediately preceding Ash Wednesday. With typical ingenuity and panache, however, Cariocas have managed to stretch the party into an event lasting several months, culminating in the all-night feast of color and sound that is the **Samba School Parade,** where tens of thousands of costumed dancers, thousands of percussionists, and hundreds of gorgeous performers atop dozens of floats all move in choreographed harmony to the nonstop rhythm of samba.

If you're not able to attend Carnaval itself, **rehearsals**—which usually start in mid-September or early October—are an absolute must, and the closest you'll get to the real thing. Even if you are in town for Carnaval, attending a rehearsal will give you a great appreciation of the logistics involved in putting together the parade, plus you'll learn all the words and dance moves. (See "Watching a Rehearsal," below.)

In the 2 weeks leading up to the big event, you'll begin to see the **blocos.** These are community groups—usually associated with a particular neighborhood or sometimes with a bar—who go around the neighborhood, playing music and singing and dancing through the streets. Their instruments and costumes easily identify the official bloco members, but everyone is welcome and encouraged to follow along and add to the merriment. A number of blocos are so well known that they draw throngs of

The Samba Parade Grounds

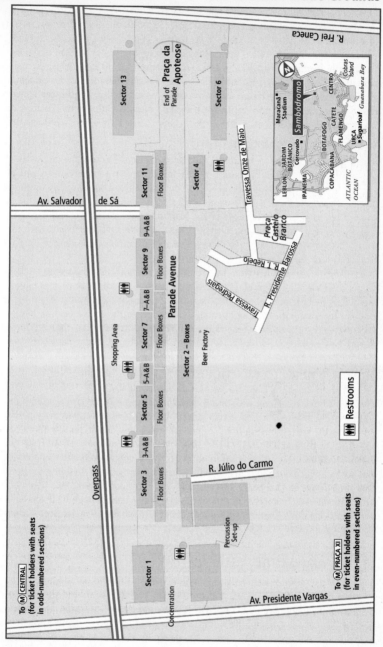

followers in the tens of thousands. The **Banda de Carmen Miranda** in Ipanema with its extravagant drag queens is a hoot. (See "Hanging with the Blocos," below, for a list of popular blocos.)

Carnaval finally kicks off on the Friday before Ash Wednesday with an explosion of lavish **balls** *(bailes)*. Originally the *bailes* were reserved for the elite, while the masses partied it up with vulgar splendor in the streets. Today, they're still a pricey affair and the **Copacabana Palace Ball** remains *the* society event in Rio. The **blocos** also kick into high gear once Carnaval arrives with several groups parading every day from Saturday through Tuesday.

WATCHING THE SAMBA PARADE

Then, there is the *pièce de résistance:* the **Samba School Parade,** the event that the samba schools work, plan, and sweat over for an entire year. Starting Sunday and continuing through Monday night, the 14 top-ranked samba schools (really community groups whose sole focus is the parade) compete for the honor of putting on the best show. The competition takes place in the **Sambodromo,** a 1.5km (1-mile) long concrete parade ground built in the center of Rio for this once-a-year event. Each night over 60,000 spectators watch the contest live, while millions more tune in on TV to catch this feast for the senses.

Even before the parade starts, the streets surrounding the **Sambodromo** are closed to car traffic, while the grounds around this stadium are transformed into Carnaval Central. A main stage hosts a variety of acts and performances, and hundreds of vendors set up shop with food and drinks. This *terreirão do samba* (samba land), as Riotur calls it, is open the weekend prior to Carnaval, from Friday through Tuesday during Carnaval, and then again for the Saturday afterward for the Parade of Champions. Contact **Riotur** (© 021/2217-7575) for more detailed program information.

HOW & WHERE TO GET TICKETS   It is next to impossible to buy tickets directly from Liesa, the **Liga das Escolas de Samba** (© 021/2253-7676; www.liesa. com.br). The tickets go on sale a few months before carnival and always sell out in 20 minutes. The few tourist tickets that remain Liesa sells at an extraordinary markup. Most tourists are left buying from scalpers or travel agencies. Reputable travel agencies include **Blumar** (© 021/2142-9300; www.blumar.com.br) and **BIT** (© 021/ 2256-5657; www.bitourism.com), both of which sell good tickets at reasonable rates, but both of which often sell out early. If you've got your heart set on seeing the parade, buy your tickets by October or at the latest November preceding the year you want to go. In recent years, a number of Internet agencies have sprung up, but all are too new to have enough of a track record for us to call them reliable. **Rio Services Carnaval**

⌐Tips   A Parade-Day Preview

On the day of each parade, the schools arrive outside the parade grounds to assemble their floats, props, and other gear. The streets around the Sambodromo, including Avenida Presidente Vargas, are closed for traffic, and pedestrians can stroll watching the schools put finishing touches on a year's worth of work. A great opportunity to take a close-up look at the floats, take pictures, and meet some of the people who put it all together.

(www.rio-carnival.net), at least sells through PayPal, which may offer some protection, but it's still very much buyer beware (Anyone who successfully does this, let me know. Their prices are genuinely cheap.) As a next to last resort, try your hotel, but expect to pay a hefty premium for this service. As a last resort, you can try the scalpers outside the stadium (The scalpers will find you as you come out any of the Metrô stops near the Sambodromo.) Be careful! Each ticket consists of a magnetic plastic card and an attached paper slip—you need both to enter. The best deals come after the first couple of schools have paraded (say 11pm) when the scalpers start to get a little desperate.

Depending on the agency, or the desperation of your scalper, tickets for the bleachers begin at around R$190 (US$95/£51) for section 4, and rise to R$500 (US$250/ £135) for section 7. Chairs in a front row box (*frisa*) start at R$900 (US$450/£243) in section 4 and R$1,600 (US$800/£432) in section 7. These are base prices. Many agencies charge much more.

Note: Avoid the tour agencies offering a "package" that includes transportation to and from the Sambodromo, at a very hefty markup. These transfers are not only unnecessary, they're actually a disadvantage. Getting to the parade, the easiest, safest quickest route is by Metrô. Due to street closures, buses will take much, much longer to reach the stadium. Coming home, there are plenty of taxis outside the Sambodromo, and you can leave whenever you want. If you've booked a package, you're expected to wait on the bus until 7am when the last school finishes before you can go home.

General seating is in concrete bleachers, with no space assigned. Your ticket gives you access to the section. After that it's up to you to find a spot and squeeze in. There are pillows for sale, or you can bring your own. The exception to the hard concrete rule is in section 9, the tourist section, where there are numbered assigned places. The advantages are obvious. The disadvantage is that you miss out on some of the *joie de vivre* that comes with being surrounded by hundreds of happy partying Brazilians.

In addition to the bleachers, there are front row boxes, called *frisas* in Portuguese. These are comfortable chairs that sit in a strip of boxes located at ground level along the parade route. There are six seats to a box (three rows of two) and seating is assigned. The frisas have the advantage of closeness and assigned seating. The disadvantages are a higher price tag and—some say—being too close to really appreciate the whole of the spectacle (like sitting in the very front row at a musical or movie).

Besides frisas and bleachers, there are the exclusive VIP boxes. However, if you can wangle an invitation to one of those, you don't need any help from us.

Whether you choose bleacher or frisa, the best sections are 5, 7, and 9. These place you near the middle of the parade avenue, allowing you to see up and down as the schools come through. Avoid sitting at the start or the end of the Avenida (sections 1, 3, 4, 6, and 13).

If you have tickets you can head directly to the Sambodromo. The parade grounds are divided into sections (see map on p. 145): even-numbered sections can be accessed from the Central Station side (Metrô: Central); odd-numbered sections can be accessed from the Praça XI side (Metrô: Praça XI). Don't worry, there are lots of police and staff around to point you in the right direction.

The parade starts at 9pm, but unless you want to stake out a particular spot you may as well take your time arriving, because the event will continue nonstop until about 7 or 8am. We recommend leaving a bit early as well to avoid the big crunch at the end when the entire crowd tries to squeeze through a narrow set of revolving gates. Food and drinks are available inside the Sambodromo. Though prices aren't outrageous, it's

---

Tips **Carnaval Redux**

If you miss the parade during Carnaval, attend the Parade of Champions on the Saturday after Carnaval. The five top schools give an encore to close the Sambadrome Carnaval season. Tickets go on sale the Thursday after Carnaval. At R$80 (US$40/£22) and up for a good spot, they're considerably less expensive than the original event. Contact the **Liga das Escolas de Samba** (© 021/2253-7676), **Alô Rio** (© 021/2542-8080), or **Blumar** (© 021/2511-3636; www.blumar.com.br) for ticket sales.

---

a serious pain elbowing your way back and forth from your seat: Grab something at one of the many inexpensive kiosks outside the Sambodromo before you head in.

A FEW HELPFUL HINTS

Whether you are attending a rehearsal, following a bloco, or watching the parade, here are a few helpful hints to ensure you have a good time.

- Dress casually and comfortably. The weather is usually hot and humid so a tank top or bikini top and shorts are fine. Comfortable shoes are a must as you will be on your feet for hours, dancing and jumping to the music.
- Pack light. A purse or any extra accessories are not recommended, especially at the rehearsals and the blocos as you will be dancing and moving around. When watching the parade you can bring a small bag or knapsack and leave it at your feet, but the lighter you travel the better. Make sure you bring enough cash for the evening, some form of ID (driver's license or some other picture ID that is not your passport), and maybe a small camera you can tuck into your pocket. Leave jewelry and other valuables at home.
- The events themselves are very safe, but be aware of pickpockets in large crowds. At the end of the event, take a taxi or walk with the crowds, avoiding any deserted streets or unfamiliar neighborhoods.
- Keep in mind that prices will be slightly higher, cabs may add a premium, and drinks and food at the parade and some other venues may be higher than what you are used to in Brazil.
- Plan to have enough cash for the entire Carnaval period. All financial institutions close for the duration, and it's not unusual for bank machines to run out of money.

PARTICIPATING IN THE PARADE

If you think watching the parade from up close sounds pretty amazing, imagine being in it. Every year, the samba schools open up positions for outsiders to participate in the parade. Putting on this extravaganza is an expensive proposition, and by selling the costumes and the right to parade, the school is able to recuperate some of its costs. But outside paraders are also needed for artistic and competitive reasons. To score high points the school needs to have enough people to fill the Avenida and make the parade look full and colorful. A low turnout can make the school lose critical points.

To parade (*desfilar* in Portuguese) you need to commit to a school and buy a costume (about R$500–R$900/US$250–US$450/£135–£243), which you can often do online. Some sites are in English as well as Portuguese; if not, look under *fantasia* (costume). Depending on the school, they may courier the costume or arrange for a pickup downtown just before the parade, or you may have to make the trek out to wherever they are.

For an added charge, a number of agencies in Rio will organize it all for you, getting you in with a school and arranging the costume. **Blumar** (© **021/2142-9300; www.blumar.com.br**) can organize the whole event for you for about R$900 (US$450/£243). For other organizations, contact **Alô Rio** (© **021/2542-8080**).

As a participant in the parade you do not automatically get a ticket to watch the rest of the event. If you want to see the other schools you need to purchase a separate ticket. If your school finishes in the top five there will be a repeat performance in the Parade of Champions, held on the Saturday after Carnaval. If you are not able to parade again, consider donating your costume to a fellow traveler or keen Brazilian.

WATCHING A REHEARSAL

Every Saturday from September (or even as early as Aug) until Carnaval, each samba school holds a general samba rehearsal *(ensaio)* at its home base. The band and key people come out and practice their theme song over and over to perfection. It may sound a tad repetitious, but you'd be amazed how a good band playing the same song over and over can generate a *really* great party. People dance for hours, taking a break now and then for snacks and beer. The income generated goes toward the group's floats and costumes. By the end of the night (and these rehearsals go until the wee hours) everyone knows the words to the song and has—hopefully—turned into an ardent fan who will cheer this particular school on at the parade. (General rehearsals usually don't involve costumes or practicing dance routines.) In December and January, the schools also hold dress rehearsals and technical rehearsals at the Sambodromo. Check with Riotur for dates and times.

Most of the samba schools are based in the poorer and quite distant suburbs, but a number of schools such as **Mangueira, Salgueiro, Vila Isabel, and Rocinha** are very accessible and no more than an R$30 (US$15/£8) cab ride from Copacabana. Nor should you worry overly much about safety. Rehearsals take place in an open-air space called a *quadra* that looks like a large gymnasium. There is always security, and the rehearsals are very well attended. Plan to arrive anytime after 11pm. When you are ready to leave there'll be lots of taxis around. Just don't go wandering off into the neighborhood, unless you're familiar with the area. Many hotels will organize tours to the samba school rehearsals, but unless you prefer to go with a group it's not really necessary and certainly a lot cheaper to go on your own.

Tip: A number of the famous schools that are located on the outskirts of the city will hold special rehearsals in the Zona Sul. The ones organized by Beija Flor and Grande Rio are the most popular, often attended by models, actors, and other VIPs. For an authentic experience, it's still better to go to the actual school.

To find out more about specific schools, rehearsals, or participating in the parade, contact the **Liga das Escolas de Samba** (© **021/2253-7676; www.liesa.com.br**). If you can't find anyone there who speaks English, contact Alô Rio for assistance (© **021/2542-8080**). Or you can try contacting one of the samba schools directly; below you'll find a partial list:

- **Mangueira** (Rio's most favorite samba school and close to downtown), Rua Visconde de Niterói 1072, Mangueira (© **021/3872-6786; www.mangueira.com.br**).
- **Beija-flor** (far from downtown but a crowd favorite and winner in 2003, 2004, 2005, and 2007), Rua Pracinha Walace Paes Leme 1025, Nilópolis (© **021/2791-2866; www.beija-flor.com.br**).

> **Tips Carnaval Behind the Scenes**
>
> In 2005 the Cidade do Samba (Samba city) in downtown Rio was inaugurated. This large warehouse-style construction provides the samba schools with a space to build their floats and work on their costumes. The location is not too far from the parade ground, making it more convenient for schools to transport their huge floats when it is their turn to parade. Visitors can have a look behind the scenes and see what it takes to put this event together. Twice a month, on Thursdays, the Cidade do Samba also hosts a musical performance giving viewers a taste of the parade. These shows are really designed for tourists and don't have anything of the authenticity that the rehearsals at the actual schools have, but if this is your only opportunity to get a taste of Carnaval it may worth it. Open Tuesday through Saturday 10am to 5pm for visits (R$10/US$5/£3). The evening musical performances are always held on a Thursday, starting at 9pm. Admission includes a buffet dinner, R$150 (US$75/£40) or R$75 (US$38/£20) for Rio residents (proof of residency required). For more information and to check on scheduling, please contact the **Liga das Escolas de Samba** (© 021/2253-7676) or **Alô Rio** (© 021/2542-8080) or check www.sambacity.info.

- **Imperatriz** (the winner in 1999, 2000, and 2001), Rua Prof. Lacê 235, Ramos (© **021/2270-8037;** www.imperatrizleopoldinense.com.br).
- **Portela,** Rua Clara Nunes 81, Madureira (© **021/2489-6440;** www.portelaweb.com.br).
- **Rocinha** (young school, located in the Zona Sul close to Ipanema and Leblon), Rua Bertha Lutz 80, São Conrado (© **021/3205-3303;** www.academicosdarocinha.com.br).
- **Salgueiro** (close to downtown, very popular), Rua Silva Telles 104, Andaraí (© **021/2238-5564;** www.salgueiro.com.br).
- **Vila Isabel** (close to downtown, mostly locals and very untouristy, winner in 2006) Boulevard 28 de Setembro 382, Vila Isabel (© **021/3181-4869;** www.gresunidosdevilaisabel.com.br).

HANGING WITH THE BLOCOS

To experience the real street Carnaval, don't miss the parading blocos. The key to the popularity of the blocos is the informality; everyone is welcome, and you don't need a costume, just comfortable clothes and shoes. (Bear in mind, however, that the informality extends to scheduling. If your group doesn't start on time, grab a beer and chill—they'll show eventually.) Different blocos do have certain styles or attract specific groups, so pick one that suits you and have fun. Riotur publishes an excellent brochure called *Bandas, Blocos and Ensaios,* available through Alô Rio (© **021/2542-8080**). Also available from Riotur, Av. Princesa Isabel 183, Copacabana (© **021/2217-7563**), is the *Rio Incomparavel* brochure, which has a full listing of events. While traditionally Rio blocos have been free of charge, in recent years a few have picked up on the Salvador practice of charging a small fee and issuing participants a T-shirt to serve as a show of support and a very visible proof of purchase.

Some of the best blocos to look for are **Bloco Cacique de Ramos** and **Cordão do Bola Preta** in Centro; **Barbas** and **Bloco de Segunda** in Botafogo; **Bloco do Bip Bip** and **Banda Santa Clara** in Copacabana; Bloco **Meu Bem Volto Já** in Leme; and **Banda de Ipanema, Banda da Carmen Miranda,** and **Simpatia é Quase Amor** in Ipanema.

Moments *Reveillon:* New Year's Eve in Rio

Trust Brazilians to throw a party where everyone is welcome and admission is free. At Rio's annual New Year's Eve extravaganza, millions pack the beach for an all-night festival of music, food, and fun, punctuated by spectacular fireworks.

Arrive early and enjoy a New Year's buffet at one of the scores of restaurants or hotels along the beachfront Avenida Atlântica. Music kicks off at 8pm, as people make their way down to the beach until every square inch of sand is packed. By midnight, more than 2 million have joined the countdown. As the clock strikes midnight, the fireworks begin. Five barges moored off Copacabana plus more in Leme, Ipanema, Flamengo, Paquetá, and the Forte de Copacabana, at the end of the beach, flood the sky with a shower of reds, greens, purples, yellows, and golds. When the last whistling spark falls into the sea, bands fire up their instruments and welcome in the new year with a concert that goes on until wee hours. Many stay all night and grab a spot on the sand when they tire. The event is perfectly safe.

During the party, followers of the Afro-Brazilian religion Candomblé mark Reveillon in their own way. New Year's Eve is an important moment in Candomblé, a time when followers make offerings to the powerful sea goddess Yemanjá. Along the beach circles of women dressed all in white light candles and prepare small boats loaded with flowers, mirrors, trinkets, and perfumes. They launch the boats into the surf in hopes of obtaining Yemanjá's favor for the year to come.

Cariocas traditionally wear white on New Year's Eve; it's the color of peace and the color worn by devotees of Candomblé to honor Yemanjá. Don a pair of white shorts and a T-shirt, but don't forget your swimsuit. The traditional New Year's Eve "polar bear swim" will be even more tempting when the temperature is a balmy 105°F (40°C). Many Cariocas will also buy flowers to take to the beach and offer these to Yemanjá by tossing them in the ocean.

The best way to get to the event is by subway (buy tickets in advance to avoid lines). Most streets in Copacabana are closed to traffic; parking anywhere near the beach is impossible. For more details on the schedule contact Alô Rio (© **021/2542-8080**).

BAILES

More formal than the blocos, the samba balls *(bailes)* are where you go to see and be seen. Traditionally reserved for Rio's elite, some—such as the Copacabana Palace ball—remain the height of elegance, while others have become raunchy and risqué bacchanals. Numerous clubs around town host Carnaval balls.

Among the most fabulous is the notorious **Baile Vermelho e Preto (Red and Black Costume Ball)** held every year on Carnaval Friday in honor of Rio's most popular soccer club, Flamengo. It's known for both the beauty of the female attendees and the skimpiness of their costumes. The **Baile do Preto Branco (Black and White Ball)**, also on Carnaval Friday, takes place at the Clube Botafogo. For both events contact **Alô Rio** (© **021/2542-8080**) for details and ticket information. The popular Copacabana nightclub **Le Boy** (see club listings under "Rio After Dark," earlier in this chapter) organizes a differently themed ball every night during Carnaval, Friday through Tuesday included. These balls are gay-friendly but not gay-only. Call © **021/2240-3338.** The prime gay event—and one of Rio's most famous balls—is the Tuesday night **Gala Gay** at the Scala nightclub, Av. Afranio de Melo Franco 296, Leblon (© **021/2239-4448**). TV stations vie for position by the red carpet, a la Oscar night.

But the grand slam of all Carnaval balls is the Saturday night extravaganza at the Copacabana Palace Hotel, the **Baile do Copa,** which plays host to the crème de la crème of Rio's and Brazil's high society. This is the ball of politicians, diplomats, models, business tycoons, and local and international movie stars. Tickets start at R$600 (US$300/£162) per person and sell out quickly. Call © **021/2548-7070** for details.

6

Side Trips from Rio de Janeiro

Two of the greatest joys of Rio are its mountains and its beaches. Side trips from the cidade maravilhosa explore these two features in greater detail. On weekends and holidays, many head north to the beach resorts dotting the warm Atlantic coast. First and most famous of these is the town of **Búzios,** "discovered" in the 1960s by a bikini-wearing Brigitte Bardot. Now it's a haven for Rio socialites, visiting Argentines, and anyone else who loves their beaches Brazilian-style—civilized, with a beachside table in sight, and a caipirinha in hand.

Heading inland, one finds the summer refuge of an earlier, pre-beach generation, the mountain resort. The prettiest of these is also the closest: **Petrópolis,** the former summer capital of Emperor Pedro II. Just an hour from Rio, this green, graceful refuge is a place of peaceful strolls, great museums, and mountain hikes in the Atlantic rainforest. Beyond Petrópolis, in the highlands of the interior, lies an architectural wonderland: the **Historical Cities of Minas Gerais.** Built during the gold boom of the 18th century, the cities of **Ouro Prêto, Mariana,** and **Tiradentes** are gems of high baroque architecture; thanks to the later gold-mining bust, most have been preserved in their original condition. Several of these cities have excellent hiking nearby, but the main joys here are quiet and largely visual. It's enough to simply contemplate the beauty of the surrounding mountains and the architectural creativity of man.

Want your history served up with a splash of ocean? The perfect blend can be found in the former colonial port of **Paraty.** Situated almost halfway between Rio and São Paulo, this beautiful historic town had its heyday in the 18th and 19th centuries as a prime transshipment point for gold and later for coffee. Visitors can sail the bays and visit the surrounding sandy beaches and islands in the daytime, and at night wander the cobblestone streets of this UNESCO World Heritage Site, in search of architectural beauty or just some very fine dining.

1 Búzios

It's anyone's guess how small or sleepy the fishing town of Búzios truly was when French starlet Brigitte Bardot stumbled onto its sandy beaches in 1964, but it's certain that in the years since the little town used the publicity to turn itself into Rio's premier beach resort. In the summer the town is packed; many Carioca celebrities own places here, and Argentines continue to invade with a gusto not seen since the Falklands. Despite the influx, the town has managed to retain a good deal of the charm of its fishing-village past.

Búzios (the town's full name is Armação de Búzios) sits on the tip of a long, beach-rich peninsula jutting out into the clear blue Atlantic. The sheer number of beaches close to town makes it easy to experience Brazilian beach culture firsthand. **Geribá**

Beach is the place for surfing. Quiet and calm and very deep, **Ferruda Beach** is perfect for a lazy afternoon snorkel. Far from town are more isolated spots to steal a quiet moment with a special beach friend, while right in town on **Ossos Beach** you can sip a caipirinha at a beachside cafe and pretend for a moment you're young, rich, and beautiful. In this South American Saint-Tropez, everyone else certainly is.

Finally, on top of serious inquisitions into beach culture, there are more trivial pursuits such as diving, sailing, windsurfing, fine cuisine, and endless opportunities to shop. And at night, everyone comes to the busy, bar- and cafe-lined **Rua das Pedras** to stroll, primp, drink, and party.

ESSENTIALS
VISITOR INFORMATION
The **Búzios Tourism Secretariat** operates an information kiosk on the downtown Praça Santos Dumont 111 (© **0800/24-999** or 022/2623-2099); it's open daily from 9am to 10pm. Two good websites on Búzios are **www.buziosonline.com.br** and **www.buziosturismo.com**.

GETTING THERE
BY CAR Búzios is about a 2-hour drive from Rio de Janeiro. Leaving Rio, follow the signs to Niterói to cross the 16km-long (10-mile) Rio-Niterói bridge. Remember to have R$2.90 (US$1.50/£.75) handy to pay the toll. Across the bridge, stay in the left lane and take the Rio Bonito exit. Once close to Rio Bonito, take the Via Lagos to Araruama/Cabo Frio and follow the signs to the RJ-106 and Búzios. Note that the Via Lagos is also a toll road (R$6.40 (US$3.20/£1.70) on weekdays, R$9.80 (US$4.90/£2.65) on weekends).

BY VAN/TAXI **Malizia Tours** in Búzios (© 022/2623-1226 or 022/2623-2622; malizia@mar.com.br) offers transfer to/from Rio by van and taxi. Cost in a 15-person air-conditioned minibus is R$50 (US$25/£14) per person one-way. Pickup can be at your hotel or from the airport.

BY BUS **Auto Viação 1001** (© **0300/313-1001;** www.autoviacao1001.com.br) has departures seven times a day from Rio's main bus station (**Novo Rio Rodoviaria,** Av. Francisco Bicalho 1, Santo Cristo; © **021/3849-5001**). Cost of the 3-hour trip is R$20 (US$10/£5.40). In Búzios, buses arrive (and depart) at the Búzios Bus Station (© **022/2623-2050**) on Estrada da Usina, corner of Rua Manoel de Carvalho, a 10-minute walk from the center of town.

GETTING AROUND
BY WATER TAXI Water taxis are an efficient and fun way to get around, but they run only during daylight hours and only on the protected side of the bay, from João Fernandes to Tartaruga. To catch a water taxi you can hail one from the beach or the pier in town or phone (© **022/2620-8018**). When being dropped off by water taxi, you can set a time for pickup. From Centro to Azeda beach costs R$5 (US$2.50/ £1.35) per person and from Centro to João Fernandes beach R$8 (US$4/£2.15) per person. Taxis carry up to seven people.

BY TAXI Taxis can be hailed at the *ponto* in Praça Santos Dumont (© **022/2623-2160**) or by calling Búzios Rádio Táxi (© **022/2623-1911**).

BY RENTAL CAR **Rent a Car 24 horas,** Estrada de Búzios 815 (© **022/2623-1556;** rentacar24horas@mar.com.br). Cost starts at R$110 (US$55/£30) per day for a Fiat Palio with air-conditioning. Includes unlimited mileage and insurance.

Side Trips from Rio de Janeiro

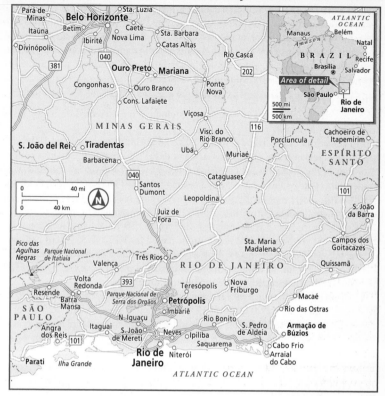

FAST FACTS: BÚZIOS

BANKING Banco do Brasil, Rua Manuel de Carvalho 73 (4 blocks from Rua das Pedras). Open Monday through Friday from 11am to 6pm. ATMs are open 24 hours.

INTERNET ACCESS Búzios Cybar, Shopping de Búzios, loja 4, corner of Rua Turibe (☎ 022/2623-2969). Cost is R$8 (US$4/£2.15) per 30 minutes.

EXPLORING BÚZIOS
HITTING THE BEACHES

The charm of Búzios lies largely in its beaches, the 20 stretches of sand large and small within a few kilometers of the old town. Thanks to the irregular topography of this rugged little peninsula, each beach is set off from the other and has developed its own beach personality. Farthest from the old town is **Manguinhos** beach. Sheltered from the heavy surf, this gentle beach is where many learn to sail and windsurf. A short hop over the neck of the peninsula lies **Geribá** beach, a wonderful long stretch of sand facing out toward the open ocean. This is the beach for surfing, boogie boarding, and windsurfing (see "Outdoor Activities & Watersports," below). Closer to town is **Ferradura** or **Horseshoe** beach. Nestled between rocky headlands in a beautiful horseshoe bay, this beach offers calm, crystal-clear waters, making it the perfect place for a long lazy afternoon's snorkel. Tiny and beautiful, **Olho de Boi** or **Bull's Eye** beach is tucked away on its own at the far end of a small ecological reserve. It can only be reached by a 20-minute walk from surfers' favorite **Brava** beach. Thanks to this isolation, Bull's Eye beach has been adopted by Búzios' clothing-optional crowd. Back on the calm inland side of the peninsula, **João Fernandes** and the pocket-size **João Fernandinho** beaches are busy, happening places lined with beachside cafes and full of people intent on getting and showing off their tans.

OUTDOOR ACTIVITIES & WATERSPORTS

Most everything in the way of watersports equipment can be rented in Búzios, generally right on the beach.

On **Ferradura** beach, **Happy Surf** (𝒞 **022/2623-3389**) rents **sailboards, lasers** (a type of one-person sailboat), **Hobie Cats,** and **kayaks.** Happy Surf also gives **courses.** A 6-hour beginner's **sailboard** course costs R$150 (US$75/£40). For more advanced students there are 1- and 2-hour courses costing from R$35 to R$60 (US$18–US$30/ £9.50–£16). Lasers rent for R$35 (US$18/£9.50) per half-hour, R$45 (US$23/£12) with instructor. Hobie Cats rent for R$25 (US$13/£7) per half-hour, R$40 (US$20/ £11) with instructor. Kayaks rent for R$5 (US$2.50/£1.35) per half-hour, R$8 (US$4/£2.15) per hour. Paddle boats can be rented for R$22 (US$11/£6) per hour.

The following equipment is available at **João Fernandes Beach: kayak rental,** R$5 (US$2.50/£1.35) for 30 minutes; **mask and snorkel package,** R$12 (US$6/£3.25) per hour; and **sailboard,** R$30 (US$15/£8) per hour.

On **Manguinhos** beach, two clubs rent lasers and sailboards: Búzios Vela Club, Rua Maurício Dutra 303 (𝒞 **022/2623-1237**), and Yucas Beach Club, Rua Maurício Dutra 356 (𝒞 **022/2623-2001**). Prices similar to those above. Manguinhos is also a popular **kite-surfing** location. Intensive weekend courses are available for R$400 (US$200/£108), including gear and 8 hours of instruction. To book a lesson call Búzios Kite Surfing School (𝒞 **022/2633-0396**).

BOATING   Schooner trips are a great way to spend a day in Búzios. A small fleet of converted fishing schooners makes a circuit of about eight of Búzios' beaches plus three offshore islands. On board you trundle along in the sunshine eating complimentary fresh fruit and drinking free caipirinhas (or mineral water). At any of the beaches you're free to get off, hang out and swim for a bit, and then hop back on the next schooner (from your company) that comes along. There are enough boats that you usually don't have to wait long. One company is **Malizia Tour** (𝒞 **022/2623-1226**), but there's really no need to seek them out. Just walk along Rua das Pedras anywhere near the pier, and you're guaranteed to be approached by a schooner tout. The exact price depends on how many of you there are and how hard you negotiate, but competition between various schooner operators keeps things fairly competitive. Expect to pay from R$30 to R$50 (US$15–US$25/£8–£14) for a half-day's cruise.

DIVING   The islands just off Búzios are—along with Angra dos Reis and Arraial do Cabo—some of the best diving spots within a 1-day drive of Rio. Diving takes place at a number of islands about 45 minutes off the coast. Water temperature is normally around 72°F (22°C). Visibility ranges from 10 to 15m (30–50 ft.). Coral formations are fairly basic—mostly soft coral—but there are always lots of parrotfish, and there are often sea turtles (green and hawksbill) and stingrays of considerable size.

Casa Mar, Rua das Pedras 242 (𝒞 **022/2623-2441;** www.casamar.com.br), offers a full range of services including cylinder refill and courses all the way from basic to nitrox. For a certified diver, a two-dive excursion costs R$110 (US$55/£30) or R$150

(US$75/£40) if you need to rent all the equipment such as a regulator, BCD (buoy-ancy control device), wet suit, and mask/fins/snorkel. For those wanting to get their diving license, a 4-day PADI open-water course costs R$850 (US$475/£230). If you just want to try diving, there are also introduction dives—you practice in the pool first and then the dive instructor takes you out for a controlled one-on-one dive in the open ocean—for R$180 (US$90/£49). Non-divers who come on the boat pay R$80 (US$40/£22).

GOLF   The **Búzios Golf Club & Resort** (© 022/2629-1240; www.buziosgolfe. com.br) is located just in from Manguinhos beach. Greens fees for this 18-hole course are R$165 (US$83/£45) per day for unlimited golf. No carts allowed, but caddies are available.

SURFING   Geribá and Tocuns beaches are the best surfing options. They're located on the way in to Búzios, about 5km (3 miles) from downtown. Closer to town is the smaller Brava beach, which also often has good waves. Note that board rentals are currently unavailable in Búzios.

BIKING   Hard-core mountain bikers would likely find it a little tame, but Búzios is an excellent place for gentle, recreational off-road cycling. There are lots of trails accessible only to pedestrians and cyclists. **Armação Bikes,** Manoel De Carvalho 229 (© 022/9213-4597), and **Bike-Tour,** Rua das Pedras 266, loja 4 (© 022/2623-6365), both rent bikes and can provide trail maps and even guides. Cost is around R$15 (US$7.50/£4) per hour, R$40 (US$20/£11) per day.

ADVENTURE SPORTS   **Canoar,** Travessa Oscar Lopez 63, loja 02 (© 022/2623-2551), runs **nature treks, rappelling trips,** and **rafting expeditions** in the Serramar region, about 30 minutes inland from Búzios. A 2-hour trek to a waterfall along the Pai João Trail costs R$30 (US$15/£8), transfer and light lunch included. A 3-hour rappelling trip, including a descent down a 25m (82-ft.) cliff face, costs R$56 (US$28/£15), transfer and light lunch included. Rafting trips leave twice daily, at 9am and 2pm. Participants descend 5km (3 miles) down a Class III river in either six-person or two-person inflatable rafts. Cost is R$60 (US$30/£16). Minimum age is 12.

HORSEBACK RIDING   **Canoar,** Travessa Oscar Lopez 63, loja 02 (© 022/2623-2551), runs "eco" horseback trips in the Atlantic rainforest. Horses are very calm, and riders carefully monitored. A 2-hour trip costs R$40 (US$20/£11).

WHERE TO STAY

Búzios is known for its pousadas, similar to North American B&Bs. These small, often owner-operated hotels provide excellent personalized service. By avoiding high season (Dec–Mar and July) and weekends throughout the year, you should be able to get a discount, although you will still end up paying more at a pousada in Búzios than you would anywhere else in Brazil.

VERY EXPENSIVE

Colonna Park Hotel ★★   Colonna Park Hotel offers a superb setting, straddling the hill between the beaches of João Fernando (the most happening beach in town) and João Fernandinho. Rooms in this sprawling Mediterranean-style mansion are spacious and elegantly furnished in cool tones of white and blue. All feature pleasant sitting areas. Forty-eight of the 63 rooms provide an ocean view. If you're in the mood for a splurge, try suite no. 20; it comes with Jacuzzi tub and a large deck with a view of both beaches.

Praia de João Fernandes, Armação de Búzios, RJ. ℂ 022/2623-2245. Fax 022/2623-2923. www.colonna.com.br. 63 units (showers only). High season R$480 (US$240/£130) double no view, R$520 (US$260/£140) double with view, R$570 (US$285/£154) suite; low season R$340 (US$170/£92) double no view, R$370 (US$185/£100) double with view, R$420 (US$210/£113) suite. Extra person an additional 30% of room rate. Children under 4 stay free in parent's room, over 4 R$40–R$90 (US$20–US$45/£11–£24) extra. AE, DC, MC, V. **Amenities:** 2 restaurants; bar; outdoor pool; sauna; game room; service; massage; laundry service. *In room:* A/C, TV, minibar, fridge, hair dryer, safe.

La Boheme ⭐ (Kids)   At the beginning of João Fernandes Beach, La Boheme overlooks the beach and the ocean from its hillside vantage point. The apartments all offer beautiful views and are within walking distance of the main village and the beaches. All are very spacious and feature kitchenettes, perfect for groups or families traveling with children. A few are split-level suites and sleep up to seven people; the other apartments are on one level only, accommodating up to four people comfortably. The pool area includes a great children's pool, and the beach, about 90m (300 ft.) below the hotel, is safe enough even for the little ones, with almost no waves and perfect bathtub-like temperatures.

Praia de João Fernandes, lote 1, Armação de Búzios, 28950-000 RJ. ℂ 022/2623-1744. www.labohemehotel.com. 32 units (showers only). R$250–R$320 (US$105–US$133/£52–£66) double; R$380 (US$190/£103) in 1-bedroom apartment that sleeps up to 4 people; R$620–R$880 (US$310–US$440/£167–£238) double in an apartment that sleeps up to 7 people. Children under 5 stay free in parent's room, 5 and over R$50 (US$25/£14) extra. AE, DC, MC, V. Free parking. **Amenities:** Restaurant; 2 pools; tour desk; car rental; room service; laundry service. *In room:* A/C, TV, kitchen, minibar, safe.

Pousada Byblos ⭐⭐   Tucked away on Orla Bardot, Byblos is in a quiet spot yet just a 5-minute walk from the nightlife and restaurants of the busy Rua das Pedras. The rooms are spacious, have comfortable beds, and offer either an ocean or garden view. The garden rooms are pleasant and have the advantage of being nice and quiet. The best rooms are the oceanview rooms on the top two floors. Both feature balconies. These cost the same as oceanview rooms without a balcony, so make sure you specify when you book. Two of the oceanview rooms have been upgraded to a super deluxe status and feature a Jacuzzi tub for two. The top floor of the pousada boasts a fabulous rooftop deck with a small swimming pool and a lounge. This pousada is not for people who have difficulty with stairs as access is on narrow spiral stairways.

Rua Alto do Humaitá 14, Praia da Armação, Armação de Búzios, 28925-000 RJ. ℂ 022/2623-1162. Fax 022/2623-2828. 21 units (showers only). Dec–Mar R$396 (US$198/£107) standard room (garden view), R$506 (US$253/£137) deluxe room (ocean view), R$598 (US$299/£161) super deluxe double; Apr–Nov R$288 (US$144/£78) standard room (garden view), R$378 (US$189/£102) deluxe room (ocean view), R$426 (US$213/£115) super deluxe double. Extra person 30% extra. Children 2 and under stay free in parent's room. AE, DC, MC, V. **Amenities:** Restaurant; bar; pool; tour desk; room service; laundry service. *In room:* A/C, TV, minibar, fridge, safe.

MODERATE

Búzios Internacional Apart Hotel (Value) (Kids)   One of the few relatively inexpensive options in town, this modern apart-hotel is located just a few blocks from Rua das Pedras. Units are all self-contained flats equipped with a living room with foldout couch, kitchen, and either one or two bedrooms. These are an excellent option for a family traveling together. All units are pleasantly if simply furnished and come with a balcony and hammock looking out over a central garden. The complex also boasts a swimming pool, sauna, game room and bar. Rentals are either calculated by day or by the week. Prices for two are comparable to the less expensive pousadas, but if there are more than three people (up to a maximum of six) savings can be significant. Discounts for 7-day stays available.

Estrada da Usina Velha 99, Armação de Búzios, 28980-000 RJ. ℰ/fax **022/2537-3876**. www.buziosbeach.com.br. 44 units. High season (mid-Dec to Mar) R$240 (US$120/£65) for 2, R$300 (US$150/£81) for 4. Low season (rest of year excluding holidays) R$200 (US$100/£54) for 2, R$250 (US$125/£67) for 4. AE, V. Free parking. **Amenities:** Pool; laundry. *In room:* A/C, TV, kitchen, minibar, fridge, hair dryer, safe.

WHERE TO DINE

Buzin KILO   One of the better kilo restaurants, Buzin offers a large buffet of excellent salads, antipasto, and vegetables. The grill serves up a variety of cuts of steak, grilled to your preference. Of course, being right by the sea the restaurant also includes a daily selection of fresh seafood and fish in its offerings.

Rua Manoel Turibe de Farias 273. ℰ **022/2633-7051**. Reservations not accepted. Main courses R$38 (US$19/£10) per kilo. AE, V. Daily noon–midnight.

Estancia Don Juan STEAKHOUSE   The Don loves only meat: the menu features *linguiça* (smoked sausage) and numerous exquisite beef cuts such as *picanha,* entrecôte, and *olho de bife.* Side dishes such as broccoli, baked potatoes, or carrots must be ordered separately. Fish flesh is also acceptable: The Don offers a toothsome catch of the day served with hollandaise sauce, capers, or balsamic vinaigrette. You can eat your meat on a lovely flowered patio, or in a multilevel hacienda dripping with atmosphere. Wines by the glass are not offered, but a number of South American reds (R$40–R$120/US$20–US$60/£11–£32) are sold by the bottle. On Tuesday evenings at 9pm, the Estancia features a live tango show.

Rua das Pedras 178. ℰ **022/2623-2169**. Reservations accepted. Main courses R$34–R$52 (US$17–US$26/£9–£14) for 2. AE, DC, MC, V. Mon–Tues 6pm–midnight; Wed–Sun noon–2am.

Patio Havana ⭑⭑ INTERNATIONAL   By the same owners as the Estancia Don Juan, the Patio Havana offers not only a restaurant but also a cigar shop, bar, lounge, and wine bar. The specialty is seafood. The seafood pasta and grilled lobster in a butter-and-lemon sauce are outstanding. The menu includes many other options including seven different kinds of carpaccios, excellent salads (almost a meal in themselves), and tasty sandwiches. The kitchen also turns out some great steak dishes. Look for the Filet do Pastor, a tender steak stuffed with goat cheese and served with a Dijon mustard sauce. The lounge hosts live music, usually bossa nova, samba, blues, or jazz. Thursday is salsa night. The music with free dance lesson kicks off at 9:30pm.

Rua das Pedras 101. ℰ **022/2623-2169**. R$28–R$52 (US$14–US$26/£7.50–£14). AE, DC, MC, V. Daily 6pm–midnight (later on Fri–Sat and holidays).

Sawasdee THAI   Sawasdee is one of only a handful of Thai restaurants in all of Brazil, so it's the perfect spot to indulge that craving for some satay skewers with spicy peanut sauce or a steaming bowl of Tom Kha Gai, a fragrant coconut soup with lemon grass and coconut. Main courses have a definite seafood focus. Try the prawns and fresh pineapple in Thai curry or the prawns with shitake mushrooms in oyster sauce. Spiciness has been toned down significantly for Brazilian customers so if you like it hot, tell the kitchen to spice it up.

Av. José Bento Ribeiro Dantas 500, Praia da Armação. ℰ **022/2623-4644**. www.sawasdee.com.br. Main courses R$32–R$58 (US$16–US$29/£9–£16). AE, DC, MC, V. Sun–Tues 6pm–midnight; Fri–Sat 6pm–1:30am. Closed Wed–Thurs Mar–July.

BÚZIOS AFTER DARK

If you're looking for a night out, **Rua das Pedras** is the place to crawl. This 4,000-foot-long street boasts pubs, bars, discos, and restaurants open on weekends until 5am.

One of the most popular spots is the Mexican bar and disco **Zapata.** To simply sit, sip a drink, and check out the action, the place to be is **Ponto Bar,** which serves Japanese food accompanied by the sounds of long-in-the-tooth rockers such as the Rolling Stones and Eric Clapton. If you prefer your entertainment live, there's **Patio Havana** (see above), which features a nightly selection of jazz, blues, and MPB (Musica Popular Brasileira). Should you get bored of the band, you can wander out to the oceanside patio, light up a cigar, and enjoy the nighttime view. To dance until you drop, there's no better place than disco **Privilege.** But remember, don't bother showing up until 1 or 2am. Two popular Rio bars have set up shop in Buzios recently; both **Devassa** and **Conversa Fiada** serve up good beer and excellent pub food.

2 Petrópolis (★)

Known as *Cidade Imperial* (the Imperial City), Petrópolis is one of Rio de Janeiro's premier mountain resorts, located 720m (2,400 ft.) above sea level. Though only an hour from Rio, its quiet and calm put it light-years from the hectic pace of the city. The lovely tree-lined streets, the palaces, mansions, and museums can be comfortably explored on foot or by horse and buggy, and the mountain air ensures a pleasant climate year-round. Once just a stopover on the gold route between Minas Gerais and Rio de Janeiro, its fine location and cool climate drew the attention of Emperor Dom Pedro II, who in 1843 founded the city of Petrópolis and built his summer palace (now the Imperial Museum) on a piece of land acquired by his father. Construction of the first railway in 1854 opened up easy access to the new city. Many of Brazil's merchant nobility—industrialists, coffee moguls, and politicians—built their summer residences here, turning Petrópolis into the de facto summer capital. Even after independence in 1889, Petrópolis maintained its prestige. In 1904 the former residence of the Baron of Rio Negro became the official summer residence of the president of the Republic.

Nowadays Petrópolis is a favorite weekend getaway for Cariocas: in the summer to escape the heat and humidity of the city, in the fall and winter for a chance to experience "really cold" weather, wear winter clothes, eat fondue, and sit by the fireplace. The historic part of the city, centered around the Imperial Museum and the Cathedral, contains the majority of the monuments and museums. Tree-lined canals and large squares give the small city a remarkably pleasant atmosphere; the side streets are worth exploring just to have a peek at the many mansions and villas. Particularly nice are Avenida Koeler and Avenida Ipiranga as far as the Casa Petrópolis.

In addition to the Cariocas's noble pursuit of culture and nature, they also flock here to visit the **Rua Teresa,** the best shopping street in Brazil. The area around Petrópolis has many textile factories, and the Rua Teresa has become the prime retail and wholesale outlet for cotton and knitwear at unbelievably low prices.

Petrópolis makes an easy day trip from Rio, but to experience the atmosphere of the city and take in some mountain air, it's better to spend the night. The region has a number of beautiful pousadas, excellent restaurants, and is close to a national park with excellent hiking trails.

ESSENTIALS
GETTING THERE
BY BUS   Unica/Facil (© 021/2263-8792) offers daily service from Rio to Petrópolis. The trip takes 1 hour and 15 minutes. Buses leave every 15 minutes Monday

Tips When Not to Go

The absolute worst day to visit Petrópolis is Monday; most attractions are closed, and shops at the Rua Teresa only open at 2pm. Some attractions are also closed on Tuesday, and many restaurants are closed Monday through Wednesday. The best days to visit are Wednesday through Friday. Weekends can be busy, so book accommodations ahead of time. Avoid holidays as museum lines and traffic can be very bad.

through Friday between 5:15am and midnight. On Saturday and Sunday buses leave at 5:30am, 6:15am, and 7am and then every 15 minutes until approximately 10pm. Tickets cost R$14 (US$7/£4). Buses depart from the main bus station in Rio, **Novo Rio Rodoviaria,** Av. Francisco Bicalho 1, Santo Cristo (© 021/2291-5151). Buses arrive at the new bus station in Petrópolis on the outskirts of the city. A short taxi ride will take you to all the attractions.

VISITOR INFORMATION
Petrotur has a number of offices around town. The main office is at Av. Koeler 245 Centro, Petrópolis (© 024/2243-9300 or 024/2246-9377). Kiosks are located at Rua do Imperador (by the Obelisk) and Casa do Barão de Mauá, both open daily from 9am to 5pm. Ask for the English version of the excellent "Petrópolis Imperial Sightseeing" brochure. It comes with a map and opening hours of each of the attractions. Petrotur also has a free tourism information line—call © 0800/241-516 without a phone card at no charge; the line is open Monday and Tuesday from 9am to 6:30pm, Wednesday through Saturday from 9am to 8pm, Sunday and holidays from 9am to 4pm.

The **Banco do Brasil** branch is located on the Rua do Imperador 940 (corner of Rua Alencar Lima).

GETTING AROUND
All the sites in the historic center are within walking distance of the bus station and each other. There is no need to drive or take a taxi.

BY RENTAL CAR Useful only if you're thinking of checking out some of the nearby national parks. In Petrópolis cars can be rented from **Imperial Coop,** Rua do Imperador 288, Centro (© 024/2246-0066).

BY TAXI For trips outside the city center, to pousadas or restaurants, phone (© 0800/241-516) for taxi service or just hail one of the many circulating taxis.

BY HORSE & BUGGY A great way to see the city without doing all the walking. Buggies depart only from the main entrance of the Museu Imperial. (Buggies in front of other attractions are waiting for their clients to come back from their visit.) You have two options for sightseeing: the first tour, R$50 (US$25/£14) per buggy for up to six people, stops at the Cathedral, Palácio de Crystal, Casa de Santos Dumont, Palácio Rio Negro, and Palácio Barão de Mauá, allowing you to get off and visit each site while the buggy waits. It takes about an hour and a half. On the second, cheaper option you cover the same route, but the buggy never stops so you see the sights only from the outside. Cost is R$40 (US$20/£11) for up to six people, and it takes about 30 minutes. Tours run year-round, Tuesday through Sunday. Please note that the tour does not include admission to any of the museums along the way.

EXPLORING PETRÓPOLIS

The historic heart of Petrópolis can easily be explored on foot: The city is fairly flat and extremely safe; even traffic is less hectic than in Rio. Following the directions below will take you to most points of interest. A more detailed description of the most important sights is also included below.

Starting on the corners of Avenida Ipiranga and Tiradentes, the first thing you see is the **Cathedral São Pedro de Alcantara,** a neo-Gothic church named for both the patron saint of the Empire and—not coincidentally—the Emperor Dom Pedro II himself. Construction began in 1876, but the celebratory first Mass wasn't held until 1925. Just inside the main doors to the right is the Imperial Chapel containing the remains of the Emperor Dom Pedro II, the Empress Dona Teresa, their daughter Princess Isabel, and her husband (whose name no one remembers). The princess, who often ruled during her father's many trips abroad, lived in the beautiful mansion immediately across the street, now known as the **Casa da Princesa Isabel.** Continuing along the Avenida Koeler as it follows the tree-lined canal, it's a 5-minute walk to the beautiful **Praça da Liberdade.** The bridge in front of this square offers the best view of the cathedral and the canal. Just behind the Praça da Liberdade is the **Museu Casa de Santos Dumont** (see below). From here follow Avenida Roberto Silveira, then turn right on Rua Alfredo Pachá to the **Palácio de Cristal,** Rua Alfredo Pachá s/n (✆ 024/2247-3721), open Tuesday through Sunday from 9am to 6:30pm. Commissioned by Princesa Isabel and built in France, the structure was inaugurated in 1894 as an agricultural exhibition hall. Nowadays, the palace is used for cultural events and exhibits (see "Special Events," below). Crossing the bridge to Avenida Piabanha, you come to the **Casa Barão de Mauá,** Praça da Confluencia s/n (✆ 024/2242-4300). Built in 1854 in neoclassical style by the industrial baron who constructed Brazil's first railway, the house is open for guided visits Monday though Saturday from 9am to 6pm and on Sunday and holidays from 9am to 4pm. Only a small number of personal belongings have been preserved (the high-flying baron was forced to sell off his possessions just prior to his death to pay off his many debts). The columns surrounding the winter garden are solid iron, made by the baron himself. Admission is free.

The Petrotur information kiosk inside the building has a great brochure in English that features a map plus a listing of all the attractions with their opening hours.

Continue by taking Rua 13 de Maio—right across the street from the Casa Barão de Mauá—toward the cathedral and then turning left on Avenida Ipiranga at the intersection just before the cathedral. Along this street are a number of interesting buildings as well as some gorgeous mansions and villas. Standing on the right side of the street at no. 346 is the 1816 **Igreja Luterana,** the oldest church in Petrópolis (open for visitation only during Sun morning service at 10am). On the left side of the street at no. 405 is the **Casa Rui Barbosa,** the summer residence of the liberal journalist, politician, and positivist who helped found the First Republic. A bit farther along the Avenida Ipiranga at no. 716 is the lovely **Casa de Petrópolis,** a museum, cultural center, restaurant, and garden (see below). From here it's a simple matter to retrace your steps to the cathedral.

Casa de Petrópolis ✶✶   Guided tours of this beautifully preserved house will take you through numerous salons lavishly decorated with satin curtains and wallpaper, gold-leaf chandeliers, and ornate and beautiful furniture. The banquet room is a marvel of jacaranda wood—the room's generous palette of colors is the result of judicious use of variously colored jacaranda subspecies. The rest of the house is used for concerts and exhibits. Weekly concerts take place on Saturday night at 8pm; tickets cost R$15 (US$7.50/£4). The lovely garden is also well worth a look. Allow 1 hour.

Rua Ipiranga 716. © 024/2242-0653. Admission R$5 (US$2.50/£1.35). Thurs–Mon noon–7pm.

Museu Casa de Santos Dumont ⭑   Who invented and flew the first airplane? Santos Dumont! Brazil's most famous aviator was the first in the world in 1906 to take off and land under his own power (unlike the Wright brothers, who used a catapult for takeoff on their first flight at Kitty Hawk). Dumont's creativity extended well beyond aviation. Among many other things, he also invented the wristwatch. Flying in balloons and blimps, he needed a watch at hand so he tied his pocket watch with a scarf to his wrist. Later he took the idea to his jeweler friend Cartier in Paris, who developed the first wrist strap. The Paris design house still comes out with a new watch design every year named "Santos." On display in this house are a number of bits of personal memorabilia: the medallions he earned for his many flight projects; his photos, books, and letters; and the Brazilian flag he carried with him on every flight. In the bathroom there's another Dumont original: the first hot shower in Brazil, heated by alcohol. Expect to spend 20 minutes. Helpful guides happily provide information in English.

Rua do Encanto 22. © 024/2247-3158. Admission R$5 (US$2.50/£1.35). Tues–Sun 9:30am–5pm.

Museu Imperial ⭑⭑   Built by Dom Pedro II in 1845 as his summer palace, the much-loved Museu Imperial is now Petrópolis's premier museum. (On Sun and holidays the line can be fierce.) The self-guided visits take you through numerous ground-floor salons decorated with period furniture, household items, and lovely paintings and drawings depicting life and landscapes of 19th-century Rio. Best of all is Brazil's equivalent of the crown jewels: Dom Pedro II's crown, weighing almost 4 pounds, encrusted with 639 diamonds and 77 pearls. Upstairs, visitors can see the bedrooms, including lovely baby cribs made out of jacaranda wood and decorated with bronze and ivory—fit for a pair of princesses. In the garden, the palace's coach house has a beautiful collection of 18th- and 19th-century carriages. The highlight is the royal carriage, painted in gold and pulled by eight horses. Expect to spend 1½ hours.

Rua da Imperatriz 220. © 024/2237-8000. Free admission to gardens; museum R$8 (US$4/£2) adults, R$4 (US$2/£1) children 7–14, free for children under 7. Tues–Sun 11am–5pm.

Palácio Rio Negro   Built by the coffee mogul Barão de Rio Negro in 1890, the palace has served as the summer residence of Brazilian presidents from 1903 onward. The rest of the year it functions as a cultural center. Most of the furniture inside is Portuguese baroque—dark, heavy, and beautifully carved. The hardwood floors are particularly ornate. Each room has a different pattern; the dining room floor is done in a coffee-bean pattern. Upstairs many of the rooms bear the stamp of particular presidents. Juscelino Kubitschek (the builder of Brasilia) put in an en-suite bathroom and modern all-white built-in closet. In the annex is a movie theater, added in 1968 by then-president Costa Silva.

Av. Koeler 255. © 024/2246-9380. Admission R$4 (US$2/£1). Wed–Sun 9:30am–5pm.

OUTDOOR ACTIVITIES

HIKING   Petrópolis has great hiking in the hills surrounding the town. For information on day hikes contact **Petrotur** (© **0800/241-516** or 024/2243-9300). **Açu Expedições** (© **024/2221-3832;** www.cabanasacu.com.br) offers guided day hikes and overnight trips as well as rafting, rappelling, horseback riding, and rock climbing.

Rio Hiking (✆ **021/2552-9204** or 021/9721-0594) also organizes a variety of hiking trips in the Petrópolis region, with transportation to and from Rio included. A day trip can combine a short hike with some sightseeing of Petrópolis (R$180/US$90/£49 per person) or you can opt for a 2-day hiking trip in the national park of Serra dos Orgãos close to Petrópolis (R$440/US$220/£119).

HORSEBACK RIDING   Contact the **Açu Expedições** for horseback riding (✆ **024/2221-3832**). See more details on Açu Expedições above. They can recommend and customize a trek for you according to your skills and interests.

SPECIAL EVENTS

To honor the German immigrants who played an important role in the early days of Petrópolis, the city holds **Bauernfest,** an annual festival celebrating German music, culture, and food. It is held yearly on the last weekend of June and the first week of July. Contact Petrotur for more information (✆ **0800/241-516**).

Making the most of Petrópolis's reputation as a winter destination, the **Festival de Inverno (Winter Music Festival)** takes place in the last 2 weeks of July at the Palácio de Crystal, Palácio Rio Negro, Centro Cultural Raul de Leoni, and Praça da Liberdade. For information contact ✆ **0800/241-516** or 024/2231-3011.

WHERE TO STAY

Overnight visitors to Petrópolis can choose to stay at hotels or pousadas in the historic part of town, or head farther out and find a nice hotel in the hills and valleys close to town. The advantage of staying downtown is that all the attractions are easily accessible on foot. If you choose to stay farther out it's always a good idea to contact your pousada for instructions on how to get there; some can arrange for pickup or send a taxi. Unlike many other Brazilian destinations, Petrópolis does not have a pronounced low or high season.

Casablanca Hotel Imperial 🌟 *Value*   More central would be almost impossible. Located next door to the Museu Imperial on one of Petrópolis's fine canals, Casablanca is within easy walking distance of all the city's historic sights. The hotel consists of the original mansion and a modern annex. The nicest rooms are the deluxe ones on the second floor of the original building. These have sky-high ceilings, airconditioning, bathtubs, and antique dark-wood furniture. On the same floor there is also a lovely reading lounge with a fireplace looking out over the canal. The standard rooms with showers only—in the annex and on the ground floor of the main house—are pleasant but lack the same level of character. The only drawback to this hotel's central location is the neighboring school; it gets very noisy during recess.

Rua da Imperatriz 286, Petrópolis, 25610-320 RJ. ✆ 024/2242-6662. www.casablancahotel.com.br. 43 units (7 with bathtub, 36 with shower only). R$180 (US$90/£49) standard double; R$220 (US$110/£59) deluxe double. Extra bed R$60 (US$30/£16). Children 6 and older R$35 (US$18/£9.50). AE, DC, MC, V. Free parking. **Amenities:** Pool; sauna; game room; limited room service; laundry service. *In room:* A/C (in *luxo* rooms only—standard rooms w/fans), TV, minibar.

Pousada Monte Imperial Koeller   This cute inn is located on one of the prettiest boulevards in Petrópolis, amid many of the historic buildings. Some of the rooms have a balcony and offer pleasant views of the gardens. Other rooms look out over the historic Casa da Princesa Isabel mansion next door. All rooms are nicely decorated and feature comfortable beds and Egyptian cotton sheets. Breakfast is included.

Av. Koeller 99, Petrópolis, RJ. ✆ 024/2243-4330. www.pousadamonteimperial.com.br. 11 units (showers only). R$195–R$230 (US$97–US$115/£53–£62) Extra person R$60 (US$30/£16). Children's rate negotiable. AE, DC, MC, V. Free parking. **Amenities:** Laundry service. *In room:* TV, minibar, fridge.

Solar do Imperio ⭐⭐⭐ Fit for a king, or a princess to be more precise, the Solar do Imperio is a lovingly restored neoclassical palace built in 1875, and home for a time to Brazil's Princess Isabela. Now, commoners can experience the regal elegance of this villa in the heart of Petrópolis. Upgraded, as much as possible, to modern standards, the rooms boast air-conditioning and heat, king-size beds with down comforters and pillows. Guests can choose between the *Real* suite or the Imperial suite, the basic difference being the size of the room; *Real* suites are much more spacious and have soaring high ceilings. Amenities, however, are the same in all rooms. The hotel also boasts a beautifully restored reading room, and an elegant veranda and garden—a royal experience indeed.

Av. Koeler 376, Petrópolis, RJ. ℂ 024/2103-3000. www.solardoimperio.com.br. 16 units. R$390–R$590 (US$195– US$245/£105–£159), suite Imperial double; R$490–R$625 (US$245–US$312/£132–£169) suite Real double. AE, DC, MC, V. Free parking. **Amenities:** Restaurant; bar; pool; sauna; game room; limited room service; laundry service. *In room:* A/C, TV, minibar, hair dryer, safe.

WHERE TO DINE

Petrópolis offers a range of dining opportunities, from schnitzel to sushi to *churrasco.* Check opening times carefully, though, as a number of restaurants are closed Monday through Wednesday or Monday through Thursday.

Churrascaria Majoricá ⭐ CHURRASCO A traditional-looking *churrascaria* with wood panels and booths, Majoricá is a local favorite when it comes to a good steak. Make your choice: T-bone, *picanha,* entrecôte, half and half (tenderloin pork and beef), or grilled chicken. Just as delicious is the shrimp skewer with roasted vegetables and the prawn stroganoff. Most dishes serve two people. Small steak orders are also available; add a side plate or two and you have a perfect meal for one.

Rua do Imperador 754. ℂ 024/2242-2498. R$18–R$34 (US$9–US$17/£5–£9) steak; R$26–R$48 (US$13–US$24/ £7–£13) seafood dishes. AE, MC, V. Sun–Thurs 11am–10pm; Fri–Sat 11am–11pm.

Luigi ⭐ ITALIAN Lovers of simple Italian food will enjoy Luigi's. The large menu lists pasta and sauce separately, allowing guests to mix and match. There are also a variety of stuffed pastas such as cannelloni, ravioli, and lasagna. For a lighter meal, creamy onion or broccoli soup and the option of the salad buffet is perfect. This large buffet offers salad in the broad definition of the word, including cold cuts, cheeses, quiches, and sliced roast beef. In the evenings the restaurant serves excellent pizzas.

Praça Rui Barbosa 185, Centro. ℂ 024/2246-0279. www.massasluigi.com.br. R$16–R$38 (US$8–US$19/£4–£10). AE, DC, MC, V. Sun–Thurs 11am–midnight; Fri–Sat 11am–1am.

Petit Palais Tea Room ⭐⭐ TEA/CAFE Tucked away in the corner of the gardens surrounding the museum, this lovely tearoom is the perfect place for lunch. Head toward the coach house and follow the path slightly downhill to the left. Full tea service is available, including cakes, pies, croissants, madeleines, toast, jam, cold cuts, and pâté. For a smaller lunch or snack the restaurant also serves a variety of quiches, omelets, soups, and sandwiches, as well as pastas such as the Gorgonzola with nuts or the shrimp with fresh tomato sauce.

Rua da Imperatriz 220. ℂ 024/2244-7912. Main lunch courses R$14–R$26 (US$7–US$13/£4–£7); full tea R$39 (US$20/£11). No credit cards. Tues–Wed noon–7pm; Thurs noon–8pm; Fri–Sat noon–midnight; Sun noon–7pm.

Paladar KILO Just a block from the Santos Dumont Museum, the Paladar restaurant is great for a quick and inexpensive lunch. From 11am to 4pm the restaurant puts out a great spread including a variety of salads, pasta, roast beef, chicken, beans, and other dishes. The selection varies from day to day. You make your own plate and then make sure it gets weighed before you sit down to eat.

Rua Barão do Amazonas 25. © 024/2243-1143. Main courses R$20 (US$10/£5.40) per kilo. AE, MC, V. Tues–Sun 11am–4pm.

3 Ouro Prêto ★★★

The inland state of Minas Gerais struck it rich on gold just about the time the baroque style reached its elaborate architectural height. Newly wealthy citizens needed something to blow their money on, and they turned to architecture. The result? Several small cities boasting cobblestone streets, soaring palaces, and elaborate churches that rival St. Petersburg or Prague.

The largest of these is the hilltop town of **Ouro Prêto;** its cobblestone streets wander up and down hills crowned with more than a dozen ornately carved and elaborately decorated baroque churches. Each corner turns on new surprises: mansions, fountains, ruins, beautiful terraced gardens, and towers glowing with colored tiles. Once known as Vila Rica (the rich town), Ouro Prêto begs to be explored on foot. Yes, the cobblestone streets can get quite steep, but the rewards are worth it. Only on foot can you appreciate the rich details of the perfectly preserved houses, gaze at the intricately carved fountains, and steal glimpses of courtyards and living rooms. The monuments and museums can be visited in 2 days, allowing plenty of time to stroll and explore.

ESSENTIALS
GETTING THERE
Ouro Prêto is 410km (254 miles) from Rio de Janeiro and 635km (393 miles) from São Paulo.

Drivers from Rio de Janeiro take the BR-040 highway as far as Conselheiro Lafaiete, then follow the Estrada Real to Ouro Prêto. From São Paulo follow the BR-381

The Inconfidência Mineira

Ouro Prêto has a special place in Brazilian history for its role in the Inconfidência Mineira (1788–92), a failed rebellion against the Portuguese Crown. The movement started as a protest against the 20% royal tax on gold production. A group of intellectuals (doctors, writers, and poets) began meeting with the idea of taking some sort of action. The ringleader was a dentist named Joaquim José da Silva Xavier, also known as Tiradentes (literally, "the teeth puller"). Unfortunately, before the group formulated a plan, someone betrayed their existence, and in 1789, Tiradentes and 11 of his confederates were arrested. All were condemned to death. The viceregal governor commuted the sentences of the other 11 and sent them into exile. Tiradentes was hanged as an example, his body cut in four pieces, and each piece put on display. Nowadays, the Inconfidência is interpreted as Brazil's first uprising against Portuguese rule, and Tiradentes as Brazil's first martyr in the struggle for independence.

Ouro Prêto

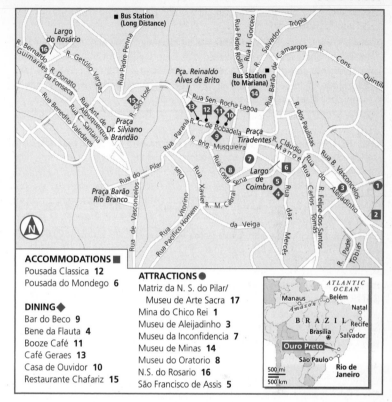

ACCOMMODATIONS ■
Pousada Classica **12**
Pousada do Mondego **6**

DINING ◆
Bar do Beco **9**
Bene da Flauta **4**
Booze Café **11**
Café Geraes **13**
Casa de Ouvidor **10**
Restaurante Chafariz **15**

ATTRACTIONS ●
Matriz da N. S. do Pilar/
　Museu de Arte Sacra **17**
Mina do Chico Rei **1**
Museu de Aleijadinho **3**
Museu da Inconfidencia **7**
Museu de Minas **14**
Museu do Oratorio **8**
N.S. do Rosario **16**
São Francisco de Assis **5**

to Lavras and then take the BR-265 to Barbacena. In Barbacena take the BR-040 in the direction of Belo Horizonte.

For those who have little time or maybe a leg left on their air pass, there is the option of **flying** to Belo Horizonte's Pampulha or Confins airport (Pampulha is about 40km [25 miles] closer to Ouro Prêto than Confins airport). Gol, Tam, and Varig all fly from Rio, São Paulo, and other cities to Belo Horizonte. Gol's Internet specials cost around R$190 (US$95/£51) for a one-way flight from Rio or São Paulo. From the airport it's possible to negotiate with a taxi to take you straight to Ouro Prêto for a set fee (expect to pay around R$100/US$50/£27, depending on your bargaining skills) or you can take the bus (see below).

Regular buses connect from Rio (7 hr.), São Paulo (11 hr.), and Belo Horizonte (2 hr.) to Ouro Prêto. Bus company **Util** runs a nightly 11:30pm bus from Rio to Ouro Prêto, arriving first thing in the morning (② **021/2518-1133** in Rio, or 031/3551-3166 in Ouro Prêto); tickets costs R$65 (US$33/£18) for a regular seat and R$125 (US$63/£34) for a comfortable almost bedlike seat *(leito)*. **Cristo Rei** has three daily departures between São Paulo Bresser Station (② **011/3692-4073**) and Ouro Prêto (② **031/3551-1777**). **Passaro Verde** runs at least 20 buses a day between Belo Horizonte and Ouro Prêto (② **031/3551-1081**). Tickets range from R$16 to R$70 (US$8–US$35/£4–19). The Ouro Prêto bus station is a R$10 (US$5/£3) taxi ride

> ### Tips When to Go
>
> Avoid visiting Ouro Prêto and Mariana on Monday, as the majority of churches, museums, and attractions are closed. The best days to visit Mariana are Friday or Sunday so you can take in the organ concert at the Catedral da Sé. To take advantage of lower room rates, visit Tuesday through Friday. Everything is open but not as busy as on the weekends.

from the historic core. *Tip:* Many of the taxi drivers will also agree to a full- or half-day sightseeing rate. This is an ideal option for visiting Mariana or getting out into the countryside.

TOURIST INFORMATION

Ouro Prêto Tourist Information is at Rua Claudio Manuel 61 (© 031/3559-3544); hours are daily from 8am to 6pm.

For tour guides, contact the **Ouro Prêto Tour Guide Association** at © 031/3551-2655. A 4-hour English-language tour of Ouro Prêto (with up to 10 people) costs R$100 (US$50/£27).

FAST FACTS: OURO PRÊTO

BANK Banco do Brasil, Rua São José 189 (© 031/3551-2237), has a 24-hour ATM. This branch will also exchange U.S. dollars. Almost next door, the **HSBC,** Rua São José 201 (© 031/3551-2048), also has ATMs.

INTERNET ACCESS Cyber House, Rua Conde Bobadela 109 (© 031/3552-2808), is open daily from 10am to 8pm.

CITY LAYOUT

Ouro Prêto is a city of twisting, turning streets that seem to change names at every corner, but despite this it's remarkably hard to get lost. Thanks to the ever-present incline you can usually pick out your destination—be it church, museum, or square—either above or below you and figure out a route to get there. The main square in the center of the city is the **Praça Tiradentes.** The **Museu da Inconfidência** stands on one side of the square and the **University of Ouro Prêto** on the other. Running downhill out of the square are two parallel streets—**Rua Sen. Rocha Lagoa** and **Rua Conde de Bobadela** (aka Rua Direita)—packed with restaurants, pubs, and shops. Following those streets will lead via a number of twists and turns first to the **Praça Reinaldo Alves de Brito** with its lovely sculpted fountain, and below that to the **Igreja Matriz N.S. do Pilar.** Below that again—possibly on the Rua Antonio Albuquerque, though there are several other routes—stands the lovely **Igreja N.S. do Rosario.**

Head downhill on the other side of Praça Tiradentes, and you'll come to the Largo de Coimbra, site of the **Igreja São Francisco de Assis.** Continue following the street down the hillside to the next important church, the **Matriz N.S. da Conceição** and the next-door **Aleijadinho Museum.** Past this church, strolling along **Rua Bernardo Vasconcelos,** the street crosses a lovely stone bridge before it starts to climb very steeply. At the top—the view is worth the effort, but if you're feeling lazy you can always take a cab from the main square for R$6 (US$3/£1.50—stands the **Matriz Santa Efigenia dos Prêtos,** built by communities of slaves who were not permitted to worship in other churches. Notice some of the Afro-Brazilian motifs, such as shells and goat horns. Retracing your steps down the steep street, you will be rewarded with a beautiful view of the city.

Bring good walking shoes. All the streets are cobblestone, and the sidewalks and steps are often carved out of uneven stones.

TOP ATTRACTIONS

If you can only take museums in small dosages, save your energies for the Museu de Arte Sacra in Mariana, well worth a visit.

Matriz da N.S. do Pilar/Museu de Arte Sacra ⊕ You may want to shield your eyes from the glitter of the over 400 kilograms of gold that were used to decorate this church. Completed in 1786, it was built at the height of Brazilian baroque, when the phrase "less is more" would have evoked only laughter. More is more! And more there is: angels and cherubim everywhere, all of them dripping in gold. Recently opened in the basement, the Museu de Arte Sacra is disappointingly small for a town of Ouro Prêto's significance.

Praça Mons, Castilho Barbosa. ✆ **031/3551-4736**. R$4 (US$2/£1). Tues–Sun 9–11am and noon–5pm.

Mina do Chico Rei *(Kids* Touring this former mine in the heart of Ouro Prêto gives you a visceral feel for what life as a miner must have been like. Not for the claustrophobic, this self-guided tour lets you wander some of the narrow underground tunnels, poking your nose along the way in some of the wall cavities where miners would store their finds during the day. Deeper in the mine a mineral room shows various types of stone from this area, including the reddish-brown mineral that held most of Ouro Prêto's gold. Allow 45 minutes.

Rua D. Silverio 108. ✆ **031/3552-2866**. R$6 (US$3/£1.60) adults, free for children under 8. Daily 8am–5pm.

Museu da Inconfidência *(Overrated* As interesting as the building is—it was the city council and jail where the conspirators were imprisoned—the museum itself is seriously lacking in content. The ground floor houses nothing but a mumbo jumbo of

---

The Incredible Aleijadinho

It's impossible to go anywhere in Ouro Prêto (or any of the other historic cities, for that matter) and not hear the name or see the work of *Aleijadinho.* Brazil's finest baroque artist, he carved much of the marble and other stonework decorating many of the finest churches both in Ouro Prêto and in the other historical cities. (The church of São Francisco de Assis has some particularly fine examples of his work.) His signal achievements are all the more remarkable given that Aleijadinho worked without the use of his hands. The son of a Portuguese architect and a black slave woman, Antonio Francisco Lisboa was born in 1738, inheriting the name Aleijadinho in his 20s when a debilitating disease—probably leprosy—left his hands and legs crippled. Undaunted, Aleijadinho carried on working, even as his body degenerated to the point where his apprentices had to strap hammer and chisel to his wrists. He died in 1814, having completed his last sculpture just 2 years previously.

locks, keys, lamps, and other artifacts from the time of the Inconfidência. One of the back rooms contains the remains of the Inconfidentes (as many as could be repatriated posthumously) and a tribute to their role in Brazilian history. However, this museum is mostly of interest to Brazilians who come for the mystique that surrounds the whole Inconfidência episode. Considering there is little explanation to begin with, and none of it in English, you may want to give this one a miss. Allow 30 minutes.

Praça Tiradentes s/n. Ⓒ 031/3551-1121. R$6 (US$3/£1.60) adults, R$3 (US$1.50/£.80) youth 10–18, free for children under 10. Tues–Sun noon–5:30pm.

Museu de Aleijadinho   Many of Aleijadinho's best works are in the churches around the city, leaving this museum (entered through the Matriz N.S. da Conceição) with odds and ends and smaller pieces, often oratories and statues of saints. However, the displays do provide the opportunity to take a close-up look at some of the master sculptor's work. The faces of the statues seem almost alive, and the creases and folds of their clothes resemble soft flowing fabric instead of wood. Those hoping to find out more about the artist himself will be disappointed. Not much is known beyond his work, and the museum hasn't really bothered to delve into the artist as a person. On your way out, have a peek inside the church; Aleijadinho's father carved many of the angels, and both father and son are buried in the church. Aleijadinho's tomb is located on the right-hand side underneath the first altar. Allow 45 minutes. Your ticket is also good for the São Francisco de Assis church (see below).

Praça Antonio Dias s/n. Ⓒ 031/3551-4661. Admission R$5 (US$2.50/£1.35). Tues–Sat 8:30am–noon and 1:30–5pm; Sun noon–5pm.

Museu de Minas ⚡ *Kids*   Part modern showroom, part old-fashioned museum, but well worth a visit. Unless you are into natural history, most people skip the ground-floor collection of stuffed animals and critters preserved in formaldehyde: The highlight of the museum is its mineral collection. The most valuable and interesting pieces are displayed on the ground floor in a flashy showroom, with perfect lighting and dramatic black backdrops. Opals, emeralds, topaz, quartz, and close to 2,000 lesser-known varieties can be seen. The remainder of the mineral collection is housed upstairs in an old-fashioned lab room with hundreds of small wooden cabinets containing 18,000 samples. To show how these samples were extracted, there's a collection of modern equipment and original tools from the past. Allow 1½ hours.

Praça Tiradentes 20. ⒸZ 031/3559-1597. R$5 (US$2.50/£1.35) adults, free for children under 6. Tues–Sun noon–5pm.

Tips   **Choose Your Guide Wisely**

The square in front of the São Francisco de Assis church is particularly notorious for the guides that try to sell their services to visitors entering the church. Some are incredibly knowledgeable and will greatly add to your experience; others are trained only in spewing completely useless facts and can't answer any questions. If interested in a guide, check with the tourist information office on the Praça Tiradentes, or when negotiating with a freelancer be clear on the amount and the length of time (will he/she just give information on one church or visit a number of monuments with you?).

Fun Fact **Huh?**

This quote was taken from one of the English-language guides for sale in Ouro Prêto: *"The constructive process of the temple began in 1733, reaching the decade of 80, when the frontispiece was concluded with base in Manoel Francisco's risk."* Buyer beware!

Museu do Oratorio ★★★ What is an oratory? Visit here and ye shall see. One of the loveliest museums in Ouro Prêto, the Museu do Oratorio displays a comprehensive collection of oratories, which are in fact little mini-altars, used by people so they could pray without having to go to church. The museum showcases home, travel, and work oratories. All are works of art, elaborately decorated and painted. Some are small enough to tuck into your pocket or bag for traveling, while others may have stood in a living room or bedroom. Nuns often made them as fundraisers for the convent. The Afro-Brazilian oratories are decorated with flowers and shells from the Candomblé religion and usually portray black saints such as Santa Efigenia. Allow 45 minutes.

Rua Brog. Musqueira s/n (next to the Igreja do Carmo). ✆ 031/3551-5369. www.oratorio.com.br. Admission R$3 (US$1.50/£.80). Daily 9:30am–5:30pm.

Nossa Senhora do Rosario ★★ Not one of the more famous churches but certainly one of the more interesting ones, the N.S. do Rosario was built by slaves who were forbidden to worship elsewhere. Rumor has it that they smuggled tiny bits of gold from the diggings to put toward the building of their church. Constructed over a period of 30 years, the church was finally completed in 1792. Strikingly elegant and very unusual in Brazilian baroque, the church was built in the shape of an ellipse, with beautiful soft curves. Unlike the rich folks' churches, this one stands out for its simplicity. In lieu of gold, the altars are beautifully painted and dedicated to black saints such as Santo Elesbão and São Benedito. The Sunday Mass is held at 4pm. Visitors welcome.

Largo do Rosario s/n. ✆ 031/3551-4736. Free admission. Tues–Sat 9am–5pm; Sun 1:30–5pm.

São Francisco de Assis ★★★ Completed in 1794, the São Francisco de Assis church is one of the top contenders for most beautiful church in Ouro Prêto, if not the whole of Brazil. Most of the artwork was done by Aleijadinho, who was invited by the Franciscan brotherhood to design and decorate the church. His elaborate soapstone carvings, including the pulpits and altars, are simply unbelievable. The baptismal font in the sacristy alone took him 3 years to make! The paintings are by Atayde, who was also responsible for the ceiling mural of the Virgin Mary in heaven, surrounded by cherubs and musicians. One interesting aspect of the architecture is the way the two towers flanking the church at the front were actually set back so that when you stand directly in front of the church, nothing takes away from the intricately carved entrance.

Largo de Coimbra s/n. ✆ 031/3551-4661. R$5 (US$2.50/£1.35). Tues–Sun 8:30am–noon and 1:30–5pm. Your ticket is also good for the Aleijadinho Museum.

WHERE TO STAY

One of the busiest times of the year in Ouro Prêto is during Easter week (Semana Santa). The many processions, events, and concerts make it a worthwhile visit, but reserve accommodations at least a few weeks in advance. Carnaval is also a busy time of the year as many flock to take part in the lively street celebrations. Prices go up significantly.

Luxor Ouro Prêto Pousada ★★   This lovely 200-year-old colonial mansion has been transformed by the Luxor group into a fabulous cozy inn. All 19 rooms are decorated with antique period furniture, some original works by *Mineira* artist Chanina or 18th-century replicas. Both the superior rooms and the suites look out over the Santa Efigencia and N.S. das Mercês churches. The standard rooms come either with a double bed or two twin beds and several of the bathrooms feature a bathtub. The suites are much bigger and have a separate sitting room. The hotel restaurant serves very decent *Mineiro* food.

Rua Dr. Alfredo Beata 16 (Praça Antônio Dias), Ouro Prêto, 35400-000 MG. ℂ 031/3551-2244. www.luxorhoteis. com.br. 19 units. R225 (US$108/£61) standard double; R$300 (US$150/£81) suite double. Extra person add R$50 (US$25/£14). Children 6 and under stay free in parent's room. AE, DC, MC, V. **Amenities:** Restaurant; bar; game room; concierge; tour desk; limited room service; laundry. *In room:* A/C, TV, dataport, minibar, safe.

Pousada Classica ★★   A fascinating blend of old and new, the Pousada Classica is in an old baroque mansion that's been gutted and completely renovated. The lobby is modern and spacious with large glass doors (in place of the original dark shutters). The rooms are very pleasant with high ceilings, hardwood floors, and elegant furnishings, mixing modern amenities with the classic features of the building. The difference in price for a deluxe double and a super deluxe room or a suite is so small that you may as well go for the spacious suite with the whirlpool tub and the prime view. The standard and deluxe rooms don't have tubs, but the showers are brand-new and spotlessly clean.

Rua Conde de Bobadela 96, Ouro Prêto, MG. ℂ 031/3551-3663. Fax 031/3551-6593. www.pousadaclassica.com.br. 27 units (standard and deluxe rooms with shower only). R$240–R$250 (US$120–US$125/£65–£68) standard and deluxe double; R$280 (US$140/£76) suite double. 35% discount on weekdays and low season. Extra person add 25%. Children 5 and under stay free in parent's room. V. Free parking. **Amenities:** Restaurant; concierge; tour desk; limited room service; laundry. *In room:* A/C, TV, dataport, minibar, fridge.

Pousada do Mondego ★★   Located in the heart of Ouro Prêto, the Pousada do Mondego looks out over the Largo de Coimbra and the São Francisco de Assis church. The 24 units in this 250-year-old pousada are spread out over three floors. The prime rooms are the suites or deluxe units on the second floor overlooking the square and the city below. These rooms are spacious and elegant, with hardwood floors, a four-poster bed, sofa, and large dressers. The superior rooms are also quite nice—the beamed ceilings give the rooms a cozy feel—but the view is of the internal courtyard. Avoid the standard rooms, as these have low ceilings and no view at all. Service is outstanding (the pousada belongs to the high-quality Roteiros de Charme association), so it's not surprising that rooms are often booked; call in advance.

Largo de Coimbra 38, Ouro Prêto, 35400-000 MG. ℂ 031/3551-2040. Fax 031/3551-3094. http://mondego.com.br. 24 units (shower only). R$160 (US$80/£43) standard double; R$220 (US$110/£60) superior double; R$280 (US$140/£76) deluxe double. Extra person R$40 (US$20/£11). Children 5 and under stay free in parent's room. AE, DC, MC, V. Free parking. **Amenities:** Concierge; tour desk; limited room service; laundry. *In room:* TV, minibar.

WHERE TO DINE

The food in Minas Gerais is renowned in Brazil for its heartiness and simplicity. The favorite dishes are rich stews and bean dishes with pork. Two typical Minas dishes are *Tutu á Mineira* and *feijão tropeiro*. In *Tutu* the beans are cooked, mashed, cooked again (similar to Mexican refried beans), and served with roasted pork, sausages, bacon, collard greens, egg, and rice with side dishes. The *feijão tropeiro* is fairly similar except the beans are kept whole and mixed with cassava flour. Two other traditional dishes are made with chicken: *frango a molho pardo* and *frango com quiabo*. *Frango a molho pardo,* originally a Portuguese dish, is a stew made with fresh chicken blood—a little gruesome sounding but surprisingly tasty. Do try this dish; maybe have a small bite at one of the kilo restaurants. The other chicken dish is a rich tomato stew with okra. You'll find these four dishes in almost every Minas restaurant. The servings are always enough for two.

Bené da Flauta 🍴🍴 BRAZILIAN Although the chefs consider their menu Mineiro food with a contemporary twist, you will find plenty of other options. A great appetizer is the antipasto dish with roasted tomatoes and eggplant in olive oil, served with a basket of bread. Main courses are still far from being light cuisine but include options such as a veal *osso buco* with risotto or a grilled tournedos steak with creamy piemontese rice. The 18th-century building itself has a lovely history; right next to Ouro Prêto's monumental São Francisco de Assis church, it is here that painter Athayde had his atelier when he was working on the artwork for the church. The gorgeous dining room is decorated in beautiful antiques.

Rua São Francisco 32. © **031/3551-1036.** Reservations recommended on weekends. Main courses R$22–R$38 (US$11–US$19/£6–£10). DC, MC, V. Daily noon–11pm.

Cafe Geraes 🍴 CAFE Cafe Geraes is the perfect little cafe, and with only a dozen tables it is always busy. The best spot is on the mezzanine level overlooking the bar where you can still see part of the original clay and straw wall. Geraes serves delicious *caldos* (thick soups) together with a thick slice of home-baked potato bread. To nibble, you can order appetizers of salami, olives, and crackers. Or you can skip ahead and go straight for dessert. The strudels and pies are excellent and served with a generous dollop of fresh cream.

Rua Direita 122, Centro. © **031/3551-5097.** R$12–R$24 (US$6–US$12/£3.25–£6.50). No credit cards. Sun–Thurs 11am–11pm; Fri–Sat 11am–1am.

Casa do Ouvidor 🍴🍴 BRAZILIAN The Casa do Ouvidor is one of the best restaurants for trying out local cuisine. Located on the second floor above the Rua Direita, this elegant dining room basks in the warm glow cast from candles and numerous antique lamps. The menu includes the four typical Mineiro dishes. Some lighter items such as a grilled chicken breast and a beef brochette are offered, but I was on a mission and ordered the *Tutu á Mineira*. The dish was everything I expected and more; the beans were mashed to almost a paste, accompanied by a juicy grilled sausage, tender pork loin, and crispy roasted bacon bits. A side order of rice, a boiled egg, and thinly shredded, stir-fried greens completed my feast. Dessert, not a chance!

Rua Direita 42, Centro. © **031/3551-2141.** Main courses R$22–R$36 (US$11–US$18/£6–£10) for 2. AE, DC, MC, V. Daily 11am–3pm and 7–10pm.

Restaurante Chafariz 🍴 *Finds* BRAZILIAN The dining room of the Chafariz does a great job blending old with new. Housed in the former residence of Ouro Prêto's beloved poet Alphonsus de Guimaraens, the restaurant looks like an antiques shop with large armoires, wrought-iron chandeliers, and large wooden tables. In contrast, the heavy ceiling beams are painted in cheerful colors, and the glass art is positively funky. Open for lunch only, the restaurant serves an excellent buffet of the best of Minas food as well as a good selection of salads. Dessert is always included, and at the end of your meal, the waiter will bring a complimentary glass of liquor made from the tiny red *jabuticaba* fruit.

Rua São José 167. ⓒ 031/3551-2828. Main courses R$24 (US$12/£6.50) buffet. DC, MC, V. Daily 11am–4pm.

OURO PRÊTO AFTER DARK

Bar do Beco *(Moments)*   If I lived in Ouro Prêto, I think I'd come to Bar do Beco every day and slowly work my way through the cachaça menu. With at least 65 varieties in stock at any given time, this bar is the perfect spot to embark on a taste trip. The bar special, the ice-cold Milagre de Minas, is made in-house with a secret 15-spice formula. The bartender also makes some wicked cachaça cocktails such as *da paixão* with Milagre de Minas, blue Curaçao, passion-fruit juice, and rose petals. With its smooth stone floors and low overhead beams, the bar has the feel of an old tavern. Opens at 6pm. Travessa do Arieira 15. ⓒ 031/3551-1429. No credit cards.

Booze Café Concerto *(Finds)*   A great spot to duck into after 9pm on a Friday or Saturday to catch some live music. Bands hail mostly from Minas Gerais and play MPB, blues, or jazz. The cafe itself is a large basement room with exposed brick walls, round windows that look out into the alley, and amazing glass art behind the bar. Daily 11am to midnight. Rua Direita 42, subsolo (basement). ⓒ 031/3551-1482. R$5 (US$2.50/£1.35) cover Fri–Sat. No credit cards.

4 Mariana (★)

Unlike Ouro Prêto, Mariana is not a perfectly preserved historic town but rather a town with a perfectly preserved historic section. Unlike its larger neighbor, Mariana also still has active mining on the outskirts of the city. The historic part of Mariana makes a pleasant half-day trip from Ouro Prêto. The monuments, museums, and churches can be seen in a few hours, and the trip by bus is only 30 minutes.

GETTING THERE   Buses depart from Ouro Prêto for Mariana every 30 minutes between 5:30am and 11:30pm from behind the Museu de Minas (Rua Barão Camargos). The trip costs R$2 (US$1/£.50), takes approximately 30 minutes, and drops you in the center of Mariana. A much more scenic way to get to Mariana is by steam train. Originally built in 1883, the 18km (11 miles) of track that connect the two towns have recently been restored. The trip takes an hour; make sure you sit on the right hand side as you leave Ouro Prêto to get the best views of the landscape. Also if you sit in the rear of the train you can take some great photos of the front carriages as the track curves. Departures Ouro Prêto to Mariana Friday to Sunday at 11am and 4pm. Return from Mariana to Ouro Prêto only at 2pm. Visitors can return by bus or arrange a taxi. One-way fare: adults R$18 (US$9/£5), children 6 to 10 pay R$15 (US$7.50/£4); ⓒ 031/3551-7310.

VISITOR INFORMATION   Bring some information on Mariana from Ouro Prêto's tourist information as the office here, located at Praça Tancredo Neves s/n

---

(Tips) **When to Go**

Time your visit to Mariana for the Friday (11am) or Sunday (12:15pm) concert, performed on the exquisite 18th-century organ at the Catedral da Sé.

(© **031/3557-1158**), is notoriously unreliable. It's supposed to be open daily 8am to 5pm, but don't count on it.

EXPLORING MARIANA

From the bus stop, it is an easy stroll to all of Mariana's sights. Built according to a city plan in 1743, the old part of town has an easy-to-follow grid pattern. Following **Rua Josafia Macedo** out and then the parallel **Rua Dom Viçoso** back to the **Praça Cláudio Manuel** makes for a perfect loop. Starting off on **Rua Josafia Macedo,** the first stop of interest is Mariana's **Pelourinho** at the Praça Minas Gerais. This square is one of the few in Brazil that has kept the *pelourinho* (flogging post) to attest to this bloody era of Brazilian history; the locals claim the square is haunted. Surrounding the Pelourinho are the **Igreja São Francisco de Assis,** viewable upon request, the **Igreja N.S. do Carmo,** currently undergoing renovations after a recent fire, and the former jail and city council. Both churches were built in the late 18th century and are lovely examples of the local baroque architecture. Continuing up the street, now known as **Rua D. Silverio,** it is a pleasant 20-minute stroll to the top of the hill where the **Basilica de São Pedro dos Clerigos** overlooks the city from its vantage point. Coming back down, zigzagging through the side streets with beautifully preserved colonial houses, make your way to the **Praça Gomes Freire,** the main gathering place for locals. On the corner of the square you can still see one of the original drinking troughs used for watering the horses. After visiting the **Museu de Arte Sacra** and the **Catedral Basilica da Sé,** loop back to the bus station via the short **Rua Direita,** observing the colorful two-story houses.

Catedral Basilica da Sé ✦✦   Well worth a visit, this lovely cathedral is the oldest church in Mariana, completed in 1750. Some famous Brazilian baroque artists worked on the decorations: Aleijadinho's father carved many of the altars, Atayde painted a number of pieces, and the baptismal font in the sacristy was made by Aleijadinho himself. The stunning chandeliers in the center of the church are pure Bohemian crystal, imported from Germany. The organ, a gift from Dom. João V, has been fully restored after a 70-year silence. Every Friday and Sunday the organist holds a 40-minute concert, followed by a detailed explanation of the organ itself.

Praça Claudio Manuel s/n. © **031/3557-1216.** Church visit R$2 (US$1/£.50); admission to concerts R$12 (US$6/£3.25). Tues–Sun 9am–noon and 2–6pm. Concerts take place Fri 11am and Sun 12:15pm.

Museu de Arte Sacra ✦✦✦   Although unassuming from the outside, the colonial mansion behind the cathedral houses one of the best collections of sacred art in Brazil. The vast collection is beautifully displayed and illuminated, and the stone floors and thick walls of the building create the appropriate stately ambience. On the ground floor you will find a large collection of silver and gold artifacts: crowns, diadems, crucifixes, and chalices. Also on display are intrinsically decorated *custodias*—a type of chalice used only for the host—as well as lanterns and processional crosses. Upstairs there's a collection of statues made by Aleijadinho, as well as a portrait of the artist done by Atayde. What makes the work of this baroque artist so vibrant is the painstaking effort he put in to preparing his canvasses and paint. Often working on wood, he started with a white layer to bring out the luminosity in the paint, followed by an ocher layer, and then a white, almost transparent layer to increase the dark and light contrast. In his paints, Atayde blended in gold dust, red dirt, coal dust, and metal shavings.

Rua Frei Durão 49. © **031/3557-3259.** R$5 (US$2.50/£1.35) ages 5 and over, free for children under 5. Tues–Sun 9am–noon and 1:30–5pm.

WHERE TO DINE

Most of Mariana's restaurants do not open for lunch except on weekends and holidays. A great lunch spot, open daily 11am to 3pm and popular with local families on Sunday, is the kilo restaurant **Lua Cheia,** Rua Dom Viçoso 26 (© **031/3557-3232**). Two more upscale choices are **Tambaú,** Travessa São Francisco 26 (© **031/3557-1780**), serving tapas and great Brazilian finger foods, and **Bistrô,** Rua Salamão Ibrahim 61A (© **031/3557-4138**), for sushi, pasta, and pizzas. Both only open for lunch on the weekends.

5 Tiradentes ★★★

Surely one of the loveliest little towns in all of Brazil, Tiradentes doesn't "wow" like Ouro Prêto, doesn't seduce like Salvador or charm like Olinda, but it quietly wins you over and before you know it you, too, will be head over heels in love. Nestled at the foot of the Serra de São José, it's a place where time has stood still. When the last mine closed in 1830, people moved away and the town was left as if frozen in amber. A heritage designation early on in 1938 kept any further development at bay.

The town has only a few dozen streets and can easily be seen in a day, but why rush? See the sights, browse the fabulous antiques and jewelry stores, enjoy the fine dining, or just stroll the streets. Despite its size and isolation, Tiradentes has a well-developed tourism infrastructure. In high season and on weekends the town gets hopping; if you prefer peace and quiet, stick to weekdays for your visit.

GETTING THERE As there are no direct long-distance buses to Tiradentes, visitors must travel to São João del Rei first and from the rodoviaria connect with one of the 11 buses a day that cover the 14km (8½ miles) to Tiradentes in 20 minutes and cost R$2 (US$1/£.50). Regular buses connect São João del Rei to São Paulo and Rio de Janeiro. The Paraibuna line runs at least three buses a day to Rio. The Vale do Ouro line has five buses a day to São Paulo, and one bus leaves for Ouro Prêto every day at 5:30pm.

In a pinch one can always take a taxi, for about R$50 (US$25/£14). For taxi service contact © **032/3355-1466** or 032/3355-1100. The Tiradentes Rodoviaria is within walking distance of most pousadas.

To arrive in style, take the 115-year-old narrow-gauge steam train, called **Maria Fumaça (Smoking Mary)** ★★, from São João del Rei (© **032/3371-8485**). Following the Rio das Mortes, the train takes 35 minutes to reach Tiradentes's rail station. Trains depart São João del Rei Friday through Sunday and holidays at 10am and 3pm, and from Tiradentes at 1pm and 5pm. One-way tickets cost R$14 (US$7/£3.75) adults, R$10 (US$5/£3) children 6 to 10. The train station is a short taxi ride or a 10-minute walk from the historic center of town.

VISITOR INFORMATION The **tourist office** is located at Largo das Forras 71 (© **032/3355-1212**), and open daily from 9am to 5:30pm.

EXPLORING THE TOWN

The list of attractions may seem small, but that's because the town itself is the main attraction. The only way to experience Tiradentes is on foot, getting lost in the little streets, absorbing the breathtaking architecture.

A STROLL AROUND TOWN

Start at the **Largo das Forras,** the large tree-lined square in the center of town. This is where the tourist office is located (open daily 9am–5:30pm) and where, if you really

---

Moments **Mengoooooooooo!**

It was the day after Sunday's big game in Rio's Maracanã stadium: Flamengo won the match, making it a shoe-in (well, a cleat-in) for the Carioca cup. As I strolled through Tiradentes's sleepy streets I heard a car coming, the first one in 2 hours, and as it drove by I heard a loud "Mengoooooooo"—the drawn-out call of Flamengo fans—and turned to see three guys in Flamengo shirts, with the black-and-red flag proudly draped over the hood. Back in the main square, I was just in time to see residents put up a few tables, pull some *cervejas* from the trunk and dance, and sing to the boom box, belting out Flamengo tunes. Even 1 day later—and no matter where you are—a victory by Brazil's most beloved team is always a good excuse for a party.

---

don't want to hoof it, you can hire a buggy and horse to do the hoofing for you (R$20/US$10/£5.40) for a 45-minute tour. Walk to the corner next to the tourism office, and you'll see the beautifully restored post office. Continuing up that street (Rua Resende Costas) you start to climb a bit, and soon to the right you will be able to catch breathtaking views of the Serra de São José. Stay on the street (now renamed Rua Direita) until you come to the **N.S. do Rosário dos Prêtos** on your right. The oldest church in town, it was built entirely by Tiradentes's slave community. It's definitely worth a peek inside. The stars and moon painted on the ceiling refer to the fact that most of the construction had to be done at night, after the enslaved had completed their forced labor. The individually painted wooden panels on the ceiling represent the mysteries of the rosary. From here, instead of continuing up along Rua Direta, duck into the alley behind the church, and it will lead to the **Largo do Sol** and **Museu de Padre Toledo.** One of the *inconfidentes,* Padre Toledo lived in this house until he was arrested and exiled to Lisbon. The museum, unfortunately, doesn't tell much of the padre's story; instead, it's mostly a mishmash of furniture, paintings, oratories, and household objects. Stay on the Rua Padre Toledo as it leads up the hill to the **Matriz de Santo Antônio** church (see listing below). Take the street to the right of the Matriz and continue farther up the hill to the church of **Santissima Trinidade.** This church stands out for its simplicity: no fancy ornaments, no gold, not even a clock tower. But for an over-the-top display of faith, look no further than the room of miracles around the back of the church. The place where the faithful give thanks for cures and interventions is packed from top to bottom with letters, photos, wax and plastic body parts, and every piece of orthopedic equipment imaginable. Right next door is the holy shop of saints where you can purchase a statue of just about any saint in the calendar. Retrace your steps down the hill and continue past the Matriz to the charming little **Largo do Ô.** Beyond that, just across the bridge is the large **Chafariz de Sao José** where residents used to obtain their water. Walking back toward the main Largo das Forras along the **Rua Direita** will take you through Tiradentes's gallery row. Many artists live and work here; painters, furniture makers, silversmiths, and craftspeople make high-quality pieces at reasonable prices. Typical souvenirs include locally made cachaça, sweets and preserves, silver jewelry, paintings, and quilts and rugs.

Matriz de Santo Antônio ⭑   One of the richest churches in Minas Gerais, the Matriz has recently been renovated and looks as good as new. Aleijadinho sculpted the front entrance, portraying a shield with the Lamb of God. The interior is completely plastered with gold; the main altar seems positively ablaze. The sacristy is worth a look for the paintings by Manuel Victor de Jesus representing scenes from the Old Testament. The steps of the church offer one of the best views in the city. On Friday, Saturday, and Sunday there is a sound-and-light show that tells the history of the church (R$5/US$2.50/£1.35). The show begins at 8pm.

Rua da Camara s/n. No phone. R$2 (US$1/£50). Daily 9am–5pm.

OUTDOOR ACTIVITIES

HIKING   The hills around Tiradentes and São João del Rei offer some spectacular hiking and walking trails. Local company **Lazer e Aventura** (⊘ **032/3371-7956;** www.lazereaventura.com) specializes in trips in the region. One of the more popular hikes goes up to the top of the Serra de São José and offers fabulous views of the surrounding valleys. The company also runs a jeep tour, which follows a trail along the base of the hills through some stands of Atlantic forest and takes you through some small villages. More adventurous types can try out rappelling or caving as well. Most tours last about 4 hours and require just an average level of fitness. All transportation is included and prices range from R$30 to R$40 (US$15–US$20/£8–£11) per person.

WHERE TO STAY

Pousada Pé da Serra   Run by a friendly family, this pousada sits only 150m (500 ft.) from the bus station directly behind the São Francisco de Paulo church. Thanks to the boost provided by a small ridge, five of the nine rooms offer sweeping views of the mountains and the town itself. The rooms are very basic and simple, no phones and no fancy furnishings, but the location makes up for a lot: Guests have use of a cozy sitting room with a fireplace and bar, and on sunny days can enjoy the large garden with a swimming pool.

Rua Nicolau Panzera 51, Tiradentes, 36325-000 MG. ⊘ 032/3355-1107. www.pedaserra.com.br. 9 units (showers only). R$150 (US$75/£40) double. Extra person add R$30 (US$15/£8). Children 6 and under stay free in parent's room. V. Free parking. **Amenities:** Bar; outdoor pool. *In room:* TV, minibar, fridge, no phone.

Pousada Tres Portas   Named after the three double doors forming the entryway, this lovely pousada is located within the historic town. Just off the main square, the views of the Serra São Jose are quite beautiful. The best room has a full view of the Serra and is furnished with a beautiful four-poster bed. The other rooms have partial views and are also very pleasant, featuring lovely antiques, hardwood floors, and colorful bedspreads on comfortable beds. All guests have the use of the lounge, a great spot to relax by the crackling fire. On weekends the pousada works with a 2-night minimum, but on weekdays there is a 30% discount and no minimum length of stay.

Rua Direita 280A, Tiradentes, 36325-000 MG. ⊘ 032/3355-1444. Fax 032/3355-1184. www.pousadatresportas. com.br. 9 units (showers only). R$220–R$275 (US$110–US$138/£60–£75) double. Extra person over 12, add 50%. Children 2 and under stay free in parent's room, ages 3–12 add 20%. MC, V. Free parking. **Amenities:** Restaurant; bar; small indoor heated pool; sauna; laundry. *In room:* TV, minibar, fridge, no phone.

Solar da Ponte ⭐⭐⭐   Though for very different reasons, the Solar da Ponte is much like the Eagles' Hotel California—you may never leave. Located in the heart of Tiradentes, this member of the Roteiro de Charme group of pousadas is the perfect home base for exploring this historic town. The 12 rooms are all uniquely furnished with antiques, harmonious color schemes, fresh flowers, and comfortable couches and chairs. The standard rooms overlook the street and the stone bridge that the pousada is named after, while the superior rooms face out over the garden. The pousada also has a comfortable reading room with ample literature in English and a large fireplace for chilly evenings. The restaurant in the garden room serves a scrumptious breakfast with fresh warm rolls, eggs, cold cuts, cake, and fresh fruit, all on beautiful dishes made by a local artist. In the afternoon, the restaurant offers complimentary tea.

Praça das Mercês s/n, Tiradentes, 36325-000 MG. (© 032/3355-1255. www.solardaponte.com.br or www.roteiros decharme.com.br. 18 units (showers only). High season R$300 (US$150/£81) standard double; R$500 (US$250/£135) superior. Extra person R$70 (US$35/£19). In low season 20%–30% discount. AE, DC, MC, V. Free parking. Children must be older than 12. **Amenities:** Outdoor pool; sauna; game room; concierge; laundry. *In room:* TV, dataport, mini-bar, fridge, coffeemaker, hair dryer.

WHERE TO DINE

Tiradentes is quite sophisticated when it comes to restaurants. Most specialize in traditional Mineiro cuisine (see "Ouro Prêto," earlier in this chapter, for more details on the dishes). Every year, at the end of August, the city hosts a culinary festival and provides a wonderful opportunity for local chefs to show off their skills. During the off season check ahead for opening hours, particularly Sunday through Tuesday.

Many interesting restaurants can be found just by strolling along Tiradentes's streets. The top restaurants in town all specialize in local cuisine. **Estalagem do Sabor,** Rua Min. Gabriel Passos 280 (© 032/3355-1144), is well known for its hearty regional fare. In addition to basic chicken and meat stews, try the *Mané sem Jaleco,* a dish that combines rice with beans, sliced kale, bacon, eggs, and pork tenderloin; lean cuisine it ain't. **Viradas do Largo,** Rua do Moinho 11 (© 032/3355-1111), is another local favorite that has made a name for itself with outstanding Mineiro dishes. Many of the dishes are made with herbs and vegetables from the restaurant's own garden. Keep in mind that portions are generous, more so than in other restaurants; often a dish will feed four people. Appetizers include handmade pork or chicken sausages. For Mineiro cuisine with a modern twist check out the restaurant **Tragaluz,** Rua Direita 52 (© 032/3355-1424). Here you will also find some of the meat stews but with shitake instead of cabbage and served with a side of mashed inhame (a Brazilian root vegetable) instead of rice. Desserts are creative; for example, the staple goiabada (guava paste) is served fried with a sprinkling of cashew nuts and cream cheese.

Minas is almost as famous for its food as it is for the outstanding cachaça (hard liquor made from sugar-cane juice) it produces. **Dona Xepa** ✹✹, Rua Ministro Gabriel Passos 26A (© 032/3355-1767), offers an extensive cachaça menu; many of the brands boast florid and poetic names. For example, try Minha Deusa (My Goddess), a fruit-flavored variety of cachaça. One of the best cachaças around is Havana. Aged in balsamic barrels and made in small quantities, it is considered the champagne of cachaças. And, yes, it is possible to enjoy cuisines other than Mineiro cooking in Tiradentes. Overlooking the Ponte do Solar, **Sapore d'Italia** ✹, Rua Francisco de Paula 13 (© 032/3355-1487), cooks up some excellent Italian dishes. The menu offers a good selection of pasta dishes such as cannelloni with ham, penne with Calabrese sausage, or lasagna. The wine list includes mostly Portuguese, French, and Italian reds, all reasonably priced.

6 Paraty ✹✹✹

The main attraction of Paraty is its historic core, a UNESCO World Heritage Site with beautifully preserved colonial architecture. In contrast to the ornate baroque opulence of Ouro Prêto, Paraty was a port, a working-class kind of town. The architecture is simple and colonial. Even the churches and municipal buildings seemed to have been built more for daily use than as a statement of wealth.

Paraty first grew in importance in the 1800s when it became the main shipping port for the gold from the mines of Minas Gerais. The gold was transported down windy trails and cobblestone roads from Ouro Prêto to the coast, where it was loaded on ships sailing for Portugal. Once gold became scarce, Paraty switched to coffee, but with the abolishment of slavery in 1888, that too dried up and Paraty faded to near oblivion; the population fell from 16,000 in its glory days to 600 in the early 1900s. From a heritage perspective it was the city's saving grace.

In 1966 the historic colonial center of Paraty was declared a UNESCO World Heritage Site. To preserve its unique pre-modern character, cars were banished from the old colonial core. In the heart of the city it's pedestrians only. Radical as that may sound, it actually works rather well. Boat tours of the surrounding islands leave from the dock in the city center. Day trips into the surrounding hills include transportation.

The region surrounding the city adds much to Paraty's quiet beauty. The hills are still mostly covered in lush green coastal rainforest, and the waters around Paraty, dotted with 65 islands, are tropical turquoise, warm, and crystal clear, perfect for snorkeling, swimming, or scuba diving. If you only have time to visit one of the historic towns, Paraty makes a fine (long) 1-day or easy overnight destination from either Rio or São Paulo.

ESSENTIALS

VISITOR INFORMATION

The official **Paraty Tourist Information,** Av. Roberto Silveira 1 on the corner of Rua Domingos Gonçalves de Abreu (© **024/3371-1222;** www.paraty.com.br), is open daily 9am to 9pm. **Paraty Tours** operates an information kiosk downtown, just a block down from the historic center at Av. Roberto da Silveira 11 (© **024/3371-1222;** www.paratytours.com.br). They provide general tourist information as well as suggestions on hotels, tours, and excursions.

GETTING THERE

BY BUS   Paraty is easily accessible by bus. From Rio de Janeiro, there are two bus companies with daily departures: **Costa Verde** (© **024/3371-1177**) or **Normandy** (© **024/3371-1277**); both depart from the main bus station in Rio (Novo Rio). The trip takes approximately 4 hours and costs R$36 (US$19/£10). From São Paulo five buses depart daily from Tietê station with **Reunidas** (© **024/3371-1196**). The trip takes about 6 hours and costs R$28 (US$14/£7.50).

BY PRIVATE TRANSFER   **Paraty Tours** (© **024/3371-1222;** www.paratytours.com.br) offers private transfers with set times for a minimum of two people at 8:30am, 12:30pm, and 5pm. Airport pickups anytime between 8:30am and 5pm. Rates per person R$125 (US$63/£34). For three people or more you can set your own pickup time.

GETTING AROUND

ON FOOT   The historic center of Paraty is perfect for exploring on foot. The city center is closed to cars (parking is on the outskirts), making walking a traffic-free dream. Wear comfortable shoes as the big cobblestones make for a bumpy stroll.

BY TAXI   Taxis in Paraty can be hailed outside of the car-free historic city center, or call ✆ **024/9999-9075.**

BY RENTAL CAR   To explore the surrounding area on your own, you can rent a car from **Atrium,** Rua do Comércio 26 (✆ **024/3371-1295**).

FAST FACTS: PARATY

BANKING   **Banco do Brasil,** Av. Roberto Silveira s/n (✆ **024/3371-1379**), is open Monday through Friday 10am to 3pm. ATMs are open 24 hours.

INTERNET ACCESS   **Paraty Web Internet Access** is located inside the Quero Mais Restaurant, Rua Marechal Deodoro 243 (✆ **024/3371-7375**). Connection cost is R$4 (US$2/£1.35) per hour.

EXPLORING PARATY

EXPLORING THE HISTORIC CENTER

Start your exploration of Paraty at the main pier at the bottom of **Rua da Lapa.** Fishing boats come and go, as well as frequent schooner excursions. Turn and face the city and you will see the postcard-perfect vista of Paraty: the **Santa Rita** church framed by a background of lush green hills. The church was built by freed slaves in 1722 and despite its plain exterior, displays some fine rococo artwork. The church also houses the small **Museum of Sacred Art** (Wed–Sun 10am–noon and 2–5pm; R$4/US$2/£1.35). It's worth a quick peek, though it can't compare to some of the fine art on display in Ouro Prêto or Mariana. The building just to the left of the church was once the town jail; now it's home to the city library and historical institute. Paraty's biggest and most ornate church, the **Igreja da Matriz,** stands on the Praça da Matriz, close to the River Perequê-Açu. What started with a small chapel in 1646 became a bigger church in 1712 and was finally replaced with the current large neoclassical building, completed in 1873. The **Casa da Cultura** (Rua Dona Geralda) was originally built in 1754 as a private residence and warehouse. Later it housed the town's public school. In the 1990s, the city restored it to serve as a cultural center and exhibit space.

OUTDOOR ACTIVITIES

BOATING   Just beyond the muddy Paraty waterfront, the coast is dotted with more than 60 islands, many lush and green, surrounded by turquoise water. It shouldn't be surprising then that schooner trips are extremely popular. The pier in the city center is the main departure point. Boats leave daily, weather permitting, and take you on a 5- to 6-hour tour, stopping several times for a swim or snorkel and a lunch break. **Paraty Tours** (✆ **024/3371-1327**) and **Saveiro Porto Seguro** (✆ **024/3371-1254**) are just two of several companies that have daily departures at 11am (as well as 10am and noon in high season); the cost is R$25 (US$13/£7) for adults, free for children under 5, R$15 (US$7.50/£4) for 5- to 10-year-olds. To explore the bay at a more leisurely pace, Paraty tours offers a kayak tour. The 6-hour paddle provides plenty of opportunity for checking out some of the islands and beaches. Cost is R$60 (US$30/£16) per person, including a guide and all the equipment (minimum of two people).

DIVING   The islands around Paraty have some decent diving and cater to a variety of levels. Most operators take you to the many islands around Angra dos Reis (up the coast from Paraty). Two dive companies in town are **Alpha Dive,** Praça da Bandeira

1, centro histórico ((C) **024/3371-2798**), and **Paraty Tours,** Av. Roberto da Silveira 11 ((C) **024/3371-1327**). Both offer a full range of services, including cylinder refill and courses, and an introductory dive if you do not have a license. For a certified diver, a two-dive excursion costs approximately R$150 (US$75/£41). This rate includes all the equipment such as a regulator, BC (buoyancy control), wet suit, and mask/fins/snorkel.

BIKING   A mountain bike is the perfect way to reach some of the waterfalls in the surrounding hills or some of the beaches just a 10km (6½-mile) ride out of town. **Paraty Tours,** Av. Roberto da Silveira 11 ((C) **024/3371-1327**), rents bikes by the hour for R$6 (US$3/£1.60) or by the day for R$30 (US$15/£8). Maps are provided.

HIKING   In the surrounding hills one can still find stretches of the old wagon trail that was used to bring the gold from Ouro Prêto down to the coast. Parts of the old cobblestone trail have been restored and are accessible to hikers. **Caminho do Ouro (Gold Trail)** offers an easy trek along this historic route. The full-day tour leaves Thursday through Sunday at 10am and includes a guide and transportation from Paraty. R$35 (US$18/£9.50) per person, children 4 to 10 half price. Their booking office is located inside the Teatro Espaço, Rua Dona Geralda 327 ((C) **024/3371-1575;** www.caminhodoouro.com.br). If you want a more serious hike, consider a 2- or 3-day trip. **Rio Hiking** ((C) **021/9874-3698;** www.riohiking.com.br) offers excellent hiking trips along the beaches and through the coastal rainforest on the peninsula just south of Paraty, Paraty-Mirim. Transportation from Rio de Janeiro and rustic accommodations are included (2-day trip R$440/US$220/£119 per person, and 3-day trip R$660/US$330/£178). **Paraty Tours,** Av. Roberto da Silveira 11 ((C) **024/3371-1327**), offers a number of short guided hikes to the isolated beaches at Trinidade and Praia do Sono (R$35–R$45/US$18–US$23/£9.50–£12 per person). Transportation is by jeep and includes several stops.

HORSEBACK RIDING   **Paraty Tours,** Av. Roberto da Silveira 11 ((C) **024/3371-1327**), can organize horseback rides in the local hills. Groups can be as small as two people with a minimum of a 3-hour ride (R$90/US$45/£24 per person).

WHERE TO STAY

Paraty's historic center is jampacked with pousadas, similar to North American B&Bs. Of course, retrofitting modern accommodations into 18th-century buildings requires some adaptations. Don't expect fancy plumbing or high-speed Internet. Stairways are narrow and steep and there is no parking, as all cars have to remain outside the historic core. What you do get are charming bed-and-breakfasts in beautiful heritage buildings. Most of the pousadas really play up the history and are thus decorated with lovely antique furniture, comfortable lounges, and pleasant inner courtyards. Paraty is surprisingly affordable, even more so if you travel during the week instead of the weekend.

EXPENSIVE

Pousada Art Urquijo ⭐⭐⭐   Probably Paraty's most unusual pousada, Art Urquijo is a true labor of love by the owner, artist Luz Urquijo. Her bold and colorful artwork is prominently displayed throughout the pousada. Guests are greeted with classical music and asked to take their shoes off and help themselves to comfortable slippers. Luz has paid a lot of attention to detail and each of her six rooms is unique. Our favorite is Sofia; this room looks out over the rooftops toward the ocean and has a small deck. Probably the most unique room is Xul; as the ceilings are a bit low, Luz has used a Japanese bed (low on the floor) and mats and pillows to decorate. All rooms come with a very tiny private bathroom. Despite the absence of air-conditioning, the building is airy and cool. This pousada is not for people who have a difficulty with stairs; the higher floors can only be reached via a narrow winding staircase.

Rua Dona Geralda 79, Paraty, 23970-000 RJ. ⓒ/fax **024/3371-1362**. www.urquijo.com.br. 6 units (showers only). High season R$310–R$370 (US$155–US$185/£84–£100); low season R$290–R$330 (US$145–US$165/£78–£89). Rooms accommodate doubles only. V. No children under 12. **Amenities:** Bar; small pool; laundry service. *In room:* TV, minibar, no phone.

MODERATE
Pousada da Marquesa ✦ A lovely sprawling colonial mansion, Pousada da Marquesa offers affordable accommodations with some great amenities. The pousada actually consists of two buildings, the original main building and an annex along the side with its apartments and a large veranda overlooking the garden and swimming pool. These rooms are on ground level and perfect for those who don't want to climb the steep and narrow stairs. All rooms are simply and nicely furnished and the common rooms have beautiful antiques. A swimming pool and garden offer a perfect refuge on hot summer days.

Rua Dona Geralda 99, Paraty, 23970-000 RJ. ⓒ **024/3371-1263**. Fax 024/3371-1299. www.pousadamarquesa. com.br. 28 units (showers only). Dec–Mar R$300–R$340 (US$150–US$170/£81–£92) double; Apr–Nov R$190 (US$95/£51) double. Extra person 30%–50% extra. Children 6 and under stay free in parent's room. MC, V. Free street parking. **Amenities:** Bar; pool; laundry service. *In room:* A/C, TV, minibar, safe.

Pousada Porto Imperial One of the largest pousadas in the city center, Porto Imperial still feels like a small inn, despite its 51 rooms. The decorations throughout the pousada are quite impressive, blending antique furniture with modern folk art and tropical colors. In contrast, the rooms are very simply decorated with plain wooden furniture and bedding. The inner courtyard hides a lovely garden and swimming pool as well as a sauna.

Rua Tenente Francisco Antonio s/n (across from the Matriz church), Paraty, 23970-000 RJ. ⓒ **024/3371-2323**. Fax 024/3371-2111. www.portotel.com.br. 51 units. Low season R$200 (US$100/£54) standard double; R$240 (US$120/ £65) superior double. High season R$320 (US$160/£86) standard double; R$425 (US$213/£115) superior double. Children 2–12 R$40 (US$20/£11). AE, DC, MC, V. Free street parking. **Amenities:** Pool; sauna; limited room service; laundry. *In room:* A/C, TV, dataport, minibar, safe.

WHERE TO DINE
Arco da Velha COFFEE SHOP For your morning shot of caffeine or afternoon aperitif (or vice versa, depending on your preference), try this lovely coffee/antiques/ cigar shop. It's the perfect place to sit back and have a drink or a bite and rest your legs from wandering the cobblestones. Besides a delicious sweets menu, Arco da Velha also has an extensive cigar and whiskey collection, and while you're there you can browse the lovely store.

Rua Samuel Costa 176. ⓒ **024/3371-2546**. Everything under R$15 (US$7.50/£4), except for the cigars. No credit cards. Daily 10am–8pm.

Banana da Terra BRAZILIAN This beautiful little restaurant on one of Paraty's side streets offers exotic combinations of seafood and tropical ingredients. *Ponta Negra* is a fabulous fish dish served in a coconut sauce with shrimp. Another dish stars the lowly squid dolled up with a banana-and-cheese stuffing and served in coconut milk.

Another seafood favorite is the risotto with squid, crab, and prawns spiced with ginger and chutney. Desserts include banana sweets or baked banana.

Rua Dr. Samuel Costa 198. ② **024/3371-1725.** Main courses R$21–R$48 (US$8.75–US$20/£4.40–£10) for 2. AE, DC, MC. Wed–Mon noon–4pm and 7pm–midnight. In the off season closed for lunch on Mon and Wed–Thurs.

Kontiki SEAFOOD   If you thought only millionaires got to go for lunch on a private island, you're missing out. Kontiki restaurant is only a 10-minute boat ride from Paraty, on the tiny Ilha Duas Irmãs (two sisters island). In the daytime, the restaurant operates a shuttle service from the pier in Paraty. Just ask for the Kontiki transfer. In the evenings the restaurant will only open with a minimum of 10 people (in total) so call in your reservations and they will confirm if there's enough to open the restaurant. The menu is Mediterranean seafood, including lots of fresh prawns, crab, and fish. Pastas with seafood are also a good option as well as the authentic Spanish *paella,* a saffron rice dish with meat and seafood. The restaurant's two large verandas look out over the bay and the mainland. In the daytime showers are available in case you want to rinse off after a swim.

Ilha Duas Irmãs. ② **022/3371-1666.** Main courses R$34–R$68 (US$17–US$34/£9–£18). MC, V. In the low season Mon–Tues and Fri–Sun 10am–5:30pm; daily 10am–5:30pm in summer.

Restaurante Refúgio BRAZILIAN   A refuge indeed, Restaurante Refúgio is tucked away from the busy streets and offers a large patio overlooking the harbor of Paraty. The specialty here is seafood. As an appetizer, try the *camarão casadinho* (a large deep-fried prawn stuffed with a spicy farofa and dried shrimp filling), a regional specialty found only in Paraty. For a main course, try the fish or seafood moquecas (stews with coconut milk and palm oil).

Praça do Porto 1, on the waterfront. ② **022/3371-2447.** Main courses R$25–R$38 (US$11–US$16/£5.50–£8). DC, MC, V. Daily noon–11pm.

PARATY AFTER DARK

Paraty is not a wild party town (that's Búzios). The crowd's a bit older, the nightlife more laid-back. Enjoy some live music, have some drinks, and chat with the other folks who are quite likely visiting as well.

One of the more popular live-music venues is the **Café Paraty,** Rua do Comércio 253 (② **024/3371-1464**). It bills itself as a restaurant—and the food is pretty decent—but the place really gets hopping later in the evening, after 10pm or so. The restaurant has a small stage and the excellent bands usually play covers of popular Brazilian music. Daily 9am to midnight.

Moments Cachaça Festival

The region around Paraty is very well known for its cachaça (also known as *pinga*), the Brazilian booze made from sugar cane. There are several distilleries nearby, and each year, on the third weekend of August, the city celebrates the Festival da Pinga. Events include live music and lots and lots of tastings. *Tip:* If you miss the festival, make sure to stop at the **Emporio da Cachaça,** a specialty store with over 300 types of cachaça from all over Brazil. Rua dr. Samuel Costa 22 (② **024/3371-6329**).

Festivals Galore

Paraty is trying to establish itself as the Festival Town (see above for the Cachaça Festival). So far the town has very successfully started up a writer's festival, flippantly referred to as the FLIP (Festa Literária Internacional de Paraty). This event takes place in early July and includes numerous well-known foreign authors. For more details on upcoming FLIPs see www.flip.org.br. Book early if you plan to attend the FLIP! This event has quickly become the toast of the town and it's even outselling New Year's or carnival! In the third week of October, the city hosts a small but well attended International Film Festival. Contact the tourist information office (✆ 024/3371-1222) for details.

Another popular spot in the evenings is **Porto da Pinga,** Rua da Matriz 12 (✆ **024/9907-4370**). This bistro specializes in local cachaças. Live music nightly; a great spot to go and try some of the regionally produced firewater. Should you find one you particularly like, you can pick up some extra to take home from their on-site *cachaçaria.* Another restaurant doing double duty as a bar is the **Margarida Café,** Praça do Chafariz (✆ **024/3371-2441**). Both the restaurant and bar are very nice and on weekends there is always live Brazilian music, a perfect spot to enjoy a nightcap after dinner.

7

Settling into São Paulo

Look out the window as your plane descends to São Paulo's airport, and you'll see nothing but high-rises as far as the eye can see. It's a truly awesome sight.

Now the largest metropolis in South America—and, with 17 million people spread over 3,000 square miles, the third-largest city in the world—São Paulo nevertheless sprang from humble beginnings. In 1554, Jesuit priests founded a mission on a small hill, strategically close to the River Tietê. The mission developed into a small trading post and then, in the 17th and early 18th century, into a jumping-off point for Bandeirante expeditions traveling into the interior. In 1711 the little market town was incorporated as the city of São Paulo. The seeds of its future prosperity showed up just 12 years later with the arrival of the first coffee plants in Brazil.

The climate and soil surrounding São Paulo turned out to be perfect for coffee. With the arrival of the railway in 1867, large-scale cultivation exploded. São Paulo became one of the largest coffee exporters in the world.

When slavery was abolished in Brazil in 1888, coffee growers started looking toward immigrant labor. Italians and Japanese and, later, eastern Europeans, Spanish, Portuguese, and Germans, made the trek to São Paulo. To this day São Paulo remains the most culturally diverse city in Brazil.

In the mid-1950s São Paulo surpassed Rio in population and kept growing. Foreign investment by car companies such as Ford, GM, and Volkswagen transformed the city into South America's largest car manufacturer.

Unfortunately, little foresight and only rudimentary planning were devoted to the growth of the city. So although wages are the highest in the country, São Paulo's traffic regularly snarls into nearly endless traffic jams.

Prospective visitors often hear of this chaos and shy away from Brazil's big city, which is a shame. Visitors to São Paulo get all the benefits of a sophisticated, cosmopolitan city—they can eat at the finest restaurants in Brazil, shop at boutiques that even New York doesn't have, browse high-end art galleries, check out top-name Brazilian bands almost any night of the week, and take advantage of one of Brazil's most dynamic nightlife scenes to party until the wee-est of hours. And they can do all this, without ever experiencing the big drawback to this city, which is traffic.

The challenge to living in São is the commute. Visitors get a free pass. Stay in the Jardins, Higienópolis, or Centro, and all the sights and shops and galleries and restaurants are within easy reach. The word *commute* need never enter your consciousness.

Best of all, time in São Paulo is a chance to get to know that subspecies of Brazilian known as the Paulista. They're proud of their work ethic and their "un-Brazilian" efficiency. Lacking beaches and mountains, Paulistas have devoted themselves

entirely to urban pursuits. They domi-
nate Brazilian politics. They run Brazilian
business. Dining out is an almost religious observance. And in São Paulo, the
music and nightlife never end.

1 São Paulo Essentials

ARRIVING

BY PLANE Most international airlines fly through São Paulo. Even those heading for Rio often change planes or stop in São Paulo first. There are two main airports. International flights arrive at **Guarulhos Airport** (© 011/6445-2945), 30km (19 miles) northeast of the city. Paulistas will also refer to this airport as Cumbica. São Paulo has a duty-free shop upon arrival **before clearing Customs,** where you can purchase up to US$500 (£270) of goods. Once you have cleared Customs you can change money or traveler's checks or use an ATM to obtain cash in Reais (R$). The **American Express** office is open daily from 6:30am to 10:30pm and is located in Terminal 1 arrivals. The **Banco do Brasil** charges a US$20/£11) flat rate for traveler's check transactions and US$5/£2.70 flat rate for cash transactions. ATMs compatible with Visa/PLUS are in Terminal 1 arrivals.

From **Guarulhos Airport** to the city, travelers can either take a taxi or a bus. Prepaid taxi fares are available with **Taxi Guarucoop** (© 011/6440-7070). Sample fares: Congonhas Airport R$84 (US$42/£23), São Paulo Centro and Tietê R$66 (US$33/£18), and Jardims and Avenida Paulista R$74 (US$36/£20). One can also take a regular metered taxi; if traffic is good, these taxis are a little cheaper, but when traffic backs up the prepaid ride turns out to be a much better deal.

The **Airport Service** (© 011/6445-2505) operates four different shuttle bus routes: to Congonhas Airport, to Praça da República, to Avenida Paulista (stopping at major hotels along the street), and to the Rodoviario Tietê (bus station). Cost is R$24 (US$12/£6.50), and each route takes about 50 minutes (if traffic is good). Shuttles depart daily every 30 minutes from 6am to 11pm, and then hourly overnight.

Congonhas, São Paulo's domestic airport, is within the city limits south of Centro. It is used by seven national airlines for their domestic flights. From Congonhas it is a 15- to 20-minute taxi ride to Jardins or Avenida Paulista. Prepaid taxis to Centro or Jardins cost R$28 to R$38 (US$14–US$19/£7.50–£10). A regular metered taxi can cost as little as R$24 (US$12/£6.50) or as much as R$40 (US$20/£11), depending on traffic. The **Airport Service** (© 011/6445-2505) operates shuttle buses to Congonhas Airport, Praça da República, and the Rodoviaria Tietê (bus station). Cost is R$24 (US$12/£6.50), and the trip takes about an hour. Shuttles depart daily about every 30 minutes from 6am to 11pm, and then hourly overnight.

BY BUS São Paulo has four bus terminals (*rodoviaria*). All are connected to the Metrô system. **Barra Funda,** near the Barra Funda Metrô, serves buses to the interior of São Paulo, northern Paraná, and Mato Grosso. **Bresser,** next to the Bresser Metrô, provides buses to Minas Gerais. **Jabaquara,** next to the Jabaquara Metrô, provides transportation to Santos and the south coast. The **Rodoviaria Tietê** (for buses to Rio and connections to Paraguay, Uruguay, and Argentina) is by far the largest and most important bus station, located on the Tietê Metrô stop. Buses depart from here to Rio, and most major Brazilian cities, as well as international destinations. The general information number is © 011/3235-0322.

São Paulo Airport Woes

Over the last year, the airport situation in São Paulo has been, to say the least, chaotic—delays, cancellations, work-to-rule actions, and more. With every airline in the country using São Paulo as its hub, the small domestic airport of Congonhas has hopelessly outgrown its facilities; its short runways mean planes often can't take off or land in bad weather, which only adds to the chaos. Major renovations and runway repairs have been undertaken, but in the meantime the government has also imposed flight restrictions, and transferred a large number of domestic flights to the large international airport of Guarulhos. This has the advantage of plenty of space and modern airport facilities. The drawback is that Garulhos is located far outside the city limits, and São Paulo traffic can be a nightmare. On a rainy Thursday night around rush hour it took us a full 2 hours to drive from Congonhas to Guarulhos.

The upshot of all this is that if you have the option of booking a connection through another city, avoid São Paulo altogether. If you do have to connect through São Paulo, allow plenty of time for your connections (at least 2 hours, 3 if you have to shuttle during rush hour between Congonhas and Guarulhos. Finally, try to schedule your flight for early in the day, as delays to pile up and problems compound as the day goes on.

VISITOR INFORMATION

São Paulo's visitor information booths are of limited use. They offer a free city map and a city booklet with limited sightseeing information (but 30 pages of ads for escort services). Staff will attempt to answer your questions, but there's little information to pick up and browse.

Both the city of São Paulo and the state of São Paulo provide tourist information at Guarulhos. The state info booths, **SET** (✆ 011/6445-2380), can be found in Terminals 1 and 2 in the arrivals section and are open daily from 7am to 9pm. The city's booth, **CIT,** is open Monday through Friday from 8am to 10pm and Saturday and Sunday from 9am to 9pm. Booths in Terminals 1 and 2 are open daily from 7am to 7pm. **CIT** (at the airport or in the city) often has copies of the excellent free map, *Mapa das Artes,* which not only shows streets and subways but also gives the location of the city's most interesting public and private art galleries.

The **CIT booths** (Central de Informações Turisticas) are located downtown at **Praça da República,** in front of Rua 7 de Abril (✆ 011/3231-2922; daily 9am–6pm); and **Avenida Paulista,** in front of Trianon Park (✆ 011/3251-0970; Mon–Fri 9am–6pm, Sat–Sun 10am–4pm). The **SET** (State Information Booths) can be found at **Rua XV de Novembro** 347, Centro (✆ 011/3231-44-5), open daily from 9am to 6pm, and across from the Teatro Municipal in the **Shopping Light,** Rua Coronel Xavier de Toledo 23, Centro (✆ 011/6445-2380), open Monday through Friday only from 9am to 6pm.

CITY LAYOUT

Some 17 million people make their home in and around São Paulo. It's a daunting number. But for all its ridiculous sprawl there's a charm to South America's biggest city, and getting around the areas of interest is neither difficult nor especially stressful. For a more detailed description of São Paulo's neighborhoods, see "Neighborhoods to Explore," in chapter 8.

CENTRO   The old heart of the city stands around **Praça da Sé,** atop what was once a small hill circled by a pair of small rivers. Little remains of that original city; Paulistas take a manic joy in knocking buildings down almost as soon as they go up. The neo-Gothic **Catedral da Sé** dates to only 1912. Evidence of the city's age can be seen only in downtown's narrow and irregular streets. **Rua Direita,** São Paulo's original main street, leads through this maze to a viaduct crossing over a busy freeway that now occupies the Anhangabaú valley and goes into the "newer" section of the old town. This area, centered on leafy green **Praça República,** contains government buildings plus office buildings from the '20s to the '40s (and later). Back at the edge of the Anhangabaú valley stands the ornate **Teatro Municipal,** a Parisian-style opera house still heavily used for concerts and theater. The Anhangabaú River, which once separated the two halves of downtown, was long ago filled and covered with a freeway, which in turn has been covered over by a broad and open city plaza—the **Parque Anhangabaú**—which effectively rejoins the two halves of downtown. Together, these two halves of the old inner city are known as **Centro.**

HIGIENÓPOLIS   Immediately west of Centro is one of São Paulo's original upscale suburbs, **Higienópolis.** Though long since swallowed up in the city, Higienópolis remains a green and leafy enclave with some good restaurants and the city's **Museum of Brazilian Art,** also known as **FAAP.**

LIBERDADE & BIXIGA   To the south of Centro are two turn-of-the-20th-century working-class neighborhoods long adopted by immigrants. Due south of Centro is **Liberdade,** said to have the largest **Japanese** population of any city outside Japan. In addition to great food and interesting shopping, Liberdade is also home to the **Museum of Japanese Immigration.** Southwest of Centro lies **Bela Vista,** more often referred to as **Bixiga.** This is São Paulo's **Little Italy.** Bela Vista in turn butts up against São Paulo's proudest street, the **Avenida Paulista.**

AVENIDA PAULISTA   Long and straight and set on a ridge above surrounding neighborhoods, the **Avenida Paulista** boasts rank upon rank of skyscrapers, the headquarters of the city's banking and financial interests. On the adjacent side streets are numerous hotels catering to business travelers. Halfway along the street is São Paulo's top-notch **Museum of Art,** known by its Portuguese acronym as **MASP.** Avenida Paulista marks the border between the old working-class areas and the new middle-class neighborhoods.

JARDINS   Extending southwest from Avenida Paulista are a series of upscale neighborhoods developed in the '20s according to the best Garden City principles and accordingly named gardens (*jardins*) to emphasize their green and leafy separation from the gritty urban core. Though each area has a particular name—**Jardim Paulista, Jardim America, Cerqueira Cesar, Jardim Europa**—Paulistas tend to refer to them as a group as **Jardins.**

What these areas offer is a bit of calm, some terrific restaurants, and the best shopping in São Paulo. Particularly noteworthy is the **Rua Augusta,** which intersects the

Avenida Paulista at the Consolação Metrô stop and continues southwest through the heart of the Jardins. The few square blocks where **Rua Augusta** is intersected by **Alameda Lorena** and **Rua Oscar Freire** is the apex of the city's upscale shopping scene, São Paulo's Rodeo Drive.

Rua Augusta continues on straight through the Jardins, changing names as it goes to **Avenida Columbia** and then **Avenida Europa** and finally **Avenida Cidade Jardim.** At this point it intersects with **Avenida Brigadeiro Faria Lima.** Though a much less fashionable street, Avenida Brig. Faria Lima is home to a number of large shopping malls; the most important is Shopping Iguatemi. Following Avenida Brig. Faria Lima northwest leads to another Jardim-like area called **Pinheiros;** going the opposite direction leads to **Itaim Bibi** and then to a fun and slightly funky area of restaurants, clubs, and cafes called **Vila Olímpia.**

THE PARK   The last key element to São Paulo is a green space—**Ibirapuera Park.** Located immediately south of Jardim Paulista, Ibirapuera is to São Paulo what Central Park is to New York. It's a place for strolling, lazy sun-tanning, outdoor concerts, and the view to a couple of the city's top cultural facilities, including the **Modern Art Museum** and the **São Paulo Bienal.**

GETTING AROUND

São Paulo has a convenient public transportation system, and many of its tourist-oriented neighborhoods are compact enough for a stroll. However, at night it's safest to take a taxi to and from your destination.

ON FOOT   Though São Paulo itself is huge, many of the neighborhoods that make up the city are compact enough to be easily explored on foot. This is especially true of the more pleasant neighborhoods such as Centro, Higienópolis, Jardins, Vila Madalena, and Ibirapuera. During the day the city is quite safe; in the evening the safest neighborhoods are Jardins, Higienópolis, and the residential areas of the city. Best avoided are the quiet side streets of Centro, particularly the empty shopping streets around Praça Sé, Bexiga, and around Luz station.

BY SUBWAY   The Metrô is the easiest way to get around São Paulo. There are three lines: the North-South line, East-West line, and the line that travels underneath the Avenida Paulista. The two main lines converge at Sé station, the busiest station of all. These two lines run daily from 5am until midnight. The line under Avenida Paulista meets the North-South line at Paraiso and Ana Rosa stations and runs daily from 6am to 10pm. It is usually a lot quicker to take the Metrô as close as possible to your destination—even if it means a bit more of a walk or a short taxi ride—than taking the bus all the way. Metrô tickets cost R$2.30 (US$1.15/£.60) for a single ride. For more information contact © **011/3286-0111.**

BY BUS   Good as Sao Paulo's Metrô is, there are some places you can only get to by bus. São Paulo buses are plentiful and frequent, but the city's sprawling layout and

---

(Tips   Watch Out for Rogue Motorcyclists

São Paulo has the highest number of motorcycles in the country, most of them used by couriers. Be careful; even when traffic is backed up motorcycles will ride at high speeds weaving in between stopped cars.

lack of landmarks can make the system hard to navigate. The routing information on the front and sides of the buses works the same as in Rio (see "By Bus" in chapter 4 for details). A few useful routes are listed below (more are given with particular attractions and restaurants), but there will be many others running along similar routes. Buses cost R$2.30 (US$1.15/£.60), and you pay as you board through the front of the bus. Bus drivers generally won't stop unless you wave your hand to flag them down. Some useful routes are:

- No. 702P, Belém-Pinheiros: From Praça da República along Rua Augusta, then north on Avenida Brigadeiro Faria Lima into Pinheiros.
- No. 701U, Jaçanã-Butantã-USP: From Praça República along Avenida Ipiranga, Rua da Consolação, and Avenida Rebouças to Buntantã and the University of São Paulo.
- No. 5100, 5131: From Brigadeiro Metrô station, along Avenida Brig. Luis Antonio to Ibirapuera Park.
- No. 5175, 5178: From Ibirapuera Park (opposite main gate) along Avenida Pedro Alvares Cabral to Brigadeiro Metrô station.

The bottom line? If possible we recommend going by Metrô.

BY TAXI   Taxis are a great way to get around São Paulo, and an absolute must late at night. You can hail one anywhere on the street, and taxi stands are usually found on main intersections, next to malls, squares, and parks. To order a taxi at a specific time, call a radio taxi. **Rádio Táxi Vermelho e Branco** (the name means "red-and-white") can be reached at © 011/3146-4000. Cost depends on traffic, so the following prices are only guidelines: From Centro to Avenida Paulista, R$15 (US$7.50/£4); from Avenida Paulista to Vila Olímpia, R$26 to R$32 (US$13–US$16/£7–£8.50); from Avenida Paulista to Higienópolis, R$18 (US$9/£5).

BY CAR   Driving in São Paulo is for the daring, the foolish, or the infinitely patient; traffic is always chaotic and frequently snarled and slow, particularly during rainstorms when the streets flood. Oh, and parking is expensive and difficult to find. São Paulo's appalling traffic has given rise to the world's largest fleet of civilian helicopters that ferry commuting executives in from their suburban homes.

For those who do want to give it a try, several car companies are listed below under "Fast Facts: São Paulo." Note that in an attempt to declog the streets the city has brought in a traffic rotation system. Cars with a license plate that ends in 1 or 2 are not allowed to drive in the city on Monday; plates ending in 3 or 4 are banned on Tuesday, no plates ending in 5 or 6 on Thursday, and on Friday 9s and 0s are off the streets. These restrictions are in effect between 7 and 10am and 5 and 8pm. Service vehicles are excluded from this regulation. Fines are steep, and photo radar and police keep track of cars as they enter the city.

FAST FACTS: São Paulo

American Express Hotel Sheraton Mofarrej, Alameda Santos 1437, Cerqueira Cesar (© 011/3741-8478), Monday to Friday 9:30am to 5:30pm; and Guarulhos International Airport (© 0800/702-0777), daily 6:30am to 10pm.
Area Codes The area code for São Paulo is 011.

Banks & Currency Exchange Most banks are located on the Avenida Paulista. **Banco do Brasil,** Av. Paulista 2163 (ⓒ **011/3066-9322**); Rua São João 32, Centro (ⓒ **011/3234-1646**); and Guarulhos International Airport, daily 6am to 10pm (ⓒ **011/6445-2223**). **Bank Boston,** Av. Paulista 800 (ⓒ **011/3285-3477**), Monday to Friday 11am to 3pm. **Citibank,** Av. Paulista 1111 (ⓒ **011/5576-1000**), Monday to Friday 11am to 3pm.

Business Hours See "Fast Facts: Brazil" (p. 38).

Car Rentals **Avis,** Aeroporto de Congonhas (ⓒ **011/5090-9300**); **Hertz,** Rua da Consolação 307 (ⓒ **0800/701-7300**); **Localiza,** Rua da Consolação 419 (ⓒ **0800/ 992-000** or 011/3231-3055); and **Unidas,** Rua da Consolação 355 (ⓒ **0800/121-121** or 011/4001-2222). Rates start at R$90 (US$45/£24) per day for a small (Fiat Palio, Ford Ka) car with air-conditioning and unlimited mileage. Insurance adds R$30 (US$15/£8) per day.

Consulates *Australia,* Al. Min. Rocha Azevedo 456 (ⓒ **011/3085-6247**); *Canada,* Av. das Nações Unidas 12901 (ⓒ **011/5509-4321**); *United States,* Rua Henri Dunant 500, Chácara Santo Antonio (ⓒ **011/5186-7000**); *Great Britain,* Rua Ferreira de Araujo 741 (ⓒ **011/3094-2700**); *New Zealand,* Al. Campinas 579, 15th floor (ⓒ **011/288-0307**).

Dentist Dr. Marcelo Erlich, open 24 hours, English spoken, Rua Sergipe 401, suite 403, Higienópolis (ⓒ **011/3214-1332** or 011/9935-8666).

Electricity Generally 110V; some hotels have both 110 and 220 volts.

Emergencies Police ⓒ **190**; Fire Brigade and Ambulance ⓒ **193.**

Hospitals **Albert Einstein Hospital,** Av. Albert Einstein 627, Morumbi (ⓒ **011/ 3747-0307**); and **Hospital das Clinicas,** 255 Av. Doutor Eneias de Carvalho Aguiar s/n (ⓒ **011/3069-6000**). Ask your hotel for a referral to the nearest clinic.

Internet Access Internet access in São Paulo is easy to find in bookstores and Internet cafes. In Pinheiros: **FNAC Centro Cultural,** Praça dos Omaguás (ⓒ **011/ 4501-3000**), daily 10am to 10pm, R$12 (US$6/£3.25) per hour. Very inexpensive are the Monkey franchises. You'll find one just off Avenida Paulista: **Monkey,** Alameda Santos 1217, corner of Pamplona (ⓒ **011/3253-8627**), daily 9am to 6am, R$4 (US$2/£1) per hour. Another **Monkey Cyber Café** is conveniently located across from the Shopping Higienópolis, Rua Aracaju 66 (ⓒ **011/3668-5674**). Monday to Saturday 9:30am to 10pm and Sunday 1 to 9pm. R$4 (US$2/£1) per hour.

Laundry & Dry Cleaning A laundromat is called a *lavanderia.* For dry cleaning ask for *a seco.* **Quality Cleaners** does dry cleaning and laundry, Rua Jose Maria Lisboa 879, Jardim Paulista (ⓒ **011/3885-9772**). **Bright Laundrettes** has a 2-hour express service or an overnight service, Al. Joaquim Eugenio Lima 1696, Cerqueira Cesar (ⓒ **011/3887-0973**).

Mail Downtown: Rua Libero Badero 595, Centro (ⓒ **011/3838-7009**), and Rua Haddock Lobo 566, Cerqueira Cesar (ⓒ **011/3838-8632**). The branch at the international airport of Guarulhos is open 24 hours.

Pharmacies Pharmacies are called farmacia or drogaria in Portuguese. The following are open 24 hours: **Drogaria São Paulo,** Rua Augusta 2699, Cerqueira Cesar (ⓒ **011/3083-0319**); **Drogasil,** Av. Brigadeiro Faria Lima 2726, Jardim

Europa (© **011/3812-6276**); and **Droga Raia**, Av. São Luis 35, Centro (© **011/ 3259-3311**). Most pharmacies will deliver 24 hours a day, usually for a small surcharge (R$4–R$10/US$2–US$5/£1–£3); contact your hotel's front desk to place an order at the nearest one.

Police Emergency number © **190**. Tourist Police, Av. São Luis 92 (1 block from Praça da República), Centro (© **011/3214-0209**), and Rua São Bento 380, fifth floor, Centro (© **011/3107-5642**).

Safety During the day the tourist areas are generally safe for walking; in the evening the safest neighborhoods are Jardins, Higienópolis, and the residential areas of the city. At night it's best to avoid the quiet side streets of Centro, particularly the empty shopping streets around Praça da Sé and Bixiga. The area around the Praça da Luz is definitely to be avoided after dark. At night, traveling by taxi is strongly recommended—don't rely on public transportation. The U.S. State Department has reported incidences of armed robbery and widespread pickpocketing in São Paulo, though this has not been our experience. As in any large metropolitan area with great disparities between rich and poor, it's wise to observe common-sense precautions: Don't flash jewelry or cash, and stick to well-lit and well-traveled thoroughfares.

Taxes The city of São Paulo charges a 5% accommodations tax, collected by the hotel operators. This amount will be added to your bill. There are no other taxes on retail items or goods.

Time Zone São Paulo is 3 hours behind GMT (as is Rio de Janeiro).

Visa Renewal You can extend your visa at the Policia Federal, Av. Prestes Maia 700, Centro (© **011/223-7177**, ext. 231); Monday to Friday 10am to 4pm. The fee is R$63 (US$32/£17), and you may need to show evidence of sufficient funds to cover your stay as well as a return ticket.

Weather São Paulo's summers, December through March, are hot and humid. Temperatures rise to the high 90s (mid-30s Celsius). In the spring and fall, the temperatures stay between the high 70s and 90s (mid-20s to mid-30s Celsius). In the winter, June through August, it can cool off to a minimum of 59°F (15°C), but during the day temperatures can sometimes rise to the 70s or mid-80s (20s°C). Those traveling to São Paulo between May and September should bring some cold-weather clothes, the equivalent of what someone would wear in New York or London in the fall. Most rain tends to fall in the summer (Dec–Feb); January is especially wet. When it rains heavily the city is prone to flooding, particularly the area around the Tietê River.

2 Where to Stay

As the financial and business hub of Brazil, São Paulo has many excellent hotels at very affordable rates. Hotels tend to cluster around the financial district of the Avenida Paulista, and in the upscale shopping and restaurant district Jardins. Jardins is one of the safest areas of the city, and even at night one can comfortably go for a stroll. Women traveling alone will feel completely comfortable in this part of town.

São Paulo attracts business travelers Monday through Friday and then sits empty from Friday afternoon to Monday morning. Hotels try to lure weekend travelers with museum or shopping packages, but capacity still far exceeds demand and prices drop up to 50% or even more. Hotels will often throw in free breakfasts and dinners, and checkout can be as late as 6pm on a Sunday evening.

Many visitors to São Paulo prefer to stay in an apart-hotel. These hotels usually offer suites: one- or two-bedroom apartments with fully furnished kitchens. The benefit is much lower prices; even the most expensive apart-hotels are still significantly cheaper than a luxury hotel, and the units are much larger than a standard hotel room. You do give up a few of the amenities that you would get in a top-notch hotel, but the majority of apart-hotels still offer breakfast, parking, a small gym, sauna, and swimming pool as well as limited room service.

CENTRO

Staying in Centro you're close to the fun and movement of downtown; many of the attractions are within walking distance, and public transit to other regions is very accessible. The drawback is that at night, Centro empties out. Dining and nightlife options are limited, and parts of downtown transform into red-light districts, particularly around the Rua Augusta and Praça da República. However, the savings can be significant, especially on weekends when hotels often slash their prices in half.

EXPENSIVE

Bourbon São Paulo Business Hotel ⭐ *Value*   An elegant, slightly Parisian-style building on the outside, on the inside the Bourbon has been kept thoroughly up-to-date and comfortable. Superior rooms come in two types. Those with a queen-size bed are of a good size, with a small breakfast table and full-length mirror. Bathrooms are large and bright, but feature only showers. Superior rooms with two single beds are similar but a little smaller. Both room types unfortunately lack any kind of desk. Junior suites are quite spacious, with a queen-size bed and an anteroom set up as a small office, plus a sizable bathroom with bathtubs and showers. Depending on demand the Bourbon often reduces listed rates by up to 50%.

Av. Vieira de Carvalho 99, Centro, 01210-010 SP. © **0800/118-181** or 011/3337-2000. Fax 011/3337-1414. www. bourbon.com.br. 129 units. R$200 (US$100/£54) double; R$250 (US$125/£67) junior suite. 50% discount weekends and slow periods. Extra person add about 25%. Children 6 and under stay free in parent's room. AE, DC, MC, V. Parking 1 block away, R$15 (US$7.50/£4) per day. Metrô: República. **Amenities:** Restaurant; bar; weight room; sauna; business center (free Internet); room service; laundry; dry cleaning; 7 nonsmoking floors. *In room:* A/C, TV, free high-speed Internet, minibar, fridge, hair dryer, safe.

Normandie Design Hotel ⭐ *Finds*   Unfortunately the location is not top-notch, especially at night this area is not great but the hotel makes up for a lot: sleek, stylish, cool—from the moment you walk through the large metal doors you know this place is different. The lobby is completely white: white counters, white bar, white floor, and white ceiling, with just touches of chrome throughout. The rooms, in contrast, have black accents; the curtains, the furniture, the headstand, even the bedding are all black, although the staff will substitute a white duvet if it's all too black for you. The bathrooms are beautiful and spacious, with counters of elegant marble. As for the suites, the master suite with its king-size bed and sitting room is worth the extra money. Rooms for travelers with disabilities or allergies are available.

Av. Ipiranga 1187, Centro, São Paulo, 01039-000 SP. © **0800/99-1902** or 011/3311-9855. Fax 011/228-3157. www.normandiedesign.com.br. 171 units (showers only). R$135 (US$67/£36) standard double; R$200–R$250

Where to Stay & Dine in São Paulo Centro

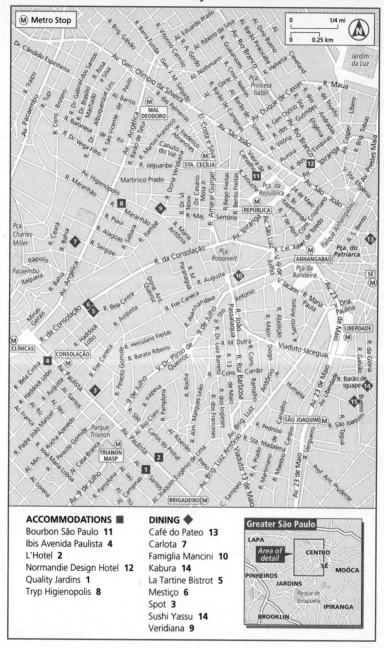

ACCOMMODATIONS ■

Bourbon São Paulo **11**
Ibis Avenida Paulista **4**
L'Hotel **2**
Normandie Design Hotel **12**
Quality Jardins **1**
Tryp Higienopolis **8**

DINING ◆

Café do Pateo **13**
Carlota **7**
Famiglia Mancini **10**
Kabura **14**
La Tartine Bistrot **5**
Mestiço **6**
Spot **3**
Sushi Yassu **14**
Veridiana **9**

(US$100 US$125/£54–£67) suite double. Internet and weekend specials offer standard rooms as low as R$120 (US$60/£32). Extra person R$60 (US$30/£16). Children 5 and under stay free in parent's room; over 5 add 25%. AE, DC, MC, V. Parking R$15 (US$7.50/£4) per day. Metrô: República. **Amenities:** Restaurant; bar; concierge; tour desk; car rental; business center; 24-hr. room service; laundry; nonsmoking rooms. *In room:* A/C, TV, dataport, minibar, fridge, hair dryer, safe.

AVENIDA PAULISTA

The hotels around Avenida Paulista cater to business travelers and executives who spend most of their time in the city's financial district. They're high-end and expense account–friendly. However, on weekends the rates drop almost in half; visitors can treat themselves to a great hotel at a bargain price. Metrô connections make it easy to travel back and forth from this area. From Paulista it is only a short walk or quick cab ride to the upscale neighborhood of Jardins (see below).

VERY EXPENSIVE

L'Hotel ★★★   Just off the Avenida Paulista, L'Hotel is one of São Paulo's most elegant boutique hotels. The plain and modern facade does not do justice to the chic interior. L'Hotel's interior is warm and welcoming and with only 80 rooms, the service is attentive and friendly. Rooms are luxuriously furnished with elegant antique furniture, a queen- or king-size bed with top-quality linen, goose down pillows and a pleasant well-lit work space. Bathrooms feature bathtubs, lovely Spanish marble finishings, and high-end l'Occitane amenities. The suites feature a separate sitting room with a comfortable couch and armchair, a stereo, and cordless phone. There's a small but well-designed fitness center, a spa, a small heated indoor pool, and a business center. The hotel also has an excellent in-house bakery in case you want to grab a quick bite. Please note that the prices listed below are the high season rack rates. Call or e-mail for discount rates. Weekend packages, including welcome drink, can often be booked for as low as R$600 (US$300/£162) for 2 nights.

Alameda Campinas 266, Jardim Paulista, 01404-000 SP. (✆ **0800/13-0080** or 011/2183-0500. Fax 011/2183-0505. www.lhotel.com.br. 80 units. R$825 (US$412/£223) double; R$1,200 (US$600/£324) double suites. Children 12 and under stay free in parent's room. Extra person 25%. AE, DC, MC, V. Valet parking. Metrô: MASP. **Amenities:** Restaurant; bar; small indoor pool; fitness center; business center; 24-hr. room service; laundry; dry cleaning; nonsmoking floors. *In room:* A/C, TV, dataport, minibar, hair dryer, electronic safe.

EXPENSIVE

Quality Jardins ★   The Quality Jardins offers some of the best affordable accommodations just off the Avenida Paulista. Rooms are a cross between a studio and a regular hotel room, featuring a desk and TV on a swivel in order to separate the sitting area from the sleeping area. The furnishings are modern and pleasant with light colors, blond wood, and comfortable lighting. The hotel offers three categories of rooms: superior, deluxe, and premium. The difference is mainly in the improved bathroom amenities and the turndown service and bathrobe that come with the premium rooms. Unless you get a free upgrade, it's not worth the money. The hotel has a good-size fitness room with saunas and an outdoor pool.

Alameda Campinas 540, São Paulo, 01404-000 SP. (✆ **0800/555-855** or 011/2182-0400. Fax 011/2182-0401. www. atlanticahotels.com.br. 220 units (showers only). R$185–R$210 (US$92–US$105/£50–£57) superior double; R$215–R$245 (US$107–US$122/£58–£66) deluxe double; R$245–R$310 (US$122–US$155/£66–£84) premium double. Extra person add R$30 (US$15/£8). Children 5 and under stay free in parent's room. AE, DC, MC, V. Free parking. Metrô: Trianon-MASP. **Amenities:** Restaurant; indoor pool; health club; sauna; concierge; business center; room service; laundry; nonsmoking floors. *In room:* A/C, TV, dataport, minibar, hair dryer, safe.

MODERATE

Ibis Avenida Paulista *Value*   The Accor group's budget Ibis brand offers predictable but quality accommodations in the heart of the business district. All 236 rooms are standard, identically furnished with good firm double or twin beds, a desk, and a shower. Breakfast is not included but can be ordered at the restaurant for R$9 (US$4.50/£2.50). This is a nonsmoking hotel.

Av. Paulista 2355, Cerqueira Cesar, 01420-002 SP. © 011/3523-3000. Fax 011/3523-3030. www.accorhotels. com.br. 236 units. R$129 (US$65/£35) double. Children 12 and under stay free in parent's room. AE, DC, MC, V. Free parking. Metrô: Consolação. **Amenities:** Restaurant; limited room service; laundry; nonsmoking floor; rooms for those w/limited mobility. *In room:* A/C, TV, dataport, minibar, safe.

JARDINS

One of the most pleasant hotel neighborhoods in São Paulo, Jardins offers less traffic and streets lined with restaurants, shops, and cafes. Indeed, this area offers the best high-end shopping and some of the best restaurants and nightlife in the city. The disadvantage is you're not on a Metrô line. A bus to Avenida Paulista (and the Metrô) along Rua Augusta will take 15 to 25 minutes; a bus into Centro will take 20 to 45 minutes. The area is safe and pleasant at night.

VERY EXPENSIVE

Emiliano ✦✦✦   Though more expensive than almost any other hotel in São Paulo, the Emiliano is a bargain compared to what a room like this would cost in New York or Paris. It's five-star treatment all the way, from the welcome massage to the minibar stocked according to your preference, to the personalized selection of pillows, carefully fluffed and placed on your Egyptian cotton sheets. The Emiliano offers two types of rooms: deluxe studios and suites, The studios (really just a large room) are marginally cheaper, but is this really the time to skimp? The prime rooms are the fabulous, spacious suites. These come decorated with designer furniture and feature original artwork and the latest home entertainment electronics. The bed is king-size and the bathroom is a minispa in itself; toiletries are customized to your skin type and you can sit back and relax in the claw-foot tub, maybe watch a little TV, or contemplate life on your heated toilet seat.

Rua Oscar Freire 384, Cerqueira César, 01426-000 SP. © 011/3069-4369. Fax 011/3068-4398. www.emiliano. com.br. 57 units. R$800 (US$400/£216) double room; R$1,400 (US$700/£378) double suite. Special packages are available. Please check the website. Extra person add 30%. Children 10 and under stay free in parent's room. AE, DC, MC, V. Free parking. **Amenities:** Restaurant; upscale lobby bar; small exercise room; outstanding spa; concierge; business center; salon; 24-hr. room service; massage; babysitting service; laundry; dry cleaning; nonsmoking floors. *In room:* A/C, TV, dataport, minibar, hair dryer, safe.

Fasano ✦✦✦   The Fasano family, successful São Paulo restaurateurs, decided several years ago to apply their hospitality experience to the hotel industry. In 2003, the São Paulo Fasano opened its doors, followed in 2007 by the Rio de Janeiro Fasano (designed by Phillipe Starck, see p. 64). The hotel is decorated with elegant 1930s period furniture, combined with clean modern design elements. All 50 rooms and 10 suites are beautifully appointed with sober, modern furniture, hardwood floors, Persian rugs, Venetian blinds and feature a king-size bed with 500-thread Egyptian cotton sheets and goose down pillows. The white marble bathrooms feature deluxe touches such as l'Occitane amenities and a towel warmer. As you move up the categories, the rooms get progressively bigger and more luxurious. The deluxe room is bigger than the superior room and has a sitting area and a bathtub in addition to the shower. The suite is more than twice the size of the superior room and features a separate living room with a plasma TV and Bang & Olufsen sound system; the spacious bathroom also has a Jacuzzi tub. Of course in terms of food, guests are in excellent hands here. The hotel's signature restaurant, Fasano, is one of the top Italian restaurants in South America, and breakfast and room service are prepared by the chef of the Nonno Ruggero, the hotel's upscale trattoria.

Rua Vitório Fasano 88, Cerqueira César, 01426-000 SP. © **011/3896-4000.** Fax 011/3896-4155. www.fasano. com.br. 57 units. R$800 (US$400/£216) superior double room; R$990 (US$495/£243) deluxe double room; R$1,400 (US$700/£378) double suite. Extra person add 30%. Children 6 and under stay free in parent's room. AE, DC, MC, V. Free parking. **Amenities:** 2 restaurants; upscale jazz bar; small exercise room; small spa; concierge; business center; salon; 24-hr. room service; massage; babysitting service; laundry; dry cleaning; nonsmoking floors. *In room:* A/C, TV, dataport, minibar, hair dryer, safe.

EXPENSIVE

Mercure São Paulo Jardins 🖈   A pleasant modern hotel, everything is crisp and clean, the decoration Scandinavian modern with blond wood, simple design, and lots of light. Rooms are spacious with king-size beds, a couple of small sitting chairs, and a good-size maple-wood desk with desk lamp and phone and power jacks for laptops. Bathrooms have nice fixtures but are functionally compact. More than half the hotel rooms are nonsmoking. The leisure area is small, offering only an indoor pool and sauna, but the Mercure's location is excellent, only a hop and a skip to the Avenida Paulista and a 15-minute walk downhill to the best shopping and dining in Jardins.

Alameda Itu 1151, Cerqueira César, 01421-001 SP. © **0800/703-7000** or 011/3089-7555. Fax 011/3089-7550. www.accorhotels.com.br. 126 units (showers only). R$260 (US$130/£70) double weekdays; R$168 (US$84/£45) double weekends. No triple rooms are available. Children 10 and under stay free in parent's room. AE, DC, MC, V. Free parking. Metrô: Consolação. **Amenities:** Restaurant; laptop-friendly bar; small pool; 24-hr. room service; laundry; dry cleaning; nonsmoking floors. *In room:* A/C, TV, dataport, minibar, hair dryer, safe.

MODERATE

Quality Suites Imperial Hall 🖈🖈   On the corner of Oscar Freire and Consolação, the Imperial Hall sits in the heart of São Paulo's toniest neighborhood, surrounded by restaurants, designer boutiques, and trendy shops. The building is new, and the 190 rooms are modern and pleasantly furnished. Built with the business traveler in mind, the hotel offers firm beds, large closets, a small kitchen, in-room high-speed Internet, and a large desk with easy access to lots of plugs. The Master Rooms on the 13th to 19th floors feature balconies and a few perks such as bathrobes and clock radios. As they only cost a fraction more, they're worth reserving. There's also a floor exclusively for women travelers.

Rua da Consolação 3555, Jardins, São Paulo, 01416-001 SP. © **011/2137-4555.** Fax 011/2137-4560. www.atlantica hotels.com.br. 190 units. R$285 (US$143/£77) master R$215 (US$107/£58) double. Extra person add 25%. Children 6 and under stay free in parent's room. AE, DC, MC, V. Free parking. **Amenities:** Restaurant; rooftop pool; small weight room; sauna; spa; business center; 24-hr. room service; laundry; nonsmoking rooms; women-only floor. *In room:* A/C, TV, dataport, kitchen, safe.

Regent Park Hotel 🖈   This small apart-hotel is situated on one of the best-known streets in Jardins. The neighborhood is quite safe, and packed with shops, cafes, and restaurants. The majority of units in this hotel are one-bedroom suites, but two-bedroom suites are available as well. The furnishings are a little dated, with '80s rustic wood, but everything is very well maintained and clean, and all the suites have a full kitchen. The staff is exceptionally friendly and helpful, and business travelers will appreciate the small and efficient business center.

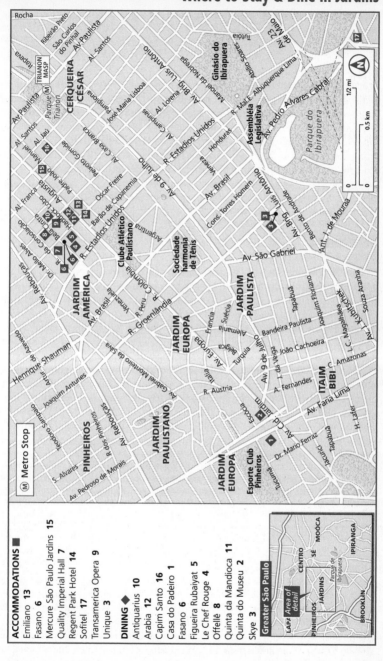

ACCOMMODATIONS ■

Emiliano **13**
Fasano **6**
Mercure São Paulo Jardins **15**
Quality Imperial Hall **7**
Regent Park Hotel **14**
Sofitel **17**
Transamerica Opera **9**
Unique **3**

DINING ◆

Antiquarius **10**
Arabia **12**
Capim Santo **16**
Casa do Padeiro **1**
Fasano **6**
Figueira Rubaiyat **5**
Le Chef Rouge **4**
Offellè **8**
Quinta da Mandioca **11**
Quinta do Museu **2**
Skye **3**

Ⓜ Metro Stop

Greater São Paulo

Area of detail

LAPA   PINHEIROS   JARDINS   SÉ   MOOCA   CENTRO   Parque do Ibirapuera   IPIRANGA   BROOKLIN

Rua Oscar Freire 533, Jardins, 01426-001. ✆ **011/3064-3666**. www.regent.com.br. 70 units. 1-bedroom R$215–R$260 (US$107–US$130/£58–£70); 2-bedroom R$385 (US$192/£104). Weekend discounts are available. Extra person R$40 (US$20/£11). Children under 5 stay free in parent's room. Free parking. AE, MC, V. Bus: 702P. **Amenities:** Restaurant; outdoor rooftop pool; small weight room; sauna; concierge; tour desk; business center; limited room service; laundry; nonsmoking rooms. *In room:* A/C, TV, dataport, kitchen, minibar, fridge, safe.

Transamerica Opera ✪ (*Value*)   The bargain of the century happens to be in the heart of the city's best neighborhood. The Opera offers spacious flats, featuring a separate sitting room with comfy couch and TV and small dinette table, plus a good-size work desk with lamp and lots of plugs, plus a bedroom with firm queen-size bed and vast closets and full-length mirror, plus a kitchenette with stove and fridge, all for less than many hotels charge for just a bed. True, the furnishings are a tad dated, but on the plus side, step out the door and you're in the heart of the Jardims shopping district.

Alameda Lorena 1748, Cerqueira César, 04003-010 SP. ✆ **011/3062-2666**. Fax 011/3062-2662. www.transamerica flats.com.br. 96 units. R$205 (US$102/£55) double. Discounts available on weekends. Children 10 and under stay free in parent's room. AE, DC, MC, V. Free parking. Metrô: Consolação. **Amenities:** Restaurant; bar; room service; small pool; small gym; sauna; laundry; nonsmoking floors. *In room:* A/C, TV, high-speed Internet, kitchenette, minibar, safe.

ELSEWHERE
VERY EXPENSIVE
Sofitel São Paulo ✪✪✪   The combination of French sophistication and Brazilian hospitality results in one fine hotel. Owned by the French Accor group that also manages a large number of apart-hotels in the city, the Sofitel is the luxury flagship of the chain. Located just across from Ibirapuera Park, the hotel is ideal for those who like to start the day with a nice walk or a vigorous game of tennis; this is one of the few hotels in the city with its own courts. A quick cab ride will take you into Jardins and Centro, or a helicopter can pick you up from the hotel's helipad. The guest rooms are quite spacious and elegantly appointed in cheerful yellow-gold and greens. A sitting area and desk provide plenty of space to spread out. Breakfast is not included, but strategically placed in the lobby is a *boulangerie* that sells croissants and other French pastries. Not a bad way to start your morning. Those traveling on a weekend can often book a room online for rates as low as R$250 to R$300 (US$125–US$150/£68–£81)!

Rua Sena Madureira 1355, Ibirapuera, São Paulo, 04021-051 SP. ✆ **0800/703-7003** or 011/5574-1100. www.accor. com.br. 219 units. R$530–R$680 (US$265–US$340/£72–£184) deluxe double; R$715 (US$357/£193) junior suite double. Extra person add 25%. Children 10 and under stay free in parents' room. AE, DC, MC, V. Free parking. Bus: 5126. **Amenities:** Restaurant (French); bar; outdoor pool; tennis courts; health club; sauna; concierge; tour desk; car rental; business center; 24-hr. room service; massage; babysitting; laundry; dry cleaning; nonsmoking floors; executive-level room.

Unique ✪✪✪   Unique truly is. In form this latest São Paulo design hotel is a teetering verdigris-colored disk, chopped off at the top to make a roof deck, and propped up at either end by a pair of concrete pillars hanging down like unfurled banners. Large round portholes gazing out the side of this slice give Unique something of the air of a boat, though an abandoned *Martian Chronicles* kind of craft. Inside it's all high design, from the lobby bar The Wall (the only cocktail lounge I've yet seen stocked with its own small library of expensive architecture books) to the rooms and suites that feature white-on-white decor, queen-size beds with luscious bedding, sparkling bathrooms with Jacuzzi tubs, clever desk space, and a plethora of room gadgets including electric blinds, 48-inch flatscreen TV/DVDs, lots of light options, and a console to control it all. Suites are all located on the rim of the disk so their outer walls rise in one seamless curve from floor to ceiling. Room views are excellent, but the ultimate view is from the rooftop pool and lounge where on one side you see Ibirapuera Park, and on the other, the ridgeline run of skyscrapers on Avenida Paulista. The hotel has just completed a state-of-the-art fitness center and indoor heated pool with slide-in entrance.

Av. Brigadeiro Luis Antônio 4700, Jardim Paulista, 01402-002 SP. © 011/3055-4700. Fax 011/3889-8100. www.hotel unique.com.br. 95 units. R$800 (US$400/£216) double; R$1,200–R$1,400 (US$600–US$700/£324–£378) suite. AE, DC, MC, V. Parking R$15 (US$7.50–£4) daily. Metrô: Brigadeiro. Amenities: Rooftop restaurant; rooftop pool; concierge; room service. In room: A/C, flatscreen TV/DVD, high-speed Internet, minibar, fridge, laptop-size safe w/electrical outlet, CD.

HIGIENOPOLIS

Often overlooked by visitors, Higienópolis is a quiet, green, and pretty residential neighborhood with some excellent restaurants and shops located just a hop and a skip from Centro; a 20-minute walk from the Tryp Higienópolis takes you to the Praça da República. Better yet, prices are much lower than in Jardins.

MODERATE

Tryp Higienópolis ✹✹✹ *Value*   Elegant and luxurious, the Tryp Higienópolis (also referred to as the Meliá Confort) looks more like a high-end condominium than a hotel. The rooms are amazing. Much bigger than your average hotel rooms, these are bright and beautifully furnished with modern decor and colors. Rooms come in standard and superior. The only difference is that superior rooms have a balcony. Otherwise, both are the same spacious size, and come with a king-size bed and a large desk and comfy chair. Unusual for São Paulo, the hotel offers a partially covered pool as well as a large sun deck. As if all of that weren't enough, prices are a steal; Internet rates often go as low as R$150 (US$75/£40)!

Rua Maranhão 371, Higienópolis, São Paulo, 01404-002 SP. © 011/3665-8200. www.solmelia.com. 252 units. R$155 (US$77/£42) standard or superior double. Extra person add R$40 (US$20/£11). Children 6 and under stay free in parent's room. AE, DC, MC, V. Free parking. Metrô: Marechal Deodoro. Amenities: Restaurant; bar; pool; exercise room; sauna; concierge; business center; limited room service; laundry; nonsmoking floors. In room: A/C, TV, dataport, minibar, hair dryer, safe.

3 Where to Dine

São Paulo is the gourmet capital of Brazil. It's the city with the money to attract the country's best chefs, with the clientele to pay the tab at the most outstanding restaurants. Plus, with no beaches or mountains to play on, Paulistas amuse themselves by eating out. People dress up for dinner here (or more than they would elsewhere in the country) and usually go out around 9 or 10pm *at the earliest*. It's becoming more common for restaurants to accept reservations, but many still don't. If waiting for a table drives you to distraction, better to arrive unfashionably early at 8pm.

The variety of cuisine is larger than anywhere in the country. Like New York or Toronto, São Paulo is a city of immigrants. Many of the city's best restaurants are Italian. However, the city has a number of top Middle Eastern restaurants, as well as the best Japanese food in the country, plus Spanish, Portuguese, Bahian, and even Thai cuisine. *Churrascarias* are always a favorite, as are lunchtime kilo spots, which mad-for-work Paulistas see as the perfect way to fuel up for long hours at the office.

The *Guia São Paulo*, the entertainment listing published in the Friday *Folha de São Paulo* newspaper, contains a detailed restaurant section, handy for confirming hours and phone numbers. Also note that the long street names are often abbreviated by Paulistas; for example, the Rua José Maria Lisboa may also be known as Rua Lisboa.

CENTRO

For a map of restaurants in this area, see the map "Where to Stay & Dine in São Paulo Centro," earlier in this chapter.

MODERATE

Famiglia Mancini 🌟🌟 ITALIAN   You'll find a lineup at this São Paulo institution almost every night of the week. Luckily, this cantina-style restaurant with its small tables with traditional red-and-white checkered tablecloths is bigger than it seems and the wait is never too long. Start your meal off at the antipasto buffet where you can choose from a sizable spread of olives, cold cuts, marinated vegetables, cheeses, quail eggs, and salads. With that on your plate you'll have the energy to tackle the enormous pasta menu. There's every kind of pasta you could dream of, and more than 30 different sauces to match. There are also stuffed pastas such as cannelloni, ravioli, and lasagna. Portions are huge; they serve at least two people, often three. Desserts are uninspiring, but most people are too stuffed to contemplate eating more.

Rua Avanhandava 81, Centro. ✆ 011/3256-4320. Reservations not accepted. Main courses R$34–R$68 (US$17–US$34/£9–£18) for 2. AE, DC, MC, V. Sun–Wed 11:30am–1am; Thurs 11:30am–2am; Fri–Sat 11:30am–3am. Metrô: Anhagabau.

INEXPENSIVE

Alaska *(Finds* DESSERT   One of the city's favorite ice-cream parlors, Alaska has been serving over 30 homemade flavors for over 95 years. Flavor-wise it's fairly traditional: lots of chocolates, vanilla, and fruits. Also on the menu are excellent ice-cream desserts such as a banana split, peach melba, or the Alaska: almost a meal with a choice of two toppings, *farofa*, peach slices, and cookies.

Rua Doutor Rafael de Barros 70, Paraiso. ✆ 011/3889-8676. Everything under R$12 (US$6/£3.25). No credit cards. Sun–Thurs 9am–midnight; Fri–Sat 9am–2am. Metrô: Brigadeiro.

Café do Pateo 🌟🌟 *(Value* CAFE   Tired of the hustle and bustle of São Paulo? Tuck away into this great cafe hidden inside the Patio do Colegio, the place where the city was founded. The cafe serves up outstanding coffees, sweets, quiches, sandwiches, and pasta.

Pátio do Colégio 2. ✆ 011/3106-4303. R$12–R$26 (US$6–US$13/£3.25–£7). No credit cards. Tues–Sun 9am–5pm. Metrô: Sé.

AVENIDA PAULISTA

VERY EXPENSIVE

Antiquarius 🌟🌟🌟 PORTUGUESE   Antiquarius offers the perfect elegant setting to savor Portuguese cuisine served up with style and tradition. The menu offers dishes that are hard to find outside Portugal, such as the *cataplana de peixes e frutos do mar,* a rich stew of seafood and fish, with bacon and sausage thrown in for seasoning, all served in a traditional pot resembling a wok with a lid. Another traditional seafood favorite is *açorda*—crab, shrimp, and mussels baked together in a clay dish, with an egg on top of the food for decoration. Then there's the cod *(bacalhau),* which has been a staple of Portuguese cooking since long before Columbus set sail. The wine list leans to higher-end reds, with a large selection drawn mostly from Portugal and France.

Alameda Lorena 1884, Jardim Paulista. ✆ 011/3064-8686. Main courses R$62–R$110 (US$31–US$55/£17–£30). DC, MC, V. Mon 7pm–1am; Tues–Fri noon–3pm and 7pm–1am; Sat noon–2am; Sun noon–6pm. Metrô: Trianon-MASP.

EXPENSIVE

Spot 🌟 BRAZILIAN   More than 10 years old and still trendy, Spot seems to be the exception to the rule that all that is hip soon melts into air. The daytime crowd consists of mostly well-dressed office workers or businesspeople on expense-account lunch meetings. It's the evening crowd, however, that keeps Spot buzzing when musicians, designers, models, and other trendy types crowd in to this glass-enclosed downtown cocoon to flirt, schmooze, and preen. The food is pretty decent; pasta dishes, such as a penne with melon, salads (try the Spot Salad—lettuce, Gorgonzola, dried pears, and nuts), grilled salmon, and tuna with vegetables are offered. It may just be that Spot's owners have created a perpetual motion machine: The young and beautiful flock to see the young and beautiful, who flock to see the young and beautiful, and so on. . . .

Rua Min. Rocha Azevedo 72, Cerqueira Cesar. ✆ 011/3283-0946. Reservations accepted only until 9pm. Main courses R$28–R$46 (US$14–US$23/£7.50–£13). AE, DC, MC, V. Mon–Fri noon–3pm and 8pm–1am; Sat–Sun 1–4:30pm and 8pm–1am. Metrô: Trianon-MASP.

MODERATE

Mestiço ★★ *Value* THAI/BAHIAN Two women, two flavors, one hip eatery. Mestiço is run by a woman from Bahia and her partner from Thailand—each brings her own culinary traditions to bear in the cuisine. Traditional Thai noodle salads sit side by side on the menu with *acarajé,* a Bahian fast food made with beans and shrimp and served with hot sauce. The salads are outstanding; the Malibu comes stuffed with tuna, carrots, rucula, lettuce, and mango in a balsamic-honey dressing while the Cubana boasts squid, palm hearts, grilled banana, and an intriguing variety of lettuces. For more substantial meals there are Thai dishes like chicken with shiitake mushrooms in ginger sauce, and grilled prawns with roasted peanuts in a sweet-and-sour sauce. The room is quite pleasant, lots of light wood with high ceilings, dimmed lights, and soft yellow walls decorated with exotic photos and masks. Service is friendly, and the prices are very reasonable. Alas, we're not the only ones to have discovered this restaurant; in the evenings, especially on weekends, the wait can be at least an hour.

Rua Fernando de Albuquerque 277, Consolação. ✆ 011/3256-3165. www.mestico.com.br. Reservations accepted. R$20–R$45 (US$8.40–US$19/£4.20–£9). AE, DC, MC, V. Sun–Thurs noon–midnight; Fri–Sat noon–2am. Metrô: Consolação.

La Tartine Bistrot FRENCH We actually only tried this because of the fierce lineup at next-door Mestiço, but we're glad we did. True, there was a wait here as well, but we could pass the time drinking cocktails in the comfortable and quirky upstairs bar. Both bar and restaurant have a great funky atmosphere, decorated with a profusion of cast-off items—plastic lunch boxes, shower curtains, tacky postcards, posters, and mismatched furniture—that only a talented decorator could turn into something other than a yard sale. But somehow it works. The menu lists only a handful of items, mostly simple bistro fare, including several types of quiche with side salads, steak and baked potato, coq au vin, and croque-monsieur sandwiches. The dessert menu is even smaller and consists of apple pie and chocolate petit gâteau; we can vouch for both.

Rua Fernando de Albuquerque 267, Consolação. ✆ 011/3250-2090. Main courses R$16–R$28 (US$85–US$14/£4–£7.50). V. Mon–Sat 7:30pm–12:30am. Metrô: Consolação.

LIBERDADE
EXPENSIVE

Sushi Yassu ★★ JAPANESE The second generation owners of this traditional Liberdade standard bearer are trying to introduce some new and different dishes to the Paulista palate. Customers can try the grilled white tuna or anchovy, in salt or with a sweetened soy sauce, a steaming bowl of udon noodle soup in a rich broth with seafood or tempura vegetables. There's of course a large variety of sushi and sashimi dishes, as well as the stir-fried teppanyaki and yakisoba noodles with meat and vegetables. Expect a bit of a wait on Sunday afternoons when this restaurant is a popular lunch destination for those visiting the Liberdade street market.

Rua Tomas Gonzaga 98, Liberdade. ℭ 011/3209-6622. Main courses R$14–R$36 (US$7–US$18/£4–£10). AE, DC, MC, V. Tues–Fri 11:30am–3pm and 6–11pm; Sat noon–4pm and 6pm–midnight; Sun noon–10pm. Metrô: Liberdade.

MODERATE

Kabura JAPANESE   Twenty years and still going strong, Kabura offers late-night dining in the heart of São Paulo's little Japan. The restaurant serves up the usual Japanese faves—sushi, sashimi, donburi, and tempura—all at a reasonable price. The food is fresh, and the portions are generous. For an interesting cold appetizer try the sashimi made from Brazilian top picanha beef. An excellent hot appetizer is the plate with six breaded and crunchy deep-fried oysters.

Rua Galvão Bueno 54, Liberdade, Sao Paulo. ℭ 011/3277-2918. Reservations accepted. R$18–R$39 (US$9–US$20/£5–£11). No credit cards. Mon–Sat 7pm–2am. Metrô: Liberdade.

JARDINS/ITAIM BIBI

For a map of restaurants in this area, see the map "Where to Stay & Dine in Jardins," earlier in this chapter.

VERY EXPENSIVE

Fasano ✿✿✿ ITALIAN   As the owner of what has long been considered the best Italian restaurant in the country, Rogerio Fasano doesn't seem the least bit intimidated about living up to expectations. It helps to have a beautiful restaurant. Located in the Fasano hotel, the dining room combines black marble and dark furniture with exquisite lighting to create an intimate and warm ambience. The mainstay of the menu is dishes from northern Italy, more specifically Lombardy, from where the Fasanos originally hailed. However, over the last few years, chef Salvatore Loi has been diversifying the menu with dishes from other Italian regions. Start off with a traditional tomato soup with prawns and Italian bread or try the antipasto. Pasta courses include favorites such as the delicate pumpkin tortelli, a hearty duck ravioli in orange sauce, or try one of the risottos with Tuscan sausage and white beans or with marinated tuna. For mains, the menu offers excellent meat and seafood options. Choose from classic veal cutlets, roasted lamb, filetto alla Rossini with foie gras and truffles, or perhaps a lighter choice, the grilled tuna steak with Sicilian lemon. Diners can also opt for the five-course tasting menu and let Chef Salvatore take them on a gastronomic journey around Italy.

Rua Vittorio Fasano 88, Cerqueira Cesar. ℭ 011/3062-4000. Main courses R$98–R$160 (US$49–US$80/£27–£43). 5-course tasting menu R$240 (US$120/£65). AE, DC, MC, V. Mon–Sat 7:30pm–1am. Bus: 206E.

Figueira Rubaiyat ✿✿✿ BRAZILIAN/STEAK   The most beautiful restaurant in the city, Figueira (fig tree) Rubaiyat is built around the spreading limbs of a magnificent old fig tree. Seating can either be "outside" in the gazebo around the tree boughs or inside in the lovely restaurant. Rubaiyat's specialty is beef. Indeed, it serves the best prime beef in São Paulo, all of it raised with care at the owner's private cattle ranch. For the non-carnivorous, the Figueira also offers a wide variety of top-notch Mediterranean seafood dishes, such as paella, codfish, and grilled prawns.

Rua Haddock Lobo 1738, Cerqueira Cesar. ℭ 011/3063-3888. Main courses R$44–R$89 (US$22–US$40/£12–£24). V. Mon–Fri noon–3:30pm and 7pm–midnight; Sat–Sun noon–12:30am. Bus: 206E.

EXPENSIVE

Arabia 👬 MIDDLE EASTERN   A spacious and modern restaurant just 1 block off the stylish Rua Augusta, Arabia serves up a range of favorites from Lebanon. In addition to the daily specials, there's a tasting menu that changes regularly. At R$38 (US$16/£8) it's a great way to sample some of the chef's best. The main menu includes Moroccan rice with roasted almonds and chicken, or the signature stuffed artichoke bottoms with ground beef, accompanied by rice with almonds. As an appetizer or a light meal, try the *mezze,* the Lebanese equivalent of tapas. Served for two, three, or four people, each tray comes with at least half a dozen tasters of the most popular dishes such as hummus, falafel, tabbouleh salad, and a generous serving of fresh pita.

Rua Haddock Lobo 1397, Cerqueira Cesar. ✆ 011/3061-2203. www.arabia.com.br. R$20–R$46 (US$10–US$23/ £5.50–£13). AE, DC, MC. Mon–Thurs noon–3:30pm and 7pm–midnight; Fri noon–3:30pm and 7pm–1am; Sat–Sun noon–midnight. Bus: 206E.

Capim Santo 👬 BRAZILIAN   Modeled after the Capim Santo restaurant in Bahia, the São Paulo version is set in a lovely garden with lush mango trees and plenty of outside tables. The specialty is seafood. Try the robalo fish with a crust of cashew nuts and a side of vatapá shrimp stew, or the perfectly tender grilled tuna. Another delicious dish is the stew of prawns in coconut milk, served in a hollowed-out pumpkin. Homemade pastas come in a variety of seafood combinations, or for a vegetarian option try the mini-cannelloni stuffed with asparagus, ricotta, and tomato confit. Desserts include some favorites with a tropical twist, such as the guava crème brûlée or the tarte tartin with banana. At lunchtime, you can also opt for the excellent buffet with 15 salads and more than 10 hot dishes, including seafood, chicken, and pasta. Dessert included (R$35/US$18/£9.50 on weekdays and R$48/US$24/£13 on weekends and holidays).

Rua Ministro Rocha Azevedo 471, Cerqueira César. ✆ 011/3068-8486. www.restaurantecapimsanto.com.br. Main courses R$26–R$49 (US$13–US$25/£7–£13). AE. Tues–Sat noon–3pm and 7pm–midnight; Sun 12:30–4:30pm. Metrô: MASP.

Le Chef Rouge 👬 FRENCH   Listening to the *chansons* in Chef Rouge's cozy dining room, you could easily believe that you were somewhere on the Left Bank (although waiters here are friendly, attentive, and speak English). The menu includes a number of delicious salads such as the green salad with warm goat cheese or the greens with warm mushrooms and a balsamic dressing. We visited on a cold winter evening and were pleased with the hearty dishes such as the *trois filets aux trois sauces,* a trio of juicy grilled steaks each served with a different sauce and the *canard à l'orange,* thin slices of duck with just a tiny bit of crisp fat for flavor, served in a sweet-savory orange sauce on a bed of wafer-thin potato chips. The wine list leans heavily toward expensive French bottles, but a small selection of Chilean cabernet sauvignon and Shiraz can make for an affordable evening. For dessert we opted for a cheese plate, a wonderful change from sweet Brazilian desserts.

Rua Bela Cintra 2238, Cerqueira César. ✆ 011/3081-7539. www.chefrouge.com.br. R$32–R$58 (US$16–US$29/ £9–£16). AE, DC, MC, V. Tues–Sat noon–3:30pm and 7pm–midnight; Sun noon–5pm and 7pm–midnight.

MODERATE

Quinta da Mandioca 👬 BRAZILIAN   For some Brazilian-style "home-cooking" check out Quinta da Mandioca. This cute rustic-looking restaurant serves up some excellent steaks and salads and a few typically Brazilian dishes such as the *picadinho,* a spicy beef stew topped with a poached egg and served with baked banana, farofa, and rice. On Saturday the Quinta puts out an excellent *feijoada* buffet with all the trimmings such as rice, baked bananas, farofa, sliced oranges, and sautéed green cabbage. If you just want a quick snack or lunch, there's also a great sandwich menu.

Rua Oscar Freire 726, Cerqueira Cesar. ℂ 011/3064-4999. Main courses R$14–R$34 (US$7–US$17/£4–£9). AE, DC, MC, V. Sun–Thurs noon–11pm; Fri–Sat noon–1am.

Quinta do Museu ⊛⊛ (Finds) (Kids) BRAZILIAN/BISTRO   The Quinta do Museu is housed in the Museu Casa Brasileira's kitchen; seating is in the old dining room or, better yet, on the back patio under the shade of a spreading rubber tree overlooking the garden. The kitchen prepares a good selection of light lunches including grilled salmon, pastas, salads, and sandwiches. There's a large lawn where kids can run around while adults enjoy their lunch in peace. The garden is also a lovely spot for just a coffee and dessert. From Tuesday to Saturday, the restaurant serves a full afternoon tea (3:30–6pm). The hearty spread includes tea and fruit juice accompanied by a selection of sandwiches, quiches, cake, brownies, and other goodies (R$35/US$18/£9.50 per person).

Av. Brigadeiro Faria Lima 2705, Jardim Europa. ℂ 011/3031-0005. Main courses R$12–R$28 (US$6–US$14/£3.25–£7.50). AE, DC, MC, V. Tues–Sat noon–3:30pm lunch; Tues–Fri 3:30–6pm afternoon tea; Sun noon–5pm lunch (museum Tues–Sun 1–6pm). Bus: 5100 or 5119.

INEXPENSIVE

Casa do Padeiro CAFE   Open 24 hours a day, the Casa do Padeiro (Baker's House) dishes up way more than just bread. It's the perfect spot to grab a light meal any time of the day. This branch of the cafe/restaurant chain serves salads, sandwiches, pasta meals, and sweets. The coffee bar is excellent, serving up fresh espresso, café au lait, cappuccinos, and other hot beverages.

Av. Brigadeiro Faria Lima 2776, Jardim Paulistano. ℂ 011/3812-1233. Everything under R$15 (US$7.50/£4). AE, MC, V. Daily 24 hr. Bus: 5100 or 5119.

Offellê ICE CREAM   Offellê's display case shows a dazzling rainbow of Italian gelato-style ice cream. The chocolate flavors are rich and creamy; try the chocolate and mint or the chocolate with hazelnut. Exceptionally yummy. The fruit flavors are made with fresh fruit and range from the tropical passion fruit to more "foreign and exotic" raspberry and blackberry fruits of the forest.

Alameda Lorena 1784, Cerqueira Cesar. ℂ 011/3088-8127. Everything under R$12 (US$6/£3.25). V. Daily 1–11pm. Bus: 206E.

VILA MADALENA
EXPENSIVE

Kabuki ⊛⊛ JAPANESE   Romantic and rustic-chic are adjectives not usually associated with Japanese restaurants but Kabuki is an exception. The candlelit dining room is furnished with lovely dark wood, and the exposed brick walls are adorned with tasteful artwork. Mellow music is on hand in the evenings. For those who just want to nibble there's a large menu of cold and hot appetizers such as sautéed shitake or shimeji mushrooms, deep-fried prawn, and an assortment of grilled skewers with meat, seafood, or vegetables. Main courses include a large variety of sushi and sashimi combos, tempuras, yakisoba noodles, and grilled meats. Interesting dessert options include the flambéed mango and banana or tempura ice cream, a wonderful sensation of a hot, crunchy crust and a soft, cold, creamy center.

Rua Girassol 384, Vila Madalena. ℂ 011/3814-5131. Reservations accepted. Dinner R$22–R$70 (US$11–US$35/£6–£19). AE, DC, MC, V. Mon 7–11pm; Tues–Sun noon–3pm. Metrô: Vila Madalena.

Santa Gula ★★ *Finds* ITALIAN   One of the quaintest restaurants in São Paulo, Santa Gula is in the backyard of an old house. Entering off the Rua Fidalga, a fairy-tale lane with lush tropical plants, banana trees, and flickering candlelight leads to a dining room that, with its handmade furniture and rustic decorations, gives the restaurant the feel of a simple Tuscan villa. The kitchen serves up a mix of Italian and Brazilian flavors—think risotto with palm hearts or pasta stuffed with *carne seca* (a flavorful dried meat) and pumpkin purée. Equally intriguing is the duck with red-wine sauce and a pineapple risotto; for meat lovers, the steaks arrive grilled to perfection. For dessert, don't pass up on the Brazil nut pie or the sweet coconut with tapioca mousse and tangerine sorbet.

Rua Fidalga 340, Vila Madalena. ℂ 011/3812-7815. Reservations recommended. Dinner R$26–R$40 (US$13–US$20/£7–£11). AE, DC, MC, V. Mon 8pm–midnight; Tues–Thurs noon–3pm and 8pm–1am; Fri–Sat noon–4pm and 8pm–2am; Sun noon–5pm. Metrô: Vila Madalena.

MODERATE

Santa Pizza ★ *Value* ITALIAN/PIZZA   With over 40 varieties of pie to choose from at Santa Pizza, it may take you an eternity to make up your mind. There are many of the more traditional combinations such as tomato, ham, basil, cheese, and onion, or the Portuguesa with olives and eggs. Brazilians, however, have a real thing for sweet and savory when it comes to pizza—witness the Gorgonzola cheese with pineapple pizza, or the smoked bacon, mozzarella, tomato, and mango chutney combo. For something truly unique, try the banana with mozzarella with sugar and cinnamon.

Rua Harmonia 117, Vila Madalena. ℂ 011/3816-7848. Main courses R$26–R$37 (US$13–US$19/£7–£10). AE, DC, MC, V. Mon–Wed 7pm–midnight; Thurs–Sun 7pm–1am. Metrô: Vila Madalena.

INEXPENSIVE

Deliparis CAFE   A combination of cafe and bakery, Deliparis has an excellent selection of freshly baked breads to go, including loaves made with olives, nuts, or multigrain. Most people, however, prefer to linger in the cafe with a tea or cappuccino and order some of the delicious fruit tarts, quiches, or brioches. If these aren't sweet enough for you, Deliparis also bakes excellent pies and divine cakes: Think banana cake with almonds or creamy chocolate ganache.

Rua Harmonia 484, Vila Madalena. ℂ 011/3816-5911. Everything under R$12 (US$5/£2.50). No credit cards. Daily 7am–10pm. Bus: 473T.

HIGIENÓPOLIS
EXPENSIVE

Carlota ★★ *Finds* BRAZILIAN   A phenomenal success in the male-dominated world of Brazilian gourmet chefs, owner and chef Carla Pernambuco earned her stripes in New York before coming home to Brazil and starting her own restaurant. Her cuisine blends the ethnic flavors of cosmopolitan New York and her own Italian heritage with fresh Brazilian ingredients to create dishes such as the *camarão pacifico:* shrimp grilled with sesame seeds and Thai chile sauce on a bed of vegetable-fried rice. She pulls off a great grilled duck with Dijon mustard on mashed mandioc, and the beef with balsamic port sauce and a fig risotto is also outstanding. For a lighter meal there are several pasta options, such as the ravioli stuffed with brie or codfish. Reservations are not accepted; expect a long wait on most nights after 9pm.

Rua Sergipe 753, Higienópolis. ℂ 011/3661-8670. Main courses R$35–R$68 (US$18–US$34/£9.50–£18). AE, DC, MC, V. Mon 7pm–midnight; Tues–Thurs noon–4pm and 7pm–midnight; Fri–Sat noon–1am; Sun noon–6pm. Bus: 8107.

Veridiana (Finds) PIZZA   So trendy is Veridiana that it does not have a name on the door, but not to worry—you can't miss the beautiful rust-colored heritage building on the corner of Avenida Higienópolis and Rua da Veridiana (the valet-parking guys give it away). This beautifully restored building, originally from 1903, is one of the most elegant pizzerias we have ever seen. The menu offers pizza at its most traditional—thin crusts, and just a few quality ingredients per pizza. The grande serves two people, and you can order different combos on each half of the pizza.

Rua da Veridiana 661, Higienópolis. ℂ 011/3120-5050. Main courses R$26–R$48 (US$13–US$24/£7–£13). AE, DC, MC, V. Sun–Thurs 7pm–12:30am; Fri–Sat 7pm–1:30am. Metrô: Santa Cecilia.

MODERATE

The Higienópolis Dining Triangle   Smack in the middle of Higienópolis just behind the **FAAP** sits the delightful **Praça Vila Boim.** A lovely three-sided square with beautiful trees, the *praça* offers a number of great casual dining options. Sushi lovers will be pleased to find **Sushi Papaia** (Praça Vila Boim 93; ℂ 011/3666-2086). The menu offers a variety of sushi and sashimi; the restaurant also serves heaping plates of *yakisoba* noodles and sizzling *teppanyaki* stir-fries. If you're in the mood for a perfectly grilled steak, look no further than the **Empório Natan** (Praça Vila Boim 73; ℂ 011/ 3828-1402). This new restaurant specializes in Argentine and Angus steaks. In the mood for carbs? Try **Piola** (Praça Vila Boim 49; ℂ 011/3663-6539). This pizzeria is almost as famous for its edgy, industrial-chic decor as it is for its pizza. The 30 combos, including the Rimini (smoked salmon and ricotta) and the Mantova (mozzarella, brie, fresh tomatoes, and arugula), are sure to please everyone.

ELSEWHERE
EXPENSIVE

Skye (Finds) BRAZILIAN   Even if you aren't staying at the Unique, it is worth coming to Skye for lunch and dinner. Not only to experience this fantastic hotel, nicknamed "*melancia*" (watermelon) for its interesting shape, but also to enjoy the rooftop restaurant. The views of the São Paulo skyline are spectacular, and this modern lounge/restaurant serves up creative and innovative Brazilian cuisine. The menu constantly changes but a few of the recent dishes have included chicken breast with mushrooms, wasabi purée and ginger broth, and duck confit with a malbec and rucula risotto. For a more Asian twist there is a grilled salmon with yakisoba and a full sushi bar that serves up excellent sushi and sashimi. Desserts are more than worth splurging on. For a rich and creamy choice try the mascarpone mousse with guava compote and caramelized cashews or the pear pie with ginger and pistachios in a tangy tangerine sauce. In the evenings the lounge is one of the city's hot spots and a popular celebrity hang out. The restaurant only accepts reservations for hotel guests.

Av. Brigadeiro Luis Antonio 4700, Jardim Paulista (inside the Unique Hotel). ℂ 011/3055-4702. Main courses R$42–R$69 (US$21–US$35/£11–£19). AE, DC, MC, V. Daily noon–4pm and 7pm–1am.

8

Exploring São Paulo

Rio is a beauty. But São Paulo—São Paulo is a city.

—Marlene Dietrich

What was once a little market town in the cool high plateau has jumped its bounds and sprawled for the hills in all directions. São Paulo is now not only the largest city in Brazil, but it's also the largest in Latin America and the third or fourth largest in the world. What assembles and drives this vast assemblage of people is commerce. The city and surrounding municipalities account for an incredible 65% of Brazil's GDP. When Paulistas do take a break from work they devote much the same energy to leisure. The city boasts some of the best galleries and museums in the country. It has by far the best cuisine and some of the best nightlife. And despite the seeming chaos, remain for a few days and you'll discover, as Paulistas have, that the city could not be otherwise; somehow São Paulo makes sense.

SUGGESTED SÃO PAULO ITINERARIES

If You Have ❶ Day

Get to know South America's largest city. Wander the busy pedestrian streets of the old downtown neighborhood of **Centro.** In the constant commercial chatter you'll feel, see, and hear Paulistas at their best: buying, selling, and trading. Ascend to the top of the Banespa building for a 360-degree view of the city. Have a coffee at the Patio do Colegio. In the afternoon take the Metrô out to the **Avenida Paulista.** Bask in the wealth and power a bit, then go see some fine art at the **MASP.** In the evening take advantage of your presence in Brazil's culinary capital and go out for dinner at a truly fine restaurant like the **Antiquarius** or **Figueira Rubaiyat.**

If You Have ❷ Days

Get some culture. Anyone interested in modern Brazilian architecture should see the **Monument to Latin America.** Those interested in seeing Brazilian art should check out the **Pinacoteca do Estado,** or

for older work the **Museu de Arte Sacra.** Reward yourself with an afternoon shopping in the green and leafy **Jardins** neighborhood. The intersection of **Rua Augusta** and **Oscar Freire** is perhaps the most exclusive shopping enclave in all Brazil. The neighborhood is also one of São Paulo's culinary hot spots. For a taste of the diversity in this most cosmopolitan of cities, seek out a Bahian dinner at **Capim Santo,** a French meal at Le **Chef Rouge,** or something Middle Eastern at **Arabia.**

If You Have ❸ Days

Set off to explore the Japanese neighborhood of **Liberdade,** topped off with a fine Japanese lunch. Walk off those calories with an afternoon in **Ibirapuera Park.** Stroll the pathways, rent a bicycle, and enjoy the people-watching. That night, check out some of the clubs or bars in **Vila Olímpia,** starting the evening with a *chopp* (draft beer) and some *picanha* at **Rabo do Peixe.**

1 The Top Attractions

Museu da Lingua Portuguesa ⭐⭐   The Museum of the Portuguese Language is everything you'd want in a museum; it's creative, interesting, interactive, visually fabulous, and fun. This probably explains why in the short time it's been open it has become São Paulo's most popular museum. The only drawback? No English signage. However, anybody with a basic understanding of Portuguese, or an interest in the language, will enjoy the experience.

The most magnificent display tells the history of the Portuguese language, as it slowly developed from Latin, only much later to be influenced by Arabic, eventually by African and Indian words and later by French and English. On the right side a giant timeline and several interactive displays impart a myriad of interesting facts, on the left, a giant 100m-long (328-ft.) screen runs the full length of this former train station showing images and clips relating to unique Portuguese words associated with cultural events such as carnival, religion, soccer, music, and so on. Allow 2 hours.

Tip: The popularity of the museum is such that on weekdays it is packed with schoolchildren, and on weekends with families and Brazilian tourists. Either way, it's best to arrive either early or else late in the afternoon (after 4pm!)

Praça Luz s/n Administration ☎ 011/3326-0775. www.museudalinguaportuguesa.org.br. R$4/US$2/£1. Tues–Sun 10am–6pm. Metrô: Estação Luz.

Ibirapuera Park ⭐⭐   Blessed with over 2 million square meters of green space, São Paulo's version of Central Park offers quite a bit to see and do. You can wander the paths beside pleasant lagoons or rent a bicycle (R$6/US$3/£1.50 per hour) and cycle the pathways. Every Sunday morning there's a **free outdoor concert** in the park's Praça da Paz. Sunday from 10am to 4pm you can take advantage of the **Bosque de Leitura,** a kind of free outdoor lending library that lets you borrow magazines or books (including many in English) to read in the park for the duration of day. In the corner near Gate 3 there's the **Museu de Arte Moderna (Museum of Modern Art;** see listing, below). Just nearby there's the excellent **Museu Afro Brasil** (see listing, below) and the **OCA Auditorium,** a flying saucer–shaped building that often hosts traveling art exhibits.

Administration ☎ 011/5574-5177. Free admission. Daily 5am–midnight. Bus: 5100 or 5131 from Metrô Brigadeiro.

Monument to Latin America ⭐⭐   Shy of a visit to Brasilia, this is the best place to see Brazilian modernism in all its concrete austerity. Designed by famed Brazilian architect Oscar Niemeyer, the monument consists of a vast field of concrete dotted about the edges with perfectly geometrical concrete pavilions originally painted blinding white, but long since streaked by the rain. The two pavilions of most interest to visitors unimpressed by architecture are the Art Gallery and the Hall of Creativity. The Art Gallery hosts changing fine-art exhibits, whereas the Hall of Creativity is a permanent home to a fun and fascinating display of folk art from across the length and breadth of Latin America. Back outside, in the center of all this hard-edged mathematical purity stands Niemeyer's first attempt at sculpture, a giant concrete hand, its palm incised with a blood-red map of Latin America.

Av. Auro Soares de Moura Andrade 664, Barra Funda (next to the Barra Funda Metrô stop). ☎ 011/3823-4600. www.memorial.org.br. Free admission. Tues–Fri 9am–8pm; Sat–Sun 9am–6pm. Metrô: Barra Funda.

Museu Afro Brasil ⭐⭐   Brazil has the largest black population outside of Africa, so it's curious that only in the past decade or so has black or Afro consciousness really

---

Tips **Check Out the Antiques Market**

Every Sunday from 10am to 5pm there's an antiques fair in the courtyard beneath the MASP building. Dealers are registered, and the quality is often good. Plus, it's the only time you'll ever find anybody voluntarily occupying that open space.

---

begun to take root. This new museum—one of the most popular cultural institutions to open in São Paulo in recent years—is dedicated to showing the cultural achievements of Africans and their descendants enslaved in Brazil. If you think you might be letting yourself in for a hectoring guilt-inducing lecture, think again. The museum is not a *cri de coeur* over the injustice and hardship of slavery but rather a celebration of the art and accomplishments of the African diaspora. Displays show short biographies of writers or painters or politicians who were black, including lots of their artwork and artifacts. Displays are gorgeous—particularly the art and photography—and the museum has wonderful natural light. Allow an hour.

Parque do Ibirapuera. (C) 011/5579-0593. Free admission. Tues–Sun 10am–5:30pm. Bus: 5100 or 5131 from Metrô Brigadeiro.

Museu Arte Brasileira/FAAP 🍴   Don't let the name fool you. What this majestic and slightly pompous building (think Mussolini monumental) in quiet Higienópolis plays host to is not Brazilian art, but an ever-changing parade of grand international exhibits. The grand hall and both wings of the museum are transformed for each new exhibit. The museum also claims to house a number of the Brazilian greats—Portinari, Di Cavalcanti, and others—but they're never actually on display. (You may also see the museum referred to as FAAP, which is the acronym for the cultural institute where it's located.)

Rua Alagoas 903, Higienópolis. (C) 011/3662-7200. www.faap.br/museu. Admission varies from free to R$15 (US$7.50/£4) depending on exhibit. Tues–Fri 10am–8pm; Sat–Sun 1–5pm. Bus: 137T.

Museu Arte São Paulo (MASP) 🍴🍴   São Paulo's big art museum recently reorganized its galleries to give much more space to Brazilian artists. The top floor contains the permanent collection, which, as before, contains an excellent selection of Western art, from 14th-century Italian religious imagery to the early-20th-century works of Picasso. Every period and country has a representative sample—Dutch Rembrandts, English Turners, Spanish El Grecos, and French everythings (Rodin, Renoir, Degas, and Monet). But in one big change, several rooms on this floor are now dedicated to the Brazilian greats, among them Di Cavalcanti and Candido Portinari. Even better, the entire second floor of the MASP is now a temporary gallery, dedicated to changing exhibitions, again of mostly Brazilian artists. The display space is still long and fluorescent lit and kind of warehouse-y, but the art is now worth the trip.

Av. Paulista 1578, Cerqueira César. (C) 011/3251-5644. www.masp.art.br. Admission R$15 (US$7.50/£4) adults, free for seniors and children 10 and under. Tues–Sun 11am–6pm. Metrô: Trianon-MASP.

Museu Casa Brasileira 🍴   Built in 1945, this big yellow Palladian villa was long the home of Fábio da Silva Prado, the patriarch of one of São Paulo's leading families. Inside, the museum displays an assortment of haute-bourgeois artifacts from the 17th to 19th centuries: ornate jacaranda-wood furniture, fancy porcelain, silver plates, the

What to See & Do in São Paulo

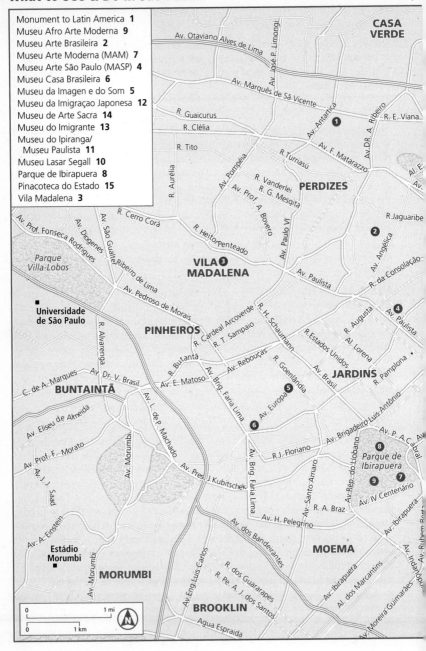

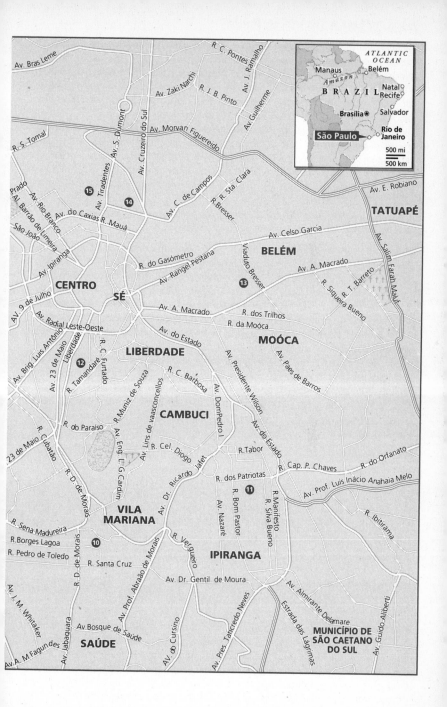

Av. Bras Leme
R. C. Pontes
Av. J. Ramalho

ATLANTIC
OCEAN
Manaus
Belém
Amazon
B R A Z I L
Natal
Recife
Brasília
Salvador
Rio de
Janeiro
São Paulo
500 mi
500 km

Av. Zaki Narchi
R. J. B. Pinto
Av. Guilherme
Av. Morvan Figuereido
Av. S. Dumont
Av. Cruzeiro do Sul
R. S. Tomal
Prado
Al. Barão de Limeira
Av. Rio Branco
São João
Av. Tiradentes
Av. do Caxias R. Mauá
Av. Ipiranga
Av. 9 de Julho
CENTRO
SÉ
Av. Radial Leste-Oeste
Av. Brig. Luís Antônio
Av. 23 de Maio
Liberdade
R. Tamandaré
R. C. Furtado
LIBERDADE
R. Muniz de Souza
R. do Paraíso
23 de Maio
R. Cubatão
R. D. de Morais
R. Eng. L. G. Cardim
Av. Lins de Vasconcellos
R. C. Barbosa
CAMBUCI
R. Cel. Diogo
Av. Dr. Ricardo Jafet
Av. Dom Pedro I
Av. Presidente Wilson
Av. do Estado
VILA
MARIANA
R. Sena Madureira
R. Borges Lagoa
R. Pedro de Toledo
R. Santa Cruz
R. Vergueiro
IPIRANGA
Av. Nazaré
R. Bom Pastor
R. dos Patriotas
R. Tabor
R. Manifesto
R. Silva Bueno
Cap. P. Chaves
R. do Orfanato
Av. Prof. Luis Inácio Anahaia Melo
R. Ibitirama
Av. J. M. Whitaker
Av. A. M. Fagundes
R. D. de Morais
R. Jabaquara
Av. Prof. Abraão de Morais
Av. Bosque de Saúde
SAÚDE
Av. do Cursino
Av. Dr. Gentil de Moura
Av. Pres. Tancredo Neves
Av. Almirante Delamare
Estrada das Lágrimas
MUNICÍPIO DE
SÃO CAETANO
DO SUL
Av. Guido Aliberti

Av. C. de Campos
R. R. Sta. Clara
R. Bresser
Av. Celso Garcia
BELÉM
Viaduto Bresser
Av. A. Macrado
Av. Salim Farah Maluf
TATUAPÉ
Av. E. Robiano
R. do Gasómetro
Av. Rangel Pestana
R. Siqueira Bueno
R. T. Barreto
Av. A. Macrado
R. dos Trilhos
R. da Moóca
MOÓCA
Av. Paes de Barros
Av. do Estado

15
14
12
13
11
10

213

token oil painting by Portinari. If you've seen similar collections elsewhere—like at Rio's Museu Chácara do Céu—there's no need to come here. If you missed out, the standard collection is well displayed in this museum. Under a new curator, the museum has also begun hosting changing exhibits, many focused on modern Brazilian design, others on innovative themes such as the idea of the house in Brazilian history and imagination. Check the website for programming details.

Tip: The best part of the museum may be the restaurant, the **Quinta do Museu,** housed in the mansion's kitchen. Seating is in the old dining room or on the back patio under the shade of a rubber tree. The menu includes light lunches, including grilled salmon, salads, and sandwiches, as well as a hearty afternoon tea (R$18–R$30/ US$9–US$15/£5–£8). Better yet, there's a large lawn where kids can run around while adults dine in peace.

Av. Brig. Faria Lima 2705, Jardim Paulistano. ⓒ 011/3032-3727. www.mcb.sp.gov.br. Admission R$4 (US$2/£1) adults, free for seniors and children 12 and under. Tues–Sun 10am–6pm. Bus: 107P.

Museu da Imagen e do Som ★★ *(Finds)*

The Museum of Image and Sound showcases the best Brazilian contemporary image-makers. Photographs in the changing exhibits are always compelling, beautifully displayed, and deeply engaged with contemporary themes such as sex, media manipulation, or marginalization. At all times they make you think. The museum's one permanent display is a 14m (45 feet) 360-degree panoramic photograph of the city of São Paul, taken between 1919 and 1921. Allow 1 hour. Call ahead to verify hours. The museum closes between exhibits, often for extended periods.

Located in an intriguing concrete building right next door, the **Museu Brasileiro da Escultura** (ⓒ 011/3081-8611; www.mube.art.br) claims to play host to traveling exhibits of Brazilian artists and sculptors, and to be open Tuesday through Sunday 10 to 7pm, but for lack of funds and organization the museum is closed more often than not.

Av. Europa 158, Jardim Europa. ⓒ 011/3062-9197. www.mis.sp.gov.br. Admission R$3/US$1.50/£.80. Tues–Sun 10am–6pm. Bus: 373T.

Museu de Arte Moderna (MAM) ★

Small but intriguing, the MAM in Ibirapuera Park has two galleries that it devotes to ever-changing exhibits of modern work, be it in the form of painting, sculpture, video, textile, or some other medium. At any one time, each of the main building's two spacious and well-lit galleries is given over to a particular artist. Check the website for upcoming exhibits. There's also a small library with an excellent collection of art books in various languages. Surrounding the museum is a **sculpture garden** featuring 28 works by different Brazilian artists. Though not often on display, much of the gallery's permanent collection is online. Check the website. Allow 45 minutes.

Parque do Ibirapuera, Gate 3. ⓒ 011/5085-1300. www.mam.org.br. Admission R$5.50 (US$2.75/£1.75) adults, free for seniors 60 and over and children 10 and under. Free Sun. Tues–Sun 10am–6pm. Bus: 5100 or 5131 from Metrô Brigadeiro.

Museu de Arte Sacra ★★

Sacred art refers to objects—chalices, crosses, statues, paintings, and sculptures—created to adorn churches or for use in Catholic services. Built in 1774, the Mosteiro da Luz (which still functions as a monastery on the upper levels) provides the perfect setting to view these works; piped-in choral music echoes through the stone corridors as light pours in from the cloister, casting a warm glow on the beautiful collection. Many of the silver objects sparkle, ostentatious testimony to the wealth of the Church. Older pieces include woodcarvings and clay statues of angels and saints. Portuguese and English texts explain the origins and name of each piece. Allow 1 hour.

Outside in the garden of the Luz convent is the **Presepio Napolitano,** a lovely miniature village composed of over 1,600 hand-painted figurines depicting life in an 18th-century Neapolitan village. Admission is included with the museum ticket.

Av. Tiradentes 676, Luz. ℂ 011/3326-1373. http://artesacra.sarasa.com.br. Admission R$4 (US$2/£1) adults, free for seniors and children 5 and under. Tues–Sun 11am–7pm. Metrô: Luz or Tirandentes.

Museu do Imigrante ★★ (Kids)

São Paulo's Ellis Island. Beginning in the 19th century, three million immigrants went through the gates of this building to start a new life in Brazil. The last group to get processed was in 1978. Today's visitors get an excellent idea of what those immigrants must have felt. The admission hall, office, hospital, and dormitories are shown in their original condition. Objects are on full display, not hidden in display cases. Another room shows how immigrants first eked out a living in their newly adopted country as masons, printers, farmers, and bakers. The upstairs has been converted into a diorama of an early-20th-century São Paulo street. On Sunday and holidays a historic train takes visitors on a short ride around the museum area. On other days you can still visit the carriages and the station area. Allow 2 hours.

Rua Visconde de Parnaiba 1316, Bras. ℂ 011/6692-1866. www.memorialdoimigrante.sp.gov.br. R$4 (US$2/£1). Train ride R$4 (US$2/£1). Tues–Sun 10am–5pm. Metrô: Estação Bresser. Take the Av. Alcantara Machado exit down the ramp and take the street to the right along the Metrô tracks (Rua Visconde de Parnaiba) for about 3 blocks.

Museu do Paulista do Ipiranga ★★

Located at the birthplace of Brazilian independence—it was here that D. Pedro I in 1822 declared Brazil's independence from Portugal—the museum is a classic European palace: a grand neoclassical building with Versailles-like gardens out front and a "wilder" botanical garden out back. The collection houses some real gems of Brazilian art and some interesting exhibits telling the history of São Paulo. There are also a number of photo exhibits showing 19th-century São Paulo as it developed. Upstairs in the grand salon hangs one of Brazil's most famous paintings, a canvas by Pedro Americo entitled *Independence or Death.* The remainder of the exhibit consists of period furniture, household objects, and clothing. On weekends, the park behind the museum is packed. No English signs. Allow 1 hour.

Praça da Independencia s/n, Ipiranga. ℂ 011/6165-8000. www.mp.usp.br. Admission R$2 (US85¢/£50) adults and children over 6, free for children 6 and under. Tues–Sun 9am–5pm. Closed statutory holidays. Bus: 4506 Jardim Celeste.

Museu Lasar Segall ★

Lovers of modern art, particularly of cubism and Klee and Kandinsky, will enjoy a visit to the Segall museum. Born in the Jewish ghetto of Vilnius in Lithuania in 1891, Segall started his painting career in Europe, but moved to Brazil in 1923. Over the years his work grew increasingly abstract and geometric. The museum was also his residence from 1932 until his death in 1957. On display are his sculptures, pen drawings, watercolors, graphite, and oil paintings. No English signs. Allow 1 hour.

Rua Berta 111, Vila Mariana. ℂ 011/5574-7322. Free admission. Tues–Sat 2–7pm; Sun 2–6pm. Metrô: Vila Mariana.

Pinacoteca do Estado ★★★

The Pinacoteca is a sunlit joy to be in, and one of the best-curated art collections in the city and the country. It's the perfect place for anyone wanting to see and understand Brazilian art. Renovated in 1997, the roof and many interior walls were removed, replaced with a latticework of glass and open

The São Paulo Bienal

Most everyone's heard of the Venice Biennale, so it's surprising how many haven't heard of the Bienal in São Paulo. Every 2 years a huge exhibition hall on the edge of Ibirapuera Park is transformed into the largest visual arts exhibition in Latin America. Most countries sponsor work by one or more of their best artists; curators choose selected others. The event takes place from September and December of even-numbered years. For information contact the **Fundação Bienal de São Paulo** (© 011/5576-7600; http://bienalsaopaulo.globo.com).

spaces, and connected by a series of catwalks. Though none of the signs are in English, the Pinacoteca does an excellent job of displaying some of the best Brazilian artists from the 19th and 20th centuries, from the landscapes of Antonio Parreiras and João da Costa to still-life painters such as Georgina de Albuquerque and João Batista Pagini. The 20th-century work starts to break free of European influence and includes interesting examples of colorful Brazilian pieces bursting with energy. The Pinacoteca's sculpture collection includes a lovely statue by Raphael Galvez entitled *O Brasileiro,* as well as works by Alfredo Ceschiatti, the artist who designed many of the sculptures in Brasilia. Allow 2 hours.

Praça da Luz 2, Luz. © 011/3229-9844. www.pinacoteca.sp.gov.br. Admission R$5 (US$2.50/£1.25) adults, R$2 (US$1/£.50) students, free for children 10 and under. Tues–Sun 10am–6pm. Guided tours leave at 10am, 11:30am, 1pm, and 2:30pm. Metrô: Luz.

2 Architectural Highlights

HISTORIC BUILDINGS & MONUMENTS

One of the few remaining relics of old São Paulo, the **Pátio de Colégio** complex sits a hop and a skip north from Praça da Sé on Rua Boa Vista, on the exact site where the original Jesuit mission was founded in 1554. Though built in 1896, the simple **Anchieta Chapel** (daily 9am–5pm) is an accurate reproduction of the original. Next door to the chapel, the newly renovated **Museu Padre Anchieta** (Tues–Sat 9am–5pm; R$5/US$2.50/£1.25) features a number of maps of São Paulo through the years, plus a large diorama of the original settlement. Better yet, at the back of the complex there's the green and quiet **Café do Páteo** (see "Take a Break," below).

Just around the corner from the Pátio do Colégio at Rua Roberto Simonsen 136 is the **Solar de Marquesa de Santos,** the 18th-century manor house of an important Paulista noblewoman. The Solar is also home to the small **City Museum** (© 011/3241-4238), which contains a number of fascinating photographs of São Paulo before and after it spilled out all over everywhere. Admission is free and it's open Tuesday through Sunday 9am to 5pm.

The pretty mansion **Casa das Rosas** (Av. Paulista 37, Centro; © 011/3285-6986; www.casadasrosas.sp.gov.br) was built in 1928 by Ramos de Azevedo, the same architect who designed the Teatro Municipal and the Pinacoteca. The house, now a cultural center, plays host to small art exhibits, while the rose garden makes for the perfect escape from the Avenida Paulista. Admission is free (Tues–Sun 10am–6pm).

On the north side of downtown, the **Estação de Luz** looks exactly like a British high Victorian railway station: Romanesque red-brick arches and cast-iron pillars support a single vault that covers four tracks and platforms. The materials and design were imported wholesale from England in 1901. It now holds Museum of the Portuguese Language (see "The Top Attractions," earlier in this chapter). Even more elaborate is the nearby **Estação Julio Prestes (Praça Julio Prestes s/n).** Built in 1931, its tall sandstone and red-brick clock tower recalls an Italian campanile. The station was recently renovated and transformed into a concert hall. Call ℂ **011/3337-5414** for programming details. (The police have been working hard to clean up the area around the Estação da Luz and the Julio Prestes cultural center. During the day it is perfectly safe, but at night it's better to take a taxi.)

The 30-story **Edifício Martinelli,** at Av. São João 33, was the city's first skyscraper, inaugurated in 1929. Stylistically it's an interesting mixture—Italian palazzo with a mansard roof—and it remains an important landmark.

In 1965, the city's Italian community reasserted its ascendancy with the 42-story **Edifício Itália,** located on Av. Ipiranga 344 near Praça República. The Itália is rigorously modern—severe as a monk, in fact—but the 41st-floor restaurant, the Terraço Itália, is a great vantage point from which to view the city.

More daring and more interesting from an architectural perspective is Oscar Niemeyer's **Copan Building,** erected in 1951 at the corner of Avenida Ipiranga and Avenida Araújo. Its scale, its celebration of raw concrete, and its curvilinear shape were all quite advanced for the time. It remains a city landmark.

CHURCHES & TEMPLES

There's been a Benedictine monastery on this site by the edge of the Anhangabaú Valley since 1600, just a few decades after São Paulo was founded. The current **Basilica de São Bento** dates to 1910 and is worth a look if you're passing by, though to tell the truth, despite all the marble, wood, and stained glass that went into the construction, the net effect is far from beautiful. Visitors may be most impressed by the German organ with 6,000 pipes. Come for High Mass on Sunday at 10am, and the service is accompanied by Gregorian chants. Open Saturday to Thursday 6am to noon and 2 to 6pm, and Friday from 2 to 6pm. Gregorian chanting is Monday and Saturday at 7am, and Sunday at 10am.

São Paulo's **Metropolitan Cathedral** is a curious structure, a blend of Byzantine and High German Gothic. Construction began in 1911, but wasn't completed until 1954. Its best feature may be the Praça da Sé out front, which is lined with stately imperial palms and occupied during the daylight hours by street preachers, some of them quite good. It's open Monday to Saturday 8am to 5pm, Sunday 8am to 1pm and 3 to 6pm.

On the other side of Centro on the Largo do Paisssandu stands the pretty yellow **Irmandade de N.S. do Rosario dos Homens Prêtos.** Built by São Paulo's freed-slave community, the church is now something of a refuge for the down and out. Homeless congregate on the steps, and inside the cream-and-ocher interior the offering and donation boxes are housed in thick steel safes.

3 Neighborhoods to Explore

São Paulo is a great city for pedestrians, and most neighborhoods can easily be explored on foot. Just be very careful when crossing the street. São Paulo has the highest number of motorcycle couriers in the country, and it's motorcycles that are responsible for the highest number of pedestrian deaths. Be particularly careful when crossing in between stopped cars; motorcycles often ride at high speed between lanes.

TAKE A BREAK

While strolling the historic part of downtown, duck into the **Pátio do Colégio.** The **Café do Páteo** (*©* **011/3105-6899**), open Tuesday to Sunday 9am to 5pm, has a lovely garden and terrace where you can rest your legs over a coffee and slice of cake.

CENTRO

The original city of São Paulo was founded in 1554 on a hilltop between two rivers, the **Tamanduatei** and the **Anhangabaú.** The original site is now occupied by a partial reproduction of the old mission called the **Pátio do Colégio.** Close by, the **Cathedral da Sé** (also called the **Metropolitan Cathedral**) was completed only in 1954, though the square it occupies—the **Praça da Sé**—has had a church on it since the city's founding. Throughout the city center, streets veer off from and intersect with each other in odd and intriguing ways.

Key architectural sights in this area include the all-white **Banespa Tower** ♠♠ and the 1920s **Martinelli Building.** Two of the key pedestrian streets are **Rua Direita** and **Rua São Bento,** which leads northward to the **São Bento Monastery.** This, too, dates from the 20th century, but the site, high on the banks of what was once the Anhangabaú River, dates back to 1600.

The river itself was long ago filled and turned into a freeway, an act of ecological madness for which the city has paid ever since with flooded roadways. Where the freeway enters downtown (opposite the monastery), it's been sunk beneath a huge civic plaza called the **Parque Anhangabaú.** At either end, the park is crossed by two high viaducts, the pedestrian-only **Santa Ifigênia Viaduct** in the north and the **Viaduto do Chá** in the south.

Going across the middle of the Parque Anhangabaú you come out on the far side in the **Praça Ramos de Azevedo,** upon which stands the pretty Beaux Arts **Teatro Municipal.** This bank of the Anhangabaú is often called **Nova Centro** or New Centro, to distinguish it from the old center, **Centro Velho,** across the way. The buildings are newer, and apartments and hotels are mixed in with the office towers. From the Teatro Municipal a number of crowded pedestrian streets—**avenidas 7 de Abril, Baron de Itapetininga,** and **24 de Maio**—lead west through downtown to the large and green **Praça República.**

Going northward from here leads through the run-down **Luz** neighborhood to the high Victorian **Luz Station** and adjacent **Luz Park.** Just nearby one also finds the **Pinocoteca do Estado** and the **Sacred Art Museum.**

LIBERDADE

One of the city's older neighborhoods, Liberdade got its name after the 1888 abolition of slavery when the neighborhood's main square, which once held the official city whipping post or *pelourinho*, was renamed **Praça da Liberdade.** Italians were the first immigrant group to settle here, but as they moved into other neighborhoods Japanese immigrants gradually moved in. The best way to experience the area is to get off at the **Liberdade** Metrô stop and take a stroll down **Rua Galvão Bueno.** In addition to pretty Japanese lamp standards, the street boasts an infinitude of mineral shops and some great sushi restaurants, as well as Japanese faces everywhere. Now very proud of its Asian heritage, Liberdade celebrates it with an excellent **Museum of Japanese Immigration** and a popular **Sunday market** on the Liberdade square.

The Museu da Imigração Japonesa ✦ features enthusiastic staff members eager to show off three floors of photographs, artifacts, and film loops telling the hundred-year history of the Japanese experience in Brazil.

Rua São Joaquim 381, Liberdade. ✆ 011/3209-5465. Admission R$5 (US$2.50/£1.35) adults, R$2.50 (US$1.25/£.70) seniors and children over 7. Tues–Sun 1:30–5:30pm.

HIGIENÓPOLIS

Higienópolis (Healthy City) owes its name to a blatant bit of developer marketing. At the beginning of the 20th century wealthier Paulistas were starting to move out of Centro to get away from the mosquito-infested swamps around the banks of the Anhangabaú River. Green and leafy Higienópolis was one of most sought-after destinations. Even today some of the elegant mansions from 80 years ago still remain. It lies on a slight rise west of Centro, centered around **Rua Higienópolis** and **Avenida Angélica.** It's here you'll find the small but restaurant-packed **Praça Vila Boim** and the **Museu de Arte Brasileira (FAAP).**

JARDINS

What is currently called Jardins (gardens) is a combination of a number of neighborhoods such as **Jardim Europa, Jardim Paulista,** and **Jardim America** that extend southwest in a regular grid pattern (mostly) from the towers and offices of the Avenida Paulista. Built after the Avenida Paulista developed at the end of the 19th century, these neighborhoods were carefully planned according to the principles of the British Garden City movement. In Jardim Paulista the lots were built with laneways for cars, and apartment buildings were not allowed. Jardim America was even more exclusive; lots were not to be subdivided, and row houses and apartment buildings were not allowed. Some of these regulations have fallen by the wayside. Jardim Europa is still home to mostly villas and mansions, but the **Rua Augusta,** which runs through the heart of the Jardins, now has many hotels and some of the best restaurants in the city. Where Rua Augusta meets **Rua Oscar Freire** is now the prime shopping area in São Paulo.

AVENIDA PAULISTA

What was once a track along a ridgeline through virgin Atlantic rainforest has come quite a way in just over 100 years. Over one million people and 100,000 cars make their way along the **Avenida Paulista** on any given business day. Even back in 1891 its original designers intended it to be a grand ceremonial boulevard. The street was then home to São Paulo's elite, the place where coffee barons and factory owners built their magnificent villas. One of these grand mansions still remains, the **Casa das Rosas** down near the Brigadeiro Metrô stop. Beginning in the '30s, however, the old mansions gave way to office buildings and then ever higher commercial skyscrapers. Collectively, they make for an impressive statement of wealth and prestige, though individually the architecture is pretty mediocre. There are two worthwhile attractions near the north end of the Avenida: the **Museu Arte São Paulo (MASP)** and, just opposite, **Siqueira Campos Park,** also called by its old name, **Trianon Park.**

PINHEIROS/ITAIM BIBI

Now prime residential neighborhoods with excellent restaurants, good hotels, and some of the city's better nightlife, these areas didn't get developed until well into the 20th century. **Itaim Bibi** is set on a large flood plain periodically swamped by the Pinheiros River.

Its first streets were laid out in the 1920s, and not until the '40s did the original 1-hectare (2½-acre) lots (used for extensive backyard orchards and gardens) begin to give way to something more urban. **Pinheiros,** too, was once a flood plain as well as a landing point for canoes delivering goods across the Pinheiros River. In 1904 a streetcar line connected this part of town to Centro, encouraging this neighborhood to grow. These streets share a principal thoroughfare, **Avenida Brig. Faria Lima.** Its wide, busy street is not as fashionable as Rua Augusta but is dotted with shopping malls such as the **Shopping Iguatemi.** Crossing Faria Lima in Pinheiros, **Avenida Rebouças** boasts a number of restaurants and bars with live music.

VILA MADALENA

Tucked away behind Pinheiros, Vila Madalena became popular in the '60s and '70s among University of São Paulo staff and students looking for affordable housing. The neighborhood still has a slightly bohemian feel, and many artists and designers have both homes and galleries here. The Vila is also one of the city's most popular dining spots, featuring many fine restaurants and a number of interesting bars. (Check our listings in chapter 7 and "São Paulo After Dark," later in this chapter, for some excellent options.) The neighborhood centers around the **Rua Purpurina,** from **Rua Harmonia** to **Rua Murato Coelho.**

4 Plazas & Parks

MARKETS

Located to the north of Praça da Sé, the **Mercado Municipal** ✦✦ (Rua da Cantareira 306) is an imposing neo-Gothic hall built in 1933. In addition to its enormous display of Brazilian fruits, vegetables, cheeses, and other food goods, the hall is noted for its huge stained-glass windows depicting scenes of coffee growing and cattle ranching. The market is open Monday through Saturday from 5am to 4pm, but is at its most active in the early morning.

Moments **Some Spectacular Views**

The pedestrian-only **Santa Ifigênia Viaduct** runs from one side of Centro to the other, high above the Parque do Anhangabaú. At the midpoint you get a wonderful view of São Paulo's old downtown.

The best view of São Paulo is from atop the **Banespa Tower** ✦✦, 24 Rua João Brícola ✆ **011/3249-7428.** Ascending to its 35th-floor observation deck, you get an incredible view—high-rise towers, 360 degrees of them, filling every inch of land for as far as the eye can see. It's open Monday through Friday from 10am to 5pm, and better yet, it's free. Bring ID to show the door guards.

Built in 1965, the 42-story **Edifício Itália** (✆ **011/2189-2929**), at Av. Ipiranga 344 near Praça da República, features a 41st-floor restaurant, the Terraço Itália, which offers a great vantage point from which to view the city. (The food's not great—stick to drinks or tea.) Cover is R$10 (US$5/£2.70), and there's a R$15 (US$7.50/£4) drink minimum. It's open Monday through Friday from 6pm to midnight, and Saturday from 6pm to 1am.

Every Sunday from 10am to 5pm the courtyard space beneath the **MASP** building on Avenida Paulista is the scene of an **antiques fair.** Dealers are registered, and the quality of the wares is often good.

Saturday and Sunday on the **Praça Dom Orione** in the Italian **Bixiga** neighborhood there's a small antiques/flea market. On Sunday on the **Praça da Liberdade** (next to the Liberdade Metrô stop) São Paulo's Japanese residents celebrate their heritage with an outdoor market featuring an excellent and inexpensive selection of Japanese cuisine. A crafts fair here also features mostly tacky Oriental knickknacks (porcelain dogs, bonsai trees, and so on).

PARKS & GARDENS

Adjacent to the Pinacoteca, the **Parque da Luz** is well worth a look. Inaugurated in 1825 as the city's botanical garden, the garden was then outside of the city limits, and locals at the time wondered whether it was wise to set aside such a large piece of land. Nowadays the park's lovely old trees contrast with the modern sculptures from the archives of the Pinacoteca that dot the park's walkways. Note that the large numbers of solitary ladies admiring the statuary are actually working girls; they're so discreetly dressed and nonaggressive they're easy to overlook. The park is heavily policed and safe during the day. It's open Tuesday through Sunday from 9am to 6pm.

Opposite the MASP is the green refuge of the **Parque Tenente Siqueira Campos,** often known by its old name of **Trianon Park.** The park is thickly planted with Atlantic rainforest vegetation, laced with walking trails, and dotted here and there with children's play areas. It's a wonderful green refuge from the bustle on Avenida Paulista and is open daily 6am to 6pm.

So much is there to see and do in the vast green space known as **Ibirapuera Park** that we've covered it under "The Top Attractions," earlier in this chapter.

OUTDOOR PLAZAS

The **Praça da Sé,** in front of the Metropolitan Cathedral, has recently been lovingly restored. Two files of imperial palms enclose a flagstone-covered courtyard with a sundial at the center. People stroll through this area, slowing or stopping to give an ear to the ever-present street preachers.

The centerpiece of new Centro, **Praça da República** is more park than square. There are numerous little walking paths winding through a thick overhang of trees in which bright green parrots screech, chatter, and chirp. There are benches to sit on, several small lagoons, a fountain, and a bandstand.

Between the Praça da República and the Praça da Sé lies the city's newest and most interesting square, the **Parque Anhangabaú.** Running an eight-lane freeway over the top of the Anhangabaú River that once flowed through Centro was probably not one of São Paulo's better planning moves, but the city recently made amends by covering a 1km (½-mile) stretch of the freeway with this beautifully landscaped urban plaza. In the daytime it's occupied by pedestrians, sun-tanners, lunch-break idlers, and clusters of folks listening to street musicians.

5 Especially for Kids

Parque da Monica (Kids)   Young kids will love the Parque da Monica, an amusement park based on the popular Brazilian cartoon character Monica. It's located at the Shopping Eldorado and easily accessible by bus. The park includes games, activities, rides, and shows geared toward kids in the 2-to-10 age range.

> ### (Kids Take a Break at Siqueira Campos
>
> Just opposite the MASP on Avenida Paulista, the lush Siqueira Campos Park has several small play areas featuring swings, teeter-totters, and slides. It's a fun and quiet refuge from the bustle of the city.

Shopping Eldorado, Av. Rebouças 3970. (© 011/3093-7766. Admission R$21 (US$11/£5.50) adults and children over 14, R$30 (US$15/£8) children 2–14. Wed–Fri 10am–5pm; Sat–Sun 10am–8pm. Bus: 6251.

Playcenter (Kids Brazil's biggest roller coaster plus a huge variety of other rides and games are all at this large amusement park, about a 20-minute walk from the Barra Funda Metrô stop.

Rua José Gomes Falcão 20, Barra Funda. (© 011/3350-0199. Admission R$24 (US$12/£6.50) with unlimited rides on most attractions, free for children 5 and under. Thurs–Sun 10am–7pm. Metrô: Barra Funda. Playcenter runs a free shuttle from Barra Funda every 30 min. during open hours. To catch the shuttle follow signs to Terminal Rodoviaria.

Zoológico (Kids This large and impressive zoo has more than 3,000 species, most in large enclosures that resemble the animals' native habitats. There are also lunch and picnic areas, and a petting zoo for smaller children. It's about 45 minutes southeast of the city. Allow 3 hours.

Av. Miugal Estéfano 4241, Água Funda. (© 011/5073-0811. www.zoologico.com.br. Admission R$10 (US$5/£2.70) adults and children over 7, free for seniors and children 7 and under. Tues–Sun 9am–5pm. Metrô: Jabaquara; catch microbus to Jardim Zoológico from Jabaquara station (R$3.30/US$1.65/£.90).

6 Organized Tours

SIGHTSEEING TOURS

Easygoing Brazil (© 011/3801-9540; www.easygoing.com.br) specializes in private tours for foreign visitors. They work with excellent English-speaking guides. The company offers a 1-day tour of São Paulo for R$150/US$75/£41 that includes the city's "must-sees" and leaves room for your interests, whether it's art, museums, fashion, parks, anything! Easygoing also runs several tours that will take you out of São Paulo—to a coffee plantation, or to the mountain resort of Campos do Jordão, or on a hike along the Cantarareira hills that look over the city (R$220–R$385/US$110–US$193/£60–£104). Prices are for a private tour for two people; with three or more the price goes down significantly. Easygoing even has a 1-day tour of Rio (though we don't recommend it unless you have absolutely no alternative). They fly you to Rio on the early flight, show you the sights, and return you to São Paulo in time for a late dinner. The tour is popular with high-powered execs who only have a day to get away. R$365/US$183/£99 not including airfare.

7 Outdoor Activities & Spectator Sports

GOLF In the western suburb of Osasco, **São Francisco Golf Club** (Av. Martin Luther King 1527, Osasco; (© 011/3681-8752; www.golfsaofrancisco.com.br) offers a 9-hole par-71 course open to the public Tuesday through Sunday from 7am to 6pm. Greens fees are R$125 (US$63/£34) weekdays, R$245 (US$123/£66) weekends and holidays. The club also rents clubs and shoes.

HORSE RACING   Races run Monday, Saturday, and Sunday at the **Jockey Clube de São Paulo** (Av. Lineu Paula Machado 1263, Cidade Jardim; © **011/2161-0240;** www.jockeysp.com.br). On Monday races start at 6pm; on Saturday and Sunday the races start at 1:30pm. Minimum bet is R$1 (US50¢/£.25). The club has a restaurant open for dinner Monday through Friday and for lunch on weekends; the bar Cantér is popular even with those who don't watch the races.

MOTOR RACING   Important races such as the **Brazil Formula 1 Grand-Prix** take place at the Autódromo de Interlagos, Av. Senador Toetônia Vilela 259. Call © **011/ 5521-9911.** Tickets for this sought-after event sell out up to 6 months in advance; try www.gpbrasil.com.br for information on upcoming dates.

SOCCER   The big clubs in town are **São Paulo** (www.saopaulofc.net), **Corinthians** (www.corinthians.com.br), **Palmeiras** (http://palmeiras.globo.com), and **Portuguesa** (www.portuguesa.com.br). Any match between these teams is likely worth seeing. So are all the state championships. Though the team websites provide details on upcoming games, deciphering soccer schedules is the stuff of serious scholarship; better to just ask your hotel clerk or bellboy if there are any big games coming up. The city's big stadium is the **Morumbi,** located in the Morumbi neighborhood at Praça Roberto Gomes Pedrosa 1 (© **011/3749-8071**).

8 Shopping in São Paulo

THE SHOPPING SCENE

Paulistas say that if you can't buy it in São Paulo, you can't buy it in Brazil. They're probably right. São Paulo has it all, from international fashion boutiques to little local crafts markets.

The city has a number of shopping areas worth exploring. **Jardins** is well known for its high-end fashion boutiques. The main shopping streets are **Rua Augusta,** the parallel **Rua Haddock Lobo,** and their cross streets: **Rua Oscar Freire** and **Alameda Lorena.** This area is packed with national and international brands, expensive clothing and jewelry, gourmet foods, and luxurious gift shops.

In **Centro** (downtown São Paulo), **Rua 25 de Março** is the place where Paulistas rich and poor browse the market stalls and small shops for inexpensive items such as belts, buttons, small toys, gadgets, towels, textiles, and socks. Keep an eye on your purse, though, as the streets are chaotic with vendors and stalls vying for space, and throngs of people making their way through.

For Oriental trinkets, there's no better place than São Paulo's Japanese neighborhood, **Liberdade.** On Sunday there's a large market with great food and a variety of market stalls selling everything from bonsai plants to porcelain Buddha statues.

Then there are the malls, which in São Paulo have been elevated to a whole other shopping experience: elegant, upscale, and refined. Sophisticated brands, boutiques, and fine dining can be found in a number of malls; the best-known ones are **Shopping Morumbi** (www.morumbishopping.com.br), **Shopping Iguatemi** (www.iguatemi saopaulo.com.br) and **Shopping Patio Higienópolis** (www.patiohigienopolis.com.br), located in upscale neighborhoods close to the city center.

And finally, there are the street markets, which are particularly popular on the weekends. With antiques, food, and flea markets, they provide a great excuse to get out, browse, haggle, and shop.

HOURS   Most stores are open from 9am to 6pm Monday through Friday and 9am to 1pm on Saturday. Malls are open from 10am to 10pm, Monday through Saturday.

MONEY   Most stores will accept credit cards, though you can often get a discount if you pay cash. Traveler's checks are not normally accepted.

SHOPPING FROM A TO Z
BOOKS
Centro Cultural FNAC   The Centro Cultural boasts several floors of books, plus a coffee shop, cybercafe, and a large music and video department. The foreign language section (English, French, Spanish, and German) is extensive, and the guidebook and map section offers a good selection. Open on Sunday. Praça dos Omaguás 34, Pinheiros ℭ 011/3579-2000. www.fnac.com.br. Bus: 6251.

Haddock Lobo Books and Magazines   Open every day until midnight, this bookstore has an excellent selection of international magazines and books, including some guidebooks. Space is at a premium in this tiny store, so if you can't find something, ask. Chances are the owner will be able to dig it out for you. Rua Haddock 1503. ℭ 011/3082-9449. http://haddocklobo.com.br. Bus: 7392.

Mille Foglie   Everything you ever wanted to read on cuisine. This bookstore/cooking school stocks over 3,000 titles on culinary topics. Many of the books are in English and there's a section on Brazilian cooking. Open Monday through Friday 11am to 8pm, and Saturday 10am to 2pm. Rua da Consolação 3542 (corner Oscar Freire), Cerqueira Cesar. ℭ 011/3083-6777. www.millefoglie.com.br. Bus: 7392.

DEPARTMENT STORE
Daslu   To call Daslu a department store doesn't really do it justice. This is shopping taken to the nth degree, shopping with a capital "S." Daslu offers 17,000 sq. m of luxurious upscale shopping. Uniformed staff guide you through the maze, while strategically placed espresso bars keep you energized with complimentary hits of caffeine. A large part of the women's department is off-limits to men. Daslu offers some of the best-known international designers such as Prada, Dolce & Gabbana, Dior, Chanel, Valentino, Armani, and Gucci as well as an array of Brazilian names, including Iodice, Forum, Maria Bonita, and beach fashions from Lenny and Rosa Chá. In addition to designer fashions, the store sells home decorating items, jewelry, sporting goods, audio and video equipment, and even cars. The service is top-notch and the restaurants and cafes throughout the store are elegant and refined. Av. Chedid Jafet 131, Vila Olimpia. ℭ 011/3841-4000. www.daslu.com.br. Taxi recommended.

FASHIONS
For Women
Clube Chocolate   Another place that doesn't quite fit neatly into the shopping category. The Clube Chocolate looks like a gallery, houses an upscale martini bar and cozy cafe, and sells a variety of renowned national and international fashions for men and women as well as plants, gift items, and home decorations. And the chocolate, you ask? The only type you'll find is the Brazilian women's clothing line sold under the Chocolate label. At least it's low-cal. Rua Oscar Freire 913, Jardins. ℭ 011/3084-1500. www.clubechocolate.com. Bus: 7110.

Santa Gema   Now in its 10th year, Santa Gema pulls in the well-heeled Paulista with an eye for international fashion. The store represents international designers such

---

Brazilian Fashion
The Jardins neighborhood is the place to find excellent Brazilian labels, including **Guaraná Brasil,** Alameda Lorena 1599 (✆ **011/3061-0182); Maria Bonita,** Rua Oscar Freire 705 (✆ **011/3063-3609);** and **Forum,** Rua Oscar Freire 916 (✆ **011/3085-6269).** For the latest beach styles check out **Rosa Chá,** Rua Oscar Freire 977 (✆ **011/3081-2793).**

---

as Christian Dior, Bijoux Givenchy, Gerard Yosca, Rodo, and Michael Golan. Rua Alameda Lorena 1616, Jardins. ✆ **011/3081-2920.** Also Rua Oscar Freire 691, Jardins. ✆ **011/3081-1533.** Bus: 7392.

Sinhá Those looking for elegant and fashionable clothing in plus sizes will have a hard time in Brazil. Most stores only stock up to size 42 (the equivalent of a North American size 12 or 14). Sinhá offers a beautifully designed collection, including evening wear, for sizes up to 52 (North American size 20). Shopping Patio Higienópolis, Av. Higienópolis 618. ✆ **011/3823-2519.** Bus: 508.

For Men
Mr. Kitsch There's nothing gaudy about this excellent collection of menswear. Though it stocks a small collection of suits and formal wear, the largest selection is of comfortable and simple casual wear. Shopping Morumbi, Av. Roque Petroni Junior 1089, Morumbi. ✆ **011/5181-9304.** Bus: 5121 or 5154.

Richard's My favorite men's store in all of Brazil. From stylish and elegant suits to comfortable casual wear, khakis, button-down shirts, and T-shirts, these clothes are high quality and come in great vibrant colors. Av. Higienópolis 615, Shopping Higienópolis. ✆ **011/3823-2733.** Bus: 508.

FOOD
Casa Santa Luzia The size of a grocery store, Santa Luzia is stuffed with imported products that can be next to impossible to find anywhere else in Brazil, including cold cuts, pastas, sauces, and cheeses, as well as sweets and desserts; the mango-and-passion-fruit-flavored minigâteaus are to die for! Alameda Lorena 1471 (corner with Rua Augusta), Jardins. ✆ **011/3897-5000.** Bus: 7392.

GALLERIES
Britto It's hard to miss Britto's colorful and bold pop-art style. The store sells original and limited-edition prints of Britto's work, as well as accessories such as mugs and mouse pads decorated with his work. Rua Oscar Freire 562, Cerqueira Cesar. ✆ **011/3062-7350.** Bus: 7392.

Galeria Fortes Vilaça This gallery represents over 20 Brazilian and international artists who work in Brazil. Exhibits range from paintings to installation art, sculpture, and mixed media. Rua Fradique Coutinho 1500, Vila Madalena. ✆ **011/3032-7066.** Metrô: Vila Madalena.

Galeria Luisa Strina One of the older contemporary art galleries in town, Luisa Strina now showcases work from a number of young national and international artists. This gallery usually has interesting exhibits of artwork done in various media: paintings, bronze, glass, or photo art. Rua Oscar Freire 502, Jardins. ✆ **011/3088-2471.**

Tips **Online Gallery Guide**

For information on the city's galleries pick up a copy of the *Mapa das Artes São Paulo* at the tourist office or check www.mapadasartes.com.br.

Monica Filgueiras de Almeida   This gallery specializes in the same media as Galeria Luisa Strina and usually displays a good variety of contemporary pieces, mostly of Brazilian artists. Rua Bela Sintra 1533. ✆ 011/3081-9492.

GIFTS & SOUVENIRS

Arte Tribal   Make sure to explore this little alleyway store off the trendy Rua Augusta. The front of the store displays Brazilian native art: necklaces, pottery, baskets, bags, and woodcarvings. In the rear of the store and on the walls of the alleyway, shoppers find crafts from native people all over the world, though most of the works are African. Rua Augusta 2481. ✆ 011/3081-8170. Bus: 7392.

Art India   Souvenirs and handicrafts made by Indians from tribes across Brazil. There are beautiful necklaces made from colorful seeds and household items such as wooden spoons, bowls, and baskets or pottery. Rua Augusta 1371, loja 119, Cerqueira Cesar. ✆ 011/3283-2102. Metrô: Consolação.

JEWELRY

Joalheria Esplanada   Most of us would be happy just browsing this beautiful upscale jewelry store. A favorite among many Paulistas, this shop has been around for over 70 years. Rua Augusta 2777. ✆ 011/3081-5230. Bus: 7392.

Petra Brazilis   A specialist in Brazilian gemstones, Petra has the usual birds and chess sets, but there's also some fine jewelry. Loose stones are also available. Alameda Itú 215, Jardins. ✆ 011/251-3805. Bus: 7392.

MALLS & SHOPPING CENTERS

Shopping Iguatemi   One of the more elegant malls in town, Iguatemi houses many exclusive brand names such as Bally, Tiffany's, and Louis Vuitton. On the top floor of the mall are a movie theater and a number of food courts and full-service restaurants. The building is fully wheelchair-accessible. Av. Brigadeiro Faria Lima 2232, Jardim Paulistano. ✆ 011/3038-6000. www.iguatemisaopaulo.com.br. Bus: 775 or 637G.

Shopping Patio Higienópolis   Shopping-mad Paulistas are demanding when it comes to malls. This is one of their favorites. Built in 1999, the entrance resembles a Victorian crystal palace, with large glass and wrought-iron doors and awnings. No department stores or large chains are in this mall; the shops are mostly high-end boutiques. The mall also has a children's play area. Av. Higienópolis 615. ✆ 011/3823-2300. www.patiohigienopolis.com.br. Bus: 508 (from Paulista or Liberdade).

MARKETS

Mercado das Pulgas   This flea market (*pulgas* are fleas in Portuguese) attracts a wide variety of merchants, buskers, musicians, and shoppers. The variety on offer is huge: junk, good-quality antiques, secondhand clothing, crafts, and whatever else people think of putting out for sale. Open Saturday from 9am to 5pm. Praça Benedito Calixto, Pinheiros. No phone. Bus: 778J.

Mercado Municipal Built in the 1930s, this gorgeous market hall with its sky-lights and stained-glass windows is a fabulous setting for one of the city's largest produce and food markets. Open Monday to Saturday from 5am to 4pm, the hall is packed with vendors selling vegetables, fresh fish, meats, fruits, and herbs. The food section is a popular place to grab a *cafezinho* or a sandwich. Rua da Cantareira 306, Centro. ✆ 011/3326-3401. Metrô: São Bento.

MUSIC

Casa Amadeus A great selection of Brazilian sheet music and very helpful staff. There's also a good variety of musical instruments: *cavaquinhos* (a Brazilian mandolin), percussion instruments, and hand-held rattles and shakers. Av. Ipiranga 1129, Centro. ✆ 011/228-0098. Metrô: Republica.

Saraiva Megastore Saraiva sells books, magazines, and stationery as well as CDs, videos, and DVDs. The CD collection is large, though limited to the commercially successful artists. Shopping Morumbi, Av. Roque Petroni Junior 1089, Brooklin. ✆ 011/5542-0336. Bus: 5121 or 5154.

PERFUMES

O Boticario Long before aromatherapy became a household term, O Boticario was already using fresh flowers and herbs to create its light fragrances. It now has a line of body products and makeup, but the bestsellers are still the perfumes. Rua Augusta 2887, Cerqueira Cesar. ✆ 011/3898-2973. Bus: 7392.

SHOES

Banana Price You'll find a huge collection of national and international designers at low prices, such as heavily discounted collections of Nine West, Red's, Massimo, and Dilly. Other leather products available include bags, purses, and belts. Alameda Lorena 1604. ✆ 011/3081-3460. Bus: 7392.

9 São Paulo After Dark

If Sinatra had known about São Paulo, he would never have given the "city that never sleeps" title to New York. Most Paulistas won't even *set foot* in a club until midnight. Take a cab into Vila Olímpia around the witching hour, and you'll find yourself in a traffic jam formed by everyone just heading out for the evening.

Less casual than Cariocas, Paulistas love to dress up when going out. Women are partial to black or other dark colors. Men are less formal. Good casual is fine, but jeans and running shoes likely won't make it past the door at many clubs.

To catch the big names in Brazilian music, São Paulo is the place. The city gets more of the stars, playing more often, than any other city in Brazil. São Paulo also offers a variety of theater, dance, opera, and classical music.

WHERE TO GO FOR INFO An excellent source of arts and entertainment information is the *Guia da Folha,* an entertainment guide published in the Friday *Folha de São Paulo* newspaper. In addition to theater and concert listings, it includes bars and restaurants (with updated hours and phone numbers) as well as exhibits and special events. On the first page is a useful overview of all the free events that week, titled in Portuguese *é gratis.* The guide also includes details on upcoming concerts (*shows* in Portuguese) and events at nightclubs *(casas noturnas). Veja* magazine (Brazil's equivalent of *Newsweek*) comes out every week on Sunday and includes a separate entertainment guide called *Veja São Paulo;* many hotels provide this insert for free. For vultures of high culture, the cultural department of the state government puts out a listing magazine every month, *Revista Cultural,* with details on classical music, dance, theater, and exhibits.

THE PERFORMING ARTS

São Paulo is considered—both by Paulistas and grudgingly by Cariocas—to be the cultural capital of Brazil. The classical music scene is excellent, and the theater scene positively thriving. The majority of high culture takes place at just two halls. The **Teatro Municipal** is the more traditional and arguably the more luxurious of the two. Built in 1903 in the heart of the old downtown, this Parisian-style opera house is said to have near-perfect acoustics. The **Sala São Paulo** is the main hall in the recently renovated Estação Julio Prestes, a grand old Victorian railway station that has been completely restored and adapted for use as a cultural center. Both halls put on a rich program of classical music, dance, opera, and theater. For free performances, check for the "gratis" listings in the *Revista Cultural.*

THEATER

Ibirapuera Park   The largest park in the city is a popular venue for free outdoor concerts. Check the listings guides for dates and details on upcoming shows. Av. Pedro Alvares Cabral (gate 10) or Av. República do Libano (gate 8). Bus: 675C from Ana Rosa Metrô stop, or 775 to Santa Cruz Metrô stop.

Sala São Paulo   This venue is one of the hottest tickets in town, no matter the show. The setting is glorious, in the soaring main hall of a grand Victorian railway station that's found a second life as a cultural center. Acoustical engineers did a brilliant job on the adaptation. The hall sounds great, and Paulistas just can't get enough of it. The São Paulo Symphony Orchestra (www.osesp.art.br) now makes their home here. The inexpensive Saturday afternoon concerts often sell out. For concert information, check the website under *"programmação e ingressos."* Praça Julio Prestes s/n. 𝄞 011/3367-9500. www.salasaopaulo.art.br. Tickets R$25–R$100 (US$13–US$50/£7–£27). Metrô: Luz.

Teatro Municipal   This elegant 19th-century building provides the perfect backdrop for any performance, be it ballet, concert, or opera. São Paulo's city opera company, ballet company, and symphonic orchestra all make their homes here and put on regular performances. The theater is also home to a pair of choral companies, an experimental orchestra, and a music school. So popular is the teatro that it's in use nearly every night and many days of the week. Check the website listings (look under "programmação") for lunchtime concerts, the perfect way to break up a day of sightseeing or shopping. Praça Ramos de Azevedo s/n. 𝄞 011/3223-8698. http://portal.prefeitura.sp. gov.br/secretarias/cultura/theatromunicipal. Metrô: Anhangabaú.

MUSIC & DANCE CLUBS

Large and varied, São Paulo's nightlife scene is also quite spread out, with little entertainment clusters in neighborhoods all over town; barhopping is really more like car hopping. Best to pick a neighborhood, enjoy dinner, and then grab a drink or catch a show at a club nearby so you don't waste time and cab dollars stuck in one of São Paulo's late-night traffic jams. **Vila Olímpia** is where the 18- to 30-year-olds go for nightlife, with a number of large dance clubs and some of the city's best bars (see sidebar below). **Vila Madalena** is more in vogue with the 25- to 45-year-olds who enjoy bars and restaurants more than dance clubs.

> ### *Tips* **In São Paulo, Know Your Club Lingo!**
> The word *boate* or *boite* used in Rio for a nightclub or dance club refers in São Paulo almost exclusively to a strip or sex club.

As in most Brazilian cities, many bars and clubs charge a drink minimum instead of or in addition to a cover charge. Patrons receive a slip of paper on arrival. All your expenses are recorded on the card and tallied up when you leave. Lose the card and you get charged a steep maximum fee (the assumption being that you've been on a bender all night).

LIVE MUSIC

Bourbon Street Music Club   In the land of samba, forró, and *axé*, it can be hard to find a club with blues and jazz on the menu. Such is Bourbon Street. This midsize venue is a safe bet almost any night of the week (closed Sun–Mon) for bossa nova, jazz, funk, or even salsa. Anything but samba. Doors open at 9pm; the show starts at 10:30pm (11:30pm on Fri and Sat). Rua dos Chanes 127, Moema. ℂ **011/5561-1643**. Cover R$15–R$35 (US$6.15–US$15/£3–£7.50). Bus: 5154.

Grazie a Dio!   One of the best known bars and bistros in Vila Madalena, Grazie a Dio! is also one of the best places in the city for live music almost any day of the week. Bands vary from night to night. Expect anything from pop to samba-rock to salsa or merengue. Shows start at 10pm and cover rarely exceeds R$15 (US$7.50/£4). Open Sunday through Thursday 8pm to 1am, Friday through Saturday 8pm to 2am. Rua Girassol 67, Vila Madalena. ℂ **011/3031-6568**. www.grazieadio.com.br. Metrô: Vila Madalena.

Piu Piu   After 19 years this popular downtown venue still hops with a range of Brazilian contemporary artists, from rock to samba to jazz. Tickets run from R$10 to R$20 (US$5–US$10/£2.50–£5.50). Check www.cafepiupiu.com.br for listings. Rua Treze de Maio 134, Bela Vista. ℂ **011/3258-8066**. Metrô: Brigadeiro.

Tom Brasil   Exclusively dedicated to Brazilian music, Tom Brasil has recently been voted best MPB venue in São Paulo. Now in a new custom-built complex, it hosts big names such as Cassia Eller, Elba Ramalho, and Jorge Ben. Ticket prices range from R$35 to R$100 (US$18–US$50/£9.50–£27). Rua Bragançao Paulista 1281, Chácara Santo Antonio. ℂ **011/2163-2120**. www.tombr.com.br. Bus: 675N.

Samba   The music on offer should be no surprise at this Vila Madelaina hot spot. In case there was any doubt, the interior features a 16m-long (52-ft.) wall collage of photos of famous sambistas of yore. Wednesdays onward the house moves to the sound of live samba. Saturday afternoon, there's music plus a traditional feijoada lunch, from 1pm onward. Open Wednesday to Sunday 7pm to 2am. Rua Fidalga 308, Vila Madalena. ℂ **011/3819-4619**. Cover R$10–R$20 (US$5–US$10/£2.70–£5.40). Bus: 109P.

DANCE CLUBS

Azucar   Hot, hot, hot. The latest hit on São Paulo's club scene is Cuban club Azucar. Salsa, merengue, and other Latin beats get the crowd going. It opens at 7pm every day of the week, but things really get happening after midnight. The stiff drink minimum attracts a more mature (25- to 45-year-olds) and attractive crowd. Rua Mario Feraz 423, Itaim Bibi. ℂ **011/3078-3130**. www.azucar.com.br. Cover R$25–R$35 (US$13–US$18/£7–£9.50). Bus: 107P.

Love Club   A lotta love indeed for lovers of electronic music. Brazilian and international celebrity DJs make regular appearances here and spin techno and house. Maybe one exception is DJ Heron on Wednesday, who heats things up with his rhythmic Carioca funk. Open Tuesday through Friday midnight to 6am and Saturday midnight to 10am. Rua Pequetita 189, Vila Olímpia. ℂ 011/3044-1613. www.loveclub.com.br. Cover R$30–R$60 (US$15–US$30/£8–16). Bus: 675N.

D-Edge   São Paulo's newest, hottest dance club features wall-long flashing monster woofers, a *Saturday Night Fever* flashing disco floor, and some of the hottest heaviest funk beats this side of Birmingham. The crowd possesses youth, money, and ecstasy in abundance. Open Tuesday through Friday midnight to 6am and Saturday midnight to 10am. Alameda Olga 170, Barra Funda ℂ 011/3667-8334. www.d-edge.com.br. Drink minimum R$50–R$60 (US$25–US$30/£14–16). Bus: 115P.

LOUNGES, BARS & PUBS
LOUNGES

Bar des Arts   The place to go on a third date or when you're trying to convince that would-be partner that—appearances aside—you really do have a sweet and sensitive side. Set in a large garden beneath mature trees, the tables surround an Italian marble fountain whose soft gurgling combines with the flickering candlelight to create a feeling of magic. Open Tuesday through Sunday noon to 1am. Rua Pedro Humberto 9, Chacara Itaim (behind the gas station). ℂ 011/3078-0828. www.bardesarts.com.br. Bus: 106A.

Lotus   Any club that puts the coordinates of its Heli point on its website has to be pretty upscale. São Paulo's hottest club is modeled after the New York Lotus and is a modern and sleek lap of luxury geared to attract the city's high rollers. So far so good. The beautiful and rich have been flocking here en masse, so take advantage of the exchange rate and your exotic foreign accent and head down to the São Paulo World Trade Center. Open Wednesday and Friday through Saturday from 11pm to 4am (or later). Av. Nações Unidas 12551, 2nd floor of the WTC, Brooklin. ℂ 011/3078-3625. www.lotussp.com.br. Drink minimum: women R$40 (US$20/£11), men R$80 (US$40/£22). Taxi recommended.

Trianon Piano Bar   One of the city's more elegant lounges in the luxurious Maksoud Plaza hotel, the Trianon Bar makes everyone feel like a millionaire. Just sit back in the plush surroundings, order a whiskey from the 140 or so brands available, and sip it slowly from your crystal glass. Live music Tuesday through Saturday from 7 to 10pm. Open Monday through Saturday 6pm to 1am. Alameda Campinas 150, Bela Vista. ℂ 011/3145-8000. Metrô: Trianon-MASP.

BARS & PUBS

Bar Brahma   Since 1948, Bar Brahma has been the meeting place for intellectuals, musicians, politicians, and businessmen. Renovations have restored the original wooden and bronze furnishings, and the chandeliers once again illuminate the crowds that gather to chat and drink beer. Open daily 11am to 2am. Av. São João 677, Centro. ℂ 011/3333-0855. www.barbrahmasp.com. Metrô: República.

Bar Municipal   In the bubbling little locale around the Rua Aspicuelta, this little bar is the favorite of the beautiful 25-to-35s, who quaff chopp and sip delicately from long neck Stella Artois, while munching panini and calabresa, admiring the giant photos of the Teatro Municipal and the beauty of their fellow patrons. Weekends from 6 to 11pm there's live MPB and samba. Rua Aspicuelta 578 Fiandeiras, Pinheiros ℂ 011/ 3812-0492. Cover R$10–R$20 (US$5–US$10/£2.70–£5.40) Bus: 6401.

Happenin' Hood: Vila Olímpia

The most happening nighttime neighborhood in São Paulo is currently Vila Olímpia. Packed with clubs and bars, it's always busy, even on weeknights. Many of the more popular bars are concentrated on the **Rua Prof. Atilio Innocenti**. At Atilio Innocenti 780 is the **Buena Vista Club** (✆ 012/3045-5245; www.buenavistaclub.com.br). Despite the name, the music is only a little Cuban and a lot Brazilian, live from Wednesday to Saturday. **Bar Favela** (Prof. Atilio Innocenti 419; ✆ 011/3848-6988; www.barfavela.com.br) is anything but downscale. This hip bar attracts a happening crowd who come to see and be seen. **Athilio Music** (Rua Prof. Atilio Innocenti 618; ✆ 011/3044-0206; www.athiliomusic.com.br) is a split-personality kind of place, with a sports bar in the front and a dance club hidden in back. The cover is R$5 to R$20 (US$2.50–US$10/£1.35–£5.50). Also on the Atilio Innocenti is **Pennélope** (Rua Prof. Atilio Innocenti 380; ✆ 011/3842-3802). Larger than some of the other bars, Pennélope has a small stage for live music and a couple of DJs who keep the crowd happy.

Bossa Nueva   Many bars in São Paulo seem to have a Rio theme. Coincidence? Carioca envy? We're not sure, but Bossa Nueva is no different. The vast back wall shows a floor-to-ceiling photo of 1960s Copacabana. The bar itself has a pleasant casual atmosphere, with small tables downstairs awash in mellow music. If you're a little puzzled over the picture, don't worry, it's not the booze; the wall photo is a reverse mirror image of the original. Open Tuesday through Friday 5pm to 3am, Saturday and Sunday noon to until the last person leaves. Rua Wisard 138, Vila Madalena. ✆ 011/3814-4164. www.bossanueva.com.br. Metrô: Vila Madalena.

Fidel   With a name like Fidel you expect cigars and green fatigues. And that's what you get. This intimate bar is decorated with black-and-white photos of the revolution and lots of cigar paraphernalia. The music is a blend of Latin, bossa nova, and Brazilian. Most evenings feature live music (cover R$8/US$4/£2). The menu has some excellent pub food, plus mojitos and cubanitos. Open Tuesday through Thursday 5:30pm to 1:30am, Friday and Saturday 5:30pm to 3am. Rua Girassol 398, Vila Madalena. ✆ 011/3812-4225. Metrô: Vila Madalena.

Jacaré Grill ⚘ (Value) BRAZILIAN   Should the Jacaré Grill be classified as a restaurant or a bar? We're not sure. The food is excellent—lots of appetizers (the curry empanadas are scrumptious), delicious salads and grilled meats, chicken skewers with ginger and soya marinade, and pork tenderloins with a mango chutney. On the other hand, the reason locals flock here, particularly on weekend afternoons, is to see and be seen, flirt, talk, and meet friends. The two large patios on opposite street corners offer maximum exposure to your fellow patio mates. Open Tuesday through Friday noon to midnight, Saturday and Sunday noon to 8pm. Rua Harmonia 321–337, Vila Madalena. ✆ 011/3816-0400. www.jacaregrill.com.br. R$15–R$35 (US$7.50–US$18/£4–£9.50). AE, DC, MC, V. Metrô: Vila Madalena.

Pirajá   São Paulo's attempt at re-creating the typical Rio botequim gets points for verisimilitude. Lots of tables on the sidewalk, lots of people out for a beer and a chat with friends, while eternally surly waiters serve up a never-ending stream of chopp. Undeniably Paulista, however, are both the fashion sense of the crowd and the high quality of the food. Nibbles include an outstanding cold-cut buffet with a huge variety of cheeses, olives, sun-dried tomatoes, and marinated mushrooms. Open Monday through Wednesday 5pm to 3am, Thursday and Friday 5pm to 4am, Saturday noon to 4am, and Sunday noon to 7pm. Av. Brigadeiro Faria Lima 64, Pinheiros. ⓒ 011/3815-6881. www.piraja.com.br. No cover.Bus: 7214.

Rabo do Peixe   If there is such a thing as a typical Brazilian pub, this would be it. The patio fans out on all sides, and tables are packed every day. The food that'll put all pub food to shame is the grilled *picanha* (beef) served on a sizzling cast-iron skillet (R$36/US$15/£7.50). Open Tuesday and Wednesday 5pm to 2am, Thursday through Saturday noon to 3am, and Sunday noon to 1am. Rua Nova Cidade 99, Vila Olímpia. ⓒ 011/3845-2296. Bus: 6404.

GAY & LESBIAN BARS

Director's Gourmet   A little low-key bar in Jardins, the Director's Gourmet (a reference to the film posters used as decorations) attracts a mellow crowd of mostly men. A DJ spins some tunes to add to the atmosphere but this is by no means a dance club. Open Tuesday through Saturday 10pm to 3am, Sunday from 9pm to 3am. Rua Alameda Franca 1552, Cerqueira Cesar. ⓒ 011/3064-7958.

Farol Madalena   Although GLS, the emphasis in this busy little club is definitely on the *L* for lesbian. The bar has live Brazilian music on most evenings Wednesday through Sunday. Open Tuesday through Saturday 7pm to 1am, Sunday 4pm to midnight. Rua Jericó 179, Vila Madalena. ⓒ 011/3032-6470. www.farolmadalena.com.br. Cover R$7 (US$3.50/£1.75). Metrô: Vila Madalena.

Vermont Itaim   On the ground floor of a commercial building, the Vermont is one of the relatively few GLS bars outside the Jardins. There's live music most nights—MPB on Wednesdays, danceable pop Thursday though Saturdays. The boys predominate through the week and on Saturday, but Sundays the girls take over with a 9-woman samba band. The drink menu leans to sweet and fluffy cocktails. Open Monday to Thursday 6:30pm to 2am, Friday to Saturday 8pm to 4am, Sunday 4:30pm to midnight. Cover R$10 (US$5/£2.70) Friday from 8pm onward, Saturday R$15 (US$7.5/£4) from 8pm, Sunday from 4:30pm. Rua Pedroso Alvarenga 1192, Itaim Bìbi. ⓒ 011/3071-1320.

9

Salvador & the Best of Bahia

A visit to Salvador is a chance to step back in time, to stroll through a perfectly preserved city from the 16th and 17th centuries. It's a chance to experience Brazil's close connection to Africa—to taste this connection in the food, hear it in the music, see it in the faces of the people. All of these elements—architecture, food, and music—mix together in Pelourinho, the restored colonial heart of the city of Salvador.

Beyond Salvador, a trip to Bahia is a chance to stock up on two of Brazil's greatest non-exportable products—sand and sunshine. The beaches of Bahia are some of Brazil's most varied and beautiful. They come blessed by sunshine, lapped by a warm southern ocean, and infused with a laid-back spirit that is uniquely Bahian.

The Italian navigator Amerigo Vespucci—the one who later gave his name to a pair of continents—was the first European to set eyes on the Baía de Todos os Santos, the beautiful bay around which Salvador now stands. He arrived in the service of the king of Portugal on November 1, 1501.

By 1549, the new city and colony of Salvador was important enough that the Portuguese king dispatched royal governor Tomé de Souza together with a small army to protect it from the French and Dutch.

The wealth of the new colony was not in silver or gold, but something almost as lucrative: sugar. Sugar cane thrived in the Northeast. As plantations grew, the Portuguese planters found themselves starved for labor, and so plunged headfirst into the slave trade. By the mid–19th century close to 5 million slaves had been taken from Africa to Brazil.

The wealth earned by that trade is evident in the grand mansions and golden churches in Pelourinho. The legacy of the slave trade is also reflected in the population. Modern Salvador is a city of two million, and approximately 80% of its people are of Afro-Brazilian descent.

This heritage has had an enormous influence on Salvador's culture, food, religion, and especially its music. Even in a country as musical as Brazil, Bahia stands out. The last 2 decades have seen an explosion in music that draws on African influences. A new term has been coined to describe an Afro-Brazilian blend of upbeat dance music: *axé*, from the Yorubá word for energy. Musical groups such as Olodum and Timbalada have blended complex African drumming rhythms with reggae melodies, while adding a dose of social activism to the mix.

Capoeira, the balletic mix of martial arts and dance, is now seen on almost every Salvador street corner. The West African religious practice of Candomblé is also emerging from generations in the shadows.

This same 20-year period has seen the resurrection of Salvador's Pelourinho neighborhood. Derelict until as recently as the '80s, Pelourinho—the 16th-century heart of what was once the richest city on the Atlantic coast—has been painstakingly brought back to its former glory.

And then there's Carnaval. Over a million people now come out to dance and revel their way through the city's streets. Salvador may soon claim to hold the biggest street party in the world.

1 Salvador Essentials

ARRIVING

BY PLANE **Varig** (© 071/4003-7000), **Gol** (© 0300/115-2121), and **TAM** (© 071/4002-5700) all fly from Rio, São Paulo, Recife, Brasilia, and other places with connections.

The modern **Aeroporto Deputado Luis Eduardo Magalhães** (© 071/3204-1010), Salvador's international airport, is 32km (20 miles) from downtown. The bank machines are all in the arrivals hall area, to the right at the end of the corridor (past the office for Costa do Sauípe). Cambio Gradual offers 24-hour money-changing services.

To reach your hotel, **Coometas** taxi (© 071/3244-4500) offers prepaid fares. The trip to **Pelourinho** costs R$75 (US$38/£20), to **Ondina** R$65 (US$33/£18), and to the northern beaches (such as **Itapuã**), R$35 (US$18/£9.50). Regular taxis are cheaper; on the meter a taxi from the airport to Pelourinho costs around R$60 (US$30/£16).

If you have very little luggage, an inexpensive airport-to-Pelourinho bus runs along the coast, stopping close to (though not at) most of the hotels located along the beach road. Its final stop is Praça da Sé on the edge of Pelourinho. The bus runs daily from 7am to 8pm; cost is R$6 (US$3/£1.60).

BY BUS Bus travelers go through the **Terminal Rodoviaria de Salvador Armando Viana de Castro,** usually simply known as **Rodoviaria.** It's located at Av. ACM (Antônio Carlos Magalhães) 4362, Iguatemi (© 071/3460-8300). For ticket information and schedules, travelers need to contact the specific bus company directly. However, the general bus station number will tell you which company to phone. **Itapemirim** (© 071/3392-3944) travels to Recife and Rio de Janeiro; **Real Expresso** (© 071/3246-8355) has scheduled service to Lençóis for people traveling to the Chapada Diamantina (see "Side Trips from Salvador," later in this chapter); **São Geraldo** travels to destinations like Natal and São Paulo (© 071/3244-0366).

VISITOR INFORMATION

Note: All telephone numbers in Salvador now have eight digits, but you will still find lots of pamphlets, flyers, and other printed materials showing numbers that have not been updated. To get the correct eight-digit number, just add a "3" to the beginning of the older seven-digit number.

Bahiatursa, the state's tourist information service, has booths and kiosks throughout the city. The staff is friendly, although as of press time they had no useful brochures and pamphlets because the new state government was going to redo all of the materials. However, they should be able to help you with general information. There are Bahiatursa booths at the following locations: **Salvador International Airport** in the arrivals hall (© 071/3204-1244), open daily from 7am to 10:30pm; **Rodoviaria** (© 071/3450-3871), open daily from 8am to 9pm; **Mercado Modelo,** Praça Cayru 250, Cidade Baixa (© 071/3241-0242), open daily Monday through Saturday 9am to 2pm; and **Pelourinho,** Rua das Laranjeiras 12 (© 071/3321-2463 or 071/3321-2133), open daily from 8:30am to 10pm. The office at Pelourinho has

Greater Salvador

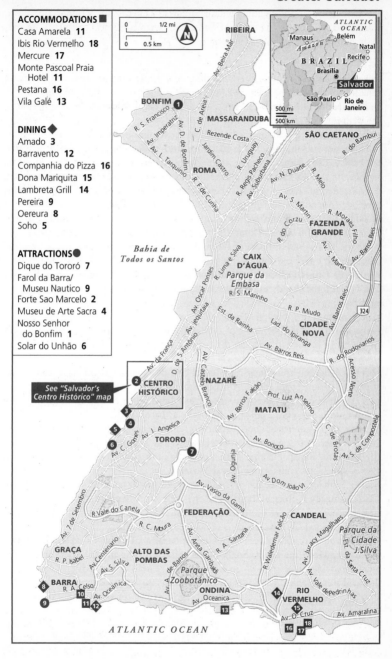

See "Salvador's Centro Histórico" map

Bahia de Todos os Santos

ATLANTIC OCEAN

RIBEIRA

BONFIM

MASSARANDUBA

SÃO CAETANO

ROMA

FAZENDA GRANDE

CAIX D'ÁGUA
Parque da Embasa

CIDADE NOVA

CENTRO HISTÓRICO

NAZARÉ

MATATU

TORORO

FEDERAÇÃO

CANDEAL

Parque da Cidade J.Silva

GRAÇA

ALTO DAS POMBAS

Parque Zoobotánico

ONDINA

RIO VERMELHO

BARRA

ATLANTIC OCEAN

Inset map
ATLANTIC OCEAN
Manaus
Belém
Natal
Recife
B R A Z I L
Brasília
São Paulo
Salvador
Rio de Janeiro

the best stock of information and pamphlets. The city of Salvador site (www.emtursa.ba.gov.br) and the state of Bahia site (www.bahiatursa.ba.gov.br) are both quite informative.

CITY LAYOUT

Salvador is an easy city to get around. Picture a wedge thrusting out into the ocean. One side of the wedge borders the Atlantic Ocean, the other side borders the bay (the **Baía de Todos os Santos**). The two sides meet at **Farol da Barra,** the skinny point of the wedge.

Perched on a high cliff on the bay side of the wedge one finds **Pelourinho,** the historic old downtown. This area is also sometimes referred to as the **centro histórico,** or as the **Cidade Alta,** the upper town. This is Salvador's chief area of interest. At the foot of the cliff lies **Comércio,** a modern area of commercial office towers. This area is also sometimes known as the **Cidade Baixa,** or lower town. Upper town and lower town are connected via a cliff-side elevator, the **Elevator Lacerda.** Except for the fun of riding the elevator, and visiting a large crafts market called the **Mercado Modelo,** there's little reason to visit Comércio (the downtown business neighborhood).

About 8km (5 miles) north of Pelourinho, the **Bonfim** peninsula juts out into the bay. Located on a headland on this peninsula is one of Salvador's most famous landmarks, the **Church of Our Lord of Bonfim,** source of many reputed miracles. The area between the church and Pelourinho is occupied by port, rail yards, and working-class housing.

Just outside the southern border of Pelourinho one finds the **Avenida Sete de Setembro.** This is the beginning of a street that will, under various names, travel south to the point of the wedge, turn the corner, and travel out along the Atlantic coast through increasingly upscale beach neighborhoods to the border of Salvador and beyond. At its beginning near Pelourinho, Sete de Setembro is a modern commercial street with many small shops. A little farther south as it enters **Vitória,** it becomes more residential. Below that, the street drops down to the coast and continues by the ocean until it reaches the point of the wedge at **Farol de Barra.**

Barra has a number of good restaurants, and a few good hotels, and on the point where All Saints Bay meets the Atlantic, a tall white lighthouse, called in Portuguese the **Farol de Barra.** On that same point sits the sizable **Forte Santo Antônio de Barra,** which also contains the **Naval Museum.**

As it rounds the corner, the oceanside road changes its name to **Avenida Oceanica.** (Well, officially it changes its name to Av. Presidente Vargas, but that name is used only sparingly.) The road continues past a number of good hotels to the oceanside neighborhood of **Ondina.** From here out, road names change frequently, and neighborhoods come thick and fast: **Vermelho, Amaralina, Pituba, Costa Azul, Pituaçu, Piatã, Itapuã,** all the way to **Stella Maris** adjacent to the airport. There are pleasant

---

Tips Be Kind to Your Feet in Salvador

Wear comfortable shoes when walking around Salvador; high heels are both imprudent and uncomfortable on the large, uneven cobblestones and steep streets.

⌒ **Tips Know the Hours for Exchanging Money**

Please note that most banks will change money only during certain hours, often 11am to 2pm.

---

ocean beaches all along this stretch. Particularly noteworthy is the beachside park named **Jardim de Alah.**

GETTING AROUND

ON FOOT   Large parts of Salvador are pedestrian-friendly. Pelourinho can only really be experienced on foot and is a stroller's dream. The narrow streets and cobblestone alleys open onto large squares with baroque churches; the stately mansions and homes now house shops, galleries, and wonderful little restaurants.

The Cidade Baixa, around the Mercado Modelo, and the commercial heart of Salvador in Comércio are also pedestrian-friendly neighborhoods, but less safe at night and on weekends, when they get quite deserted. All the beaches make great strolls; just grab a bus or taxi to get out there and then hit the pavement or sand.

BY BUS   Salvador's neighborhoods of interest all hug the ocean and are connected by one main avenue that winds along the coast and then leads into downtown, ending just steps from the historic center. Once downtown all the attractions are within walking distance of each other. As long as you have a general idea of the order of the beaches, you should be able to find your destination, as a bus from downtown traveling to the far-off beach of Itapuã via Ondina will automatically stop at all the beaches in between. Buses are marked by name; the main buses for travelers going from any of the beach neighborhoods to downtown are marked PRAÇA DA SÉ for Pelourinho or COMÉRCIO for the lower town. To travel to the city's main bus station (or the large mall across from the bus station) take buses marked IGUATEMI. When leaving downtown for the beaches, take a bus that says VIA ORLA, which means along the coast, and make sure that the bus's final destination lies beyond the beach neighborhood you want to reach. Along the coast, you have the option of taking a regular bus, R$1.80 (US90¢/£.50) or an air-conditioned bus, called a *frescão* (fresh one) for R$4 to R$6 (US$2–US$3/£1.10–£1.60). These are more comfortable, but then again if there are three or four of you, a *frescão* is almost the same price as a taxi.

BY TAXI   Local taxis can be hailed on the street or from any taxi stand. To book a radio taxi contact **Radiotaxi** (✆ **071/3243-4333**) or **LigueTaxi** (✆ **071/3357-7777**). You usually pay a surcharge of R$3 to R$5 (US$1.50–US$2.50/£.80–£1.35), but these taxis have air-conditioning and are usually new vehicles. Also, these two companies accept credit cards and can be reserved ahead of time.

BY CAR   There is no need to drive in Salvador; the historic center of Pelourinho has no parking, and many of the streets are closed for traffic. To get between the city and the beaches, buses are quick and convenient, and taxis are cheap and readily available. Outside of Salvador, a car can be useful; see "Car Rentals" under "Fast Facts: Salvador," below, for information.

FAST FACTS: Salvador

Area Code The area code for Salvador is **071.**

Business Hours Stores are open 9am to 6pm Monday through Saturday, and closed on Sundays. Pelourinho's stores open Sunday afternoon. Shopping centers open Monday through Saturday from 10am to 8pm; on Sunday most malls are closed except for the movie theater. Banks are open Monday through Friday from 9am to 3pm but hours for exchanging money may be restricted to 11am to 2pm.

Car Rentals **Avis,** Av. Presidente Vargas 3097, Ondina (© **0800/198-456** or 071/3369-9100); **Hertz,** Salvador International Airport (© **0800/701-7300** or 071/3377-3633); **Localiza,** Av. Presidente Vargas 3057, Rio Vermelho (© **0800/792-000** or 071/3332-1999); and **Unidas,** Salvador International Airport (© 071/3377-1244).

Currency Exchange & Banks **Banco do Brasil,** Praça Padre Anchieta 11, Pelourinho (© **071/3321-9334**), or Rua Miguel Bournier 4, Barra Avenida, parallel to the Avenida Oceanica (© **071/3264-5099**). **Citibank,** Rua Miguel Calmon 555, Comércio, close to the Mercado Modelo (© **071/3241-4745**), or Av. Almirante Marques Leão 71, Barra (© **071/4009-6310**). All have 24-hour ATMs.

Dentist **Salvadent** is a 24-hour dental clinic, Rua Conde Filho 87, Graça. (© **071/3332-9393; Emergency Number** © **071/8818-9603**).

Emergencies Police dial © **190;** fire and ambulance dial © **193.**

Hospitals **Hospital Portugues,** Av. Princesa Isabel 2, Barra (© **071/3203-5700**) or **Hospital Aliança,** Av. Juracy Magalhães 2096, Rio Vermelho (© **071/3350-5600**).

Internet Access **Bahia Café.com,** Praça da Sé 20, Centro (© **071/3322-1266**); **Internet Café.com,** Rua João de Deus 2, Pelourinho (© **071/3331-2147**) and Av. Sete de Setembro 3713, Barra (© **071/3264-3941**); and **Pelourinho Virtual,** Largo do Pelourinho 2 (© **071/3323-0427**). Most are open daily, and rates range from R$6 to R$10 (US$3–US$5/£1.60–£2.70) per hour.

Laundry & Dry Cleaning Laundromats are called *lavanderia,* and for dry cleaning ask for *a seco.* **Laundromat,** Av. Sete de Setembro 2721, Vitória (© **071/3237-5776**) is a do-it-yourself laundry service.

Mail Downtown: Rua Visconde de Cairu 250, by the Mercado Modelo (© **071/3346-9518**); Pelourinho, Largo do Cruzeiro de São Francisco (© **071/3321-8787**). There is also a post office at the international airport.

Maps The tourist office has an excellent Salvador map for R$5 (US$2.50/£1.35) and free booklets with small maps of the main tourist areas.

Pharmacies Try **Farmacia do Farol,** Av. Sete de Setembro 4347, Barra (© **071/3264-7355**); or **Farmacia Santana,** Av. Antônio Carlos Magalhães 4362, at the bus station (© **071/3450-3599**), open 24 hours. Most pharmacies will also deliver 24 hours a day. Call © **136** to find the nearest pharmacy.

Restrooms Public washrooms are scarce, except during big events like Carnaval when the city provides chemical toilets. Your best bet is to try a hotel or ask nicely at a restaurant.

Safety Salvador's main sightseeing areas are heavily policed and safe, even at night. Still, it pays to follow some common-sense precautions. Don't carry valuables or excessive amounts of cash, or display expensive camera equipment unnecessarily. At night, stick to the main streets where there is more foot traffic and surveillance. The Cidade Baixa around the Mercado Modelo and the commercial heart of Salvador in Comércio are less safe at night, and mostly deserted on the weekends.

Taxes The city of Salvador charges a 5% accommodations tax, collected by hotel operators. This amount will be added to your bill. There are no other taxes on retail items or goods.

Time Zone Salvador is on the same time zone as Rio de Janeiro and São Paulo, 3 hours behind GMT. Due to out-of-sync daylight saving in the Northern and Southern Hemisphere, Salvador can be in the same time zone as New York (approximately May–Sept) or 2 hours ahead of New York (Oct–April).

Visa Renewal If you need to extend your visa go to the **Policia Federal,** Av. Oscar Pontes 339, lower city (© **071/3319-6082**). The fee is R$69 (US$35/£18), and you may need to show your return ticket and evidence of sufficient funds to cover the remainder of your stay.

Weather Salvador has a tropical climate, with an average temperature of 78°F (26°C) year-round. With over 2,220 hours of sunshine a year, there is little precipitation; most of it falls between April and August when brief heavy showers are common. Summer clothes can be worn year-round, and fashions are very casual. But even in summer there is often a cool breeze coming in off the ocean. If you plan to go to the interior (Chapada Diamantina) or do a lot of boating, bring a few pieces of warm clothing.

2 Where to Stay

In days of yore, Salvador's top-quality hotels were all located close to the beach, a 15-to-30-minute drive from historic Pelourinho. In recent years, in response to the ever-increasing number of foreign visitors, a number of pousadas have opened up on the edge of Pelourinho, most of them located in restored historic buildings. Visitors now have a much greater range of options, though the central dilemma remains: You have to decide between staying in something old in Pelourinho or something new on the coast, at 20-minute drive from downtown.

Salvador's peak season ranges from mid-December to early March and maxes out during Carnaval. Hotels make big bucks during this time of year by jacking up their prices to insane heights, usually demanding payment in full upon reservation and requiring a minimum stay of 4 or 5 nights. Most Carnaval packages start at R$1,500 (US$625/£338) and go up to R$4,000 (US$1,666/£900). Even at these prices, rooms often sell out by October or November. The most popular Carnaval hotels are in Barra, as they are right on the beach and the parade route.

Once Carnaval is out of the way, occupancy rates drop significantly, and your bargaining powers increase enormously. In the off season (Apr–June and Aug–Nov) it's worth shopping around, as some hotels give as much as a 50% discount, especially if you are staying a couple of nights.

Tips Prices Skyrocket for Carnaval

Please note that none of the prices listed below, even those for high season, remotely reflect the room cost during Carnaval. Most of the hotels have web-sites with information on special Carnaval packages that you can check out as early as September. Consult with the hotels directly or contact a tour company like Brazil Nuts (www.brazilnuts.com).

PELOURINHO

The advantage to staying in Pelourinho is that you get to stay in restored 18th-century buildings, and you're minutes from the bustle and fun of the old city. The disadvantages? Rooms are older and quirkier, parking is difficult, and on Saturday night you're just minutes from the bustle and noise of the old city.

VERY EXPENSIVE

Convento do Carmo ✦✦✦   Finally Pelourinho has the boutique hotel it deserves. Located at the top of a steep cobblestone street leading up from largo Pelourinho itself, the Convento has the perfect location on the outside, and luxurious accommodations inside. Indeed, considering the original 17th-century convent was designed to shield its residents from the pleasures of the flesh, the conversion carried out by the Portuguese Pestana group did a remarkable job leading the old girl back into the lap of luxury. All rooms come with a large comfy queen fitted out with softest of linens and piled high with a cornucopia of pillows. (For those tempted into working, there's also a big wooden desk, free high-speed Internet, and flatscreen TV). Bathrooms—converted monks cells, still with massive walls and thick wooden shutters—feature delightful rainfall showers, l'Occitane beauty products, plus a frosted window looking onto the cloister, where at night the fountain gushes quietly. The conversion respected the original architecture as much as possible, and for that reason there is no standard room layout. That said, the deluxe rooms are certainly all larger—the deluxe rooms on the third floor are a particular bargain; at no extra charge you get more space for a small sitting lounge plus a higher ceiling raftered with ancient wood beams. The hotel's common areas—the round tiled pool and restaurant in the cloister, the lounge tucked into one of the arcades, the large library—are a delight; at night, subtle lighting is used to show off the convent to lovely effect.

Rua do Carmo 1, centro histórico, Salvador, 40030-170 BA. ✆/fax **071/3327-8400.** www.pousadas.pt. 79 units. R$470 (US$235/£127) double; R$600 (US$300/£162) luxury double. Extra person add R$50 (US$25/£14). Children 9 and under stay free in parent's room. AE, DC, MC, V. Parking R$25/US$12.5/£7 daily. Bus: Praça de Sé. **Amenities:** Restaurant; bar; outdoor pool; small health club; library; spa; concierge; tour desk; car rental; business center; 24-hr. room service; massage; laundry; nonsmoking rooms. *In room:* A/C, TV, dataport, minibar, hair dryer, safe.

Solar dos Deuses ✦✦   Truly in the heart of Pelourinho, the Solar dos Deuses overlooks the square in front of the São Francisco church. This lovely pousada has seven rooms, each one decorated in honor of an orixá, the African deities of the candomblé. All rooms are elegantly furnished with period furniture and feature lovely high ceilings, hardwood floors and large windows looking out over the square or side street just off the square. Most of the rooms have king-size beds. Breakfast is served in the privacy of your own room at the time of your choice. The biggest room, Oxalá, can accommodate three or four people comfortably. Due to its central location this pousada is not for early sleepers.

Largo Cruzeiro de São Francisco 12, centro histórico, Salvador, 40020-280 BA. © 071/3320-3251. www.solardos deuses.com.br. 7 units. R$260 (US$130/£70) standard double; R$300 (US$150/£81) luxury double. Children 6 and under stay free in parent's room. MC, V. Parking unavailable. Bus: Praça de Sé. **Amenities:** Laundry. In room: A/C, TV, minibar, safe.

Pousada Redfish 👁👁   The Redfish is located in a gorgeous renovated colonial home and managed to keep the features that provide that old colonial feeling, including spacious rooms with high ceilings and tall windows. Standard rooms feature two queen-size beds with new firm mattresses, high ceilings, plus spacious bathrooms and a small balcony. (Avoid the two "garden" standard rooms that are just outside the breakfast area.) Room no. 6 is the largest standard room. No. 5 is the smallest. The luxury rooms have a vast king-size bed plus a second single bed, leather arm chair, armoire, and vaulted ceiling, plus a large veranda with fresh ocean breezes and a view of the city. On the ground floor a gallery features the artwork of the owner.

Ladeira do Boqueirão 1, centro histórico, Salvador, 40030-170 BA. ©/fax **071/3243-8473**. www.hotelredfish.com. 8 units. R$240 (US$120/£65) standard double; R$300 (US$150/£81) luxury double. Extra person add R$50 (US$25/£14). Children 6 and under stay free in parent's room. MC, V. Parking unavailable. Bus: Praça de Sé. **Amenities:** Laundry. In room: A/C, minibar, safe.

EXPENSIVE

Pousada do Pilar 👁👁   One of the "newcomers" to Pelourinho, this beautiful heritage building has been gutted and renovated, giving rooms a modern feel and bringing them fully up to modern standards. All 12 rooms are huge and come with all the modern facilities such as air-conditioning, nice en-suite bathrooms, and good lighting. Seven of the rooms have a veranda and face out over the port and the ocean. The remaining five rooms have a small balcony (standing room only) and look out over the street. A wonderful breakfast with regional cakes is served on the rooftop patio overlooking Salvador's waterfront. The location of the pousada is perfect for exploring Pelourinho; the main square is only a 10-minute walk downhill. Unlike most Pelourinho hotels, the Pousada do Pilar has an elevator.

Rua Direita de Santo Antônio 24, centro histórico, Salvador, 40301-280 BA. © **071/3241-2033**. Fax 071/3241-3844. www.pousadadopilar.com. 12 units. City view R$230 (US$115/£62); ocean view and veranda R$270 (US$135/£73). Children 5 and under stay free in parent's room. Extra bed R$60 (US$30/£16). AE, DC, MC, V. Bus: Praça de Sé. **Amenities:** Laundry. In room: A/C, TV, minibar, safe.

Studio do Carmo   As close as you can get to Pelourinho without sleeping on the square. Located on the Ladeira do Carmo just steps past the Largo Pelourinho, this pousada offers four bright rooms with double beds and hardwood floors, plus a breakfast table and small kitchenette. The decor includes original artwork, much of it on loan from the gallery downstairs. Showers are clean and small, but functional. There's no air-conditioning but each room does have a large fan over the bed. Room nos. 1 and 3 have a view out over the steps in front of the N.S. do Passo church. Room nos. 2 and 4 look back over the rooftops of Pelourinho; the view's not as nice, but these rooms get a better breeze. Breakfast is brought to your room on a tray each morning.

Ladeira do Carmo 17, centro histórico, Salvador, 40301-410 BA. © **071/3243-0646**. www.studiodocarmo.com.br. 4 units. R$150 (US$75/£40) double. Children under 6 stay free in parent's room. V. No Parking. Bus: Praça de Sé. In room: Kitchenette w/toaster oven, fridge, sink, coffeemaker.

BARRA

Barra offers sea, sun, and a good bit of fun in neighborhood restaurants and cafes, while Pelourinho remains in easy striking distance. A number of hotels line the Avenida Oceanica (Av. Presidente Vargas), offering fabulous views of the beach and lighthouse; others are located just around the corner from the lighthouse where the Avenida Oceanica becomes Avenida Sete de Setembro.

EXPENSIVE

Monte Pascoal Praia Hotel ⟨⟨ *Value*   Fabulously located across from Barra beach and recently completely renovated, the Monte Pascoal Praia offers great value. All rooms come with a king-size bed or two double beds—great for families traveling with young children. Every room has a balcony and at least a partial view of the ocean. The 32 rooms with a full ocean view cost an additional 25%. The one room that has been fully adapted for travelers with disabilities has wide doorways, handrails, an adapted toilet, and a chair for use in the shower. This hotel is incredibly popular during Carnaval, as its pool deck overlooks the main parade route and the beach is just 45m (150 ft.) across the street.

Av. Oceanica 591, Barra, Salvador, 40170-010 BA. ⟨⟨ **071/2103-4000.** Fax 071/3245-4436. www.montepascoal. com.br. 80 units. R$200–R$250 (US$100–US$125/£54–£68) double standard; R$220–R$300 (US$110–US$150/ £59–£81) double ocean view. Extra person R$60 (US$30/£16). Seasonal discounts available. Children under 6 stay free in parent's room. AE, DC, MC, V. Parking R$12 (US$6/£3.35) per day. **Amenities:** Restaurant; bar; outdoor pool; fitness room; sauna; game room; small business center (computer, Internet, fax, and printing) w/24-hr. access; salon; 24-hr. room service; laundry service. *In room:* A/C, TV, dataport, minibar, hair dryer, safe.

MODERATE

Casa Amarela ⟨⟨ *Value*   You can't miss the yellow house (the Casa Amarela) on Barra beach. It is also called Hospederia de la Habana but when you arrive at the bright canary-yellow house you can see why that name never caught on. This pleasant and comfortable inn offers one of the best deals along the Salvador waterfront. All 13 rooms have views of the bay, private bathrooms, and are clean and simply furnished. An excellent breakfast is included in the price. The pousada also has a garden, a small bar, and a lovely veranda, perfect for enjoying a drink before you head out for dinner. The Casa Amarela is right on the major carnival parade route so book early if you plan to be here to celebrate Salvador's largest event of the year.

Av. Oceânica 84, Barra, Salvador, 40170-010 BA. ⟨⟨ **071/3237-5105.** www.hospederiadelahabana.com.br. 13 units. R$110 (US$55/£30) double. Children under 6 stay free in parent's room. No credit cards. Street parking. **Amenities:** Bar; laundry service; Internet access. *In room:* A/C, TV.

ONDINA/RIO VERMELHO

Ondina begins just around the bend from Barra on the open Atlantic coast. A number of good hotels are located right on the waterfront; some even have private beaches. However, because the hotels have cut off public access to the waterfront, Ondina is not as pleasant a beach neighborhood as Barra and the rocks make swimming difficult, if not downright dangerous. **Rio Vermelho** is just beyond Ondina and boasts a lively restaurant and nightlife scene, centered around its main square, with hotels set far enough away from the nightlife to guarantee a good night's sleep.

VERY EXPENSIVE

Pestana Bahia ⟨⟨⟨   Formerly the Meridien, the Pestana Bahia is positively buzzing after its extensive makeover. Set on an outcrop overlooking Rio Vermelho, its privileged location guarantees all 430 units an ocean view. The rooms on the 2nd through the 17th floors are superior, the ones on the 18th to the 22nd floors are deluxe. The difference is really in the small details; the deluxe rooms have bathtubs, 29-inch TVs, and a couch. Other than that the rooms are identical, very spacious with modern and funky decorations. Furnishings and artwork have splashes of green and orange, making for very pleasant rooms. The outdoor pool and sun deck overlook the beach; the Pestana's beach service includes towels, chairs, umbrellas, and drinks. The hotel is about a R$20 (US$10/£5.40) cab ride from Pelourinho and just a 10-minute walk from Rio Vermelho's happening nightlife scene.

Rua Fonte do Boi, Rio Vermelho, Salvador, 41940-360 BA. © **071/3453-8005.** Fax 071/3453-8066. www.pestana hotels.com.br. 430 units. R$295 (US$148/£80) superior double; R$375 (US$188/£101) deluxe double. Extra person add 30%. Children 12 and under stay free in parent's room. AE, DC, MC, V. Free parking. Bus: Rio Vermelho. **Amenities:** 3 restaurants; bar; large outdoor pool; small health club; concierge; tour desk; car rental; business center; salon; 24-hr. room service; massage; laundry; nonsmoking floors. *In room:* A/C, TV, dataport, minibar, safe.

Vila Galé ★★   Originally built to house a Holiday Inn, the hotel was bought by the Portuguese Vila Galé hotel chain and has been upgraded to their high standards. Located on a point just between Barra and Ondina, the Vila Galé offers luxury and elegance. The rooms are quite spacious and fit two double beds or a king-size bed, a comfortable chair, and a big desk. All rooms on the first floor have a veranda. Standard rooms look out over the street behind the hotel; superior rooms have gorgeous ocean views. The hotel also has a number of suites, the best of which is the Oceano, which consists of a large L-shaped room with curved windows that look out over the ocean. Although they are elegantly furnished and offer extras such as a Jacuzzi tub, 29-inch TV, and DVD, they are just big rooms; you don't get a separate bedroom. The staff provides excellent customer service.

Rua Morro Escravo Miguel 320, Ondina, Salvador, 40140-610 BA. © **0800/284-8818** or 071/3263-8888. Fax 071/ 3263-8800. www.vilagale.com.br. 224 units. High season R$400 (US$200/£108) standard double; R$495 (US$248/ £134) superior double; R$580 (US$290/£157) suite double. Low season discounts 25%. Special rates for Carnaval and New Year's. Children 6 and under stay free in parent's room. AE, DC, MC, V. Parking R$5 (US$2/£1). **Amenities:** Restaurant; bar; outdoor pool; business center; 24-hr. room service; laundry; nonsmoking rooms. *In room:* A/C, TV, dataport, minibar, hair dryer, safe.

EXPENSIVE

Mercure ★★   The Mercure is one of two newest hotels in Rio Vermelho. It's located right on the water and just next door to the Pestana. This hotel is an excellent option for those who want more comfort and a higher standard of service and amenities than a budget hotel would provide, without going high-end. All 175 rooms have a modern and clean look with tile floors, oak-colored furniture, and red or blue accents. The rooms are spacious and come with a desk, two phone lines, and free high-speed Internet. The superior rooms face the city and the adjacent Ibis hotel; the deluxe rooms look out over the swimming pool and ocean. As the price difference between the two is minimal, it's worth reserving a room with a view. Breakfast costs an extra R$19 (US$9.50/£5).

Rua Fonte do Boi 215, Rio Vermelho, Salvador, 41940-360 BA. © **071/3172-9200.** Fax 071/3741-8201. Toll-free reservations 0800/703-7000. www.accorhotels.com.br. 175 units. R$215 (US$108/£58) superior double; R$246 (US$123/£66) deluxe double. Extra person add 25%. Children 6 and under stay free in parent's room. AE, DC, MC, V. Parking R$8 (US$4/£2) per day. Bus: Rio Vermelho. **Amenities:** Restaurant; bar; large outdoor pool; small health club; concierge; tour desk; business center; room service; massage; laundry; nonsmoking floors; rooms for travelers w/limited mobility. *In room:* A/C, TV, dataport, minibar, hair dryer, safe.

INEXPENSIVE

Ibis Rio Vermelho ⭐   The Ibis provides inexpensive accommodations without giving up too much comfort. The no-frills brand of the Accor group (same owners as the Mercure next door) specializes in clean and plain rooms with quality basics such as firm beds with good linens, a desk or work table, and a hot shower. The rates are low because the hotel doesn't charge you for a lot of fancy services that aren't always used by guests, such as dry cleaning, gift shop, business center, buffet breakfast, or valet parking. You even have the possibility of getting an ocean view at bargain rates; there is no price difference between the rooms that look toward the ocean so request one when you reserve or check in. Breakfast, not included, costs R$9 (US$4.50/£2.45).

Rua Fonte do Boi 215, Rio Vermelho, Salvador, 41940-360 BA. ℃ **071/3330-8300.** Fax 071/3330-8301. www.accor hotels.com.br. 252 units. R$119 (US$60/£32) double. Extra person add 30%. Children 12 and under stay free in parent's room. AE, DC, MC, V. Bus: Rio Vermelho. **Amenities:** Restaurant; bar; tour desk; partial room service; laundry; nonsmoking floors. *In room:* A/C, TV, dataport, minibar, safe.

3 Where to Dine

Bahian cuisine is truly regional, with its own ingredients and flavors not seen elsewhere in Brazil. The coastal version of Bahian cooking is rich in seafood and the distinct African flavors of dendê oil, dried shrimp, and coconut milk. These ingredients are combined into fragrant stews loaded with prawns, oysters, crab, or fish and finished with a handful of fresh cilantro and tangy lime juice. You can't say you have been to Bahia without trying a *moqueca de siri-mole* (stew with soft-shell crab), a *vatapá*, the famous *bobó de camarão,* and the popular *acarajé.*

PELOURINHO

Pelô, as the locals call Pelourinho, is not the place to go for fine dining, but you will find decent Bahian food and of course plenty of atmosphere. Located mostly in historic colonial houses, restaurants in Pelô provide the perfect backdrop for the exotic flavors of Salvador. Any night is a good night, though Tuesday and weekends are the most bustling. For a map of restaurants in this area, see the map "Salvador's Centro Histórico," later in this chapter.

EXPENSIVE

Sorriso da Dadá *Overrated* BAHIAN   Dadá has made quite a name for herself. Brazilians and foreigners come from far and wide to taste her food, journalists write articles about her, and gourmet magazines rave about her cozy restaurant. And after coming here year after year we were a bit disappointed this last time. Nothing is wrong with the food, thankfully. However, the restaurant was looking a bit run-down and service was inattentive. The ambience was more cafeteria than cozy restaurant and the portions were not what they used to be. Considering the prices she charges—typically 25% more than other restaurants—we were disappointed. It could just be that she has

---

⟮*Tips* **A Meal Built for Two**

Remember that except in fine dining the portions are very generous; one main course is usually enough for two people. When in doubt ask the waiter *"Dá para dois?"* (Does it serve two?)

A Glossary of Bahian Dishes

Rich with African influences, Bahian cuisine comes with its own ingredients and terminology. Here is a list of the most common dishes and ingredients:

Abará (ah-bah-*rah*): Usually made by *Baianas* on the street, this is a tamale-like wrap made with bean paste, onions, and dendê oil, cooked in a banana leaf, and served with ginger and dried shrimp sauce.

Acarajé (ah-kah-rah-*zhey*): Similar to the *abará* in that the dough is made with mashed beans, but the *acarajé* is deep-fried in dendê oil and stuffed with a shrimp sauce, hot peppers, and onion-tomato vinaigrette.

Bobó de camarão (boh-*boh* dje cah-mah-*roun*): A stew made with shrimp, cassava paste, onion, tomato, cilantro, coconut milk, and dendê oil.

Dendê oil (den-*de*): The key ingredient for Bahian food, this oil comes from the dendê palm tree and has a characteristic red color.

Ensopado (en-so-*pah*-do): A lighter version of a *moqueca* (see next entry) made without the dendê oil.

Moqueca (moo-*keck*-ah): Bahia's most popular dish, the ingredients include any kind of seafood stewed with coconut milk, lime juice, cilantro, onion, and tomato. Though the taste is similar, this stew is much thinner than a *bobó*.

Pirão (pee-*roun*): As popular as *farofa* in the rest of Brazil, this dish looks more like a polenta or porridge. Cassava flour is added to a seafood broth and cooked until it thickens.

Vatapá (vah-tah-*pah*): One of the richest dishes, the *vatapá* is a stew made with fish, onion, tomato, cilantro, lime juice, dried shrimp, ground-up cashew nuts, peanuts, ginger, and coconut milk. The sauce is thickened with bread.

been too busy expanding her food empire, opening new restaurants, and writing books. However, the lack of attention shows and that's a shame.

Rua Frei Vicente 5, Pelourinho. ✆ 071/3321-9642. Main courses R$36–R$68 (US$18–US$34/£10–£18) for 2. AE, DC, MC, V. Daily 11am–midnight. Bus: Praça da Sé.

MODERATE

Jardim das Delicias ★ *Finds* BRAZILIAN/CAFE   The Jardim das Delicias (Garden of Delights) is appropriately named. Tucked away inside an antiques store on the ground floor of a colonial house in Pelourinho, this lovely courtyard restaurant is the perfect getaway from the bustle and crowding of Pelourinho. The restaurant serves a full Bahian menu, including moquecas, bobó de camarão, and even foods from the interior such as beans with smoked meat and sausage. In the evenings there is live music. However, the Jardim is also very nice for just a drink (the caipirinha made with cashew fruit is delicious) or a coffee and some sweets. Just pick something from the display of delicious cakes and pies, or order some waffles with a generous scoop of ice cream. That should give you the boost you need for further exploring.

Rua João de Deus 12, Pelourinho. ✆ 071/3321-1449. Main courses R$20–R$50 (US$10–US$25/£5.40–£14); the more expensive dishes serve 2. Sweets and desserts are all under R$10 (US$5/£2.70). AE, DC, MC, V. Daily noon–midnight. Bus: Praça da Sé.

Mama Bahia Salvador ⭐ STEAK   Rip-off Tommy Hilfiger logo aside, this lovely steak restaurant serves up excellent grilled meats and fish. The house specialty, filet Mama Bahia, is a generous portion of grilled filet served with tagliatelli pasta in a Spanish tomato sauce with olives and peppers. There's also *picanha,* chicken, filet mignon, and other cuts. All are served a la carte—you order the side dishes separately with a choice of salad, rice, *farofa,* or garlic bread. All this red meat calls for good wine, and the list includes a great selection of reds for less than R$90 (US$38/£19), mostly from Chile and Argentina.

Rua Alfredo Brito 21, Pelourinho. ⓒ 071/3322-4397. Main courses R$20–R$38 (US$10–US$19/£5.40–£10). AE, MC, V. Daily 11am–midnight. Bus: Praça da Sé.

INEXPENSIVE

A Cubana ⭐ *Finds* DESSERT   It's only right that a city with an abundance of tropical fruits and a year-round warm climate would have great ice cream. One of the oldest *sorveterias* (ice-cream parlors) in town, A Cubana can be found in the heart of Pelourinho. The menu is not huge, only 28 homemade flavors at any given time; the owners say they prefer quality to quantity. Try the unusual fruit flavors such as *jáca* (jack fruit) or *cupuaçu,* a fruit only found in the Northeast and the Amazon.

Rua Alfredo de Brito 12, Pelourinho. **Note:** There is also an A Cubana store right next to the upper exit of the Lacerda elevator. ⓒ 071/3321-6162. Everything under R$12 (US$6/£3.25). No credit cards. Daily 8am–10pm. Bus: Praça da Sé.

COMÉRCIO

Located at the foot of a cliff directly below Pelourinho, the business and marina district of Comércio is fine for wandering in the daytime during office hours, but come

---

Acarajés & Abarás

Everywhere you go in Salvador you'll see *Baianas*—women dressed in the traditional white hoop skirt, lace blouse, and turban—sitting behind big cooking pots serving up *acarajés* and *abarás,* falafel-like snacks made with beans, onions, and dendê oil, either deep-fried *(acarajés)* or cooked in a banana leaf and served with ginger and dried shrimp sauce *(abarás).*

Although the costume is always the same, there are *Baianas,* and there are *Baianas.* Each has her regular spot, sometimes inherited from a mother or aunt. **Abará de Dona Olga** in Pelourinho on Travessa Agostinho Gomes—in front of the Moderna Funeral Home—has been serving up *abará* for over 50 years, daily from 5pm to 3am. Outside of Pelourinho, by the lighthouse Farol da Barra, look for **Acarajé do Farol Celia.** This lady also sells excellent coconut sweets, daily from 1 to 11pm. At the end of Barra beach, next to Barravento restaurant, is **Acarajé de Dona Jó,** open Tuesday through Friday from 4 to 10pm and Saturday and Sunday from 9am to 6pm. The queen of all *acarajés* is **Dinha,** who runs the **Casa da Dinha** ⭐⭐, Rua João Gomes 25, Rio Vermelho (ⓒ 071/3334-0525); she has traded in her metal tray for a little restaurant but still sells the best *acarajés* in town. Also worth trying are the moquecas—25 combinations of fish and seafood. Open Tuesday through Saturday from noon to 4pm and 6pm to midnight, and Sunday from noon to 6pm.

evening the workers head home and the streets become quiet and empty. We recommend taking a taxi instead of walking.

VERY EXPENSIVE

Amado 🎯🎯 CONTEMPORARY   Ultimately cool waterfront dining—the room is vast and gorgeous, mixing wood and stone and glass with open views over the waterside deck and the harbor and bay beyond. The cuisine takes traditional Bahian ingredients—mandioc and seafood principally—and puts them to use in innovate ways, always with lovely presentation. For starters we had *lambrettas* (a local shellfish) in white wine, *rolinhos de camarão* (little shrimp rolls), and a salad of octopus and sweet potato. For mains we threw ourselves completely into the ocean, trying the giant squid stuffed with shrimp and leek in a Provençal sauce, the shrimp in a Gorgonzola and pistachio sauce, and a broiled *badejo* filet in a crust of cashews with an okra tapenade, and banana purée on the side. The cashew crust made the fish perhaps a tad drier than it ought to have been—but that is but a minor complaint in what was all in all a sophisticated and delicious parade of seafood dishes. For those not into fish, the menu boasts an equally intriguing array of chicken and beef creations. The wine list is a little on the pricey side—nothing good for under R$100/US$50/£27, though they do eminently acceptable champagne in the R$40 (US$20/£11) range. Service is young, pretty, and efficient.

Av. do Contorno 660, Comércio. ☎ 071/3322-3520. www.amadobahia.com.br. Reservations recommended on weekends and in high season. Main courses R$30–R$46 (US$15–US$23/£8–£12). AE, DC, MC, V. Mon–Sat noon–3pm and 7pm–midnight; Sun noon–4pm. Taking a taxi is recommended. Even though it's not too far from the Mercado Modelo, the street is dark and very quiet at night.

Trapiche Adelaide 🎯🎯🎯 ITALIAN/FRENCH   Dining at Trapiche Adelaide is a visual experience. The restaurant sits on pilings over the water, and features floor-to-ceiling windows looking out over the bay. The food is as impressive as the view. The menu has a definite Italian/French twist with dishes such as the grilled *Robalo* fish with herbs in an extra-virgin olive oil or the grilled sole with fresh asparagus and orange-basil sauce. However, there is a tropical influence as well; worth trying are the prawns with mustard and pineapple sauce or the *carne seca* (sun-dried meat) with pumpkin purée served with crisp cassava. The outstanding wine list features bottles from Italy, Portugal, Chile, and Argentina; many are available by the glass. Desserts are tempting, too. Try the green apple pie with cashew nuts and ice cream, or the caramelized mango, banana, and apple in a puff pastry.

Praça do Tupinambás 2, Av. Contorno, Comércio. ☎ 071/3326-2211. www.trapicheadelaide.com.br. Reservations required on weekends, recommended in high season. No shorts or tank tops allowed at night. Main courses R$38–R$60 (US$19–US$30/£10–£16). AE, DC, MC, V. Mon–Thurs noon–4pm and 7pm–1am; Fri–Sat and holidays noon–1am; Sun noon–4pm. Taking a taxi is recommended. Even though it's not too far from the Mercado Modelo, the street is dark and very quiet at night.

EXPENSIVE

SOHO 🎯🎯🎯 JAPANESE   Judging from the crowd on a Wednesday night at SOHO, the Soteropolitanos (as residents of Salvador are called) have taken to sushi like fish to water. Located inside the Bahia Marina, SOHO sits right at the waterline. The patio is particularly pleasant—it's worth waiting for an outside table. The large menu offers most of the usual Japanese suspects—sushis, sashimis, tempuras, yakisobas, and grilled meat teryakis. But what earns this restaurant an above-average rating are intriguing local dishes such as the *shake lounge* (salmon sashimi with orange sauce, lime, and balsamic

> ### *Fun Fact* How Sweet It Is: Bahian Desserts
>
> To say that Brazilians have a sweet tooth is like saying Italians are fond of pasta. Most Brazilian desserts are just a few ingredients shy of pure sugar—not surprising, given that Brazil was once the world's largest sugar producer. Visitors often find desserts overwhelmingly sweet, and nowhere is this truer than in the sugar capital of Bahia. From the Portuguese, Bahians inherited the habit of making sweets with egg yolks; they then combined this with coconuts imported from Africa and the perfect dessert was born.
>
> Most traditional sweets are just variations on those three ingredients: *Cocada*, the little clusters of coconut you see everywhere, are nothing more than grated coconut with white or burned sugar; *quindim*, something between a pudding and a pie, is made with coconut, an incredible number of egg yolks (at least 10 per tiny serving!), and sugar; *manjar*, a soft pudding often served with plum sauce, combines sugar, coconut milk, and milk. My personal favorite is *Baba de Moça*—coconut milk, egg yolks, and sugar syrup. The name translates as "girl drool."

vinegar) and the *uramaki shake* (salmon with green onion and sesame seeds). Also worth trying are the *marina maki* (a salmon and prawn roll flambéed in cachaça) and the *kyo* (a lightly grilled tuna and nira in a thick soya sauce). The *gunkon especial* (warm grilled mushrooms rolled in a slice of salmon) was so good we ordered it three times. Many of the hot dishes such as the yakisoba noodles are large enough to share, especially after a couple of the sashimi and sushi appetizers.

Av. do Contorno s/n, inside the Bahia Marina, Comércio. © 071/3322-4554. Reservations recommended. Main courses R$18–R$36 (US$9–US$18/£5–£10). AE, DC, MC, V. Mon 7pm–midnight; Tues–Sun noon–3pm and 7pm–midnight. Taking a taxi is recommended. Even though it is not too far from the Mercado Modelo, the street is dark and very quiet at night.

MODERATE

Camafeu de Oxossi *⊛* BAHIAN   The Camafeu de Oxossi and the Maria de São Pedro restaurants share the lovely large patio upstairs in the Mercado Modelo. However, they have two very separate owners and two very separate bank accounts, which explains why when you first walk in, two equally keen and friendly *Baianas* try to persuade you to sit in their restaurant. Does it really matter where you eat? I couldn't tell the difference; both menus serve up traditional Bahian food, including nine types of moquecas. Shunned by locals, these restaurants are geared to tourists who are wandering the Mercado Modelo browsing for souvenirs, but the food is still fine and the views over the bay and the São Marcelo Fort are worth the price of admission.

Praça Visc. De Cayru 250, Mercado Modelo, Comércio. © 071/3242-9751. Main courses R$24–R$48 (US$12–US$24/£6.50–£13) for 2. AE, DC, MC, V. Mon and Wed 9:30am–7:30pm; Tues and Thurs–Sat 11am–7pm; Sun 11am–4pm. Bus: Praça da Sé, then take the Elevator Lacerda to the lower city.

BARRA

This beach neighborhood is a popular dining destination for locals; with the many hotels concentrated in this area, it is always a lively spot in the evening. For the best views, you can't beat the patio of **Barravento** (see below).

EXPENSIVE

Pereira 🅐🅐 BRAZILIAN This beautiful faux-rustic modern restaurant with exposed brick and expansive glass walls opens up to a lovely patio overlooking the ocean and seawall in Barra. It's an excellent destination, whether it's for lunch, dinner, or just a drink and some tapas. In addition to the typical Brazilian snacks such as deep-fried cod or prawn dumplings *(bolinho de bacalhau* and *pastel de camarão)*, you'll find bruschetta with ham and goat cheese or grilled squid in teriyaki sauce. Main courses range from pastas and risottos to grilled seafood and steak. The restaurant has a large wine list with a number of affordable Portuguese, French, and Italian wines in the R$40-to-R$90 (US$17–US$38/£11–£24) range. Pereira is especially busy on weekends when Salvador's young and beautiful gather to preen and be seen. *Tip:* Right next door is the Japanese eatery Sato, run by the same owners. Don't bother. If you really want Japanese go to SOHO (see above).

Av. Sete de Setembro 3959, Porto da Barra. ℂ 071/3264-6464. Main courses R$32–R$48 (US$16–US$24/£8.50–£13). AE, DC, MC, V. Mon–Wed 6pm–midnight; Thurs–Sun noon–3pm and 6pm–midnight. Bus: Barra or via Orla.

MODERATE

Barravento 🅐 BAHIAN Underneath a large sail-shaped roof, Barravento offers alfresco dining on a beach patio overlooking all of the beach as far as the Farol da Barra. The menu includes a large selection of typical Bahian dishes such as *moquecas*, *marriscadas* (seafood stews), and grilled fish. One dish that every Baiano will recommend is the *moqueca de siri-mole* (soft-shell crab). If you're not in the mood for a full meal, Barravento serves a variety of appetizers such as *casquinha de siri* (spiced crabmeat) and fish pastries; the view is complimentary.

Av. Getulio Vargas 814 (aka Av. Oceanica), Barra. ℂ 071/3247-2577. Main courses R$18–R$38 (US$9–US$19/ £5–£10); all dishes for 2. DC, MC, V. Daily noon–midnight (if busy, open later on weekends and in high season). Bus: Barra or via Orla.

RIO VERMELHO

Over the last few years, Rio Vermelho has grown into a bustling, lively restaurant destination. You will find several excellent options and most are centered around the main square, Praça Brigadeiro Farias Rocha, so you can stroll around and see what strikes your fancy. We have included a few reviews of restaurants that may easily be overlooked but are worth visiting.

MODERATE

Companhia da Pizza PIZZA One of the best pizzerias in town, and also one of the most happening restaurants in Rio Vermelho. In the evenings you may have to wait for a table but it is worth snagging one on the patio so you have a prime people-watching spot. The menu includes more than 50 flavors of pizza, sweet and savory. Unless you order one of the pizzas with a filled crust you get a traditional thin-crusted "São Paulo-style" pizza. Flavors to try include the chicken with palm heart, rucula (with sun-dried tomato and mozzarella), or the spicy Baiana, with pepperoni, calabresa pepper, and ground beef.

Praça Brigadeiro Farias Rocha s/n, Rio Vermelho. ℂ 071/3334-6276. Main courses R$20–R$42 (US$10–US$21/ £5.40–£11) for 2. AE, V. Sun–Thurs 5:30pm–1am; Fri–Sat 5:30pm–2am. Bus: Rio Vermelho.

Dona Mariquita BRAZILIAN Tucked away in a little laneway opposite the main square, this small restaurant is full of surprises. First up, all of Dona Mariquita, pleasant patio included, is beautifully decorated with high-quality Northeastern crafts and artwork. Then there are the delicious caipiroscas. We highly recommend the umbu-caja, combining two typical Northeastern fruits into one outstanding cocktail. And last but not least there is the food. Start off with the pastel, puffy fried savory meat dumpling served with a hot pepper jam. Main courses include specialties from the coast (seafood and fish moquecas and bobó) as well as interior dishes such as a bean stew and *carne seca* (sun-dried beef). On Friday evenings there is live music.

Rua do Meio 178, Rio Vermelho. ⒸⒻ **071/3334-6947.** Main courses R$28–R$36 (US$14–US$18/£7.50–£10) for 2. AE, V. Tues noon–3pm; Wed–Sat noon–3pm and 6pm–midnight. Bus: Rio Vermelho.

Lambreta Grill BRAZILIAN/SEAFOOD   Hidden at the top of a steep street, the Lambreta Grill is well worth the trip. Japanese chef Fukino runs one of the most popular yet laid-back seafood restaurants in town. The restaurant decor is ultra-basic, but wait until you taste the food! Lambretas are small oysters, and the best way to try them is to order the appetizer plate where you get a dozen of the little mollusks with various toppings including sun-dried tomato, curry sauce, garlic, or calabresa pepper. For the main course try the grilled seafood. Our favorite was the seafood symphony—*sinfonia de frutos do mar;* a piping hot steel griddle is brought to your table, piled high with juicy and tender morsels of squid, prawns, mussels, and octopus, served with a side of potatoes and palm heart. If you like octopus, try the *polvo a la mode* for some of the plumpest and most tender octopus you'll ever taste. *Note:* This small street can be hard to find. It runs uphill off the main waterfront street beyond a popular bar called Extudo (give that as a reference to your taxi driver).

Rua Alexandre Gusmão 70, Rio Vermelho. ⒸⒻ **071/3335-0107.** Main courses R$35–R$50 (US$18–US$25/£9.50–£14) for 2. AE, MC, V. Mon–Sat 6pm–2am. Bus: Rio Vermelho.

4 Exploring Salvador

Brazil's first capital city, Salvador serves simultaneously as the repository of the country's historical heritage and the source of much that is new and vibrant in its culture. Nothing symbolizes this dual role better than Pelourinho. The historic core of Salvador, Pelourinho is a perfectly preserved urban gem from the 16th and 17th centuries, the capital of one of the grandest and richest colonial dominions in the Americas. Pelourinho today boasts a wealth of richly decorated baroque churches, tiny squares, and fine old colonial mansions. By day, one could wander its cobblestone streets for hours.

At night, Pelourinho assumes its cultural role. Small squares and larger praças come alive with bands, singers, and concerts. Many tourists attend, certainly, but so do an equal or even greater number of Salvadorans. Bahia has long been the cultural wellspring of Brazil, the source of what's new in music. Since its revitalization in the '80s, Pelourinho has established itself as one of Salvador's main stages. Unfortunately, the new state government has cut much of the funding for cultural events, and the wonderful programming that kept Pelourinho hopping almost any night of the week has disappeared. Individual bars and restaurants have stepped in to fill the gap, however, and now schedule their own entertainment and events. Check with the Bahiatursa office in Pelourinho for upcoming concerts or shows.

Outside the old city there are several good museums, great arts and crafts, and the glittering Baía de Todos os Santos, the bay that attracted the Portuguese to Salvador in the first place. Just beyond the bay, warm Atlantic Ocean beaches stretch unbroken from the Farol de Barra lighthouse some 80km (50 miles) up the coast to Praia do Forte.

Salvador's Centro Histórico

DINING ◆
A Cubana **5**
Camafeu de Oxossi **3**
Jardim das Delicias **12**
Mama Bahia Salvador **13**
Sorriso da Dada **11**
Trapiche Adelaide **1**

ACCOMMODATIONS ■
Convento do Carmo **20**
Pousada do Pilar **21**
Pousada Redfish **22**
Solar dos Deuses **9**
Studio do Carmo **19**

ATTRACTIONS ●
Casa de Jorge Amado **16**
Catedral Basilica **7**
Elevator Lacerda **6**
Forte Sao Marcelo **2**
Igreja de São Francisco **10**

Largo Pelourinho **17**
Mercado Modelo **4**
Museu Afro-Brasileiro **8**
Museu da Cidade **15**
Museu Tempostal **14**
Nossa Senhora do Rosário dos Pretos **18**

SUGGESTED SIGHTSEEING ITINERARIES

If You Have ❶ Day

If 1 day is all you've got, you better get moving! Exploring the district of Pelourinho is a must. You could spend hours in this neighborhood admiring the colorful colonial mansions and impressive baroque churches. Wander down and marvel at the gilded splendor of the Igreja São Francisco. See Nossa Senhora do Rosario dos Pretos, then take the Lacerda to the Cidade Baixa. Bargain hard at the Mercado Modelo. In the evening go munch on a moqueca or some other Bahian delicacy. Then wander the old town, enjoying the music and energy of Pelourinho by night.

If You Have ❷ Days

Begin day 2 by viewing some of Brazil's best Catholic art at the Museu de Arte Sacra. Then for a taste of the faith that produced such splendor, visit the most famous church in Salvador, Nosso Senhor do Bonfim. Afterward go for a stroll along Boa Viagem Beach and Forte Monte Serrat for the best views of the city and—if it's a weekend—some great people-watching as well. Be at the Farol de Barra around about 5pm in time to grab a drink and admire what will almost surely be a spectacular sunset. Have dinner in one of Barra's many restaurants, or splurge on a waterfront dinner at Soho or Trapiche Adelaide, or else wander down the shore a bit and have dinner on the beach.

> ### *Tips* Take It Easy on Sundays
>
> Sundays are pretty slow in Salvador. Everyone's been up partying until 5 in the morning, so next to nobody is on the street. The Cidade Baixa and the Mercado Modelo are virtually deserted, and even Pelourinho isn't much fun until the evening. In short, it's a good day to do as the locals do and head to the beach.

If You Have ❸ Days

Get some R & R by spending the day at one of Salvador's beaches enjoying the sunshine and fresh seafood at the *barracas*. On weekends, Flamengo and Stella Maris are the prime locations. Or take a schooner tour and enjoy the view of Salvador from the water, exploring the islands and beaches in the Bay of All Saints at the same time. In the evening head to the newly trendy Rio Vermelho neighborhood for a fine seafood dinner or casual pizza, then join the people-watching on Praca Brigadeiro arias Rocha, or if it's Tuesday night head to Pelourinho for the weekly Terça da Bençáo (Blessed Tuesday) party.

If You Have ❹ Days or More

Catch a catamaran to the small beach community of Morro de São Paulo, where life is simple and the beaches are fabulous. Or to really get away from the hustle and bustle, go one island farther down to the tiny, quiet, gorgeous beach at Boi Peba. For a more mountainous experience, head inland to the hills and trails of the Chapada Diamantina, which has great hiking and exploring.

THE TOP ATTRACTIONS
A VISIT TO PELOURINHO 𝒜𝒜𝒜

Make your first stop the Bahiatursa office, located at Rua das Laranjeiras (℃ 071/3321-2133) to pick up maps.

In 1985 the historic core of colonial Salvador was designated a UNESCO World Heritage Site by the United Nations. It's well merited. One could spend years getting to know the history of the churches, squares, and colorful colonial mansions in this old part of the city. What follows is but a brief introduction. The place to start a tour of Pelourinho is in the main square, called the **Terreiro de Jesus.** Dominating the west end of the square is the 17th-century **Catedral Basílica** (see listing below). Flanking the cathedral is the neoclassical **Antiga Faculdade de Medicina** (see listing for Museu Afro-Brasileiro/Faculdade de Medicina, below), now home to the excellent Afro-Brazilian Museum. Also on the north side of the square is the smaller baroque **Igreja São Pedro dos Clerigos** (Mon–Fri 1–5pm). Facing the cathedral at the far end of the *terreiro* is the **Igreja de Ordem Terceiro de São Domingos de Gusmão.** Built between 1713 and 1734, this baroque church suffered through an 1870s renovation that destroyed most of its fine interior painting and tile work. On the south side of this church there's a wide cobblestone street with a tall cross in the middle. This is the **Praça Anchieta.** The saint on the cross is São Francisco de Xavier, patron saint of Salvador. At the far end of this little praça stand two of the most impressive churches in the city. The large two-towered one on the right is the **Igreja de São Francisco** (see listing below); the central element is the surrounding **Convento de São Francisco.** Next to it is the **Igreja de Ordem Terceira de São Francisco,** immediately recognizable by its ornately carved sandstone facade. Inside (the church is open Mon–Fri

8am–noon and 1–5pm) there's a small green cloister, around the outside of which there's some fine blue Portuguese tile.

Back at the Terreiro de Jesus, the two streets on either side of the Church of São Pedro (Rua Joao de Deus and Rua Alfredo de Brito) both run downhill to the **Largo Pelourinho.** This small, steeply sloping triangular square gets its name from the whipping post that used to stand at the top end. This was where slaves and criminals were flogged. The smaller building at the top of the square, now the **Casa de Jorge Amado** (see listing below), used to serve as the city's slave market. Looking downhill, on the right-hand side of the largo you'll find the blue and creamy yellow **Nossa Senora do Rosário dos Pretos** (Mon–Fri 7:30am–6pm, Sat–Sun 7:30am–noon). Literally translated as Our Lady of the Rosary of the Blacks, the high baroque structure was erected over the course of the 18th century by and for the African slaves who represented the backbone of Salvador's sugar economy. Today, much of the congregation is still of African descent; new paintings inside show the Passion of Christ with an all-black Holy Family, and drums have largely taken the place of the organ in church services (the Tues 5:30pm Mass is particularly well attended). At the far end of the square is the tiny **Praça de Reggae.** At the lowest point of the Largo Pelourinho a narrow street leads steeply uphill to a trio of old baroque churches, the **Igreja de Carmo,** the **Igreja de Ordem Terceiro de Carmo,** and the **Igreja do Santissimo Santo do Passo.** Only the Ordem Terceiro is open, and the views back over the city are only okay, so it's likely better to retrace your steps and explore one of the other delights of Pelourinho, its hidden interior courtyards. There are four of them: the **Praça de Arte, Cultura e Memoria;** the **Praça Tereza Batista;** the **Praça Pedro Arcanjo;** and the **Praça Quincas Berro d'Água.** Their entrances branch off the little streets between the Largo Pelourinho and the Terreiro de Jesus. During the day they contain cafes and artisan booths and museums. At night, nearly every one features a band.

ATTRACTIONS IN PELOURINHO

Casa de Jorge Amado   Though Jorge Amado was long one of Brazil's most beloved writers (he died in 2001 at the age of 93), there's not really much to see in his former house, now a museum dedicated to his memory. The ground-floor cafe has a

---

Tips   Consider a Freelance Guide

In Pelourinho freelance tour guides armed with ID badges will approach you and try to sell you on a tour of the old town. Some are indeed accredited tour guides; others just have fake IDs. It's nearly impossible to distinguish one from the other, nor is it really that critical; many of the independent guides are excellent. Prices are negotiable, depending on the size of the group, length of tour, time of year, time of the day, and your interests (churches, culture, architecture, museums, and so on). Typically you can expect to pay R$50 (US$25/£14) for a 4-hour tour with two people. It's not a bad idea to test your prospective guide before engaging him. Ask him to give you a quick spiel on whatever sight is close at hand. If he seems to know his stuff and you can understand his English, go ahead and hire him. If you want to make sure you're hiring an accredited guide, stop by the **Singtur (guide association)** office, Praça José Anchieta 12, second floor, Pelourinho (© **071/3322-1017**).

collage of his book covers, showing the wide range of languages into which his dozens of works have been translated. On the upper floors, the text-heavy exhibits that tell the story of Amado's life are written exclusively in Portuguese. Better to just read one of his books. His most popular works are all set in Bahia. *Dona Flor and Her Two Husbands* is set in Pelourinho. *Gabriela, Clove and Cinnamon* (my personal favorite), and *Tieta do Agreste* take place in provincial towns farther south. *Gabriela, Tieta,* and *Dona Flor* have all been made into movies starring the luscious Sonia Braga.

Largo do Pelourinho 51, Pelourinho. © 071/3321-0122. Free admission. Mon–Sat 10am–6pm. Bus: Praça da Sé.

Catedral Basílica 𝕮   Fresh from a thorough restoration in 1996, the 17th-century basilica that dominates Terreiro de Jesus square now looks as good as it did when it was first erected by the Jesuits in 1672. The craftsmanship found inside is impressive. Beautifully ornate, the many altars are made from cedar and covered with a thin layer of gold; the high altar alone consists of 18 gold-covered pillars. The image of Christ the Savior above the transept is the largest wood sculpture in Brazil. Like much of the carving work in the church, it was likely the work of trained slaves; look closely at some of the altars and you'll notice symbols of the Candomblé religion such as small fishtails, a tribute to Yemanjá, the goddess of the sea. The Basilica hosts "Barroco na Bahia," baroque chamber concerts on Sunday at 11am.

Terreiro de Jesus s/n, Pelourinho. © 071/3321-4573. Admission R$2 (US$1/£.50). Daily 8–11:30am and 2–5:30pm. Bus: Praça da Sé.

Igreja de São Francisco 𝕮𝕮𝕮   At a time when Salvador was the biggest port in South America and Portugal still vied with Spain and Holland for the title of world's richest empire, the sugar barons of Salvador decided to splurge a little and let folks know that their colony had *arrived.* Beginning in 1708 and continuing until 1723, they took more than 100 kilograms of gold and slathered it over every available knob and curlicue in the richly carved interior of this high-baroque church. The result could hardly be called beautiful—works of the nouveaux riches seldom are—but by God, it's impressive. The inside fairly gleams; on nights when the doors are open it casts a yellow sheen all the way up to Terreiro de Jesus. If you can, time your visit on a Tuesday toward dusk (5:30pm-ish). The church will be packed with parishioners coming for a blessing, while outside wealthy matrons seeking the special favor of Saint Francis will be passing out little loaves of bread to a veritable mosh pit of Salvador's poor. On Monday, Wednesday, and Saturday, at 11:30am and 4pm, there is an impressive sound-and-light show in the church.

Next door, the **Ordem Terceira de São Francisco church** (Mon–Fri 8am–noon and 1–5pm) has a gorgeous sandstone facade on the outside, and on the inside some fine blue tile and a rather silly hall of saints. Allow an hour for both churches.

Largo Cruzeiro de S. Francisco s/n (off Terreiro de Jesus). © 071/3322-6430. Admission R$3 (US$1.50/£.80). Mon–Sat 8am–5:30pm; Sun 7am–5pm. Bus: Praça da Sé.

Museu Afro-Brasileiro/Faculdade de Medicina 𝕮   This fine old building (built in 1808) is now home to the Museu Afro-Brasileiro, which attempts to show the development of the Afro-Brazilian culture that arose as African slaves settled in Brazil. Particularly good is the large portion of the exhibit space dedicated to the Candomblé religion, explaining the meaning and characteristics of each god *(Orixá)* and the role it plays in the community. Make sure to ask for one of the English-language binders at the entrance—they contain translations of all of the displays. In the back room, 27 huge carved wood panels—the work of noted Bahian artist Carybé—portray the

> *Tips* **Ups and Downs**
>
> The quickest way to move between Pelourinho and the cidade baixa (lower city) is via the **Lacerda elevator,** which takes you from the Praça Tomé de Sousa to the praça Visconde de Cairu, almost across from the Mercado modelo. You can also use the **Plano Inclinado do Pilar,** a funicular railway farther down the Rua Direita de Santo Antônio, past the Carmo convent. Restored in 2006, the *plano inclinado* drops you at the Mercado do Ouro. And at US10¢ a ride you don't have to worry about blowing your transportation budget.

Orixás and the animal and symbol that goes with each. The museum staff can also provide information on Candomblé celebrations. Allow 30 to 45 minutes.

Two other small museums that were once located in this building, the **Memorial de Medicina** and the **Museu de Arqueologia e Etnologia,** have been closed with no reopening date foreseen.

Antiga Faculdade de Medicina, Terreiro de Jesus s/n, Pelourinho (just to the right of the basilica). ℂ **071/3321-2013.** Admission R$5 (US$2.50/£1.35). Mon–Fri 9am–6pm; Sat–Sun 10am–5pm. Bus: Praça da Sé.

Museu da Cidade *(Overrated*   I love city museums. Poring over old maps and photographs to see how a city grew and what people were wearing at a particular time fascinates me. In this case, however, curators have done such an uninspired job it's hardly worth the effort. The museum has some old photos and a few maps, but there's not much in the way of signage and what little there is certainly is not in English. There's also a display on Candomblé featuring various Orixás, but for that you're better off going to the Afro-Brasilian museum.

Largo do Pelourinho 3. ℂ **071/3321-1967.** Free admission. Mon and Wed–Sat 9:30am–6:30pm; Sun 9am–1pm. Bus: Praça de Sé.

Museu Tempostal ✦   Did you know the postcard was invented by Emmanuel Hermann? The Austrian professor first put a paper backing on a photograph and tossed it in the mail in 1869. By 1880, they were legal post in Brazil. In 1904 the first colored card appeared. Useless trivia? Well, maybe. But considering how many of these things are sent and received throughout the world, it's a wonder how little thought they get. This fun little museum boasts a large collection of postcards dating from the 1880s to the 1990s. Most are of Salvador itself; viewing the collection is a wonderful way to see how the city grew and changed. Indeed, it's much better than the city museum. There's also a collection of cards from the turn of the last century; even during the Belle Epoque people liked to have photos taken of themselves in silly costumes.

Rua Gregório dos Matos 33. ℂ **071/3117-6383.** Free admission. Tues–Fri 10am–6pm; Sat–Sun 1–7pm. Closed Mon. Bus: Praça de Sé.

IN CENTRO
Museu de Arte Sacra ✦✦✦   This small but splendid museum displays one of Brazil's best collections of Catholic art. The artifacts are shown in the former Convent of Saint Teresa of Avila, a simple, beautiful building that itself counts as an artwork. The galleries enclose a small green cloister in the center of which a tiny fountain gurgles quietly. The collection includes oil paintings, oratorios (a cabinet containing a

crucifix), metalwork, and lots of wooden statues of saints. In general the cabinetry is better than the carving: The jacaranda-wood oratorios are things of beauty, while the wooden saints seemed to have kept the same look of stunned piety through more than 2 centuries. If you're pressed for time, head for the two rooms of silver at the back. Walk through these rooms and you can see how Brazilian silversmiths refined their technique, as the rather crude—but massive—works of the 18th century changed and developed until by the early 19th century, Brazilian artists were producing reliquaries, processional crosses, and crucifixes of astonishing refinement. Allow 1½ hours.

Rua do Sodré 276. ℭ 071/3243-6310. www.mas.ufba.br. Admission R$5 (US$2.50/£1.35) adults, R$3 (US$1.50/ £.80) students with valid ID, free for children under 7. Mon–Fri 11:30am–5:30pm. Located just south of Pelourinho. From Praça de Sé walk 10 min. south on Av. Carlos Gomes, turn right and walk downhill on Ladeira Santa Teresa for 45m (150 ft.). Bus: Praça de Sé.

IN CIDADE BAIXA

Forte São Marcelo 𝒢   For years we have admired this perfectly round fort (Jorge Amado referred to it as "the belly button of Bahia") at the entrance of the lower city, thinking how cool it would be to visit it. And now that it has been restored and we visited we discovered that sometimes things look better from a distance. Originally built in 1650 and modified to its current configuration in 1812, it is still pretty cool to be able to set foot in the fort and have a look around, but it is not worth more than a 30-minute visit. There are a few exhibits on the history of the forts of Salvador (there used to be over 30; now 17 remain). For those who want to stretch their visit, a good restaurant called Buccaneros is inside the ramparts. Boats go ferry visitors from shore regularly, leaving from inside the Centro Nautico (across from the Mercado Modelo, where also the catamarans to Morro de São Paulo leave from). If you are eating at the restaurant you are not required to pay the museum fee. Please inform the ticket office.

Acess from the Terminal Maritimo da Bahia (across from the Mercado Modelo), Cidade Baixa. ℭ 071/3495-8359. www.fortesaomarcelo.com.br. R$10 (US$5/£2.70), R$5 (US$2.50/£1.35) children 7 and older, free for children under 7. Tues–Sun 9am–6pm. Bus: Comércio.

Mercado Modelo 𝒢   There's no sense pretending you're not a tourist in the Mercado Modelo. If you're here, you are. Still, it's a fun place to wander. This former Customs building and slave warehouse burned to the ground in 1984 and was then rebuilt in its original 19th-century style. It houses just about everything Bahia has to offer in terms of arts and crafts and souvenirs. Merchants in the little stalls certainly want your business, but they're not annoying about it. Instead, in the best Brazilian tradition, they'll invite you in to look around, press you if you seem interested, drop their prices if you hesitate (bargain hard in here!), and concede gracefully if you decline.

Praça Cayru, Comércio (just across from the elevator). ℭ 071/3243-6543. Mon–Sat 8am–7pm; Sun 8am–noon. Bus: Comércio.

Solar do Unhão 𝒢𝒢   An old sugar mill, the Solar consists of a number of beautifully preserved heritage buildings centered around a lovely stone courtyard that dates back to the 18th century. Half the fun is just to wander around and explore the various buildings set on the waterfront (the views are fabulous). The main building houses a small modern art museum; you'll find some works of Portinari and Di Cavalcanti among the works on display. Taking the path to the right of the main building will lead you above the rocks to the sculpture garden with works by Caribé and Mario

> ## *Moments* Catch the Sunset at Barra
>
> Barra Point is the prime sunset spot in all of Salvador; 30 minutes before sunset the crowds start to gather and stake out their spots at the foot of the lighthouse. Even better, though, is the cafe on the fort's upper ramparts, where from the comfort of your patio table you can watch the sun sink slowly behind the island of Itaparica.

Cravo. The rest of the small collection is housed in a side building behind the sculpture garden. Expect to spend 1 to 2 hours.

Tip: There's a nightly dinner and folklore show in the Solar's restaurant. Yes, it's touristy, but the food is good and the dancers top-quality. Shows start Monday through Saturday at 8:30pm and cost R$76 (US$38/£21).

Av. do Contorno 8, Cidade Baixa. © 071/3329-0660. Free admission. Tues–Sun 1–7pm. It is best to take a taxi from the Mercado Modelo or Pelourinho.

IN BARRA

Museu Nautico da Bahia/Farol da Barra/Forte de Santo Antônio ⓡ The lighthouse, fort, and museum are mostly worth a visit for the views over the Bay of All Saints. Erected in 1534, the Forte de Santo Antônio da Barra was the first and most important Portuguese fortress protecting Salvador. It thus had the honor of being taken by the invading Dutch in 1624, and retaken the following year by a combined Portuguese and Spanish fleet. You can wander the halls and admire the military architecture, but there's no signage on the history of the fort. The museum inside the lighthouse contains a small collection of maps and charts, navigational instruments, and a number of archaeological finds from wrecks that the lighthouse obviously didn't help. Signage here is in English and Portuguese.

Farol da Barra, Praia da Barra s/n, Barra. © 071/3264-3296. Admission R$6 (US$3/£1.60). Mon 8:30am–noon; Tues–Sun 9am–7pm museum, 9am–10pm cafe. Bus: Barra or Via Orla.

IN BONFIM

Nosso Senhor do Bonfim ⓡⓡ Salvador's most famous church has a reputation for granting miracles. Tourists and faithful alike thus flock to this relatively plain 18th-century church on a small peninsula just north of downtown. (You'll be swamped on arrival by kids selling *fitas*, the colorful ribbons that people tie around their wrist for good luck; you may as well buy a dozen and get it over with.) Step inside and you'll likely be distracted from the tall barrel vault and blue wall tiles by the fervor of the people offering up their prayers. To see the extent of this devotion, go to the Room of Miracles at the back where people give thanks for miracles by donating valuable or important objects. Definitely eye-catching are the numerous hanging body parts—models made of wood, plastic, even gold. This church also plays a very important role in the Candomblé religion and is dedicated to Oxalá, one of the highest deities. This is where in January one of Salvador's most significant syncretist religious events takes place, the famous washing of the steps.

Largo do Bonfim. © 071/3312-0196. Free admission. Tues–Sun 6:30am–noon and 2–6pm. Located about 8km (5 miles)—or a R$18 (US$9/£5) taxi ride—north of Pelourinho on the Bonfim Peninsula. Bus: Catch a Bonfim bus at Praça de Sé or at the bottom of the Elevator Lacerda in Comércio.

Moments **The Spectacle of Lavagem do Bonfim**

One of the most impressive demonstrations of faith (Catholic and Candomblé) takes place every year on the third Thursday of January on the steps of N.S. do Bonfim. Beloved because he offers protection even to non-Catholics, N.S. do Bonfim is associated by Candomblé followers with Oxalá, the supreme ruler and one of the most important *Orixás* (deities). On the day of the Lavagem, hundreds of women in their best Bahian outfits (hoop skirts, white turbans, lovely white lace blouses, and colorful jewelry) parade 8km (5 miles) from the N.S. Conceção de Praia in the lower city out to the N.S. do Bonfim. They carry jugs of perfumed water, and are serenaded on the way by the music of the Sons of Gandhi bloco. Vendors sell food and drinks, and thousands of spectators follow along. At the church, the barefoot *Baianas* go about scrubbing the steps with brooms. The Catholic Church does not approve of this event and keeps its doors shut on this day. Once the actual washing is completed, the party in front of the church lasts well into the night with music, *capoeira,* and plenty of food and drink.

ARCHITECTURAL HIGHLIGHTS
HISTORIC BUILDINGS & MONUMENTS

The old town of **Pelourinho** was recognized in 1985 as a UNESCO World Heritage Site. See "A Visit to Pelourinho," earlier in this chapter, for descriptions of some of the hundreds of interesting structures in this neighborhood.

At the top of the cliff at the edge of Pelourinho one finds the **Praça Tomé de Souza,** flanked on one side by a glass-cube-on-stilts that houses the city hall, on the other side by the neoclassical **Palácio Rio Branco** ⚜, and on the cliff face by the Art Deco **Elevator Lacerda** ⚜. The original 80-meter- (236-foot)-tall elevator was built in 1872 to whisk people between the upper and lower city. The present Art Deco look was added in 1930, when the old mechanism was replaced with hydraulics. The elevator was also then re-christened "Lacerda" in honor of the original engineer. Open daily from 5am to midnight. Admission is R$.10 (US5¢/£.03), the cheapest ride in town.

FORTS

After taking Salvador back from the Dutch in 1625, the Portuguese went on a bit of a fort-building binge. Fortresses small and large were built or strengthened all along the Bay of All Saints. Perhaps the city's most famous fort is the perfectly round **Forte de São Marcelo,** built in 1625 in the Bay of All Saints directly opposite the lower town. The current low thick walls were built in 1738. Jorge Amado called the fort "the belly button of Bahia." It was recently restored and is now open for visits (Tues–Sun 9am–6pm). South of Pelourinho stand two forts fairly close to each other. The **Forte de São Diogo** saw a great deal of action during the second Dutch invasion of 1638. Inside, there's a small model of the system of forts protecting the city. Open Tuesday through Sunday from 9:30am to noon and 1:30 to 5:30pm. The **Forte de Santa Maria** is located on Avenida Sete de Setembro just a bit north of the Farol de Barra point. Its complement of large guns is still in position. Open Tuesday through Friday from 8am to 6pm, and Saturday from 8am to noon. The city's most important fortress, the **Forte de Santo Antônio** ⚜ (see listing above), was built in 1583, taken by the Dutch in 1624, retaken by the Portuguese in 1625, and rebuilt into its current form in 1702. Open Tuesday through Sunday from 9am to 7pm (to 9pm in summer).

CHURCHES & TEMPLES

Salvador has a wealth of beautiful old churches, so many in fact that a couple in the centro histórico stand abandoned, sizable trees growing from their ornate baroque bell towers. Some of the best churches are covered in the sections under either Pelourinho or Bonfim. One not covered but that's still worth mentioning is **Nossa Senhora da Conceição da Praia,** Largo de Conceição de Praia (© **071/3242-0545**). Open Tuesday through Friday from 6:30 to 11:30am and 3 to 5:30pm, and Saturday through Monday from 6:30 to 11:30am. Located in the Lower City a couple hundred feet south (left) of the Elevator Lacerda, the building was prefabricated in Portugal, shipped in parts to Salvador, and erected in 1736. On the third Thursday in January a huge procession of white-clad *Baianas* sets off from this church—water jars on their heads—on their 8km (5-mile) trek to the Church of N.S. do Bonfim, where with great ceremony they wash the church steps.

NEIGHBORHOODS TO EXPLORE
PELOURINHO 🐾🐾🐾

The historic heart of the city, Pelourinho is a delight to explore. Indeed, it's so worthwhile, we have already covered it under "The Top Attractions," earlier in this chapter.

COMÉRCIO

The Cidade Baixa (lower city) was always the commercial center of Salvador. In the 16th century people preferred to live in the cooler heights of Pelourinho and keep their offices and warehouses on the waterfront below. The concept is the same today, but Comércio, as the area is known, is now planted thick with stubby commercial high-rises. The Elevator Lacerda is the easiest way to access this area—though there's really little of interest down here except the ferry docks and the crafts fair in the **Mercado Modelo.** A number of steep, shabby alleys also connect the lower city to the upper city, but it's safer to take the elevator.

VITÓRIA

This quiet and green neighborhood lies immediately south of Pelourinho. It has some lesser city landmarks such as the **Castro Alves Theatre** and **Campo Grande Square.**

BARRA 🐾🐾

The most popular beach neighborhood close to town, Barra is a neighborhood of restaurants and small shops located south of the city center just where the coastline makes a sharp turn to the east. Many hotels are located here, and in the evenings, locals and tourists mingle in the bars and restaurants. Sights in the area include the **Farol da Barra (Barra Lighthouse)** and the smaller **Forte Santa Maria.** The prime attraction, however, is the sunset; small crowds gather to watch the show.

BONFIM/MONTE SERRAT 🐾

Located on a small peninsula that juts out into the bay, Bonfim is home to the **Church of Nosso Senhor do Bonfim,** one of the most important religious sites in the city. Beloved by both Catholics and Candomblé worshipers (who revere their equivalent deity of Oxalá), the hilltop church draws huge crowds who come to pray or ask for miracles. The **Washing of the Steps,** which takes place on the third Thursday in January, is one of the year's most colorful religious events. The neighborhoods

Understanding Candomblé & the *Terreiros*

The religion of Candomblé is practiced throughout Brazil, but its roots are deepest in Salvador, where it forms an important part of community life. The practice originated with slaves brought to Brazil from West Africa; they believed in a pantheon of gods and goddesses *(Orixás)* who embodied natural forces such as wind, storm, ocean, and fire. Each Orixá had its own rituals, colors, habits, and even a day of the week associated with his or her worship. A believer who is prepared and trained can become possessed by a certain Orixá and form a link between humankind and the gods.

In Catholic Brazil, the practice of Candomblé was prohibited. Willing or no, Brazilian slaves were converted to Catholicism. Though they weren't allowed inside white churches, the slaves watching from without soon recognized aspects of their *Orixás* in various Catholic saints. By translating each of their gods into an equivalent saint, Candomblé followers found they could continue their native worship under the very noses of their Catholic priests and masters.

Oxalá, the creator and supreme ruler, thus became the Senhor do Bonfim; *Iansã*, the Orixá of wind and storms, resembled Santa Barbara; *Yemanjá*, the queen of the ocean and fresh water, seemed to have the same privileged position as Our Lady of Conception. Unlike the saints, Orixás are far from perfect; Yemanjá, for example, is notoriously vain and jealous. However, in the process of syncretizing Roman and West African practice, much that was Catholic was adopted, and the result is that Candomblé is now something uniquely Brazilian.

Actual Candomblé ceremonies are fun and fascinating—singing, chanting, and drumming, plus wonderful foods and perfumes are all used in order to please the Orixás and encourage them to come and possess some of the believers present. When a person goes into a trance and receives an Orixá, his or her movements, gestures, and voice change to reflect those of the Orixá. The language used in Candomblé is Yoruba, a West African language still spoken in large parts of Nigeria.

of Bonfim, Ribeira, and Monte Serat are now mostly home to the lower middle class and working poor, but started out originally as a summer destination with cottages and summer homes. The other worthwhile sight is the **Forte de Monte Serrat,** which offers fabulous views of Salvador. On Sunday the seawall is packed with families and teenagers out for a stroll.

ONDINA, RIO VERMELHO & BEACHES ☞

Once past Ondina, the coast is an almost uninterrupted string of beaches. Most neighborhoods are very modern and new, with little attraction beyond the beach itself. Popular beaches include Rio Vermelho, Praia dos Artistas, Praia de Piatã, Praia de Itapuã, Praia de Stella Maris, and Praia do Flamengo. **Rio Vermelho** is home to some of the city's best waterfront hotels, and has recently evolved into one of Salvador's prime nightlife enclaves. The area around the Praça Brigadeiro Farias Rocha is great for evening people-watching.

There are many *terreiros* (areas of worship) in Salvador, though most are located in poorer neighborhoods far from downtown. Many accept visitors provided they follow a few basic rules: no revealing clothing (shorts and miniskirts are out); white clothing is preferred; no video or picture taking; visitors cannot participate but only observe. This last is especially important. As inviting as the food or dancing may look, these practices are part of a religious ceremony for believers only. Real *terreiros* will not quote an admission price, but may ask for and will definitely appreciate a donation, to be given to the Mãe or Pai de Santo, the spiritual leader of the *terreiro*.

To attend a Candomblé session check with the Afro Brazilian Federation: **Federação Baiana de Culto Afro Brasileiro,** Rua Alfredo de Brito 39, second floor, Pelourinho (© **071/3321-1444**). Another good resource is the Afro-Brazilian museum in Pelourinho (© **071/3321-0383**).

Many tour guides and hotel concierges can arrange for you to attend a Candomblé session, although some services will be more touristy than others. If you only have a few days, this may be your only option. If you have more time and want to try harder to find an authentic ceremony, contact the *terreiros* listed below or get in touch with **Tatur Turismo** (© **071/3450-7216;** www.tatur.com.br) before your arrival to find out on which dates ceremonies take place.

Terreiros that accept visitors include **Menininha do Gantois,** Alto do Gantois 23, Federação (© **071/3331-9231;** service led by Mãe Carmem); popular with artists and visiting celebrities is **Ilê Axé Opô Afonjá,** Rua Direita de São Gonçalo do Retiro 245, Cabula (© **071/3384-6800**); and **Casa Branca,** Av. Vasco da Gama 463, Vasco da Gama (close to Rio Vermelho) (© **071/3334-2900;** the oldest *terreiro* still in use, dating back to 1836). Always take a taxi to the *terreiro;* some are in less safe neighborhoods, and addresses can be hard to find.

BEACHES & PARKS

BEACHES   With over 48km (30 miles) of beaches within the city limits, finding a beach is much less trouble than deciding which one to go to. Here follows a short description of the main beaches: The beaches on the bay side of town (**Boa Viagem** and **Monte Serrat**) are not recommended for sunbathing but can be fun places to walk, watch a pickup soccer game, or have a beer. On weekends the **Forte de Monte Serrat** is crowded with working-class families having a day out.

Barra is the closest clean beach area to downtown. **Porto da Barra** is the beach on the bay side of the lighthouse, whereas **Farol da Barra** is on the ocean side. Both beaches have calm and protected waters and are great for swimming. Just around the bend you will come to **Praia de Ondina,** the first of the true ocean beaches. It's popular with the many visitors who stay in the Ondina hotels, but only because of its proximity; the beach itself is narrow and cut off from Avenida Atlântica by shade-throwing

Moments **Spend an Easy Sunday at Boa Viagem Beach**

Salvador, we discovered, is deserted on Sunday. No one in Pelourinho. No one at N.S. do Bonfim church. It wasn't until we wandered down the hill through the equally deserted Boa Viagem neighborhood that we discovered where everyone was. At the beach. The place was packed with flirting teens and moms with lawn chairs and little kids with beach balls and inflatable orca whales. We snagged a couple of beers from a passing vendor and watched a pickup soccer game for a while, waving now and again at the folks a little surprised to see a couple of pale-skinned *gringos* on an unfashionable working-class beach. Then we continued along the shoreline to an old fort where a cafe with tables sat on a tiny bit of sand below a tall stone seawall. While the tide rolled slowly in we watched a dad and young son make sand breasts (it started out as a sand castle but evolved into a Lara Croft–size bosom), flinching now and again when neighborhood kids would take a run along the top of the seawall, plant both feet, and do double forward somersaults into the sea.

hotel towers. **Praia de Amaralina** is as much known for the excellent food stalls as for the excellent surf and windsurfing conditions; the strong seas make it less ideal for swimming. **Praia dos Artistas** is highly recommended for swimmers and has waves gentle enough for children. **Praia do Corsario** is very popular with the fit crowd; lots of people come to jog and play volleyball or soccer. At low tide the reefs form natural swimming pools. **Praia de Piatã** has that tropical paradise look with lots of palm trees and kiosks offering cold drinks and perfect seafood snacks. One of the prettier beaches, **Itapuã,** has inspired many a song, including one by Vinicius de Moraes. Fishermen still bring their rafts in at the end of the day. The most recently trendy beaches are the ones the farthest from downtown; **Praia de Stella Maris** and **Flamengo** are where the young and beautiful gather on the weekends. **Stella Maris** combines calm stretches that are perfect for swimming with some rougher spots where the surfers can do their thing. *Barracas* are springing up fast and furious to keep up with the crowds. The buses from downtown that are marked VIA ORLA will follow the coastal road connecting all the beaches until their final destination. Sit on the right-hand side, check it out, and get off when you see the beach you like. Keep in mind that on weekdays, especially in the low season, the beaches that are farther out can be quite deserted. On those days it's better to stick to beaches close to town, such as Barra or Porto da Barra.

SPECTACULAR VIEWS

The classic viewpoint in Salvador is from the **Farol de Barra,** the lighthouse at the point where the Atlantic Ocean meets the Bay of All Saints. The view here, of course, is not of the city but of the sunset. People start gathering in the park around the lighthouse about a half-hour beforehand.

The best place to see the city itself is from the **Forte de Monte Serrat (Forte São Felipe),** located at the foot of the tall headland upon which the Bonfim Church stands. From here you can look back across a small stretch of bay at the lower town, the old city on the cliffs above, and behind that the high-rises of modern Salvador.

There are also a couple of good places on the cliff tops to look out over the bay. One is in **Praça Tomé de Souza,** next to the modern city hall and the **Elevator**

Lacerda. To have a view with a fine lunch to go with it, go to either of the two restaurants on the top-floor balcony of the **Mercado Modelo.** Both have decent Bahian food and killer views of the bay.

ESPECIALLY FOR KIDS

A number of the city parks provide plenty of recreational opportunities for kids and adults alike. In **Dique do Tororó Park,** Av. Marechal Costa e Silva s/n (℗ 071/3382-0847), kayaks and paddleboats are available for rent. This pleasant park is also known for the set of 20-foot-tall sculptures of eight Orixás in the middle of the lake. In the evening these are beautifully illuminated.

Pituaçu Park, Av. Otavio Mangabeira s/n, Pituaçu, across from Pituaçu beach (℗ 071/3231-2829), contains a 2,500 hectare (1,000-acre-plus) reserve of Atlantic rainforest. In addition to the native species there are lots of palms, cashews, mangos, and *dendezeiros* (the small dendê palm tree). This popular recreational park has 18km (11 miles) of cycle trails (plus bikes for rent) and a children's playground.

ORGANIZED TOURS

Tour operators around town operate a fairly standard package of tours. A reliable company is **Tatur** (℗ 071/3450-7216; www.tatur.com.br). The half-day city tours include either a visit to **Pelourinho** or a more panoramic tour to the **lighthouse and the beaches.** They range from R$40 to R$60 (US$20–US$30/£11–£16). **Full-day schooner tours** in the Bay of All Saints usually stop at **Ilha dos Frades** and **Itaparica.** Cost is about R$50 to R$60 (US$25–US$30/£14–£16). A number of evening tours include dinner and a folklore show, or a visit to a **Candomblé** ceremony. Prices range from R$60 to R$120 (US$30–US$60/£16–£32). Farther afield, full-day tours to **Praia do Forte** or **Morro de São Paulo** depart Salvador almost every day.

Praia do Forte costs R$60 to R$120 (US$30–US$60/£16–£32), whereas a day trip to Morro de São Paulo starts at R$120 (US$60/£32) for the catamaran option or up to R$350 (US$175/£95) for the plane option. To book any of these tours, contact **Tatur** (℗ 071/3450-7216; www.tatur.com.br).

TOUR GUIDES Salvador's attractions are so easily accessible that it's not really necessary to take an organized city tour. For Pelourinho it is a much better deal to book a tour guide through **Singtur,** the guiding association, Praça José Anchieta 12, second floor, Pelourinho (℗ 071/3322-1017). Two people can hire a guide for a few hours starting at R$30 (US$15/£8), depending on your negotiation skills, for a tour customized to your interests. You want churches, you want views, or you want Afro-Brazilian art? Just let the guides know what you would like to see before you book.

BOAT TOURS Definitely worth the money, the schooner trips in the Bay of All Saints depart daily from the dock in Comércio. The city views from the water are fabulous, and the beaches at Ilha do Frade and Itaparica are quite refreshing. Plus, if you've been wandering around the city for a day or two, it's a great feeling to be out on the water. To book a schooner trip contact **Tatur** (℗ 071/3450-7216) or **Prive Tur** (℗ 071/3338-1320). Prices range from R$50 to R$75 (US$25–US$38/£14–£20) including pickup and drop-off at your hotel.

SPECIALTY TOURS For more specialized tours contact **Tatur** (℗ 071/3450-7216; www.tatur.com.br). This company offers a number of interesting multiday customized excursions such as African-heritage tours, folklore, history, or even archaeological tours to Bahia's interior.

Moments The Ever-Present *Capoeira*

In Salvador, it is physically impossible not to witness the Brazilian martial art known as *capoeira*. Particularly around Pelourinho you're bound to hear the sounds of the drums and the metallic drone of the *berimbau* (a banjo-like instrument) as you walk around and catch a glimpse of two opponents spinning and kicking in a graceful half-fight, half-dance.

Though its origins are somewhat murky, most agree that *capoeira* evolved from rituals brought to Brazil by slaves from what is now Angola. The story goes that the slave owners were intimidated by the martial-arts rituals practiced by these tribes, and so tried to ban *capoeira* outright. The Africans then came up with a less-threatening form of the martial art, with a lot of moves that are more dance and acrobatics than martial arts. *Capoeira* was eventually outlawed anyway and its practitioners forced underground.

The practice never really went away, however, and with the changing times the public became more tolerant of *capoeira*. Finally in the '50s, *capoeira* received the establishment seal of approval when President Getulio Vargas referred to it as the only "true Brazilian sport."

OUTDOOR ACTIVITIES

DIVING   The coast and bay around Salvador have some interesting dive spots, including reefs and shipwrecks. Daily outings, trips, and times vary according to the tides and weather conditions. The prices are pretty competitive; expect to pay around R$100 (US$50/£27) for a dive trip excluding equipment, and R$160 (US$80/£43) for a dive trip including full equipment rental. The trip includes two dives. Contact **Dive Bahia,** Av. Sete de Setembro 3809, Barra (© **071/3264-3820;** www.divebahia. com.br), for more information.

GOLF   The **Sofitel Hotel** has a golf course that is open to the general public. The 18-hole course is located in Itapuã and subject to availability, as guests have preferred tee times. Greens fees are R$65 (US$33/£18) for 9 holes and R$120 (US$60/£32) to play the full 18-hole course. Contact the Sofitel at © **071/3374-8500** or the golf club directly at © **071/3374-9296.**

SPECTATOR SPORTS

CAPOEIRA   There are a few good schools in Pelourinho where you can either watch or learn *capoeira* (see "The Ever-Present *Capoeira*," above). **Mestre Bimba's** academy, located on the Rua das Laranjeiras 1, Pelourinho (© **071/3492-3197;** www. capoeiramestrebimba.com.br), is the best known and is well set up to receive foreign students of all levels of experience, even those who want to try it for the first time. Visitors are welcome to have a look during lessons, but to see some good capoeira it is best to visit during the demonstrations Tuesday through Saturday, from 7 to 8pm. In high season there is a second demonstration at 8pm. The school asks for a small contribution to take pictures and to support the school, which offers free classes to children from low-income communities. For those interested in taking a lesson, the academy offers 1-hour lessons for R$15 (US$7.50/£4) per person, no experience required (wear long comfortable pants and a T-shirt or tank top). If you buy a package of 5 or 10 lessons the price drops to R$10 (US$5/£2.70) per lesson. The groups are very small, never more than three or four students per teacher. Contact the academy to schedule a lesson.

Another popular school is the **Associação Brasileira de Capoeira Angola,** Rua Gregorio de Matos 38, Pelourinho (© **071/3321-3087**). This school also holds lessons and regular demonstrations in Pelourinho. Each class costs R$20 (US$10/£5.40) or you can purchase a package of six lessons for R$75 (US$38/£20). Contact the office for more details.

Many of the "spontaneous" capoeira demonstrations that take place around Pelourinho and the Mercado de Modelo are held for the benefit of tourists. They're fun to watch, but keep in mind that if you look on for a while and especially if you take pictures, you're expected to contribute some money to the group. Depending on how good the show is and how long I watch, I usually give between R$5 and R$10 (US$2.50–US$5/£1.35–£2.70).

To watch a more authentic presentation visit the **Forte de Santo Antonio Alem do Carmo,** aka the *Capoeira Fort.* Located at the very end of the Rua Direita de Santo Antonio, the fort is home to the capoeira academy of **Mestre João Pequeno de Pastinha** (© **071/3321-7587**). Events here take place on Tuesday, Thursday, and Saturday from 7:30 to 9:30pm and on Sunday from 5:30 to 7:30pm.

SOCCER The most popular spectator sport in town is soccer. The **Otavio Mangabeira Stadium,** built in the '50s, holds 80,000 people and hosts many important games. The big local teams are **Esporte Clube Bahia** and **Esporte Clube Vitória.** Contact the tourist information for details on upcoming games or contact the stadium at © **071/3243-3322.**

5 Shopping

Salvador offers wonderful shopping and some of the best crafts in all of Brazil. The best buys include crafts made out of wood, ceramics, or leather; musical instruments; and CDs of *axé* music. Remember to always bargain.

ART

Pricey but unique pieces can be bought at the many galleries in Pelourinho. **Galeria 13,** Rua Santa Isabel 13 (© **071/3242-7783**), has a large exhibit space with regular showings of work by local artists. **Galeria de Arte Bel Borba,** Rua Luis Viana 14 (© **071/3243-9370**), specializes in the sculptures and paintings by Bel Borba; his work is colorful and fresh. For top-of-the-line names check out **Oxum Casa de Arte,** Rua Gregorio de Matos 18 (© **071/3321-0617**). The large collection of art includes work by Mario Cravo and Carybé, who did the large wood panels of the Orixás in the Afro-Brazilian museum. The **Fundação Pierre Verger,** in honor of the French photographer and ethnologist who specialized in Afro-Brazilian culture, displays a fabulous collection of his works and sells Verger's amazing photo books, Rua da Misericordia 9, centro histórico (© **071/3321-2341**).

ARTS & CRAFTS

Instituto de Artesanato Visconde de Mauá Founded by the government to promote and support regional artists, the institute is an excellent place to get a feel for Bahian arts and crafts. There are weavings, hammocks, furniture, woodcarvings, and ceramics. Prices are fixed. To see future artists at work take a peek at the third floor, where students learn the traditional arts through workshops and apprenticeships. Just as any American can grow up to be president, every Baiano has the potential to be an artist. As the saying goes, *"O baiano não nasce, estreia"*—a Baiano isn't born, he premiers. Institute and shop are open Monday and Wednesday through Friday 8am to 7pm, and Tuesday 8am to 6pm. The shop is also open Saturday and Sunday 10am to 4pm. Rua Gregorio de Matos s/n, Pelourinho. ✆ 071/3321-5638. Bus: Praça da Sé.

Mercado Modelo   Souvenir junkies will think they have died and gone to heaven. Located in the former Customs building, the Mercado Modelo has around 300 merchants selling a large variety of souvenirs: leather goods, hammocks, musical instruments, masks, carvings, Orixás, paintings, terra-cotta figurines, jewelry, lace, and much more. Open Monday through Saturday 8am to 7pm and Sunday 8am to noon. Praça Cayru, Comércio (just across from the Elevator Lacerda). ✆ 071/3243-6543. Bus: Comércio.

MUSIC

Aurisom   To pick up the latest *axé* or Afro-reggae tunes, stop in at Aurisom. The compilation CDs of *axé* music that come out every summer give you the best of a whole crop of Bahian artists. This store also has a fabulous selection of LPs of old Brazilian music. Praça da Sé 22, Pelourinho. ✆ 071/3322-6893. Bus: Praça da Sé.

Midialouca   This small music store in the heart of Rio Vermelho, near the Ibis hotel, has a huge collection of Bahian and Brazilian music. In addition to DVDs and CDs, you will also find books on music and arts and songbooks. Best of all, the store is open daily from 8am to midnight! Perfect for a browse before heading out for dinner. Rua da Fonte do Boi 81, Rio Vermelho. ✆ 071/3334-2077. Bus: Rio Vermelho (or beaches beyond).

Oficina de Investigação Musical   The *berimbau* must be the most purchased souvenir of all judging from the number of tourists I see leaving with these odd-shaped instruments under their arms. More portable and just as interesting are some of the drums, rattles, and tambourines used in Afro-Bahian rhythms. The shop is closed Sunday. Rua Alfredo Brito 24, Pelourinho. ✆ 071/3322-2386. Bus: Praça da Sé.

SHOPPING MALLS

Salvador has a number of shopping malls outside of the downtown core. **Shopping Barra,** Av. Centenario 2992, Barra (✆ 071/3339-8222) is just a few blocks from the Farol da Barra; it's open Monday through Friday from 10am to 10pm and Saturday from 9am to 8pm. A bit farther out, next to the bus station, is one of the larger malls, **Shopping Iguatemi,** Av. Tancredo Neves 148, Pituba (✆ 071/3350-5060). Open Monday through Friday from 10am to 10pm and Saturday from 9am to 9pm. Take buses marked RODOVIARIA. Here you'll find everything you need: clothing, souvenirs, books, and CDs, as well as movie theaters and an excellent food court.

SOUVENIRS

For above average souvenir T-shirts check out these stores: **Litoral Norte,** Rua Gregorio de Matos 30 (✆ 071/3322-3781), sells a beautiful collection of T-shirts and also has some lovely hand-painted hammocks; **Boutique Ilê Aiyê,** Rua Francisco Muniz Barreto 16 (✆ 071/3321-4193), sells CDs and T-shirts and other merchandise with the Ilê Aiyê band's logo, and part of the funds support the group's educational program; **Projeto Axé,** Rua das Laranjeiras 9 (✆ 071/3321-7869), is a nonprofit organization that sells great skirts, shorts, kangas, blouses, and other clothing to raise funds to support projects for street children.

Entre Dedos   This little shop sells every kind of Havaiana, as the Brazilians call the colorful flip-flops that are now popular around the world. Havaiana actually refers to the brand name that made this footwear popular many years ago. You'll find an amazing selection here, including special-editions with images of endangered species and artwork. Rua Inácio Acioly 7, Pelourinho. (© 071/3321-1383. Bus: Praça da Sé.

Lembranças da Fé   For a different kind of souvenir try this store, which specializes in religious articles. Only in Bahia would you see saints sitting happily side by side with Orixás. Take time to browse the interesting herb mixes, shells, and cards used in Candomblé celebrations. Rua João de Deus 24, Pelourinho. (© 071/3321-0006. Bus: Praça da Sé.

SWEETS

Cafelier Santissimo   This lovely store fits into so many categories: cafe, bookstore, antiques shop, and souvenir store, but the great thing is that you can look at all the lovely objects, admire the view, and enjoy a delicious sweet or baked good. Rua do Carmo 50, Pelourinho. (© 071/3242-5151. Bus: Praça da Sé.

Delícias Bahia   Souvenirs bought here may not last until you get home. The shop has a large selection of coconut sweets, chocolates, jams, and candied fruit as well as over 100 different kinds of liquors flavored with fruit (try the banana or cupuaçu flavor), creamy condensed milk, or spices. Rua Inacio Accioli 9, Pelourinho. (© 071/3241-0775. Bus: Praça da Sé.

6 Salvador After Dark

Night owls won't lack for options in Salvador. The old city center of Pelourinho hums with music, people, and a lively mix of activities that Brazilians call *movimento*. Farther out along the beaches music venues are bigger and more geared toward the club crowd, but it is still easy to find places with live music, particularly in the new nightlife enclave of Rio Vermelho. True, the "high arts" of theater, dance, and classical music do suffer a bit in Bahia, but with everything else going on, odds are you won't notice. The scene in Bahia is very laid-back and casual; you won't find any upscale yuppie pretensions here, unless you look really hard.

THE PERFORMING ARTS

Teatro Castro Alves   Home to the Bahian Symphony Orchestra and the Balé (ballet) de Castro Alves, this is your best bet for catching fine-arts performances. Occasionally this venue also serves as a concert hall for popular Brazilian musicians or local music acts. Check the schedule for upcoming events. Praça Dois de Julho s/n, Campo Grande. (© 071/3339-8000. www.tca.ba.gov.br. Admission varies from R$10–R$60 (US$5–US$30/£2.70–£16). Bus: Praça da Sé or Campo Grande.

Teatro Sesi Rio Vermelho   One of the best places to see contemporary bands is the beach neighborhood of Rio Vermelho. The Teatro Sesi Rio Vemelho is housed in a renovated heritage building and specializes in bringing in local and Brazilian acts. Music varies from jazz to blues to MPB (Musica Popular Brasileira) and even pop. Rua Borges dos Reis 9, Rio Vermelho. (© 071/3335-1529. www.sesi.fieb.org.br/teatrosesi. Tickets range a fair bit from act to act, but you can expect usually to pay R$15–R$40 (US$8–US$20/£4–£11). Bus: Praia Flamengo or Pituba.

Teatro Vila Velha   Much loved by locals, the Teatro Vila Velha has played an important role in the cultural life of Salvador. Caetano Veloso, Gal Costa, Maria Bethania, and Gilberto Gil all performed here in the early days of their careers. These

> ### *Tips* If It's Tuesday, It Must Be Terça da Bênção
>
> Tuesday is known in Pelourinho as Terça da Bênção (Blessed Tuesday). It's the day parishioners of the São Francisco de Assis Church give out bread and donations to the poor. Somehow, this simple act of charity has grown into a happening street party that kicks off every Tuesday after the 6pm Mass. If you want to attend Mass before the festivities kick off, you can attend the one held at the São Francisco church. Much more interesting is the one held at N.S do Rosário dos Pretos, a more eclectic service attended by the church's black parishioners. The square of Terreiro de Jesus is packed with tables, chairs, and dozens of vendors selling beer and pop; others fire up their barbecues and sell some of the best beef and chicken skewers I've ever had in Brazil. Up and down the streets of Pelourinho, music seems to pour from every corner as bands play in little largos or cafes crank their stereos. Inside Praça Teresa Batista, Olodum holds its traditional Tuesday show. Outside a crowd gathers to listen for free to the pounding drum sounds that carry clearly even through thick stone walls. Down in Largo Pelourinho less-established blocos often gather to try out their routines on the crowd. It's the best free show in town. Unlike the weekend street scene, this party ends relatively early. By midnight everyone heads home. Even Baianos have to get up early sometimes.

days, it's home to two theater companies and one modern dance company—Viladança. For performances or other events such as MPB, *choro*, or *pagode* concerts, check the schedule. Tickets are inexpensive. Passeio Publico s/n, Gamboa de Cima. © 071/ 3336-1384. www.teatrovilavelha.com.br. Admission R$10–R$25 (US$5–US$13/£2.70–£7). Bus: Campo Grande or Praça da Sé.

MUSIC & DANCE CLUBS
PELOURINHO
In the evenings, Pelourinho often comes alive with music. Two of the most popular venues for concerts are the Praça Quincas Berro D'Agua and the Largo Pedro Archanjo. Check with the Bahiatursa office in Pelourinho or look in the newspaper for information on events (programming has become a bit spottier, alas, since a new state government cut back on cultural funding).

LIVE MUSIC
Praça do Reggae   In Pelourinho, reggae lives on. The Rasta flag flies proudly, dreadlocks are common features, and Bob is still a hero, if not a full-on prophet. A combination of three bars—Negros Bar, Bar do Reggae, and Cravo Rastafari—Praça do Reggae is reggae central. It doesn't really matter which one of the three you pick; all put out Jamaican-laced tunes, and most of the action is outside anyway with live music every Friday and Saturday. Open Tuesday through Sunday 7pm to 1am. Ladeiro do Pelourinho, by the N.S. dos Rosarios dos Pretos Church, Pelourinho. No phone. R$5–R$12 (US$2.50–US$8/£1.35–£3.25) cover for the band. Bus: Praça da Sé.

DANCE CLUBS
Lotus   Upscale Club Lotus is the second Brazilian endeavor of the fancy New York dance club (the other one is in São Paulo). This is where you are most likely to rub

shoulders with Brazilian celebrities such as Ivete Sangalo. Of course they will most likely be in the VIP area on the second floor, but the lounge and dance floor are not too shabby either. Music ranges from hip-hop (also called "Black music" in Brazil) to pop and dance. Rua Marques de Leão 46, Barra. ℂ 071/3264-6787. R$20–R$30 (US$10–US$15/ £5.40–£8). Bus: Barra.

Boomerangue   Salvador's hottest dance club and live music venue, at least for now. This two-story club (decorated with boomerangs, hence the name) often features two different bands or may feature one band and a DJ. Open Friday and Saturday only, doors open at 10pm but don't bother to get there before midnight. Rua da Paciência 307, Rio Vermelho. ℂ 071/3334-6640. R$10–R$25 (US$5–US$13/£2.70–£7). Bus: Rio Vermelho.

BARS & PUBS

Bahia Café   The Bahia Café is a very popular bar close to Centro. The view is spectacular—the large open bar overlooks the bay and there are plenty of seats on the sprawling patio. There is live music on Tuesday (acoustic guitar and voice) and Thursday (reggae). After midnight on Friday and Saturday, the tables are removed to make room for a dance floor. Open Tuesday through Thursday 5:30pm to 1am, Friday and Saturday 5:30pm to 3am. Quartel dos Aflitos s/n (the entrance is at the very end of the square, walk toward the viewpoint). ℂ 071/3328-1332. Minimum consumption R$10–R$20 (US$5–US$10/£2.70– £5.40), cover R$6 (US$3/£1.60). Bus: Praça da Sé.

Bar da Ponta ★★★ *Finds*   Built of glass and set at the very end of a long pier by the waterfront Trapiche Adelaide, this bar boasts a sweeping view of the Bay of All Saints, making it a prime sunset spot, particularly on Thursday and Friday afternoons during happy hour. The wine list and ultra-modern decor attract a 30-something yuppie crowd who stay long after the sun goes down. Appetizers come from the kitchen of the excellent Trapiche restaurant next door. Open Monday through Thursday 6pm to 1am and Friday to Saturday 5:30pm to 2am. Praça dos Tupinambas 2, Av. Contorno. ℂ 071/ 3326-2211. Taxi recommended from the Mercado Modelo or Praça Castro Alves.

Finds The Mission of Olodum

Olodum is one of the best-known blocos in Salvador, maybe in all of Brazil. Founded in 1979, Olodum started as a recreational group for residents of Pelourinho who had few options during Carnaval. More than 20 years later, Olodum has grown into a cultural phenomenon with international fame, not to mention its own nifty logo, a peace sign filled with reggae colors. The group's mandate is to preserve and value black culture and heritage, and fight all forms of racism and violence. One of the ways they pursue this is through work with young children and teens in some of the poorer neighborhoods of Salvador. Over 150 kids are involved in Olodum-sponsored cultural activities. The money raised by international performances and recordings made with people like Paul Simon help fund the group's educational activities. Every Tuesday night the group performs at the Praça Teresa Batista starting at 8pm. Contact the Olodum office at ℂ 071/3321-5010 or www.olodum.com.br for information on concerts and Carnaval rehearsals, or stop in at the gift shop located at Rua Gregorio de Matos 22, Pelourinho.

Café do Farol 🦐🦐 *Finds*   You can't get a better view than this. The Café do Farol is inside the lighthouse at Barra, and the patio has one of the most amazing views of the ocean and the city of Salvador. You can come here for a drink or enjoy a meal or a snack: Popular and inexpensive choices are the sweet or savory crepes. To access the cafe you must pay admission to the museum (R$6/US$3/£1.60). Open Tuesday through Sunday 9am to 10pm. Praia da Barra s/n, Barra (inside the lighthouse). ✆ **071/3267-8881.**

Cantina da Lua 🦐   So what if you and every other tourist in town are on this patio? It happens to be one of the loveliest and largest patios on the Praça Terreiro de Jesus, offering the best view of all the activity on the square: the *capoeiristas* sweating in the sun, the hawkers selling souvenirs, and the dressed-up *Baianas* posing for pictures. In the evening it seems like all of Salvador strolls through this square. Open daily 11am until last customer. Praça Quinze de Novembro 2, Pelourinho. ✆ **071/3322-4041.** Bus: Praça da Sé.

GAY & LESBIAN BARS

A great resource for gay travelers, the **Grupo Gay da Bahia,** Rua Frei Vicente 24, Pelourinho (✆ **071/3321-1848;** www.ggb.org.br), has information on tourism and recreational opportunities in Salvador as well as on local social issues and community activism. Salvador has a small but growing Pride Parade that is usually held in the spring, in September. Of course the parade includes lots of music and the trio eletrico sound trucks. Famous Bahian artists such as Daniela Mercury and Ivete Sangalo have taken part in previous years. Check the Grupo Gay da Bahia for details on the date. A very popular event during Carnaval is the election of the best Gay Costume. This event takes place in front of the Salvador city hall and includes drag queen performances and lots of music. One of the more popular Carnaval blocos that counts on a huge gay following is the **Bloco dos Mascarados** (✆ **071/3237-0066**), led by Bahian singer Margaret Menezes. Rehearsals take place from November until Carnaval. Check with the tourist office for the dates and locations of these *ensaios.*

Salvador's gay scene is not as open as in Rio de Janeiro, but two popular hangouts are Saturday late afternoon at Porto da Barra beach and Sunday at the Barraca Aruba, a beach kiosk at Praia dos Artistas. In town, Avenida Sete de Setembro, from Praça da Sé to Campo Grande—particularly around the Praça da Piedade, as well as Pelhourino's Praça Pedro Arcanjo, are known cruising areas.

The dance club at **Queens Clube,** Rua Teodoro Sampaio 160, just behind the Biblioteca Nacional (✆ **071/328-6220**) is open Friday and Saturday midnight to 6am. The sex shop, DVD rentals, and movie screening rooms are open Monday through Saturday 3 to 10pm. Also popular, **Off Club,** Rua Dias d'Avilla 33, Barra (✆ **071/3267-6215;** www.offclub.com.br), attracts a mixed crowd of both male and female clubbers. Open Thursday through Sunday; on Friday the DJs play eclectic flashback hits, while Saturday is house and techno night; the other nights are a mishmash with go-go boys, drag queens, and other performers. Doors don't open until 11:30pm. **Espaço Originally,** Rua Marques de Queluz 43, Pituaçu (✆ **071/3497-0002**), is open only on Sundays from 5pm to 2am, and is very popular with women. There are usually two local bands each night and occasionally shows will include famous Brazilian artists.

7 Carnaval in Salvador

Carnaval is Salvador's biggest party of the year. Over a million and a half people (locals and tourists) join in to celebrate. In contrast to Rio's more spectator-oriented celebration, the focus in Salvador is on participation. There are no samba schools

---

Tips Some Carnaval Do's and Don'ts

Do not bring any valuables with you; bring a photocopy of your passport or driver's license instead of the real thing. Buy a disposable camera that tucks into your pocket. Only bring as much money as you think you'll need and spread it out; put some in your pocket and a few bills in your shoe. Do not underestimate the heat, and drink sufficient water or coconut milk. Don't dress up: For blocos just wear your *abadá,* shorts, and running shoes; otherwise shorts and a tank top will do just fine.

---

with outlandish costumes and big floats—in fact, there is hardly any samba at all. The beat of choice is *axé* or Afro *axé,* the unique Bahian rhythm that combines African percussion with Caribbean reggae and Brazilian energy. The action is out on the streets with the blocos.

In Rio, blocos are a group of locals who gather up a few instruments for an impromptu parade. In Salvador, blocos started out years ago as flatbed trucks with bands and sound systems, leading people on an extended dance through the streets. The concept's still the same, but as the number of participants has grown, Salvador blocos have evolved into more highly organized affairs. All now follow set routes. Many have corporate sponsorship. Some even belong to production companies. Your dancing-through-the-streets-of-Salvador experience now comes with a huge sound system, security guards, and a support vehicle with washrooms and first-aid attendants. Unavoidably, it also comes with a price tag.

The revelers that follow a bloco must buy a T-shirt *(abadá)* to identify themselves. In return they get to sing and dance behind the music truck in a large cordoned-off area, staffed by security guards who keep troublemakers out. Following the revelers is the support car with a first-aid attendant, bar, and washrooms (to which only *abadá* wearers have access). If you follow the entire route you can expect to be on your feet for at least 6 hours. Most blocos parade 3 days in a row, and your *abadá* gives you the right to come all 3 days if you've got the stamina. It is also possible to purchase an *abadá* for just 1 day.

Carnaval officially begins at 8pm on the Thursday evening before Ash Wednesday, when the mayor of Salvador hands the keys of the city over to King Momo, who will rule for the next 5 days.

BLOCOS

Blocos all follow one of three set parade routes and start at designated times. Most blocos will take 4 to 6 hours to complete the course. The routes are **Osmar, Dodô,** and **Batatinha.** (Osmar and Dodô are named after the two musicians who first came up with the *trio eletrico* idea of mounting the band on a flatbed truck in the '50s.) The 7km-long (4¼-mile) **Osmar route** starts at Rua Araujo Pinha in Campo Grande, goes up Avenida Sete de Setembro as far as Praça Castro Alves, and returns to Campo Grande via Avenida Carlos Gomes. The **Dodô route** was designed in the '80s to accommodate the increased number of blocos. It follows the coastal road from Ponto da Barra to Ondina Beach. **Batatinha** is the preferred route for the percussion-heavy Afro *axé* blocos as well as the colorful drag queen blocos. Sticking close to the historic center, Batatinha runs from Praça da Sé to the Praça Municipal, then to Praça Castro

---

Tips Carnaval Central

The most convenient location of the Central do Carnaval is in the heart of Pelourinho, Rua Gregorio de Matos 13 (corner of the Rua Laranjeiras), © 071/ 3321-9365. Other locations can be found at the Shopping Iguatemi and Shopping Barra. Book early as some of the popular blocos sell out by August!

Alves, and finishes up in Campo Grande. The blocos parade from Friday to Tuesday, some on 3 days, others on 4. Order and start times vary, so pick up an updated calendar just before Carnaval at one of the tourist offices.

The best resource for all Carnaval programming is the state tourism agency Bahiatursa (www.bahiatursa.ba.gov.br); they can inform you about all the parades and events that are taking place around town. In addition to the regular tourist information offices (see "Visitor Information," earlier in this chapter) they have booths with English-speaking staff along the three parade routes. Another great resource on sale at newsstands is the *Guia do Ocio,* a monthly arts and entertainment magazine that publishes an amazingly detailed Carnaval edition, R$5 (US$2.10/£1.20).

See the list below to help you decide which blocos you would like to follow. To purchase an *abadá,* contact the bloco directly or else call the Central do Carnaval (© 071/3372-6000; www.centraldocarnaval.com.br); they represent at least a dozen of the most popular blocos. The average prices for the *abadás* ranges from R$400 to R$900 (US$200–US$450/£108–£243) for 2 or 3 days. The Central can also sell you an *abadá* for a day if you don't want to commit to the entire 3 days or want to try different blocos.

Ara Ketu Though it's getting more and more known across Brazil, Ara Ketu's roots remain in Salvador where the group works with community organizations and runs music and theater workshops for disadvantaged children and teens.

Blocos Axé Many of the blocos *axé* originated in the poorer and overwhelmingly black neighborhoods on the outskirts of Salvador. With the recent revival of black culture and pride, these blocos have become more and more popular and are now part of the mainstream events. The most popular ones are Ilê Aiyê, Olodum, Filhos de Ghandi, Ara Ketu, and Filhas de Oxum.

Camaleão Founded in 1978 by a group of university students, Camaleão parades Sunday through Tuesday along the Osmar route. Chiclete com Banana is the lead attraction, one of the most popular Bahian bands. This bloco was a recent winner of the best bloco and best band award and also takes first place in being the most expensive bloco. The 2008 *abadás* for all 3 days topped out at R$1,800 (US$900/£486).

Cerveja e Cia Given that Ivete Sangalo's producer owns this bloco, it only makes sense that Sangalo—Bahia's new musical sensation—is the star attraction. The bloco parades Thursday through Saturday along the Dodô beach route.

Filhos de Ghandi Popular during Carnaval for its symbolic message of peace, this bloco is instantly recognizable for the white Ghandi costumes worn by its 10,000 all-male followers. The bloco parades Sunday through Tuesday (along the Osmar route Sun and Mon and along the Dodô on Tues). To purchase an *Abadá* (the Ghandi uniform) contact © 071/3321-7073.

Ilê Aiyê One of the most traditional Afro blocos, Ilê only lets blacks parade, but everyone is welcome to watch and cheer. Its music is a wonderful blend of reggae and percussion; the drums are phenomenal. The group parades on Saturday, Sunday, and Tuesday along the Osmar route. For *abadás* contact © **071/3388-4969.**

Olodum Internationally known, Olodum's popularity draws huge crowds. The music is fun, some reggae, a little bit of samba, and lots of drums. Olodum always provides a great show. The group parades on 4 days, Friday and Sunday through Tuesday. *Abadás* can be purchased at the store in Pelourinho, Rua das Laranjeiras 30, or contact © **071/3321-5010.**

Papa One of the older blocos, Papa was founded in 1979, it has since a few years been led by the wildly popular local group Babado Novo. Since this group has taken Brazil by storm it has become one of the most popular blocos, and attracts mostly young people. Immensely popular lead singer Claudia Leite puts on quite a show.

REHEARSALS

Though less organized and structured than the samba school rehearsals in Rio, a small number of blocos do meet regularly in the months leading up to Carnaval. For some this is also an important money generator, and admission can cost as much as R$60 (US$30/£16). However, if you won't be in Salvador during Carnaval, these rehearsals are highly recommended.

The most popular rehearsals are those run by **Olodum.** On Tuesday nights the group meets at the Praça Teresa Batista s/n, Pelourinho (© **071/3321-3208**). Tickets are R$20 (US$10/£5.40). Unfortunately the ticket does not allow in-and-out privileges, and Olodum's rehearsal coincides with Terça da Bênção, one of the most fun nights in Pelourinho when there are bands and events galore. It's a bit of a tossup over which is more fun. On Sundays Olodum holds a free rehearsal starting at 6pm at the Largo do Pelô. Several of Salvador's big names such as **Araketu, Ivete Sangalo,** and **Vixe Mainha** will hold regular rehearsals in the months leading up to Carnaval. If you are in Salvador between October and Carnaval, check with the tourist office for details on *ensaios* (rehearsals).

Some great online resources for Carnaval are available on the Web. Though in Portuguese only, they will certainly give you an idea of what things look like: the official

---

Tips Commitment Shy?

Instead of committing to one specific bloco and following along for hours, you can also get a seat in the stands that line the parade route and watch all the blocos go by. Tickets for box seats *(camarote)* or tables are expensive. The Central de Carnaval sells tickets to box seats at three different venues; prices range from R$150 to R$390 (US$75–US$195/£40–£105) per person a day. The ticket often includes drinks, food, and entertainment. To reserve a seat in one of the bleachers that line the parade route, contact the city hall at © **071/3450-2711** or the Central do Carnaval at © **071/3372-6000.** These go for much less than the box seats, about R$80 to R$130 (US$40–US$65/£22–£35) per day but don't include any of the fancy trappings, just a seat. Some hotels also set up their own bleachers like the Monte Pascoal in Barra.

(Moments) The End of Carnaval: It Ain't Over 'til it's Over

In most cities Carnaval comes to a quiet end as partygoers run out of steam in the early hours of Ash Wednesday and finally flop into bed. In Salvador, the party goes out with a bang. Although this event is an informal one, it takes place every year at the Praça Castro Alves. At the meeting of the trios *(encontro dos trio eletricos)*, a few of the blocos that have finished their parade meet to compete for the last bit of energy the crowd has to offer. Usually the party keeps going until the sun comes up. Last year Caetano Veloso and Carlinhos Brown were among the prominent musicians who came out for the grand finale and packed the square with tens of thousands of people.

---

city site, www.carnaval.salvador.ba.gov.br, has pictures, important phone numbers, programming details and maps; www.centraldocarnaval.com.br has *abadás* for sale and provides detailed scheduling and program information. For more information, contact the *Central do Carnaval* at ✆ 071/3372-6000.

8 Side Trips from Salvador

PRAIA DO FORTE

Even as recently as 10 years ago Praia do Forte was a sleepy little fishing town with a handful of streets (none of them paved), no banks, no post office, no business hours, a couple of small pousadas, and a tiny seaside church. Then a firestorm of real estate speculation swept the coast, bringing massive new resorts, upscale hotels, chain restaurants, and expensive clothing boutiques. Then the main street was covered with interlocking paving stones, festooned with signs brought to you by Visa, and flanked by shop windows of brightly lit plate glass offering R$300 (US$150/£81) bikinis and the chance to act now and secure your place in the latest and best condominium real estate opportunity on the coast.

Why anyone would come all this way to stroll a mall-ified street looking at the same chain stores found in any big shopping mall is beyond me. Indeed, what the people pushing all this development seem to have overlooked is that the attraction of Praia do Forte was never its beach—which is nice but not exceptional for Brazil—but rather the low-key laid-back charm of the place. Now that that's gone, there's hardly any reason to visit Praia do Forte at all. There are much prettier and still practically unspoiled beaches and small towns south of Salvador.

The Projeto Tamar sea turtle project is still there. If it's the right season and the turtles are hatching it may be worth making a short day trip to see the hatchlings make their mad dash for the sea (see Projeto Tamar below). But if you're looking for a beach experience near Salvador, head south to Morro São Paulo or Boipeba or farther down to Barra Grande.

GETTING TO KNOW THE TURTLES

Projeto Tamar   The sea turtle organization Tamar is Brazil's one big environmental success story. Starting out as a poor and unloved environment agency in the early '80s, Tamar has since come into the mainstream, forming alliances with the Brazilian environment agency IBAMA and with Petrobras, Brazil's national oil company, and making its SOS (Save Our Sea turtles) symbol a mainstay of posters, billboards, and

Side Trips from Salvador

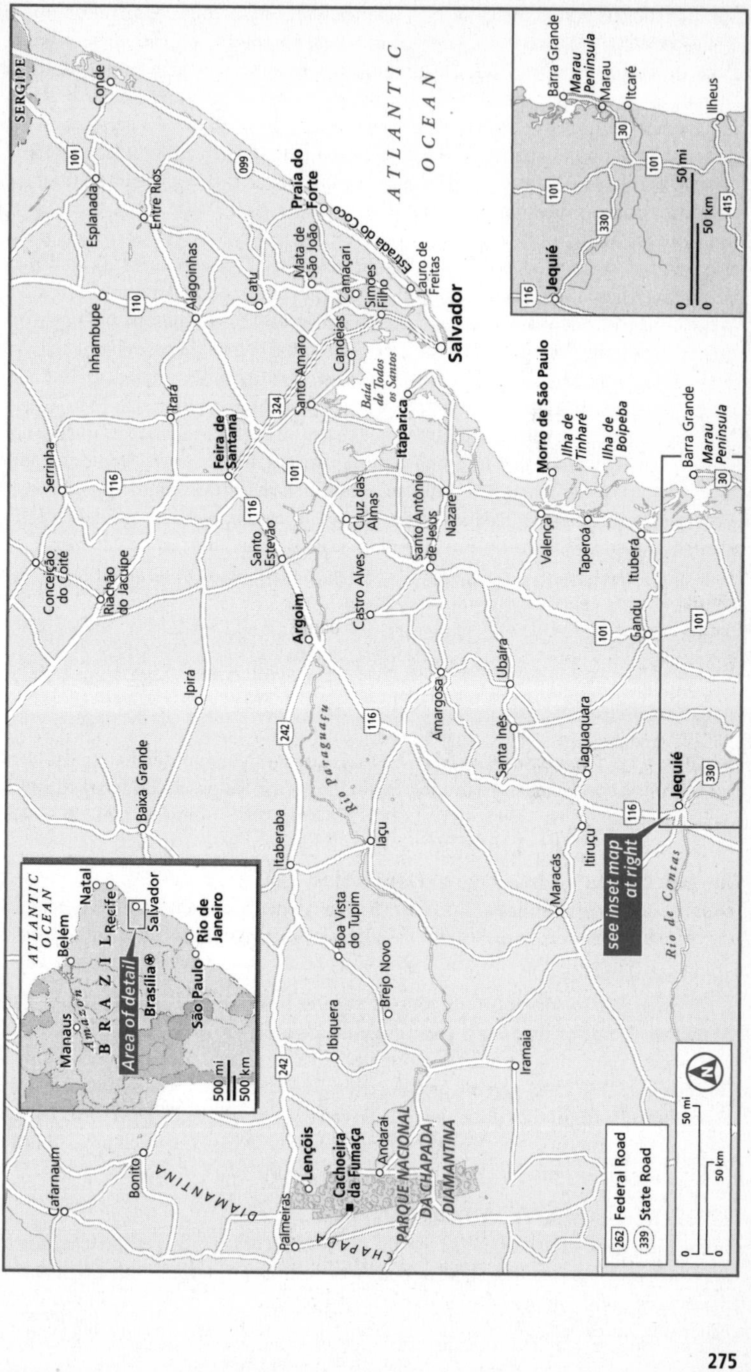

ATLANTIC OCEAN
SERGIPE
Conde
Esplanada
Entre Rios
Alagoinhas
Inhambupe
Catu
Praia do Forte
Mata de São João
Camaçari
Estrada do Coco
Simões Filho
Lauro de Freitas
Salvador
Candeias
Santo Amaro
Baía de Todos os Santos
Itaparica
Irará
Feira de Santana
Serrinha
Conceição do Coité
Riachão do Jacuípe
Santo Estevão
Cruz das Almas
Santo Antônio de Jesus
Nazaré
Morro de São Paulo
Ilha de Tinharé
Ilha de Boipeba
Valença
Taperoá
Ituberá
Gandu
Barra Grande
Marau Peninsula
Castro Alves
Argoim
Ipirá
Amargosa
Ubaíra
Santa Inês
Jaguaquara
Jequié
Itiruçu
Maracás
Rio de Contas
see inset map at right
Baixa Grande
Rio Paraguaçu
Itaberaba
Iaçu
Boa Vista do Tupim
Brejo Novo
Ibiquera
Iramaia
Lençóis
Cachoeira da Fumaça
Andaraí
PARQUE NACIONAL DA CHAPADA DIAMANTINA
CHAPADA DIAMANTINA
Palmeiras
Bonito
Cafarnaum
Marau
Itacaré
Ilheus
Manaus
Belém
Natal
Recife
Salvador
Rio de Janeiro
São Paulo
Brasília
BRAZIL
Amazon
Area of detail
500 mi
500 km
262 Federal Road
339 State Road
0
50 mi
50 km

bumper stickers across the country. Tamar now has numerous conservation outposts along the Brazilian coast, with one of the most important on the nursery beach at Praia de Forte. Most evenings, beginning in December and continuing until mid-March, three different species of sea turtles swim ashore, clamber up the beach, and dig a small pit into which they deposit anywhere from 50 to 200 eggs. Each night, teams of Tamar biologists sweep the beach looking for laying turtles. If the mother has chosen a suitable nest site, the biologists simply cover the eggs with a chicken-wire screen for added protection and mark the spot with a tall white stake. If the eggs are too close to the high-tide line or too near human habitation, Tamar collects the eggs and transfers them to its incubation site nearby. Fifty days later, more or less, the little turtlings hatch, dig their way up through the sand, and make a mad scramble to the sea. Nationwide, Tamar has to date released over three million hatchlings. Unfortunately, it's tough being a sea turtle. Only 1 out of 100 hatchlings will return 35 years later to the same beach to begin the cycle again. Visitors to the Tamar site in Praia do Forte see turtles from days-old hatchlings to 20-year-old adolescents. (There's also a kid-friendly video, a cafe, and a gift shop.) Better still, on certain nights during laying season, visitors are allowed to watch mother turtles lay. Best of all, from late January to the end of April, Tamar lets visitors witness the little turtles hatch out and make for the ocean. Exactly when depends on the turtles, of course, but during February there's a hatch-and-scramble nearly every evening, usually timed for just before sunset.

Av. do Farol s/n, Praia de Forte, BA 48280-000. (C) 071/3676-1045. www.projetotamar.org.br. Admission R$8 (US$4/£2.15) adults, free for children under 5. Daily 9am–6pm.

Getting There

By Car Praia do Forte is only 50km (31 miles) north of Salvador on the Estrada do Coco highway, which starts just past Itapoã beach by the airport. Exits are very well marked.

By Bus The **Nossa Senhora das Graças** bus company provides regular service between Praia do Forte and Salvador, leaving from the Salvador Rodoviaria. Buses run almost every hour between 6am and 6pm. For exact times phone (C) **071/3676-1607.** Fares are R$8 (US$4/£2.15). The trip takes 2½ hours.

By Taxi Centro Turistico ((C) **071/3676-1091** or 071/9989-9864; www.prdoforte. com.br) offers transfers to Praia do Forte from anywhere in the city of Salvador for R$65 (US$33/£18) per person or R$60 (US$30/£16) per person from Salvador airport.

Accommodations

If for whatever reason you find yourself staying in Praia do Forte, **Pousada Ogum Marinho,** Alameida do Sol s/n (near Projeto Tamar) ((C) **071/3676-1165;** www.ogum marinho.com.br), has comfortable doubles with a veranda and air-conditioning for R$200 (US$100/£54), parking and breakfast included. Fancier and quieter but more expensive is **Rufugio da Vila,** Aldeia dos Pescadores Qd. 39 ((C) **071/3676-0114;** www. refugiodavila.com.br). The Refugio offers a pool and pleasant garden area, plus king-size beds, parking, and breakfast for R$380 (US$190/£103) double.

LENÇÓIS & CHAPADA DIAMANTINA

In the hinterland of Salvador, just outside of the town of Lençóis, lies the Chapada Diamantina, or Diamond Highlands. Valleys of lush green dotted with bright tropical flowers surround a mountain range of twisted red-rock formations reminiscent of the American Southwest. Numerous small rivers carve their way through the highlands, splashing over waterfalls and natural slides. There are also numerous caves, some many kilometers long. Many are quite popular, some just being discovered, some restricted yet to geologists who are trying to figure out just how they and the rock formations they contain were formed.

The gateway community of Lençóis is an old colonial town of stone streets and little churches, with cellphone towers the only real sign of the modern world. The attractions here are entirely natural. People walk the highlands, explore caves, mountain bike old miners' tracks, and swim in natural pools and waterfalls.

ESSENTIALS
Getting There

BY CAR   The main Chapada town of Lençóis is 427km (265 miles) from Salvador. Take BR-324 to Feira to Santana, turn onto BR-116 to Argoim and then BR-242 to Lençóis. The road is paved the entire way, but the asphalt breaks up in places on the BR-242.

BY BUS   Real Expresso (© **0800/617-325;** www.realexpresso.com.br) makes the approximately 5-hour journey between Salvador and Lençóis at a cost of R$45 (US$23/£12). Buses depart the Salvador Rodoviaria for Lençóis daily at 11:30pm (arriving at 5am) and 7am (arriving 1pm). From Lençóis, buses depart the bus station on Av. Senhor dos Passos s/n (© **075/3334-1112**) for Salvador daily at 7:30am and 11:30pm.

VISITOR INFORMATION   In Lençóis, the local tourism agency **Sectur Lençóis,** Av. Sr. dos Passos s/n, opposite the Portal Lençóis Hotel on the far side of the river from the main square (© **075/3334-1327**), has pamphlets on tours and attractions in the area, and a color brochure on the Chapada for sale for R$10 (US$5/£2.70). Staff speaks Portuguese only.

The official city tourism website is www.guialencois.com. In English, there's a reasonably good website with geology, trail maps, and more at www.gd.com.br/candomba/english.

Two worthwhile books on the Chapada Diamantina are *A Visitor's Guide to the Chapada Diamantina Mountains* by Roy Fuchs and *Trilhas e Caminhos: Circuito do Diamante* by Roberto Sapucaia, worth it just for the top-quality topographic map. (See the website that goes with the book: www.trilhasecaminhos.com.br.) Both books are usually available in Lençóis at Loja Dois Irmaos on the main square, or in bookstores in Salvador.

GETTING AROUND   All parts of Lençóis can be reached by foot in less than 15 minutes. Excursions to the many caves and waterfalls in the area all include transport (see below). Car rental is best done in Salvador.

FAST FACTS   The **Banco do Brasil,** Praça Horario de Matos 56 (main square), is open Monday through Friday from 9am to 1pm. ATM is open 24 hours—PLUS/Visa only. There's Internet access at **Pede Trilha,** Rua Miguel Calmon s/n, opposite the market hall (© **075/3334-1124**); it's open daily from 8am to 10pm. Connection costs R$6 (US$3/£1.65) per hour. For laundry, there's **Lavandaria Lençóis** on Rua 10 de Novembro 8 (© **075/3334-1694**). Cost is R$8 (US$4/£2) per kilogram to wash and dry. For first-aid and medical supplies there's **Pharmacia Maciel,** Av. 7 de Setembro 50 (© **075/3334-1224**), open daily from 8am to 8:30pm (will close Sat and Sun afternoons if business is slow). The post office is at Av. Sete de Setembro 18. Open Monday through Friday from 9am to 5pm.

EXPLORING THE TOWN & BEYOND

The town of Lençóis is a tiny colonial gem, but it won't take more than an hour to see it all. After that, it's out into the highlands to see what the natural world has to offer. There are a number of excellent hikes in the area, leading either to waterfalls or mountaintop viewpoints. Some of these sights are far enough to require transportation, but quite a few you can find with your own two feet.

From the bridge in Lençóis a trail leads up beside the Lençóis River to the **Serrano swimming hole** and **Primavera Falls.** An hour's walk south of town will lead you to the **Riberão de Meio** rock slide, a huge natural waterslide flanked by many natural swimming holes. A long (8-hr.) hike up this same river leads to the **Sossego** canyon and **waterfall.**

The most famous waterfall in the park is **Cachoeira de Fumaça (Waterfall of Smoke),** so called because the thin stream of water slipping over the 335m (1,100-ft.) precipice fades into a fine mist before it reaches the ground.

The park is also known for its mesa-like mountain formations. The most famous are **Morro do Pai Inácio** (located right next to BR-242 west of Lençóis), the 1,067m (3,500-ft.) **Morro do Camelo,** and the 1,403m (4,600-ft.) **Monte Tabor** (also called **Marrão**). All have trails to the top, and from the flat top of any one, you have the entire Chapada spread at your feet.

Caves are a fascinating aspect of the Chapada Diamantina Park. Some of the best-known ones in the area include **Gruta de Lapão,** a rare sandstone-and-quartzite cave over 1km (½ mile) long from end to end. It's located about 5km (3 miles) from Lençóis. Farther afield one finds a number of the more traditional limestone caves, with rock flowers, stalagmites, and stalactites. The prettiest cavern may be **Gruta da Lapa Doce,** which extends 850m (2,788 ft.) underground. In the same area is **Gruta da Pritinha,** where an underground river emerges into the sun. Inside there's a large pool where you can dive and swim. Nearby is the small **Gruta Azul.** Late in the afternoon when the sun reaches into this cave, the water glows cobalt blue.

OUTDOOR ACTIVITIES

When the weather gets hot (and it does), take to natural swimming pools. Close to Lençóis, and so popular that there are now beer and refreshment stands lining its banks, is the **Mucugezinho River.** Below these stands on the same river is a deep cold pool called the **Poço de Diablo.** South of Lençóis, near the town of Andaraí, there's an underground pool with crystal-clear water and excellent limestone formations called the **Poço Azul,** where swimming is allowed.

Swimming is not allowed at the **Poço Encantado,** and it's a long way from anywhere down some pretty bad roads, but it's worth seeing anyway. It's a large underground cavern with crystal-clear water. Between April and August light reaches down through a hole in the cavern wall, and the water glows electric blue.

For wildlife watchers there's the **Marimbus** wetland. In addition to lots of caiman, it boasts capybaras and a wide variety of colorful bird life.

BIKING   **Rony Bike** (© 075/3334-1700) offers guided mountain bike trips and also rents bikes. Owner **Rony Oliverira** has lived in the area for over 10 years and biked every possible trail. The cost for one person including a bike and guide is R$75 (US$38/£20) per day. Itineraries can be customized to suit all interests and abilities. **Adilson Trilhas, Passeios e Bikes,** Praça Samuel Sales 32 (© 075/3334-1319), is another option for mountain-bike tours and rentals.

HIKING   Trails in the Chapada Diamantina are universally good. Many of them are old miners' supply routes. Signage is nonexistent. Carry a map, compass, and some spare food and water (locals insist the water from the highlands is drinkable, but there are enough cattle still pastured up there that I have my doubts). If in doubt of your trail-finding skills, bring a guide along. It's an old tradition in this area, and there are a fair number of good guides. Try the tour agencies below or contact the guide association directly: **ACVL** (Associação dos Conductores de Visitores no Lençóis), Av. General Viveiros 61, across the river by the Cantos dos Aguas Hotel (℡ **075/3334-1425**). **Roy Funch Specialized and Personalized Guide Services** (℡ **075/3334-1305**) is another source of guide information. Roy is American, but has lived in the area for years.

There are dozens of hikes in the Chapada Diamantina. The following are just suggestions. A short hike up the Lençóis River from the bridge will take you to the **Serrano** swimming holes, composed of little pools of pink conglomerate rock. About .5km (.25 mile) farther up the river, there's the larger **Hartley natural pool.** A short, pretty walk beyond that a small tributary comes in from the right, the **Grizante Creek.** Follow that up and you'll come to **Primavera Falls.**

An hour's walk south of town will lead you to the **Ribeirão de Meio** natural waterslide. The waterslide is also the trail head for a long (8-hr.) hike along the banks of the Ribeirão River to **Sossego Canyon** and **Sossego Falls.**

A good day hike that will take you through the heart of the Chapada is the 25km (16-mile) trek from the **Capão Valley to Lençóis** (or vice versa). Done from Lençóis, it's possible to get an 8am bus to Palmeiras (R$6/US$3/£1.65) on the far side of the Chapada, then hire a cab to take you over the rough gravel road to the trail head (R$40/US$20/£11). The mostly level hike takes about 8 hours and provides some excellent views along the way back to the village.

HORSEBACK RIDING   For horseback riding, find one-armed **Taurino Sousa Alcantera** in his souvenir shop at Rua das Pedras s/n, about halfway up the street (℡ **075/3334-1403**). Itineraries include a 5-hour ride to the **Rio Capivara** (R$60/US$30/£16 per person), a short 40-minute ride to **Ribeirão de Meio** (R$30/US$15/£8 per person) where you can then play on the natural waterslide, and an 18km (11-mile) day-long ride through several rivers to the **Rio Roncador** (R$90/US$45/£24 per person).

RAPPELLING   A popular sport in Brazil, rappelling is the act of lowering yourself down a length of rope with a harness and a locking carabiner. You can rappel down a cliff face, a waterfall, into a cave, whatever. In Lençóis, the rappelling specialist is **Nativos da Chapada,** Rua Miguel Calmon 29 (℡ **075/3334-1314** shop, or 075/9960-0131 cellphone; www.nativosdachapada.com.br). The company offers a number of different rappel outings, ranging from a 30m (98-ft.) drop down the **Alto da Primavera Cliff** (R$70/US$35/£19) to a 48m (157-ft.) descent into the **Gruta do Lapão Cave** (R$75/US$38/£20) to a 150m (492-ft.) descent from the **Pai Inácio Mesa** (R$95/US$48/£26), to a soaking 50m (164-ft.) drop through the waters of **Mosquito Falls** (R$95/US$48/£26). On most outings you get to make six descents. Cash only.

TOUR OPERATORS   **Lentur,** Avenida Sete de Setembro (℡ **075/3334-1271;** www.lentur.com.br), offers seven different **guided minivan tours** to just about all of the local caves, springs, waterfalls, and mesas (Lapa Doce, Gruta Azul, Poço do Diable, Poço Encantado, and so on). Tours are in eight-passenger minivans. They begin at 8:30am and end at 6pm, and include a light lunch. Minimum group size is four. Cost for each tour is R$65 (US$33/£18), including the services of a Portuguese-speaking guide. An English-speaking guide costs R$90 (US$45/£24) total, with that cost divided by however many require his services.

Lentur also does **guided trail hikes** for groups of up to six people. Included is a guide and transportation to and from the trail head. The prices range from R$60 to R$120 (US$30–US$60/£16–£32) per day for the trip (not per person). Trips include the 1-hour walk to **Ribeirão de Meio,** the 3-hour walk to **Sossego Falls,** the 4-hour walk to and through **Lapão Cave** (bring a flashlight), the 8-hour walk from **Capão to Lençóis,** and the 5-hour walk from **Pai Inácio Mesa to Lençóis.** There is also a 3-day hike to Cachoeira da Fumaça in the center of the Chapada. Cost is R$110 (US$55/£30) per person per day, including meals and guide. A sleeping bag is required.

On the main square, **Venturas & Aventuras,** Praça Horácio de Matos 16 (© **075/3334-1304;** www.venturas.com.br), is run by English-speaking guides. Slightly less volume-oriented than the above two companies, they are also somewhat more expensive. In addition to 1-day trips, this company also offers a number of 2- and 5-day trekking packages.

Ecotrekking (© **071/3358-6057;** www.ecotrekkingaventuras.com.br) specializes in multiday hikes in the Chapada. The company has a shop in Lençóis. Praça Horácio de Matos 656 (© **075/3334-1491**).

SHOPPING

Dois Irmãos, Praça Horario de Matos 3, on the main square (© **075/3334-1405;** www.doisirmaos.com.br)—open from 8am to 10pm daily, Visa and cash only—sells high-quality trekking and hiking gear: boots, backpacks, sandals, sleeping bags, and so on. If you're looking for souvenirs, the Diamantina region is famous for semiprecious stones, which local craftsmen make into interesting jewelry. One good shop is **Casa das Pedras,** Rua das Pedras 129 (© **075/3334-1434**). On the main square, photographer Calil Neto runs a small shop (**Calil Neto Fotografia;** Praça Horácio de Matos 82; © **075/3334-1950**) displaying his beautiful Ansel Adams–like photographs of the Diamantina highlands. Open daily from 7 to 10pm. No credit cards.

WHERE TO STAY

Lençóis has everything from the cheap and simple to wonderful pousadas to top-service resorts. Note that in the off season (Mar–June and Aug–Nov), all of the establishments below will cut prices from 10% to 40%.

EXPENSIVE

Canto das Aguas Hotel ⟨ Located just below the stone bridge leading to the town square, the Canto occupies a series of terraces cascading downward to a pool and patio that rest by the edge of the riverbank. The standard rooms (the old wing) are vaguely dark and dank, but the special rooms in the new wing are lovely, bright, and spacious; they each come with a queen-size bed and foldout sofa, a nook with a small sitting table, a good-size bathroom and, overlooking the river, a veranda upon which to sling your hammock. The only special rooms to avoid are nos. 210 and 211, which lack a river view. The hotel is part of the Roteiros de Charme, an association of top-quality inns and pousadas.

Av. Senhor dos Passos s/n, Lençóis, 46960-000 BA. ©/fax **075/334-1154.** www.lencois.com.br. 44 units. R$180 (US$90/£43) standard double; R$220 (US$110/£59) special double; R$260 (US$130/£70) suite double. Extra person add 20%. Children 6 and under stay free in parent's room. AE, DC, MC, V. Free parking. **Amenities:** Restaurant; bar; pool; game room; 24-hr. room service; laundry. *In room:* A/C, TV, minibar, fridge, hair dryer, safe.

MODERATE

Casa de Geleia   Try the jams. Lia, wife of owner Ze Carlos, makes fabulous home-made jams and chutneys—hence the name of this green and pleasant pousada. There are two older rooms and four newer ones. All are spacious but simply furnished, fea-turing single beds with slightly mushy mattresses. Bathrooms in all are large and bright. All have private verandas above a large garden that overlooks the town. Views from the older rooms are slightly better, but all are still excellent. Owner Ze Carlos is an avid birder and speaks fine English. Note that Casa prefers things quiet and peace-ful; those with children under 10 may want to look elsewhere.

Rua Gen Viveiros 187, Lençóis, 46960-000 BA. © 075/3334-1151. www.casadageleia.com.br. 6 units (showers only). R$110 (US$55/£30) double. Extra person add about R$40 (US$20/£11). No credit cards. Free parking. **Ameni-ties:** Large garden. *In room:* Fan, TV, fridge, no phone.

Estalagem Alcino ★★ *Finds*   Every town should have such a pousada. Housed in a replica of a 19th-century colonial house, there's antique furniture inside and comfort-able nooks upstairs and down to hide out and peruse the sizable book collection. Out back, on the far side of a well-manicured pocket garden, is where the owner keeps his pottery workshop and kiln. The garden is where breakfast is served, and it is a tour de force; the cook brings out delicious local specialties until the table is covered with plates and platters. Next morning she does the same again, but no dish ever seems to appear twice. The only drawback to the Estalagem is the shared bathrooms, one for the two rooms upstairs and one for two of the rooms downstairs. Considering all the other advantages, it's a minor complaint.

Rua Tombe Surrão 139, Lençóis, 46960-000 BA. ©/fax 075/3334-1171. 8 units, 5 with shared bathroom (showers only). R$90–R$150 (US$45–US$75/£24–£40) double. Children 6 and under stay free in parent's room. DC, MC. Street parking. **Amenities:** Garden; common lounge. *In room:* Fridge, no phone.

WHERE TO DINE

Picanha na Praça, Praça Otaviano Alves 62, Lençóis (© **075/3334-1248**), serves up the best Brazilian steak sizzling hot and done to perfection. If you don't like steak, there's not much point in coming, and the side dishes are the usual forgettable assort-ment of Brazilian carbohydrates. But mmmmm, that *picanha* is good. Open daily from 1 to 11pm. **Neco's Bar,** Praça Clarim Pacheco 15 (© **075/3334-1179**), serves regional cuisine—the favorites of the local area. Seafood is almost nonexistent up here. Instead, chefs make use of dried, often salted beef and a variety of strong spices. Open daily from noon to 10pm.

MORRO DE SÃO PAULO/ILHA DE BOIPEBA

To really get away from it all (as if the rest of Bahia wasn't relaxed enough) consider the ultimate beach holiday in Morro de São Paulo or, even more remote, the little village of Boipeba. Built on an island only accessible by boat or plane, these small beachside vil-lages are blissfully isolated—no cars, no lights, no motorcars, though luxuries abound. Still, the main mode of transportation is your feet; wheelbarrows double as taxis trans-porting everything from luggage to food and drinks for the evening beach party.

By sea, the best approach is by catamaran, leaving from behind the Mercado Mod-elo in downtown Salvador. A 2½-hour boat ride brings you to Morro (as the locals refer to it), located on the island of Tinharé. As you approach you'll notice the outline of a large hill (*morro* is hill in Portuguese) and the remnants of an old fort. Upon arrival locals with wheelbarrows vie for your business, offering to take your bags to your pousada for R$5 to R$10 (US$2.50–US$5/£1.35–£2.70) per bag—bargain hard and you should be able to get it for R$10 (US$5/£2.70) per wheelbarrow. A steep uphill trail takes you from the docks to the main village, which consists of only a handful of sand-covered streets. The main (sand-covered) street, called Broadway, leads from the main square down to the beaches. The beach at the bottom of the main street is called First Beach (Primeira Praia), followed by Second Beach (Segunda Praia), Third Beach (Terceira Praia), and so on. Most of the pousadas are on Second and Third beaches. The island itself is still lush and green, and the beaches vary from busy and fun to almost deserted.

ESSENTIALS
None of the addresses in Morro de São Paulo have street numbers, but there are only a handful of streets and locals are very helpful with directions. For visitor information stop by the **CIT** (Central de Informações Turisticas), Praça Aureliano Lima s/n (© **075/3652-1083**). This office can assist you with accommodations and transportation as well as book excursions. It also has a number of Internet terminals and doubles as the post office. An excellent website on the area is www.morrodesaopaulo.com.br.

Getting There
BY CAR   As no cars are allowed on the island, drivers will have to leave their vehicles in Valença, the nearest city to the island.

BY BUS   From Salvador, **Viação Camurujipe** (© **075/3642-3280**) runs a daily service to Valença (approximately 4 hr.). From Valença there are at least two ferry options: the regular service, **Bio Tur** (© **075/3652-1062**), takes about 2 hours and costs R$4 (US$2/£1). The fast ferry, **Atobás** (© **075/3641-3011**), costs R$10 (US$5/£2.70) and takes 45 minutes. In high season you will find a number of other boats offering transportation.

BY CATAMARAN   The most direct route to Morro de São Paulo is via the catamaran departing from downtown Salvador; the Terminal Maritimo do Mercado Modelo is just across the street from the Mercado Modelo. There are several daily departures: 8:30am, Lancha Ilhabela (© **071/9118-2393** or 071/9132-8262); 1:30pm, Catamarã Farol do Morro (© **071/3319-4570**); and at 9am and 2pm, Catamarã Biotur (© **071/3641-3327**). Each costs R$50 (US$25/£14) and takes about 2 hours. The boats return from Morro de São Paulo at 9am (Farol do Morro), 11:30am (Biotur), and 2pm (Ilhabela). Note that the sea can get rough, and voyagers on this boat often get seasick.

BY PLANE   The quickest way to get to Morro de São Paulo is to fly. Both **Addey** (© **071/3377-1993**) and **Aerostar** (© **071/3377-4406**) offers at least three flights a day, more on weekends and in high season; one-way fare is R$198 (US$99/£53), and flying time is 30 minutes. Flights depart and arrive at Salvador's international airport, making for convenient connections with onward flights.

SPECIAL EVENTS   For New Year's and Carnaval book a few months ahead. Most pousadas work with 5-night packages, and prices rise significantly. It's also when the island fills to capacity and even beyond.

FAST FACTS
There are no banks in Morro de São Paulo, but there is one Banco do Brasil ATM. It is a good idea to bring some extra cash just in case the ATM doesn't work. Most pousadas and restaurants accept credit cards. In a pinch, they will also exchange small-denomination U.S. dollars ($10s and $20s).

HITTING THE BEACH & EXPLORING THE TOWN

The main attraction of Morro de São Paulo is the beach, or better, the beaches. Each has a unique flavor. **First Beach** is mostly residential; **Second Beach** has lots of pousadas and people. This is where you'll find vendors, watersports, and restaurants and nightlife after sundown. **Third Beach** is quite narrow; at high tide it almost disappears. It is much quieter, perfect for a stroll. **Fourth Beach** is the (almost) deserted island tropical beach—wide, white sand, palm trees, and a few small restaurants. The town itself consists of just a few streets and the main square. During the day it's pretty quiet, as most people hang out at the beach. In the evening, a crafts market starts up, attracting both locals and tourists to the main square. The restaurants surrounding the main square fill up with diners feasting on local seafood dishes. More active pursuits include boating, horseback riding, and hiking. There are a number of interesting local excursions. See below for more information.

OUTDOOR ACTIVITIES

Marlins, Rua da Prainha s/n (© 075/3652-1242), the island's main tour operator, offers a number of trips. The most popular is the **8-hour boat trip** around the island with plenty of stops for swimming or snorkeling. Another great boat tour goes out to **Ilha de Boibepa** (a small island off the main island; see below for more details). Tours cost R$50 (US$25/£14) per person, lunch not included. More active trips include **hikes** to waterfalls or a **walk** along the cliffs and beach to Gamboa for R$20 to R$30 (US$10–US$15/£5.40–£8) per person.

Another operator that offers a number of interesting activities is **Quarta Praia Sul,** Rua da Prainha 75 (along the trail that connects Second and First beach) (© 075/3652-1284; www.quartapraiasul.com.br). The focus of this young company is to introduce visitors to a nature experience. One of the more interesting walking tours is the Trilha do Mar (Ocean trail), which takes hikers through the three main ecosystems of the region: the Atlantic rainforest, the mangroves, and the beach. Guides point out flora and fauna and explain how the ecosystems function. Cost is R$25 (US$13/£7). Other tours include horseback riding, various hikes, and boat tours. This tour operator also offers excellent, inexpensive accommodations packages at the Anima Hotel (see review below under "Where to Stay").

Along Third and Fourth beaches you will find a number of local **horseback** tour operators; the common rate is R$15 (US$7.50/£4) per person per hour. The best time to go is early in the morning, around 9am or 10am when the horses are fresh.

For scuba diving contact **Companhia do Mergulho,** Pousada Farol do Morro, Primeira Praia (© 075/3652-1200). Conditions are best in the summer months (Dec–Jan). In the winter (June–Sept), when the rains are heavy, visibility can be poor. A double dive with all equipment included costs R$150 (US$75/£40). The dive store also rents out masks and snorkels for R$10 (US$5/£2.70)

Tip: Don't be late for the sunset: One of the best spots in Morro de São Paulo to watch the sunset is from the old fort next to the catamaran quay. From the docks take the path toward the left above the cliffs; it's an easy 15-minute walk. The fort, originally built in 1630 and expanded in 1728, is extremely photogenic; the red rocks glow in the rich light of the setting sun and keen spotters will often see dolphins or whales from their vantage point above the rocks.

SHOPPING

Bring enough toiletries, sunscreen, and personal items to last for your entire stay, as these tend to be pricey in Morro de São Paulo. Every evening in the main square there's a crafts market with some beautiful items for sale, well worth browsing.

WHERE TO STAY

Morro de São Paulo is not a luxury destination; although there are many lovely pousadas; most tend to be small, simple, and casual. Amenities are minimal.

Anima Hotel 🕏🕏   Brand-new in 2005, the lovely Anima hotel sits in splendid isolation on the outer reaches of Fourth Beach, to date the farthest outpost of tourist civilization on that still largely pristine stretch of sand. Everything in the new Anima has been built with taste and care. A small swimming pool faces the beach, and a comfortable lounge and sitting area was made from local palm and coco fibers. The owners have left out coffee-table books and examples of local artwork on tables and bookshelves. Accommodations are in self-contained bungalows. Some face the sea; others hide back in the coconut groves. All feature comfortable queen-size beds with top-quality linens, big windows, high ceilings, rattan chairs for relaxing, and hammocks on the balconies for relaxing even more. Bathrooms are large, bright, and modern, with showers. Two of the bungalows feature private outdoor Jacuzzis. All the bungalows are exquisitely decorated with local artwork and crafts. The only disadvantage to staying here is the long hike back to the village.

Praia do Encanto (Quarta Praia), Morro de São Paulo, 45428-000 BA. ℂ 075/3652-2077. Fax 075/3652-1397. www. animahotel.com. 9 units. High season R$260–R$310 (US$130–US$155/£70–£84) double; low season R$210–R$260 (US$105–US$130/£57–£70) double. Extra person add about 20%. Children 7 and under stay free in parent's room. AE, V. **Amenities:** Restaurant; bar; pool; Jacuzzi; laundry; beachfront. *In room:* A/C, TV, DVD, CD, minibar, fridge, no phone.

Pousada o Casarão 🕏🕏   In the heart of the village overlooking the main square, this pousada can be deceptive. From the sandy street it appears to be (just) a beautiful heritage building (though one with quite a pedigree—it was here that the Emperor D. Pedro II stayed when he visited in 1859.) What you can't see from the street is the lush back garden with nine bungalows set against the sloping hillside. Each is decorated in a different style—Indonesian, Japanese, Indian, African—with rich furnishings and artwork. The best bungalows are nos. 15 and 16. Located at the top of the property, these look out over the gardens, the square, and the ocean.

Praça Aureliano Lima s/n, Morro de São Paulo, BA 45428-000. ℂ/fax 075/3652-1022. www.ocasarao.net 16 units (6 rooms and 10 bungalows). Units in the main building R$130–R$150 (US$65–US$75/£35–£40) double; bungalows R$140–R$210 (US$70–US$105/£38–£57) double (showers only). Extra person add R$40 (US$20/£11). Children 5 and under stay free in parent's room. AE, DC, MC, V. **Amenities:** Restaurant; bar; 2 outdoor pools; sauna; massage; laundry. *In room:* A/C, TV, minibar, no phone.

Vila Guaiamú 🕏🕏🕏   Vila Guaiamú may just have the perfect location in Morro. Far enough from the village for total peace and quiet, yet close enough that within 10 minutes you can be dancing the night away. This lovely pousada consists of 24 cabins set among the lush green gardens (through which skulk the cute little species of burrowing freshwater crab that gives the vila its name). All have verandas with hammocks and are simply furnished. Cabins come in standard or deluxe, the only difference being the air-conditioning and television in the deluxe rooms. The pousada is located halfway down Terceira Praia, about a 20-minute walk from the village.

Terceira Praia, Morro de São Paulo, 45400-000 BA. ℂ 075/3652-1035. Fax 075/3483-1073. www.vilaguaiamu.com.br. 24 units (showers only). High season R$210 (US$105/£57) double; R$120–R$160 (US$60–US$80/£32–£43) double.

Extra person add R$40 (US$20/£11). Children 5 and under stay free in parent's room. AE, V. Closed May–June. **Amenities:** Restaurant; bar; laundry; massage; beachfront. *In room:* A/C, TV (in 12 rooms only), minibar, no phone.

WHERE TO DINE

For a small village in the middle of nowhere, Morro de São Paulo has a surprising number of excellent restaurants. The main street of the village, Broadway, is lined with eateries. Although most are open for lunch, it's in the evening that things really get hopping. **Restaurante e Pizzaria Bianco e Nero** (© 075/3652-1097) sells some of the world's best pizza, hot out of the wood-burning oven. It also offers a number of excellent seafood, grilled meat and chicken, and pasta dishes; closed Monday. The restaurant has a large outdoor patio overlooking the street. Almost across from the pizzeria is **Sabor da Terra** (© 075/3652-1156), famous for its generous portions of outstanding *moquecas* and *bobó de camarão* (prawn stew). Meat eaters can order the *picanha na chapa,* tender steak served at your own table grill. The tables on the veranda (if you can snag one) offer great views of the main street. One of the prettiest viewpoints in town is that of **O Casarão** (© 075/3652-1022), overlooking the main square. The menu offers a number of excellent fish and seafood dishes (portions serve two people) including *moquecas* and grilled fish. Closed Sunday.

Note: All restaurants mentioned above accept Visa or MasterCard. However, bring extra cash when dining out because the online authorization can be fickle and sometimes service is unavailable.

NIGHTLIFE

Surprise, surprise, Morro's nightlife is centered around the beach. If you do want to make a night of it, it's wise to take a nap before starting out—things only get hopping around 1am. While most people are having dinner in the main village, browsing the crafts market in the square, or sampling a dessert from the stalls on *Broadway,* the locals are busy setting up their drinks stands on Second Beach. Around midnight, the village empties out and people head to the nightclubs at the end of Second Beach: **Ponta da Lua** or **Praia Clube Caitá.** These are pretty casual affairs—sand-covered dance floors and lots of open-air space right by the beach. The atmosphere is great, with locals and tourists mingling (there is, of course, nowhere else to go). The fruit-laden bar *barracas* specialize in caipirinhas or *batidas* made with the fresh fruit on display. Just point to your favorite fruits, pick your booze of choice (vodka, cachaça, or rum), and it all goes in the blender, coming out as a delicious cocktail.

BARRA GRANDE/MARAU PENINSULA

Once you get a taste for this part of Bahia you may want to explore farther south. The Marau Peninsula is a magical place where deserted beaches and unspoiled scenery are still easily found. The main village of Barra Grande sits at the very top of the peninsula that juts out into the Bay of Camamu, the third-largest bay in all Brazil. Part of what has helped preserve the beaches in this region is the limited access. Wedged in between the Atlantic on the east and the enormous bay and its many islands on the west there are no real roads to speak of (although Itacaré is only 50km/31 miles from Barra Grande, it is a 5-hr. drive in a 4×4) so visitors arrive by boat from Camamu or by plane from Morro de São Paulo or Salvador. What they come for are the miles and miles and miles (and miles!) of unspoiled beaches, the beautiful bay and islands, mangroves and lagoons, the Atlantic rainforest and bromeliads, and the excellent food and accommodations. Most visitors stay in or near Barra Grande. Here you will find a number of excellent bed-and-breakfasts and several great restaurants set amid lots of

Visiting Boipeba Island 𝕽𝕽𝕽

Although most people visit Boipeba on a day trip from Morro de São Paulo, the island is worth a longer visit. A half-hour boat trip south of Morro de São Paulo, Boipeba is often described as "Morro 20 years ago." And indeed, after spending some time in Boipeba, Morro will come to seem "big" and "busy" in comparison. The advantage of spending the night is that, as soon as the day-trippers head back for Morro, you have the beach pretty much to yourself. The island offers enough to see that you can easily spend 2 or 3 days exploring. A variety of coastal hikes will lead you to other, more remote beaches. For a full day of hiking, you can traverse the length of the island to reach a fishing village on the southern tip. Instead of walking back you can arrange for a boat to bring you back to Boca da Barra. The Rio Inferno estuary is also worth exploring for its birdlife and the beauty of its vegetation and sweeping vistas of ocean and river. For photos and information check www.boipeba.tur.br.

If you want to stay overnight it's a good idea to reserve ahead, particularly in high season. The few pousadas here are all quite small. We recommend staying at the lovely **Pousada Santa Clara** 𝕽𝕽𝕽, Boca da Barra (© 075/3653-6085; www.santaclaraboipeba.com). Rates range from R$80 to R$170 (US$40–US$85/ £22–£46), depending on size of room and time of year. Built and managed by two American brothers—Mark and Charles—the pousada combines Brazilian warmth and luxury with American customer service and amenities, and is only steps from the beach. Each room is uniquely decorated with beautiful artwork and Mark's original photos. The pousada has an outstanding restaurant, which serves a three-course gourmet breakfast (complimentary for guests). At night the restaurant is open to the public and serves creative and fresh regional dishes. There is also a beautiful reading room and library stuffed with English-language books, as well as a massage bungalow. Just make sure you ask Charles or Mark to nag you about taking at least one tour because it would be a shame if you missed out on seeing the rest of this lovely island

Getting There: The quickest way to reach Boipeba is by plane. **Addey** (© 071/ 3377-1993) offers three flights a day from Salvador to Boipeba with a minimum of two passengers (R$290/US$145/£78 per person). The landing strip is on Fazenda Pontal, just across the river from Boca da Barra. Transfer from the air strip to the village (a 5-min. crossing) is included. Boipeba can easily be reached by boat from Morro de São Paulo (2 hr. by boat). The cheapest transfer option is to go with a day tour that leaves Morro around 9:30am and reaches Boipeba in time for lunch. This is perfect in combination with staying in Morro for a few days. Those who don't want to go through Morro and come or return directly to Salvador, can take the ferry from downtown Salvador to Itaparica (there are at least 5 ferries a day). Upon arrival, the buses to Valença meet the ferry passengers and it takes about 2 hours to reach Valença, and another 15 minutes to reach Graciosa. Two bus companies cover this route: **Cidade do Sol** and **Aguia Branca**. It is possible to catch a boat to Boipeba from either Valença (4½ hr.) or Graciosa (2½ hr.). Charles can also arrange to have a private boat bring you over, or arrange a car and driver to meet you at the Itaparica ferry at quite reasonable rates, especially if three or four people divide the bill.

green in a cute sleepy village with streets made of sand. A must-see day trip, or even better as an overnight visit, is Taipu de Fora, listed as one of the most beautiful beaches in Brazil (see box: p. 290). Relax on this stretch of glorious beach framed by thousands of palm trees, swim in the natural pools at low tide, or explore the lagoon and beaches to the south.

ESSENTIALS

One of the best resources for planning your trip to Barra Grande and Taipu de Fora is **Turismo Taipu** (⟨C⟩ **073/3258-9051** or 071/9962-6222; www.taiputurismo.com.br). The owner, Tatiana Pugliese, speaks excellent English, has lived here for years, and knows the area like the back of her hand. She and her staff can set up transfers, accommodations, and sightseeing.

Getting There

BY CAR   There is effectively no car access. Cars aren't allowed on the ferry (see below). From the south, the only road access is hard-core 4×4 territory.

BY BUS   From Salvador, the best route is to take the ferry from Salvador to Bom Despacho on Itaparica island (approximately 1 hr.). From there you can connect with a bus that will take you to Camamu 180km (112 miles) away. Both **Viação Camuru-jipe** (⟨C⟩ **073/3255-2508**) and **Aguia Branca** (⟨C⟩ **073/3255-1823**) run a daily service to Camamu from Bom Despacho Valença (approximately 4 hr.; tickets cost R$16/US$8/£4.30). Then from Camamu you catch another ferry to Barra Grande. You can either take the regular ferry (every hour, between 7am and 5:30pm, R$5/£2.50/£1.35 per person), which takes an hour and a half or a fast boat that will get you there in 35 minutes; departures at 7am, 9am, 1pm, and 4:30pm. Tickets are R$25 (US$13/£7) per person.

BY PLANE   The quickest way to get to Barra Grande is to fly from Salvador straight to Barra Grande airport (well, dirt air field). The trip is fast and the route is very scenic as you fly over Salvador, cross the bay of All Saints and enjoy fabulous views of Morro, Boipeba, and the beaches farther south. **Aerostar** (⟨C⟩ **071/3377-4406;** www.aerostar.com.br) offers flights on Sunday, Wednesday, and Friday, leaving Salvador International airport at 1pm, arriving in Barra Grande an hour later (tickets are R$300/US$150/£81, children 2–10 are half price). Aerostar also offers flights between Morro de São Paulo and Barra Grande on Sunday, Wednesday, and Friday (R$195/US$98/£53 per person). The other option is to fly to Ilheus. There are daily flights by **TAM** (⟨C⟩ **071/4002-5700**) and **Gol** (⟨C⟩ **0300/115-2121**). From Ilheus you need to then travel to Camamu and take the ferry (see information above).

SPECIAL EVENTS   Only during New Year's and Carnaval does this region get really full. To visit during this period please book a few months ahead. Better in the off season, when you have the beaches practically to yourself.

FAST FACTS

There are no banks or bank machines in Barra Grande. Most pousadas and a number of restaurants accept credit cards (mostly MasterCard and Visa) but it is a good idea to bring plenty of cash. You will find the Lan House Barra Internet cafe in the main square, across from the church. Open daily from 8am to 10pm; R$8 (US$4/£2).

HITTING THE BEACH & EXPLORING THE TOWN

The main attractions of Barra Grande are the beach and the glorious bay that bathes the peninsula. The beaches in Barra Grande proper are pretty enough and make for a great sunset spot. The pousadas listed below are right on the beach so you can just set out and explore as far as you feel like going. The town itself consists of three main streets and a few cross streets and can be explored in an hour or so. However this is best done at night when the cozy restaurants and charming patios add a warm glow to the sultry evening. In high season the town is livelier, with live music and a few more bars. However, we enjoyed the calm and quiet off-season atmosphere. In the daytime you are best off exploring some of the farther beaches such as Taipu de Fora, or setting off on a boat tour of the bay and the many islands. See below for a description of some interesting local excursions.

OUTDOOR ACTIVITIES

Taipu Turismo (© 073/3258-9051), the island's main tour operator, offers a number of trips. The most popular is the **8-hour boat trip** around the Bay of Camamu, the third-largest bay in Brazil, with several stops at some of the islands for swimming or snorkeling, and a visit to Cajaíba, the wooden boat center of the region. Other boat tours can be combined with a visit to Camamu, the region's main town, a hike to a waterfall, or a visit to a *quilombo* community, a settlement founded by runaway slaves. Another great tour goes out to **Taipu de Fora** (one of the region's most beautiful beaches; see below for more details), where you can snorkel in the natural pools that form at low tide. The tour by 4×4 takes you across the peninsula's back roads to the Cassange lagoon and the Bromeliad trail. These are not just your boring run-of-the-mill bromeliads. These are humongous alien-looking bromeliad creatures perched high in the treetops that grow to the size of a family sedan. Tours range from R$35 (US$18/£9.50) per person, lunch not included, for a boat tour to R$120 (US$60/£32) for a full day tour, including a hike.

SHOPPING

Bring enough toiletries, sunscreen, and personal items to last for your entire stay, as there is very little available here. In the evening there is a small craft market where local artisans make lovely lampshades and other decorative items of natural materials.

WHERE TO STAY

Barra Grande has a surprising number of excellent pousadas and even a high-end resort.

VERY EXPENSIVE

Kiaroa 🐾🐾   The Kiaroa offers the most luxurious accommodations in the region. This seaside resort is set on a gorgeous stretch of beach amid a lovely lush garden; all the bungalows are tastefully furnished in a tropical style, using lots of rustic natural materials and fabrics and colorful artwork. All of the bungalows are spacious and beautiful, perfect for a romantic getaway. The deluxe bungalows come with a private swimming pool and a separate sitting room, two bathrooms with Jacuzzi tub, and a large-screen plasma TV. The apartments are significantly smaller, somewhat noisy, and frankly not worth the money. Splurge or stay elsewhere. A new high-end spa has just been opened. The rates listed are rack rates. Breakfast and dinner included. Contact a travel operator like Brazil Nuts or Tatur in Salvador for more affordable packages.

Praia da Bombaça, Barra Grande, 45.445-000 BA. © 073/3258-6212. For reservations contact © 071/3272-1320. www.kiaroa.com.br. 10 bungalows and 14 apartments. R$988 (US$494/£267) double apartment; R$1,500–R$1,800 (US$750–US$900/£405–£486) double bungalow; R$2,200 (US$1,100/£594) double deluxe bungalow. Accepts children only over the age of 14. AE, DC, MC, V. **Amenities:** Restaurant; bar; large outdoor pool; tennis court; spa; tour desk; business center; room service; laundry; beachfront. *In room:* A/C, TV, DVD, CD, wireless Internet, minibar, hair dryer, safe.

Pousada Barra Bella ★★ *(Kids)*　Barra Bella offers affordable and child-friendly accommodations, right on the beach and within walking distance of the amenities in the village. The pousada features a large garden with plenty of play room and a swimming pool. All rooms are nicely furnished with colorful touches and local artwork. Many look out toward the ocean, and the duplex mezzanine room and the master room are each big enough to comfortably accommodate a family of four or five.

Rua Vasco Neto s/n, Barra Grande, 454428-000 BA. ☎ 073/3258-6298. www.pousadabarrabella.com.br. 13 units (showers only). Low season R$140–R$160 (US$70–US$80/£38–£22) standard double; R$180–R$200 (US$90–US$100/£49–£54) mezzanine or master double. High season R$240 (US$120/£65) standard double; R$290 (US$145/£78) mezzanine or master double. Extra person add 25%. Children 5 and under stay free in parent's room. AE, V. Closed May–June. **Amenities:** Restaurant; bar; outdoor swimming pool; beachfront. *In room:* A/C, TV, minibar, hair dryer, safe.

Pousada Ponta do Mutá ★★　Another affordable and pleasant pousada, Ponta do Mutá is centrally located between the village and the beach. All rooms have a veranda with a hammock and look out either over the garden (the lower ones) or the ocean and garden (the top ones). The pousada is set in a lovely garden with several pleasant sitting (or snoozing) areas in the shade or overlooking the beach. Kayaks are available free of charge.

Rua do Anjo s/n, Barra Grande, BA 45428-000. ☎ 073/3258-6028. www.pousadapontadomuta.com.br. 10 units. Low season R$130–R$160 (US$65–US$80/£35–£43) double; high season R$220 (US$110/£59) double (showers only). Extra person add 25%. Children 5 and under stay free in parent's room. AE, DC, MC, V. **Amenities:** Restaurant; tour desk; laundry. *In room:* A/C, TV, wireless Internet, minibar, hair dryer, safe.

WHERE TO DINE

Barra Grande has a number of excellent restaurants. In fact, if you are only staying for 1 or 2 nights, one of the challenges will be choosing which place to try!

Whatever you do, don't miss **Donanna's** restaurant, Rua do Anjo s/n (☎ **073/ 3258-6109**), just past the pousada Ponta do Mutá. This simple restaurant serves up delicious local seafood. Make sure to order the salada de polvo (octopus salad), the best we ever had! Other dishes worth trying include the grilled lobster, fried fish, and bobó. Dona Anna herself shops, cooks, looks after the guests, and brews a mean espresso. A great place for dinner, **Café Latino,** Rua Dr. Chiquinho 19 (☎ **073/ 3258-6188**), is a cozy bistro/eatery run by a Brazilian-Argentine couple. They serve up excellent homemade pastas, have a decent wine list, and also make delicious specialty coffees and desserts. Even if you don't have dinner here it is worth going for a dessert coffee. For a local home-cooked meal visit **a Tapera,** Rua Dra. Lili s/n (☎ **073/3258-6119**). The only dish to order here is the moqueca, the house specialty. Keep in mind that portions are generous so you can easily share a main course, especially if you have an appetizer such as the casquinha de siri made with shredded crabmeat baked in a clay dish. During the off season please check for opening hours.

Note: All restaurants mentioned above accept Visa or MasterCard. However, bring extra cash when dining out because the online authorization can be fickle and sometimes service is unavailable.

ITACARÉ

The small town of Itacaré is nestled at the mouth of the Rio das Contas, the river that separates the mainland from the southern tip of Marau peninsula. Once a thriving export center of cacau, the town's economic activities now focus mostly on tourism, taking advantage of the exceptional natural beauty of this region. Unlike the coast north of here, where long beaches lined with groves of palm trees form the landscape,

Visiting Taipu de Fora ☆☆☆

Often sold as part of a day tour from Barra Grande, Taipu de Fora is well worth an overnight stay, particularly if you like your beaches endless, gorgeous, and empty. This vast wide strand is framed by thick groves of palm trees, dotted in just a few spots with pousadas. When the day-trippers leave you have the place to yourself. Time your visit during the full moon and you may very well believe you have found paradise. Go for a stroll, enjoy a swim (at low tide there area some impressive natural pools; a mask and snorkel can be rented on the beach for R$10/US$5/£2.70), enjoy a delicious grilled seafood platter at the **Bar das Meninas** (𝄐 073/3258-9035; www.bardas meninas.com.br), and try one of the many delicious fruit *roscas* (vodka and fruit juice cocktails).

There are two good options for an overnight stay. We recommend the **Village Taipu** (see the site of Bar das meninas for pictures), a pleasant house with ocean view and only two rooms—a studio that sleeps two (R$120/US$60/£32) and a one-bedroom suite that sleeps four people (R$240/US$120/£64). Breakfast is served on the Bar das Meninas lovely beachside patio. Another good option is to stay at the **Pousada Taipu de Fora** (𝄐 073/3258-6278; www.taipudefora.com.br). This 28-room pousada also looks out over the ocean and provides more comfortable accommodations with some amenities such as room service, rooms for disabled travelers, and recreation for children. Rooms range from R$250 to R$315 (US$125–US$158/£68–£85).

Itacaré is set in lush Atlantic rainforest and its small beaches are tucked away in bays protected by rocks and hills. Best of all, most beaches can only be reached on foot, on scenic trails through the forest, keeping most development (still) at bay. The ocean here is often quite rough with big waves, making it a surfer's paradise. For the non-surfer, Itacaré offers lovely unspoiled beaches, great short hikes, and excellent accommodations and dining.

Getting There

BY CAR   Itacaré is a great place to have your wheels. The roads are in great shape and most of the beaches are a short drive outside of the city. You can either rent a car in Itacaré or at the airport in Ilheus and drive the 64km (40 miles) north on your own. The BR-001 has recently been repaired and the drive takes you along a windy road through the beautiful Atlantic rainforest.

BY BUS   Rota (𝄐 073/3251-2181) offers regular bus service between Ilheus and Itacaré. Buses go every hour, between 7am and 7pm. Tickets are R$7 (US$3.50/£2).

BY PLANE   The nearest airport to Itacré is in Ilheus. There are daily flights by **TAM** (𝄐 071/4002-5700) and **Gol** (𝄐 0300/115-2121). From Ilheus it is 64km (40 miles) to Itacaré. Many pousadas can arrange transportation. Eco Trip (𝄐 073/3251-2191; www.ecotrip.tur.br) also offers a private transfer service from the airport in Ilheus to Itacaré for R$120 for two people (US$60/£32).

FAST FACTS

There is only a Bradesco bank machine in Itacaré in the Praça do Forum so it's wise to bring some extra cash in case it's down or doesn't accept your card. Most restaurants, hotels, and tour companies accept credit cards (MasterCard and Visa are most commonly accepted). Internet cafes are everywhere, especially along the Rua Pedro Longo where you will find at least six cybercafes.

HITTING THE BEACH & EXPLORING THE TOWN

The main attraction of Itacaré is the beach, or rather the beaches. In town, the most popular beach is **Praia da Concha,** which is also where a number of pousadas are concentrated. Especially in the summer this is a lively evening destination, as people meet at the beach bars to listen to music and dance. From there it is only a 5-minute drive or a 15- to 20-minute walk to the "city beaches" of **Resende, Tiririca, Costa,** and finally **Ribeira** where the road ends and the trail to the more isolated beaches starts. Starting here, just south of the main village there begins a string of lovely small beaches, each tucked away in its cove, separated from the next by steep hills and rocks. The only way to reach any one of these beaches is to hike from the trail head down to the ocean. Most trails are short (20–45 min.) and your reward is a practically unspoiled beach framed by stands of Atlantic rainforest. From the trail head past Ribeira beach, a 45-minute walk through the forest takes you to the first of the more rugged ocean beaches, **Prainha.** At the end of Prainha, you can pick up the trail again and continue to the next beach over, **São Jose.** Trail guides who hang out at the parking lot will try to frighten you into contracting their services with tales of multiple trails and confusing pathways, but it's really quite straightforward. To reach the more popular beaches farther south, such as **Engenhoca** (a surfers' and hippie favorite), **Havaizinho** (with more gentle surf, better for swimming) and **Itacarezinho** (a 5km-long/3-mile sandy beach), you need to drive out on the main highway to the appropriate trail head (usually well marked), and then walk from there. From the Havaizinho trail head the walk to Havaizinho takes about 15 minutes, while the walk to Engenhoca takes about 25 minutes. The trail head for Itacarézinho is a little farther south on the highway. It too is well marked, but there's a R$10 (US$5/£2.70) parking fee. The walk to the beach takes about 20 minutes. Bring water, plenty of sunscreen, and anything else that you are likely to need, especially in the low season, because you will find almost no services at these beaches.

OUTDOOR ACTIVITIES

Besides surfing, Itacaré offers a number of other outdoor activities. The town is at the mouth of the Contas river and there are several excursions, either by kayak or by fast boat upriver to explore the estuary, the mangrove forests, the side channels, and the waterfalls upstream. Even farther upriver there is rafting, but don't expect serious wild water. The Atlantic rainforest also offers some interesting tours. Tree climbing has become very popular. Well, tree climbing with the help of walkways, as you make your way through the forest, overcoming obstacles and challenging yourself in a fun climbing game. If you are not traveling to the Marau peninsula you can take a day tour by jeep to explore across the river (not recommended for people with back problems; the dirt road is in very poor shape and the trip is uncomfortable). Local eco-tourism operator **Eco Trip** (✆: **073/3251-2191;** www.ecotrip.tur.br) offers all these activities. Trips range from R$60 (US$20/£16) for a kayak trip to R$140 (US$70/£38) for the jeep tour or R$120 (US$60/£32) for the tree climbing (these prices are for two people).

Tips **Renting a Car**

Car rental costs approximately R$100 (US$50/£27) per day for unlimited mileage. For insurance add another R$30 (US$15/£8). If you are arriving in Ilheus, your best plan is to rent a car at the airport. All the major companies (plus some really obscure local ones) are represented here. Some are in the arrivals hall (**Hertz** ⓒ **073/3231-5042** and **Localiza** ⓒ **073/3231-8007**) and a dozen more are out across the street from the airport. Prices are very similar so we recommend going with a well-known company that offers decent service.

SHOPPING

Bring enough toiletries, sunscreen, and personal items to last for your entire stay, as there is very little available here. In the evening there is a small craft market where local artisans make lovely lampshades and other decorative items of natural materials.

WHERE TO STAY

Despite all the surfers and younger travelers, Itacaré is not a cheap destination. The best accommodations within walking distance of the amenities and nightlife in the village are in Praia da Concha.

VERY EXPENSIVE

Txai 𝒜𝒜𝒜   For the ultimate in luxury accommodations check in at the Txai, a resort carefully built to make the most of a stunning location. Set on Jacarezinho beach (approximately 18km/11 miles from Itacaré), the bungalows and facilities are spread out to offer fabulous views and privacy. The most luxurious bungalow comes with a private pool, but even the standard ones are spacious and elegantly furnished. All rooms feature a king-size bed, a sofa, CD player, an outside shower, and veranda. The hotel's leisure area is beautiful with several swimming pools and decks, an exclusive spa, and of course, the beach. Except for the occasional hiker or surfer, guests have the entire long strand all to themselves.

Rodovia Ilhéus-Itacaré BR 101, Km 48, BA. ⓒ **073/2101-5000.** For reservations ⓒ 011/6858-777. www.txai. com.br. 40 units. Rack rates apartment R$875–R$1,050 (US$438–US$525/£236–£283) double; standard bungalow R$1,250 (US$625/£338) double. Children 3 and under stay free in parent's room. AE, DC, MC, V. **Amenities:** 2 restaurants; 4 bars; 2 large pools; children's pool; game room; health club; tennis; spa; sauna; Jacuzzi; concierge; tour desk; business center; room service; massage; laundry; nonsmoking floors; beachfront; rooms for travelers w/limited mobility. *In room:* A/C, TV, DVD, CD, minibar, fridge, no phone.

EXPENSIVE

Aldeia do Mar 𝒜𝒜   The Aldeia do Mar is fabulously located at the very end of Praia da Concha, the prime sunset spot! The chalets come in three categories that differ in size but offer identical amenities; all feature a veranda and new, firm mattresses, and are pleasantly furnished in bright colors. The hotel has a spacious lawn, a beach volleyball court, and a large swimming pool, and is located right on the beach. Kayaks can be rented to explore the gentle waters of the inlet.

Praia da Concha, Itacaré, BA 45530-000. ⓒ/fax **073/3251-2230.** www.aldeiadomar.tur.br. 13 units. Veranda chalet R$400–R$440 (US$200–US$220/£108–£119); Master chalet R$440–R$488 (US$220–US$244/£119–£132); Aldeia chalet R$514–R$560 (US$257–US$230/£139–£151) double. Extra person 20%. Children 5 and under stay free in parent's room. AE, DC, MC, V. **Amenities:** Restaurant; bar; outdoor pool; laundry; beachfront. *In room:* A/C, TV, minibar.

The Perfect Resort ★★★

On a beach not so far away, in fact only a 50km (31-mile) drive south of Ilheus, there stands the perfect resort, **Fazenda da Lagoa,** Rodovia Una-Ilheus Km 18 (© **073/3236-6046;** www.fazendadalagoa.com.br). Set on what is for all intents and purposes an island, the resort has been carefully hidden away at the end of an unmarked dirt road, beyond which you come to a river that you have to cross by boat. A labor of love of a Rio designer and her husband, the Fazenda offers luxurious accommodations without being over-the-top. Staying at the Fazenda you feel like you're visiting a friend, albeit a friend with oodles of money and exquisite taste. What makes this place so special? First of all it's the only pousada, and one of only a handful of buildings, on a beautiful 10km-long (6-mile) stretch of beach. Then there are the fabulous 140 sq. m (460-sq.-ft.) bungalows with king-size beds, large decks, outside (and inside) showers, a beautiful swimming pool, and a lovely main lounge with an outstanding library. There is a small spa, an excellent restaurant, and only 14 bungalows, which means you never have to worry about the crowds. If you can tear yourself away from the lap of luxury (and nobody says that you have to) you can borrow bikes at low tide and ride out along the beach. Or you can take a short hike to the private lagoon with crystal-clear water and enjoy a swim, a paddle, or simply sunbathe or snooze on the wooden deck, then dig into a delicious picnic lunch that the staff will prepare for you in advance. And did I mention that you have the beach practically to yourself? At the Fazenda da Lagoa, the isolation is truly splendid. Low-season rates R$650 to R$850 (US$325–US$425/£175–£230); high season R$800 to R$1,150 (US$400–US$575/£175–£300). Children under 3 stay free, 3–8 years R$150 (US$75/£40).

Pousada Sage Point ★★   The Sage Point is tucked away at the far right corner of Tiririca beach, on a privileged spot above the rocks overlooking the ocean. The pousada is a lovely wooden treehouse-style structure spread out over several levels; each room is different and uniquely furnished. All but one has a veranda or deck. The less expensive rooms are set higher up and a little farther from the beach (still within view though). The pousada's best room is Sereia (mermaid) room, set on the very point, with panoramic views of the ocean and the beach. This duplex apartment has a fabulous deck and Jacuzzi tub. All rooms have a fan, but if you must have air-conditioning, request one of the two rooms that do. Despite its isolated feel, Tiririca beach is still within a 20-minute walk of the main village. Breakfast is served on the lovely deck overlooking the beach.

Praia de Tiririca, Itacaré, 45530-000 BA. © **073/3251-2030.** www.pousadasagepoint.com.br. 17 units (showers only). High season R$298–R$398 (US$149–US$199/£80–£107) double; R$698 (US$349/£188) suite double. Low season R$180–R$290 (US$90–US$145/£49–£78). Children 5 and under stay free in parent's room. AE, DC, MC, V. **Amenities:** Restaurant; bar; laundry; massage; beachfront. *In room:* A/C (2 rooms only), fan, minibar, safe.

WHERE TO DINE

Itacaré has a number of excellent restaurants that specialize in Bahian food. The village is small enough that you can go for a stroll and see what appeals to you before you decide. The town's finest restaurant is **Dedo de Moça,** Rua Plinio Soares 26 (© **073/3251-3372**). In addition to serving up local fish and seafood with a twist, such as grilled fish with mango chutney and bobo de camarão with Asian spices, you will also find excellent chicken and steak dishes on the menu. For excellent pizzas, try **Beco das Flores,** Rua Lodonio Almeida 108 (© **073/3251-3121**). Not only are the wood oven–baked pizzas delicious, the restaurant has a great atmosphere and courtyard seating.

Along Rua Pedro Longo you will find probably a dozen restaurants that serve up Bahian food, sandwiches, crepes, and burgers. One that stands out for the quality of the food (and drinks too; the caipiroscas are delicious!) is **O Restaurante,** Rua Pedro Longo 170 (© **073/3251-2012**). This plain and unpretentious restaurant serves up some of the best moquecas and bobós in town. Portions are huge so order wisely. In addition to seafood, the restaurant serves pasta and outstanding Argentine steaks.

Note: All restaurants mentioned above accept Visa or MasterCard. However, bring extra cash when dining out because the online authorization can be fickle and sometimes service is unavailable.

10

Recife & Olinda

Recife and Olinda stand within sight of each other on Brazil's Northeast coast, one city on a hilltop, the other in a river mouth, one founded by the Portuguese, the other by the Dutch.

Recife, in keeping with the commercial character of its Dutch founders, is busy, flat, efficient. Modern. Recife is the second-largest city in Brazil's Northeast, and aside from a small but pretty historical core, it's not really worth a visit, at least not in comparison with Salvador or São Luis.

Then there's Olinda. Founded by the Portuguese in 1530 on a steep hill over-looking the harbor, Olinda grew rich and proud on sugar exports. The Dutch at the time were keen to move in on the sugar business, so after trying (and failing) to take Salvador in 1624, they arrived in Pernambuco in 1630, took its capital, Olinda, and with the exception of a few churches, utterly destroyed it. In need of a capital of their own, the Dutch abandoned the ruins of Olinda, and set to work draining and diking the islands at the mouth of the harbor.

Their new city of Mauritstad quickly turned into a bustling commercial center. When the Dutch were expelled in the 1654, the Portuguese rebuilt Olinda as a matter of pride, but the center of the region had shifted. The former Dutch city was renamed Recife, after the long coral reefs that menace the harbor. By the 19th century, Recife had far outgrown Olinda; the older town was left blissfully free of development pressures, still in its largely pristine 17th-century condition.

Restoration work began on Olinda in the 1970s. In 1982 its lovingly preserved historic core was declared a UNESCO World Heritage Site. Unlike Salvador's Pelourinho, however, Olinda feels very much lived in. Walk its streets and you'll come across kids playing soccer on a patch of hard-packed dirt, women carrying groceries, perhaps artists in courtyards carving interesting-looking woodwork. The city is hilly but distances are short, and with so much to capture your attention, it's a joy to explore.

Recife has tried to follow Salvador's example by restoring its colonial downtown and promoting the area as a music and nightlife center, but its efforts haven't been as successful. Old Recife is worth a visit if you're here; it's not worth a trip in itself.

The same can be said for the beaches south of Recife. Most are beautiful—Porto de Galinhas is gorgeous, a laid-back town with long, wide beaches, and hotels that cost but a fraction of larger resorts.

1 Essentials

ARRIVING

BY PLANE   **Varig** (© 4003-7000), **Gol** (© 0300/115-2121), and **TAM** (© 4002-5700) all have flights to Recife. Visitors fly into Recife's **Aeroporto Internacional dos Guararapes,** Praça Ministro Salgado Filho s/n, Boa Viagem (© 081/3464-4188), about 12km (7½ miles) south of the city center and just a few kilometers from the beachside hotels in Boa Viagem. A taxi to Boa Viagem costs R$14 to R$22 (US$7–US$11/£3.75–£6) and to Olinda, R$45 to R$60 (US$23–US$30/£12–£16). You'll find a queue for **Taxi Coopseta Aeroporto** (© 081/3464-4153) on the arrivals level. For visitors staying in Boa Viagem, the regular airport bus, no. 33 or 42, leaves every 15 minutes and passes within 1 block of most hotels along the beach; the fare is R$1.50 (US75¢/£.40).

BY BUS   Buses arrive at Recife's **Terminal Integrado de Passageiros (TIP),** Rodovia BR-232, Km 15, Curado (© 081/3452-1999), 14km (8½ miles) west of downtown. A Metrô connects the bus station to downtown Recife's station, Estação Central. *Note:* Buses from Recife to Olinda or to Porto de Galinhas leave from downtown and Boa Viagem, not from this station.

VISITOR INFORMATION

Recife's airport has a **tourist information booth** at the arrivals level that's open daily from 8am to 6pm (© 081/3462-4960). The best information booth is at Praça Boa Viagem, open daily from 8am to 8pm (© 081/3463-3621). The staff is helpful and will provide an excellent free map of Recife.

In Olinda, the tourist information office is located near the Largo do Amparo on Rua do Bonsucesso 183 (© 081/3439-9434), open daily from 9am to 6pm. There is also a kiosk at the Praça do Carmo, where the buses from Recife arrive.

CITY LAYOUT

Recife's layout of downtown can be a little confusing as it is made up of various islands that are connected by several bridges. Downtown Recife consists of three main areas: **Bairro do Recife** (often called Recife Antigo, or Old Recife), **Santo Antônio,** and **Boa Vista/Santo Amaro.** Recife Antigo is the oldest part of the city, founded by the Dutch in the 1630s. Ongoing renovations are reviving and revitalizing this area, a la Pelourinho in Salvador (see chapter 9). An area of at least 15 city blocks centered on the **Rua da Bom Jesus** has been restored to its former glory. The best time to experience this area is during the weekends when it is at its liveliest.

Three bridges connect Old Recife with **Santo Antônio.** It's one of Recife's main commercial areas, and the home of many of its most interesting sights. Narrow streets packed with shops and vendors surround beautiful baroque churches and plazas. On weekdays this part of downtown just hops, particularly the narrow and twisting streets around the **Patio de São Pedro.** The principal street in Santo Antônio is **Avenida Dantas Barreto,** a wide boulevard that runs down the spine of the island. Buses to and from downtown leave from this street, either from **Praça da Independencia,** where Dantas Barreto meets Rua Primeiro de Março, or from farther up opposite **N.S. de Carmo Basilica.**

West of Santo Antônio on the mainland lie the modern and not very interesting office districts of **Boa Vista** and **Santo Amaro.**

The main beach and residential area of Recife starts just south of downtown and carries on uninterrupted for many miles. The first stretch, where **Avenida Boa**

Recife & Olinda at a Glance

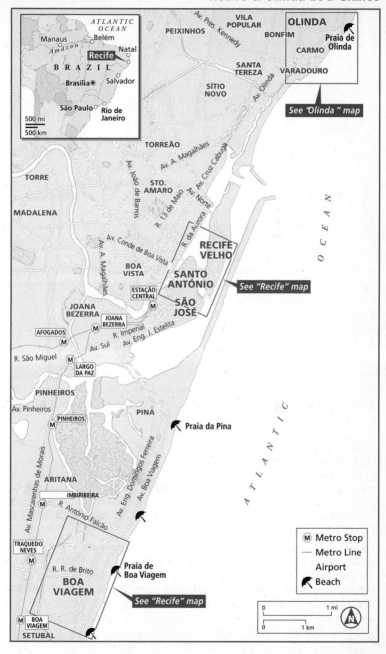

ATLANTIC OCEAN

Manaus   Belém
Amazon   Natal
BRAZIL   Recife
Brasília⊛   Salvador
          São Paulo   Rio de Janeiro

500 mi
500 km

VILA POPULAR
Av. Pres. Kennedy
PEIXINHOS
OLINDA
BONFIM   Praia de Olinda
CARMO
SANTA TEREZA
VARADOURO
SÍTIO NOVO
Av. Olinda

See 'Olinda" map

TORREÃO
Av. A. Magalhães
Av. Cruz Cabugá
TORRE
Av. João de Barros
STO. AMARO
R. 13 de Maio
Av. Norte
MADALENA
R. da Aurora
Av. Conde de Boa Vista
RECIFE VELHO
Av. A. Magalhães
BOA VISTA
SANTO ANTÓNIO
ESTAÇÃO CENTRAL
See "Recife" map
JOANA BEZERRA
SÃO JOSÉ
JOANA BEZERRA
R. Imperial
AFOGADOS
Av. Sul   Av. Eng. J. Estelita
R. São Miguel
LARGO DA PAZ

O C E A N

PINHEIROS
Av. Pinheiros
PINA
PINHEIROS
Praia da Pina

A T L A N T I C

Av. Mascarenhas de Morais
ARITANA
IMBIRIBEIRA
Av. Eng. Domingos Ferreira
Av. Boa Viagem
R. António Falcão
TRAQUEDO NEVES
Praia de Boa Viagem
R. R. de Brito
BOA VIAGEM
See "Recife" map
BOA VIAGEM
SETUBAL

Ⓜ Metro Stop
— Metro Line
  Airport
🏖 Beach

0   1 mi
0   1 km

N

(*Tips*) Stay Alert for Sharks

BATHERS IN THIS AREA ARE AT A GREATER RISK OF SHARK ATTACK reads a sign on Boa Viagem beach. But greater than what, exactly? Those who don't go in the water? The first recorded shark attack occurred on Boa Viagem beach 14 years ago. Since then there have been numerous others, some of them fatal. Locals say the new port built just south of Recife forced the sharks out of their usual habitat and moved them up the coast. Attacks have decreased lately due to more public awareness, but caution is still required on Pina, Boa Viagem, and Piedade beaches. Follow the directions of lifeguards and don't go beyond the reefs.

Viagem begins, is called **Pina.** The area around **Polo Pina** is a popular nightlife spot with some bars and restaurants. Farther along the beach the neighborhood name changes to **Boa Viagem.** This is the city's main hotel area. The beach itself is pleasant and clean but unfortunately the area has the highest number of shark attacks in all of Brazil. At low tide the reefs that lie just off the coast are easily visible in the perfectly clear blue water.

   Olinda lies atop a hill, 7km (4¼ miles) north of downtown. Regular buses make the trip in about 30 minutes. You'll arrive at the **Praça do Carmo** bus station at the foot of Olinda. From there it's all uphill. The town is small enough that directions aren't really necessary. Keep strolling and you'll see everything.

GETTING AROUND

BY BUS   From Boa Viagem, regular buses run along Avenida Domingos Ferreira into downtown, about a 20-minute trip. Those marked CONDE DA BOA VISTA will loop through Boa Vista and into Santo Antônio via the Duarte Coelho Bridge, stopping at Praça da Independencia. Some of these buses continue across the Mauricio de Nassau bridge into Old Recife (ask the ticket seller). If not, it's only a 10-minute walk. Once downtown, all sights are easily reachable on foot.

   From Boa Viagem, two regular buses travel directly to and from Olinda's Praça do Carmo bus station: SETUBAL-PRINCIPE and SETUBAL-CONDE DA BOA VISTA. The trip takes about 50 minutes.

   From Olinda, all buses depart from the bus station on Praça do Carmo. Buses marked RIO DOCE go to Santo Antônio, stopping on Avenida Nossa Senhora do Carmo. Buses marked JARDIM ATLANTICO also go to Santo Antônio but stop in front of the post office on Rua Siqueira Campos. The trip takes about 30 minutes. All buses cost R$2.30 (US$1.30/£.60).

BY TAXI   Taxis are quick and reliable and can be hailed anywhere or booked by phone. Your hotel will usually hail a more expensive radio taxi; to catch a regular one just grab one on the street. **Coopseta Aeroporto** (② 081/3464-4153) specializes in airport service. Both **Ligue-taxi** (② 081/3428-6830) and **Tele-Taxi** (② 081/3429-4242) can be booked ahead of time.

BY METRÔ   There's a Metrô in Recife, but it's not useful to tourists. The stations are too far from Boa Viagem to walk, and given the time required to take a bus to the Metrô station, you might as well take the bus straight into downtown.

FAST FACTS: Recife & Olinda

Area Codes The area code for Recife and Olinda is **081.**

Banks **Banco do Brasil:** in Recife—Rua Barão De Souza Leão 440, Boa Viagem (© **081/3462-3777**); in Olinda—Av. Getulio Vargas 1470, Bairro Novo (© **081/ 3439-1344**).

Car Rentals **Avis** (© **0800/118-066** or 081/3462-5069); **Localiza** (© **0800/312- 121** or 081/3341-2082); **Unidas** (© **081/3461-4661**).

Consulates **United States,** Rua Gonçalves Maia 163, Boa Vista (© **081/3416- 3050**); *Great Britain* (Honorary), Av. Conselheiro Aguiar 2941, Boa Viagem (© **081/3465-0230**).

Currency Exchange **Monaco Cambio,** Praça Joaquim Nabuco 19, Santo Antônio (© **081/3424-3727**); and **Colmeia Cambio,** Rua dos Navegantes 783, Boa Viagem (© **081/3465-3822**).

Dentist Clinica Odontologica, Rua Ademar da Costa Almeida 130, Piedade (© **081/3341-3341**).

Emergencies Dial © **190** for police, © **193** for fire and ambulance. Tourist Police, Praça Min. Salgado Filho s/n (at the airport) (© **081/3303-7217**).

Hospitals **Centro Hospitalar Albert Sabin,** Rua Senador José Henrique 141, Ilha do Leite (© **081/3421-5411**).

Internet Access **Olind@.com Cyber Café,** Praça João Pessoa 15, Carmo, Olinda (© **081/3429-4365**), charges R$6 (US$3/£1.60) per hour. **Recife Internet,** Shopping Guararapes, Av. Barreto de Menezes 800, Piedade (© **081/3464-2107**), charges R$8 (US$4/£2.15) per hour.

Pharmacies **Farmacia dos Pobres,** Av. Conselheiro Aguiar 3595, Boa Viagem (© **081/3301-3117;** www.fp.com.br). Open 24 hours.

Visa Renewal Go to the **Policia Federal,** Cais do Apolo 321, Bairro do Recife (© **081/3425-4026**). You may need to show both a return ticket and evidence of sufficient funds to cover the remainder of your stay.

Weather Recife, just below the Equator, has a pleasant, warm climate year-round, with average temperatures of 82°F (28°C). Most rain falls in winter (July–Sept). The most pleasant months are March through June; it's warm but not as hot as in December through February.

2 Where to Stay

Just a 20-minute bus ride from downtown, the beach neighborhood of Boa Viagem offers a variety of hotels, some good restaurants, and a bit of nightlife, all within easy access of the beach. Unfortunately, none of the hotels in Recife really stands out. However, whatever Recife lacks in interesting hotels, Olinda more than makes up for with a number of gorgeous pousadas, most in buildings 200 years old or more. Olinda also has some of the best restaurants in the area, and there's great daytime sightseeing. It's easy to understand why, increasingly, more visitors are choosing to stay in Olinda and explore the city from there. A bus between Olinda and Recife takes about 30 minutes and taxis are affordable as well.

BOA VIAGEM/PIEDADE

Recife's main hotel neighborhoods for tourists are Boa Viagem and Piedade. Both are on the same stretch of beach; Boa Viagem is the closest you can get to downtown and Olinda while still being in a safe neighborhood on a lovely, clean beach. Most of the hotels are located within 3 blocks of the water, if not directly on the beachside Avenida Boa Viagem. From late March to June and August through October, rates can drop 50%, sometimes even more.

VERY EXPENSIVE

Beach Class Suites 🐾🐾🐾   The only bright light in Boa Viagem, this brand-new tower with bright and spacious rooms offers the best accommodations in town, at a lower rate than some of the five-star properties. All rooms are decorated with modern furniture, predominantly white with some splashes of colorful art. A number of the rooms have balconies; some also have a small kitchen with a microwave and coffeemaker. A nice feature is the women's-only floor, ideal for women traveling alone. In-room amenities include free broadband Internet. The hotel also has a fitness center and outdoor pool overlooking the beach. Internet rates offer as much as 50% savings over the rack rate.

Av. Boa Viagem 1906, Boa Viagem, Recife, 51011-000 PE. 📞 **0800/55-5855** or 081/2121-2626. www.atlanticahotels. com.br. 145 units (showers only). R$390 (US$195/£105) double, Internet special R$170–R$230 (US$85–US$115/ £46–£62). Extra person in room add 25%. Children 7 and under stay free in parent's room. AE, DC, MC, V. Free parking. Bus: Boa Viagem. **Amenities:** Restaurant; bar; outdoor pool; sauna; exercise room; business center; room service; laundry; nonsmoking rooms. *In room:* A/C, TV, dataport, minibar, hair dryer, safe.

Recife Palace Hotel 🐾🐾🐾   Size does matter. Recife's top hotel, the Recife Palace offers a prime location across the street from Boa Viagem beach, and the largest rooms in all of Recife. The amenities of a five-star hotel don't hurt. Recent renovations have left rooms looking fabulous: fresh and modern with pleasant lighting, blond-wood furniture, and soft-toned colors. Each room has a bathtub and a partial view (superior room) or full view (deluxe room) of the ocean, but again, it's the spaciousness that most impresses: ample closet space and a desk large enough for two people to work side by side. The suites are even bigger, but aren't worth the extra money.

Av. Boa Viagem 4070, Recife, 51012-000 PE. 📞 **0800/702-8383** or 081/4009-2500. Fax 081/3465-2525. www.lucsim hoteis.com.br. 295 units. R$260–R$350 (US$130–US$175/£70–£95) superior double; R$310–R$400 (US$155–US$200/£84–£108) deluxe double; R$475–R$600 (US$238–US$300/£128–£162) suite. Check Internet for off-season discounts. Children under 12 stay free in parent's room, over 12 are charged 25% of room rate. AE, MC, V. Bus: Boa Viagem. **Amenities:** 2 restaurants; disco; bar; pool; gym; sauna; tour desk; concierge; car rental; business center; salon; room service; babysitting; laundry; dry cleaning; rooms for those w/limited mobility. *In room:* A/C, TV, dataport, minibar, fridge, hair dryer, safe.

EXPENSIVE

Blue Tree Towers 🐾 *Kids*   This excellent modern hotel is located south of Boa Viagem in Piedade, the adjacent beach neighborhood. All 180 rooms have an ocean view and a private balcony. To seriously splurge, book on of the duplex suites with private swimming pool and sauna. In the low season (Sept to mid-Dec and Mar–June) these can be had for as little as R$335 (US$167/£90). The hotel is right on the beach and offers excellent services such as chairs, umbrellas, towels, and refreshments. Families traveling with children will also appreciate the fabulous swimming pool and sun deck, with ocean view, of course!

Av. Bernardo Vieira de Melo 550, Praia da Piedade, Recife, 54310-001 PE. 📞 **0800/15-0505** or 081/3468-1255. Fax 081/3468-2466. www.bluetree.com.br. 180 units (showers only). R$160–R$240 (US$80–US$120/£43–£65) double;

Recife

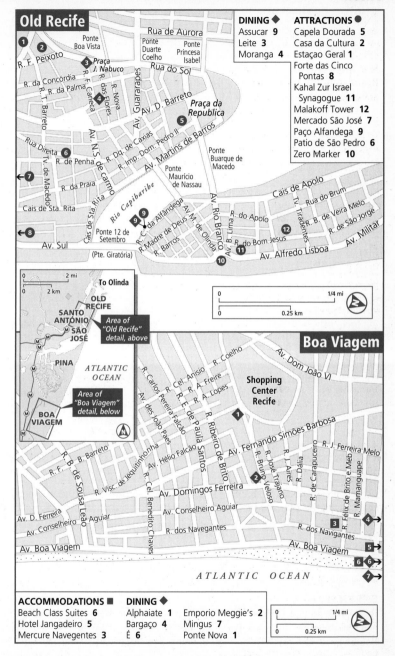

Old Recife

Rua de Aurora

Ponte Boa Vista

Ponte Duarte Coelho

Ponte Princesa Isabel

DINING ◆
Assucar **9**
Leite **3**
Moranga **4**

ATTRACTIONS ●
Capela Dourada **5**
Casa da Cultura **2**
Estaçao Geral **1**
Forte das Cinco Pontas **8**
Kahal Zur Israel Synagogue **11**
Malakoff Tower **12**
Mercado São José **7**
Paço Alfandega **9**
Patio de São Pedro **6**
Zero Marker **10**

Praça J. Nabuco

R. F. Peixoto

R. da Concórdia

R. da Palma

R. T. Barreto

R. F. Caneca

R. Nova

das Flores

Av. Guararapes

Rua do Sol

Av. D. Barreto

Praça da Republica

Rua Direita

Av. N.S. de Carmo

R. Dq. de Caxias

R. Imp. Dom. Pedro II

Av. Martins de Barros

R. de Penha

Tv. de Macêdo

R. da Praia

R. da Carmo

Cais de Sta. Rita

Cais de Sta. Rita

Ponte Maurício de Nassau

Ponte Buarque de Macedo

Rio Capibaribe

R. C. da Alfandega

Av. M. de Olinda

R. Madre de Deus

R. Barros

Av. Rio Branco

R. B. Lima

R. do Apolo

Cais de Apolo

Tv. Tiradentes

Rua do Brum

R. B. de Veira Melo

R. de São Jorge

Av. Militar

Av. Alfredo Lisboa

Av. Sul

Ponte 12 de Setembro

(Pte. Giratória)

R. do Bom Jesus

Map Legend

0 — 2 mi
0 — 2 km

To Olinda

OLD RECIFE

SANTO ANTÔNIO

SÃO JOSÉ

Area of "Old Recife" detail, above

PINA

ATLANTIC OCEAN

Area of "Boa Viagem" detail, below

BOA VIAGEM

0 — 1/4 mi
0 — 0.25 km

Boa Viagem

Av. Dom João VI

R. Coelho

R. Cel. Anisio

R. Carlos Pereira Falcão

R. A. Freire

R. E. de Paula Santos

R. A. Lopes

Av. des João Paes

R. Ribeiro de Brito

Shopping Center Recife

Av. Fernando Simões Barbosa

R. José Traiano

R. Bruno Veloso

R. J. Ferreira Melo

R. Dália

R. J. Aires

R. de Carapuceiro

R. Félix de Brito e Meb

R. Mamanguape

R. F. B. B. Barreto

R. B. de Sousa Leão

R. Visc. de Jequitinhonha

R. Hélio Falcão

R. Cel. Benedito Chaves

Av. Domingos Ferreira

Av. Conselheiro Aguiar

R. dos Navegantes

R. dos Navegantes

Av. D. Ferreira

Av. Conselheiro Leão Aguiar

Av. Boa Viagem

Av. Boa Viagem

ATLANTIC OCEAN

0 — 1/4 mi
0 — 0.25 km

ACCOMMODATIONS ■
Beach Class Suites **6**
Hotel Jangadeiro **5**
Mercure Navegentes **3**

DINING ◆
Alphaiate **1**
Bargaço **4**
É **6**
Emporio Meggie's **2**
Mingus **7**
Ponte Nova **1**

R$335–R$500 (US$167–US$250/£90–£135) suite. Extra person in room add 25%. Children 12 and under stay free in parent's room. AE, DC, MC, V. Paid parking (R$10/US$5/£2.70). Bus: Piedade. **Amenities:** Restaurant; bar; large pool; children's pool; fitness center; sauna; tour desk; car rental; room service; laundry; nonsmoking rooms. *In room:* A/C, TV, dataport, minibar, fridge, hair dryer, safe.

MODERATE

Hotel Jangadeiro ★★ (Value) Overlooking Boa Viagem beach, Hotel Jangadeiro offers the best value for money in this upscale neighborhood. This small, pleasant hotel has been recently renovated and the rooms are spacious and bright. It's worth paying a little bit extra for the oceanview rooms; all come with balconies and offer stunning views of Boa Viagem beach. The standard rooms look out onto the neighboring buildings, or have a partial ocean view but lack the balcony. Bathrooms come with showers only but are spotless and modern.

Av. Boa Viagem 3114, Boa Viagem, Recife, 51020-001 PE. ℂ 081/3465-3544. Fax 081/3466-5786. www.jangadeiro hotel.com.br. 93 units (showers only). R$110–R$190 (US$55–US$95/£30–£51) standard double; R$200–R$280 (US$100–US$140/£54–£76) oceanview double; significant discounts in the low season. Children under 8 stay free in parent's room, over 8 extra bed 25%. AE, MC, V. Free parking. **Amenities:** Restaurant; small rooftop pool; room service; laundry service. *In room:* A/C, TV, dataport, minibar, fridge.

Mercure Navegantes ★★ (Kids) The Mercure is located on a quiet street just 1 block from Boa Viagem beach. What the hotel lacks in charm, it makes up for with the usual high standards of the French hotel group Accor; this apart-hotel may be the best deal around. Hotel apartments are configured either as a one-bedroom or a studio. The one-bedrooms are perfect for families traveling with children—the sofa bed in the living room easily accommodates two people. All rooms come with a balcony, kitchen, dining table, and sitting area. Those on the 13th floor or higher even get an ocean view. The hotel also has two swimming pools, a business center, and free parking. The only drawback is that the bathrooms are on the small side and depending on the rate and conditions, breakfast isn't always included. Internet specials can be as low as R$110 to R$155 (US$55–US$78/£30–£42) for a double studio room, even in high season.

Rua dos Navegants 1706, Boa Viagem, Recife, 51021-040 PE. ℂ 0800/703-7000 or 081/4009-1185. Fax 081/4009-1148. www.accorhotels.com.br. 73 units (showers only). R$135 (US$68/£36) studio double; R$185 (US$93/£50) suite. Extra person in room add 25%. Children 8 and under stay free in parent's room. AE, DC, MC, V. Free parking. Bus: Boa Viagem. **Amenities:** Restaurant; bar; small pool; weight room; room service; laundry; nonsmoking rooms. *In room:* A/C, TV, dataport, fridge, hair dryer, safe.

OLINDA

Olinda's pousadas, located in the city's historic center, provide charming and comfortable accommodations. Staying in a 200-year-old building does mean giving up a few modern conveniences (especially elevators), but in return these pousadas offer personalized, attentive service and beautifully furnished digs in a unique setting.

Note: There are no buses running within Olinda, as it is a small hillside neighborhood. However, all restaurants, accommodations, and attractions are within walking distance from the main bus station.

EXPENSIVE

Hotel 7 Colinas ★★★ (Kids) Set on the grounds of a former sugar plantation, the hotel has beautiful lush gardens and the best leisure area of any hotel in the region. Rooms are divided over a few low-rise buildings and all come with verandas that overlook the garden. Rustic room interiors feature tile floors and dark wood furniture. Even the smaller standard rooms are still very pleasant. The hotel's large outdoor pool is set in the lovely garden, with lots of space for kids to run and play, and there's a

Olinda

pleasant bar and restaurant. It may be hard to tear yourself away to see the sights of Olinda just steps away.

Ladeira de São Francisco 307, Olinda 53020-170 PE. ©/fax **081/3439-6055**. www.hotel7colinas.com.br. 45 units (showers only). R$230–R$270 (US$115–US$73/£62–£73) standard double; R$260–R$360 (US$130–US$180/£70–£97) deluxe double. Extra person add about 25%. Children 5 and under stay free in parent's room, children 6-12 pay 15%. AE, MC, V. Free parking. Bus: Rio Doce. **Amenities:** Restaurant; large outdoor pool; children's pool; laundry. *In room:* A/C, TV, minibar, safe.

Pousada do Amparo ◈◈◈   The most charming place to stay in all of greater Olinda is this concatenation of two 200-year-old colonial buildings in the heart of historic Olinda. Views down the hillside from the sumptuous back garden and pool deck are fabulous. Inside, tile floors, heavy ceiling beams, and lots of dark colonial furniture create a period feel. The addition of light wells and an internal courtyard space have given the building a wonderfully sunlit feel. Rooms come in several configurations; most are quite spacious, and several have verandas. All are furnished with a combination of antiques and modern artwork. The three rooms that face directly onto the street are a bit noisy and better avoided. The best room is the Alto da Sé, on the top floor; it has its own small balcony with a fabulous view, a hammock, and a Jacuzzi tub. *Tip:* The downstairs **Restaurante Flor de Coco** (Tues–Sun 6pm–1am) is one of the better ones in Olinda.

Rua do Amparo 199, Olinda, 53020-170 PE. © **081/3439-1749.** Fax 081/3419-6889. www.pousadadoamparo.com.br. 18 units (showers only). R$240 (US$120/£65) standard double; R$360–R$460 (US$180–US$230/£97–£124) deluxe double. Extra person add about 25%. Children 10 and under stay free in parent's room. V. Street parking. Bus: Rio Doce. **Amenities:** Restaurant; small pool; children's pool; sauna; car rental; laundry. *In room:* A/C, TV, minibar, safe.

MODERATE

Pousada dos Quatro Cantos ✪   A lovely large colonial building, this pousada takes up the entire block, hence the name (*quatro cantos* means "four corners"). The best rooms are the three deluxe rooms that offer a view of the pool or the city. Also very nice are the newly upgraded deluxe superior rooms that have a jetted tub. The best room is the Veranda Suite, a spacious chamber overlooking the garden. The two rooms on the ground floor lack air-conditioning and bathrooms, and they're next to the lobby. An annex across the garden contains five more rooms, which are comfortable but lack character.

Rua Prudente de Morais 441, Carmo, Olinda PE. © **081/3429-0220.** www.pousada4cantos.com.br. 17 units (showers only). Annex room double, no bathroom, no A/C, fan only R$95 (US$47/£26); standard room double R$140 (US$70/£38); deluxe and deluxe superior double R$190–R$250 (US$95–US$113/£51–£68). Seasonal discounts up to 20%. Extra bed add 25%. Children 5 and under stay free in parent's room. MC, V. Street parking. Bus: Boa Viagem. **Amenities:** Small outdoor pool; car rental; laundry. *In room:* A/C, TV, fridge.

INEXPENSIVE

Pousada D'Olinda *Value*   A mere 100 years old—just a baby compared to the other buildings on the square—the Pousada D'Olinda has an excellent location and reasonable prices. The rooms are very simple; don't expect a fancy heritage building as most of the rooms are in the modern annex. However it is hard to beat these prices: R$75 (US$38/£20) for a room with a fan and R$95 (US$48/£26) for one with air-conditioning. The pousada even has a small pool and restaurant, and the staff is helpful with booking transportation and excursions.

Praça João Alfredo/Rua Prudente de Morais 178, Olinda, 53110 PE. ©/fax **081/3493-6011.** www.pousadadolinda. com.br. 18 units, 3 with shared bathroom (showers only). R$75–R$120 (US$38–US$60/£20–£32) double room. Children under 7 stay free in parent's room, over 7 pay R$15 (US$7.50/£4). No credit cards. Street parking. **Amenities:** Restaurant; bar; small pool. *In room:* A/C (in 12 rooms; fan only in 6 rooms), TV, fridge.

3 Where to Dine

CENTRO

Recife's historic downtown is a bustling and fascinating part of the city during business hours. Most of the restaurants in Centro cater to a business and office-lunch crowd and are closed at night and on weekends. The best spot in the evening is in Old Recife around the Rua do Bom Jesus, where most bars serve full meals or excellent appetizers. See "Recife & Olinda After Dark," later in this chapter, for more information.

EXPENSIVE

Leite ✪✪ BRAZILIAN   Leite was founded in 1886, and year after year it gets listed as one of the city's top restaurants. Inside it's an oasis of old-world elegance—a mirrored room decorated with dark wood paneling, the tables set with fine linen and china. It has a large menu with numerous steak dishes including *filet a Dijon,* a grilled steak with mustard sauce and rice with broccoli. Fish dishes include sole in almond sauce and prawns in coconut milk with onions and tomatoes. The kitchen also serves Portuguese dishes such as *bacalhau á moda,* a grilled cod filet with onions, potatoes, olives, and garlic. The most popular dessert is the *cartola*, a fried banana with cheese, sprinkled with sugar and cinnamon.

Praça Joaquim Nabuco 147, Santo Antônio. ℂ **081/3224-7977**. R$26–R$45 (US$13–US$23/£7–£11). DC, MC, V. Sun–Fri lunch only, 11:30am–4pm.

MODERATE

Assucár REGIONAL   We don't often recommend restaurants in shopping malls but then Paço Alfandega is not just any mall. The view from the top-floor dining room is fabulous, and the kitchen serves up modern, regional cuisine with plenty of seafood, grilled fish, and steak dishes. The delicious *couvert* (appetizer plate) features an inventive bean broth cooked with just a dash of cachaça. Main dishes include classic regional fare such as carne-de-sol, grilled fish with banana purée, as well as risottos and chicken. For dessert, Assucár serves a table of sweets—*a mesa de doces*—for only R$10 (US$5/£2.70) per person. The best part of dinner, however, is the panoramic view over the Capibaribe River. It's worth waiting at the bar to get a window table.

Cais da Alfandega 35, Recife Antigo (top floor of the mall). ℂ **081/3419-7582**. Reservations recommended on Fri–Sat evenings. Main courses R$24–R$39 (US$12–US$19/£6.50–£11). AE, DC, MC, V. Mon–Tues noon–10pm; Wed–Sat noon–midnight; Sun noon–6:30pm.

Moranga KILO   Moranga's claim to fame is its excellent stuffed *moranga* (stew served in a pumpkin). Pumpkins can be filled with fish, seafood, palm-heart cream, or *carne de sol*, a tasty dried meat. In addition, the excellent self-service buffet offers at least 10 salads and 15 hot dishes. There's also a great selection of desserts, including *rocambole* (a light rolled cake with chocolate or guava filling) to help you linger a bit over your *cafezinho* before hitting the pavement.

Rua das Flores 129, Centro. ℂ **081/3224-1573**. Buffet R$26 (US$13/£7) per kilo. AE, V. Mon–Fri 11am–3pm.

BOA VIAGEM
EXPENSIVE

Bargaço 𝄞𝄞 SEAFOOD/FISH   A Recife institution, the Bargaço restaurant is *the* place in town for seafood. The restaurant is housed in a beautiful mansion that looks out over the ocean. The menu includes such offerings as grilled fish and garlic-fried shrimp, but we recommend ordering those as an appetizer in order to save room for a *moqueca*. The menu features eight varieties, including lobster, octopus, shrimp, fish, or crab, but it's the Bahian *moqueca* dish that made this restaurant famous. If you can't decide, try the seafood combination *moqueca mixta*. These main courses are big enough for two. Your best bet for dessert is the *cocada*, a typical Bahian sweet made with sugar, more sugar, and coconut.

Av. Boa Viagem 670, Boa Viagem. ℂ **081/3465-1847**. On weekends reservations recommended. R$39–R$68 (US$19–US$34/£11–£18), most dishes serve 2 people. DC, MC, V. Sun–Thurs noon–midnight; Fri–Sat noon–1am. Bus: Boa Viagem.

É 𝄞𝄞 CONTEMPORARY   Recife's best restaurant of the year takes you on a culinary tour of some interesting cuisines. Chef Douglas van der Ley loves to play with techniques and flavors from all across the world, and his dishes reveal touches of Vietnamese, Thai, Japanese, Italian, and French cuisine. Some interesting dishes you will find on the menu include *Fillet Ban Chá* (grilled beef medallions served on pasta with a Dijon, miso, and green tea sauce) and the Thai prawns (deep-fried and served with a sweet-and-sour honey sauce). É offers a surprising variety of dishes with foie gras. In fact, the restaurant is the third-largest consumer of the product in Brazil! Try the *Filet* *do Chef,* a beef medallion served with slices of foie gras and a fig compôte on pasta, or the *Filet ao patê de foie,* grilled beef with a foie gras pâté and port sauce, served with a cheese petit gâteau and sweet potato. The kitchen is open late, until 1:30am.

Rua do Atlântico 147, Boa Viagem. (C) 081/3325-9323. www.egastronomia.com.br. On weekends reservations recommended. R$36–R$52 (US$18–US$26/£10–£14). AE, DC, MC. Tues–Sat 8pm-1:30am. Bus: Boa Viagem.

Mingus 🐦🐦 CONTEMPORARY   Almost across the street from É is another popular new restaurant, Mingus. Named in honor of jazz bassist and composer Charles Mingus, the restaurant is beautifully decorated with photos and musical instruments. However, it is the harmony in the kitchen that has people raving about this place. Mingus serves up excellent contemporary cuisine, combining honest ingredients with just enough spice to make it interesting without stealing the show. Try the grilled lamb with shiitake mushrooms and baby potatoes, or the grilled partridge with linguine au poivre. Seafood lovers will also be pleased with dishes such as the grilled fish in cashew crust with leek risotto or the salmon with a ham and melon risotto. Desserts are deliciously decadent and worth lingering over . . . especially the warm apple compôte with a cashew crust and vanilla ice cream or the warm chocolate biscuit with nuts and chocolate mousse topped with rich crème anglaise and red fruit.

Rua do Atlântico 102, Boa Viagem. (C) 081/3465-4000. www.mingus.com.br. Reservations recommended in the evening. R$29–R$48 (US$15–US$24/£8–£13). DC, MC, V. Sun–Mon noon–3:30pm; Tues–Sat noon–3:30pm and 7pm–midnight. Bus: Boa Viagem.

Ponte Nova 🐦🐦 CONTEMPORARY   Considering how many restaurants fail after the first year, it is wonderful to not only see this newcomer doing well but aspiring to new heights. Not only is Ponte Nova one of the best restaurants in town, its young chef Joca Pontes has just been voted Best Chef of Recife in 2007 by *Veja Magazine.* Of course it helps to have a good-looking restaurant; the interior combines warm wood tones with cool marble floors, plus tables with crepe-lined tablecloths and fresh flower arrangements. The menu has some French influences but is mostly a regional cuisine that can be best described as "contemporary." Start your meal with the *pasteis de camarão* (shrimp dumplings) or the more elaborate *mini-rotoloni,* grilled eggplant stuffed with a mixture of ricotta, sun-dried tomatoes, and herbs. Mains include *Camurim,* a grilled fish marinated in lemon grass and herbs. The chef's baby, however, is the lamb, which is marinated for 4 hours in rosemary and honey before being grilled and served with an apricot risotto. Desserts include a traditional crème brûlée served with a lime zest. More creative is the flambéed pear in cachaça, or the rich strawberry cappuccino—strawberries topped with vanilla ice cream and a layer of mascarpone, finished with a crumble.

Rua Bruno Veloso 528. Boa Viagem. (C) 081/3327-7226. Reservations recommended in the evening. R$23–R$38 (US$12–US$19/£6–£10). AE, DC, MC, V. Mon–Sat 7:30pm–midnight; Fri noon–4pm. Taxi recommended.

MODERATE

Alphaiate 🐦🐦 STEAK   The Alphaiate is the perfect spot to take a break from eating fish and seafood. Located in Boa Viagem, the restaurant faces the ocean and offers indoor as well as covered alfresco dining. Even if you don't feel like a full meal, the Alphaiate is great for just a beer and snack. The beer list includes over 20 options, and a variety of the steaks come in appetizer format. Also good for nibbling are the pork spareribs, served with farofa and vinaigrette sauce. Main courses will often feed two people. The most popular dish is the picanha steak for two, served with a side of

> ### (*Finds*) Try a Tapioca Pancake
>
> Thursday through Sunday from 2 to 10pm, there's a small market at the Praça da Boa Viagem. Though the crafts are nothing special, the **tapioca pancakes** are worth writing home about. These small pancakes are made from scratch with tapioca flour; it's kind of fun to watch the women pour the tiny tapioca grains on the skillet and see a pancake slowly take form. Served either sweet (with coconut and condensed milk) or savory (with cheese), these are mighty addictive little treats.

farofa, rice, and beans. Individual plates include the minifilet with Madeira sauce, served with a side of Alfredo pasta.

Rua Artur Muniz 82, Boa Viagem. (*C*) **081/3465-7588.** R$16–R$46 (US$8–US$23/£4.50–£13), more expensive dishes serve 2 people. DC, MC, V. Sun–Wed 11am–midnight; Thurs 11am–1am; Fri–Sat 11am–2am. Bus: Boa Viagem.

INEXPENSIVE
Empório Meggies (★ *Finds*) CAFE/DELI   This fabulous deli, bakery, wine store, and cheese shop is the perfect place for a quick snack, a glass of wine, or sipping an espresso. The deli also offers a great selection of items to go. True, the modern glass-and-concrete building is not exactly cozy, but with its great food and excellent hours it is quickly becoming a favorite neighborhood pit stop.

Rua Domingos Ferreira 3814, Boa Viagem. (*C*) **081/3326-9587.** R$20 (US$10/£5.50) and under. MC, V. Mon–Wed and Sat 9am–8pm; Thurs–Fri 9am–midnight; Sun 9am–3pm. Bus: Boa Viagem.

OLINDA
Who'd-a-thought artists could cook? Long known as an artistic center, Olinda has recently begun to establish itself as the best place for fine dining in Recife.

EXPENSIVE
Kwetu (★★★ *Finds*) FRENCH   Don't discard this little restaurant just because it isn't on the hillside. Located in a lovely house by the water, Kwetu offers an intimate indoor setting or alfresco dining in the garden looking out over the ocean. Belgian owner and chef Brigitte Anckaert knows her way around the kitchen. To start off, order one of the fresh salads such as the *Breton* with greens, cheese, and seafood, or the *coquille* with fish and prawns in white-wine au gratin. Kwetu is probably one of the few places in Recife where you can order rabbit stew, the *Lapin a Catalana*, with white wine, tomatoes, herbs, and red peppers. Also worthwhile is the *frango archiduc*, chicken with fresh mushrooms, parsley, and lime. The restaurant offers paella for two (R$40/US$17/£8.50) on Sunday, and mussels on Thursday. A plate of the bivalves, steamed in white wine and herbs, will set you back R$30 (US$15/£8). For dessert there's the *très* French Dame Blanche, a large glass of vanilla ice cream with hot chocolate sauce.

Rua Manoel Borba 338, just behind the Praça do Jacaré, Olinda. (*C*) **081/3439-8867.** R$26–R$38 (US$13–US$19/£7–£10). DC, MC, V. Mon and Wed–Thurs 6pm–midnight; Fri–Sat noon–4pm and 6:30pm–midnight; Sun noon–9pm. Taxi recommended.

Mourisco (★) BRAZILIAN   Located in one of the oldest residences in Olinda, Mourisco has been a restaurant for the last 40 years. The best tables are in the front room, overlooking the pleasant João Alfredo Square. The menu includes traditional Brazilian dishes like *galinha cabidela* or *galinha molho pardo*. Both terms are used to describe chicken cooked in its own blood to make a rich sauce. Give it a try if you dare—it's absolutely delicious. Other menu choices include *camarão Mourisco,* shrimp with white cream sauce and corn, or the catch of the day cooked in a rich coconut sauce until it is soft enough to melt in your mouth.

Praça Cons. João Alfredo 7, Carmo, Olinda. ⓒ 081/3429-1390. R$19–R$45 (US$9.50–US$23/£5–£12). AE, MC, V. Daily noon–3pm and 7pm–midnight.

MODERATE

Don Francisco ★★★ *Finds* ITALIAN   This little restaurant serves up some of the best Italian food in town. Owner and chef Francesco Caretta takes care of the kitchen, and his wife Norma looks after the dining room and welcomes guests into the cozy restaurant. Many of the herbs and vegetables come from their organic garden. For starters there is the homemade minestrone soup, a rich and satisfying blend of 20 vegetables. Another delicious appetizer is the grilled eggplant with fresh ricotta and basil, served with homemade bread. The pastas are made from scratch by Francesco and served with simple sauces. You choose whether you prefer the tagliatelle, ravioli, or rondelle and pick one of the sauces such as the organic pesto, fungi mushrooms, Gorgonzola, or tomato with basil and ricotta. The menu always includes a traditional and a vegetarian lasagna. All desserts, except for the ice cream, are also made in Don Francisco's kitchen. He is particularly proud of the tiramisu, which is made with fresh mascarpone, and the apple pie with cinnamon ice cream. It's impossible to resist when he insists.

Rua Prudente de Moraes 358, Olinda. ⓒ 081/3429-3852. R$15–R$26 (US$7.50–US$13/£4–£7). V. Mon–Fri noon–3pm and 7–11pm; Sat 7pm–midnight.

Goya ★★ BRAZILIAN/SEAFOOD   Although there are a variety of outstanding restaurants on the Rua do Amparo, Goya seems to take the regional cuisine one inventive step further. The menu showcases the best seafood in combination with tropical fruits and regional ingredients. One of the most creative dishes is the *Lagosta ao Goya,* pieces of lobster flambéed in cachaça and served with pineapple and mashed *maca-xeira* (manioc). The prawn salad with pineapple, mango, and melon is served in a pineapple and topped with a cashew dressing. The atmosphere is bustling and pleasant, and the service is knowledgeable and friendly.

Rua do Amparo 157, Olinda. ⓒ 081/3439-4875. Reservations accepted. Main courses R$18–R$36 (US$9–US$18/£5–£10). AE, DC, MC, V. Mon noon–5pm and 6pm–midnight; Wed–Sat 6pm–midnight; Sun noon–5pm. Bus: Rio Doce.

Oficina do Sabor ★★★ BRAZILIAN   You can expect the Oficina to be busy—this restaurant's well-deserved reputation has spread far beyond Olinda. The most popular dishes are the *Jerimums,* a local variety of pumpkin. Bestsellers include the *Jerimum recheado com camarão ao maracuja* (pumpkin filled with prawn and passion-fruit sauce). Another popular dish is the *Jerimum recheado com lagosta ao coco* (pumpkin filled with lobster in coconut milk). Inside, the Oficina is a beautifully decorated space in a lovely restored building—but that's just icing on the pumpkin. The patio offers gorgeous views of Olinda.

Rua do Amparo 335, Olinda. ⓒ 081/3429-3331. www.oficinadosabor.com.br. Reservations recommended for weekends. R$34–R$60 (US$17–US$30/£9–£16), most dishes serve 2. AE, DC, MC, V. Tues–Fri noon–4pm and 6pm–midnight; Sat noon–1am; Sun noon–5pm.

INEXPENSIVE

Creperia *Value* CREPES   Set in a lovely house just across from the church on the Praça João Alfredo, the Creperia serves up—surprise, surprise—crepes. The menu offers a variety of savory and sweet crepes. Perfect for a quick lunch or snack, try the Ilha de Marajó, made with melted mozzarella cheese, arugula, and sun-dried tomatoes. The prawns with curry sauce are also tasty. For a sweet treat or dessert, there's the Cartola, a crepe filled with cheese, banana, and cinnamon or coconut and chocolate sauce. In addition to crepes, the kitchen serves up salads and fruit juices. The restaurant has a great patio.

Praça João Alfredo 168, Carmo, Olinda. ℂ **081/3429-2935.** Everything under R$15 (US$6.25/£3). DC, MC, V. Tues–Sun 11am–11pm.

4 Exploring Recife & Olinda

The allure of both Olinda and Recife lies not so much in particular sights as in the urban fabric. In Olinda, while no particular church merits a special trip, the ensemble of 300- and 400-year-old architecture makes for a memorable stroll. If your time is limited, head first for Olinda, making sure to go up to the Igreja da Sé for the best views.

Downtown Recife has a number of interesting monuments and buildings to see; the Zero Marker makes a fine starting point. From there it's a nice stroll through restored Old Recife (make sure to walk down Rua do Bom Jesus and take a peek from the Malakoff Tower). Then cross the bridge to Santo Antônio; the commercial heart of Recife is as packed with vendors and food stands as any Asian market. Staying in Boa Viagem makes it easy to fit in a morning swim and stroll on the beach. If you need more sand time than that, remember that small, laid-back Porto de Galinhas boasts one of the finest beaches in the Northeast (see "A Side Trip to Porto de Galinhas," later in this chapter).

Moments **The Passion Play at Nova Jerusalem**

If you're in the Recife area in the 10 days leading up to Easter, don't miss the **passion play in Nova Jerusalem, Fazenda Nova** ⊛⊛. More than 500 actors and extras assemble on nine different stages to act out the last days in the life of Christ. The specially built theater is massive—the size of 12 football fields, with tall towers and thick walls resembling old Jerusalem. The play's been going since 1968, but in recent years it's become much more popular; well-known actors and actresses now take the coveted roles of Jesus, Mary, Pontius Pilate, and Judas. What makes it worth the trip to Fazenda Nova, 190km (118 miles) from Recife, is the street fair and festival that accompanies the play. Performances start on the Saturday of the week before Easter. Good Friday and Hallelujah Saturday (the day before Easter) are the most popular nights. Up to 8,000 people make the trip out to Nova Jerusalem each night. Tickets cost R$30 to R$40 (US$15–US$20/£8–£11). Performances start at 6pm and finish at 9pm. For up-to-date info on actors and starts, see the play website: www.novajerusalem.com.br. For day tours, contact **Luck Viagens** (ℂ **081/3302-6222;** www.luckviagens.com.br; R$75/US$37/£20 for tour and ticket), or **Caravana Turismo** (ℂ **081/3221-1623;** R$50/US$25/£14 for day trip plus ticket).

HIGHLIGHTS OF OLINDA

The only way to truly explore Olinda is by hitting the cobblestones and setting off on foot. It's hard to get lost in the historic part of the city. The hilltop **Igreja da Sé** dominates the city to the west, while the ocean is always visible to the east; Recife's skyline stands out to the south. Most attractions are open daily; churches usually open from 8am to 5pm, with a 2-hour closure for lunch from noon to 2pm. Sunday and Monday are pretty quiet. If you like it more lively and bustling, visit on Friday and Saturday.

Buses from Recife will drop you off at the Praça do Carmo, dominated by the lovely **N.S. do Carmo church** ✸. This more-than-400-year-old church has finally undergone a much-needed renovation. It's worth peeking in to see the huge ornate jacaranda-wood altar. The large leafy square on the front side of the church is known as **Praça da Abolição (abolition square)** because of the statues of Princess Isabel, who was responsible for abolishing slavery in 1888. Follow Avenida da Liberdade, and you'll pass by the 1590 Church of **São Pedro Apostolo** before turning right and walking up the steep **Ladeira da Sé** to the **Igreja da Sé** ✸.

Alternatively, from N.S. do Carmo you can swing to your right on the Rua Sá Francisco, which leads to the **Convento de São Francisco** ✸✸ (R$1/US40¢/£.20; closed Sat afternoon and all day Sun). Built in 1577, this was the first Franciscan monastery in Brazil. It's worth ducking in to see the life history of Jesus in the N.S. das Neves, done in Portuguese blue tile.

From the Convento São Francisco, the Travessia São Francisco leads up to the Ladeira de Sé and the **Igreja da Sé.** Originally built in 1537, this now rather austere church is more interesting for what it's suffered over the years than anything else. A series of photographs and drawings just inside the main door shows the church's various incarnations.

The square in front of the Igreja da Sé provides the best view in town. You see the red-tiled roofs and church towers of Olinda, and thick stands of tropical trees set against the sparkling blue ocean below. Farther south you get great views of Recife's skyline all the way to Boa Viagem. It's a good place to ponder Recife, Olinda, and the nations that made them. The Portuguese, coming from cities like Lisbon, founded Olinda on a hilltop. The Dutch, with models like Amsterdam in mind, founded Recife on a bit of mudflat by the river mouth. The Dutch choice proved the more practical. But the Portuguese city is far more beautiful.

The square in front of the Igreja da Sé has a great crafts market and excellent food stalls selling fresh tapioca pancakes and shots of flavored cachaça. Nearby, at Rua Bispo Coutinho 726, you'll find the **Museu de Arte Sacra de Pernambuco** (Tues–Fri

---

Tips Give Your Guide a Test Drive

In most of the squares, especially at the Praça do Carmo, young guides will offer their services for a fee (usually around R$25/US$13/£7). Many are former street children trained by the city as tour guides. Some are good; some are hopeless. If you're interested, test out your prospective guide, if only to make sure you can understand his English. Hiring a tour guide protects you from being hassled by other guides and vendors. If you're lucky, they may also show you the city's nooks and crannies.

Tips **Olinda, City of Artists**

Every year, the Olinda hosts a large open house event, called Olinda, Arte em Toda Parte (Olinda, Art Everywhere). During the last 10 days of November, the city's artists open their studio doors to visitors and a number of special events, exhibits, and cultural presentations take place. For more information check the website www.olindaarteemtodaparte.com.br or stop by the tourist information center at the Largo do Amparo on Rua do Bonsucesso 183 (© 081/3439-9434), open daily from 9am to 6pm.

9am–12:45pm). It's not one of the great ones; if you saw the sacred art museums in Salvador or São Paulo, skip this one.

The very steep **Ladeira da Misericordia** leads down toward the **Rua do Amparo** ☆☆. This is one of Olinda's prettiest streets, featuring small, brightly colored colonial houses packed with galleries, restaurants, and shops. The **Largo do Amparo** ☆ has the feel of a little Mexican square. On the square itself, **N.S. do Amparo** (built 1613) features two bell towers (a sign they could afford to pay the bell-tower tax back in the old days) on the outside, and some nice tiles and gold work inside. Farther up the hillside, **N.S. do Rosario dos Pretos** and **São João Batista** have nothing inside worth hoofing it up the hill.

Leaving the square and following Rua Amparo until it becomes **Rua Treze de Maio,** you come to the **Mamulengo Puppet Museum** ☆ (© 081/3429-6214; Tues–Fri 10am–5pm, Sat–Sun 11am–5pm; free admission). The small three-floor museum assembles puppets used in Northeastern folk drama. Puppet characters come in a wide variety of shapes and sizes. Some have hidden levers that cause them to stick out their tongues (or other, ruder appendages). Almost next door, the **Museu de Arte Contemporânea de Pernambuco (Museum of Contemporary Art; © 081/3429-2587)** has next to nothing inside.

Farther down, following **Rua São Bento** leads to the **Mosteiro de São Bento.** Built in 1582, this monastery is still home to 27 Benedictine monks, and only the church is open to the public.

From the monastery, **Rua XV de Novembro** leads down to the **Largo do Varadouro;** the large crafts market **Mercado Eufrasio Barbosa** is worth a visit. Those returning to Recife can take a bus from this square instead of returning to the Praça do Carmo.

HIGHLIGHTS OF RECIFE

The place to start a tour of Recife is at the **Zero Marker** in the heart of Old Recife. Gaze out toward the ocean from here, and about 90m (300 ft.) offshore you'll see the long low reef from which the city draws its name. On the reef sits a strange tall green pillar capped with something that could charitably be said to resemble a tulip. This more than slightly phallic monument is the work of an eccentric ceramics artist named **Francisco Brennand.** If you're interested in seeing more, he has a large estate on the far edge of town (**Oficina Cerâmica Francisco Brennand,** Avenida Cachangá, Varzea; © 081/3271-2466; Mon–Fri 8am–6pm) brimming with weird and wonderful ceramic creations, many of them long, hard, and potent-looking (see attractions below).

A block back from the Zero Marker is the **Rua do Bom Jesus.** The street and this whole island are the oldest part of Recife, founded not by the Portuguese but by the

Dutch. The reconstructed **Kahal Zur Synagogue,** rebuilt on the foundations of the first synagogue in the Americas, is worth a visit. On weekends this part of the city is a fun area to visit for free outdoor concerts. The center of the nocturnal activity is the **Praça Artur Oscar.** At the north end of the square the tall thing like a Norman castle is the **Malakoff Tower,** a former astrological observatory now open as a public viewing platform.

From here north all the way to Forte Brum, Old Recife reverts from antique to just plain old—run-down and a little slummy. The fort at the end of the 5-block walk isn't special enough to warrant the trip, so head back to **Avenida Rio Branco,** and cross the Buarge de Macedo bridge to **Santo Antônio.**

This area, too, was the work of the Dutch. In the heyday of the Dutch colony Santo Antônio was called Mauritsopolis, after the founder and ruler, Enlightenment prince Maurits van Nassau. The large green neoclassical square almost at the foot of the bridge was once Nassau's private estate, but is now the **Praça da República** ★. It's one of Recife's most graceful public areas.

Just behind the Beaux Arts **Palácio da Justiça** on Rua do Imperador Dom Pedro II, you pass by the **Capela Dourada** (see below). Then, turning right on Rua Primeiro do Março, you come to a big blue-and-white Beaux Arts confection of a building that has, since the 1880s, been home to the city's premier paper, the *Diário de Pernambuco.* Across the street is the **Praça da Independencia,** a good place to catch a bus, but of no interest otherwise.

Crossing Primeiro do Marco and sneaking south through the fun maze of narrow streets (parallel to but not on Av. Dantas Barreto) you will come—provided you find **Rua do Fogo** on the far side of **Avenida N.S. do Carmo**—to the **Pátio de São Pedro,** a popular outdoor music venue.

The **Concatedral de São Pedro de Clérigos** is a classic example of Portuguese colonial baroque. Nice as it is, however, it's the patio that makes the spot special. This broad cobblestone square is enclosed by dozens of small, restored shops, all gaily painted in bright pinks, blues, and greens.

Crossing Avenida Dantas Barreto from here you would come to the **N.S. do Carmo Basilica,** which would be worth a quick look before continuing for a few more blocks to the **Casa da Cultura** (see below) and the **Estação Geral.**

As it turns out, however, the little shops surrounding the patio are a great place to grab a chopp (cold Brazilian draft) and have a seat at—what else?—a patio table. Toward the end of the day the place fills up with the one-for-the-road crowd; there's often a band. This is a good place to cease exploring for a while.

Capela Dourada ★   The Golden Chapel is aptly named. The altar is a two-story arch of jacaranda and cedar, all gilt with gold. Christ hangs on a golden cross with gold and silver rays shining out behind his head. The chapel is part of a Franciscan complex that includes a small sacred art museum with a few nice pieces of gold and silver work. Also worth a look is the **Church of the Ordem Terceiro de São Francisco.** One wall of this church is decorated with a rather disturbing oil painting showing Franciscan monks getting crucified. Someone else obviously took a dislike to it; the face of every soldier has been scraped away. Don't miss the **church archives** behind the altar. The cabinets are 3 meters (12 feet) high and made of solid jacaranda—gorgeous craftsmanship.

Rua do Imperador Dom Pedro II 206, Santo Antônio. ✆ 081/3224-0530. Admission R$2 (US$1/£.50) adults, free for children 7 and under. Mon–Fri 8–11:30am and 2–5pm; Sat 8–11:30am. Bus: Conde da Boa Vista.

Casa da Cultura ☆   This former penitentiary has only barely changed since its prison days; the cells, still with their original numbers, are now occupied by souvenir shops. You'll find a good selection of local crafts: ceramics, woodcarvings, leather sandals, lace, and clothing. Prices are reasonable, but a bit of bargaining is expected. There's still more than frisson of dread as you climb the heavy iron catwalks and duck through a thick doorway into one of the old cells. Good thing there's nothing more frightening than handicrafts inside.

Rua Floriano Peixoto, Santo Antônio. ℭ 081/3224-2850. Mon–Sat 9am–6pm; Sun 10am–5pm. Bus: Conde de Boa Vista.

Centro Cultural Judaico de Pernambuco/Kahal Zur Israel Synagogue ☆☆
This reconstructed synagogue is built on the foundations of the original Kahal Zur Israel synagogue, built in the 1640s when Recife was ruled by religiously tolerant Holland. With the end of Dutch rule in 1654 many of Recife's Jews fled to New Amsterdam (later New York), and the synagogue was confiscated and sold. Over the centuries, evidence of the temple all but disappeared. In the late 1990s, traces of the old synagogue were discovered in the form of a *mikve,* or ritual bath. The reconstructed building is not a replica of the original but more a monument that honors the Jewish community in Recife. The museum tells the history of Jews in Recife. On the ground floor you can see the remains of the 17th-century temple. The second floor houses the actual synagogue; and if you aren't familiar with Jewish traditions, a guide will show you around. The third floor has a TV lounge where staff will play an excellent documentary (with English subtitles) on the history of the Jews in Recife and the rebuilding of the synagogue. Expect to spend an hour.

Rua do Bom Jesus 197, Bairro do Recife. ℭ 081/3224-2128. Tues–Fri 9am–5pm; Sun 3–7pm. R$4 (US$2/£1). Bus: Conde de Boa Vista.

Forte das Cinco Pontas/City Museum ☆☆   Perhaps the most curious thing about the "Fort of Five Points" is that it only has four. The original Dutch fort built in 1630 had five, but the Portuguese leveled that fort and rebuilt in their traditional four-pointed style. The fort today has been wonderfully restored; you can wander the ramparts at will. Unfortunately, the city has crept out far past this once seaside installation, leaving the fort outflanked by a freeway. The excellent city museum, which takes up two wings of the fort, has two rooms devoted to the Dutch period, including a wealth of maps and drawings of the early colony.

Largo dos Cinco Pontas, Bairro de São José. ℭ 081/3224-8492. Admission R$3 (US$1.50/£.80) adults, R$1.50 (US75¢/£.40) students and seniors, free for children 7 and under. Mon–Fri 9am–6pm; Sat–Sun 1–5pm. Bus: São Jose.

Oficina Cerâmica Francisco Brennand ☆☆   Although somewhat off the beaten track, this ceramics workshop/museum is more than worth the price of admission. The lifelong work of ceramic artist Francisco Brennand is on display at this sprawling

---

⟨Tips⟩ All in the Family

Don't confuse the Oficina Cerâmica Francisco Brennand with the nearby Instituto Ricardo Brennand (Al. Antônio Brennand, Várzea. ℭ 084/2121-0352; Tues–Sun 1–5pm)! This large museum contains mostly European art, such as a large collection of weapons and an exhibit on the 17th-century Dutch occupation of Recife. Out of the two, the ceramics museum is by far the most fascinating.

Tips   **Where to Find the Most Spectacular Views**

No one should miss the view from the front steps of the **Igreja da Sé** in Olinda. Look out over the red-tile roofs and church towers of the old Portuguese city, the white sand, and bright blue of beach and sea. In Old Recife it's worth taking the elevator to the top of the restored **Malakoff Tower,** an old astronomical observatory on Praça Artur Oscar. It's only four stories high, but the view of the low-rise old city is still good. Open Tuesday through Sunday from 3 to 8pm; free admission.

---

estate/workshop. Although famous for some notorious giant phallic sculptures, his collection is so much more and includes thousands of sculptures, tiles, and pieces of ceramic art, as well as drawings. His work is beautifully displayed in several buildings as well as various outdoor settings. The Burle Marx garden was designed by the landscape artist himself and decorated with Brennand statues.

Propriedade Santos Cosme e Damião s/n, Várzea. (℃ 81/3271-2466. www.brennand.com.br. Admission R$4 (US$2/£1). Mon–Fri 8am–5pm. Taxi recommended.

ESPECIALLY FOR KIDS

Veneza Water Park *Kids*   Just 10km (6¼ miles) north of Olinda, the Veneza Water Park is a great place to frolic. There are slides, pools, a wave pool, water volleyball, Jacuzzis, and many other types of aquatic entertainment. Special family and group rates apply.

Praia Maria Farinha. (℃ 081/3436-6363 or 081/3436-8845. www.venezawaterpark.com.br. Individual ticket R$39 (US$20/£11) adult, child 1–1.4m (3–4½ ft.) tall R$29 (US$15/£8), free for children under 1m (3 ft.). Daily 9–5pm. Bus: to Maria Farinha beach. Catch bus from Terminal Av. Dantas Barreto across from N.S. do Carmo church. A taxi from Olinda would cost approximately R$18–R$25 (US$9–US$13/£5–£7).

ORGANIZED TOURS

BOAT TOURS   Recife's location on a series of islands makes a boat tour a good way to see the town. **Catamaran Tours** (℃ **081/3424-2845** or 081/3424-8930; www.catamarantours.com.br) offers sightseeing tours on broad, comfortable catamarans. Historic tours of 1½ hours show the old city. Full-day tours head up the coast to visit Fort Orange and the beaches of Itamaracá. The city tour costs R$22 to R$30 (US$11–US$15/£6–£8); the 6-hour Itamaracá tour costs R$35 (US$18/£9.50). Children ages 6 to 10 pay half price. Tours depart from Avenida Sul, 50m (164 ft.) past the Forte Cinco Pontas. Exact departure times depend on the tide. Call ahead to confirm.

BUS TOURS   **Luck Viagens** (℃ **081/3464-4800;** www.luckviagens.com.br) offers a range of bus tours. There's a 4-hour city tour that shows the highlights of Recife and Olinda (R$30/US$15/£8). There's also a full-day tour to Itamaracá island, R$75 (US$38/£28), where the Dutch built Fort Orange in 1631, and day trips to Porto de Galinhas for the best beaches and snorkeling in the area, R$65 (US$33/£18).

OUTDOOR ACTIVITIES

Wreck divers will be in heaven; at least 15 wrecks are diveable and within easy reach. For excursions contact **Projeto Mar,** Rua Bernardino Pessoa 410, Boa Viagem (℃ **081/3326-0162;** www.projetomar.com.br). Two dives including all the gear cost R$130 (US$65/£35); a non-diving companion pays R$30 (US$15/£8).

5 Shopping in Recife & Olinda

In Recife's downtown neighborhood of Santo Antônio, the streets around the **Pátio São Pedro** and in between **Avenida N.S. do Carmo** and **Rua Primeiro de Março** are all jampacked with little shops. Some of the alleys are so narrow that they resemble Asian street markets. The best time to explore is weekdays during office hours; in the evening this part of town is deserted. Larger, more fashionable stores are located just on the other side of the Duarte Coelho Bridge on **Avenida Conde da Boa Vista.** There are large modern malls located out in Boa Viagem as well as the new Paço Alfandega, the restored 18th-century Customs hall in Old Recife.

Olinda's historic downtown also offers prime shopping: Two markets sell excellent souvenirs (see below), and you will find many more galleries and interesting shops once you start to explore the winding streets.

GIFTS & SOUVENIRS   In Olinda there are two excellent markets for local handicrafts. **Mercado Eufrasio Barbosa** (also called Mercado Varadouro) is located in the former Customs house at Sigismundo Gonçalves s/n (© **081/3439-1415**). Open Monday through Saturday from 9am to 6pm, this market has great souvenirs at reasonable prices. Up the hill close to the Praça João Alfredo is the **Mercado Ribeira,** Bernardo Vieira de Melo s/n (© **081/3439-2964**), which is open daily from 9am to 6pm. The merchants there specialize in religious arts, paintings, woodcarvings, and regional crafts.

Olinda is jampacked with studios and ateliers that are open to the public. If you like colorful artwork, visit **Sergio Vilanova's** studio on the Rua do Amparo 224 (© **081/3439-7629**). His work is all in the *Naïf* style, using lots of bold and bright colors. Artist **Simone Simonek's** work is much more subtle; Rua Prudente de Morais 256 (© **081/3439-8561**). She works in water colors and *nanquim* (ink on paper). Her hand-painted shirts, tablecloths, and other textiles are lovely and affordable. More expensive but worth checking out is the **Estação Quatro Cantos,** Rua Bernardo Vieira de Melo 134 (© **081/3429-7575**).

In Recife, a great shop with above-average souvenirs is **Paranambuco,** Rua do Bom Jesus 215 (© **081/3424-1689**). The best spot for picking up local crafts is in the **Casa**

Tips The Ultimate Craft Market

A 2-hour drive inland from Recife, Caruaru is famous for its artisans and craft market. Over 40,000 people a week travel to this interior town to shop for souvenirs. Local artists specialize in colorful clay figurines that represent elements from everyday life. Luck Viagens (© **081/3464-4800**; www.luckviagens.com.br) offers tours twice a week on Thursday and Saturday costing R$70 (US$35/£9.50) per person, including lunch. Children under 8 pay half. The tour includes a visit to the market and a number of the ateliers. The tour also stops in Nova Jerusalem for lunch and a visit to the huge outdoor stage where the Passion Play takes place every Easter. Caruaru is also famous for throwing one of the best *Festa Juninas* in the country. Held in June, it's a combination of a harvest festival, a tribute to Saint John (São João), and a big forró party. Caruaru is one big Festa Junina with bonfires, group dances, games, and a lot of forró. If you're here in June, check with Luck Viagens for evening tours to Caruaru.

da Cultura (see above), Rua Floriano Peixoto s/n, next to the train station (© 081/ 3224-2850). This former jail has been converted into a large handicrafts market, with the former cells now occupied by dozens of souvenir shops. Those who are staying in Boa Viagem can visit the large crafts market on the Praça Boa Viagem; Monday through Friday 3 to 11pm and 8am to 11pm on weekends.

MALLS & SHOPPING CENTERS   Shopping Center Recife, Rua Padre Carapuceiro 777, Boa Viagem (© 081/3464-6123; www.shopping-recife.com.br), is a modern mall; all buses heading downtown stop here. Farther along the beach where Boa Viagem becomes Piedade there's another pleasant mall, **Shopping Center Guararapes,** Av. Barreto Menezes 800, Piedade (© 081/3464-2211; www.shopping-guararapes.com.br). The most beautiful mall is the **Shopping Paço Alfandega,** Cais da Alfandega 35, Recife Antigo (© 081/3419-7500). Housed in the restored 18th-century Customs building, this is one of the city's prime shopping destinations. The bookstore **Livraria da Cultura** has an above-average selection of English-language books. Malls are open Monday through Friday from 10am to 10pm and Saturday from 10am to 8pm.

MARKETS   A bustling fruit-and-vegetable market in a lovely old iron and glass building, the **Mercado de São José, Praça Dom Vital s/n, Santo Antônio (no phone), is a great place to browse. Vendors sell locally made hammocks, baskets, ceramics, and lace. Hours are Monday through Saturday from 6am to 5:30pm and Sunday from 6am to noon.

6 Recife & Olinda After Dark

THE PERFORMING ARTS

Recife's prime theater venue is the elegant **Teatro Princesa Isabel,** Praça da República s/n (© 081/3224-1020), built in 1850. Just reopened after years of renovations, it's worth checking local listings for events held at this lovely venue.

CLUBS & BARS

Recife's historic downtown has undergone a complete face-lift, becoming a cultural and entertainment district. Activities center around the **Rua do Bom Jesus;** lined with at least 15 bars and restaurants, this is one of the best places in town Thursday through Saturday and Sunday afternoons. Free concerts add to the entertainment, and on Sunday there's a street market.

One of Old Recife's nicest bars is the **Arsenal do Chopp,** Praça Artur Oscar 59, at the corner of Rua do Bom Jesus (© 081/3224-6259). Most tables are spread out over the sidewalk; for a quiet spot grab a table inside. The bar opens daily at 4:30pm. Recife's hottest dance club is **Cuba do Capibaribe,** Shopping Paço Alfandega, Recife Antigo (© 081/3419-7502; www.cubadocapibaribe.com.br). This Cuba-inspired bar serves up a great mojito to the sound of live Latin and salsa music, Thursday through Saturday. Another great venue downtown is the **Patio de São Pedro.** Beautifully restored, this square now hosts a variety of free outdoor music events. On Tuesday, locals gather for the Terça Negra, an event with Afoxé music, a style with heavy African influences. On Saturday, a younger crowd gathers to dance to *maracatu, mangue beat,* and other regional tunes. Events start at 7 or 8pm.

In Boa Viagem the favorite nightspot is **Polo Pina,** a few square blocks around Pina beach and Avenida Herculano Bandeira de Melo. Recently named the best bar in Recife, **Biruta Bar,** Rua Bem-te-Vi, Pina (© 081/3326-5151; www.birutabar.com.br), features a large veranda looking out over the ocean, making it the perfect setting for a special date. On Thursday, Biruta presents blues bands and on Friday there's forró. For more live music head out to the **Uk Pub,** Rua Francisco da Cunha 165, Boa Viagem (© 081/3465-1088). Open Tuesday through Sunday, there is live music (samba, rock, pop) every night except Wednesday. It also boasts a great beer menu with more than 50 specialties. Cover ranges from R$5 to R$15 (US$2.50–US$7.50/£1.35–£4). The best night for dancing at **Boratcho,** Av. Herculano Bandeira 513 (inside Galeria Joana d'Arc) (© 081/3327-1168), is Thursday when DJs play a variety of music, including samba-rock and regional rhythms. **Boteco,** Av. Boa Viagem 1660, Boa Viagem (© 081/3325-1428), is a popular destination almost any night of the week. Serving the best beer in town, the bar is often packed with locals stopping by for an ice-cold chopp. Open daily.

Olinda is not known for its nightlife; most folks settle for wine and conversation over a late-night supper. One of the best spots for a drink or a stroll is the **Alto da Sé.** On weekends (Sun evening especially), locals flock to this prime view spot to grab a drink or some food from the many stalls and just hang out for an impromptu outdoor party. Olinda's cutest hole-in-the-wall spot is **Bodega de Veio,** Rua do Amparo 212 (© 081/3429-0185). It's just a small bar/old-fashioned convenience store where people put their drinks on the counter or sit on the sidewalk. Saturday features live forró. Note that this is not a late-night place; last round is at 11pm. Brand-new is the **Casa Maloca,** Rua Amparo 183 (© 081/3429-7811), an antiques store with a restaurant at the very back, the lovely **Bar Olindita.** Guests can sit at a long bar or funky tables scattered about the room. The best spots are on the patio, looking out toward Recife.

GAY & LESBIAN BARS   **Metropole,** Rua das Ninfas 125, Boa Vista (© 081/3423-0123), is a huge gay club for men with a bar, dance floor, and video room. Regular shows include go-go boys, strippers, and drag queen performances; it's open Friday and Saturday from 10pm until at least 5am. Another popular gay venue is the **SPTZ,** Rua Joaquim Nabuco 534, Graças (© 081/3223-9100). Open Tuesday through Sunday, from 6pm until at least 4am.

7 A Side Trip to Porto de Galinhas ★★★

Porto de Galinhas is one of the nicest beach destinations in all the Northeast. Known for its crystal-clear water, its lovely beaches, and the tidal pools that form in the nearby reefs, the region is a perfect water playground for adults and children. Development has been kept resolutely small-scale. There are no high-rises, mostly small pousadas and low-rise hotels. The town boasts perhaps six streets: enough for a dozen restaurants, a bank, some surf shops, and some beachside bars. Colorful *jangadas* (one-sail fishing rafts) come and go all day, and the beachside restaurants and cafes are packed with people soaking up rays.

ESSENTIALS
GETTING THERE
By Car   Porto de Galinhas is just 70km (43 miles) south of Recife, an hour by car. From Recife take BR-101 south until it connects with the PE-60, then look for the turnoff for the PE-38 that leads to Porto de Galinhas. Exits are well marked but the road has heavy traffic and is in very poor shape. If you are just driving to Porto de Galinhas it's not worth renting a car.

By Bus   Buses to Porto de Galinhas leave daily from 6:30am to 6:30pm every hour on the half-hour from the Avenida Dantas Barreto bus terminal in downtown Recife (across from N.S. do Carmo). Tickets are R$8 (US$4/£2.15) and the drive takes about 2 hours. A number of these buses go through Boa Viagem and all stop at the airport on the way. From Porto de Galinhas to Recife buses depart daily once an hour from 5:40am to 5:40pm.

By Taxi   A taxi from Recife airport or downtown will cost from R$80 to R$120 (US$40–US$60/£21–£34) for up to four people and luggage. The price will depend on your bargaining skills. Don't go on the meter, though. Agree on a price beforehand. Many hotels and pousadas can book a taxi service for you at a reasonable rate.

VISITOR INFORMATION   The **tourist office** is at Rua da Esperança 188 (*©* **081/ 3552-1480;** www.portodegalinhas.com.br). Hours are Monday through Friday from 9am to 5pm, Saturday and Sunday from 9am to 3pm.

GETTING AROUND   A minivan shuttle runs from the village to Pontal do Cupe and back, stopping by request at hotels and pousadas along the way. Departures are more or less half-hourly from the Petrobras station on Rua da Esperança (R$1/ US50¢/£.25).

There are taxi stands *(ponto de taxi)* for dune buggy taxis in the village and halfway down the beach in front of the Armação do Porto hotel. One-way fare is R$15 (US$7.50/£4) from the village to either Cupe or Maracaípi beach. If you're planning to spend time at Maracaípi beach, it's a good idea to set a pickup time with your driver as it can be difficult to find a buggy to return. A full-day rental, including driver and up to four passengers, costs R$110 (US$55/£30). In the unlikely event you can't find a buggy, contact **APCI Buggy** (*©* **081/3552-1930**).

FAST FACTS   Banco do Brasil, Via Porto de Galinhas s/n (*©* **081/3552-1855**), has a 24-hour ATM. The bank is open Monday through Friday from 10am to 4pm. There is also a **Banco 24 Horas** ATM inside the Petrobras Gas Station, open from 7am to 10pm. Internet access is available at **Pé No Mangue,** Rua da Esperança 101, second floor; cost is R$9 (US$4.50/£2.50) per hour.

EXPLORING THE TOWN

The main attraction at Porto de Galinhas is the beach, whether you swim, surf, snorkel, or snooze. **Cupe** beach stretches 4km (2½ miles) north from town; it's wide and warm, punctuated at either end by small coral reefs full of fish. Around the point in the other direction, **Maracaípi** beach regularly hosts national and international surfing competitions. Even better, thanks to a nature reserve backing most of the beach, about the only development on Maracaípi is a few *barracas* selling fruit juice and fresh-steamed crab. And if the beach gets dull, you can take nature hikes, trips to nearby islands, or dive trips to offshore reefs.

BUGGY TOURS   The best way to see the local beaches is to head out in a buggy. The most popular tour is the Ponta-a-Ponta, which takes you to four different beaches from the northern end of Porto de Galinhas to the southern end. A full-day trip costs R$110 (US$55/£30), leaving from your hotel or from Avenida Beira Mar at the main square. Contact the buggy drivers at *©* **081/9192-0280.** You can fit four in a buggy, but you'll likely have more fun with just two or three so that one person doesn't have to sit in the boring passenger seat. Included in the tour is a stop at the mangroves of Pontal do Maracaípe. This protected nature reserve is home to several species of sea horses that live among the roots of the mangroves. Small rafts (R$8/US$4/£2 per person) take up to 10 people on a gentle float through the mangroves. The guide will don a mask and dive into the water looking for sea horses, which he captures in a glass jar. You get a good look at the little critters before they are returned to their natural habitat.

OUTDOOR ACTIVITIES & ADVENTURE SPORTS

The specialist in soft adventure in town is the firm **Pé no Mangue,** Rua da Esperança 101, first floor (② **081/3552-1935** or 081/9211-1450; www.penomangue.com.br), run by a congenial pair of young São Paulo refugees. They have a wide range of outings, all under R$50 (US$25/£14), including guide and transfer.

Tip: Check in with Pé no Mangue upon arrival as many tours depend both on the tide and on having enough participants. Let the staff know what you are interested in, and they can make recommendations and put together a small group.

Their 2½-hour guided **nature hikes** through Atlantic rainforest or low-lying mangrove forest cost R$20 (US$10/£5.50); a 2-hour **kayak tour,** usually timed to coincide with sunset, down a wide slow mangrove-lined river to the sea, is R$30 (US$15/£8); 2-hour **horseback rides** on gentle horses through the rainforest cost R$30 (US$15/£8); a **snorkeling by starlight** trip in the natural pools just offshore costs R$40 (US$20/£11), which includes guide, mask, snorkel, wet suit, and flashlight; several **boat trips,** ranging from a 3-hour *jangada* trip to the less-visited coral reefs off Maracaípi to 4- and 6-hour trips to offshore islands and local beaches, cost R$30 to R$50 (US$15–US$25/£8–£14). One of the most popular destinations is the trip to Ilha de Santo Aleixo and Praia dos Carneiros. Both are to the south of Porto de Galinhas and offer plenty of nice scenery, swimming, and snorkeling.

DIVING   Though most people opt for tide-pool snorkeling (see next entry), there are a number of dive sites in the surrounding area. Contact **Porto Point,** Praça Av. Beira Mar s/n (② **081/3552-1111**), for charters. Expect to pay R$90 to R$150 (US$45–US$75/£24–£41), including gear and two dives. Beginners can do an introductory lesson and dive for R$110 (US$55/£30). No credit cards.

SNORKELING   The coast just off Porto de Galinhas is lined with coral reefs. At low tide they form natural pools that trap hundreds of tropical fishes. With a mask and snorkel you just hop in and check out what's doing. The water is warm year-round (75°F–82°F/24°C–28°C) and the pools are never more than a few meters deep. Most pools are close enough that you could swim out, but another fun way of getting close is by taking a *jangada.* These one-sail fishing rafts are the boat of choice for local fishermen. For R$6 (US$3/£1.50) per person, local sailors will take you out to the best pools, and provide you with a mask, snorkel, and some bread to lure in the fish. Check the tide tables at your hotel for low tide; early morning is best if you want to avoid crowds.

If you want to play in the water by yourself, you can rent a **mask/snorkel** combo for R$10 (US$5/£2.50) per day at **Porto Point,** Av. Beira Mar s/n (② **081/3552-1111**). They also offer tours to the natural pools in the daytime (RS$30/US$15/£8) or at night (R$40/US$20/£11), including equipment and guide.

WHERE TO STAY

Porto de Galinhas is gloriously free of sun-blocking high-rises. Accommodations are mostly in small family-run pousadas and a few larger cabana-style hotels. In recent years, a number of bigger resorts have sprung up, but even these have been kept to a reasonable scale and are located farther from the town. Prices are low, especially considering the high quality of the accommodations. In town, you'll be close to the action—too close perhaps in high season when the streets are packed until the wee hours. Staying a bit farther out will ensure a peaceful night's sleep and access to a quiet stretch of beach. The disadvantage is that it's a R$10-to-R$15 (US$5–US$7.50/£2–£4) taxi or buggy ride every time you come to town. However, most tours will provide pickup and drop-off at your hotel. In high season, particularly on the weekend, reservations for accommodations are required.

EXPENSIVE

Tabajuba 🏖🏖 Owned by the same couple who run the Tabapitanga, the Tabajuba specializes in affordable honeymoon packages or romantic getaways for young couples. The pousada is colorful and playfully decorated in a rustic, tropical beach-house style and set right on the beach. Children under 12 are not allowed. It's a 30-minute stroll to the center of Porto de Galinhas, very romantic on a starlit night. All rooms have the same colorful furnishings and come with air-conditioning and fan. The best rooms are those on the second floor, which have a small balcony and more of a sea view. The entire facility is nonsmoking.

Av. Beira Mar s/n, Porto de Galinhas, PE. ℭ 081/3552-1049. Fax 081/3552-1006. www.tabajuba.com.br. 25 units (showers only). High season R$260 (US$130/£70) double; low season R$160–R$200 (US$80–US$100/£43–£54) double. Extra person add 25%. Only children older than 12 are allowed. AE, MC, V. Free parking. **Amenities:** Restaurant; pool; reading room; beachfront terrace. *In room:* A/C, TV, minibar, phone.

Tabapitanga 🏖🏖🏖 *Kids* A member of the high-end Roteiros de Charme Association, the Tabapitanga offers gorgeous accommodations on the beach just 5km (3 miles) from the village. Rooms are in one- or two-story chalets. All rooms are spacious and decorated with unique, colorful artwork. Furnishings are luxurious; the rooms have king-size beds, large flatscreen TVs, and big bathrooms. Each room also comes with a veranda or deck with patio furniture and a hammock. The least expensive rooms are set in the lovely garden. The newer two-story units offer a view of the ocean but the best units are the *frente mar* rooms with unobstructed views. The hotel has beach service as well as a great pool. A fabulous breakfast is included. Lunch and dinner are optional. The attentive staff is happy to book a variety of reasonably priced tours. The pousada also offers transfers at a reasonable price: R$16 (US$8/£4.30) round-trip Porto de Galinhas or R$90 (US$45/£24) airport service for up to four people.

Praia Pontal do Cupe, Porto de Galinhas, PE. ℭ 081/3552-1037. Fax 081/3552-1037. www.tabapitanga.com.br. 43 units. High season R$450 (US$225/£122) double ocean view, R$300–R$365 (US$150–US$183/£81–£99) double garden or partial ocean view; low season R$360 (US$180/£80) double ocean view, R$240 (US$120/£65) double garden or partial ocean view. No triples. Children 10 and under stay free in parent's room. AE, DC, MC, V. Free parking. **Amenities:** Restaurant; bar; 1 outdoor pool; children's play area; game room; massage room; tour desk; laundry; nonsmoking facility. *In room:* A/C, TV, minibar, fridge, safe.

MODERATE

Pousada Beira Mar 🏖🏖 This pousada is both on the beach *(beira mar)*, and in the heart of Porto de Galinhas. The Swiss owners have further capitalized on the location by putting a large patio with deck chairs and bar service seaside. At high tide you can feel the waves smash into the seawall. The three upstairs deluxe rooms (nos. 10, 11, and 12) have huge private terraces equipped with laze-the-day-away hammocks. The eight standard rooms lack terraces, but they are still roomier than the local norm and come with firm top-quality mattresses. The small budget room should be avoided. All guests have equal access to the deck, the sun, and the view of the *jangada* fleet setting sail.

Av. Beira Mar 12, Porto de Galinhas, PE 55590-000. ℭ/fax 081/3552-1052. www.pousadabeiramar.com.br. (15% discount for Internet bookings). 12 units (showers only). High season R$220 (US$110/£60) deluxe double, R$155 (US$77/£42) standard double; low season R$140 (US$70/£38) deluxe double, R$90 (US$45/£24) standard double.

Extra person add R$25 (US$13/£7). Children 5 and under stay free in parent's room. AE, V. Free parking. **Amenities:** Restaurant; bar; game room; beachfront terrace. *In room:* A/C, TV, minibar, safe, no phone.

Pousada Canto do Porto ✦✦   Pousada Canto do Porto is a great option for those who want to stay close to the village without being smack in the middle of things. Only a 5-minute walk from the main square, the pousada is set right on the beach and has 14 rooms. The nicest is the deluxe oceanview panorama suite, which offers primo views from its large wraparound veranda. The king-size bed and Jacuzzi are just icing on the cake. The more affordable master suites have a partial ocean view and a veranda. The only rooms to avoid are the small standard ones. These are set back behind the pousada in an annex and have no verandas or views.

Av. Beira Mar s/n, Porto de Galinhas, PE. ✆ 081/3552-2165. www.pousadacantodoporto.com.br. 20 units. High season R$200–R$230 (US$100–US$115/£54–£62) deluxe or master double, R$140–R$180 (US$70–US$90/£38–£49) standard double; low season R$140–R$180 (US$70–US$90/£38–£49) deluxe or master double; R$110–R$140 (US$55–US$70/£30–£38) standard double. Children under 7 stay free in parent's room, over 7 R$30 (US$15/£8). AE, V. Free street parking. **Amenities:** Bar. *In room:* A/C, TV, minibar, fridge, no phone.

WHERE TO DINE

Beijupirá ✦✦✦ (Finds) SEAFOOD   One of the best restaurants in the region, Beijupirá is also one of the loveliest, set in a garden aglow with hundreds of candles and lanterns. Everything about this restaurant is creative and fun; from the funky decorations to the phenomenally inventive kitchen. The dishes combine either seafood or chicken with a range of interesting spices that blend together sweet and savory. The *beijupitanga* combines grilled *beijupirá* fish with a sweet-tart pitanga sauce (a sour cherrylike fruit) and a side of rice with cashew nuts. The *camarulu* is a generous portion of grilled prawns with a glazing of cane molasses and rice with passion fruit. Also popular is the *Beijumanga*, grilled fish with sesame seeds and coconut rice, flambéed bananas, and a mango sauce. For non-seafood eaters there's the *Galinhatrololo*, grilled chicken breast with bacon and banana, served with cashews, raisins, and rice. Desserts are sweet and luscious; the all-time favorite (and we tried several) is the *cajuendy*, made with dried cashew fruits topped with cheese and honey, flambéed with cinnamon liquor.

Rua Beijupirá s/n, Porto de Galinhas. ✆ 081/3552-2354. www.beijupira.com.br. Reservations required on weekends and holidays. Main courses R$26–R$38 (US$13–US$19/£7–£10). AE, DC, MC, V. Daily noon–midnight.

Peixe na Telha ✦✦ SEAFOOD   Peixe na Telha offers one of the best patios in town, with a terrific view of the beach and fleet of jangadas. The menu offers regional fish and seafood dishes such as *moqueca* stews with coconut milk and red palm oil and *bobó de camarão*, a thick stew made with prawns and manioc. The house special is the *peixe na telha* (fish served on a red roof tile) accompanied with rice and *pirão*, a purée made of seafood broth, manioc flour, and spices. Bring your friends because this dish serves at least three people.

Av. Beira Mar s/n, Porto de Galinhas. ✆ 081/3552-1877. Main courses R$38–R$52 (US$19–US$26/£10–£14), dishes serve 2 to 3 people. AE, DC, MC, V. Daily 11am–10pm.

Picanha Tio Dadá CHURRASCO   Turf on the surf. Tio Dadá serves up fine Brazilian *picanha* on a great patio, just steps from the beach. The meat comes to your table sizzling on its own grill. Vegetables include potatoes, french fries, and *farofa*. There are other cuts besides *picanha*, plus lamb, chicken, fish, and seafood. Forget the wine list—there isn't one—just order a cold Brazilian chopp.

Rua da Esperança 167, Porto de Galinhas. ✆ 081/3552-1319. Main courses R$27–R$38 (US$14–US$19/£7.25–£10). MC, V. Daily 11am–midnight.

11

Natal

Natal is a city built on sand. It blows across the city streets and piles up in drifts like snow. It lines the city's beaches, lies beneath the city's foundations, landscapes the city's parks, and piles up in towering dunes that form the city's picture-postcard views. Outside Natal, the sand dunes spread in mountainous dune ranges that stretch for miles.

Perhaps because sand is not the most fertile of foundations, Natal has been an oft-overlooked sandlot of a city for much of its history, noticed by the powers that be only when some other power tried to take it away.

The Portuguese founded a town on the banks of the Potengi River to drive out the French. To hold the territory, the Portuguese built Forte dos Reis Magos in 1599. The fort's foundation was celebrated with a Mass on December 25, 1599, and so the city was named Natal (the Portuguese word for Christmas). After that, the Portuguese pretty much ignored the place. By 1757 there were a whopping 120 buildings in the area, among them a church and a prison.

Natal first came to American notice in the early 1940s. The U.S. had just entered the war against the Axis powers and sleepy little Natal—the closest land base to North Africa—was suddenly a place of world significance. Franklin Roosevelt paid a visit, meeting with Brazilian President Getulio Vargas to work out the details of Brazil's war effort. There's a famous picture of the two presidents, riding through the streets of Natal in an open limousine, sand barely visible beneath the wheels.

Natal became the "Trampoline of Victory," an air and communications base providing cover for the Allied invasion of North Africa. According to local folklore, one lasting legacy of that period was a new Brazilian dance step. Wanting to make the American airmen welcome, the Brazilians invited them to local dances, and developed a simplified two-step rhythm the rather club-footed Yanks could handle. They titled the dances "For All." The dance spread all over the Northeast, while the name got shortened to *forró*.

Only recently, as Europeans and Americans began to discover the true value of sand and endless sunshine, has Natal has really begun to blossom.

Why visit? Natal offers endless beaches for surfing and tanning, and dunes, glorious dunes, hundreds of feet high and spilling down to within inches of the seashore. To the north of the city the dunes pile up so high locals have begun to make use of them in a wide variety of peculiar and original sports. You can ski or toboggan down them, rope-slide from the top of them, camel ride across them, and buggy ride over, up, down, and all around them.

North and south of Natal the beaches stretch for hundreds of miles, dotted now and again with fishing villages and only lightly touched by tourism. The preferred method of transport in these regions is by dune buggy. Offshore—at places up the coast such as Maracajaú—wide coral reefs lie in shallow water, great places to spend a day snorkeling.

And everywhere you go, north and south and in the city, there's sand.

1 Natal Essentials

ARRIVING

BY PLANE   TAM (toll-free ℂ **0800/570-5700** or 084/4002-5700); **Gol** (ℂ **0300/115-2121**); and **Varig** (ℂ **084/4003-7000**) offer flights that arrive and depart daily from all major cities in Brazil.

All flights arrive at **Aeroporto Augusto Severo,** Rua Eduardo Gomes s/n (ℂ **084/3643-1000**), about 15km (9¼ miles) from downtown and just a few miles from Ponta Negra beach. Taxis from the airport are about R$25 to R$30 (US$13–US$15/£7–£8) to Ponta Negra and R$35 (US$18/£9.50) to Praia dos Artistas, close to downtown. City buses marked VIA COSTEIRA will also stop in Ponta Negra before continuing along the coastal highway to downtown.

BY BUS   Long-distance buses arrive at the **Rodoviaria,** Av. Cap. Mor Gouveia 1237, Cidade Esperança (ℂ **084/3232-7310**), about 5km (3 miles) from downtown and Ponta Negra beach.

VISITOR INFORMATION

Natal's **airport** has a tourist information center (ℂ **084/3643-1811**) in the arrivals hall, open daily from 9am to 5pm. The **main tourist information center** is in Natal's Centro de Turismo, Rua Aderbal de Figueiredo 980, Petrópolis (ℂ **084/3211-6149**). See "Shopping in Natal," later in the chapter for more details.

CITY LAYOUT

A small downtown aside, Natal is a postwar creation; in many ways it resembles the modern, sprawling, car-centric cities of the southwestern United States. The original city was founded on a peninsula between the Potengi River and the Atlantic Ocean. Just off the tip of the peninsula, where ocean and river meet, the original **Forte de Reis Magos** still stands, a forgotten bit of the 17th century. Where the fort's causeway touches the mainland the 21st century begins—a modern oceanside boulevard that under various names runs from here south through the length of the city and out into the dunes beyond. About 3km (1¾ miles) south of the fort the street is called **Avenida Presidente Café Filho,** and the surrounding neighborhood is **Praia dos Artistas.** From here the road climbs a bit, becoming **Avenida Governo Silvio Pedroso,** then **Via Costeira,** which runs for some 9km (5½ miles) between the ocean and a vast nature preserve called **Parque das Dunas.** There are a number of five-star resort hotels nestled in between the parkway and the ocean. Where the park ends, the road swings away from the beach a bit and becomes **Avenida Engenheiro Roberto Freire,** the backbone of the city's best beach neighborhood, **Ponta Negra.** Avenida Roberto Freire itself is a wide, busy, and rather ugly artery, but the streets leading off it down to the ocean are quiet and pleasant, lined with hotels and pousadas. The beach itself has no traffic at all along this stretch, just a pedestrian walkway and seawall, punctuated by beachside kiosks or *barracas.* About two-thirds of the way along the lovely 3km (1¾-mile) beach, Avenida Roberto Freire drops downhill to the waterfront and becomes **Avenida Erivan França,** a busy beachside boulevard lined with pubs and restaurants

Natal

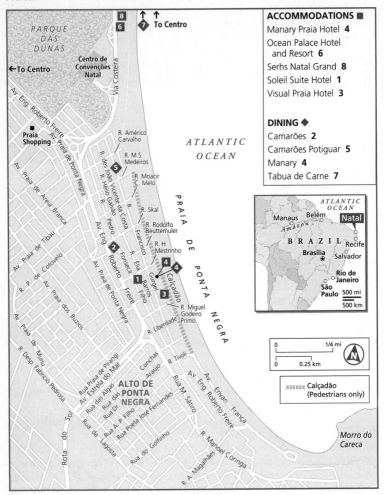

↑ ↑
7 To Centro
←To Centro

PARQUE
DAS
DUNAS

Centro de
Convenções
Natal

8
6
7 To Centro

Via Costeira

Av. Eng. Roberto Freire

Praia
Shopping

Av. Praia de Ponta Negra

Av. Praia de Areia Branca

R. Américo
Carvalho

R. M.S.
Medeiros

R. Moacir
C. Melo

R. des João Vicente da Costa

R. Hélio Galvão

Av. Eng.
Pedro

R. Skal

R. Rodolfo
Beuttemuler

R. H.
Mestrinho

R. Ella Francisco

Av. Praia de Tibau

R. P. de Cotovelo

Av. Praia dos Búzios

Av. Praia de Ponta Negra

Av. Eng. Roberto Freire

Fonseca

R. Guaros Filho

Gugel

Calçadão

R. Miguel
Godeiro
Primo

R. Liberdade

ATLANTIC
OCEAN

PRAIA DE PONTA NEGRA

5

2
4
4
1
3

Av. Praia de Piranji

Rua Praia de Pirang

Av. Estrela do Mar

Rua das Algas

Rua das Conchas

Rua Dr. Araújo

Rua A.P. Filho

Rua M. Satiro

Av. Eng. Erivan França

R. Tivoli

ALTO DE
PONTA
NEGRA

R. Desp. Fabrício Pedrosa

Rota do Sol

Rua da Lagosta

Rua Poeta José Fernandes

Rua do Golfinho

R. Manoel Coringa

R. A. Magalhães

Morro do
Careca

ACCOMMODATIONS ■

Manary Praia Hotel **4**

Ocean Palace Hotel
  and Resort **6**

Serhs Natal Grand **8**

Soleil Suite Hotel **1**

Visual Praia Hotel **3**

DINING ◆

Camarões **2**

Camarões Potiguar **5**

Manary **4**

Tabua de Carne **7**

ATLANTIC
OCEAN

Manaus Belém   Natal

Amazon

B R A Z I L   Recife

Brasília

Brasília ✳   Salvador

Rio de
Janeiro

São
Paulo   500 mi

500 km

0   1/4 mi
0   0.25 km

N

Calçadão
(Pedestrians only)

and nightclubs that runs all the way to **Morro do Careca (Bald Mountain),** the 117m (390-ft.) sand dune that overlooks the beach.

Going the other direction from the Forte dos Reis Magos, along the banks of the **Rio Potengi,** you pass the abutments of a bridge (now in its seventh year of construction) that may some day lead across the river to **Genipabu,** as well as the terminal for the ferries that actually do cross the river. The road then climbs and enters **Centro,** also called the **Cidade Alta,** the commercial heart of Natal. Centro has a few old squares—the **Praça André de Albuquerque** and **Praça Sete de Setembro.** The main street is **Avenida Rio Branco.**

North of Natal, the dunes and beaches begin as soon as you cross the river. This area is called the **Litoral Norte** (north coast). The first settlement in the Literal Norte is the quiet village of **Genipabu,** about 25km (16 miles) north of downtown Natal.

Once a fishing village, Genipabu now caters to tourists who come to swim at the beach and buggy and climb through the huge surrounding dunes.

South of Ponta Negra there's a long stretch of beaches known as the **Litoral Sul** (south coast), with something for everyone. **Búzios** beach is excellent for snorkellers, while **Barra de Tabatinga** is a surfer's hot spot. Capping off the string of south coast beaches is **Praia da Pipa,** a gorgeous stretch of sand and a small destination in its own right.

GETTING AROUND

BY BUS   The bus is a quick and efficient way to travel from Ponta Negra to Centro and vice versa. In Ponta Negra, buses run along Estrada Ponta Negra. For downtown, look for buses marked CENTRO or CIDADE ALTA. There are two routes. Buses with signs saying VIA COSTEIRA follow the coast as far as Praia dos Artistas and then cut across to Centro. Other CENTRO buses use the inland route along Avenida Prudente de Morais or Avenida Hermes da Fonseca. To return to Ponta Negra, any bus that says PONTA NEGRA or even VIA COSTEIRA will do. You enter buses through the front. Fare is R$1.80 (US75¢/£.40).

BY TAXI   You can hail a taxi anywhere. To reserve one, phone **Disk Taxi Natal** (© 084/3223-7388) or **CoopTax** (© 0800/84-2255). A taxi from Ponta Negra to downtown will cost about R$25 to R$30 (US$13–US$15/£7–£8).

BY CAR   Natal is an easy city for driving; streets are wide, traffic is light, and parking not much of a problem. See "Fast Facts: Natal," below, for car-rental information. You can rent a car to drive up or down the coast, but you'll have more fun if you rent a buggy with a driver who can take you off-road.

FAST FACTS: Natal

Car Rental   **Localiza** (© 0800/979-2000 or 084/3643-1557); **Avis** (© 0800/725-2847 or 084/3644-2503); **Unidas** (© 0800/121-121 or 084/3643-1222); **Hertz** (© 084/3087-1428).

Currency Exchange   Near Centro, **Banco do Brasil,** Av. Rio Branco 510, Cidade Alta (© 084/3216-4500), which also has a 24-hour ATM; and **Sunset Cambio,** Av. Hermes da Fonseca 628, Tirol (© 084/3212-2552). In Ponta Negra, **Banco do Brasil,** Rua Dr. Ernani Hugo Gomes 2700 (© 084/3219-4443, next to the Praia Shopping.

Hospitals   **Monsenhor Walfredo Gurgel,** Av. Salgado Filho s/n, Tirol (© 084/3232-7501).

Weather   Natal lies just 3 degrees from the Equator, so temperatures hover around 82°F to 93°F (28°C–34°C) year-round. The only difference between summer and winter is that in the winter (June–Aug) it tends to rain more. In summer you get 15 regular hours of sunshine a day.

---

2 Where to Stay in Natal

High season for hotels in Natal is December through February, and then again in July when Brazilians take their winter holidays. Outside of this period it is possible to obtain substantial discounts. Remember also that in Brazil you can often get a better rate if you book through a travel agent.

PONTA NEGRA

Ponta Negra is the most popular beach within the city limits. It's wide, clean, and busy, with good waves for surfing. A pleasant waterfront walkway runs along the beach, past a number of beachside restaurants and *barracas*. In the past couple of years many of the city's better restaurants have opened up branches in the area, and several new cafes, bars, and nightclubs have set up shop. All this means that if you're going to stay within the Natal city limits, Ponta Negra is really your best option. The few sights worth visiting in downtown Natal are only a 15-minute cab ride or a 30- to 40-minute trip by city bus away.

VERY EXPENSIVE

Manary Praia Hotel ✸✸✸   The best place to stay in Natal is also one of the nicest spots to rest your head in all Brazil. The Manary is done up like a Spanish hacienda, with old dark beams, red-tile roofs, and large cool flagstones on the floor. The location is also premium, with a large deck and two pools (one regular, one for children) facing out over the sea. In the rooms, the furnishings are tasteful and unique, the beds king-size, the mattresses, linen, and furniture all top-notch. All rooms come with a balcony and ocean view. For the 15 standard rooms, the view is a bit oblique, but still lovely. The nine deluxe rooms have a straight-on view. The luxury suite not only has a broad veranda facing out over the water, but it also has a Jacuzzi whirlpool. Breakfast here is memorable—a well-stocked array of fresh regional fruits and lots of regional delicacies, plus fresh-made tapioca pancakes and eggs however you like 'em. The Manary is a member of the *Roteiros de Charme*, a network of top-end pousadas and small hotels.

Rua Francisco Gurgel 9067, Praia de Ponta Negra, Natal 59090-050 RN. ℂ/fax 084/3204-2900. www.manary. com.br. 24 units. High season Nov–Feb and July R$550–R$875 (US$275–US$438/£148–£236) double. Low season R$450–R$725 (US$225–US$363/£121–£196) double. Extra person add 25%. Children 6 and under stay free in parent's room. AE, DC, MC, V. Free parking. Bus: Ponta Negra. **Amenities:** Restaurant; bar; 2 pools; game room; tour desk; business center; room service; laundry. *In room:* A/C, TV, dataport, minibar, hair dryer, safe.

EXPENSIVE

Visual Praia Hotel ✸   Located right on the seawall in Ponta Negra, the Visual Praia is kind of a mini–resort hotel, complete with a large pool deck, and waterside bar and children's play area. Of course, if it's really a full-service resort you want you'll be better off at the Ocean Palace; the advantage of the Visual Praia is its location on Ponta Negra beach and its cheaper price tag. Rooms are comfortable and beautifully furnished with blond wood and marble desktops. Just two rooms have no view and no balcony; all the other rooms range from a partial to a full ocean view. Breakfast is served on the patio overlooking the beach.

Rua Francisco Gurgel 9184, Praia Ponta Negra, Natal 59090-050 RN. ℂ 084/3646-4646. www.visualpraiahotel. com.br. 136 units (showers only). High season R$385–R$462 (US$193–US$231/£104–£125) double. Extra person add R$75 (US$38/£20). 30% discount in low season. Children up to 5 stay free in parent's room. AE, DC, MC, V. Free parking. Bus: Ponta Negra. **Amenities:** Restaurant; bar; large pool; sauna; children's pool and playground; laundry service. *In room:* A/C, TV, minibar, fridge, safe.

MODERATE

Soleil Suite Hotel   The Soleil offers excellent value for the money, with generously sized rooms and a location that's just a 3-block walk from the beach. The least expensive room, the Suite Luxo, comes with tile floors, a firm queen-size bed, couch and TV, and small kitchen table (no desk space, however), a kitchenette unit with fridge and hot plate and utensils, plus a balcony but with no view of the sea. The next step, the Suite Master, costs about 30% more and is identical except the balcony offers an ocean view. For view junkies, the extra US$20 will be worth the price. One step up again, the Suite Master Plus offers a couch that folds out to a double bed, plus French doors separating bedroom from sitting room. It's not a bad option if you have kids, but otherwise not worth the price premium. Another, more expensive family option is the top-floor Suite Executiva, which has two bedrooms plus a full kitchen and sitting/dining area and a sizable veranda. The hotel also has a small pool and another children's wading pool, neither of which is nice enough to tempt anyone away from the beach.

Rua Elia Barros 70, Praia Ponta Negra, Natal 59090-140 RN. ℂ **084/3219-5959**. www.soleilhotel.com.br. 31 units (showers only). High season Nov–Feb and July R$175–R$270 (US$88–US$135/£47–£73) double. Low season 30% discount. Extra person add 25%. Children up to 5 stay free in parent's room. AE, DC, MC, V. Free parking. Bus: Ponta Negra. **Amenities:** Restaurant; pool; children's pool; business center. *In room:* A/C, TV, minibar, fridge, safe.

VIA COSTEIRA

The Via Costeira parkway looks like a lovely place for a hotel (and it is) but there are a couple of drawbacks. Though you get outstanding views and unmatched isolation, the ocean is rougher, and there is nothing within walking distance, so you're looking at a cab ride any time you want to leave the hotel.

EXPENSIVE

Ocean Palace Beach Resort & Bungalows ★★   From the outside, the architecture the Ocean Palace is kind of squat ziggurat, but the hotel makes up for it on the inside with a lovely sunlit lobby with terrific views of the sea. Rooms are good but not outstanding (nowhere as nice as those in the Manary Praia, for example), but then that's not where the hotel has put its energy. What really makes the Ocean Palace stand out are its amenities: a vast multi-level pool complex featuring two large pools and another five wading or whirlpools, some with waterside bar, all on a lovely palm-shaded deck looking out over the crashing waves of the Atlantic. In addition there's a children's play room, saunas, spa, top-quality weight room, tennis court, squash court, and more.

As for the rooms, the basic layout is long and narrow, with a pleasant modern decor, hardwood floors, firm queen-size beds (two twins also available), a very small desk area, and smallish tiled bathroom with shower only and lots of counter space. *Superior* rooms face back over the parking lot; avoid these. What you want are the *luxo* rooms, which face out over the ocean. Luxo rooms on floors 1 to 3 feature a balcony that, while smallish, is still large enough for a deck chair or hammock. On floors 4 and 5, the balconies shrink to standing room only. Floor 6 houses the hotel's 20 suites, which really aren't much bigger than the other rooms.

The hotel's 32 seaside bungalows are comfortable enough on the inside, but packed in cheek-by-jowl almost trailer park–style in two rows along the waterfront. If you do opt for these, the *bungalôs suite* offers an unobstructed front-row view of the ocean.

Av. Via Costeira, Km 11, Praia de Ponta Negra, Natal 59090-001 RN. ℂ **084/3220-4144**. Fax 084/3219-3081. Toll-free 0800-844-144. www.oceanpalace.com.br. 315 units. R$700–R$1,000 (US$350–US$500/£189–£270) double; R$1,000–R$1,200 (US$500–US$600/£270–£324) bungalow. Extra person add 25%. Children 6 and under stay free in parent's room. Off-season discounts (20%) Sept–Oct and Mar–May. AE, DC, MC, V. Free parking. Bus: Via Costeira. **Amenities:** 2 restaurants; 2 bars; 2 larger pools and 3 smaller pools; tennis courts; 2 Jacuzzis; game room; weight room; squash courts; small spa; sauna; business center; room service; laundry; 3rd floor nonsmoking; rooms for those w/limited mobility. *In room:* A/C, TV, minibar, hair dryer, safe.

Serhs Natal Grand ✧✧✧ Little more than a year old, the Natal Grand is the newest and most luxurious of the top-end resorts strung along the ocean-side Via Costeira. Rooms are fresh, bright, and modern, all with tile floors, clean bright bathrooms, and balconies facing out over the sea. Superior rooms feature firm double beds and a small writing desk. Family rooms feature two double beds, but no extra space making them a little squished. Junior suites are more spacious, with a separate sitting room and fold-out couch, making them a good option for those traveling with kids. A couple looking to splurge, however, should opt for a Senior or even an Executive Suite, both of which feature an outdoor terrace with Jacuzzi built for two.

Recreational facilities at this Spanish-run hotel are top-notch. The entire front deck of the hotel is one sprawling wavy pool, dotted here and there with little Jacuzzi islands. The sports center offers volleyball, soccer, and basketball, while the Japanese spa offers a full range of massage and beauty treatments. The Kid's Club features a kids' pool and indoor children's recreation area. On the beach, the hotel offers volleyball and soccer, plus beach chairs and a lifeguard service. The hotel's **Tapiro Grill** is one of the better restaurants in town. The hotel was awarded Best Beach Resort in 2007 by the Guia Brasil guide.

Av. Via Costeira 6045, Praia de Ponta Negra, Natal 59090-001 RN. ✆ **084/4005-2000.** Fax 084/4005-2001. Toll-free 0800-702-2411. www.serhsnatalgrandhotel.com. 396 units. R$495–R$647 (US$248–US$324/£134–£175) double; R$800–R$1,000 (US$400–US$500/£216–£270) suite. Extra person add 25%. Children 6 and under stay free in parent's room. Off-season discounts (20%) Sept–Oct and Mar–May. AE, DC, MC, V. Free parking. Bus: Via Costeira. **Amenities:** 4 restaurants; 3 bars; 4 large outdoor pools and children's pool; 3 Jacuzzis; sports center w/weight room; volleyball; basketball; soccer courts; children's game room; Japanese spa; sauna; business center; room service; laundry; 10 wheelchair-accessible rooms. *In room:* A/C, plasma TV, Internet, minibar, hair dryer, safe.

3 Where to Dine in Natal

Natal's better restaurants have been gravitating out toward Ponta Negra. Better yet, quite a few have been moving off the busy and ugly Avenida Eng. Roberto Freire and into locations with more charm and better views. That said, there are still a couple of worthwhile places in other parts of the city.

ELSEWHERE

Mangai ✧✧ (Value) REGIONAL The ideal place to get a look and taste of *Nordestino* food, the cuisine of Brazil's dry, cattle-raising Northeast. Mangai offers a self-serve buffet—or better, a smorgasbord—featuring over 40 different Nordestino dishes, some of them traditional favorites, other wonderful inventions made using traditional local ingredients such as *carne-de-sol* (sun-dried beef), *macaxeira* (sweet manioc root), *farofa* (ground, roasted manioc root), beans, and rice. The *carne-de-sol na nata* (butter-sautéed sun-dried beef) is a house specialty. Mangai is truly best for a long leisurely lunch. After you indulge (or overindulge), take advantage of the hammocks slung throughout the establishment and settle in for a snooze. Alcoholic beverages are not available, but there is an excellent array of fruit juices.

Tip: For a real Northeastern treat, try Mangai for breakfast. Dishes include *tapioca catolé* (fresh soft cheese with shaved coconut), toasted *macaxeira* (manioc) bread, *pamonha* (a sort of sweet corn bread served in a banana leaf), *cuscuz de santa* (cornmeal covered in sun-dried beef and warm cream), plus a wide variety of exotic fruit juices.

Av. Almintos Barros 3300 (on the inland road between Ponta Negra and downtown, about halfway between the 2). ✆ **084/3206-3344.** www.mangai.com.br. Reservations not accepted. Main courses R$10–R$25 (US$5–US$13/£3–£7). V. Wed–Sun 7am–10pm. Bus: Centro.

VIA COSTEIRA

Tábua de Carne *Value* BRAZILIAN   Perched on a cliff top overlooking the beach on the Via Costeria, Tabua offers carnivorous dining at its lip-smacking best. The menu now includes such treats as lamb and pork chops and even fish (though if you're in the mood for seafood you really should go elsewhere) as well as the traditional favorites of *carne de sol* (salted sun-dried beef, a specialty of Northeastern Brazil) and chicken and good old Brazilian *picanha* (sirloin steak). For the decision-shy, there's the Tábua, a wood platter containing picanha, sausage, chicken, and *carne de sol*. Dishes here are made for two and would easily feed three. The *picanha*—a large beautiful roast cooked exactly to your specifications—melts delicately on the tongue. The wine list is of minimal length and features questionable vintages. Stick to beer or fruit juice by the half-liter earthenware jug. For Net-heads, Tábua offers one of the few Wi-Fi hotpoints in all Natal—free wireless Internet on your laptop while you're inside the restaurant. Tábua has a second location in Ponta Negra, also with Wi-Fi, though on a viewless stretch of Av. Engenheiro Roberto Freire 3241 (© **084/3642-1236**).

Av. Senador Dinarte Mariz 229. © **084/3202-5838**. www.tabuadecarne.com.br. Main courses R$18–R$32 (US$9–US$16/£5–£9) for 2. AE, DC, MC, V. Daily 11:30am–11pm. Bus: Via Costeira.

PONTA NEGRA

Camarões BRAZILIAN/SEAFOOD   With a name that means "prawns," it's not hard to guess the house specialty. Papa Jerimum prawns are served in a pumpkin, while Champagne prawns are sautéed with butter in a champagne/applesauce. The tiny creatures are also featured in sauces such as the *Espaguete de Camarão*, sautéed prawns in a creamy cognac sauce with basil served on spaghetti. Portions are generous enough to serve two people, while the restaurant's location on the ocean side of the busy Avenida Eng. Roberto Freire offers diners a view over Ponta Negra beach. The restaurant has a nonsmoking room.

Av. Eng. Roberto Freire 2610, Ponta Negra. © **084/3219-2424**. www.camaroes.com.br. R$26–R$58 (US$13–US$29/£7–£16) for 2. AE, DC, MC, V. Mon–Sat 11:30am–3:30pm and 6:30pm–midnight; Sun 11:30am–5pm. Free parking. Bus: Ponta Negra.

Camarões Potiguar BRAZILIAN/SEAFOOD   Like its parent, this new hatchling of the long-established Camarões restaurant features a menu heavy on prawns and seafood, but while the mother ship is more international, here the emphasis is on local ingredients such as pumpkin, coconut, and cashews and traditional Brazilian recipes. The architecture of this smaller space matches the new locally flavored menu—charmingly rustic, with flashes of sophistication.

Av. Eng. Roberto Freire 2610, Ponta Negra. © **084/3219-2424**. www.camaroes.com.br. R$26–R$58 (US$13–US$29/£7–£16) for 2. AE, DC, MC, V. Mon–Sat 11:30am–3:30pm and 6:30pm–midnight; Sun 11:30am–5pm. Free parking. Bus: Ponta Negra.

Manary *** SEAFOOD/REGIONAL   The best place in Natal for seafood, the Manary offers top-notch ingredients, good service, and a lovely setting—an outdoor patio overlooking the seawall and beach of Ponta Negra. Among the most tempting menu items are the *misto fritti di mare* (a platter of grilled lobster, shrimp, octopus, mussels, fish, and grilled vegetables) and the *bobó de camarão*, a rich shrimp and pumpkin stew, flavored with dendê oil and coconut milk and served hot in a hollowed-out pumpkin shell. A memorable dish. The wine list is short but serviceable.

Rua Francisco Gurgel 9067, Praia de Ponta Negra. ©/fax **084/219-2900**. www.manary.com.br. Main courses R$24–R$44 (US$12–US$22/£7–£12). AE, DC, MC, V. Daily 10am–11pm. Bus: Via Costeira

4 Exploring Natal

Natal isn't really the place to stroll around and look at the pretty old buildings. That's fine. Odds are you're here for sun and surf and some time on those famous dunes. So enjoy the beach in **Ponta Negra** for a day. Then rent a buggy and *bugreiro* (driver) and buggy up the beach and explore. Check out the monster dunes at **Genipabu.** Ride a camel, or a sand board. Head farther north and snorkel the reefs off **Maracajaú.** Try *aerobunda* where you slap your behind into a rope-sling and slide *com emoção* down into a rainwater lagoon. If that wasn't enough excitement, try sand boarding, tobogganing, dune hiking, or camel riding (see "Outdoor Activities," below). Finish the day watching a glorious sunset over the dune tops.

And don't forget the side trips. If buggying gets in your blood, do a second day trip south to **Praia da Pipa.** Or for the ultimate in buggy adventure, do a 4- or 7-day expedition from Natal 800km (500 miles) north to Fortaleza. Or strike inland and see the otherworldly rock formations at **Cariri,** and 120-million-year-old footprints in the Vale dos Dinossauros (Valley of the Dinosaurs).

TOP ATTRACTIONS IN THE CITY

Forte de Reis Magos ✿✿   Every old fort should look like this, standing proud and alone on the reefs off the tip of the city, separated from the mainland by a sand spit that at high tide sinks below 3 feet of water. Inside the fort the function of each room is carefully spelled out in Portuguese and English. The small museum in the officers' quarters has a nicely done display on the explorer Vasco de Gama, but disappointingly little on the fort itself, which saw action when the Dutch occupied it between 1633 and 1654. From the ramparts the view of the city's skyscrapers and the dunes to the north can't be beat.

Av. Pres. Café Filho s/n. ✆ 084/3502-1099. Admission R$3 (US$1.50/£.80). Daily 8am–4:30pm. No public transit.

Museu Câmara Cascudo ✿ *(Kids)*   The only noteworthy museum in Natal covers the natural history and anthropology of the state of Rio Grande do Norte. The displays are well-done reproductions, many of which you can touch. See the original *jangada* rafts made by local fishermen and walk through a fisherman's hut. Visit reproductions of Rio Grande do Norte's archaeological sites, and descend in a cave to see how these digs are carried out. Delve into a life-size salt mine. A few displays are dusty academic leftovers, including glass cases with artifacts from African religions. There are no English signs, but the displays are often self-explanatory and great for kids. Expect to spend 1 hour.

Av. Hermes da Fonseca 1398, Tirol. ✆ 084/3212-2795. Admission R$3 (US$1.50/£.80). Tues–Fri and Sun 8–11am and 2–5pm.

CENTRO NATAL

On the highlands above the port is the **Cidade Alta.** This commercial part of the city has a number of pretty squares that make for a fine stroll. The best place to begin is at the big irregular square on Rua Santo Antônio. There are actually four separate squares here, all melded together: **Praça João Maria, Praça Andrè de Albuquerque, Praça João Tibuco,** and **Praça Sete de Setembro.** The largest square is the **Praça Andrè de Albuquerque,** dominated by the **N.S. da Apresentação.** Just across from the church is the **Memorial Câmara Cascudo** ✿ (Praça Andre de Albuquerque 30; ✆ 084/3202-6425; Tues–Sun 8am–5pm; free entrance). One of Natal's most beloved sons, **Câmara Cascudo** (1898–1986), was a journalist, professor, founder of the federal university of Rio Grande do Norte, and author of the dictionary of Brazilian folklore; most Brazilian kids have read his stories of *jangadas*, fishing nets, and *Bumba meu boi* (a peasant harvest festival involving the death and miraculous resurrection of a sainted bull). The memorial shows the life of Cascudo and artifacts portraying the folklore he wrote about. It also houses all of his works and his personal library. The museum is very small, but admission is free and the proud staff (one of them is Cascudo's grandson) love receiving foreign visitors.

PARKS

The 3,400-acre **Parque das Dunas** ⋪ occupies a huge swath of Natal, from the edge of downtown all the way to Ponta Negra. To access or better understand this intriguing ecosystem, a visitor center is located at the park headquarters, Av. Alexandrino de Alencar, s/n (© **084/3201-3985;** www.parquedasdunas.rn.gov.br), from which you can set off on guided walks through the dunes. Entrance is R$2 (US$1/£.50) which includes the trail fee. (There's also a park library and exposition area, but neither is much use if you can't read Portuguese.) There are three trails: the Peroba trail is 2.4km (1.5 miles) long and takes about 1½ hours. The Ubaia trail is 4.4km (2.75 miles) long and takes about 2½ hours. The Perobina Trail is a mere 800m (2,624 ft.) but takes 40 minutes. Walks on the trails depart in the morning at 8am, 8:15am, and 8:30am, and in the afternoon at 2pm, 2:15pm, and 2:30pm. Participants must sign up for walks in advance.

TOP EXCURSIONS FROM NATAL

Buggy Expeditions ⋪⋪⋪   Untouched dunes, beaches, and lagoons stretch away north and south of Natal for hundreds of kilometers. The best and only way to see them in all their glory is to rent a dune buggy with a driver, and head out to explore. Prices are slightly negotiable but average around R$150 (US$75/£40) for a full day for up to four people. If you're in a group of fewer than four, you can pay R$38 (US$19/£10) per person and the tour operator will make up a full group, but you may want to consider paying the full rental; if you have the buggy to yourself, it stops and goes at your command.

The classic north-coast day trip crosses the Potengi River by ferry and proceeds up to **Genipabu,** where you have the chance to ride camels or slide down the dunes on a sand board (see "Outdoor Activities," below). From there you float your buggy across another small stream on a tiny raft and carry on up the beach to **Jucumã,** where you can try your bum at *aerobunda* (see "Outdoor Activities," below).

From there, it's another 35km (22 miles) of wide flat sand until you get to **Maracajaú,** a magic spot where at low tide you can snorkel in the natural pools in the offshore coral reef. (Buggy tours normally time the tour so that you arrive at low tide.)

At one or two points on the trip back, you'll have to float your buggy over estuaries on little wooden rafts. At the end of the day, the driver will take you to Genipabu to see the sun set over the dunes. (The tour used to end with a wild ride through the extreme Dune Park, but the park has been closed for the past couple of years, first due to a legal dispute between the buggy drivers and a supposed Dune Park owner, then later after the government expropriated the park, due to an ongoing environmental assessment. There are plans to reopen the park to licensed buggy drivers, but as yet nothing has been finalized.)

The classic south-coast trip heads south along 55km (34 miles) of coast and sand to **Praia da Pipa.** Along the way, buggies pass along numerous gorgeous beaches, among them **Búzios, Barra de Tabatinga, Barreta,** and **Tibau do Sul.** It's possible with a full day tour (about R$150/US$75/£40 per buggy) to stop in at several and still enjoy time at Pipa itself. Better still, head south and spend a few days in the Pipa, a pretty former fishing village of small pousadas and cobblestone streets.

There are lots of buggy drivers in Natal. An excellent longtime *bugreiro* who speaks English is **Kadmo Donato** of **Buggy & Cia** (© 084/9982-3162 or 084/9416-2222; www.buggyecia.com.br). There is also **Buggy Tour** (© 084/3086-2258) and in Genipabu, **Villa do Sol** (© 084/3225-2132).

SNORKELING THE POOLS AT MARACAJAÚ 🐟🐟   The coast north and south of Natal is hemmed with shallow coral reefs that make for perfect snorkeling. Nowhere are they more impressive than in Maracajaú, about 1 hour north of Natal. A stop here is often included in a full-day buggy tour; if not, ask your buggy driver. You need to time your arrival with low tide to get the most out of your snorkeling. From the beach a boat takes you about 7km (4¼ miles) offshore to a moored diving platform. At low tide the honeycomb of reefs forms natural pools rich in tropical fish and other marine life. As the maximum depth is about 4.8m (16 ft.), these pools can be easily explored with just a mask and snorkel. The water is crystal clear and warm. Expect to spend at least 2 hours.

Note: If you've never been scuba diving, the company offers a "baptism" dive. The water is never deeper than 4.8m (16 ft.), so there is no danger of sinking or decompression. The cost is R$80 (US$40/£20) for 15 to 20 minutes.

Maracajaú Diver, Praia de Maracajaú. (© 084/3261-6200 or 084/9983-4264 (cellphone). www.maracajaudiver.com.br. Snorkeling costs R$55 (US$27/£15) for adults, R$35 (US$17/£9.50) for children 6–12, free for children under 5.

ORGANIZED TOURS

The best way to access the terrain north and south of Natal is by buggy, but if you'd prefer to travel by more comfortable 4×4, contact **Cariri Ecotours** (© 084/3206-4949; www.caririecotours.com.br). The company offers single and multiday 4×4 trips south to Praia da Pipa and north to Maracajaú. The 1-day "eco-trip" to Praia de Pipa includes a guided walk through the Atlantic rainforest and dolphin spotting at Enseada do Madeiro.

OUTDOOR ACTIVITIES

AEROBUNDA JACUMÃ   The perfect antidote to the high-tech world of the American amusement park. At Lagoa Jacumã, Litoral Norte, Km 35, there's a dune about 60m (200 ft.) high. At its foot is a big lake. At the top of the dune someone has hammered in three telephone poles to make a scaffold, then attached a thick rope from there to another peg on the far side of the lake. To execute the *aerobunda,* you slide your butt into a sling hanging from a pulley attached to the line. The attendant then lets go. You scream down toward the lake, gathering speed and momentum. Splash! Huge fun. Back on shore you hop into a rickety iron cart, wave your arm at the guy on the donkey engine, and he hauls you up the dune so you can go again. Cost is R$3 (US$1.50/£.80) per ride, and it's open daily from 8am to 5:30pm. For more information call © 084/3228-2402.

JANGADA RIDING   A *jangada* is a narrow raft made of balsa wood (nowadays augmented with Styrofoam) and equipped with just one triangular sail. Taking a *jangada* is a quiet, gentle way to get out to the small offshore reefs. These little boats are still used by local fishermen, many of whom will happily augment their income by taking you to the reefs or for a quick sail. You'll find them along Genipabu beach. Cost is R$10 (US$5/£2.50) per person for an hour or so.

SAND BOARDING   Sand boarding is worth doing as long as you believe that no sport is too stupid to be tried at least once. As snowboarders, we felt obligated. Turns out that sand doesn't glide nearly as well as snow. But then, I guess you can't snowboard in a bikini. If you're interested, look for the entrepreneurs at the south end of Genipabu beach; cost is R$5 (US$2.50/£1.50) per trip (less, if you bargain).

SURFING   The beach at Ponta Negra is a great place to learn to surf. Waves vary from small and manageable to large and exciting. Marcelo Alves of **Sem Limites** surf school is a great instructor (© **084/9418-4030** cellphone). One-on-one instruction will get you up in no time. Lessons cost R$20 (US$10/£5.50) per hour. The school is in a tent about halfway along Ponta Negra beach.

5 Shopping in Natal

GIFTS & SOUVENIRS   Just like Recife, Natal has transformed its former prison complex into a crafts market, **Centro de Turismo de Natal,** Rua Aderbal de Figueiredo 980, Petrópolis (© **084/3211-6149**). About 40 crafts shops are now housed in the cells and provide easy one-stop shopping for local crafts. The best-known items are the handmade white-linen tablecloths, and the small painted clay figurines depicting characters from folk dances such as the bumba-meu-boi. You will also find hammocks, woodwork, and lots of sweets made with sugar cane and coconut. Prices are negotiable. The market is a steep 15-minute walk from Praia dos Artistas, and is open daily from 9am to 7pm. The **tourist information booth** at the entrance is open daily from 9am to 5pm.

In Praia dos Artistas on Av. Pres. Cafe Filho s/n is the large **Centro de Artesanato da Praia dos Artistas** (© **084/3202-4971**). Dozens of booths are packed with tacky souvenir T-shirts and trinkets as well as with nice locally made handicrafts. The market is open daily from 10am to 10pm. A **smaller evening crafts market** takes place Thursday to Sunday from 6 to 10pm, near the waterfront at Rua Conselheiro de Medeiros in Praia dos Artistas.

Recently opened in Ponta Negra, the **Shopping do Artesanato Potiguar** (Av. Engenheiro Roberto Freire 8000; © **084/3215-9781**) features more than 180 shops packed with souvenirs and local handicrafts.

If you want to mix some shopping with an evening stroll, there's **Alma Brasiliera,** Rua Dr. Manoel, A.B. de Araújo 130 (© **084/3219-3174**). Located in the nightlife area of Alto de Ponta Negra, the shop has a fine selection of local crafts, though prices are higher than at the downtown Centro de Turismo.

SHOPPING MALLS   The midsize **Praia Shopping** (Av. Engenheiro Roberto 8790; © **084/3219-4323**) is located at the edge of Ponta Negra, a short cab ride (or a tiring and not all that pleasant 15- to 20-min. walk) back in the direction of downtown. Shops are open Monday through Saturday 10am to 10pm, Sunday 3 to 9pm.

6 Natal After Dark

THE PERFORMING ARTS

Capitania das Artes   The Capitania used to house the port authority. Now fully renovated, this lovely neoclassical building just a few blocks from the **Praça André de Albuquerque** has been converted into a cultural complex, site of visiting art exhibits as well as theater and musical performances. Open Monday through Friday from 8am to noon and from 2 to 6pm. Av. Camara Cascudo 434, Cidade Alta. ✆ **084/3211-6763.**

Teatro Alberto Maranhão   Built in 1904 in a mix of neoclassical and colonial, the building was completely renovated in 1990. During box-office hours you can go in and have a peek. This is the city's main theater and concert stage. Check the calendar for upcoming events. Open Tuesday through Sunday from 8am to 6pm. Praça Augusto Severo 251. ✆ **084/222-3669.**

CLUBS & BARS

Natal's nightlife scene continues to center on the Ponta Negra neighborhood. Until recently there were two separate hot spots, each with its own distinct characteristics. The waterfront **Avenida Erivan França,** at the far end of **Ponta Negra beach,** was a busy and bustling area of restaurants and bars, though with a good 70% of the action consisting of Brazilian women looking to sell their services to male charter tourists from Europe. That said, the area was perfectly safe and not especially sleazy; regular tourists could and did pass a pleasant evening there as well.

   Located up on the heights on the far side of the busy Avenida Roberto Freire, the other nightlife area, called **Alto de Ponta Negra** (located around corner of Av. Roberto Freire with Rua Dr. Manoel. A.B. de Araújo) was almost wholly free of prostitution of any kind. It was instead a pleasant and easily strollable enclave of cafes and creperies, knickknack shops, bars, and discos.

   However, beginning in late 2006, local authorities began a concerted crackdown on the sex-for-sale scene on Ponta Negra Beach. These efforts had some local success—the Avenida França is now largely deserted in the evening. Predictably, however, the trade merely moved elsewhere, in this case up the hill to Alto de Ponta Negra. The result is that Natal's now has but one nightlife area—**Alto de Ponta Negra**—with a decidedly sleazier character than in years past. As of press time, things in Natal were still in flux. Authorities may move their campaign up to Alto de Ponta Negra, or may relax their enforcement efforts, in which case the situation may revert to what it was before.

ALTO DE PONTA NEGRA

If you're in the mood for a snack before or instead of partying, **Casa de Taipa** (Rua Dr. Manoel A.P. de Araújo 130A; ✆ **084/3219-5798**) offers tapioca pancakes with over 40 different types of filling, not to mention coffee and homemade ice cream. The Casa recently won the *Veja Magazine* Best of the City award. Open daily 5pm to midnight.

Axe Caffe   Small aboveground disco offering DJ'ed tunes of house, '80s, reggae, and sometimes even forró. Open Tuesday through Saturday 10pm to 4am. Rua Manoel Augusto Bezerro 176. ✆ **084/3219-0447.** Drink minimum R$5 (US$2.50/£1.35).

Salsa Bar   One of the best spots for dancing in Alto de Ponta Negra, the Salsa Bar's open-air dance floor is packed with 20- and 30-something tourists and locals showing off their Latin moves. In addition to a wide range of cocktails and caipifrutas, the kitchen offers small snacks and excellent crepes. Open daily 7pm to 2am. Rua Manoel A.B. de Araújo 174. ℂ **084/3236-2573**. No cover.

Taverna Pub It's a mystery. Located in the basement of the ersatz castle housing Natal's youth hostel, the Taverna Pub is low and dark and sweaty and cramped, with bad acoustics and terrible sightlines. It's also the most popular spot in Alto Ponta Negra, packed Thursday to Sunday with 20- to 30-year-old locals and visitors who come to hear either DJs or local bands playing live on the teeny-tiny stage. Open daily 11pm to 4am. Rua Chile 25, Ribeira. ℂ **084/3236-3696**. www.tavernapub.com.br. Cover R$15 (US$7.50/£4).

VIA COSTEIRA
Cervejaria Via Costeira This may well be the only brewpub south of Portland and north of Sao Paulo. It's a big sprawling barn of a place, with tasty brews on tap and a credible cold-cut buffet and pub-food kind of restaurant. The crowd is a friendly mix of Brazilians and foreigners. Open daily 6pm to 1am. Via Costeira 4197A. ℂ **084/3202-1089**.

DOWNTOWN
Forró com Turista If those feet of yours want to dance forró, but you don't quite know the steps, this is the place to come. At this huge traditional forró party, held every Thursday night in the old prison courtyard of the Centro de Turismo, there are numerous instructors (both male and female) to take you in hand and show you how it's done. Forró is a bright and accordion-happy rhythm. The dance is a simple fast two-step. Open Thursday 10pm to 2am. R$15 (US$6.25/£3.05) cover. Rua Aderbal Figueiredo 980, Petrópolis (Centro de Turismo). ℂ **084/3211-6218**. www.forrocomturista.com.br.

SIDE TRIPS FROM NATAL
The Natal-to-fortaleza buggy Adventure ✿✿✿ If you can't get enough of the coast, consider the 800km (500-mile) adventure trip from Natal north along the beach to Fortaleza. On the way you'll visit 85 beaches and countless dunes, some of them massive monsters seemingly transplanted from the Sahara. You'll pass through petrified forests and pocket deserts, and float your buggy across dozens of little estuaries on rafts, and visit little fishing towns that rarely if ever see tourists. Buggy is the best and only way to do this trip, and now is the time to do it. Real estate developers have finally discovered the vast and so far largely undeveloped coastline between Natal and Fortaleza. Wait a few more years and the coast will be clogged with resort hotels. If you're really keen, continue the voyage beyond Fortaleza all the way to the Lençois Maranhenses and São Luis.

Buggy & Cia, Rua Belo Monte 213 (ℂ **084/9982-3162;** www.buggyecia.com.br) specializes in this trip. The expedition takes 4 days, usually starting from Natal. Cost is R$2,500 (US$1,250/£675) total for two people, including accommodations and breakfast plus buggy and driver. The owner, Kadmo Donato, speaks English. The website has a good map of the route and some excellent photos showing what's in store on the trip. Note that with Buggy & Cia, a driver does most or all of the driving. Some find this a disappointment, but it actually allows you to dispense with driving and spend your time drinking in the views from the prime buggy spot—above the roll-bars on the back of the buggy's chassis. The only company that does allow guests to drive is the Paris-based firm **Brésil Aventure** (www.bresil-aventure.com). However,

Bresil Aventure's trips from Natal to Fortaleza take 2 weeks, and their guides speak only French.

HEADING INLAND

The hot, dry interior of the Northeast hides some places of outstanding natural beauty: indigenous petroglyphs, rock formations as odd and impressive as many in Utah, and fossilized dinosaur footprints 120 million years old. Reaching these sights can be a challenge: distances are long, and temperatures high. Based in Natal, **Cariri Ecotours** (© 084/3206-4949; www.caririecotours.com.br) specializes in trips into this Brazilian outback. The company offers various multiple-day packages. The 4-day, 3-night Valley of the Dinosaurs package strikes inland for the far west of Paraiba state. Here, 120 million years ago, dozens of species of dinosaurs lived at the edge of a great shallow lake. The tracks they left in the mud of this lake filled with sediment and became fossilized; hundreds of tracks in this area remain clearly visible to this day. The tour then swings back toward the Cariri region, to the vast and magic rock formations at **Lajedo do Pai Mateus** and **Saca de Lã**. The expedition finishes up with a visit to one of Brazil's most significant archaeological sites, a stone wall inscribed with the symbols and artwork of a now-vanished prehistoric people. Trips can be made by either air-conditioned Land Rover or comfortable air-conditioned Fiat Duplo. Cost per person for groups of two to four people is R$2,400 (US$1,200/£648) by Fiat, R$2,955 (US$1,477/£798) by Land Rover. Most meals are included, and accommodations are at some of the finer pousadas of the interior.

PRAIA DA PIPA

Located 80km (50 miles) south of Natal by road (or a mere 55km [34 miles] if you go by beach buggy), **Praia da Pipa** is one of the most picturesque beaches in all Brazil's Northeast. This former fishing village was discovered by surfers back in the 1970s, and developed in the decades since, without yet overdeveloping. Though the town does fill up on weekends and holidays, Pipa's pousadas and hotels remain manageable and small-scale. The village of Pipa is well-known for its nighttime activity, and for the cafes and restaurants lining its cobblestone streets. Down on the long crescent beach there are natural pools and reefs for snorkeling. Traveling south from Pipa one finds a string of beaches—**Praia do Amor, Praia do Moleque**—snuggling at the foot of tall coastal cliffs. The cliff-top drive from Pipa to **Praia do Cunhaú** is spectacular.

Pipa does not lack for places to stay. Two that stand out are **Toca de Coruja** (Av. Baía dos Golfinhos 464; © 084/3246-2226; www.tocadacoruja.com.br), a *Roteiro de Charme* property that features luxurious self-contained chalets with private outdoor Jacuzzis, all in a large private garden; and **Sombra e Agua Fresca** (Rua Praia do Amor 1000; © 084/3246-2258; www.sombraeaguafresca.com.br), located on the cliff overlooking the bay, which offers large rooms and two pools with terrific views.

Excellent restaurants in Pipa include the seafood-oriented **Cruzeiro do Pescador** (Rua da Gameleira s/n; © 084/3246-2262; open daily 7–11:30pm) and for more varied fare, **Agua na Boca** (Av. Baia dos Golfinhos 687; © 084/3246-2641; open Mon–Sat 6pm–midnight).

12

Fortaleza

The capital of the state of Ceará is best known for its beaches: glorious long stretches of sand interrupted by impressive red cliffs, palm trees, dunes, and lagoons that offer a true tropical playground.

The first Portuguese settlers arrived in the area in 1603. The colony grew slowly, beset by attacks by Tabajara Indians, and later by the Dutch, who in 1637 drove out the Portuguese, only to be slaughtered in turn by the Tabajara. When the Portuguese regained control of the area in 1654, they gave the substantial five-pointed Dutch fort a new name: Fortaleza Nossa Senhora de Assunção.

Fortaleza remained a backwater until the 1820s, when Brazilian ports opened to foreign ships and the city began to grow into an important seaport, shipping cotton, cattle, and leather from the interior to England. In response to the resulting growth, city governors in 1875 commissioned a plan to transform Fortaleza into a tropical Paris, a city of broad boulevards overlaying a functional grid.

Some of this early city planning can still be seen, but much was overwhelmed in the 1950s and 1960s as migrants from the state's dry and drought-stricken interior flocked into the city, practically doubling Fortaleza's population.

Now about two million strong, the city's major industries are cashews and tourism. The Dutch, Portuguese, and other foreigners land en masse on the beaches armed with cameras and bathing suits and a fierce will to enjoy the sun and ocean. What sets Fortaleza's beaches apart from Brazil's other 8,000km (4,960 miles) of coastline is the combination of colorful cliffs and huge sand dunes, best seen in nearby communities such as Morro Branco, Canoa Quebrada, and Jericoacoara.

For first-time visitors with limited amounts of time, the best plan of attack is to spend no more than a day in the city itself, then head out to explore the nearby beach communities, particularly the isolated Sahara-like dunes of Jericoacoara.

1 Fortaleza Essentials

ARRIVING

BY PLANE   TAM (toll-free © **0800/570-5700** or 085/4002-5700); **Varig** (© **085/4003-7000**); and **Gol** (© **0300/115-2121**) have daily flights to all major cities in Brazil. Flights arrive at **Aeroporto Internacional Pinto Martins,** Av. Senador Carlos Jereissati 3000 (© **085/3477-1200**). Taxis cost about R$30 (US$15/£8) to the beaches or downtown.

BY BUS   Long-distance buses arrive at the **Rodoviaria Eng. João Tomé,** Av. Borges de Melo s/n, Fatima (© **085/3256-1025**).

VISITOR INFORMATION

The state tourism agency **Setur** has an exclusively Portuguese website at www. setur.ce.gov.br. Fortaleza's **airport** has a tourist information center (© 085/3477-1667) in the arrivals hall, open daily 6am to 11pm, where you can pick up a good map of the city for free. The **state tourist information center (Centro de Turismo do Ceará)** is located downtown at Rua Senador Pompeu 350 (© 085/3101-5508), open Monday through Saturday from 9am to 6pm, Sunday 8am to noon.

CITY LAYOUT

Located just east of the Ceará River, the commercial heart of Fortaleza—called **Centro**—is small and quite walkable, though the traffic and sidewalk vendors can make the area seem a little hectic. Starting from the waterfront **Fortaleza N.S. de Assunção,** Centro stretches inland in a grid pattern. Following the **Avenida General Sampaio** or **Rua Barão do Rio Branco** will lead you straight into Fortaleza's main shopping area, centered on a large city square, the **Praça José de Alencar.** Smaller but lovelier is the **Praça dos Leões,** just 1 block east of the Rua Barão do Rio Branco at the corner of **Rua São Paulo.**

An easy stroll to the east of Centro leads to the ocean-side neighborhood **Praia de Iracema,** the first of a long string of beaches that line the waterfront, linked together by the **Avenida Beira Mar.** (Unfortunately, none of the urban beaches is recommended for bathing.) Name aside, Iracema isn't so much a beach as an ocean-side party place. You'll find lots of restaurants and bars along the seawall, and the **Rua Tabajaras** that runs parallel to the beach is packed with nightlife and restaurants. A kilometer (½ mile) or so east of Iracema you come to the next beach neighborhood, **Meireles.** From here onward, the beachside boulevard becomes a pleasure to walk. It's wide and shaded with plenty of kiosks for a drink or snack. The nightly **crafts market** (see "Shopping in Fortaleza," later in the chapter) always attracts large crowds. **Mucuripe** is the next neighborhood to the east of Meireles. At the end of Mucuripe beach there's a small colony of fishermen and a seafood market where the catch of the day is sold fresh off the boat. Farther east, the coastline curves south. The bend contains an industrial area of little interest to visitors, but once around the bend you come to **Praia do Futuro,** the only urban beach where the water is clean enough to swim. The beach becomes quite lively on Thursday evenings and on weekends but can be deserted during the week.

GETTING AROUND

BY BUS Most visitors use the bus to go between the beach neighborhoods and Centro. In Meireles or Mucuripe you catch the bus on the street parallel to the beach (Av. Abolição). Look for buses marked MEIRELES, CAÇA E PESCA, or GRANDE CIRCULAR. Fare is R$1.80 (US90¢/£.50).

BY TAXI Taxis can be hailed almost anywhere. To order a taxi, call **Disk Rádio Táxi Ceará** (© 085/3243-8111) or **Taxi Fortaleza** (© 085/3254-5744). Fare from Meireles to Centro is about R$18 (US$9/£5), and from Mucuripe to Praia de Iracema about R$24 (US$12/£6.50).

BY CAR Within Fortaleza a car is more a nuisance than a pleasure: traffic is chaotic and parking a challenge. However, to explore outlying beaches on your own, a car is ideal. See "Fast Facts: Fortaleza," below, for car-rental information.

Fortaleza

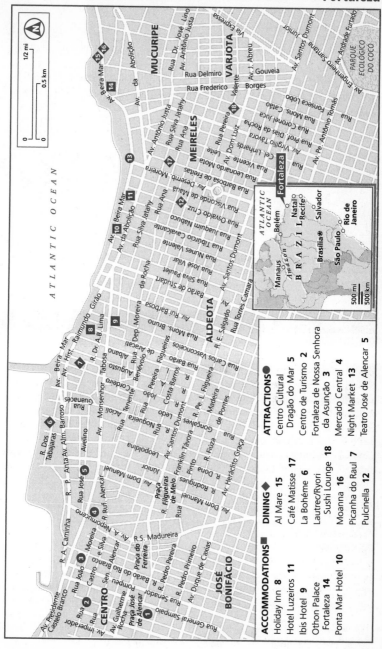

ACCOMMODATIONS ■
Holiday Inn **8**
Hotel Luzeiros **11**
Ibis Hotel **9**
Othon Palace
Fortaleza **14**
Ponta Mar Hotel **10**

DINING ◆
Al Mare **15**
Café Matisse **17**
La Bohême **6**
Lautrec/Ryori
Sushi Lounge **18**
Moanna **16**
Picanha do Raul **7**
Pulcinella **12**

ATTRACTIONS ●
Centro Cultural
Dragão do Mar **5**
Centro de Turismo **2**
Fortaleza de Nossa Senhora
da Asunção **3**
Mercado Central **4**
Night Market **13**
Teatro José de Alencar **5**

FAST FACTS: Fortaleza

American Express Inside the Via Scala Shopping, Av. Beira Mar 3960 (℃ 085/4004-7797); open Monday through Friday from 9am to 3pm.

Car Rental **Localiza** (℃ 0800/979-2000 or 085/3477-5050); **Avis** (℃ 0800/725-2847); **Unidas** (℃ 0800/121-121 or 085/3477-5373); and **Hertz** (℃ 085/3477-5055).

Currency Exchange **Banco do Brasil,** Av. Barão do Rio Branco 1515, Centro (℃ 085/3254-3266), which also has an ATM. **HSBC,** Av. Monsignor Tabosa 1200, Praia de Iracema (℃ 085/3308-1200). Both open Monday to Friday 10am to 4pm.

Hospitals **Hospital Batista Memorial,** Av. Padre Antônio Tomás 2030, Aldeota (℃ 085/ 3224-5417).

Internet Access **Cyber Café,** Av. Beira Mar 3120, Meireles (℃ 085/3242-5422) charges R$4 (US$2/£1) per hour; daily 9am–10pm. **Cyberoom Rent a Computer,** Av. Mons Tabosa 937, Centro (℃ 085/3219-6731) also charges R$4 (US$2/£1) per hour; Monday to Saturday 10am–8pm.

Weather Fortaleza has a pleasant sunny climate year-round, dry and tropical with an average temperature of 82°F (28°C); a cooling ocean breeze often takes the edge off the heat.

2 Where to Stay in Fortaleza

THE BEACHES

Most people stay within walking distance of the city beaches. The boulevards are pleasant and there are plenty of restaurants and activity along the oceanfront. The best of the beach neighborhoods is **Meireles,** which boasts a wide, well-trod boulevard by the sand, dotted with pleasant little kiosks where you can have a beer or fresh cool coconut. Meireles also has plenty of restaurants, vendors, and an excellent nightly crafts market. The beach neighborhood closest to downtown is **Praia de Iracema.** The beach here is wide and somewhat forlorn, but hotels in this neighborhood have the advantage of being within walking distance of Fortaleza's downtown attractions and the city's prime nightlife enclave. This is not the place for early sleepers. Farther east, **Mucuripe** is just a continuation of Meireles and runs all the way to a fishing colony at the eastern end of the beach.

IRACEMA
Expensive
Holiday Inn 🏨🏨   The Holiday Inn Fortaleza offers deluxe accommodations on the waterfront, a few minutes' walk from the nightlife attractions in Praia de Iracema. The 273 rooms are divided into deluxe, superior deluxe, and suites. All are spacious and have ocean views; even the most basic room is large with a queen-size bed, big desk, a pullout couch, and a separate vanity area next to the bedroom. The deluxe superior rooms are larger and come with a veranda and a king-size bed. The suites have a separate bedroom and living room with a wet bar. The furnishings are in great shape and the amenities are top-notch—the pool is especially nice.

Av. Historiador Raimundo Girão, Praia de Iracema, Fortaleza 60165-050 CE. ℃ 085/3455-5000. Fax 085/3455-5055. www.holidayfortaleza.com.br. 273 units (showers only). Dec–Mar and July R$260 (US$130/£70) deluxe double; R$325

(US$163/£88) deluxe superior double; R$390 (US$195/£105) suite double. 30%–40% discounts in low season. Extra person 30% extra. Children up to 5 stay free in parent's room. AE, DC, MC, V. Free parking. **Amenities:** Restaurant; bar; large pool; sauna; kids play room; excellent business center; room service; laundry service; nonsmoking rooms. *In room:* A/C, TV, free high-speed Internet, minibar, coffeemaker, hair dryer, safe.

Moderate

Ibis Hotel *(Value* Located a block off the water, the Ibis is the best value in Praia de Iracema. Like all Ibis hotels, the concept is basic: All rooms are identical and accommodations are comfortable but plain. Each room has a nice firm double bed, a desk, and closet space. Bathrooms are equally frills-free but are modern and spotless and come with showers only. The hotel amenities are kept to a minimum to reduce the operating costs. Breakfast is optional, R$9 (US$4.50/£2.50).

Rua Dr. Atualpa Barbosa Lima 660, Praia de Iracema, Fortaleza 60060-370 CE. *(*) 0800/703-7000 or 085/3219-2121. Fax 085/3219-0000. www.accorhotels.com.br. 171 units (showers only). R$99 (US$50/£27) double. Extra person R$18 (US$9/£5). Children up to 5 stay free in parent's room. AE, DC, MC, V. Free parking. **Amenities:** Restaurant; laundry. *In room:* A/C, TV, fridge, safe.

MEIRELES
Expensive

Hotel Luzeiros *(★★★* This is the best hotel in Fortaleza. Nearly all rooms have balconies, all have king-size beds and are elegantly furnished with dark-wood furniture set off with gold accents. White tile floors, quality linens, and high-end finishes add an air of luxury to even the most basic rooms. The prime rooms have a full ocean view *(frente mar);* the standard rooms have partial views *(vista mar).* (**Tip:** Rooms ending in 5 do NOT have balconies; avoid these.) And though we rarely judge a hotel by its lobby, the Hotel Luzeiros lobby and lobby bar are very stylish—more hip and trendy San Francisco than tropical Brazil. The swimming pool, business center, and fitness room are excellent.

Av. Beira Bar 2600, Meireles, Fortaleza 60165-121 CE. *(*) 085/3486-8585. Fax 085/3486-8587. www.hotelluzeiros. com.br. 202 units. R$270 (US$135/£73) double, partial ocean view; R$295 (US$148/£80) double, full ocean view; R$525 (US$263/£142) suite double. Extra person add about 25%. Children 6 and under stay free in parent's room. AE, DC, MC, V. Free parking. **Amenities:** Restaurant; bar; outside pool; business center; limited room service; laundry; nonsmoking rooms. *In room:* A/C, TV, dataport, minibar, safe.

Moderate

Ponta Mar Hotel What the Ponta Mar offers is a great location on Meireles beach, and good, clean, functional rooms. You'll get better value for your money at the Luzeiros, but that will cost you another R$45 to R$85 (US$23–US$43/£12–£23) per night, depending on the time of year. Rooms at the Ponta Mar are sparkling clean, with tile floors, a firm queen-size bed, a small desk and breakfast table, and floor-to-ceiling windows. Premier rooms face the street, Continental rooms face the beach. Bathrooms are modern and spotless and come with showers only.

Av. Beira Mar 2200, Meireles, Fortaleza 60165-121 CE. *(*)/fax 085/4006-2200. www.pontamar.com.br. 260 units. R$195 (US$98/£53) premier double; R$235 (US$118/£63) continental double. Extra person add 20%. Children up to 5 stay free in parent's room. AE, DC, MC, V. Free parking. **Amenities:** Restaurant; large outdoor pool; fitness room; business center; laundry. *In room:* A/C, TV, minibar, fridge, hair dryer, safe.

MUCURIPE
Moderate

Othon Palace Fortaleza *(★★* *(Value* Great location and even better value. The hotel's rooms are all beautifully furnished in blue and yellow tones and come with king-size beds; the bathrooms are done in beautiful marble. The smaller, standard rooms do not have balconies but do look out over the ocean. The deluxe rooms all have balconies and are spacious—definitely worth the price difference. The executive suites are twice the size of a deluxe apartment, with two bathrooms, a separate sitting room, and balcony, perfect for families.

Av. Beira Mar 3470, Mucuripe 60165-121 CE. © 0800/725-0505 or 085/3466-5500. Fax 085/3466-5501. www.othon hotels.com. 136 units (showers only). R$140–R$240 (US$70–US$120/£38–£65) standard double; R$160–R$290 (US$80–US$145/£43–£78) deluxe double; R$275–R$480 (US$138–US$240/£74–£130) executive suite double. Extra person add about 25%. Children 8 and under stay free in parent's room. AE, DC, MC, V. Free parking. **Amenities:** Restaurant; bar; large outdoor pool; fitness center; sauna; massage; business center; tour desk; 24-hr. room service; laundry; nonsmoking rooms. *In room:* A/C, TV, minibar, fridge, hair dryer.

3 Where to Dine in Fortaleza

Fortaleza's restaurants are surprisingly excellent. There's fine dining, including outstanding seafood at surprisingly low prices. In the main tourist zone, **Praia de Iracema,** the **Rua das Tabajaras** and its cross streets are lined with restaurants and patios. Take care, however, as many of these touristy establishments sacrifice quality for high turnover. There are some real gems, however, so with a bit of discernment it's possible to dine well. Farther out, **Meireles** and **Mucuripe** beaches offer excellent options as well. For a fun dining scene frequented mostly by Fortalezans, head to the ever-more-vibrant restaurant enclave of **Aldeota.**

If you find yourself in desperate need of a high-end coffee, try **Santa Clara Café Organico** (Rua Dragão do Mar 81; © **085/3219-6900**) located inside the Dragão do Mar cultural center. It features a range of excellent organically grown coffees and a range of chocolates and pastries. Open Tuesday through Sunday 3 to 10pm.

Al Mare ⚐ SEAFOOD   Al Mare is as spectacular as they come. The patio and dining room wrap around the main building, offering lovely views of Praia de Meireles. The decor is a tad heavy on the maritime memorabilia, but the food is excellent. For appetizers, try the tangy marinated octopus in an onion-and-herb vinaigrette or the satisfying fried calamari *(lula á milanesa).* Seafood pastas are very popular; try the spaghetti *pescatore* with squid, prawns, garlic, and tomato or the spaghetti *al vongole* with a generous serving of small clams. The most spectacular dish is the grilled seafood combination, *grelhada al mare,* a platter of grilled lobster, prawns, fish, octopus, and squid.

Av. Beira Mar 3821, Meireles. © **085/3263-3888.** Main courses R$24–R$42 (US$12–US$21/£6.50–£12) for 2; grilled seafood platters R$76–R$88 (US$38–US$44/£21–£24) for 2. AE, DC, MC, V. Tues–Sun noon–3pm and 7pm–midnight.

Café Matisse ⚐⚐ SEAFOOD/BRAZILIAN   Located just a couple blocks in from Meireles beach, this innovative restaurant is decorated in strong primary colors with lots of interesting artwork, and offers creative cuisine at reasonable prices. The dishes are refreshingly unique. The *peixe carmel* is a grilled fish served with a grape and caper sauce and a side of caramelized mushrooms and asparagus. The popular *peixe bonne femme* is a grilled filet of fish served with a béchamel sauce with mushrooms and shrimp. The wine list offers a decent selection from France, Italy, Portugal, Australia, and South America.

Rua Silva Jatahy 942, Aldeota. © **085/3242-1377.** www.cafematisse.com.br. Main courses R$18–R$42 (US$9–US$22/ £5–£12). AE, DC, MC, V. Sun–Fri noon–3pm; daily 7pm–midnight.

La Bohème ⚐⚐ SEAFOOD   One of the most beautiful restaurants in Praia de Iracema, La Bohème combines an art gallery with a restaurant and large outdoor patio. Diners can choose the white-linen table service indoors or the casual tables alfresco. The menu is the same, a delicious variety of lobster, grilled with *catupiry* cheese or

> **Tips   You Buy, We Fry**
>
> The fresh fish market in the fishing colony at the end of Mucuripe beach offers what may be the shortest distance anywhere between catch and cook. Buy fresh prawns or fish at one of the market stalls (about R$8/US$4/£2 for a half-kilo of prawns) and the stall at the corner of the market will clean, cook, and serve your meal to you on plates with rice—all for R$6/US$3/£1.50. Cold beer is extra. Open daily 2 to 10pm. No phone.

sautéed in a *moqueca* stew, or prawns prepared in a variety of ways, including flambéed and served in a pineapple shell. Other options include octopus stews *a Baiana,* with coconut milk and dendê oil. A band plays nightly from 9pm.

Av. Rua dos Tabajaras 380, Praia de Iracema. © 085/3219-3311. Main courses R$35–R$85 (US$18–US$43/ £9.50–£23) for 2 (the lobster dishes are the more expensive items). AE, DC, MC, V. Mon–Sat 5pm–1am (may close later on weekends).

Moanna ☆☆☆ FRENCH   Moanna has it all. Located on Mucuripe beach, the restaurant is absolutely gorgeous, decorated in a kind of gold-and-brown rustic chic, with a soothing waterfall against the back wall. And then there's the food. This is high-end dining with quality ingredients, creative cuisine, and excellent service, yet most dishes don't even crack the R$36 (US$15/£7.50) mark. Truly excellent is the *frango tropical,* succulent pieces of grilled chicken breast served in mango sauce with savory crepes stuffed with leek mousse. Also worth trying is the duck in an orange-and-Cointreau sauce with spinach purée. For desserts, there's a fruit carpaccio, thin slices of fruit served with a scoop of ice cream and a raspberry sauce. However, chocoholics may want to order the *último desejo* (the last wish), two slices of chocolate cookie stuffed with crème caramel served on a bed of crème anglaise with sliced strawberries and chocolate sauce. Who could ask for anything more?

Av. Beira Mar 4260, Mucuripe (inside the Golden Fortaleza Parthenon). © 085/3263-4635. R$12–R$48 (US$5–US$20/ £2.50–£10) for 2. AE, DC, MC, V. Sun–Thurs noon–1am; Fri–Sat noon–2am.

Picanha do Raul ☆ STEAK   Simple decor, simple cuisine, simply delicious. For 30 years Raul has been serving up his signature dish—400 grams of picanha steak on the grill, with side order of macaxeira (manioc), farofa, and garlic bread—in this space just off the beach in Iracema. Ice-cold beer is the beverage of choice while for dessert, there's a range of homemade fruit sweets.

Rua Joauim Alves 73, Iracema. © 085/3219-6451. R$16–R$28 (US$8–US$14/£4–£7) for 2. DC, MC, V. Mon–Sat 10am–2am; Sun 11am–10pm.

Pulcinella ☆ ITALIAN   Voted Fortaleza's best Italian year after year, this eatery features a traditional pasta menu just ever so slightly tilted toward the sea. Antipastos include sauteed shrimp and squid or salmon carpaccio. Mains include risottos and pastas with mussels, shrimp, and octopus. Stuffed ravioli dishes are more land based, including regional specialties such as sun-dried beef and locally made mussarella, or chicken and catupiry cheese. The menu includes beef and chicken dishes for those not in the mood for pasta. The wine list includes a range of mid-priced vintages from Brazil, South America, and Italy, with an added select few from Australia and France.

Rua Oswaldo Cruz 640, Aldeota. © 085/3261-3411. www.pulcinella.com.br. R$24–R$48 (US$12–US$24/£6.50–£14). AE, DC, MC, V. Mon–Thurs noon–3pm and 6:30pm–1:30am; Sat noon–2am; Sun noon–1am.

Tips Good Eating at Aldeota

The restaurant neighborhood of Aldeota is becoming ever more popular with Fortalezan locals. Just a short taxi ride from the beach hotels, the area around the Shopping Bouganvillia mall off Rua Prof. Dias da Rocha has recently seen the opening of a number of outstanding restaurants. One of the most beautiful restaurants is **Lautrec,** Shopping Buganvillia, Av. Dom Luis 1113 (© **085/3264-4020**), a small bistro offering outdoor dining and a menu of French and Italian seafood—think flambéed prawns with tarragon or grilled prawns with pesto and mozzarella. For sushi, there's **Ryori Sushi Lounge** (© **085/3224-9997**), located inside the mall itself. For a more casual night out try **Zug Choperia,** Rua Prof. Dias da Rocha 579 (© **085/3224-4193**), a lovely bar/restaurant with a large patio, live music, and fabulous appetizers, including a variety of *pasteis* or cold-cut-and-cheese platters. Just a block or so away there's excellent seafood mid-priced at **Milmares,** Rua Frederico Borges 496 (© **085/3296-1600**), while—a little more distant—**Le Parisien,** Av. Julio Abreu 131 (corner of Rua Dilmiro Gouveia) (© **085/3267-6746**) offers some of the city's best French fine dining, in an lovely room, with open-air wine bar attached for those who just want to sip a fine vintage and maybe nibble, while enjoying the live local music.

4 Exploring Fortaleza

Fortaleza's main attractions are the beaches outside of the city, including the **Morro Branco** with its multicolored cliffs, the glorious sand dunes of **Canoa Quebrada,** and the stunningly beautiful and rustic **Jericoacoara.** The city itself has a small **historic center** that's worth a visit if you have a day to spare, but it's certainly not worth the trip by itself. The best way to get out and see the beaches is to head out on a day trip to Cumbuco or Morro Branco; both are only a short distance from Fortaleza. These beaches are playgrounds for adults and children alike. Buggy tours, sand boarding, sand tobogganing, parasailing, boat rides—you name it and you can experience it, all under a hot tropical sun.

Canoa Quebrada is also within easy day-trip distance, but you may want to stay a day or two to get a better taste of the place. There are plenty of pousadas and restaurants here, and a small but active nightlife scene.

To enjoy Jericoacoara you need at least 3 or 4 days; getting there takes almost a day. This isolated beach community features Sahara-like sand dunes, stunning white beaches, plus a steady wind that makes it Brazil's windsurf capital.

THE TOP ATTRACTIONS

Canoa Quebrada *(Kids)* Every beach town should be this laid-back. But with miles and miles of soft white sand, the green-blue waters framed by low red cliffs, why shouldn't it be? The symbol of the town is a half-moon and star, representing fertility. Hippie heritage aside, locals have expanded their businesses to include **horseback riding** for R$30 (US$15/£8) per hour, **sand boarding** for R$3 (US$1.50/£.80) per trip, and especially **buggy rides** either along the beach or into the vast sand dunes piled up behind the city. The full 2½-hour buggy tour, which includes a passage along the beach and up into the dunes, costs R$180 (US$90/£49) per buggy (buggies seat two or three comfortably, four if you squish). Shorter tours ride along the cliff-top overlooking the beach, usually with a stop at a rainwater lagoon that looks like an oasis in the desert, the perfect stop for a swim or a cold beer. On the beach, *barracas* (stalls) rent out chairs and umbrellas, and food and drink is always close at hand, while local women offer scalp and shoulder massages for R$10 (US$5/£3).

Canoa Quebrada is located 156km (97 miles) east of Fortaleza. For tourism information see www.canoa-quebrada. com. To reach the community take CE-040 east to Aracati. Just past Aracati there will be a turnoff for Canoa Quebrada. For transfers to Canoa Quebrada see "Tour Operators in Fortaleza," below. By bus, the bus company Viação São Benedito (℡ 085/3272-1232) has departures from Fortaleza's central bus terminal at 8:30am, 1:40pm, and 3:40pm. Alternatively, there are 6 daily departures to the city of Aracati, located 9km (5½ miles) from Canoa. Either trip costs R$18 (US$9/£5). From Aracati it is possible to get a cab or local bus.

WHERE TO STAY

If you decide to stay, the nicest pousada in town is **Pousada Long Beach** (Rua Long Beach s/n; ℡ **085/3421-7404;** www.longbeachvillage.com.br), which features a pool deck with a fabulous view of the beach, as well as large comfortable rooms and bunga-lows. Cost is R$180 (US$90/£49) for a comfortable room, and R$240 (US$120/£65) for a self-contained double bungalow. **Pousada California,** Rua Nascer do Sol 136 (℡ **085/3421-7039;** www.californiacanoa.com), has simple but clean and comfortable doubles for R$70 to R$140 (US$35–US$70/£19–£38). The main street in town, **Broadway,** is a pedestrian cobblestone laneway chockablock with cafes, bars, and restaurants. The street remains active until early in the morning.

Cumbuco ✶✶ Located just a 45-minute drive from the city, Cumbuco is where many Fortalezans come to spend a day at the beach. The big attraction? Beach and dunes. The main activity? The dune buggy ride. If a hair-raising buggy ride is what you're after, this is the place to visit. Drivers are able to take you on a roller-coaster ride over the shifting sands, dropping down steep inclines, swerving over piles of sand as if they were minor speed bumps, and skidding and sliding at almost vertical angles off the face of the taller dunes. **Buggy rides** cost R$100 (US$50/£27) per hour for a buggy that fits two or three people comfortably. Gentler beach activities include **horseback riding** R$20 (US$10/£4.50) for 30 minutes and **boat rides** on the *jan-gada* fishing rafts for R$10 (US$5/£2.50) per 30 minutes. Cumbuco is also one of the best places on the coast for **kite surfing. Blue Wind Kiteboarding School** (℡ 085/ **8837-1132;** www.bluewindkite.com.br) offers equipment rental and lessons. If you know how to surf, 1-day rental of all equipment including wet suit runs R$200 (US$100/£54). If you want to learn, a 4-day basic course (8 hr. of instruction) costs R$750 (US$375/£203). If you want to come out early and make a day of it at the beach, the **Aldea Brasil** restaurant (℡ **085/3318-7541**) makes a good base. The restaurant has a pool, sun deck, beach chairs, and bar, all of which are available to cus-tomers on the understanding that you'll order drinks and snacks and likely lunch at the restaurant. Open daily 9am to 6pm. Should you want to stay in Cumbuco, the **Eco Paradise Hotel,** Vila dos Pescadores s/n, Cumbuco (℡ **085/3318-7750;** www. paradisecumbuco.com.br), has pleasant and comfortable suites for R$195 (US$98/ £53) per night. Remember that after dark there is absolutely nothing to do here.

Cumbuco is located 37km (23 miles) east of Fortaleza. To reach Cumbuco, follow the signs for CE-085. The turnoff for Cumbuco is 11km (7 miles) past Coité. For transfers to Cumbuco see "Tour Operators in Fortaleza," below.

Jericoacoara ✶✶✶ The pearl on the Ceará coast, Jericoacoara's attraction is par-tially its isolation. Visitors can only arrive by 4WD, preferably driven by someone who knows what he or she is doing; the 18km (11-mile) drive from Jijoca through the con-stantly shifting sands is not for the uninitiated. The payoff for those who persevere?

Tour Operators in Fortaleza

There are several good tour operators in Fortaleza including **Ernatitur**, Av. Barão de Studart 1165 (© **085/3244-9363**; www.ernanitur.com.br), **Girafatur**, Rua Tenente Benévolo 13 (© **085/3219-3255**; www.girafatur.com.br), and **Hard Tour Ecotourism**, Rua Francisco Holanda 843 ap. 203 (© **085/3224-9300** www.hardtour.com.br). All three offer transfers and tours to Cumbuco, Canoa Quebrada, Jericoacoara, Morro Branco, and Beach Park. Prices at all three are around R$30 (US$15/£8) for a city tour, R$30 (US$15/£8) for Cumbuco, R$25 (US$13/£7) for Beach Park, R$30 (US$15/£8) for Morro Branco, and R$50 (US$25/£14) for Canoa Quebrada.

Miles and miles of unspoiled beaches, rock formations, lagoons, mangroves, palm trees, and a Sahara desert landscape of beautiful dunes, some over 30m (100 ft.) tall. In recent years this formerly sleepy fishing village has gotten, if not exactly crowded, certainly much more visited. The region is now an environmental protection zone, with laws forbidding the construction of new hotels and pousadas within the protected area and guidelines for garbage and recycling. Still, in high season it can be busier than you'd expect in paradise, so plan your travel for the shoulder season (Aug–Nov and late Mar to June). Jeri (as locals call it) offers many of the same activities as other beaches on the coast. There are buggy tours, hikes, sand boarding, and visits to freshwater lagoons. However, the main attraction (in addition to the isolation) is the wind; Jeri is one of those places—like the Gorge in Oregon—with the kind of consistent near-gale beloved by top-notch windsurfers. There's a useful website at www.jericoacoara.com.br.

Clube dos Ventos (© 088/3669-2288; www.clubedosventos.com) has new, top-grade gear for rent. Price (with pre-booking) is R$122 (US$61/£33) per day, R$606 (US$303/£245) per week. Their website has details on gear and wind conditions (including a daily wind report).

GETTING THERE   There are essentially two ways to travel to Jeri—the cheaper and quicker way is by bus or minibus along the state highways (except for the last little stretch across the sand). The trip takes about 7 hours. The agencies listed in "Tour Operators in Fortaleza," above, all offer this kind of transfer. Some have packages that include a 1- or 2-night stay. The other way is to travel by Land Rover, traversing the many beautiful beaches that lie between Fortaleza and Jeri. For this kind of tour, contact **Hard Tour Ecotourism**, Rua Francisco Holanda 843 ap .203 (© **085/3224-9300;** www.hardtour.com.br), which offers both 1-day transfers, and multiday packages. On a 3-day trip, you travel by Land Rover to Jeri, doing a lot of off-road driving and stopping at scenic beaches such as Cumbuco, Lagoinha, Mundaú, and Baleia. In Jeri the next day, there are visits to the dunes and beaches and the famous rock with the hole in it (Pedra Furada). On the third day you travel back to Fortaleza by the main highway.

Keep in mind that Jeri remains a rustic spot—no fancy hotels, and amenities are pretty basic. The best hotel is undoubtedly **Mosquito Blue**, Rua da Farmacia s/n (© **088/3669-2203;** www.mosquitoblue.com.br), R$240 (US$120/£65) double.

Less expensive but still comfortable is **Recanto do Barão,** Rua do Forró 433 (© **088/ 3669-2149;** www.recantodobarao.com), R$150 (US$75/£41) double. Bring plenty of cash (in small bills), as ATMs are nonexistent and credit cards are rarely accepted.

Jericoacoara is located 300km (186 miles) west of Fortaleza. www.jericoacoara.com. From Fortaleza take the CE-085 west to Barrento and from there connect to the BR-402 to Jicoca. The last 23km (14 miles) from Jijoca are completed by buggy as regular cars are not able to handle the sand dunes and poor road conditions. If you have rented a car you can park it in Jicoca.

Morro Branco ⚭ Most visitors come to see the maze of colored sand cliffs that line the beach. Local guides (who work for a donation, anything from R$5–R$10/US$2.50– US$5/£1.50–£2.50) will take you through the maze of cliffs, showing off the spots with the best colors. A close-up look at the sand reveals incredible variations in color, ranging from almost pure white to yellow, gold, pink, orange, red, and purple. At the top of the cliff maze there are usually artisans working on new designs of the region's best-known souvenir, sand-filled glass bottles with intricate designs of colored sands.

Morro Branco is 85km (53 miles) east of Fortaleza. Take CE-040 to Beberibe, then take the turnoff for Morro Branco (it's approximately 4km/2½ miles from the main junction to the beach). For tours to Morro Branco see "Tour Operators in Fortaleza," above.

DOWNTOWN FORTALEZA

Downtown Fortaleza has some worthwhile sights if you want to take a day off from the beach. Just a short stroll from the Praia de Iracema is the area that the locals call **Casario,** a lovely collection of restored 19th-century colonial buildings, located primarily on the **Rua Dragão do Mar** and **Rua Almirante Tamandaré.** The area really comes to life at night, as most of the historic buildings house nightclubs or cafes. The new centerpiece of this area—built in a contrasting but somehow complementary contemporary style—is the **Centro Cultural Dragão do Mar,** Rua Dragão do Mar 81 (© **985/3488-8600;** www.dragaodomar.org.br; Tues–Sun 2–9:30pm). This modern cultural center is built in the shape of a mosque with a white spiraling walkway that rests on an arcade over the historic buildings on the street below. At night, the

---

⟨Kids⟩ Splish Splash

Beach Park (© **088/4012-3000;** www.beachpark.com.br) is located 29km (18 miles) outside the city on Praia de Porto de Dunas, and is the largest water park on the Northeast coast. The park features four pools—including the earthquake wave pool with 2.5m (8-ft.) waves—and a number of waterslides. The largest, the *Insano,* boasts a 41m (135-ft.) vertical drop. There are also restaurants and tennis courts for adults. Open 11am to 5pm. R$80 (US$40/£22) adults, R$70 (US$35/£19) children 12 and under. Closer to town and cheaper, though not nearly on the same scale, is **Chico do Caranguejo,** Av. Zéze Diogo 4930, © **085/ 3262-0108;** www.chicodocaranguejo.com.br (see "Fortaleza After Dark," below). More known for its Thursday night crab feast, Chico's also features a small children's water park, with a pair of waterslides and fountains, perfect for kids under 10 or so (who may well find the waves on Praia de Futuro beach a bit rough). The children's park is open daily 8am to 6:30pm; R$6 (US$3/£1.50). Restricted to kids 3 and up.

structure glows with a faint blue light. For the full range of programming at the cultural center, see www.dragaodomar.org.br.

On the waterfront there's the **Fortaleza de Nossa Senhora da Assunção,** Avenida Alberto Craveiro (*© 085/3255-1600;* daily 8–11am and 2–5pm). Built by the Dutch in 1649 (as Fort Schoonenborch) in a five-point-star shape, the fort was rechristened after the Dutch were driven from Brazil in 1654.

If you are shopping for clothes, Fortaleza is one of the cheaper cities in Brazil. One main shopping area lies on **Avenida Monsenhor Tabosa.** From Avenida Dom Manuel 6 blocks down to Rua João Cordeiro, this street is devoted almost exclusively to locally made purses, shoes, and clothing. The other shopping area is on **Rua General Sampaio, Sen. Pompeu,** and **Barão do Rio Branco,** and particularly the side streets around the **Praça José de Alencar.**

The highlight of the square is the **Teatro José de Alencar,** Praça José de Alencar s/n (*© 085/3101-2583*), open for visits Tuesday to Friday 8am to 5pm, Saturday 8 to 11:30am. At R$4 (US$2/£1), it's worth a peek. Built in 1908, the theater is a marvel of colorful high-Victorian cast-iron construction, shipped in from Scotland. The gardens, added in 1974, were designed by Burle Marx.

Shopping in Fortaleza

Ceará is known for its quality handicrafts. The most famous souvenirs are the sand-filled glass bottles. Though admittedly touristy, they are as wickedly complex as a boat-in-a-bottle. Other excellent souvenirs include handmade cotton hammocks and local craft cachaças. The **Mercado Central,** Rua Alberto Nepomuceno 199 (*© 085/3454-8586;* Mon–Sat 9am–7pm, Sun 9am–noon), is one of the best crafts markets in the city. The large circular building houses over 500 stalls and small shops selling a variety of handicrafts, including hammocks, lace, T-shirts, leather products, and sweets. Another good place to browse for crafts is the **outdoor market** that takes place nightly from 5 to 10pm in front of the new **Oasis Atlantico Hotel** in **Meireles.** The other craft you will see everywhere is lace, a tradition brought to Ceará by the Portuguese. The lace-makers (*rendeiras*) create delicate and complicated patterns, requiring enormous amounts of work, which in Fortaleza can still be bought for relatively little. Look for tablecloths, bedspreads, blouses, place mats, and numerous other items with lace trims. Good-quality lace is available at the crafts markets mentioned above, as well as at the **Centro de Turismo,** Rua Pompeu 350 (*© 085/3101-5508;* Mon–Sat 8am–6pm, Sun 8am–noon). Housed in the former city jail, it has over 100 crafts stalls (in addition to a tourist information booth that gives out a good free map). But for truly amazing creations—lace tablecloths, negligees, sheets, and pillowcases—have a look at **Nuage,** located in the Shopping Bouganvillia, Rua Prof. Dias da Rocha 579 (*© 085/3244-7971*). The large tablecloths can cost up to R$1,100 (US$550/£297) per square meter and take 8 months to make! The quality is truly outstanding.

It's July, So It Must Be Carnaval?

Fortaleza's biggest event is Fortal, or Carnaval Out-of-Season. The event takes place beginning on the Thursday of the last weekend of July, and attracts over two million revelers. If you plan to be in town, book your accommodations well in advance. Most of the events take place in Meireles on the Avenida Beira Mar, which gets closed to traffic and covered in bleachers for spectators. The event is similar to Salvador's Carnaval. Each night there are blocos, often with the same well-known artists who perform in Salvador—Olodum, Chiclete com Banada, Timbalada, and Ivete Sangalo. You can either purchase a T-shirt and follow a bloco or buy a seat in the bleachers to watch all the blocos file past. For exact dates and a list of who's playing, see www.fortal.com.br or call ℭ 085/3261-4050.

ORGANIZED TOURS/OUTDOOR ACTIVITIES

BOAT TOURS   Ceará Saveiros, across the street from Avenida Beira Mar 4293 (ℭ 085/3263-1085), runs two daily boat trips along Fortaleza's waterfront. The morning tour departs at 10am and takes in the city's main beaches. The 2-hour sunset tour leaves around 4pm.

WATERSPORTS   The urban beaches of Fortaleza have relatively calm waters and are perfect for practicing watersports. **Brothers Wind School** offers a range of equipment rentals as well as lessons. Sailors can take out a laser or Hobie Cat for R$30 (US$15/£8) per hour. Windsurfers can rent a board for R$30 (US$15/£8). You can also purchase a package of 8 hours of instruction with 10 hours of free rentals for R$160 (US$80/£43). Kayaks rent for R$10 (US$5/£2.50) an hour. Brothers is located just across the street from the Parthenon Golden Fortaleza, Av. Beira Mar 4260 in Mucuripe (ℭ **085/9984-1967;** daily 8am–5pm).

5 Fortaleza After Dark

THE PERFORMING ARTS

Teatro José de Alencar   One of the loveliest venues in Fortaleza is the high Victorian Teatro de José Alencar. Music lovers can attend classical music performances by the Eleazar de Carvalho Chamber Orquestra. Call the box office or check out www.secult.ce.gov.br under "programe-se" for schedules. Praça José de Alencar s/n, Centro. ℭ 085/3101-2583.

CLUBS & BARS

Fortaleza is well known for its nightlife, with something happening almost every night of the week. The two most happening areas are **Praia de Iracema** and the **Casario,** the historic buildings around the **Centro Cultural do Dragão,** located at **Rua Dragão do Mar** and **Rua Alm. Tamandaré.**

(*Note:* The four bars at the intersection of Rua dos Tabajaras and Tr. Iracema [Cafe del Mar, Europa, Bikini, and Kapital] are patronized exclusively by working girls and their customers. Bars in the rest of Iracema beach, and elsewhere in Fortaleza, try to prevent prostitutes from entering.)

On Monday night, everybody heads down to **Pirata,** Rua dos Tabajaras 325, Praia de Iracema (ℭ **085/4011-6161;** www.pirata.com.br). Doors open at 8pm, the band comes on at 1am, and the party continues until the wee hours. The house band plays forró, *axé,* and reggae.

Tuesdays, the crowds leave the beach and head out to Varjota, to **Arre Égua** (Rua Delmiro Gouveia 420; © **085/3267-2325**) where things catch fire with the nordeste musical style known as forró.

Lupus Bier, Rua dos Tabajaras 340 (© **085/3219-2829**), is Fortaleza's biggest and most popular microbrewery. Tables come equipped with a tap-your-own beer installation; for R$50 (US$25/£14) you get 10 liters of ice-cold lager whenever you want it. Though busy almost every night, on Wednesdays, Lupus Bier hosts an excellent and accessible regional folklore show by the group Txai. Tickets are R$20 (US$10/£5.50), and the performance starts at 8pm.

On Thursday night, locals head out to **Praia do Futuro,** southwest of Mucuripe, for a traditional evening of crab eating *(caranguejada).* Why Thursday? Nobody knows, though hanging out on a beach, eating freshly steamed crabs, drinking cold beer, and listening to a band play live *forró* (Brazilian country music) just seems to be a Thursday kind of thing. The place to be is **Chico do Caranguejo,** Av. Zéze Diogo 4930 (© **085/3262-0108;** www.chicodocaranguejo.com.br). Things warm up after 7pm. The band starts around 8:30pm. Taxi recommended.

Friday through Sunday, the options abound. The historic downtown area around the **Centro Cultural do Dragão do Mar,** Rua Dragão do Mar 81 (© **985/3488-8600;** www.dragaodomar.org.br) features at least a dozen bars and nightclubs side by side. Many have live music and almost all have wonderful patios. **O Brasileirinho,** Rua Dragão do Mar 441 (© **085/3219-3701**), has live music Thursday through Sunday. The house band plays samba from Thursday through Saturday, and on Sunday nights it's forró. The bar opens at 4pm, and the music usually starts around 10pm. Just a few doors down is **Caros Amigos,** Rua Dragão do Mar 22 (© **085/3226-6567**). The music here is more varied; Tuesday and Wednesday it's bossa nova and jazz; Thursday, Friday, and Saturday it's samba. In the same area, **Órbita,** Rua Almirante Jaceguai 93 (© **085/3453-1421**), is particularly popular on Sunday night. Cover R$5 (US$2.50/£1.35).

Close to the waterfront on the edge of the old downtown is the new and vast **Mucuripe Club,** Travessa Maranguape 108, Centro (near the Marina Park Hotel) (© **085/3254-3020;** www.mucuripe.com.br). With space for 5,000 people, this upscale disco features six different dance floors that play up to six different rhythms, usually some combination of hip-hop or house, MPB (Brazilian pop), forró, soul, and blues or jazz. Open Thursday through Saturday 9pm to 4am. Cover is about R$20 (US$10/£5.50).

13

São Luis & the Lençóis Maranhenses

It was the French, not the Portuguese, who founded the city of São Luís. In 1612 a French colony 500 strong under the command of Daniel de la Touche, Sieur de la Ravardiere, established a fortress and city that they named in honor of King Louis XIII.

Ironically enough, almost 400 years later, French and other visitors flock to São Luís because its historic center, better than almost any city in Brazil, preserves the look and feel of a traditional Portuguese city.

The northeast coast of Brazil was a void on explorers' maps when the French colonists arrived. Though Portuguese cities farther south such as Salvador and Olinda were already thriving, winds and currents conspired to isolate this part of the coastline. It was quicker to sail from Olinda to Lisbon than it was from Olinda up the coast to Belém. The French hoped to take advantage of this gap to establish a successful commercial and missionary settlement before the Portuguese even noticed.

It was not to be. The Portuguese rallied and by 1615 succeeded in driving out the would-be French colonists. Portugal took over the colony, but kept the name bestowed by the French.

São Luís's heyday came in the 18th and 19th centuries, when the city grew rich on the export of sugar, cattle, and especially cotton. Sometime in the 1820s, the fashion spread among São Luís's rich middle classes of covering their houses with Portuguese ceramic tiles. Not only were the blue, yellow, and green tiles ornate and beautiful, but they also reflected the sun and kept houses cooler. São Luís became one of the richest, most beautiful cities in the Northeast.

But in the late 1800s the Maranhão economy went into a steep decline. The end of slavery spelled the end of cheap cotton and sugar, while the city's tidal port grew too shallow for the new large ships of the steam age.

Marooned in an economic backwater, the center of São Luís—tiles and all—survived the 20th century intact. Restoration work on the city's old center began in 1989, culminating with the recognition in 1997 of the historic center of São Luís as a World Heritage Site.

Though still one of Brazil's poorer states, Maranhão has lately seen an upswing. With a new deepwater port, São Luís now serves as the export point for iron ore mined in the interior. Brazil's satellite-launching facility is located across the bay from São Luís near the city of Alcântara. Tourism is also a growing force in the economy, but remains very much in its infancy.

Visitors to São Luís can wander the streets of a beautiful colonial city without the crowds now found in Salvador. They can also savor the strong musical culture of São Luís, expressed in its love of reggae and in the yearly celebration of Bumba-meu-boi.

Farther afield, there is the chance to visit the Lençóis Maranhenses, a desert of snow-white sand dunes whose low points are full of water—truly one of the most intriguing natural landscapes in Brazil.

1 Essentials

ARRIVING

BY PLANE   **Varig** (© 098/4003-7000), **Gol** (© 0300/115-2121), and **TAM** (toll-free © 0800/570-5700 or 098/4002-5700) all have flights to São Luis. The airport, **Marechal Cunha Machado,** Av. Dos Libaneses s/n, Tirirical (© 098/3217-6101), is 13km (8 miles) from the city center. A taxi to the centro histórico costs R$40 (US$20/£11).

BY BUS   Buses arrive at the **Terminal Rodoviário de São Luis,** Av. Dos Franceses s/n, Santo Antonio (© 098/3249-2488), 10km (6 miles) from the centro histórico.

BY FERRY   Ferries to Alcântara depart from the **Terminal Hidrovário** (© 098/3232-0692), located opposite the Reviver area in the centro histórico. Ferries depart daily at 7am and 9:30am, and return at 8:30am and 4pm. Note that if the tide is out, ferries depart from the beach at Ponta D'Areia. Also, ferry departure times are only approximate. It's best to check at the ferry terminal the day before departure.

VISITOR INFORMATION

São Luis's airport has a tourist information booth in the arrivals hall that's open daily from 8am to 6pm (© 098/3244-4500). In the city there is a state tourist information office in the centro histórico on Praça Benedito Leite, Rua da Palma 53 (© 098/3212-6211), open Monday to Friday 8am to 7pm, Saturday, Sunday, and holidays 9am to 2pm. Both give out an excellent free map of the old city. The official city government tourist agency website is www.saoluis.ma.gov.br/turismo. Also worthwhile: www.guiasaoluis.com.br. The state tourism agency has a site in English: www.turismo.ma.gov.br/en/index.html.

CITY LAYOUT

The city of **São Luís** sits on the **Ilha São Luis,** a vast low-lying alluvial island that floats between two large river estuaries, the **Baia São Marcos** (to the northwest) and the **Baia São José** (to the southeast). Small tidal inlets—called *igarapés*—divide the island into numerous smaller islands and peninsulas. The oldest part of the city—called the **centro histórico**—sits on one of these peninsulas, almost completely surrounded north and south by wide igarapés.

The old city's oldest section lies at the very tip of the peninsula. It is here (tide willing) that the ferries to Alcântara dock, and where in times past ships used to unload their cargos. On maps this area is often labeled **"Praia Grande."** In recent years, as the city has poured money into renovating old buildings and bringing the old city back to life, the area has been renamed the **"Reviver."**

Roughly speaking, the Reviver runs from the ferry dock east past the old Customs house and along the cobblestone streets up the steps to the **Praça João Lisboa,** and from the small rise in the north that holds the fort and governor's palace (**Palacio dos Leões**) and south as far as the **Convento do Mêrces.**

The city has long since spread beyond the original small peninsula. Two bridges lead from the north side of the original peninsula into the newer parts of São Luis. Closest to the mouth of the estuary, the **José Sarney bridge** (named for a former Brazilian president

São Luis

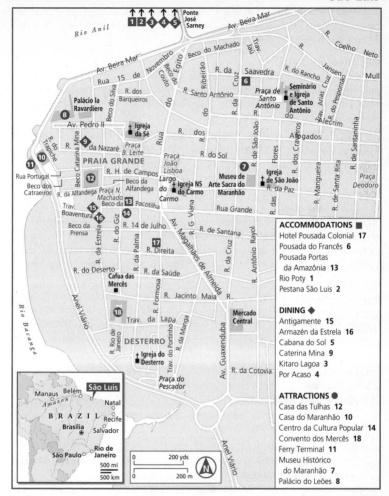

and Maranhão governor) turns into the **Avenida Castelo Branco** (named for a former president and dictator) which leads to the **São Francisco** neighborhood. This is São Luis's small central business district. It has a few banks and office towers, but is otherwise completely lacking in sights or restaurants or anything else of interest to tourists.

Beyond a roundabout at the top end of São Francisco, the road turns into **Avenida Ana Jansen,** which leads past the **Lagoa de Jansen** and then out to the first of the city's beach neighborhoods, **Ponta d'Areia.** The city recently installed a boardwalk and small park on the north side of Lagoa de Jansen, then encouraged bars and restaurants to move in, transforming the lake into one of São Luis's most popular dining and nightlife areas.

In Ponta d'Areia, the Avenida Jansen becomes **Avenida dos Holandeses,** a wide busy highway that runs parallel to the coast forming the commercial backbone for the beach neighborhoods of **Praia de São Marcos, Praia do Calhau, Praia do Caolho,** and **Praia Olho d'Agua.** Most of the hotels in these neighborhoods are located on the seaside Avenida Litorânea, which splits from Avenida dos Holandeses in Praia de São Marcos and travels out along the shoreline.

GETTING AROUND

BY BUS   São Luis is a big spread-out city, not really ideal for bus travel. Buses to the old city are marked PRAIA GRANDE. Buses to the beach neighborhoods are marked PONTA D'AREIA or PRAIA CALHAU. Buses cost R$1.80 (US90¢/£.50). You board through the front.

BY TAXI   Taxis are widely available. To reserve, phone **Cocoma** (© **098/3231-1010**) or **Coopertaxi** (© **098/3245-4404**). A taxi from Ponta D'Areia to the centro histórico costs about R$15 to R$25 (US$7.50–US$13/£4–£7).

FAST FACTS: São Luis

Area Codes   The area code for São Luis is **098.**

Banks   In the centro histórico: **Banco do Brasil** (© **098/3215-4992**) on Av. Dom. Pedro II 78, in front of the Palácio dos Leões; also **Banco do Brasil** in the Reviver at Travessa Boa Ventura 26-B (© **098/3232-8507**).

Car Rentals   **Avis** (© **0800/725-2847** or 098/3245-5957; São Luis airport); **Localiza** (© **0800/979-2000** or 098/3245-1566; São Luis airport or Av. Dos Holandeses lotes 7 e 8); **Unidas** (© **0800/121-121** or 098/3217-6190; São Luis airport).

Dentist   Clínica Odontológica Maranhão, Rua Grande 1164, Centro © **098/3232-7144.**

Emergencies   Dial © **190** for police, © **193** for fire department, © **192** for ambulance. The Tourist Police station is on Rua da Estrela 427 in the centro histórico (© **098/3214-8682**).

Hospitals   **Santa Casa de Misericórdia,** Rua do Norte 233, centro histórico (© **098/3221-0144** or 098/3232-0248).

Mail   The main post office is on Praça João Lisboa 290 in the centro histórico. There is another post office in the airport terminal. Both are open Monday through Friday 9am to 4pm.

Pharmacies   **Farmácia Gonçalves,** Rua das Hortas 379A, centro histórico (© **098/3232-1072**); **Extrafone** delivers 24 hours daily (© **0800/983-000**).

Weather   São Luis, just below the Equator, has a pleasant, warm climate year-round, with average temperatures of 82°F (28°C). Most rain falls in winter (July–Sept). The most pleasant months are March through June; it's warm but not as hot as in December through February.

---

2 Where to Stay

There are essentially two options in São Luis, the centro histórico or the beach neighborhoods such as Praia d'Areia and Praia de Calhau. The centro histórico offers beautiful surroundings, some nice restaurants, and a busy nightlife scene in the Reviver area. However, there are no full-service hotels, and the few pousadas have only a limited number of rooms. The beaches have lovely resort-style hotels, but they are a 20-minute cab ride from the attractions of the old city.

CENTRO HISTÓRICO
MODERATE
Pousada do Francês 𝒻   Pick the right room and the Francês can be a pleasant pousada conveniently located in the residential section of the centro histórico. The four nicest and most spacious rooms, the Mirante rooms (nos. 26, 27, 28, and 29) are located on the top floor on the corners of the pousada, and feature small balconies with lovely views of the river or the old city, in addition to firm queen-size beds, tile floors, and a large work space and reasonably spacious bathroom. These should be your first choice. Other double rooms (called luxo) are a little less spacious, but still feature comfortable queen-size beds and clean functional bathrooms. These are an acceptable backup, but avoid the ground-floor (single-digit) doubles, which feature windows that open directly onto the sidewalk. Then there are the rooms with no windows at all (nos. 7, 8, 21, 22, and 23), which are definitely to be avoided. Beyond the rooms, this restored colonial mansion features a lobby bar and restaurant warm and rich in bric-a-brac.

Rua 7 de Setembro 121, centro histórico, São Luis, 65010-630 MA. 𝒸 **098/3231-4844**. Fax 098/3232-0879. 29 units (showers only). Mirante R$130 (US$60/£35) double; Luxo R$107 (US$54/£29) double. Extra person in room add 25%. 20% discount in low season. Children 7 and under stay free in parent's room. AE, DC, MC, V. Street parking. **Amenities:** Restaurant; bar; laundry. In room: A/C, TV, minibar, fridge. Bus: Praia Grande.

Pousada Portas da Amazônia 𝒻𝒻   The nicest place to stay in São Luis is this renovated colonial mansion in the heart of the old city. The best rooms, called Master Suites (nos. 1, 2, 15, 16, 17, 24, 25, and 26—the best of the best is no. 16) are vast and high ceilinged, with tall colonial windows looking out on the small cobblestone square. Master Suites also feature firm queen-size beds, often raised up on a small dais. Bathrooms feature electric showers and lots of counter space. Standard rooms are not as bright or spacious, with windows facing the courtyard. Bathrooms in the standard rooms are also a tad cramped. Breakfast is excellent. Internet in the lobby costs R$4 (US$2/£1) an hour.

Rua do Giz 129, Praia Grande, São Luis, 65080-680 MA. 𝒸 **098/3222-9937**. Fax 098/3221-4193. www.portasda amazonia.com.br. 28 units. R$89 (US$45/£24) standard double; R$159 (US$80/£43) master double. Extra person add about 20%. Children 7 and under stay free in parent's room. AE, DC, MC, V. No parking. Bus: Praia Grande. **Amenities:** Internet; laundry. In room: A/C, TV, minibar, fridge.

INEXPENSIVE
Hotel Pousada Colonial   The Colonial looks gorgeous from the outside—an old colonial mansion covered with intricate Portuguese tile, but inside the rooms can be a tad cramped, the walls and floors a bit scuffed up. All rooms feature either a firm queen-size bed or two single beds, plus small functional bathrooms with showers. The two best rooms—nos. 201 and 202—have large bright windows looking out on the street. These are definitely worth the price. The worst room—no. 105—is small, dark, and moldy and should be avoided at all costs. Between these extremes, the Colonial offers clean, functional accommodations in the heart of the centro histórico. If you can, stay at the Pousada Portas de Amazônia, but if that's unavailable the Colonial is a serviceable backup.

Rua Alfonso Pena (Rua Formosa) 112, centro histórico, São Luis, 65080-680 MA. 𝒸/fax **098/3232-2834**. www.click colonial.com.br. 27 units. High season R$110 (US$55/£30) double. AE, DC, MC, V. Bus: Praia Grande. **Amenities:** Internet; room service. In room: A/C, TV, minibar, fridge.

BEACHES
EXPENSIVE

Pestana São Luis ⍟⍟ Though a little far from the centro histórico, the full-service Pestana has the advantage of a lovely location on Praia do Calhau, the city's nicest beach. Formerly the Park, the hotel was recently bought and renovated by the Pestana group. Rooms feature tile floors, firm queen-size (or two twin) beds, and a private balcony. What really sets the hotel apart, however, are its amenities—a large outdoor pool and children's pool, tennis courts, a grass soccer field—and its location on the beach. The drawback, of course, is that the sights in the centro histórico are a R$25 (US$13/ £7) cab ride away.

Av. Avicênia 10km, Praia do Calhau, São Luis, 65071-370 MA. © 098/2106-0505. Fax 098/3235-4921. www.pestana saoluis.com.br. 111 units. R$260–R$320 (US$130–US$160/£70–£86) double. Children under 8 stay free in parent's room. AE, DC, MC, V. Free parking. Bus: Praia Calhau. **Amenities:** Restaurant; bar; pool; children's pool; 3 tennis courts; children's play area; sauna; game room; soccer field; weight room; babysitting; laundry. *In room:* A/C, TV, Wi-Fi, minibar, fridge, safe.

Rio Poty ⍟ Located on the beach on Ponta D'Areia, the new Rio Poty is the best beach hotel closest to the centro histórico. The hotel's striking inverse ziggurat form means every room gets a view of the sea. Beds are queen-size (king-size in luxury rooms and suites), with tile floors, small granite desk and workspace with Internet, and clean basic bathrooms with tub and shower. The large leaf-shaped pool—with little Jacuzzi islands—fans out over a vast sun deck looking out over the beach. There is little or nothing within walking distance, but the hotel itself offers a number of restaurants and bars (including a disco). The nightlife scene by the Lagoa Jansen is but a R$5 (US$2.50/£1.35) cab ride away; getting to the centro histórico will cost about R$20 (US$10/£5.50) by cab.

Av. dos Hollandeses 4km, Praia da Ponta d"Areia, São Luis, 65077-310 MA. © 098/3215-1500. www.riopoty saoluis.com.br. 120 units. R$240–R$290 (US$120–US$145/£65–£78) double. Children under 8 stay free in parent's room. AE, DC, MC, V. Free parking. Bus: Lagoa Jansen. **Amenities:** Restaurant; bar; pool; sauna; weight room; business center; laundry. *In room:* A/C, TV, minibar, fridge.

3 Where to Dine
CENTRO HISTÓRICO

Restaurants in the centro histórico cater mostly to tourists, and they usually look better than they taste. Expect mostly Brazilian food such as *carne seca* (lightly salted dried beef), seafood stews, grilled steak with fries and farofa, or deep-fried pastries *(empanadas)*. Farther out, there are a number of good restaurants by the edge of the Lagoa de Jansen.

MODERATE

Antigamente (Overrated) BRAZILIAN Surely one of the prettiest restaurants, Antigamente is also lively and fun. The restaurant is located inside a renovated heritage building in the old city and has gorgeous mosaic floors and rustic furnishings. In the evenings it's one of the more happening restaurants, with live Brazilian music (a small cover fee is charged) out on the patio. The food, alas, is disappointing. Better to have a snack and just enjoy the atmosphere.

Rua da Estrela 220, centro histórico. © 098/3232-3964. R$12–R$39 (US$5–US$16/£2.50–£8); the more expensive dishes are for 2. MC, V. Mon–Sat 10am–3am. Live music starts at 6pm.

O Armazém da Estrela ✦ BRAZILIAN   A mix of bar, restaurant, sandwich deli, and cybercafe, housed in a lovely two-floor mansion in the heart of the old city. Most nights, there's live music.

Rua da Estrela 401, centro histórico. ✆ **098/3254-1274.** R$12–R$44 (US$6–US$22/£3.25–£12). AE, MC, V. Mon–Fri noon–midnight; Sat 6pm–1am.

INEXPENSIVE

Caterina Mina ✦ BRAZILIAN   Hidden halfway up the stairs in a tiny alley, Caterina Mina can be a little hard to find—in the evenings just follow the music coming from the *Beco* (alley). This small restaurant offers the usual variety of regional fare such as *carne de sol* (salted, sun-dried beef, more tender than carne seca), seafood stews, crab, and fish. What makes it special is its charming location in the alley, surrounded by historic buildings, some nicely fixed up and others with trees growing out of the windows. The live Brazilian music adds to the atmosphere. The band usually starts around 7pm.

Beco Caterina Mina s/n, centro histórico. ✆ **098/3221-5997.** R$15–R$28 (US$50–US$14/£4–£7.50) for 2. No credit cards. Tues–Sat noon–1:30am.

PONTA D'AREIA

Cabana do Sol ✦ BRAZILIAN   Cabana do Sol is one of São Luis's best known regional restaurants. People come in droves to try out the food here so it's a good thing the restaurant is large. The spacious open veranda-like structure can seat several hundred people but thanks to a small army of waiters things go smoothly here. The dishes are huge, often enough for three people. Very popular is the *anchova na brasa* (grilled anchovy, served with rice, farofa, and fried banana). More unusual dishes include suckling pig and roasted goat. These are served on a large platter, hot off the grill, and come with a variety of the usual side dishes including rice and farofa.

Rua João Damasceno 24, Ponta do Farol. ✆ **098/3235-2586.** R$37–R$60 (US$19–US$30/£10–£16) for 2 or 3. AE, DC, MC, V. Sun–Thurs 11am–midnight; Fri–Sat 11am–1am. Bus: Ponta D'Areia or Culhau.

LAGOA JANSEN

Kitaro Lagoa ✦ JAPANESE/BRAZILIAN   Pretty much every self-respecting Brazilian town must have a trendy Japanese restaurant, and São Luis is no different. Overlooking the lagoon, Kitaro is a zen oasis with soft lighting and modern furniture. The best tables are those that look out over the water, either inside or out on the patio. The menu covers the basics from sushi to tempura, teriyaki, and yakisoba noodles. Lately, the kitchen has been branching into regional Brazilian cuisines, including a delicious moqueca made with *jabiraca* (a local freshwater fish considered by some as tasty as cod). The restaurant has live music every night, usually starting around 9pm, and the kitchen is open late, until 3am on Friday and Saturday.

Av. Mario Meireles s/n, Lagoa de Jansen-Ponta D'Areia. ✆ **098/3268-6528.** R$18–R$39 (US$7.50–US$16/£4–£8.50). MC, V. Tues–Thurs and Sun 5pm–1am; Fri–Sat 5pm–3am. Bus: Ponta D'Areia.

Por Acaso ✦ BRAZILIAN   Just down from Kitaro, also on the lagoon, is a great casual *chopperia*. This bar/restaurant is one of the more happening places at night. Even on a Wednesday evening it was packed with locals enjoying a beer and helping themselves to the outstanding antipasto buffet. The restaurant actually has a pretty decent menu with excellent steak and seafood dishes but the buffet is a meal in itself; a selection of cheeses, cold cuts, various salads, olives, marinated eggplant, sun-dried tomato, homemade dips, fresh bread, and more. There's nothing better than snagging a table by the window, ordering a few cold chopps, and making several trips to the buffet to try out the tasty nibbles. Live music daily at 8pm (cover is only R$3/US$1.50/£.80).

Av. Mario Meireles s/n, Lagoa de Jansen-Ponta D'Areia. © 098/3233-5837. R$16–R$35 (US$6.65–US$15/£3.70–£8). MC, V. Tues–Sat 5:30pm–1am. Bus: Ponta D'Areia.

4 Exploring São Luis

TOP ATTRACTIONS

Perhaps for lack of other options, São Luis takes tourism seriously. The city does an excellent job in several small museums presenting the culture and history of the region. Many of the museums in the old city offer visually attractive and informative displays, professionally presented by engaging and informative museum guides. Even better, most of them are free.

THE CENTRO HISTÓRICO ★★★

"The Historic Center of São Luis do Maranhão is an outstanding example of a Portuguese colonial town that adapted successfully to the climatic conditions in equatorial South America and which has preserved its urban fabric, harmoniously integrated with its natural setting, to an exceptional degree." So read the UNESCO declaration, giving the historic center of São Luis a World Heritage designation in 1997.

The centro histórico formed the heart of São Luis through the 19th-century boom years, but went into decline in the 1920s. Restoration started only in 1989, under pressure from state governor Jose Sarney, and continues to today. The neighborhood still lacks modern water and sewer systems. There is also controversy over whether the historic center should be a tourist enclave or a real residential neighborhood. After fixing up buildings, the state government wants to turn them over to owners with the financial wherewithal to maintain them. That rules out the poor and working classes who for nearly a century have made the neighborhood their home. It's a problem that has not yet been resolved.

The centro histórico sits on a peninsula, almost completely surrounded north and south by wide igarapés. Twice every 24 hours the tide sucks the water from the estuary, leaving the city completely cut off from the ocean. If this seems an odd place to put a seaport, recall that the French expeditionaries who founded the city were interested mostly in defense. The old city is effectively an island, protected by the tides from large warships and their guns.

The **Reviver** area, the oldest part of the old city, lies at the very tip of the peninsula, to the east of the Jose Sarney bridge. This area contains most of the centro histórico's museums, and interesting streets and monuments.

The best plan is just to go for a stroll. There are numerous antique buildings that have been renovated into museums or tourist attractions of one kind or another. The best are given separate listings below. But just as rewarding is the fine-grained texture of the old city, and the serendipitous discovery of a lovely colonial building covered in brilliant blue or yellow tile.

The best place to start a walk is by the **Casa do Maranhão** ★★ (see below) just opposite the ferry terminal to Alcântara. The **Rua Portugal** is just around the corner. This narrow, cobblestone street features numerous restored colonial buildings from the 18th and 19th centuries, many covered in bright patterned tile. Close to the end of the street one comes to the **Casa das Tulhas** (Rua da Estrela s/n; open Mon–Fri 6am–8pm, Sat 6am–6pm, Sun 6am–1pm).

Rua Portugual dead-ends at **Rua da Estrela.** This is the heart of the Reviver area. At night this wide, tree-shaded street is full of cafes and musicians. Parallel to Rua da Estrela 1 block farther in is **Rua da Giz.** This lovely colonial street serves as a kind of crossroads leading to many more of the old city's attractions.

Turn right on Rua da Giz and proceed uphill and you come to a small formal square, **Praça Benedito Leite.** The far side of the square is formed by the **Igraja da Sé** (© **098/3222-7380;** open daily 8–11:30am and 3–6pm) and the **Bishop's Palace.** Just around the corner lies Avenida Pedro II, a broad ceremonial boulevard on which you find the **Palacio La Ravardiere,** which houses city hall, and the **Palacio dos Leões,** which was built on the foundations of the city's original fort, Fort Saint Louis. Guided visits through the upstairs salons of the Palacio dos Leões (Mon, Wed, Fri, 2:30–4pm; © **098/2108-9000**) show furniture and oil paintings from the 18th and 19th centuries, none especially distinguished.

Turn left on the Rua da Giz and you come first to the **Centro de Cultura Popular** ☆☆ (see below), and then at the far end of the street to the pretty **Convento das Mercês,** and the **Cafua das Mercês,** which is now home to the small **Museu do Negro** (Tues–Fri 9am–6pm; free admission; no phone). During the slave era, the courtyard inside the Cafua was used as an enclosure to keep slaves newly arrived from Africa penned up before they could be auctioned. A whipping post is still in evidence.

Go straight uphill from the Rua da Giz and you come to **Praça Joao Lisboa,** a rather ugly central square, with the **Teatro Arthur Azevedo** on one side. Built in 1817, the neoclassical Teatro reopened in 2006 after lengthy renovations. (Guided visits Tues–Fri 3pm; R$3/US$1.50/£.80; © **098/3218-9000**).

East of the Praça João Lisboa, the centro histórico becomes less touristed and more residential. Many of the buildings in this part of the centro histórico are just as historic and picturesque as down in the Reviver area, while the atmosphere is that of a working-class Brazilian neighborhood. In daylight hours it's a fine place to stroll and discover; however, at night it is best to be avoided. Highlights of this part of the old town include the **Museu Historico e Artistico do Maranhão** (see below), and the **Mercado Central** (daily 6am–5pm), the city's large public market, located at the far end of Avenida Magalhães de Almeida.

Casa do Maranhão ☆☆   Located in the old Customs building on the waterfront, the House of Maranhão would be better called the Museum of Bumba-meu-boi. The best and largest part of this two-floor museum depicts the rhythms and costumes of this peasant folk festival that every June takes control of the streets of São Luis (see sidebar below). Dioramas depict the various stages in the life of a bumba-meu-boi bull (birth, christening, harvest celebration in June, and death), as well as mannequins wearing the costumes and holding the instruments of the different bumba-meu-boi rhythms (called *sotaques* or accents). With luck, one of the guides will be able to speak English. If not, the dioramas and costumes are reasonably self-explanatory. Allow 1 hour.

Rua do Trapiche s/n, centro histórico. © **098/3218-9955.** Free admission. Tues–Sat 9am–6pm; Sun 2–6pm. Bus: Conde de Boa Vista.

Centro de Cultura Popular ☆☆   The arid Northeast is one of the richest sources of folklore and folk festivals in Brazil. Located in a four-story mansion in the old city,

Bumba-Meu-Boi

It's a festival celebrated throughout Brazil under a host of names—boi-bumbá, boi calemba, boi surubim, boi zumbi—but locals insist that Maranhão is Brazil's leading stronghold of bumba-meu-boi. Through music and costume and drumming, the festival tells the story of the life and death and rebirth of a magical Brazilian bull.

The bull belongs to a wealthy rancher. A peasant working for the rancher named Pai Chico steals the bull, kills it, and feeds its tongue to his pregnant girlfriend, Catirina, to satisfy her cravings. Discovering the deed, the rancher condemns Pai Chico and Catirina to death. It looks dark for the pair, but St. John warns the rancher in a dream not to kill the couple. Pai Chico and Catirina go to the *curandeiros,* the community's traditional healers, and with the help of everyone in the village, they magically drum the bull to life again.

In Maranhão, bumba-meu-boi has evolved into a kind of competition. Dozens of different groups—normally organized by neighborhood—hold their own bumba-meu-boi celebrations, competing with each other to see who can put together the best costumes and put on the best party. The music played by each group belongs to one of about five rhythms, or *sotaques* (accents), each of which has its own set of instruments. The *matraca* sotaque uses wooden blocks that musicians rap together to create complicated percussion rhythms. The *zabumba* sotaque uses only long wooden drums covered in snakeskin. Each sotaque also has its own elaborate costumes, and each group has its own magic bull.

Though made of a wire frame and papier-mâché (a dancer goes inside to act out the part of the bull) the bull is an important creature. A new bull is created each year, and the parties held by each bumba-meu-boi group mark the milestones in the magic bull's existence.

Rehearsals begin on the Saturday before Easter (these are open to the public). In early June, the bull is taken to the church to be baptized (after which there is a party). Different groups choose different dates for the christening. The most popular date is June 23, the day of São João (there is usually a party on this day). On June 29, all the bumba-meu-boi groups bring their bulls to the church of São Pedro in the Madre Deus neighborhood. And on June 30, all of São Luis comes to a halt as 200 or more bumba-meu-boi groups bring their bulls out to celebrate the feast of São Marçal, mostly in the João Paulo neighborhood.

The last step in the bull's life is the Morte do Boi, the Death of the Bull, which each group holds on a different day, anytime between June 30 and the end of December. For those who want to take part in the festivities, local papers publish the dates and locations where the different groups are celebrating the birth, blessing, life, and death of their bull.

this museum has dioramas and mannequins presenting many of these rich folk traditions. Included is bumba-meu-boi in all its various accents, as well as the rhythms such as the *tambor de crioula,* and more religious spiritual festivals such as the *Festa do Divino.* A highlight of the museum is the superb collection of photographs of folk festivals around the state, many showing the often aged matriarchs who rule these festivals decked out in all their sumptuous regalia. Guides should, but may not, speak English.

Rua do Giz 221, centro histórico. ℭ 084/3221-1557. Free admission. Tues–Fri 9am–6pm; Sat 2–6pm.

Museu Historico e Artistico do Maranhão 🏵🏵 If you want to get a sense of
how the elite of 19th-century São Luis lived, visit the Historical Museum of Maranhão. The museum is located in a mansion built in 1836, which has been restored and decorated with the heavy wood furniture, porcelain, crystal, and artwork favored by the commercial aristocracy of the time. Tours are guided, though in Portuguese only, and there is little explanatory signage. Allow 30 minutes (or more if you're an *Antiques Roadshow* person).

Rua do Sol 302, centro histórico. ℭ 098/3221-4537. Admission R$1/US50¢/£.25. Tues–Fri 9am–6pm; Sat–Sun 9–6pm. Bus: São Jose.

Alcântara 🏵🏵 A visit to Alcântara makes a great day trip. An hour's ferry ride
north across Baía São Marcos, the village of Alcântara is a curious thing, a struggling small town living inside the ruins of a once-thriving colonial city. In the boom years of the 18th and 19th centuries, Alcântara was a regional capital, the place where the merchant and plantation elite kept their families and traded their sugar and cotton. With the end of slavery in 1888 the plantation economy crashed and the merchants and planters fled, leaving the half-empty city in the hands of newly freed slaves and their descendants.

In 1948, the half-empty city was declared a historic site, primarily for its lovely collection of colonial houses with ornately decorated doors and coverings of bright Portuguese tile. Called "Windows and Doors" (in Portuguese *Portas e Janelas*), the style is both functional (the tile reflects the heat) and extraordinarily pretty.

A visit to Alcântara involves strolling down the main cobblestone street that leads from the port up the hillside through a series of small squares to a beautiful ruined church on a hilltop. Along the way there are hundreds of beautiful houses to admire, and at least six ruined churches to poke about.

There are also three fine, small museums. The best, the **Casa Historica do IPHAN Seculo XVIII (the IPHAN 18th-Century Historical House)** (Praça Gomes de Castro s/n; no phone; daily 9am–2pm) is a huge colonial mansion filled with paintings, porcelain, furniture, and all of the belongings of a rich merchant family, including the still-intact slave quarters in the interior courtyard. Guides do an excellent job telling the history of the house and the families that built it. Admission is R$1 (US50¢/£.25).

Everything in Alcântara is very laid-back. Local residents pretty much leave you to wander their city. There are a few gift shops and numerous small restaurants, which make good places to do as the locals seem to be doing—trying to keep cool in blazing heat.

Brazil's satellite-launching center is just 5km (3 miles) away, but has been off-limits to visitors since a rocket blew up on the launchpad in 2003, killing 21 technicians. There's a visitor center in the town, but it's not worth visiting.

Going to Alcântara the ferry departs daily at 7am and 9:30am. The trip takes about 1 hr. Tickets cost R$10 (US$5/£2.50). Call ☎ 098/3232-0692 for information. Tickets can be purchased on the ferry, or beforehand at the Terminal Hidrovário on the waterfront in the centro histórico. Ferries depart either from the terminal, or if the tide is out, from the sandbar by the yacht club in Ponto d'Areia. Check beforehand at the terminal. Departure subject to change and delay without notice. Returning from Alcântara, ferries depart from the Alcântara Terminal at 8:30am and 4pm. R$10 (US$5/£2.50).

ORGANIZED TOURS

Lotus Turismo (☎ 098/3221-0942; www.lotusturismo.com.br) has guided tours to Alcântara that cost R$60 (US$30/£16) per person.

5 Shopping in São Luis

The best shopping in São Luis is in the **centro histórico.** The **Reviver** area features a number of good crafts and art shops, as well as the small but intriguing indoor market called the **Casa das Tulhas** (Rua da Estrela s/n; Mon–Fri 6am–8pm, Sat 6am–6pm, Sun 6am–1pm). Higher up in the old city, the principal shopping street **Rua Grande** features an intriguing mix of national chain stores and cheaper local stores selling clothing, hardware, refrigerators, and everything else. Rua Grande is pedestrian-only for much of its length, making it pleasant for strolling and people-watching.

GIFTS & SOUVENIRS   In the Reviver area of the centro histórico there are a number of shops selling products unique to the state of Maranhão. **Arte Indigena,** Rua do Giz 66 (☎ 098/3221-2940), sells baskets, jewelry, and artwork made by Maranhão's indigenous peoples. The shop is associated with the Associação Carlo Ubbiali (www.asscarloubbiali.com.br), a nonprofit organization that works to improve the lives of Maranhão's Indians through education, advocacy, and by providing a commercial outlet for Indian products. **Casa dos Produtos Regionais,** Beco Catarina Mina 187 (☎ 098/3222-6548), is the place for those with a sweet tooth. The shop features a delicious assortment of local foodstuffs, including sweets, preserves, and liqueurs made from local fruits such as bacuri, cupuaçu, murici, and buriti. It's also a good place to stock up on moisturizing oils made from copaiba and andiroba for R$20 (US$10/£5.50) if you buy it here, or for R$200 (US$100/£54) if you buy it in a fancy eco-shop in New York or Paris. The two shops named above are open Monday through Saturday 9am to 9pm, Sunday noon to 7pm. If you like the tilework you've seen all over the old city, check out **Ateliê Mão na Massa,** Rua do Giz 117 (☎ 098/3227-0094). In addition to tiles, the workshop also features beautiful pieces of glazed pottery, as well as cheaper souvenirs. Open Monday through Saturday 9am to 6pm.

At the airport, **In Natura Handicraft** (☎ 098/3226-8435) has sophisticated purses and handbags made from palm and coconut fiber. Prices aren't rock-bottom (R$60/US$30/£16) but the same bags in Rio or São Paulo sell for R$200 (US$100/£54) and up.

MALLS & SHOPPING CENTERS   The city's biggest shopping mall, the **São Luis Shopping,** Av. Euclides Figueiredo 1000, Jaracaty (☎ 098/3251-3621), boasts a six-screen cinema, large food court, and hundreds of shops. It's located a little past the Bandeira Tribuzzi bridge leading out of the centro histórico. Open Monday through Friday from 10am to 10pm and Saturday from 10am to 8pm.

MARKETS   In the Reviver area, there's the **Casa das Tulhas** (Rua da Estrela s/n; Mon–Fri 6am–8pm, Sat 6am–6pm, Sun 6am–1pm), also known as the Feira da Praia Grande, a small but bustling indoor market with staples such as farinha and dried shrimp and fish, as well as a selection of herbs, roots, and tree barks used for a variety of medicinal purposes. The market is open daily from 7am to 6pm. At night, the **Rua da Alfândega** in the Reviver fills up with stalls selling local sweets and pastries and handmade leatherwork and basketry. A little farther from the Reviver, the much larger **Mercado Central,** Rua do Mercado s/n (corner of Rua Jacinto Maia with Av. Gua-xenduba), sells staples, fresh fish, and a wide assortment of local fruits and medicinal herbs. Open daily 6am to 4pm, but best early in the morning.

6 São Luis After Dark

CLUBS & BARS

The best place to go for some music and fun after dark in São Luis in the **Reviver** area is the centro histórico. There are close to a dozen bars, cafes, and restaurants offering music in the small area in the evening, most of it played live. Most nights of the week, something's happening—with music usually starting around 8pm and ending around 1am. Thursday through Saturday it really hops, and the music continues past 3am. On the steps in the Beco Caterina Mina, **Monteiro's Bar** (© 098/3221-5998) has live samba Tuesday through Saturday, beginning around 8pm. On Rua Estrela, **Antigamente** (© 098/3232-3964) has live MPB (Brazilian pop) every night, starting early around 6pm. The **Roots Bar,** Rua da Palma 85 (© 098/3221-7580), and **Bar do Porto** on Rua Trapiche 49 (© 098/3221-3749), both offer reggae. Both charge a nominal cover of about R$5 (US$2.50/£1.35).

For DJs and dancing downtown, there's the gay-friendly **Metalurgica SLZ,** Rua da Palma 196 (© 098/3231-8950; www.metalslz.com.br; Fri–Sat 10pm–5am).

Outside of downtown, the Lagoa da Jansen has a number of more mellow music venues, often doubling as restaurants. **Kitaro Lagoa** (Av. Mario Meireles s/n; © 098/3268-6528) has live music—usually MPB—every night starting around 9pm. Farther along the lakeshore, **Por Acaso** (Av. Mario Meireles s/n; © 098/3233-5837) is a great casual *chopperia* offering live music daily at 8pm. Cover is only R$3 (US$1.50/£.80).

GAY & LESBIAN BARS   The **Observatório** is one of the oldest gay and lesbian clubs in São Luis and is a great place to dance the night away downtown. Rua da Estrela 370A, Beco da Prensa (© 098/3222-5151). Open Friday and Saturday 11pm to 6am.

7 A Side Trip to the Lençóis Maranhenses

The 155,000-hectare (383,000-acre) **Parque Nacional Lençóis Maranhenses** offers an intriguing and spectacular landscape seen nowhere else on earth—a vast desert formed of tall, snow-white sand dunes, interwoven with beautiful pools of turquoise rainwater. The dunes are formed by the region's strong coastal winds. During the December-to-May rainy season, over 1,500 millimeters (60 in.) of rain falls and col-lects in the basins between dunes forming countless blue freshwater lagoons. In June, when the water levels are at their highest, the dunes look like a giant mosaic of white interspersed with sparkling dots of blue, turquoise, and green.

Visitors can enter the park only on foot. The town of Barreirinhas, just outside the park, is the jumping-off spot for exploring the park and the surrounding region. The best season is June through September, when the rainwater lagoons are deepest, most swimmable, and most spectacular, and the weather warm and dry. By December and January, the water has all but evaporated, leaving only desert.

ESSENTIALS
GETTING THERE

By Car Barreirinhas is 250km (155 miles) from São Luis, along the BR-135 and MA-402 highways. Both highways were recently paved and are in good shape.

By Bus **VanExpress** (© 098/3256-4027 or cell 098/8122-9912) offers daily service to and from Barreirinhas by comfortable air-conditioned minivan. The trip costs R$30 (US$15/£8) per person and takes 3 to 4 hours. Pickup is at your hotel. Vans depart São Luis anywhere from 5 to 9am (depending on demand). Vans depart Barreirinhas daily at 5pm. **Cisne Branco** (© 098/3243-2847) has regular non-air-conditioned buses three times daily in both directions, departing from either the São Luis rodoviaria, or the rodoviaria in Barreirinhas. The trip takes from 4 to 6 hours. Cost is R$19 (US$9.50/£5).

By Plane **Litoranea Taxi Aéreo** (© 098/3108-6181; www.voelitoranea.com.br) has flights to and from Barreirinhas every day except Thursday, leaving at 7am, 9am, and 11am. Cost of the 40-minute flight is R$250 (US$125/£68). On both the way in and on the way back, pilots fly low over the Lençóis national park, providing a fabulous view of the dunes from the air. If you take this flight, there is no need to do a sightseeing flight from Barreirinhas.

VISITOR INFORMATION There is no **tourist office** in Barreirinhas. There is a useful website for Lençóis Park at www.parquelencois.com.br. The tourism agency **Ecodunas** (© 098/3349-0545; www.ecodunas.com.br) is open daily from 9am to 6m and has a helpful staff. The office is on Rua Inácio Lins 164, in the center of town. The official city tourism website is www.barreirinhas.ma.gov.br. The state tourism website is www.turismo.ma.gov.br/en/index.html.

GETTING AROUND There are taxi stands in the city center. A taxi from the center to an outlying hotel costs R$12 (US$6/£3.25). A motorcycle taxi costs R$4 (US$2/£1) from center to hotel. Call © 098/3349-0687, or cell 098/9111-5609.

FAST FACTS **Banco do Brasil,** Av. Joaquim Soeiro De Carvalho s/n (© 098/3349-1172), has a 24-hour ATM. The bank is open Monday through Friday 9am to 2pm. Internet access at **Sol e Lua Cybercafe,** Av. Beira Mar s/n. Open Monday to Saturday 8am to noon and 1:30 to 11pm, R$4 (US$2/£1) an hour, but the connection is unreliable.

EXPLORING THE TOWN

Barreirinhas doesn't take long to see. The Rio Preguiças loops its way through town. There is a pleasant boulevard with numerous restaurants and cafes facing the river, and next to that a big dune where locals swim. Most pousadas are located on the banks of the river a little out of town.

EXPLORING THE DUNES

Exploring the great shifting mass of glorious white dunes is the whole point of coming here. Local company **Ecodunas** (© 098/3349-0545 local, or 098/9112-5224; www.ecodunas.com.br) has a number of ways to get you into the dunes:

- **Hikes:** The most popular is a **half-day trip** by 4×4 to **Lagoa Bonita.** The dirt road travels by increasingly rough sand trails to the park entrance, after which you climb into the dunes and hike for about 2 hours, allowing for plenty of time to swim in a couple of small rainwater lagoons. Cost is R$45 (US$23/£12).

The half-day trip can be done in the morning, but in the afternoon it's cooler and you get to see the sunset. Variations on this trip go to other nearby lakes such as Lagoa Azul and Lagoa Paraiso. **Longer hikes** with customized itineraries can be arranged by consultation with Ecodunas. Guides are quite cheap at R$80 (US$40/£22) per day for up to three people. A 4×4 and driver—to drop you off or pick you up at a trail head—costs R$300 (US$150/£81) per day.

- **4 Wheel ATV trips:** These full-day trips zoom up and down the dunes at the very fringes of the national park (ATVs aren't allowed inside the park boundaries), covering the roughly 30km (19 miles) between Barreirinhas and Atins on the coast. A full-day trip costs R$350 (US$175/£95) per ATV, which fits two people.
- **Scenic Flights:** If you haven't flown into Barreirinhas with **Litoranea Taxi Aéreo** (see "By Plane," above) then a scenic flight is highly recommended. Cost of a 30-minute scenic flight is R$140 (US$70/£38) per person, with a minimum of three people. Flights are best in the morning.

TRIPS TO CABURÉ & MANDACARU   At the mouth of the Rio Preguiças there are two tiny villages sandwiched between the Lençóis dunes and the ocean. **Mandacaru** is a small fishing village close to the mouth of the river. **Caburé** is a narrow neck of pure sand perhaps 200m (650 ft.) wide, with crashing surf on one side and the lazy Rio Preguiças on the other. What started as simple camps on this windswept piece of geography have since grown into a small collection of pousadas and restaurants.

One popular option for visiting these areas is to take a day trip by boat from Barreirinhas. The trip descends the river, stopping at the Smaller (Pequenos) Lençóis on the way. This sand dune area is still growing, and you can see where the advancing sand is eating away at the riverside forest. The trip stops in at Caburé for lunch, with time in **Mandacaru** to wander this tiny picturesque village and climb the 45m-tall (150-ft.) lighthouse for a view of the national park, before returning to Barreirinhas. The tour can be arranged with **Ecodunas** (© **098/3349-0545**) or with local boat skipper **Rondomar** (© **098/9602-5177**). Both charge R$50 (US$25/£14), lunch not included.

Many people opt to spend the night in Caburé. This allows time the next day to make a walking expedition into the Lençóis dunes along the coast beyond Atins. **Rondomar** (© **098/9602-5177**) is the specialist with this trip. The route takes you through several beautiful and completely isolated small lakes before stopping at the **Restaurante de Luzia** (no phone, no address), a tiny palm-frond covered shack at the ocean side that serves an orgiastic feast of giant prawns for R$15 (US$7.50/£4) per person. Cost of this coastal dune expedition is around R$100 (US$50/£27) for up to four people, prawn lunch not included, with departure from Caburé. You can arrange the entire trip (boat from Barreirinhas, coastal day trip, and boat back to Barreirinhas) with Ecodunas, or with Rondomar.

If you decide to stay in Caburé, there are several rustic pousadas. The sandspit has no electricity, so it's generators only and at 10pm it's lights out, candles on. **Pousada Porto Buriti** (© **098/3349-1802** or cell 098/9984-0088) is slightly overpriced at R$120 to R$140 (US$60–US$70/£33–£38) double. Its 10 small chalets are only slightly nicer than others in the area, but double the price. **Pousada de Paulo** (© **098/9965-9931**) has simple clean rooms with small verandas for R$60 (US$30/£16) double. All pousadas have only unheated showers. Both of these pousadas have good, simple restaurants.

WATERSPORTS

In other parts of the world, **Boia Cross** is called "floating down the river in a inner-tube." **Ecodunas** (© 098/3349-0545; www.ecodunas.com.br) offers a half-day float. The trip there and back is 90 minutes each way, and you spend 2 hours floating downstream. Cost is R$200 (US$100/£54) for a car with up to six people.

PACKAGE TOURS

Several companies specialize in multiday packages. These can be as simple as transportation to and excursions in Lençóis, or as complicated as multiday jeep excursions to the Lençóis and then through the Parnaiba delta all the way to Jeircoacoara. For details contact **Ecodunas** (© 098/3349-0545; www.ecodunas.com.br), **Barratur** (© 098/3349-1779), or **Ecotrilha** (© 098/3349-0372).

WHERE TO STAY

Barreirinhas's two best pousadas are a little outside the town, a short ride by cab or moto-taxi. Though not nearly as nice, there are two options in town. The **Pousada Buriti** (© 098/3349-1800) is a sort of motor-court motel. Rooms are quite large, but they're motel blocks surrounding a hot, treeless, courtyard parking lot. However, there is a pool and children's play area. The **Pousada Beira Rio** (© 098/3349-0579) is a three-story hotel by the riverside. Rooms are simple and clean, with tile floors and small balconies overlooking the river.

EXPENSIVE

Porto Preguiças Resort ★★ *Kids*   The only luxury accommodations available in Barreirinhas, the Porto Preguiças Resort has 30 chalets set on a nicely landscaped piece of land by the river Preguiças. The leisure areas of the resort are extremely nicely done. There's a gorgeous lagoon-shaped swimming pool with a sand-covered bottom, a hammock "central" for relaxing by the river, an authentic bacchi game area, and a big beautiful restaurant and bar area. The chalets—which should be set by themselves off among the trees—are clumped together cheek by jowl. Inside, the chalets are spacious (many come with king-size beds) with large bathrooms with hot showers. Furnishings are rustic and simple. In short, the resort is very nice, though perhaps not worth what they're charging.

Carnaubal Velho 2km (1 mile) from town, Barreirinhas, MA 65590-000. © **098/3349-1220.** Fax 098/3349-0620. www.portopreguicas.com.br. 34 units (showers only). High season R$350 (US$175/£95) double; low season R$295 (US$148/£80) double. Extra person add 25%. Children 5 and under stay free in parent's room. AE, DC, MC, V. Free parking. **Amenities:** Restaurant; bar; outdoor pools; river beach; sauna; kids playground; game room; kayaks; laundry. *In room:* A/C, TV, minibar, fridge.

MODERATE

Pousada Encantes do Nordeste ★★ *Value*   Located just on the outskirts of town, the Pousada Encantes do Nordeste has a natural charm that makes it one of the nicest pousadas in the region. The chalets are set on a gently sloping hillside. The garden is beautiful and lush with a hammock for two to enjoy a lazy nap in the hot afternoon. A short trail leads to the river Preguiças. The rooms are very pleasant with nice, comfortable beds, air-conditioning, and television. There's even a closed-circuit DVD system that allows you to pick out a movie and watch it in your room (nights in Barreirinhas can be slow). The staff at the pousada is very friendly and helpful in hooking you up with all the excursions. All tours include pickup and drop-off at the pousada so the only time you will need a taxi is to go for dinner in town.

Rua Principal s/n Barreirinhas, MA 65590-000. (Ⓒ 098/3349-0288 or (São Paulo) 011/3331-3434. www.encantesdo nordeste.com.br. 11 units (showers only). R$130–R$150 (US$54–US$63/£35–£40) double chalet. Extra person R$50 (US$25/£14). Children 6 and under stay free in parent's room. AE, V. Free parking. **Amenities:** Restaurant; bar; game room; garden. *In room:* A/C, TV, minibar, safe, hammock, no phone.

WHERE TO DINE

For a town as small as Barreirinhas there are a surprising number of restaurants. Most of them have a fairly similar menu, involving grilled steak and seafood. The nicest restaurants are on the Avenida Beira Mar, the street that runs along the riverside. Next to and above the water—a number of tables are on the floating pier—is the **Tropical Marina Restaurant,** Av. Beira Mar s/n (Ⓒ 098/3349-1143). The best dish here is prawn moqueca with coconut milk and palm oil. For R$25 (US$13/£7) you get a clay pot full of fragrant stew packed with shrimp that serves two people. The menu also includes steak dishes, pasta, and grilled fish. For lunch, the Marina serves up an inexpensive and tasty kilo buffet, one of the few places where you can grab a quick hot lunch. Another nice waterfront restaurant is the **Barlavento,** Av. Beira Mar s/n (no phone), close to the Terraço Preguiças on the Avenida Beira Mar. The kitchen serves up grilled chicken and some steak dishes, as well as fish. Worth trying are the grilled fish with prawn sauce and the grilled fish in a passion-fruit sauce. Finally, for a more elegant night out try the restaurant at the **Porto Preguiças Resort,** Estrada do Carnaubal s/n (Ⓒ 098/3349-1220). Start off with a drink or a cocktail from the best-stocked bar in Maranhão. If you are hungry, order the *peixada* seafood stew with seabass; the generous portion will easily feed three people. To make it a special occasion, call ahead and order the lamb in coconut milk or the free-range chicken stew. These dishes require 4 hours notice as they are made from scratch but are worth the wait.

14

The Amazon: Manaus & Belém

It was a lost Spanish conquistador who gave a name to the largest river and rainforest on earth. In 1541 Francisco de Orellana returned after a year's absence with an account of a vast new river and of attacks by hostile Indians, some of them lead by bands of female warriors. In Europe, these women warriors were taken to be the last remaining members of that tribe whose queen Achilles slew at Troy. Land and river both were named for this likely mythical tribe—the Amazons.

Three centuries later, it was a British explorer, Alfred Russell Wallace, who first noted what is today very likely the Amazon's greatest claim to fame—its diversity. The Amazon rainforest has more biodiversity—more species of plants and animals per given patch of forest—than any ecosystem on earth. Being a naturalist, Wallace also proposed an explanation. It was due, he believed, to the Amazon's extraordinary number of rivers, streams, and channels, which effectively cut the forest up into millions of small islands. Marooned and isolated, a separated single species would evolve into many new species.

So logical did this seem that only in the past 10 years did scientists try to test it out. At which point they discovered it, too, was a myth. The reason for the Amazon's diversity has once again retreated into mystery.

The Brazilian Amazon today remains one of the most isolated, most sparsely populated regions on earth. Yet it is also home to more than four million people. Tarzan myths aside, most of them live not in the jungle, but in cities. Indeed, the state of Amazonas is one of the most urbanized in Brazil.

The Amazon's two principal cities are Manaus and Belém, capitals of the states of Amazonas and Pará, respectively. Belém sits at the mouth of the river, Manaus at the spot where the two principal tributaries—the Rio Negro and the Solimões—join to form the Amazon. Belém is the older, more civilized of the two, with colonial architecture, forts, stately churches, and a sense of itself as the natural senior partner, somehow left behind by a brash new upstart. The upstart, Manaus, has in the past 50 years grown from a city of a few hundred thousand to a near metropolis of almost two million. There's an exciting, frontier feel to Manaus. Belém offers history, excellent food, and much better nightlife. Manaus offers a sense of its own future and an opportunity to step into the vastness of the tropical rainforest.

A visit to the Amazon is a chance to penetrate the mystery, to experience the tangle of myth and reality firsthand.

1 Manaus

On the surface, Manaus looks a lot like other Brazilian cities. The old downtown is shabby and bustling. Along the shoreline in the upscale Ponta Negra area you'll find the familiar beachside high-rises, kiosks, and same wide streets. But stop for a moment

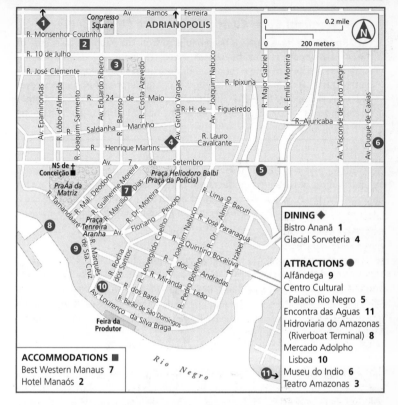

ADRIANOPOLIS

Congresso Square

Av. Ramos Ferreira

R. Monsenhor Coutinho

R. 10 de Julho

R. José Clemente

Av. Eduardo Ribeiro

R. 24 de Costa Azevedo

R. de Maio

R. H. de Figueiredo

Joaquim Nabuco

R. Ipixuna

R. Major Gabriel

R. Emílio Moreira

Av. Visconde de Porto Alegre

Av. Duque de Caxias

R. Ajuricaba

Av. Epaminondas

Av. Lôbo d'Almada

R. Joaquim Sarmento

R. Barroso

R. Saldanha Marinho

Av. Getúlio Vargas

R. Henrique Martins

R. Lauro Cavalcante

NS de Conceição

Av. 7 de Setembro

PraÁa da Matriz

R. Tamandaré

R. Mal. Deodoro

R. Guilherme Moreira

R. Marcílio Dias

Praça Heliodoro Balbi (Praça da Polícia)

R. Dr. Moreira

R. Floriano Peixoto

R. Lima

R. José Paranaguá

R. Almino Bacuri

Praça Tenreira Aranha

R. de Marques de Sta. Cruz

R. Rocha dos Santos

R. Leovegildo Coelho

Av. Joaquim Nabuco

R. Quintino Bocaiuva

R. Dr. Izabel

R. Miranda Leão

R. Pedro Botelho

R. dos Andradas

R. dos Barés

R. Barão de São Domingos

Av. Lourenço da Silva Braga

Feira da Produtor

Rio Negro

DINING ◆
Bistro Ananã 1
Glacial Sorveteria 4

ATTRACTIONS ●
Alfândega 9
Centro Cultural
  Palacio Rio Negro 5
Encontra das Aguas 11
Hidroviaria do Amazonas
  (Riverboat Terminal) 8
Mercado Adolpho
  Lisboa 10
Museu do Indio 6
Teatro Amazonas 3

ACCOMMODATIONS ■
Best Western Manaus 7
Hotel Manaós 2

0 — 0.2 mile
0 — 200 meters

and contemplate: You're in the middle of nowhere with 1,000 miles of forest in every direction.

Inhabitants of the largest city in the Amazon, Manaus's 1.6 million people live on the shores of the Rio Negro, just upstream from where it joins the Rio Solimões to become the Amazon. Though first settled in the 1600s, there's a frontier feel to the place.

Near the end of the 19th century, when the Amazon was the world's only rubber supplier, there was a 30-year boom in rubber and Manaus got rich indeed. Some of the city's finest buildings date back to this time, among them the Customs house and the famous Teatro Amazonas. The boom ended around 1910, some years after an enterprising Brit stole some Amazon rubber seeds and planted them in new plantations in Malaya (modern-day Malaysia).

The city's next boom came in 1966, when Manaus was declared a free-trade zone. Electronics assembly plants sprouted across the city, and workers poured in to staff the factories. In the space of just a few years the city's population doubled to half a million. The retail traffic dried up in the early '90s when the government reduced import tariffs, but with the free-trade zone still in place, manufacturing of electronics carries on.

These days, the city's biggest employer is the Brazilian army, which has jungle-training schools, listening stations, and a substantial standing force stationed in the

---

Tips **Warning! Steer Clear of Aggressive Airport Touts**

The airport touts have (finally!) been banished from the baggage claim area of the Manaus airport, so now they accost newcomers in the arrivals hall, offering every type of city and jungle tour. *Do not book with these people!* Their standard MO is to ask what you're interested in doing. Surprise, surprise, whatever you want to do, they have that tour. Once you pay, they resell you to another operator doing the standard 50-people-on-the-boat Meeting of the Waters day tour. Complain all you like—you'll never get your money back.

---

city—all to preserve Brazilian sovereignty over the Amazon. Tourism has also expanded, most of it focused on the rainforest. Manaus is the main departure point for trips into the Amazon. We've reviewed numerous options for exploring the forest, from comfortable lodges to luxury cruises to simple expeditions by kayak.

ESSENTIALS
GETTING THERE
BY PLANE   TAM (toll-free ℃ **0800/570-5700** or 092/4002-5700; www.tam. com.br), **Gol** (℃ **0300/115-2121;** www.voegol.com.br), and **Varig** (℃ **092/4003-7000;** www.varig.com.br) have flights from major cities in Brazil. Flights from Rio or São Paulo take about 5 hours. In addition, both TAM and **Lloyd Aéreo Boliviano** (℃ **092/3633-4711;** www.labairlines.com.bo) have daily flights to Manaus from Miami.

Manaus's international airport, **Eduardo Gomes,** Avenida Santos Dumont (℃ **092/ 3652-1212**), is 17km (10 miles) from downtown. There's a **Tourist Information** desk in the arrivals hall (℃ **092/3652-1120**) with free maps of the city and some information on hotels and tours; it's open daily from 7am to 11pm. A taxi to Manaus Centro will cost about R$45 (US$25/£12). You also have the option of taking a **regular city bus,** no. 306 to Centro, for R$1.80 (US75¢/£.35). Guests of the Tropical can take the **Fontur shuttle,** for R$15 (US$7.5/£4) per person. There is a small currency exchange at the airport as well as Banco do Brasil and HSBC ATMs connected to the Visa/PLUS systems.

BY BOAT   Boats dock at the new **Hidroviaria do Amazonas (Riverboat Terminal)** (℃ **092/3621-4310**) in the middle of downtown at Rua Marquês de Santa Cruz 25. There is an information desk inside the front door where you can find out about arrival and departure times, and a ticket kiosk where you buy tickets. Boats for **Belém** normally depart Wednesday and Friday at noon. The trip downstream takes 4 days, upstream travel takes 5 days. Delays are not uncommon. For information on the 5-day journey from Belém to Manaus, see "By Riverboat" in "Belém Essentials: Arriving" (p. 397). Cost of a first-class hammock spot (on the upper deck) is R$245 (US$123/£66). Hammocks are not supplied. Buy one in Manaus (see "Shopping," later in this chapter). Cabins cost R$750 to R$900 (US$375–US$450/£203–£243). Good, simple meals and filtered water are supplied on the boat at no extra cost. From the terminal it's a short walk or taxi ride, R$10 to R$15 (US$5–US$7.50/£2.70–£4), to the downtown hotels. To the Tropical Manaus it's a 20-minute taxi ride R$50 (US$25/£14) or 40-minute bus ride, no. 120 from Centro.

Tip: If you have some competence in Portuguese, you can negotiate a 10% to 20% cheaper fare by going directly to a riverboat, most of which dock downstream by the quay opposite the Mercado Municipal.

There is now also a new fast catamaran to Santarem, which takes approximately 12 hours to make the journey downstream. The catamaran departs from the quay opposite the Mercado Municipal.

VISITOR INFORMATION

The city tourist information agency, **Manaustur,** Av. Sete de Setembro 157 (✆ **092/ 3622-4986**), is open Monday through Friday 9am to 6pm, but it's inconveniently in a run-down part of the port. Stop in at the airport instead.

The tourism information desk at the airport is open from 7am to 11pm and located in the arrivals hall (✆ **092/3652-1120**). They can provide city maps, brochures, hotel information, and telephone numbers of tour operators.

Equally useful, the State of Amazonas tourism agency, **AmazonasTur,** has an info center at Rua Saldanha Marinho 321 (near the Opera House) (✆ **092/3233-1928;** www.amazonastur.am.gov.br), which is open Monday through Friday from 9am to 6pm. There are also free public bathrooms here.

CITY LAYOUT

The city is the river. Downtown, all activity gravitates toward the waterfront on the Rio Negro, and it's there that you really feel the heart of the city. The entire city is plotted in an easy-to-follow grid pattern; in the oldest part of town—which occupies a peninsula at the river's edge—the grid runs at a slight angle to that of the rest of the city. The **port** and the **municipal market (mercado municipal)** both face the river. The main attractions for visitors concentrate in a 20-block radius around the port and are easily accessible on foot. The downtown **bus terminal** is directly in front of the port; on the other side there's the busy and newly renovated **Praça da Matriz.** To the east of the square are a number of narrow parallel streets, centered on **Rua Guilherme Moreira,** that form Manaus's main downtown **shopping district.** The busy east-west **Avenida Sete de Setembro** marks the end of the oldest section of downtown. From here north, the grid angles slightly, and things get less interesting. The only real sight of interest is the **Teatro Amazonas,** 4 blocks farther north on **Rua Barroso.** The entire downtown area is safe during the day; just watch your purse and wallet in the crowds. In the evening stay on the main squares and avenues. Avoid the port area and the side streets along the *iguarapés* (river channels) at night; small slums have settled along the riverbed, particularly to the east and northeast of downtown. From the downtown core the city sprawls inland and along the river. **Ponta Negra Beach,** about 18km (11 miles) from downtown, is one of the more upscale neighborhoods where the beachfront has become a popular nightlife-and-entertainment area. This is also where you'll find the **Tropical Manaus.** A good part of the beach disappears in the wet season (Jan–Apr), but the food stands and entertainment stay. In the dry season the beach is a great place to swim and suntan on the shores of the Rio Negro.

GETTING AROUND

BY BUS   From the Tropical Manaus to downtown, take bus no. 120 (R$1.80/ US90¢/£.50); the trip takes 35 to 40 minutes. The bus stops at the **Praça da Matriz,** which is within easy walking distance of all downtown attractions. To get to the Ceasa Port from downtown, take the CEASA bus from Praça da Matriz.

BY TAXI   Taxis can be hailed on the street or reserved for a specific time by phoning ahead. For the airport contact **Coopertaxi** (© 092/3652-1544 or 092/3652-1568). In town, phone **Tele-Rádio Táxi** at © **092/3633-3211.** You're most likely to use taxis if you are staying at the Tropical and going back and forth to downtown. For this trip taxis all quote the same price—currently R$50 (US$25/£14)—and don't run the meter. If you negotiate you can often knock R$10 (US$5/£2.70) off the price, but make sure you bargain before getting in the cab.

BY CAR   Renting a car in Manaus makes little sense. In the city all the sights are within walking distance. Outside of the city it's, you know, a jungle.

FAST FACTS: Manaus

Car Rentals **Avis** (© **0800/725-2847** or 092/3652-1579). **Localiza** (© **0800/979-2000** or 092/3652-1176).

Consulates *United States,* virtual presence post only: http://virtual.embaixada-americana.org.br/manaus; *Great Britain* (Honorary), Rua Poraquê 240, Distrito Industrial (© **092/3613-1819**).

Currency Exchange **Banco do Brasil,** Rua Guilherme Moreira 315, Centro (© **092/3621-5500**); **Cortês Câmbio,** Av. Sete de Setembro 1199, Centro (© **092/ 3622-4222;** www.cortez.com.br); or Amazonas Shopping (© **092/3642-2525**).

Dentist **Clínica Odontológica Ortomax,** Av. Joaquim Nabuco 2285 (© **092/ 3633-3121,** or cell 092/9964-5211).

Hospitals **Pronto Socorro e Hospital dos Acidentados,** Av. Joaquim Nabuco 1755, Centro (© **092/3663-2200**).

Internet Access The **Tropical Manaus** has an Internet cafe open daily from 9am to 10pm; charge is R$18 (US$9/£5) per hour. In Centro, try **Amazon Cyber Café,** Av. Getulio Vargas 626 (© **092/3232-9068**). Open Monday through Friday 9am to 11pm, Saturday from 10am to 8pm, and Sunday from 1 to 8pm; R$4 (US$2/£1) per hour.

Time Zone Manaus is 1 hour behind São Paulo and Rio de Janeiro.

Weather It's hot year-round—hot and muggy and rainy from December through March (86°F–96°F/30°C–36°C) and just plain hot the rest of the year. The wet season (Dec–Mar) is the best time to experience the flooded forest; the river rises and brings boats and canoes up to eye level with the treetops. The dry season (Aug–Nov) is wonderful for exploring the forest and beaches that appear when the water recedes.

WHERE TO STAY
CENTRO
Expensive

Best Western Lord Manaus ⚘   Located within walking distance of all the main sites, this hotel is convenient for those who are only in town for a night before heading into the forest. The area is not great at night when most of the businesses close, but there are a few restaurants around. The hotel is similar to North American Best

Westerns. The rooms have recently been upgraded. All come with tile floors and new furnishings and have bright, modern colors. The suites aren't worth the extra money.

Rua Marcilio Dias 217, Centro, Manaus, 69005-270 AM. © 0800/761-5001 or 092/3622-2844. www.bestwestern. com.br. 102 units (showers only). Standard R$280 (US$140/£76); suite double R$310 (US$155/£84). You can usually negotiate a 30% discount on these rates. Extra bed R$45–R$75 (US$23–US$38/£12–£20). Children under 6 stay free in parent's room. AE, DC, MC, V. Free parking. **Amenities:** Restaurant; bar; tour desk; room service; laundry service; nonsmoking floor. *In room:* A/C, TV, dataport, minibar, fridge.

Moderate

Hotel Manaós Situated cater-cornered from the Opera House, the Manaós provides something rare in the Amazon—basic clean accommodations at a moderate price. Rooms come in two flavors: two singles, or a double and a single. The price is the same for both. Bathrooms are extremely clean and bright (consider wearing your shades in the shower). Best of all for those in the know, room nos. 304 through 311 and 204 through 211 provide the kind of view of the Opera House for which other hotels charge hundreds extra.

Av. Eduardo Ribeiro 881, Centro, Manaus, AM 69010-001. © 092/3633-5744. Fax 092/232-4443. www.hotelmanaos. com.br. 39 units (showers only). R$150 (US$75/£41) double. 10% discount for stays of more than 1 night. No triple rooms available. Children 6 and under stay free in parent's room. AE, DC, MC, V. Free parking. **Amenities:** Restaurant; room service; laundry. *In room:* A/C, TV, minibar.

PONTA NEGRA

Located 20km (12 miles) from downtown, the Tropical Manaus is the best place to stay in Manaus. Better yet, it's located on Ponta Negra Beach, a popular nightlife district on the banks of the Rio Negro. Of all the hotels in Brazil, this one is definitely worth the splurge.

Very Expensive

Tropical Manaus 🐟🐟🐟 After the Copacabana Palace, this is the most famous hotel in Brazil. Built on the shores of the Rio Negro, within its own little patch of rainforest, the Tropical is a destination in itself. Outside there's a zoo, children's play area, archery range (lessons complimentary), a jogging trail, beach volleyball, soccer fields, horseback riding, and the list goes on. The large pool complex includes a wave pool. Inside, the original wing of the hotel is referred to as *ala colonial,* in contrast to the more modern *ala moderna.* Where you stay is more a matter of preference than quality. The colonial rooms have more character, with beautiful dark-wood furniture and hardwood floors, but they can also be a bit musty. The more modern wing is pleasantly furnished with carpets and contemporary decor in light colors. All rooms are a good size with high ceilings and large windows, and the bathrooms are spacious and modern, with showers and bathtubs. The deluxe rooms come with a balcony and more space. To really splurge, go for the *suite nobre* (R$930/US$465/£251), elegantly furnished with a large sitting room and Jacuzzi tub in the bathroom. The junior suites are not a great deal, especially compared to the spacious deluxe rooms. The rates below are the Internet rates. A travel agent may do better.

Av. Coronel Texeira 1320, Ponta Negra, Manaus, 69029-120 AM. © 0800/701-2670 or 092/3659-5000. Fax 092/ 3658-5026. www.tropicalhotel.com.br. 601 units. Standard or superior double R$365–R$400 (US$183–US$200/ £99–£108); deluxe double R$510 (US$255/£138); junior suite double R$930 (US$465/£251). There is often a 10%–30% discount on these rates. Extra person add 25%. Children 10 and under stay free in parent's room. AE, DC, MC, V. Bus: 120. **Amenities:** 3 restaurants; 2 bars; disco; large pool complex; tennis courts; health club; spa; sauna; watersports rental; children's program; game room; concierge; tour desk; car rental; business center; shopping arcade; salon; room service; massage; babysitting; laundry; dry cleaning; nonsmoking rooms and floors. *In room:* A/C, TV, dataport, minibar, fridge, hair dryer, safe.

Tropical Manaus Business ★★★   Located right on the shore of the Rio Negro, the Tropical Business is the newest addition to the Tropical complex. Whereas the *old* Tropical oozes elegance and conjures up visions of explorers ready to take off on a jungle adventure, the new Tropical is all business. Bright and sleek, the hotel offers modern and spacious rooms with king-size beds, high-speed Internet, efficient air-conditioning and phone system, 21st-century plumbing, electronic safes, and fabulous views of the Rio Negro. The suite experience is identical to the regular rooms; the only added feature is the veranda overlooking the river. As perks, the hotel offers a free shuttle service to the airport and downtown and free 24-hour access to the business center. The hotel has a large outdoor pool and sun deck overlooking the Rio Negro and a state-of-the-art fitness center. Guests may also use all facilities of the old Tropical as well.

Av. Coronel Texeira 1320, Ponta Negra, Manaus, 69037-000 AM. ⓒ **0800/701-2670** or 092/2123-3000. Fax 092/2123-3021. www.tropicalhotel.com.br. 184 units. Standard double R$425 (US$213/£115); suite double R$497 (US$249/£134). Inquire about discounts for Varig ticket-holders and Amex cardholders. Extra person add 25%. Children 10 and under stay free in parent's room. AE, DC, MC, V. Bus: 120. **Amenities:** Restaurant; 2 bars; large outdoor pool; health club; sauna; concierge; tour desk; car rental; business center; room service; laundry; dry cleaning; nonsmoking rooms and floors. *In room:* A/C, TV, dataport, minibar, hair dryer, safe.

ELSEWHERE

Mango Guest House ★   The Mango is a nice small guesthouse, unfortunately located in a boring walled-off suburb about halfway between downtown and Ponta Negra. Rooms are simple, small, and pleasant, with tile floors, firm single or double beds, and clean, functional bathrooms with super-hot showers. All rooms have a small veranda that looks out on a grassy courtyard and small pool, and the guesthouse has several nice lounges and sitting rooms and free Internet access. The Mango is perfect for those who just need to spend a night in Manaus. All tours pick up and drop off, and the guesthouse will happily store your excess luggage while you are off in the rainforest. It's less than perfect for those who want to explore Manaus—there is no public transit, and the guesthouse is a R$30 (US$15/£8) ride from either Ponta Negra or downtown. Tell taxi drivers the guesthouse is in Kissia Dois, off Rua Jacira Reis, which runs off Rua Darcy Vargas. Even then, don't be surprised if they get lost.

Rua Flavio Espirito Santo 1, Kissia II, 69040-250 AM. ⓒ **092/3656-6033.** Fax 092/3656-6101. www.naturesafaris.com.br. 14 units. Standard double R$150 (US$75/£41). Extra person add 25%. Credit cards only when booking online or via travel agency: AE, DC, MC, V. No credit cards accepted at the guesthouse. No public transit. **Amenities:** Restaurant; outdoor pool; free shared Internet terminal. *In room:* A/C, fridge.

Mercure Apartments Manaus ★   Where the business travelers stay in Manaus. Located in Adrianópolis—fast becoming the city's restaurant hot spot—this new member of the well-respected Mercure chain offers comfortable clean rooms with tile floors and a single queen-size or two twin beds, plus a small functional work desk with plug ins for laptops and high-speed Internet. The hotel is only 4 years old, so everything has a new feel, and as with all Mercure properties the service is brisk and efficient. There's a small, pretty rooftop pool with a view of nothing much, and a good quality fitness center with personal trainers in attendance, and Jacuzzi for relaxing in afterward.

Av. da Recife 1000, Adrianópolis, 69040-250 AM. ⓒ **092/2101-1100.** Fax 092/2101-1101. www.accorhotels.com.br. 109 units. Superior double R$350 (US$175/£95). Extra person add 25%. AE, DC, MC, V. Bus: 118. **Amenities:** Restaurant; bar; rooftop pool; fitness center; Jacuzzi; room service; laundry. *In room:* A/C, TV, minibar, fridge, high-speed Internet.

Hot Spot in Adrianópolis

In the past year or so, the upscale neighborhood of Adrianópolis has emerged as Manaus' culinary hot spot, with a number of fine restaurants in a relatively concentrated area. In addition to the **Village** (one of the city's best, reviewed above), there's top quality (and top dollar) Portuguese cuisine at **Casa do Bacalhau** (Rua Paraíba 1587-A; © 092/3642-1723; open for dinner Mon–Sat 7pm–midnight, and for lunch Tues–Sun 11:30am–3pm). For local—and more affordable—Amazonian dishes there's **Choupana** (Av. Recife 790; © 092/3635-3878; Wed–Sat 11am–3pm, 6:30–11pm, Sun noon–4pm). Even cheaper, and arguably more fun, is **Açaí e Companhia** (Rua Acre; © 092/3653-3637; daily noon–midnight), a kind of outdoor kiosk which specializes in local fish dishes such as jambu and tambaqui. On Friday and Saturday evening there's live music. Korean food is hard to find anywhere in Brazil, much less in the middle of the rainforest, and yet in Adrianópolis there's **Ara** (Av. Recife 1005, casa 1; © 092/3234-2650; daily 11am–2pm and 6–10pm), as well as Japanese food at **Suzuran** (Rua Teresina 155; © 092/3234-1693; daily 11am–2pm and 6–10pm)

WHERE TO DINE
ADRIANÓPOLIS

Village BRAZILIAN   One of the city's best restaurants, the Village is a dining destination for the city's elite. The menu covers a vast range, with seafood and fish dishes, risottos and pastas, meat, chicken, and lamb dishes all on offer. The chef's approach has a slight Italian tinge, while the use of Brazilian ingredients (such as catupiry cheese with Bahian prawns) gives the dishes their local flavor. The wine list is likely the most extensive in Manaus.

Rua Recife 948, Adrianópolis. © 092/3234-3296. www.villagerestaurante.com.br. Main courses R$24–R$48 (US$12–US$24/£6.50–£13). AE, DC, MC, V. Mon–Sat noon–3pm and 6pm–midnight.

CENTRO

Bistrô Ananã BRAZILIAN   This charming little bistro prepares dishes with Amazonian ingredients that you won't find anywhere else. The signature dish is rack of tambaqui (fish) ribs in a chutney of tucupi, with Bahian risotto and a farofa of local bananas.

Travessa Padre Ghisland, 38, Centro (near the Colégio Dom Bosco). © 092/3234-0056. Main courses R$24–R$48 (US$12–US$24/£6.50–£13). AE, MC, V. Wed–Sat 7:30pm–midnight.

Glacial Sorveteria DESSERT   One of the best ways to try many of the exotic fruits of the Amazon is in the form of ice cream. Some suggested flavors are *cupuaçu, açai, jaca, bacaba,* and *graviola.* Grab a couple of flavors and taste away. There is another shop in Ponta Negra (© 092/3658-3980).

Av. Getulio Vargas 161, Centro. © 092/3233-4172. www.glacial.com.br. R$4.50–R$9 (US$2.25–US$4.50/£1.20–£2.50). No credit cards. Mon–Thurs 8am–11pm; Fri–Sun 8am–11:30pm.

PONTA NEGRA

Ponta Negra offers a number of nighttime dining options, none outstanding in terms of food, but most in very pleasant surroundings. On the waterfront, **Laranjinha** (© 092/3658-5483; Mon–Sat 5pm–3am, Sun 5pm–5am) has a great patio and makes

The Lowdown on Amazonian Cuisine

Amazonian dishes mix a dollop of Portuguese and a dash of African flavors with native traditions and lots of local ingredients. The star attraction in most dishes is fish, fresh from the Amazon's many tributaries. It's worth visiting the market in Manaus just to see what these creatures look like. Make sure you try at least the *tucunaré;* the meat is so tasty it's best served plainly grilled. *Pirarucú* is known as the codfish of the Amazon. It can be salted and used just like *bacalhau. Tambaqui* and *paçu* also have delicious firm flesh that works well in stews and broths. One popular stew is **caldeirada.** Often made with *tucanaré,* the rich broth is spiced with onion, tomato, peppers, and herbs. Very different is the **pato no tucupi**, a duck dish stewed with *tucupí,* the juice of fermented and spiced cassava. *Tacacá* is a delicious native soup, made with the yellow *tucupí* cassava, *murupí* peppers, and garlic, onion, and dried shrimp. You'll often see this for sale on the streets, traditionally served in a gourd cup. To add kick to your food, try some **murupí** pepper sauce.

The region is also rich in fruits, many of which can only be found in the Amazon, most of which do not even have English names. The citrus-like **bacuri,** with its soft spongelike skin and white flesh, is addictive; like Christmas mandarins, you can't eat just one. The most commonly eaten fruit is **cupuaçu.** This large round fruit, like a small pale coconut, has an odd sweet-and-sour taste at first bite, like it's almost *too* ripe. But you'll learn to savor it in desserts and juices. *Tucumã* is a small hard fruit similar to an unripe peach. Locals eat slices of it on bread. At lodges it's also a favorite of half-tame monkeys and parrots who will snag one whenever they get a chance. **Açai** is a popular fruit, but it can't be eaten raw; the berries are first soaked and then squashed to obtain the juice. You will find it in juices and ice cream. In the jungle you'll come across fruits that you don't even see in Manaus markets. My favorite is the **mari-mari,** a snakelike vine about as long as your arm; when opened with a quick twist it reveals a row of Lifesaver-looking fruits. Green, juicy, and full of vitamins.

for fine people-watching. Most nights there's a slightly Vegas folklore show featuring beautiful young things (male and female) in skimpy "traditional" costumes. On a candlelit patio in the Tropical Manaus there's the **Karu Grill** ☆ (② **092/3659-5000**), which offers a nightly buffet with excellent regional local fish, *macaxeira* (a local root that is often cooked like a potato), soups, or grilled steak and fresh salad.

EXPLORING MANAUS

You won't need more than 2 days to see Manaus. Start your exploration at the port. The new **Riverboat Terminal** is a little too air-conditioned and anodyne, but the **Mercado Adolpho Lisboa** is a great place to see local fish and produce, not to mention local folk remedies. Farther down, the **Feira do Produtor** has every Amazon product imaginable, and the waterfront out front where boats load up is a fascinating glimpse of Amazon frontier. The **Opera House** is an extravagant, impressive testament to the legacy of the rubber boom. A half-day trip out to **The Meeting of the Waters** is a worthwhile afternoon excursion. In the evening, head to the beach at **Ponta Negra,** and stop for a cold beer or an exotic ice cream as you watch the river. And then get thee out into the Amazon. There's wild stuff to see.

THE TOP ATTRACTIONS

Centro Cultural Palaço Rio Negro *⊛⊛*   This gorgeous palace built at the height of the rubber boom has been transformed into one of the city's leading cultural centers, home to several small but excellent museums. Built by a Manaus rubber baron in the early years of the 20th century, the main palace is wonderfully ornate, with rich tropical hardwoods used for floors and doors, and banisters and moldings. Some rooms have been decorated with lovely period furnishings; others now serve as display spaces for modern Brazilian art and sculpture. The palace served as the state governor's mansion for many years; there are some artifacts from that period, but it's the building, not the history, that impresses. The entire back garden of the palace has been transformed into a permanent **People of the Forest Exhibit** *⊛*, which shows the lifestyle of people of the interior with full-size re-creations of an Indian village, a *caboclo* house, and *farinha* and rubber processing sheds. The Indian village is staffed by members of several different Amazonian tribes, and periodically throughout the day they put on a small demonstration of indigenous culture, including dances and songs of welcome. In a smaller building to one side of the palace you'll find the state art museum, the **Pinacoteca do Estado** *⊛*. Though small (one floor only) it houses some fascinating and beautiful artwork from Manaus artists of the 19th and 20th centuries. The lower floor of the same building houses the **Bernardo Ramos Numismatic Museum,** which has 11 rooms full of rare coins from around the world. In another building on the grounds you'll find the **Amazon Image and Sound Library,** which has a vast collection of photographs, and audio and video recordings in various formats (DVD, VHS, Beta, vinyl), more or less cataloged, which can be viewed or listened to inside the museum. Allow 2 hours.

Av. 7 de Setembro 1540, Centro. *©* **092/3232-4450.** www.culturamazonas.am.gov.br. Free Admission. All museums in complex Tues–Fri 10am–5pm; Sat-Sun 2–6pm.

CIGS Zoo *Kids*   It's a strange place, this zoo. It's part of the army's jungle warfare–training center, and many of the animals were captured by soldiers on patrol. The animal enclosures range from the worst you've ever seen to quite sophisticated and humane habitats. One poor black jaguar is kept in a concrete-floored cage no more than two jaguar-lengths square, while the cougars are kept in sizable enclosures with grass and a small pond. The collection is tremendous: black and spotted jaguars, cougars and smaller cats, toucans, macaws, and more. You'll also see harpy eagles stuck in heartbreakingly small enclosures. Yet the monkey habitat is wide and well done— go figure. Allow an hour to 90 minutes.

Estrada do Ponta Negra, Km 13. *©* **092/3625-1966.** Admission R$3 (US$1.50/£.80) adults, free for children 12 and under. Tues–Sun 9am–4:30pm. Bus: 120.

The Meeting of the Waters (Encontro da Aguas) *⊛⊛*   For more than 200 years tourists have been venturing out to see this remarkable sight: The dark slow waters of the Rio Negro meet the faster muddy brown waters from the Rio Solimões, and because of differences in velocity, temperature, and salinity, the two rivers carry on side-by-side for miles, with progressively less distinct whorls and eddies marking the interface between these two rivers. It's a classic Manaus day trip, and a great excuse to get out on the Amazon. If you're booked at a lodge downstream of Manaus you'll pass through The Meeting of the Waters on the way there and back. If not, consider booking a day trip. Unfortunately, the standard day tour includes a long stop at **Lago Janauary Ecological Park.** Located about an hour from Manaus, the Lago Janauary features some elevated boardwalks weaving through the trees and giant floating Vitoria Regia lily pads. It's reasonably pretty, but generations of tourists have spoiled the place. As you arrive, hordes of small children swarm your boat thrusting various miserable rainforest creatures they've captured into your hands. Take a picture of the "cute" young urchin and his captured caiman, and you'll be paying him a photo fee, not to mention contributing to the continued depredation of local wildlife. *Note:* In the dry season (Aug–Dec), the trip through the Lago becomes impossible and tour operators will take you to the Ilha da Terra Nova instead to see the rubber trees and cocoa plantations.

All Manaus agencies offer day tours for about R$100 (US$50/£27). Try Viverde (🕾 **092/3248-9988**).

Mercado Adolpho Lisboa 🕸

The Adolpho Lisboa is beautiful iron-and-glass copy of the now-demolished market hall in Les Halles, Paris. It's a great place to see some of the local fish, fruits, and vegetables. The variety of fish is overwhelming. Not for the squeamish, the vendors cut and clean the fish on the spot with complete disregard for the tender psyche; though chopped in half, some of the larger catfish still wriggle. The fruit and vegetable section is equally fascinating. Just in case you wanted to heal thyself, stop in at one of the herb stalls. Who needs a pharmacy when the cures for diabetes, kidney failure, obesity, heart problems, and headache and impotence are all laid out in dried bunches of leaves? A number of stalls have excellent indigenous handicrafts at reasonable prices.

Rua dos Barés 46, Centro. 🕾 **092/3233-0469.** Mon–Sat 6am–6pm; Sun 6am–noon.

Museu do Indio

Spread out over six rooms, this museum presents the culture and social structure of the indigenous peoples of the Upper Rio Negro. Artifacts and clothing give an overview of their hunting and fishing traditions, as well as showing the spiritual rituals of a funeral and healing ceremony. The displays contain photos, drawings, a large number of artifacts, and occasionally models and replicas. All descriptions are in Portuguese, English, and German. Allow 1 hour.

Rua Duque de Caxias 356, Centro. 🕾 **092/3635-1922.** Admission R$5 (US$2.50/£1.35) Mon–Fri 8:30–11:30am and 2–4:30pm; Sat 8:30–11:30am.

Teatro Amazonas 🕸🕸

This is one tourist "must-see" that is actually worth seeing. This remarkable landmark was erected in the midst of the Amazon jungle in 1896 at the peak of the rubber boom. The half-hour guided tour shows off the lobby of marble and inlaid tropical hardwoods, the fine concert hall, and the romantic mural in the upstairs ballroom. Even better is to see a concert (see "Manaus After Dark," below). For the moment, the theater's official website unfortunately has no programming information.

Praça São Sebastião. 🕾 **092/3622-1880.** www.teatroamazonas.com.br. Guided 30-min. tours in English and Portuguese depart every 30 min. R$6 (US$2.50/£1.25). Mon–Sat 9am–noon and 2–4pm.

ARCHITECTURAL HIGHLIGHTS

The square and the buildings around the opera house—the **Largo de São Sebatião**— have been restored almost to their original condition. In the evenings, the city often programs free concerts here.

The pretty neoclassical **Public Library,** Rua Barroso 57, on the corner of Avenida Sete de Setembro, dates from 1870 (Mon–Fri 8am–5pm). It's worth climbing the grand central staircase to the top floor to see a large oil painting marking the end of slavery in the Amazon. Done in the best overwrought allegorical style, it positively overflows with bare-breasted Amazon princesses, each a symbolic representation of some aspect or another of the province.

The old Customs house, or **Alfândega,** on Rua Marquesa da Santa Cruz, was pre-fabricated in England, shipped to Manaus in 1912, and re-erected block by block. The tower on the water side of the building was once a lighthouse.

NEIGHBORHOODS TO EXPLORE

Downtown Manaus is a fun place to explore. Check out the waterfront behind the **Feira da Produtor** on **Avenida Lourenço da Silva Braga** to see riverboats discharging passengers or loading up with everything under the sun for the next trip up or down the river. Two blocks inland, **Rua dos Bares** is full of chandleries and hardware shops; it's also a good place to buy a hammock. Small and picturesque, **Praça Tenreiro Aranha** contains an informal outdoor crafts fair. The **Artindia** store in the center of the square is housed in a small iron-and-glass structure reminiscent of London's Crystal Palace, though on a tiny scale. The covered pedestrian mall **Rua Marechal Deodoro** is the center of Manaus's thriving downtown shopping bazaar. The triangular plaza at the corner of **Avenida Presidente Vargas** and **Avenida Sete de Setembro** is a pleasant place to relax in the shade for a spell. Like so many Brazilian squares, it goes by two names: either **Praça da Polícia** or **Praça Heliodoro Balbi.** The city's most famous sight, the **Opera House** or **Teatro Amazonas,** is but a short walk from here.

PLAZAS, PARKS & GARDENS

There are two large city parks that may be worth a visit. **Mindu Park,** Avenida Perimitral (© **092/3236-7702;** Tues–Sun 8am–5pm; bus: 511), is a 33-sq.-km (20-sq.-mile) forest reserve that is also one of the last remaining habitats of the Sauim-de-Coleira monkey, a species found only in the Manaus area. The park has walking trails with interpretive signage, a suspended treetop walkway, and an interpretation center with a library.

The **Bosque de Ciência** or Ecological Park, Rua Otávio Cabral (© **092/3643-3293;** Tues–Sun 9am–3pm; bus: 511), was created by INPA, the National Institute for Amazon Research, to promote ecological awareness. There's a small aquarium on-site with river otters and manatees.

ORGANIZED TOURS

AIR TOURS   To get an aerial view of the rainforest and the city, **Viverde,** Rua dos Cardeiros 26, Manaus (©/fax **092/3248-9988;** www.viverde.com.br), offers sightseeing flights on a floatplane that takes off from the river in front of the Tropical Manaus. The best deal is the **30-minute flight** that gives you aerial views of the city, the flooded forest, and The Meeting of the Waters, an amazing sight from the air. It costs R$450 (US$225/£121) per person with a minimum of two people. For R$900 (US$450/£243) you get a **1-hour flight** that allows you to go as far as the Anavilhanas Archipelago (more than 300 islands in the Rio Negro) and buzz some of the beaches and forest on your way back.

BUS/BOAT TOURS   The best Manaus tour operator is **Viverde,** Rua dos Cardeiros 26, Manaus (©/fax **092/3248-9988;** www.viverde.com.br). **Fontur,** located at the

Tropical Manaus, Estrada da Ponta Negra (© 092/3658-3052; www.fontur.com.br), also offers a variety of tours. Because of its location in the Tropical, Fontur is more expensive.

Both companies offer half-day **city tours,** with English-speaking guides and an air-conditioned vehicle that cover the highlights: the Opera House, the port and the market, and one museum, either the Palaçio Rio Negro or the Museu do Indio. Viverde offers a scientific city tour that includes the **Bosque de Ciência.** Cost is around R$140 (US$70/£38) per person, with two people, R$77 (US$39/£21) per person with four. They also offer full-day tours that include a visit to **The Meeting of the Waters** and boat trips to the **Anavilhanas Archipelago.**

CITY TOURS   Long the experts in deep Amazon exploration, **Amazon Mystery Tours** (© 092/3633-7844; www.amazonmysterytours.com) has recently branched out into the city, offering innovative city tours, including some that no other company has even thought of. There's a half-day **City Tour** that covers the basics, of course, including the opera house and markets and port (US$45/£24), with the option to stop in at the Palaçio Rio Negro, Cigs Zoo, or Museu do Indio (US$10/£5.40 for each add-on). In addition, guide Jean Claude has developed a **Manaus by Night** series (US$45/£24), which will take you out to a popular neighborhood to hang with locals, munch street food, and move to the sound of Manaus-based samba and pagode. The **Cultural Manaus** tours (US$45/£24) offer visitors the chance to visit a kindergarten or spend a morning with Brazilian youth being shown their part of the city; there's also a tour that allows you to spend a night with a Brazilian family (US$75/£41). And if all that's just too much culture, the company offers a day trip up to the waterfalls and caverns of **Presidente Figueiredo,** a beautiful highland area about 100km (62 miles) north of Manaus (US$125/£68). Check the website for details on new tours being developed.

SHOPPING

Downtown Manaus is one big shopping area: Vendors hawk their wares, stalls clog up the sidewalks and squares, and the streets are jampacked with little stores. The main shopping streets run behind the **Praça Tenreiro Aranha, Rua Marcilio Dias, Rua Guilherme Moreira,** and **Rua Marechal Deodoro.** The streets around the market at **Rua dos Barés** sell more household goods and hammocks. The church square, **Praça da Matriz,** has a large market during weekdays selling everything from clothing to hair accessories and bags. The city's largest mall is **Shopping Amazonas,** Av. Djalma Batista 482, Parque 10 (© 092/3642-3555; www.amazonasshopping.com.br). It's open Monday through Saturday from 10am to 10pm. Take bus no. 203, 209, or 214 from Praça da Matriz, Centro.

MARKETS

Artindia   The crafts market located on the Praça Tenreiro Aranha sells a wide variety of Indian crafts, including necklaces, bracelets, woodcarvings, baskets, and handbags. Open Monday through Saturday 8am to 6pm. Praça Tenreiro Aranha, Centro. © 092/3232-4890.

SOUVENIRS

Artesanato da Amazonia   Located across from the Opera House, this large souvenir shop offers a good selection of native arts and crafts, such as baskets, pottery, jewelry, and bags, as well as the usual T-shirts. Open Monday through Saturday 10am to 4pm. Rua Jose Clemente 500, loja A, Centro. © 092/3232-3979.

> **Tips** **Stock Up to Put Your Feet Up**
>
> Manaus is one of the cheapest places to buy a hammock. These make great souvenirs, and if you're taking a riverboat, they're indispensable. The best stores are located on the Rua dos Barés, around the Mercado Municipal. Expect to pay R$45 to R$75 (US$23–US$37/£12–£20).

Central de Artesanato Branco & Silva   Located about a 15-minute cab ride north of downtown, Central de Artesanato is worth the trek. In one location you'll find 23 handicrafts shops specializing in regional crafts. A lot of the artisans work with wood, weavings, ceramics, bark, seeds, and other organic materials. The selection is amazing, and some of the crafts are of gallery quality. Open Tuesday through Friday 9am to 6pm, Saturday 9am to 4pm. Rua Recife 1999, Parque 10. (© 092/3236-1241. By taxi only, no convenient bus route.

Native Original Products   More high-end design than knickknack stand, this gift shop specializes in high-end crafts, artwork, and furniture made with local woods and seeds. The designs are often inspired by traditional native artifacts; one candle holder is made out of a stylized spearhead set in hardwood. Open Monday through Saturday 9am to 9pm and Sunday 9am to 5pm. There are three stores, one in the Tropical Business Hotel, Av. Coronel Texeira 1320, Ponta Negra (© 092/2123-3183; www.nativeoriginal.com.br), one in the Teatro Amazonas (© 092/3622-1883), and one in the waterfront **Riverboat Terminal** at Rua Marquês de Santa Cruz 25 (© 092/3232-8020).

MANAUS AFTER DARK
THE PERFORMING ARTS
Parque Cultural Ponta Negra   Regular events and concerts take place in this large amphitheater on the Rio Negro, next to the Tropical Manaus. Contact Manaustur for information on programming (© 092/3622-4948) or just show up and wander around any evening Thursday to Saturday. Praia de Ponta Negra s/n, Ponta Negra. (© 092/3622-4948. Programming and prices vary. Call to check upcoming events.

Teatro Amazons (The Opera House)   The theater has a resident philharmonic orchestra, choir, and dance group (classic and popular dance) that perform regularly. Tickets are eminently affordable, usually around R$20 to R$40 (US$10–US$20/£2.70–£5.50). Praça São Sebastião s/n, Centro. (© 092/3232-1768. www.teatroamazonas.com.br.

CLUBS & BARS
In downtown Manaus, the best spot for an evening drink is **Bar do Armando,** Rua 10 de Julho 593 (© 092/3232-1195). Located on the square in front of the Opera House, this venerable drinking spot is the nighttime home of Manaus's artists, intellectuals, journalists, and other ne'er-do-wells. The conversation is always interesting and the beer is served icy cold. Farther down near the **Praça da Matriz,** Manaus's downtown nightlife scene degenerates into the sleazy mix of sailors and prostitutes traditional in a large port. Praça da Matriz itself remains reasonably safe, but it's best to stay off side streets like Rua Visconde de Mauá.

The city's best nightlife spot is out near the Tropical Manaus at **Ponta Negra Beach.** People stroll up and down the wide boulevard, there are regular concerts and events at the amphitheater, and a number of bars have live entertainment in the evening. One of the most popular is **Laranjinha** (© **092/3658-5483;** Mon–Sat 5pm–3am, Sun 5pm–5am) which has a great patio and stays open until the wee hours of the morning. Lower down closer to the river you'll find a whole bunch of botequins that double as *barracas* (beach kiosks) during the day when the beach is crowded and open at night for a causal beer or snack. Most places open at 5 or 6pm on weekdays and stay open until at least 1 or 2am. On weekends many venues open at 11am and stay open until 3 or 4am. Inside the Tropical Manaus, the disco **Studio Tropical Night** (© **092/3659-5000**) has DJs Thursday through Saturday.

There is a trio of popular gay bars in Centro: **Enigma's Bar,** Rua Silva Ramos 1054, Centro (© **092/3234-7985**), open Thursday through Sunday, offers live music and DJs. **Turbo Seven (TS),** Rua Vivaldo Lima 33, Centro (© **092/3232-6793**), features drag shows and go-go boys; only open on Saturday and Sunday, from 11pm onward; and **A2** (Rua Saldanha Marinho 780, Centro; © **092/3673-0112**), open Wednesday to Saturday from 11pm to 4am.

2 Introducing the Amazon
WHAT IS A RAINFOREST?

Rainforests are found throughout the world, wherever the annual rainfall is more than 2,000 millimeters (80 in.) and evenly spread throughout the year. There are rainforests in temperate zones (such as the Pacific Northwest) as well as in tropical regions. Tropical rainforests are found in a thick belt extending around the earth on either side of the Equator. The constant heat and humidity in a tropical rainforest allow trees and plants to grow year-round. Vast columns of hot, humid air rise and then condense as rain, resulting in annual rainfall of between 80 and 400 inches; annual temperatures average over 80°F (27°C).

What distinguishes the Amazon from other tropical rainforests is the sheer variety. Biologically, it is the richest and most diverse region in the world, containing about 20% of all higher plant species, roughly the same proportion of bird species, and around 10% of the world's mammals. Each type of tree may support more than 400 insect species. The Amazon is estimated to contain 2,000 species of fish—10 times the number found in European rivers—and countless varieties of reptiles. Why the Amazon should be so diverse is a question that mystifies scientists still.

Not only is it the most diverse, but the Amazon is also the largest tropical rainforest in the world, covering 3.7 million sq. km (2.3 million sq. miles) over nine countries, including Peru, Colombia, Venezuela, and Bolivia. The largest chunk, about 60%, falls within Brazil's borders.

The lifeline of the forest is the Amazon River itself, the second longest in the world and the largest in terms of water flow and drainage area. The river has over 1,000 tributaries, some of them sizeable rivers in their own right. In March and April, the water levels in these rivers rise so much that they flood the banks and the surrounding forest for months. A seasonally flooded forest is called *varzea* (on the Rio Solimões) or *igapó* (on the Rio Negro), while the upland forest that stays above water is called *terra firme.*

The annual flooding of the forest is one of the key factors in maintaining this ecosystem. As the river covers the forest floor, sometimes leaving just the treetops above water, the fish also expand their terrain and swim among the trees. These fish play a vital role in the fertilization of the forest. Many Amazonian fish are fruit eaters that feast on the nuts and seeds of the trees in the wet season. The fish feces deposit the seeds in the fertile ground of the forest, and when the waters recede, new growth occurs.

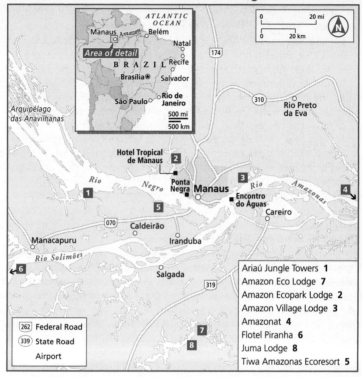

Amazon Lodges Near Manaus

Ariaú Jungle Towers **1**
Amazon Eco Lodge **7**
Amazon Ecopark Lodge **2**
Amazon Village Lodge **3**
Amazonat **4**
Flotel Piranha **6**
Juma Lodge **8**
Tiwa Amazonas Ecoresort **5**

262 Federal Road
339 State Road
Airport

The difference in water levels between wet and dry season can be as much as 40 feet. Many of the smaller side channels—called *igarapé*—and creeks that are perfectly navigable in March and April are completely dry by November.

The rainforest itself has a very defined structure. The **understory** is what you see when you hike through the forest. Shielded by the tall trees and overhead layers, the understory can be surprisingly dark. Plants, fungi, and animals found here thrive in the dark, humid conditions. The **canopy** is where a lot of the action is; birds, butterflies, and monkeys are usually up here, 60 to 90 feet above the understory. With more sunlight and less humidity, the rainforest at this height is green and lush. The **emergent** layer refers to those trees, often upwards of 120 feet, that send their crowns above the canopy to find the sunlight. Being higher also means these trees are more exposed to storms and rain. Wide buttress roots support these trees. This layering of the forest contributes to the biodiversity; each layer has its own flora and fauna that thrive in those particular conditions. Cutting through the forest opens up the understory to bright, unexpected light. The dark, humid environment vanishes, other plants and trees take over the space, and the ecological balance is thrown out of whack.

EXPLORING THE AMAZON

There are many ways to explore the Amazon. What suits you depends on how much time you have and how comfortable you want to be. Most people choose to stay at a lodge. Most are land-based, located within a few hours by boat from Manaus, and

---

(Tips) Tips for Viewing Wildlife

Wildlife viewing in the Amazon is a subtle event. It's the occasional flutter of a giant blue butterfly, the glimpse of a startled bird, or the splash as a caiman swims away from your canoe. With a keen eye you may spy snoozing bats tucked away underneath the tree branches, or a large, perfectly camouflaged iguana draped over the branch of a tree. At night a flashlight reveals the many small frogs that dot the flooded forest; a searchlight shows the hiding places of the caiman as they lie in wait, only their eyes and snout above water. What isn't subtle is the noise. It's everywhere: the tortured squawks of macaws, the high-pitched screams of monkeys high in the trees. And in the "still" of the night, the decibel levels generated by chirping cicadas and ribbiting frogs rivals that of a construction site.

---

make excursions to the surrounding area. Lodges vary in luxury but the programs offered are similar (see "Amazon Lodges," below).

Another comfortable way of seeing the Amazon is by riverboat. These range from basic to air-conditioned and luxurious. The vessel serves as your home base; you take excursions in canoes up the smaller channels. (See "Boat Trips," later in this chapter).

Regular boats that locals use to travel the river are another option. Although extremely inexpensive, these are *not* sightseeing tours; it's rare that you get close to shore, and no excursions are possible. You do meet locals traveling the river, and you'll have a front-row seat as you pull in to harbors along the way.

Specialized operators offer expedition-style trips where the emphasis is on truly experiencing the rainforest. You don't need to be in top shape for these; you just have to be able to hike or paddle a boat, and be willing to forego amenities like minibars and hot showers for a more hands-on jungle experience. One excellent adventure outfitter is **Amazon Mystery Tours** (see "Deeper into the Amazon: Expedition Tours," later in this chapter).

THE AMAZON & ECO-TOURISM: QUESTIONS TO ASK

Some visitors come away from a visit to the Amazon energized and excited by what they've seen. Others come away pissed off: The forest was degraded, the animals impossible to see, the guide had no idea what he was talking about. Some of these complaints stem from expectations set too high, from mental pictures of animal encounters developed over too many years of nature documentaries. Other times the complaints are entirely legitimate.

Eco-tourism in the Amazon is far from perfect. The section that follows will give you a better idea of what to expect, and of what to do to make your experience the best it can be. I'd also like to encourage you to use your power as a consumer to raise the level of eco-tourism as practiced in the Brazilian Amazon—for the benefit of the Amazon itself.

I love the Amazon. It's a dense, intricate, fascinating ecosystem. I also believe that eco-tourism, done right, can help endangered ecosystems throughout the world. At its best, eco-tourism teaches visitors about the ecosystem, while teaching locals that a functioning natural ecosystem is a thing of real economic value, to be guarded and preserved. Unfortunately, even after 20 years as a tourist destination, "eco-tourism" so defined has yet to develop around Manaus. Indeed, at its worst, Manaus-based eco-tourism seems to be teaching locals that you may as well chop it all down because you can show gringos any damn thing and they'll still ooh and ahh, and pay the big bucks.

It's not all bad. Some of it is very good. But things seem to have fallen into a rut, and there's no local impetus for change. Only you, the consumer, can change things, and you can do it simply by demanding more. Below I give a checklist of things to ask, and things to verify before going.

WHAT YOU WON'T GET

First, though, let's dispel the unreasonable expectations. Most lodges, for logistical reasons (food, supplies, attracting staff, ferrying people back and forth to the airport) are located no more than a half-day journey from Manaus. This rules out the "never-before-seen primeval jungle" experience. You will see houses on the riverbank and lots of other boats. In recent years as cattle prices have soared, pastureland has begun replacing forest on accessible riversides close to Manaus.

Most lodges cater to foreign tourists. For Brazilians, the Amazon is quite expensive. The majority of your fellow travelers will be European, Japanese, or North American. Like it or not, you'll be lumped in with the gringos.

Animals are hard to spot in the rainforest. You will see caiman (you may yawn at caiman by trip's end) and more than likely little pink dolphins and some species of monkeys. You will see lots of birds—kingfishers and egrets (snowy, great, and cattle), herons (gray, green, tiger), cormorants, hummingbirds, parakeets, and vultures. Macaws and toucans are also common, though not guaranteed. You *may* see sloths (I've seen one in over 10 trips to the Amazon) and capybara and agoutis as well as other small nocturnal rodents. The odds of seeing a predatory feline of any species are astonishingly small. Amphibians are also tough—those famous photos of poison arrow frogs took a lot of work and a lot of time.

On the bright side, those worried about creepy-crawlies can rest easy. Insects in the Amazon are really not that bad. There are ants (some about the size of a bumblebee), butterflies, and flying beetles and mosquitoes. In all my visits to over a dozen different parts of the forest (including a 1-week kayak trip in the far-off depths of the Amazon) I've only ever seen one snake and it was tiny and harmless.

WHAT YOU SHOULD GET

What you can expect is an opportunity to see and experience the rainforest around Manaus. Much of it is in pristine condition, and the vegetation, the range of species, and the sheer oddness of the trees and plants are truly impressive and remarkable. You can expect to learn about life on the Amazon. As the river is the main means of transportation and a major source of food, most people live on or close to it. It can be fascinating watching children going to school by canoe, seeing 4-year-olds paddle themselves around, seeing women washing their dishes or catching dinner off the decks of houses built on stilts. You can expect to learn about the ecosystem. Many of the guides are quite knowledgeable and they speak foreign languages very well, making it easy to ask questions and learn about the Amazon environment. You should expect to eat well. The lodges put on a wonderful spread of Amazonian specialties, much better than in most restaurants in town. The river fish are delicious.

HOW TO GET IT (& DO GOOD THINGS AT THE SAME TIME)

The following is a checklist of questions to ask the travel agent (or better yet the lodge manager) when researching your stay in the Amazon. The list is by no means comprehensive, but it should help you find the best available option. As importantly, by putting these questions to the operators in the Amazon, you will be educating them on what matters to foreign, ecologically minded tourists. In the listings for the lodges I've created a lodge checklist with the answers to most of these questions.

1. **How far is the lodge from Manaus?** Farther is better. Although distance does increase travel time, it also lessens the "city effect" on the animals, trees, and people.

2. **Is the lodge surrounded by a private nature reserve? Of what size?** Obviously, larger is better. In recent years as cattle prices have soared there's been a second wave of deforestation on accessible rivers close to Manaus. There's not much lodge owners can do about the Amazon as a whole, but they can work to preserve their little part. That's why we try to recommend not just lodges farther from Manaus, but lodges that are in some sort of private nature reserve that the lodge has set up and is trying to protect. I didn't include this information in the checklist simply because I have been unable to verify the legal status of various claimed reserves. You won't be able to either, but simply by asking you'll be emphasizing that this is important. Those lodges that haven't yet set up private reserves will hopefully move in that direction. Reserve sizes will likely be quoted to you in hectares. 1,000 hectares is a square about 2 miles long on a side.

3. **How big is the lodge?** Smaller is better. The more people there, the bigger the local environmental impact, the more the trails have been treaded and the animals spooked. Ten rooms is excellent, 20 acceptable, 35 pushing the limit, and 300 obscene.

4. **What is the group size?** Again, smaller is better. The larger the group, the less likely you will see animals or enjoy the forest peacefully. We have been to lodges where huge motorized canoes take 25 people out at a time. Lodges lie about group size, so I've found it more instructive to ask *"what is the maximum capacity of the boats used to take guests on outings?"* Generally, that's the group size.

5. **Are the guides trained naturalists?** Is there a biologist at the lodge? Is there a library or resource center at the lodge? Are there any nature talks? The answer to all these questions will be "no" (with the notable exception of the Mamiraua Reserve lodge). No one ever seems to have thought to hire university biology students to work as naturalists—both to train the regular guides and to give guests a deeper insight into the ecosystem. No one has ever considered hiring a full-time biologist, or even putting in a library with field guides and nature books. Hope springs eternal, however. I put in the questions because I'd like to see it happen. If enough people ask, maybe it will. And it's a good lead in to the next question.

6. **What kind of training and education do the guides have?** Your guide can make or break your experience. Unfortunately, guides vary greatly in quality. Some are truly excellent. But the main qualification seems to be an ability to speak English (or French, Italian, or what have you). Nature training comes afterward. If you're lucky, the guide will have grown up in the forest, or have gone through the army's jungle-warfare program, or have an interest in biology. I wish I could recommend a lodge with particularly good guides, but in Manaus the guides are all freelance, contracted for periods of 3 or 4 days as guests come in. Turnover is high, because pay is not great. Ask about the qualifications of your guide beforehand. Demand one that has army-jungle training, specialized nature training (above the standard guide course), or at least grew up outside of Manaus. Ask questions of your guide when you meet him to see that he is as advertised. If he's not, complain. If he is, tip him well.

7. **When do trips go out?** Trips scheduled around breakfast and supper are almost guaranteed to show nothing but forest. If you want to see animals, you have to be on the water or in the forest at sunrise or sunset; ask about early-morning or dusk excursions if you want to maximize your animal spotting odds.

8. **Are jungle-tour boats motorized or non-motorized?** If motorized, what kind of engine? Non-motorized canoes are the best, but only two lodges (the Mamiraua and the Ecopark) use these regularly. The noise of an outboard will scare off most wild creatures. However, they're justifiable if you're on the way somewhere farther off in the forest. But they should still be quiet outboards. Some lodges (the Ariaú is especially bad) use so-called *rabete* engines, unmuffled high-revving two-strokes, with the engine mounted on the drive shaft. The smell and noise of these motors are enough to make you sick; never mind the animals that you'll never get to see.

9. **What kinds of excursions are there?** The standard package of outings includes a reconnaissance tour, a jungle walk, a visit to a caboclo house, and a nighttime caiman spotting trip. These are fascinating, fun, and informative, but there could be so much more. They could set up a telescope and show you the stars (the Milky Way is incredible in the Amazon), they could take you out and show you insect life, or search for amphibians, but they don't because no one ever has, and operators in the Amazon are very conservative. So, ask the next question.

10. **Are there any excursions beyond the basic ones?** (And how much do they cost?) Maybe if enough people ask, they'll develop something.

11. **Are there canoes for guest use at the lodge?** There is inevitably a fair bit of downtime at a lodge. Tours go out early and late, leaving a big chunk of time in the middle of the day. Lodges could offer nature talks or presentations to fill this time, but they don't. Some people swim. Some snooze in their hammocks. I like to grab a small dug-out canoe and go for a paddle. The water is flat and calm, and the scenery can be fascinating. Only the floating Amazon Eco Lodge keeps a fleet of canoes on hand for guests to use. Other lodges can usually rustle one up if you make a fuss.

12. Finally, one question you should ask yourself. **How much do you want to rough it?** Can you live without air-conditioning, hot water, fridge, and TV? There is an Amazon trip for everyone, and picking the right one will greatly enhance your experience.

Forgive me if this all seems a tad didactic, but I assume that for people who have flown so far to see the Amazon, the important thing is to see the Amazon. I could be completely out to lunch on this. Certainly, the people who build and finance new lodges have concluded that what matters to people is not the quality of the nature experience but the quality of the bed. It's what has lead to the creation of places like the Tiwa, where the forest is poor and degraded but the swimming pool is excellent.

For the situation to improve, visitors will have to do one thing and one thing only—demand more. Whatever you do, don't let this explanation scare you off coming. The Amazon is a tremendous experience. But with a little effort it could be so much more. Make a pain of yourself. Ask operators if they have a biologist, if they have a library, if they have nature talks and canoes and highly trained guides. Tell them you'll go to the lodge that does. When you're there, ask for these things again. Maybe, slowly, the message will get through.

3 Amazon Lodges

Lodges are a popular way to experience something of the Amazon while keeping comfort levels high. Most are within a 3-hour boat ride from Manaus. Some are more luxurious than others, but in all, your meals are taken care of—usually hearty and healthy fare made with local fish and fruits. You will have access to a shower and toilet, and guides are there to show you around. Nearly all the lodges include the same basic package of excursions: the introductory jungle tour, the sunset and/or sunrise tour, the forest hike, the visit to a native village, the evening of caiman hunting, and the afternoon of piranha fishing (yipes!). What distinguishes one lodge from another is the size of lodge itself (smaller is better), the quality of the surrounding forest, and the quality of the guides.

Most lodges start off with a reconnaissance tour, taking you out in a motorized canoe to give you an idea what the area around the lodge looks like; this a good opportunity to check out some of the smaller channels. The **sunrise** or **sunset tour** is a great way to experience the forest at its most interesting times of the day, when animals are active and there are few disturbances around. All lodges will take guests on a **jungle hike.** This is where you really get a feel for the biodiversity of the forest; it's not the animals that make this jungle so overwhelming, it's the number of plants and trees and how these coexist. Another standard excursion is the **visit to a *caboclo* village.** *Caboclos* are river people. The visits provide a close-up look at how they build their homes, at the foods they grow, and the tools they use. Even their pets are neat; sloths and monkeys are the animals of choice. Finally there's the obligatory caiman spotting and piranha fishing. **Caiman spotting** is fun; you head out in a canoe on the river in the pitch-black night. Once you get to a good shallow area, the guide turns on the spotlight and starts looking for a caiman. The caiman should be big enough to impress the lodge-dwellers, but not *so* big that the guide can't leap into the water and wrestle it back into the boat. (That's exactly what he does.) Once it's in the boat the creature becomes the centerpiece of a short nature talk. Many enjoy **fishing for piranhas.** You put some beef on your hook and hold your rod in the water, pretty much like fishing anywhere. When you catch one, your guide will pull it off the hook—very carefully, those teeth really are razor sharp—and you'll see the little fish back at dinnertime when the kitchen serves it up grilled.

WHAT TO BRING: A CHECKLIST

Most hotels will let you store your luggage while you are away at a lodge so you don't have to carry it all with you. The smaller lodges often have a luggage limit. Whatever you leave behind, don't forget to bring the following:

- A small daypack.
- Binoculars.
- A light rain jacket.
- A few Ziploc bags to protect camera gear, notebook, and so on . . . in a sudden downpour, everything gets soaked.
- Good walking shoes.
- Sunglasses.
- Sunscreen. (The glare from the river can be quite strong.)
- Enough dry clothes; nothing dries once it's damp, so have a couple of changes of shirts and socks.

- Toiletries such as toothpaste, contact lens fluid, tampons. The lodges usually don't carry any such items.
- Medicinal items for personal use (aspirin, antacid, and so on; lodges and tour operators will have proper first-aid kits). Malaria is not an issue on the Rio Negro; the high acidity of the water prevents mosquitoes from laying their eggs.
- Anything you can't live without: chewing gum, dental floss, tissues, cookies, and the like.

BOOKING A LODGE

You can contact lodges directly or contact a tour operator who can assist you in choosing the right package. In the U.S. or Canada, your best option is to contact the experts at **Brazil Nuts** (© 800/553-9959; www.brazilnuts.com) In Manaus, contact **Viverde,** Rua dos Cardeiros 26 (© 092/3248-9988). They have an excellent English-language website (www.viverde.com.br) with detailed information on both tours and the Amazon in general. Another reputable North American agency is **South America Travel** (© 800/747-4540; www.southamerica.travel).

Note: All prices are per person and include transportation, all meals, and basic excursions. Airport transfer is usually included in the price, but always check. The policies for children vary per lodge and per season; depending on occupancy you may have bargaining power. Most lodges offer up to a 50% discount for children 12 and under; ask when making reservations. All rates are given in U.S. dollars only; most lodges work directly with foreign currencies.

LODGES CLOSE TO MANAUS

Amazon Ecopark Lodge 🐾🐾   The Amazon Ecopark is one of the better lodges close to Manaus, as long as you arrive with the right expectations. The lodge itself is about a 2-hour boat trip from Manaus and sits on a private reserve. The igarapé is of exclusive use to the lodge, which gives it a secluded feel. In the dry season there are several beaches right across from the lodge, and the vegetation is lush and beautiful. The lodge also has some natural pools for swimming, particularly nice for people who are never quite comfortable swimming in the dark waters of the Rio Negro. Most of the excursions take place in close proximity to the lodge and are done in non-motorized canoes. Paddling into the flooded forest, you'll be able to get a good sense of the sights and sounds of the jungle. The lodge also houses a rehab for monkeys that are apprehended by Brazil's environmental agency, Ibama. Guests can see the daily feedings and observe and even interact with these monkeys. Most packages include a visit to an Indian village to observe a traditional ceremony. Although undoubtedly a touristy experience, it is well done as you actually visit a small community where a number of Indian families reside. You will be able to see their traditional houses and the little plots of land where they grow and process manioc and other fruits and vegetables. The ceremony itself is also quite authentic and gives you a much better impression of the native culture than the shows put on at a lodge or a hotel. All packages include airport transfers, all meals (the food is fabulous), deluxe accommodations, and well-trained guides who speak excellent English.

Lodge Checklist: Distance: 20km (12 miles); Biome: Igapó; Size: 60; Boat Capacity: 12; Boat Motors: outboard; Canoes: Yes (canoes used for many excursions); Library: No; Biologist: No; Nature Talks: No; Other excursions: "Jungle survival training."

Reservations office in Rio © 021/2547-7742 or ©/fax 021/2256-8083. www.amazonecopark.com.br. 64 units (showers only). 3-day packages start at US$395 per person, 4-day packages US$475 per person (both these packages include a tour to The Meeting of the Waters). Children 6–12 pay 25% of rate, 13–16 pay 50% of rate. AE, DC, MC, V. **Amenities:** Restaurant; bar; pool. *In room:* A/C, fan, no phone.

Amazon Village Lodge (★) The Amazon Village is a well-run operation with its own small rainforest reserve, now alas being seriously encroached upon by ever-growing cattle operations and the beginnings of urban sprawl from the city. It's too bad, because the Amazon Village is a class act—owners treat guides well and do a good job presenting the rainforest. If at all possible, choose something farther from the city, but if you do for some reason have to be close, this would be a good option. The lodge buildings are attractively designed with local wood in the native *maloca* style, while rooms are small and clean with private toilets and showers. There is no hot water, and electricity is limited to the evening hours. There's the usual package of excursions. The lodge doesn't have a swimming pool, but you can swim in the river.

Lodge Checklist: Distance: 40km (25 miles); Biome: Igapó; Size: 36; Boat Capacity: 12; Boat Motors: outboard; canoes: Yes (1); Library: No; Biologist: No; Nature Talks: No; Other excursions: No.

Rua Ramos Ferreira 1189, sala 403, Manaus, AM 69010-120. (✆) **092/3633-1444.** Fax 092/3633-3217. www.amazon-village.com.br. 45 units (showers only). 3-day packages start at US$440 per person. AE, DC, MC, V. **Amenities:** Restaurant; bar.

Tiwa Amazonas Ecoresort The Tiwa fills an odd ecological niche, neither jungle lodge nor city hotel. It sits directly opposite the Tropical, on the far bank of the Rio Negro. Access is via fast motor launch; the trip takes about 20 minutes, and there are boats going back and forth every other hour. Each of the sizable rooms takes up half a log cabin, which are set in circles around a small pond. The hotel pool is lovely. Theoretically, the Tiwa could serve as an alternative to the Tropical—a luxury resort, just a little farther from the city. But what the Tiwa is selling itself as is a jungle lodge, with 2- and 3-day packages and the usual outings including caiman spotting and treetop walking. But the Tiwa is just simply too close to the city for that. The "forest" surrounding the lodge is a small patch of barely re-grown second-growth; walk too far and you stumble onto roads and clear cuts. If you don't have time to go to a jungle lodge, and just want a teensy-tiny taste of the Amazon, the Tiwa may be an option. Otherwise, go elsewhere.

Lodge Checklist: Distance: 8km (5 miles); Biome: Terra Firme; Size: 52; Boat Capacity: 50; Boat motor: outboard; Canoes: No; Library: No; Biologist: No; Nature Talks: No; Other excursions: Trips to Meeting of the Waters; Lago Janauary.

Caixa Postal 2575, Manaus, AM 69005-970. (✆) **092/9995-7892.** www.tiwa.com.br. 52 units (showers only). 1-night, 2-day packages US$380 double; each additional day approximately an extra US$275 double. Policy for children negotiable. AE, DC, MC, V. **Amenities:** Restaurant; bar; outdoor pool; beach; Hobie Cat rentals. *In room:* A/C, minibar, fridge, no phone.

LODGES FARTHER FROM MANAUS

Amazonat (★★) If you like space to move around, you will love the Amazonat, set on its own 900-hectare (2,223-acre) reserve of *terra firme* 160km (98 miles) east of Manaus. Amazonat is surrounded by extensive walking trails that you can roam at will. Though the lodge is not on a river, there is a lake with a beach for swimming and an orchid park with over 1,000 specimens to see and sniff and wonder at. The 3-day package includes a number of guided walks and a river trip on the Urubu for birdwatching, as well as plenty of time to explore on your own. The 4-day package includes all of the above plus a full day on the Amazon River and a visit to the Opera

House and The Meeting of the Waters. The lodge itself is set in beautiful jungle gardens and the chalets are more than comfortable. There's also a variety of specialized programs for those who want to experience more of the jungle: The Jungle Trekker package includes a variety of longer hikes and two overnight stays at a jungle camp.

Lodge Checklist: Distance: 160km (98 miles); Biome: terra firme; Size: 20; Boat Capacity: 8; Boat Motors: outboard; Canoes: No; Library: No; Biologist: No; Nature Talks: No; Other excursions: "jungle survival" excursions.

Caixa Postal 1273, Manaus, AM 69006-970. ✆ **092/3328-1183** (hotel), or ✆/fax 092/3652-1359 (reservations office). www.amazonat.com.br. 18 units (showers only). 4-day packages start at US$400 per person, 5-day packages US$645 per person. Children 6–12 pay 25% of rate, 13–16 pay 50% of rate. AE, DC, MC, V. **Amenities:** Restaurant; bar; pool. *In room:* Fan, minibar, no phone.

Amazon Eco Lodge ★★

Located just a few kilometers from the Juma Lodge (see below), the Amazon Eco Lodge has the same excellent forest surroundings, and the same long trip from Manaus. The package of outings at both lodges is also essentially the same. The one thing the Eco Lodge has over the Juma is its fleet of small canoes, always at the ready should a guest feel like going off for a paddle. The Eco Lodge floats on the lake, on top of huge log rafts, which is really quite charming. It's also a great place for river swimming. The disadvantage is that accommodations are in fairly small rooms, built in wings with wooden walls; it can get noisy. Also, toilets and showers are shared, in a shower block near the center of the raft complex. Prices at the Juma and Eco Lodge are comparable, but for the money Juma provides better value.

Lodge Checklist: Distance: 85km (53 miles); Biome: Igapó; Size: 18; Boat Capacity: 12; Boat motor: outboard; Canoes: Yes; Library: No; Biologist: No; Nature Talks: No; Other excursions: No.

Rua Flavio Espirito Santo 1, Kissia II, Manaus AM 69040-250. ✆ **092/3656-6033**. Fax 092/3656-6101. www.nature safaris.com.br. 18 units (common bathrooms and showers). 4-day, 3-night packages US$599 per person. Policy for children negotiable. AE, DC, MC, V. **Amenities:** Restaurant; bar; outdoor pool; beach; Hobie Cat rentals. *In room:* A/C, minibar, fridge, no phone.

Ariaú Amazon Towers *(Overrated)*

Avoid this place. Just don't go. The Ariaú is all that is wrong with Amazon "eco-tourism"; it is the Disneyland Ford Factory of jungle lodges. Marketing photos of treehouses and boardwalks may suggest a Swiss Family Robinson adventure, but what the Ariaú delivers is mass-market tourism, with hundreds of guests getting trundled each day along a set tourist route that has already been treaded literally tens of thousands of times. Repetition is a factor at any lodge, but the Ariaú has a serious problem of scale—there are over 300 units in place—combined with a management fixation on minimum expense and maximum profit. Although the Ariaú charges top price and has economies of scale on its side, it has never seen fit to hire a lodge biologist or open an on-site interpretation center (though there is a gym and spa, a helipad, and a jewelry boutique). Excursions are the usual, but at the Ariaú, group size runs up to 25. Trips are always in motorized canoes, equipped with noisy, fume-spewing two-stroke *rabete* motors.

Lodge Checklist: Distance: 35km (22 miles); Biome: Igapó; Size: 300; Boat Capacity: 25; Boat Motors: large rabete; Canoes: Yes (1); Library: No; Biologist: No; Nature Talks: No; Other excursions: Yes, but at steep add-on prices.

Rua Leonardo Malcher 699, Manaus, AM 69010-040. ✆ **092/3232-4160**. Fax 092/3233-5615. www.ariaut owers.com. 300 units (showers only, cold water). 3-day packages start at US$450, 4-day packages US$550. Prices are negotiable; suites can be had for as little as US$200 per package when occupancy is low. AE, DC, MC, V. **Amenities:** Restaurant; bar; pool; gym; spa; TV room; laundry service; Internet room (intermittent connection). *In room:* A/C, fridge, no phone.

Flotel Piranha ☆☆   The Flotel is unique among all the lodges in that it floats on varzea—flooded forest in the richer "white water" of the Solimões river system. White-water systems flow through younger, richer soils, and are thus richer in dissolved nutrients. Forests in the upland areas of white-water rivers have bigger, taller trees (though don't expect the trees close to the lodge to be huge—trees of the flooded forest, on both white and black rivers, don't grow to enormous sizes, simply due to the stress of getting covered for 4 months of the year in water). White-water rivers support richer, denser populations of aquatic life—more fish, and consequently, more birds. The catch in all this, of course, is that the base of the food chain is also more abundant; white-water rivers are much richer in insect life, including mosquitoes.

To avoid mosquitoes, all other lodges are on black-water rivers, but the Piranha decided that the benefit was worth the cost. And in truth, the mosquitoes aren't that bad. They're worse than on black-water lodges, certainly, but they're nowhere near as bad as they are, for example, in the hardwood forests of the eastern U.S. or Canada. You'll need repellent when you go for a walk in the forest, but out on the floating lodge it's only an issue for the 2 hours or so around sunset. The lodge has good screens on the rooms and dining areas. The benefit is you get to see and hear constant splashes from jumping fish, and see more and larger birdlife, particularly wading birds.

Rooms on this floating hotel are small but tidy and pleasant—like cabins on a ship. Beds have mosquito nets, though windows are screened. A generator powers air-conditioning in the evenings.

Lodge Checklist: Distance: 90km (56 miles); Biome: Varzea; Size: 20; Boat Capacity: 12; Boat motor: outboard; Canoes: Yes (1); Library: No; Biologist: No; Nature Talks: No, but planned for the near future; Other excursions: Horseback riding (dry season only).

Rua Flavio Espirito Santo 1, Kissia II, Manaus AM 69040-250. ✆ **092/3656-6033.** Fax 092/3656-6101. www.nature safaris.com.br. 20 units (showers only). 4-day, 3-night packages US$590 per person. Policy for children negotiable. AE, DC, MC, V. **Amenities:** Restaurant; bar; swimming platform. *In room:* A/C, no phone.

Juma Lodge ☆☆☆   One of the best of the lodges in the area, the Juma gets jungle points for its small size and its distance from Manaus. Rooms are all in comfortable small cabins built on stilts. The best rooms are the charming self-contained doubles (room nos. 9, 10, and 11) with a view out over the lake. From your veranda you can often see dolphins and caiman. Cabins are connected to the dining hall by elevated boardwalks. The Juma is located in the middle of a sizable private nature reserve, so the forest surroundings are quite well preserved. The lodge offers the standard excursions. By prior arrangement, the more adventurous can also spend a night sleeping in a hammock in the jungle. The lodge also has one dugout canoe that guests can borrow to paddle on their own. Note that the trip to the lodge from Manaus often takes longer than 3½ hours. Though the lodge quotes this figure, it's a best-case scenario, possible only when the water is highest. At other times the trip is closer to 5 or 6 hours. It's not simply dead time, though. You see lots on the way out—from forest to birds to dolphins. On the trip back you have a chance to spend time—even swim—at The Meeting of the Waters.

Lodge Checklist: Distance: 90km (56 miles); Biome: Igapó; Size: 11; Boat Capacity: 8; Boat Motors: rabete; Canoes: Yes (1); Library: No; Biologist: No; Nature Talks: No; Other excursions: Will program night walks in forest and sleepovers in forest on request.

Lago do Juma (no mailing address). ✆ **092/3245-1177** (lodge) or 092/3232-2707 (reservations office). www.juma lodge.com.br. 11 units (showers only). 3-day, 2-night packages start at US$590 per person, 4-day packages US$708 per person. Children 6–12 pay 50% of rate. AE, MC, V. **Amenities:** Restaurant; bar. *In room:* Fan, fridge, no phone.

LODGES FAR FAR FAR FROM MANAUS

Pousada Uakari in the Mamiraua ✷✷✷ The only place in the Brazilian Amazon practicing real eco-tourism, the Uakarí pousada is the eco-tourism branch of the Mamiraua Sustainable Development Institute. The Mamiraua reserve was created on the upper Amazon in 1999 in order to preserve the prime habitat of the Ukarí monkey (a primate with a bright red face and pale white fur, often called the English monkey). Initiated by the Brazilian scientist who first studied the Ukairi, the institute fosters research, while working to preserve the area by helping local inhabitants develop alternate ways of exploiting the forest. The eco-tourism operation is part of that effort. Accommodations are in small but comfortable chalets, each with its own hot shower and veranda. Excursions completely break the pattern set in other lodges. In the wet season visitors get paddled through the forest in small canoes. In the dry season tours go on walking trails. Each trip goes to a different area, and the territory has very little human impact. Nighttime excursions aim not to capture a caiman, but to show off the nocturnal animals. A local guide is always present; normally there is a trained naturalist as well. Nature talks are a nightly occurrence. The researchers working in the area have dinner one evening with guests, and share their experience. For longer stays at certain times of year, guests can accompany researchers in the field. Good as all this sounds, there are disadvantages. Guides are local people being trained in tourism; they may not be as polished. It's a lot farther to go. The ecosystem is varzea, so there are more mosquitoes. And it's very nature-focused, which isn't for everyone.

Lodge Checklist: Distance: 200km (125 miles); Biome: Varzea; Size: 10; Boat Capacity: 12; Boat Motors: outboard; Canoes: Canoes used for most excursions. No individual canoeing allowed; Library: Yes; Biologist: Yes; Nature Talks: Yes; Other excursions: Yes.

Av. Santos Dumont 1350, loja 16 (Manaus Airport), Manaus, AM 69049-000. ✆ 092/3652-1213 or (main eco-tourism line) 097/3343-4160. Fax 097/3343-2967. www.mamiraua.org.br. 10 units (showers only). 3-day, 3-night packages start at US$330, 4-day packages US$420. Price does not include plane fare to city of Tefe. AE, DC, MC, V. **Amenities:** Restaurant; bar.

Getting to Tefe: Tefe lies some 200km (125 miles) upriver of Manaus. Rico Airlines (✆ 92/4009-8333; www.voerico.com.br) has 4 flights a week to Tefe. The 1-hr. flight costs R$300/US$150/£81 one-way. Trip Airlines (✆ 0300-789-4747; www.airtrip.com.br has flights 6 days a week. Cost one-way is R$289/US$145/£78. There is also a fast ferry departing Manaus for Tefe at 7am every Wed and Sat. The journey takes about 12 hr. Cost is R$180/US$90/£49.

4 Boat Trips

On a boat-tour package, the experience is similar to that of a lodge; there are excursions on the small side channels, a sunset and sunrise tour, caiman spotting, piranha fishing, and a visit to a *caboclo* (river peasant) settlement. The difference is that in the time you're not on an excursion, you're moving on the river. There is always something to see, even if it's just the vastness of the river itself.

Viverde, Rua dos Cardeiros 26, Manaus (✆/fax **092/3248-9988;** www.viverde. com.br), can arrange boat voyages or charters. Their website has photos and descriptions of the better Manaus-based touring boats.

Amazon Clipper Cruises (✆ **092/3656-1246;** www.amazonastravel.com.br/amazon_clipper_i.html) has three old-style Amazon riverboats—the *Amazon Angler, Selly Clipper,* and *Selly Clipper II*—that make regular 3- and 4-day trips departing from the Tropical Manaus. The boats have cabins with bunk beds and private bathrooms, and in the evening the cabins have air-conditioning. The 3-day tour stays on the

Cruising the Amazon in Style

For the ultimate Amazon river experience, travelers now have the option of taking a luxury cruise ship, the *Iberostar*. For those whose first reaction is *God No! Not a cruise!* think again. The *Iberostar* does an excellent job getting guests off the boat and out into nature (in addition, of course to pampering them silly). This 75-cabin pocket cruiser started operating in June 2005. The boat offers two programs, a 3-night Solimões cruise or a 4-night Rio Negro cruise. Both are worth taking; for most people it's just a matter of which one fits better into their travel plans. The ship itself is so new that everything shines and sparkles. Cabins are beautifully appointed and feature king-size beds, large-screen TVs, a private veranda, and a luxurious bathroom. All the luxury aside, however, the cruise is actually well set up (better than many of the lodges we have visited) for making the most out of your Amazon experience. There is a well-stocked library with interesting and rare books on the environment and the region, and staff are very knowledgeable (some even have bird books to help identify species, an unheard-of thing in Brazil) and give daily presentations on the fauna and flora of the region. Excursions are made in aluminum launches with twin 240-horsepower motors, allowing you to quickly get to any place of interest. As the boat is constantly moving, you move into far more diverse territory than at a lodge. A cruise is even a luxurious way of experiencing the mosquito-ridden Solimões. The increased presence of insect life on this white-water river (they don't bother you in the daytime when you are out exploring, only around dusk) also attracts more birds and other animals. We have seen some of our best wildlife on and around the Solimões. And it's a lot easier to put up with mosquitoes if you can do so from a fancy cabin, sipping a glass of complimentary champagne.

Iberostar Grand Amazon   Rua Marquês de Santa Cruz 25, Hidroviária do Amazonas, AM 69005-050. © **092/2126-9900;** www.iberostar.com. 75 cabins (showers only). Packages start at R$715 (US$357/£175) per person, per day, including all meals, beverages (alcoholic and non-alcoholic), guides, excursions, and entertainment. AE, DC, MC, V. **Amenities:** 2 restaurants; 2 bars; 2 outdoor pools; 2 cardio machines; Jacuzzi; 24-hr. room service; laundry service; nonsmoking rooms. *In room:* A/C, TV, fridge, hair dryer, safe.

Solimões River; the 4-day tour goes up the Rio Negro. Both tours include a visit to Janauary Park and The Meeting of the Waters. The price for the 3-day Solimões tour is US$420), and the 4-day Rio Negro tour costs US$580. Children up to 12 receive a 20% discount. A newer and more luxurious boat has recently been launched, the *Amazon Clipper Premium*. The main differences are that the boat has a number of pleasant common rooms and the cabins come with real beds, not bunk beds. Rates, however, are at a premium; the 3-day Solimões package costs US$595, and the 4-day Rio Negro tour US$790.

If you want to set your own agenda, **Amazon Nut Safaris** (© **092/3248-9988;** www.viverde.com.br/amazon_nut_safaris_i.html) has a small Amazon riverboat available for charter, complete with guide and crew. The *Cassiquiari* has 10 cabins and six motor canoes, and charters for US$1,120 per day for up to eight people, plus an extra US$135 for each person over eight. The price includes food and bottled water, and activities such as piranha fishing and forest walks.

Swallows and Amazons ⚐   Swallows and Amazons is run by New Englander Mark Aitchison and his Brazilian wife, Tania. The company's core trip is a 7-day package that spends a day in Manaus and then sets off up the Rio Negro to explore the territory around the Anavilhanas Archipelago. Transportation is on company-owned traditional wooden riverboats, while exploration is done either on foot or by canoes. Accommodations are either on the riverboat or in a comfortable but basic lodge near the Anavilhanas Archipelago. Maximum group size on any trip is eight. Cost for any of the trips is about R$280 (US$140/£70) per day if you book directly. These trips run year-round; check the website for timing and availability.

Rua Quintino Bocaiuva 189, 2nd floor. Manaus, AM 69005–110. © 092/3622-1246. www.swallowsandamazons tours.com.

5 Riding the Riverboats

The old-style wood or steel-hull riverboats that ply the Amazon basin are about transport, not seeing wildlife. They stick to deeper channels, taking passengers and goods up and down the Amazon. The most popular routes are Manaus-Belém and Manaus-Santarém. Most boats have small cabins, though it's more fun just to sling your hammock on deck. Good, simple meals and filtered water are supplied on the boat at no extra cost.

Boats depart from the new **Hidroviaria do Amazonas (Riverboat Terminal)** (© **092/3621-4310**) in the middle of downtown at Rua Marquês de Santa Cruz 25. There is an information desk inside the front door where you can find out about arrival and departure times, and numerous kiosks where you buy tickets. By purchasing here, you can be sure you will not be cheated. Boats for **Belém** normally depart Wednesday and Saturday at noon. The trip downstream takes 4 days. Delays are not uncommon. Cost of a first-class hammock spot (on the upper deck) is R$275 (US$138/£74). Hammocks are not supplied. Buy one in Manaus (see "Shopping," earlier in this chapter). Cabins cost R$750 to R$850 (US$375–US$425/£202–£230). Boats for **Santarém** normally depart Tuesday and Thursday. The cost is R$125 (US$63/£34) for a first-class hammock, R$98 (US$49/£27) for a second-class hammock, and R$325 (US$362/£88) for a cabin. The trip takes about 40 hours.

6 Deeper into the Amazon: Expedition Tours

Amazon Mystery Tours ⚐⚐⚐ (Value   If you want to really explore the jungle, this is the company to go with. Amazon Mystery has the skills and experience to bring you deep into the rainforest; make your time there safe, fun, and informative; and then get you back to town again. The company has core adventures in either a kayak or speedboat descent of the Amazon tributary rivers upstream of Manaus. For the kayak adventures, a typical day includes a few hours of paddling, followed by a delicious lunch of fresh fish, followed by a hike to a waterfall or hidden cavern that few have ever seen. At night, you head out with a spotlight to search for caiman or other jungle creatures. The speedboating adventures cover much the same territory, but with less time on the river, and more time to explore the forest. The company's regular guide is a Tucano Indian with an extensive traditional knowledge of Amazon plants and animals. Participants need a basic level of physical ability—for example, you should be able to hike and paddle a small boat—but no special skills. The camping is very comfortable, the food is excellent (always important), and the company knows to bring along the little extras like folding chairs (not to mention caipirinha cocktails) that make camping civilized. You sleep in hammocks. At present, Amazon Mystery has 4- to 6-day descents on the Manacaparu river, 7-day descents of the Rio Urubu, and 10-day descents of the Jatapu river. However, the owner is always exploring new territory, so it's a good idea to check the website. The company also offers a 3-day adventure sports trip involving rappelling and white-water kayaking.

Av. Djalma Batista 385, sala 103, Manaus. ⓒ 092/3633-7844. Fax 092/3233-2780. www.amazon-outdoor.com. Prices average US$150–US$200 per person per day, which includes all airport transfers, accommodations in Manaus, equipment, drinks (alcoholic and non), meals, guides, and excursions.

7 Belém

Belém's an old city, founded in 1616 on the spot where the Amazon River reaches the sea. The first and most important building was the fort. Belém was not a commercial enterprise but a strategic investment. By controlling the mouth of the Amazon, Portugal could prevent other nations from penetrating into the vast interior, and not incidentally expand the borders of its own South American empire. Peasants and soldiers were required to feed and man the fort, along with a church and governor to keep peasants and soldiers in line. And that, give or take a tiny merchant class, was pretty much Belém for some 200 years, until in the latter half of the 1800s a Scottish engineer named Dunlop discovered vulcanized rubber, and realized it would be the perfect thing to cushion the ride on that nifty new invention, the bicycle.

Demand for rubber latex, then grown exclusively in Amazonia, soared to unimagined heights. Awash in money from rubber, Belém's unimaginative elite began importing civilization wholesale from abroad: a cast-iron market hall from Scotland; streetlights and electric trams from England; dresses and lingerie from Paris. In the copied-from-England parade ground park (now Praça da República) they built a copied-from-Italy opera house, a nice counterpoint to the copied-from-Rome basilica in the suburb of Nazaré. Everything built and bought was of the finest materials; marble, jacaranda, ebony, iron, silk, lace. Then the price of rubber crashed, and Belém never quite figured out how to bounce back. Today the city of 1.5 million survives as an export point for Amazon products.

For visitors, the chief attraction remains that 19th-century legacy. The vast Ver-o-Peso Market on the banks of the Amazon has every rainforest product imaginable available for sale. The old downtown, with its fort and cathedral and decaying stock of 19th-century buildings, provides a decent day's strolling.

Belém's cuisine is remarkable, with a mix of Amazon and seafood ingredients found nowhere else in Brazil. No visit is complete without an evening at a good Belém restaurant, and a stop at a tropical fruit-juice stand or ice-cream shop.

In a long-ago world before deforestation, the other attraction to Belém might have been the rainforest, but Pará state has chopped its forest down with such enthusiasm there's very little original forest left within easy journey of Belém.

Instead, Belém's chief wildlife attraction is the island of Marajó, the world's largest freshwater island, which sits at the mouth of the world's largest river. Occupied by buffalo ranches and prone to periodic flooding, Marajó boasts a landscape with vast flocks of colorful wading birds, caiman, and piranha.

For visitors with limited time to spend, I'd recommend no more than a day or two in Belém and then a 3- or 4-day journey to Marajó.

8 Belém Essentials

ARRIVING

BY PLANE   TAM (toll-free ✆ **0800/570-5700** or 091/4002-5700; www.tam.com.br), **Gol** (✆ **0300/115-2121;** www.voegol.com.br), and **Varig** (✆ **091/4003-7000;** www.varig.com.br). Belém's international airport, the **Aeroporto Internacional de Val-de-Cães** (✆ **091/3210-6039;** www.aeroportobelem.com), is located 22km (13 miles) from downtown. **Coopertaxi** (✆ **091/3257-1720**) operates all the taxis at the airport. The company can be reached 24/7 and accepts Visa and Master-Card. Fares to downtown (Praça da República area) average R$40 (US$20/£11). Internet is available upstairs in the departure hall in the **Kaboclas** cafe (✆ **091/3210-6371**). Cost is R$8 (US$4/£2) per hour. Open 24/7.

BY BUS   The bus station, or **Terminal Rodoviario,** is located at Av. Almirante Barroso s/n on the corner of Avenida Gov. José Malcher (✆ **091/3266-2625**). (Bus 900, CIDADE NOVA IV—VER-O-PESO from in front of The Ver-o-Peso Market or on Av. Nazaré on the bottom tip of Praça da República). Companies that run popular routes include: **Boa Esperança** (✆ **091/3266-0033**) to Natal, Recife, São Luis, and Fortaleza; **Itapemirim** (✆ **091/3226-3458**) to Salvador, São Paulo, and Rio de Janeiro; and **Transbrasiliana** (✆ **091/3226-1942**) to Brasilia and São Luis. Brazilian long-distance buses are safe, air-conditioned, and comfortable, especially the overnight ones, which have fully reclining *(leito)* or mostly reclining *(semi-leito)* seats. Tickets can be purchased only at the station.

BY RIVERBOAT   Most people choose to make the 4-day riverboat journey downstream from Manaus to Belém, but you can make the 5-day journey upstream the other way. Tickets and information are available from the riverboat company kiosks located inside the **Rodoviaria Fluvial,** Av. Marechal Hermes s/n (✆ **091/3224-6885**), located on the waterfront about a kilometer (½ mile) downstream of the Estação das Docas near the corner of Avenida Visconde de Sousa Franco. The terminal looks run-down well past the point of seedy, but it's safe enough during the day. Several boats make the journey, departing on different days of the week. **Macamazon,** Av. Boulevard Castilho França 744 (✆ **091/3222-5604**), has departures for Manaus Monday, Tuesday, Wednesday, and Friday at 6pm. Cost is R$350 (US$175/£95) for a hammock spot, R$600 (US$300/£162) for a cabin. You can often negotiate a 30% discount if you buy the day before sailing.

English-speaking agents at **Amazon Star** (✆ **091/3241-8624;** www.amazonstar.com.br) will gladly book you passage on board the NM Santarem, which departs every other Wednesday at 6pm, arriving 4 days later in Manaus. The boat stops for a day in Santarem en route, and passengers have the option of making a day trip to Altar do Chão, the beach resort on the Tapajos river.

VISITOR INFORMATION

The city and state tourism agencies, **Belémtur** and **Paratur,** have side-by-side kiosks at the airport. Both have excellent free maps of Belém. The Belémtur kiosk is open Monday through Friday 8am to 11pm, Saturday and Sunday 9am to 9pm. The Paratur kiosk is open Monday through Friday 9am to 9pm, Saturday 9am to 1pm. Paratur also has a very good Englsh-language website: www.paraturismo.pa.gov.br. In the city, **Paratur** (② 091/3212-0575) has an office near the shipping port at Praça Maestro Waldemar Henrique s/n. If you're fluent in Portuguese it's possible to stop by and have a chat with the pretty girls who staff the office, though they have little information to impart, most of it wrong or out-of-date. **Belémtur** (② 091/3283-4850; www.belem.pa.gov.br, Portuguese only) has an office at Av. Gov. José Malcher 257. The staff is equally friendly, equally unilingual, and equally less than totally useful. Both are open Monday through Friday 8am to noon and 1 to 6pm.

CITY LAYOUT

Belém was founded on a small headland where the Rio Guamá flows into Guajará Bay on the Amazon estuary. It was here in 1616 that the Portuguese erected the **Forte do Belém.** Defense taken care of, the Portuguese turned to religion, erecting both the **Catédral da Sé** and the **Igreja de Santo Alexandre** on the small square opposite the fort, **Praça Frei Caetano Brandão.** On a much larger adjacent square—**Praça Dom Pedro II**—the early city builders gave unto Caesar, erecting two palaces—the white **Palácio Lauro Sodré** and the blue **Palácio Antônio Lemos**—that would house the civil administration of the state and city, respectively. On the riverbank slightly downstream (north) is where they put **The Ver-o-Peso Market,** and next to that, the city's docklands, which have recently been renovated into a restaurant and shopping complex called the **Estação das Docas.** Running parallel to the river is the broad busy **Avenida Castilhos França.** Inland from this street is the old commercial section of the city, an area of small shops and old colonial buildings called the **Cidade Velha** or **Old City.** It's a fun area to wander during business hours, but it should be avoided in the evening and on Sundays. The northern boundary of the old city is **Avenida Presidente Vargas,** which runs inland from the waterfront uphill out of the old city to a large green square—**the Praça da República**—upon which sits the **Theatro da Paz.** At the tip of the praça, **Avenida Nazaré** veers off at an oblique angle, leading into a more upscale residential district of **Nazaré,** home to the **Basilica of Nazaré,** as well as other attractions such as the **Museum of Emilio Goeldi.** This is also the street that leads to the city's bus station.

GETTING AROUND
BY PUBLIC TRANSPORTATION

Most of Belém's main attractions are within easy walking distance of Praça da República. For destinations farther afield, Belém's buses are fast and efficient and the city's taxis are plentiful and affordable.

BY BUS   Bus fare is R$1.50 (US75¢/£.40) with no transfers. The buses' origin and destination are given on the front, while smaller signs on the front and sides give route information. Because of the many one-way streets in Belém, buses normally follow different routes going and coming, so the smaller signs list route information for the trip out—IDA—and for the return route—VOLTA. For visitors the two most useful routes are the ones that take you from either The Ver-o-Peso Market or Praça da

Belém

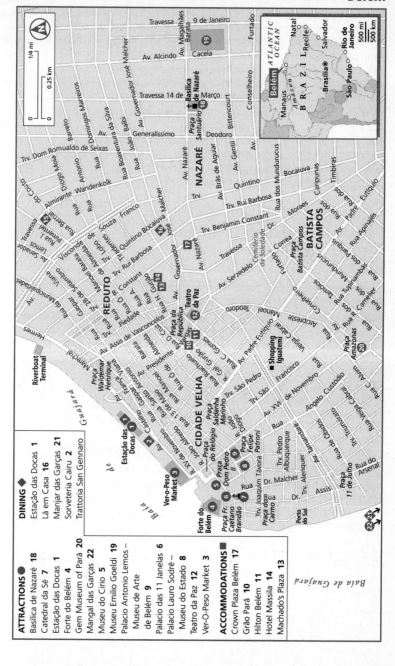

ATTRACTIONS ●

Basílica de Nazaré **18**
Catedral da Sé **7**
Estação das Docas **1**
Forte do Belém **4**
Gem Museum of Pará **20**
Mangal das Garças **22**
Museu do Círio **5**
Museu Emílio Goeldi **19**
Palacio Antonio Lemos –
Museu de Arte
de Belém **9**
Palacio das 11 Janelas **6**
Palacio Lauro Sodré –
Museu do Estado **8**
Teatro da Paz **12**
Ver-O-Peso Market **3**

ACCOMMODATIONS ■

Crown Plaza Belém **17**
Grão Pará **10**
Hilton Belém **11**
Hotel Massila **14**
Machado's Plaza **13**

DINING ◆

Estação das Docas **1**
Lá em Casa **16**
Manjar das Garças **21**
Sorveteria Cairu **2**
Trattoria San Gennaro

República out past the Nazaré Basilica, the bus station (rodoviario), and the Bosque Rodrigues Alves. The following will accomplish that, but as always there are others.

From in front of the Ver-o-Peso, the buses are: BENGUI—VER-O-PESO; CIDADE NOVA IV—VER-O-PESO AF900; JIBÓIA BRANCA—VER-O-PESO AF 986.

From Av. Pres. Vargas (Praça República), the buses are: AGUAS BRANCAS—PRES. VARGAS AU 988; CASTANHEIRA—PRES. VARGAS AG 440; ICOARACI—A. BARROSO. (This bus will also take you out to Icoaraci.)

BY TAXI   Taxis are plentiful and inexpensive. They can be hailed on the street or at numerous taxi stands. Rides are always metered. Sample fares: from the airport to Praça da República, R$40 (US$13/£6.50); from the main bus station to Praça da República, R$20 (US$10/£5.40); from Praça da República to The Ver-o-Peso Market, R$9 (US$4.50/£2.50). **Coopertaxi** (✆ **091/3257-1720** or 091/3257-1041) can be reached 24/7 and accepts Visa and MasterCard.

BY CAR   Belém drivers buckle up religiously and carefully observe posted speed limits; Belém's police enforce the rules ruthlessly. Roads and destinations are well-marked, making travel straightforward if you decide to rent a car.

FAST FACTS: Belém

Area Code   The area code for Belém is **091**.

Banks & Currency Exchange   **Banco do Brasil,** Av. Presidente Vargas 248, Comércio (✆ **021/2223-2537**). Open Monday to Friday 10am to 4pm. 24-hour ATM on-site. **Turvicam** on Praça da República, Av. Pres. Vargas 640, loja 3 (✆ **091/9609-5539**), changes cash and traveler's checks. Open Monday to Friday 8am to 6pm, Saturday 8am to 1pm.

Car Rentals   **Avis** is at the airport (✆ **091/3257-2257**) and Hotel Hilton (✆ **091/3225-1699**). Also at the airport is **Localiza** (✆ **091/3257-1541**).

Consulates   **Great Britain** (Honorary), Av. Governador Magalhães Barata 651, Room 610 (✆ **091/ 4009-0050**).

Dentist   Cliniodonto, Travessa Padre Eutiqiuio 1971 (✆ **091/3225-0413**).

Emergencies   Police ✆ **190**; fire and ambulance ✆ **192**.

Hospitals   **Hospital Ofir Loyola,** Av. Gov Magalhães Barata, 992, Nazaré (✆ **091/3249-9429**).

Internet Access   **TVTron Business Center,** in the basement of the Hotel Hilton on Praça da República (✆ **091/3225-0028**). Open Monday to Friday 7:30am to 10:30pm, Saturday and Sunday 7:30am to 6:30pm. R$10/US$5/£2.70 per hour.

Pharmacies   **Farmacia Big Ben,** Av. Serzedelo Correa 15, near Praça da República (✆ **091/3283-4145**), open Monday to Friday 8am to 10pm and Saturday 8am to 4pm. Big Ben also has an order-by-phone service (✆ **091/3241-3000**) that is open 24/7.

Safety   Pickpockets and purse snatchers are common in The Ver-o-Peso Market. They're especially fond of the two-man distract-and-snatch technique, so keep your wits about you and your bag or purse in front of you. Avoid the Old City completely on Sundays, and on weekdays after dark stick to main streets and squares (the Praça da República, Av. Pres. Vargas, and the Estação das Docas are well-lit and policed in the evening, but as always, look out for pickpockets).

Taxes Hotels add a 10% accommodations tax directly to your bill. There are no other taxes on retail items or goods.

Time Zones Belém is 3 hours behind GMT, the same as Rio.

Visa Renewal Go to the **Policia Federal**, Travess Mariz Barros, Marco (② **091/ 3246-1800**), open Monday to Friday 8 to 11:30am and 2 to 5:30pm. The fee is R$66 (US$33/£18), and you may need to show a return ticket and proof of sufficient funds to cover your stay.

Weather Belém has two seasons: hot and humid and rainy from December to May, and hot, humid, and less rainy from June to November. The daytime maximum temperature usually reaches 92°F (33°C) or slightly higher, and relative humidity is always above 90%. Rain comes in the form of short violent thundershowers, usually in the afternoon.

9 Where to Stay

Accommodations aren't Belém's strong suit. Most of the hotels in the central part of the city are too old, run-down, or seedy to be worth considering—odd for a city that sees tourism as a serious part of its future. Those listed below are really all the hotels you should consider in Belém.

EXPENSIVE

Crowne Plaza Belém 🏵🏵   Brand-new in 2006 and long overdue, the Crowne Plaza is the only truly top-notch hotel in Belém. Better yet, it's located in Nazaré, a pleasant leafy neighborhood with shops and cafes and a nice safe feel, still just a pleasant 20-minute stroll from the sights in Centro. Rooms are pleasant and modern, with tile floors and queen-size or two twin beds, dressed up in top-quality Egyptian cotton, with bathrobes and slippers for an added touch of elegance. The top three Executive floors include little extras like a complimentary daily paper, fruit plate and mineral water, and access to the Club Lounge, but considering the rooms themselves are much the same it's not really worth the price premium, unless you're in need of the ego boost that comes with calling yourself an executive.

Av. Nazaré 375, Belém, BR 66010-010. ② **0800/118-778** or 091/3202-2000. Fax 091/3202-2222. www.crowne belem.com.br. 174 units. Superior double R$390 (US$190/£105); deluxe double R$475 (US$239/£128); Executive double R$630 (US$320/£170). AE, DC, MC, V. Parking R$20 (US$10/£5.50). **Amenities:** Restaurant; bar; pool; exercise room; concierge; car rental; business center; room service; laundry service. *In room:* A/C, TV, minibar, fridge, hair dryer, iron, safe.

Hilton 🏵   A great location on the Praça República, plus a great pool and all the services that come with the Hilton brand. The standard rooms themselves—located on floors two through six—are pleasant if not outstanding, featuring a firm queen-size bed, work table, lounge chairs, a small balcony, and a bathroom with standard size tub/shower combo, a good-size counter sink, and extras like a hair dryer and makeup mirror. Superior rooms are identical, except the superior rooms are located on floors 7 through 11. The deluxe rooms, on floors 12 to 14, have not only recently been renovated, but they include access to the 14th-floor executive business lounge.

Junior suites aren't worth the cost premium, but the corner suites are. These—on floors 2 through 15—feature a furnished separate sitting room and sizable balcony with an excellent view of the Theatro da Paz.

Av. Presidente Vargas 882, Belém, BR 66017-000. (℃) **0800/780-888** or 091/4006-7000. Fax 091/3241-0844. www. hilton.com. 361 units (showers only). Standard double R$460 (US$230/£124); superior double R$480 (US$240/£130); deluxe double R$575 (US$263/£155); corner suite R$615 (US$308/£166) double. 30% discount on weekends and low season. Children under 9 stay free in parent's room. AE, DC, MC, V. Free parking. **Amenities:** Restaurant; bar; large outdoor pool; large gym; concierge; tour desk; car rental; business center; salon; room service; laundry service. *In room:* A/C, small TV, minibar, fridge, hair dryer, iron, safe.

MODERATE

Hotel Massilia (★★) (*Value*)   Considering price, quality, and location, this small hotel is the best place to stay in Belém. Unless you really need the four-star services of the Crowne Plaza or Hilton, this should be your first choice. The 10 standard rooms come with nice firm beds (either a queen-size or two singles), and are tastefully decorated with tile floors, exposed brick walls, and a writing desk made of tropical "cathedral" wood. Bathrooms are small but spotless, with showers that give lots of hot water. Upstairs the six suites, or *apartamentos,* spread out over two floors, with a small bed/couch and sitting area on the main floor, and a queen-size bed and desk in a small upstairs loft, all of it cooled by ultra-silent air-conditioning. A delicious breakfast, served outside on the patio, comes with an ever-changing variety of specialty breads.

Rua Henrique Gurjão 236, Belém, 66053-360 PA. (℃) **091/3222-2834.** Fax 091/3224-7147. www.massilia.com.br. 17 units (showers only). Standard double R$110 (US$55/£30); apartment double R$140 (US$70/£38). Extra person R$10 (US$5/£2.50). Children 6 and under stay free in parent's room. 10% discount with cash. MC, V. Free parking. **Amenities:** French restaurant; small outdoor pool. *In room:* A/C, TV, minibar, fridge, hair dryer.

Machado's Plaza (★) (*Value*)   The Machado's Plaza stands literally next door to the Massilia. This small hotel was built in 2004 and offers pleasant and new accommodations. All 36 rooms come with lots of closet space and are nicely furnished with comfortable beds (doubles or two twins) with nice linens and firm mattresses. Every room also features a desk and complimentary high-speed Internet. There are no views to speak of; most rooms look out over Rua Henrique Gurjão, a narrow street a few blocks off the Praça da República. The advantage is that it's quiet at night and you're still within easy walking of some of the city's main sights. The hotel also features a small pool and restaurant.

Rua Henrique Gurjão 200, Belém, 66053-360 PA. (℃) **091/4008-9800** or 091/4008-9816. Fax 091/4008-9817. www. machadosplazahotel.com.br. 36 units (showers only). Standard double R$160–R$220 (US$80–US$110/£43–£59). Children 6 and under stay free in parent's room. Extra person 25%. V. Free parking. **Amenities:** Restaurant; small outdoor pool. *In room:* A/C, TV, dataport, minibar, safe.

INEXPENSIVE

Hotel Grão Pará   A fabulous location on the Praça República two doors down from the Hilton; clean and reasonably comfortable rooms; and a reasonable price. Rooms are tile-floored, with a firm queen-size mattress and good linens. Rooms aren't large; space enough for a bed and small breakfast table. Bathrooms are clean and functional. Desk and service staff are friendly and professional. Given the small increase in price and vast increase in quality, the Massilia is a better bet, but if it's full, the Grão Pará is an acceptable backup.

Av. Presidente Vargas 718, Belém, 66017-000 PA. (℃) **091/3224-4100.** Fax 091/3242-8073. 150 units (showers only). Standard double R$90 (US$45/£24). Extra person R$30 (US$15/£8). Children 8 and under stay free in parent's room. AE, V. *In room:* A/C, TV, minibar, fridge.

10 Where to Dine

Blessed by geography, Belém has one of the richest cuisines in Brazil. In addition to the whole range of Amazon freshwater fish, there are saltwater species, including shrimp and crab. Beef is plentiful, as is buffalo from the island of Marajó.

Tip: On the waterfront the **Estação das Docas** (© 091/3212-5525) has a half-dozen restaurants, waterfront incarnations of some of Belém's best restaurants with locations elsewhere. The specialist in regional cuisine is **Lá em Casa** (© 091/3212-5588) (see review later in this section). The **Cappone** (© 091/3212-5666) Italian restaurant is a great spot for some pasta or risotto; sushi lovers can have a good meal on the patio at **Hatobá** (© 091/3212-3143); for a steak dinner, consider **Marujo Grill** (© 091/ 3225-5723). For a quicker regional snack, try the **As Mulatas** (© 091/3212-5300) kiosk for a bowl of tacacá soup, or the **Sorveteria Cairu** (© 091/3212-5595) for ice cream made with local Amazon fruit. You can dine on the waterfront overlooking the river, or inside in air-conditioned comfort. All six are open Monday to Friday noon to midnight, Saturday and Sunday 10am to 2am.

Lá em Casa 🍴 SEAFOOD/REGIONAL   The longtime master of local Pará cuisine, now in new location in the heart of Belém's restaurant district. The menu continues the tradition of creative use of local fruits and fish. For a sampling of local fish, try the *corridinho de peixe,* which includes fresh grilled *pirarucu,* skewers of *tambaqui,* local haddock, *filhote* in *tucupi* sauce, *pescada amarela,* and *farofa* flavored with *pirarucu.* Pará's signature dish of duck in tucupi sauce is particularly well done here. For dessert, try the tapioca balls with *cupuaçu* filling, served with *cupuaçu* ice cream.

Travessa Dom Pedro I, 546. © 091/3424-4222. Main courses R$18–R$36 (US$9–US$18/£5–£9.50). AE, DC, MC, V. Mon–Sat noon–3pm and 7–11pm; Sun noon–4pm.

Manjar das Garças 🍴🍴 SEAFOOD/REGIONAL   The excellent food at the restaurant in the Mangal das Garças park (see "The Top Attractions," p. 404) comes with complimentary views of the Guamá river. The lunch buffet is top-notch and includes a large salad bar and a variety of steak, fish, and seafood dishes such as the *filhote* in tucupí sauce or grilled calamari with onions. In the evenings, the restaurant serves an a la carte menu, specializing in fish and seafood. Dishes include local ingredients such as the grilled tucunaré with roasted palm heart in an orange sauce or the baked pescada amarela fish with a cashew-nut purée. For those who prefer steak, there's the filet mignon with a Gorgonzola risotto or the grilled beef medallions with gnocchi made from manioc flour. Desserts include several wonderful pies with tropical ice cream; try the chocolate cake with cupuaçu coulis and tapioca ice cream. The restaurant has some outside tables and makes a wonderful sunset destination.

Praça Carneiro da Rocha (inside Mangal das Garças Park). © 091/3242-1056. R$24–R$28 (US$12–US$14/ £6.50–£7.50) lunch buffet; dinner main courses R$24–R$36 (US$12–US$18/£6.50–£10). AE, MC. Sun and Tues–Wed noon–midnight; Thurs–Sat noon–3am. Taxi recommended.

Sorveteria Cairu 🍴 ICE CREAM   The specialized ice creams of the Amazon are one of Belém's treats. Made from a variety of Amazon fruits, they are delicious and exotic and not to be missed. There are numerous flavors, mostly made from fruits without English names. The best strategy is to go and sample.

Travessia 14 de Março 1570. © 091/3267-2749. Also at Estação das Docas. © 091/3212-5595. R$3–R$9 (US$1.50–US$4.50/£.80–£2.50). No credit cards. Daily 9am–9pm. Bus: Ver-o-Peso.

Trattoria San Gennaro ✹✹ ITALIAN   Trattoria San Genaro offers trendy alfresco dining in the heart of Belém's nightlife district. Don't order an appetizer but help yourself to the fabulous antipasto buffet (R$5.50/US$2.75 per 100g). As for mains, the restaurant takes great pride in making all the pasta, bread, and sauces in-house. There's a choice of three pastas; spaghetti, gnocchi, and fettuccini and sauces such as a creamy Gorgonzola, porcini mushrooms, or *romanesca* (cream, ham, mushrooms, and peas). The stuffed pastas are also excellent. We enjoyed the unusual duck ravioli in passion-fruit sauce and the prawn lasagna with Gruyère cheese. There are several excellent steak and seafood dishes. For dessert try the homemade ice creams. Flavors include pistachio, basil and papaya, white chocolate, and chocolate with hazelnut.

Av. Wandenkolk 666. ✆ 091/3241-0019. Main courses R$18–R$38 (US$9–US$19/£5–£10). MC, V. Tues–Sat 7pm–1am; Sun noon–3:30pm and 7–11:30pm. Bus: Docas.

OTHER OPTIONS

The **Umarizal** neighborhood boasts a number of excellent dining options. In addition to **Trattoria San Gennaro** (see review above) there's top-quality steak at **Picanha e Cia** (✆ 091/3224-3343), Rua Bernal do Couto 260, on the corner of Avenida Almirante Wandenkolk. The city's best pizza restaurant is **Xícara da Silva** (✆ 092/3241-0167), Av. Visconde de Souza Franco 978-A. It's a vast high-ceilinged room with a big pizza oven at the far end. For lunchtime fare, the city's best kilo spot is undoubtedly **Spazzio Verdi** ✹✹ in Nazaré, Av. Braz de Aguiar 824 (✆ 091/3241-6364). The restaurant boasts a large range of good vegetarian dishes, as well as the usual beef and chicken—all R$26 (US$13/£7) per kilo—plus an indoor patio space positively awash in lovely green foliage. In the evening, the **Boteco das Onze** (✆ 091/3224-8599), Praça Frei Caetano Brandão s/n, located on the patio of the Casa das Onze Janelas offers a lively atmosphere, good cold beer and a top quality Brazilian fare.

11 Exploring Belém

One day is likely enough to see all that Belém has to offer. *Tip:* On Tuesday, entrance is free to all Belém's museums at the fort.

THE TOP ATTRACTIONS

Forte do Presépio ✹   A wood-and-earth fort—constructed on the site of today's much more substantial installation—was the very first thing built in Belém when the Portuguese arrived in 1616. The fort was variously abandoned, rebuilt, and renamed over the years (it's also known as the Forte do Castelo and the Forte do Belém). The last major military renovation occurred in the 1850s. In the 1980s the nearly ruined fort was again restored, this time by Brazil's federal caretaker of historic sites. From the ramparts you get a wonderful view of Ver-o-Peso Market, the Catédral da Sé, and the Praça Dom Pedro II. A small museum inside the fort tells the history of the area's indigenous tribes, plus the history of the fort and the settlement of Belém. Allow 30 minutes.

Praça Frei Caetano Brandão 117. ✆ 091/4009-8828. R$2 (US$1/£.50). Wed–Sun 10am–6pm. Bus: Ver-o-Peso.

Icoaraci ✹   The central street of this seaside town close to Belém has evolved into a pottery and artisan's enclave. Belém pottery is fashioned in the style of either the **Marajóara** or **Tapajônica** tribes, Belém's indigenous inhabitants. The more ancient Marajóara tribe used angular geometric designs. **Tapajônica** pottery features countless rotund gods and animals, somewhat like Hindu sculpture. The better shops include **Anísio**

The Círio of Nazaré

Every year in Belém on the second weekend of October more than one million of the faithful gather in the streets to watch and participate in the annual *Círio of Nazaré,* a procession of an image of the Virgin of Nazaré. The procession has been taking place for more than 200 years, ever since a Belém peasant discovered an image of the Holy Virgin in the forest on the spot where the Basilica of Nazaré now stands. According to legend, the holy nature of the image was revealed when the peasant brought the image back to his hut, only to have it disappear overnight and reappear back on that same spot in the jungle. That original image has now been permanently installed in the nave of the specially built Basilica of Nazaré. Each year a replica image heads a procession of hundreds of thousands of the faithful that travels from the Basilica to the Catédral da Sé and back again.

The procession begins on the Saturday with a nautical journey, when the image departs from the beach in the village of Icoaraci and, along with a convoy of colorful floats, arrives around noon at the Estação das Docas. The image then travels to the Catédral da Sé. Sunday morning there's a Mass, and then around 7am the image departs the cathedral and begins its return journey to the Basilica of Nazaré. The 5km (3-mile) procession normally takes all day, with hundreds of thousands of the faithful following. At the end, the Virgin returns to her resting place in the square opposite the basilica, and the participants and onlookers throw themselves into a 3-week harvest festival party.

Artesanato, Travessia Soledade 740 (© **091/3227-0127;** www.anisioartesanato.com.br) and **Cultura Indigena,** Travessia Soledade 790 (© **091/3233-4583**). Both are open business hours (Mon–Sat 8am–noon and 1–6pm). At the waterfront there are more pottery options at the **Paracuri Fair,** in the waterfront **Praça de São Sebastião.** After you've shopped, go for some waterfront dining at either **Na Telha,** Rua Siqueira Mendes 263 (© **091/3227-0853**), or **Carvalho's,** Travessia do Cruzeiro 364 (© **091/3227-0065**); both are open daily 11am to midnight. **Amazon Star Turismo** (© **091/3241-8624;** www.amazonstar.com.br) offers a full-day van tour of Icoaraci for R$55 (US$27/£15) including transport and a guide to explain the pottery styles and introduce you to the potters. The public bus from Belém takes about 45 minutes.

Travesia Soledade (entire street). www.icoaraci.com.br. Daily 9am–6pm. Bus: Icoaraci, from Praça República.

Mangal das Garças ✿✿ *(Kids* A birthday present from the navy (who donated the land) to the city of Belém, the park was inaugurated in January 2005. Located on the river Guamá, the Mangal does an excellent job representing Belém's regional culture, flora, and fauna. A series of lagoons portrays the Amazonian ecosystem, starting off with a narrow igarapé creek that opens up into a larger lagoon with white herons and scarlet ibises and finally empties into mangroves. There is a large viewing platform overlooking the river and the marsh along the shore. The vegetation still needs to grow in a bit but already looks nice. The park also has an excellent restaurant (see review in "Where to Dine," p. 403), a gift shop, and a number of attractions. For R$6

(US$3/£1.50) you can see everything. This includes a 45m-tall (150-ft.) modern lighthouse that offers 360-degree views; a walk-through aviary that houses over 20 species of local birds; a butterfly world, a glass enclosed space with hundreds of butterflies flying loose; and a small but interesting navigation museum that tells the story of many river craft used on the Amazon. Allow 2 hours. *Tip:* If you want to see the birds and butterflies at their best, avoid the heat of the day. Late afternoon is great as you can combine it with a sunset stroll on the deck or a drink at the restaurant.

Praça Carneiro da Rocha (behind the Navy Arsenal), Cidade Velha. (*C*) 091/3242-5052. www.mangal.com.br. Park is free, admission only for interior facilities R$6 (US$3/£1.50). Paid facilities Tues–Sun 10–6pm, park and restaurant open later; closed on Mon. Taxi recommended.

Museu do Círio *(★)*

Two air-conditioned rooms tell the story of the Círio of Nazaré—an incredible religious spectacle held each year beginning on the second Saturday of October, during which nearly a million participants either witness or participate in a 2-day procession behind an image of the Virgin Mary. The museum explains the origins and development of the procession, from the discovery of the Virgin's image by an 18th-century peasant to the huge festival today. Included are models of the parade, images of Círio's past, and examples of floats and costumes and models of the imitation body parts offered up by the faithful. Some of the tour guides speak limited English. Allow 30 minutes.

Praça Dom Pedro II (on the side closest to the river). (*C*) 091/4009-8846. Admission R$2 (US$1/£.50). Tues–Sun 10am–6pm. Bus: Ver-o-Peso.

Museu Emílio Goeldi *(Kids)*

Brazilian zoos are also one of the few places where Brazilians and foreigners can see and learn to appreciate the creatures that inhabit this still very wild country. On the other hand, the enclosures are often achingly small. Founded in 1866 as an Amazon research institute, the Emílio Goeldi is home to a medium-size collection of birds, mammals, and reptiles, all scattered about a green and leafy park. The highlight is the aquarium, which displays a variety of rays, eels, and bizarre-looking rock turtles. The most disturbing display is the giant Amazon River otter, who swims around his enclosure screaming piteously for attention. The museum still serves as a research institute, but little of that work is visible to the public. Allow an hour.

Av. Magalhães Barata 376. (*C*) 091/3219-3369. Admission for zoo and aquarium R$3 (US$1.50/£.80); separate admission, R$1.50 (US75¢/£.40) each. Free for children 10 and under and seniors 65 and over. Tues–Sun 9am–5pm. Bus: AU 988.

The Ver-o-Peso Market *(★★★)*

The Ver-o-Peso Market is Belém's star postcard attraction. It's a vast waterside cornucopia, with just about every Amazon product available for purchase. Stroll into the original market hall—the one with the cute blue Gothic arches, imported prefab from England in 1899—and you're in an Amazon Fish World, with outrageously strange Amazon fish like the 100-kilogram catfish-like *pirapema*, all laid out on ice or on the chopping table. Outside under the canopies there are hundreds of species of Amazon fruits; most of them for sell for R$2 (US$1/£.50) per kilo or less. The love-starved can seek out the traditional medicine kiosks, where every potion and bark-derived infusion seems to heighten allure, potency, and fertility. There's also an arts-and-crafts fair with baskets, hats, spoons, and all manner of goods made from reeds and wood. When you tire of browsing, dozens of food counters sell cheap, quick eats and fresh-blended tropical fruit juices. Allow 2 hours.

Av. Castilhos França s/n. No phone. Daily 5am–2pm. Bus: Ver-o-Peso.

OTHER ATTRACTIONS

Belém's **Theatro da Paz** (© 091/4009-8750; tours every hour Mon–Fri 9am–5pm, Sat 9am–2pm; R$4/US$2/£1) is an ornate opera house modeled on Milan's La Scala theater. The inside is a rich assortment of Italian marble and tropical hardwoods, wrought iron, and gold gilt.

Located side by side on the Praça Dom Pedro II are two lovely colonial palaces. Both are worth a glance if you have time on your hands, but don't feel guilty if you miss them. The white neoclassical **Palácio Lauro Sodré** used to house the Pará state government, but is now home to the **Museu do Estado,** Praça Dom Pedro II (© **091/ 3219-1138;** Tues–Sat 10am–6pm, Sun 10am–2pm; admission R$2/US85¢/£.40, free Tues), which displays the former staterooms complete with lovely tropical furnishings. Each room is done in a different ornate style: Art Nouveau, rococo, neoclassical, and so on. The blue **Palácio Antônio Lemos** was and remains Belém's city hall, but on the second floor there's the small **Museu de Arte de Belém,** Praça Dom Pedro II (© **091/3283-4687;** Tues–Fri 10am–6pm, Sat–Sun 9am–1pm; admission R$1/ US50¢/£.25), which shows rich furniture and oil paintings from the rubber boom era. Next to the Forte do Belém, the former Church of Santo Alexandre has been converted into a small and eminently missable **Sacred Art Museum** (© 091/4009-8802; Tues–Sun 10am–6pm). There's so little on display, in fact, that it's not really worth paying the R$4 (US$2/£1) admission.

Also located beside the Forte do Belém, the yellow 11-windowed **Casa das 11 Janelas,** Praça Frei Caetano Brandão s/n (© 091/4009-8823; Tues–Sun 10am–6pm; R$2 (US$1/£.50), has two floors of contemporary art by Belém painters and sculptors.

Housed in a former hellhole of a prison, the **Gem Museum of Pará,** Praça Amazonas s/n (© **091/3230-4452;** R$4/US$2/£1; Tues–Sat 10am–8pm, Sun 3–8pm; Bus: Igautemi [but take a cab back if you buy jewelry]), is definitely quirky enough to merit a visit. The museum showcases an extraordinary variety of Pará's crystals and gems. Geologists will be in heaven. Those less than rock-happy may find it a tad much. Other cells have been leased to private jewelry companies that show off their original designs.

ARCHITECTURAL HIGHLIGHTS

The **Cidade Velha** or **Old City** opposite The Ver-o-Peso Market is a wonderful mixture of Portuguese colonial, Art Nouveau, Art Deco, and concrete-and-glass '60s modernism. This promiscuous mixing of architectural styles is the reason Belém's downtown was denied UNESCO World Heritage Site status, though Belenenses protest that the mix of styles makes their historic core all the more intriguing. The most fascinating building is the **Paris n' America** shop at **Rua Gaspar Viana 136.** At the height of the rubber boom this was the boutique for haute couture in Belém, the place where wealthy rubber barons would dress their wives and daughters. Fashions were imported from Paris, along with models to show the rather provincial Belém baronesses how the clothes ought to be worn. It's worth traipsing up the sweeping iron staircase to have a look at the still-abandoned second floor.

CHURCHES

The two most important churches in town are the **Catédral da Sé,** Praça Frei Caetano Brandão (© **091/3223-2362;** Mon 3–7:30pm, Tues–Wed and Fri 7am–noon and 2–7:30pm, Thurs 6am–7:30pm, Sat 5–8:30pm, Sun 6–11am and 5–8:30pm), and the **Basilica de Nazaré,** Praça Justo Chermont (© **091/4009-8400;** Mon–Fri

6am–7:30pm, Sat–Sun 6am–noon). Located on the square opposite the fort, the Catédral da Sé is neglected and rather dilapidated but still gorgeous inside, a mix of baroque and neoclassical with soaring vaulted ceiling and lovely Art Nouveau candelabras. However, the church that Belenenses are most proud of is the Basilica in Nazaré, located on the spot where in the late 17th century a simple *caboclo* hunter supposedly tripped over an image of the Virgin. It's from here that a replica of that original image sets off on pilgrimage during the yearly Círio of Nazaré. The original image is now permanently ensconced in the wall above the altar. Modeled on St. Peter's Basilica in Rome, the church itself, like much of Belém, is a nouveau riche rehash of things done first and better elsewhere.

PLAZAS & PARKS

The green anchor of Belém's downtown, **Praça República,** is a lovely three-sided traditional square with plentiful benches and many small patches of grass on which small children play with balls. The current classical configuration of this former military parade ground is the work of Belém's 19th-century rubber barons, who also erected the **Theatro da Paz** at the Praça's narrow end. Being snobby aristocrats, of course, they also put up a fence to keep the unwashed public out. The fence came down only after rubber prices crashed.

Just outside the old downtown, the **Praça Batista Campos** is a manicured green space shaded by huge mature mango trees, with swing sets and seesaws, walking paths, small lagoons, a band shell, folly, and lots of benches. It's well-lit and safe, populated both day and evening by young moms with kids, and young lovers necking.

PARKS & GARDENS The large, lush (16-hectare/40-acre) **Bosque Rodrigo Alves,** Av. Almirante Barroso 2305 (© **091/3276-2308;** Tues–Sun 8am–5pm; R$1/ US50¢/£.25, free for children 12 and under) is planted thick with over 2,500 Amazonian forest species. There are numerous small walking trails, an orchidarium, and a small lake with Amazonian species like turtles.

Just up street from the Museu Emílio Goeldi (see "The Top Attractions," earlier in this chapter) is the newly unveiled **Parque da Residencia,** Av. Magalhães Barata 830, corner of Travesia 3 de Maio, which occupies the former official residence of Pará's state governors. The park features fountains, a small orchid arbor, a display space with the governor's old Rolls-Royce, and a good if slightly pricey kilo restaurant, the **Restô do Parque** (© **091/3229-8000;** Tues–Sun noon–3:30pm, Wed–Sun 8–11:30pm).

ORGANIZED TOURS

The tour agency in Belém with the best and largest variety of tours is **Amazon Star Turismo,** Rua Henrique Gurjão 236 (© **091/3241-8624;** www.amazonstar.com.br). **Valeverde Turismo,** Estação das Docas, building 1 (© **091/3212-3388;** www.valeverde turismo.com.br), is another reputable agency, located at the upstream end of the Estação das Docas.

BOAT TOURS The most unique tour in Belém is the early-morning **excursion to Parrot Island** ✿✿, a small semi-flooded island a few kilometers offshore that is the bedroom of choice for hundreds of Amazonian parrots. Boats depart at 5am (4:30am hotel pickup) to arrive at the island in the gray pre-dawn. As the sky lightens, the parrots awake. They squawk, circle around to find their mates, then fly away into the dawn. Afterward the tour explores the small side channels of islands in the estuary. **Amazon Star** does this tour particularly well. The price is R$90 (US$45/£24), hotel pickup and drop-off included. For later risers, Amazon Star also has a half-day **River**

Trip through the channels and creeks of Guamá River (a tributary of the Amazon), with a stop for a guided walk in the forest. Departures are 8:30am and 2:30pm; the R$65 (US$33/£18) fee includes pickup and drop-off.

A gorgeous evening option is **Valeverde's** 1½-hour **Sunset** tour that departs at 5:30pm or the 8pm **Lights of the City** cruise, which departs nightly from the Estação das Docas and circles offshore of Belém, allowing passengers to observe as the lights come on in the city's historic churches and monuments. The price is R$35 (US$17/£9.50); cruises depart Tuesday through Sunday.

BUS TOURS   The trip to Icoaraci is highly recommended. See "The Top Attractions," earlier in this chapter. Both Amazon Star and Valeverde offer morning and an afternoon tours, about R$75 (US$37/£20) per person, 3-hour tour.

HIKING   Highly recommended for those in reasonable physical condition are **Amazon Star's trekking tours.** The **1-day tour** departs before sunrise, crossing the Guamá River to a jungle-covered section of the Amazon estuary around Boa Vista. There follows a full-day trek in the jungle, observing wildlife and visiting *caboclo* communities who make a living growing cassava and fishing. At the far end of the Acará River there's time for a rest and some swimming, followed by a sunset cruise back to Belém. Cost is R$130 (US$65/£32), guide and lunch included (July–Dec only).

WALKING TOURS   Both **Amazon Star** and **Valeverde** offer **3-hour walking tours** of old Belém with stops at major sites, including The Ver-o-Peso Market, the Theatro da Paz, and the Nazaré Basilica. Cost is R$30 (US$15/£8).

12 Belém Shopping

The specialty of Belém is **pottery,** mostly fashioned in the style of either the **Marajóara** or **Tapajônica** tribes, the indigenous inhabitants of Belém. The more ancient Marajóara tribe used angular designs, somewhat like the Aztec or the tribes of the American Southwest. Marajóara pottery features countless rotund gods and animals, somewhat like Hindu sculpture. The best place to shop for pottery is in the village of **Icoaraci** (p. 404). **The Ver-o-Peso Market** (p. 406) is one vast shoppers' paradise. In Belém's historic downtown, the **Rua Gaspar Viana** is a pretty pedestrian street with cobblestones and countless small shops selling everything from hammocks to lingerie, clothing, appliances, and bootleg CDs. The **Largo das Mercês** is a good place to look for leather sandals, belts, and handbags. For jewelry and raw gemstones, go to the **Gem Museum of Pará** (see "Other Attractions," above). For anything else, there's the three-floor **Shopping Iguatemi** mall, Travessia Padre Eutíquio 1078, Batista Campos (✆ 091/3250-5353; www.iguatemi.com.br). The mall is open Monday through Saturday 10am to 10pm, and Sunday 3 to 9pm. Bus: Shopping Iguatemi.

13 Belém After Dark

THE PERFORMING ARTS

Theatro da Paz   This Escala-in-miniature offers symphonies, chamber concerts, and light operas most weekends throughout the fall and winter (May–Sept). Tickets are reasonable, and the acoustics are very good. Check the website under "Agenda de eventos" for programming. Monday to Friday 9am to 6pm; Saturday 9am to 1pm. Av. de Paz s/n. ✆ 091/4009-8750. www.theatrodapaz.com.br. Box office ✆ 091/4009-8758. The box office is in the main lobby area.

BARS & DANCE CLUBS

The **Estação das Docas** features live music on Thursday through Sunday nights start-ing at 8pm. Belém's other nightlife area centers on the **Avenida Visconde de Sousa Franco** (usually known as **Docas Bd.**) and the surrounding small streets (notably the **Av. Almirante Wandenkolk**) located north of downtown. There are many clubs, bars, and discos in this area, close enough together that it's easy to stroll from one to the next. The better ones include the **Roxy Bar,** Av. Senador Lemos 231 (✆ **091/3224-4514**) and the intimate lounge **BBC,** Rua Jerônimo Pimentel 201 (✆ **091/3222-0562**). **Casablanca,** Av. Senador Lemos 175 (✆ **091/3224-9520**), has a large dance floor, restaurant, and bar with inventive cocktails. The **Iguana,** Av. Wandenkolk 247 (✆ **091/3225-1313**), offers DJs and dancing. R$20 (US$10/£5.50) cover.

One of the best place in for live music is Boêmio Cervejaria, **Av. Visconde de Souza Franco 555** (✆ **092/3224-0075**), located on the corner Avenida Senador Lemos in the Reduto neighborhood. Bands play MPB midweek, and rock on week-ends. R$5 (US$2.50/£1.35) cover.

If you're looking to hear local live music, try **A Pororoca,** Av. Senador Lemos 3316 (✆ **091/ 3233-7631**). This traditional show place has room for a 1,000 guests, and leans heavily toward *brega,* but also plays forró, MPB, and very occasionally samba. Cover is R$10 (US$5/£2.70) and hours are Wednesday to Sunday 10pm to 4am. Note that the outdoor **Bar do Parque** (✆ **091/3242-8798**), located in the shadow of the Theatro da Paz, is exclusively patronized by prostitutes and their customers.

14 A Side Trip to Marajó

Marajó holds the title for the world's largest river island, a vast land expanse in the mouth of the Amazon that is larger than many countries. The island has been settled for centuries so most of the original rainforest is gone. Instead, Marajó boasts low-lying, periodically flooded ranchland like that of the Pantanal. The ranches are lightly stocked with water buffalo and chock-full of incredible populations of large and col-orful birds—egrets, herons, parrots, toucans, and startling scarlet ibis, not to mention caiman and the occasional troupe of monkeys. A number of these ranches (fazendas) have opened themselves up to tourism, allowing visitors to experience the island's nature and unique way of life.

GETTING THERE   The only reason to go to Marajó is to stay at one of the hotel fazendas. Though there are two small towns—Selvaterra and Soure—close together on the eastern shore of the island, they are not in themselves worth a long ferry ride. (It's worth spending 1 night in Soure to get a feel for the local culture and community and enjoy a day at the beach, Marajó-style.) Most of the fazendas will include transporta-tion in your package, which you should arrange ahead of time either with the hotel fazenda or through a tour agency such as **Amazon Star Turismo,** Rua Henrique Gur-jão 236 (✆ **091/3241-8624;** www.amazonstar.com.br).

FERRIES   There's a **Belém-Selvaterra passenger ferry,** run by **Araparí Navegação,** Rua Siquiera Mendes 120 (✆ **091/9601-5312**), departing from Portão 10 (immedi-ately downstream of the Estação das Docas). Departures are Monday through Satur-day at 7am and 3pm, Sundays at 7am and 6pm. The trip lasts 3 hours and costs R$13 (US$6.50/£3.50). The **car ferry to Marajó,** run by HENVIL, Av. Bernardo Sayão 490 (✆ **091/3249-3400**), departs from the village of Icoaraci. Monday through Sat-urday; departures are at 5am and 7pm. Sundays 7am and 6pm. Tickets cost R$47

Moments Do Eat the Buffalo

One of the best things about Marajó is the food. Buffalo is the local specialty, and we were expecting to try a bite, but after a few days we lost track
of all the dishes that were in some way or other derived from water buffalo. We tried buffalo roast beef for our first meal. The meat is delicious,
very lean and tender, with a stronger taste than cow, though not as pronounced as lamb. For dessert we had caramel pudding made with buffalo
milk. In the evening, with the cold beer and view of the sunset, our cook
brought us slices of fresh Mozzarella di Buffalo. Only 24 hours old, the
cheese had a light, creamy taste. Another dinner started off with a rich
cheese and onion soup made with, you guessed it, buffalo cheese, followed
by a buffalo meatloaf. Our breakfast buffet included buffalo butter, buffalo
milk, buffalo cheese, and buffalo cream, in addition to waffles, omelets (no
buffalo eggs), and other goodies. Had we stayed more than a few days it
would have taken a buffalo to carry us out of there.

(US$24/£13) and can be purchased in advance at Belém's *rodoviaria* (bus station). To
reach Soure from the ferry dock in Camará is about a 30-minute bus ride (R$7/
US$3.50/£2 per person) and then a 5-minute ferry ride (free for passengers). Compe-
tition for the public bus is fierce; better to have your transport arranged beforehand
with a lodge or pousada.

LODGES

Most lodges offer similar activities. The most popular ones are horseback riding, the
perfect way to explore the flooded fields; buffalo riding, which is much more comfortable than it sounds; fishing; and bird-watching.

Fazenda N.S. do Carmo ★★   Located on the banks of the Rio Camará, this lodge
has a wonderful authentic feel. Accommodations are comfortable, clean, and basic. In
the main ranch house there are six bedrooms with simple twin beds, and three shared
bathrooms with not especially hot showers, plus a pair of sitting rooms and a shared
phone and TV. Tours cover the ranch and the nearby forest. They include horse and
buffalo riding, canoe and kayak tours on the river and smaller channels, fishing, bird-
watching, and photo safaris, plus time to kayak the river or swim in the ranch's small
freshwater lake. The package price includes all activities.

Marajó. ⓒ **091/9161-1521** (lodge) or 091/3241-2202 (reservations). 8 units (showers only, shared bathrooms). 3-
day packages start at R$850 (US$425/£229) per person, guide and transfers to Belém included. AE, DC, MC, V.
Amenities: Kayaks; horseback riding; swimming lake. *In room:* No phone.

Fazenda Sanjo ★★★ *(Kids*   Talk about arriving in style. After a 50-minute boat ride
from the ferry dock in Soure, horses await (non-riders can go by buffalo cart) for you
to ride across the flooded field to the main house of Fazenda Sanjo. This ranch offers a
wonderful rustic family experience. Ana, whose family has owned the ranch for generations, and her husband, Carlos, always look after their guests from the minute they
pick them up in Belém or at the ferry. The ranch is not luxurious but quite comfortable. The six rooms are located on the ground floor of the ranch and have comfortable

beds and screened windows. The common rooms and large decks are on the first floor, offering fabulous views of the surrounding landscape. Fazenda Sanjo still has a herd of 300 buffalos that guests can help round up in the afternoon. It's quite the experience to chase after a bunch of large water buffalos while on a horse. Guests are also welcome to observe the day-to-day activities on the ranch, such as the milking of the buffalo and cheese making. The cheese, milk, and buffalo meat are used in a lot of the dishes; the food is excellent and portions are generous. For a small fee (R$70/US$29/£14 per person), Ana and Carlos can take care of all transfers, door-to-door from your hotel to the ranch and back, including ferry tickets.

Marajó. ℂ 091/9145-4475 (lodge) or 091/3242-1385 (reservations). www.sanjo.tur.br. 6 units (showers only, shared bathrooms). 2-day packages R$450 (US$225/£121) per person; 3-day packages R$640 (US$320/£173); 4-day packages R$800 (US$400/£216). Children under 6 stay free, in parent's room children 7–12 50% discount. Daily departures. MC, V. *In room:* No phone.

Marajó Park Resort 🏵🏵 The most wild and isolated lodge, the Marajó Park is located on its own large island in the mouth of the Amazon, 6 miles off the north coast of Marajó. Access is by private plane (cost included). Facilities here are top-notch, and the grounds are huge (38,000 hectares/93,860 acres!). On the downside, the lodge is large, as is the group size on outings. Rooms are comfortable doubles with private bathrooms. The 3-day package includes the 50-minute flight over Marajó, horse and buffalo riding, a bit of sport fishing, walking safaris, boat trips out into the Amazon estuary, and a bird-watching excursion, plus downtime to enjoy the hotel's pleasant outdoor pool. Dune buggies, ATVs, and jet skis are available for rent. Five- and 7-day packages are also available, as well as specialized sport-fishing packages.

Ilha Mexiana (access by plane, departures Sun and Wed only). ℂ 091/3244-4613 (lodge) or 091/3202-7043 (reservations). Fax 091/3244-3200. www.marajoparkresort.com.br. 80 units (showers only). Packages of 3 days/2 nights start at R$2,700 (US$1,350/£729) per person, including transfers in Belém and flight to and from the ranch. Better rates may be available through a travel agent such as Amazonstar (www.amazonstar.com.br). MC, V. **Amenities:** Restaurant; bar; outdoor pool. *In room:* A/C, minibar, fridge, no phone.

SOURE

If you have an extra day, it's worth spending a night in Soure. It's a particularly charming small Brazilian town, wedged between the river and the bay. Streets are made of grass instead of dirt, and it is there that the buffalo roam. Indeed, buffalo play an important role in the life of the island and the town. Not only are they an economic resource for the farmers, but in Soure the buffalo are also put to work pulling the garbage carts, and used as transportation. There is even a squad of buffalo-mounted police. The best time to stay in Soure is on a Saturday night when locals gather in the main square, promenade along the river, eat ice cream, and often as not enjoy cultural presentations put on in the city square. One evening we lucked out and saw a presentation of carimbó, the local dance, which is a mixture of Portuguese folk dancing with Caribbean rhythms and steps.

The beaches just outside of Soure are a unique experience. The water is mostly fresh, and the tides are thoroughly impressive. At low tide, so much of the beach lies exposed that locals ride bicycles to reach the far-off water's edge. At high tide, bathers retreat to the kiosks, nestled amid the vast spreading root systems of the coastal mangrove trees.

Fazenda São Jerônimo 🏵🏵 Despite the name, this is more a bed-and-breakfast than a ranch. Located close to Soure, the São Jerônimo is a great option for those who want to visit the town, but is not an alternative to staying on an actual ranch. The rooms are simple but very nicely done; each comes with a veranda. The town of Soure is a R$15 (US$7.50/£4) taxi ride away. Behind the pousada walking trails meander through a nearby coconut plantation, and a boardwalk system leads through the mangroves, allowing you to explore on your own as far as the beach.

Rodovia Soure-Pesqueiro Km 3. ☎ **091/3741-2093**. www.marajo.tk. 5 units (showers only). R$130 (US$65/£35) double accommodations only. Packages include meals and some activities: 2-day packages R$400 (US$200/£108) per person; 3-day packages R$550 (US$275/£149). Children 5 and under stay free in parent's room, children 6–12 pay 50%. MC, V. **Amenities:** Restaurant; bar; volleyball court. *In room:* A/C, fridge, no phone.

Pousada o Canto do Francês ⭐   This pleasant pousada offers inexpensive accommodations within walking distance of "downtown" Soure. The rooms are clean and comfortable; just keep your windows closed as there are no screens and the mosquitoes can be bad at night. The pousada rents bicycles (R$10/US$5/£2.70 per day). They're the perfect way to explore the area. It's only a 20-minute ride to the beach of Barra Velha, and within an hour you can ride all the way out to Pesqueiro beach. French owner Thierry can book you on a variety of local excursions. If you've already been on a ranch the trip worth doing is the paddle through the mangroves. They're intriguing, bizarre, and fun to explore.

Sexta Rua, esquina com travessa 8 (the 6th street, corner with the 8th cross street), Soure. ☎ **091/3741-1298** or 091/8822-8746. E-mail: thcarliez@aol.com or reserve through Amazon Star, www.amazonstar.com.br. 9 units (showers only). R$65–R$80 (US$33–US$40/£18–£22). Children 5 and under stay free in parent's room, extra mattress or hammock R$20 (US$10/£5.50). No credit cards at the pousada, only when booking through Amazon Star. **Amenities:** Laundry; bicycle rental. *In room:* A/C, no phone.

15

Brasilia

There are other planned cities in the world—Washington, D.C.; Chandigarh; Canberra—but none has the daring and sheer vision of Brasilia. In the 1950s, a country that had shucked off a failed monarchy, a corrupt republic, and a police-state dictatorship decided to make a clean break from the past by creating a brand-new space for politics.

In place of the pretentious Greek columns and stone facades that other political capitals used to engender awe, designers opted for a style of clean lines and honestly exposed structure, a style in love with technology and progress and the glorious possibilities inherent in the new materials of glass and steel and concrete.

The style they chose was modernism. Brazil was blessed with some of the foremost practitioners in the world. The city plan was done by Lucio Costa. The buildings were designed by Oscar Niemeyer.

That the entire city was completed in just 4 years is thanks to the will of then-president Juscelino Kubitschek. JK (as he is known) was elected in 1956 on the promise that he'd move the capital inland from Rio de Janeiro. Few expected him to succeed.

The site, on Brazil's high interior plateau, was nothing but *cerrado*—short scrubby forest, stretching thousands of miles in every direction. It was nearly 400 miles from the nearest paved road, over 75 miles from the nearest railroad, 120 miles from the nearest airport.

Costa's plan was pure architectural modernism: Transit would be by road and car; activities were to be strictly segregated by area; residential buildings were to be identical in size and shape and appearance. Worker and manager would live in the same neighborhoods, send their children to the same schools. In place of a grid, there were but two great intersecting streets, one straight, one curved. Viewed from on high, the city looked bold and monumental—like an airplane in flight, or an arrow shooting forward into the future.

Groundbreaking began in 1957. Thousands of workers poured in from around the country. By April 21, 1960, there was enough of a city for a grand inauguration. Politicians and civil servants began the long shift inland.

In years since, Brasilia has been a source of controversy. Even as ground was being broken, urbanists were beginning to doubt the rationality of rationalist modern planning. Cities, it was being discovered, were vital, growing entities, whose true complexity could perhaps never be encompassed in a single master plan. Costa's modernist plan with its carefully designated zones for this and that now feels stifling, ill-equipped to address the vital, messy complexity of a living, growing city.

The social aspirations of the architecture also proved illusory—politicians were no less corrupt; rich and poor did not live in harmony. Instead, the rich banished the poor to a periphery beyond the greenbelt.

But if nothing else, it did succeed in shifting Brazil's focus from the coast to its vast interior.

For visitors, the attractions here are purely architectural. Brazil's best designers, architects, and artists were commissioned to create the monuments and buildings and make them beautiful. A visit to Brasilia is a chance to see and judge their success.

1 Brasilia Essentials

ARRIVING

BY PLANE **Varig** (© 061/4003-7000; www.varig.com.br), **TAM** (© 061/4002-5700; www.tam.com.br), and **Gol** (© 0300/115-2121; www.voegol.com.br) have several flights a day to Brasilia from major cities like Rio, São Paulo, and Salvador. Brasilia's airport, **Aeroporto Internacional de Brasilia—Presidente Juscelino Kubitschek** (© 061/3364-9000), is about 10km (6¼ miles) west of the Eixo Monumental. Taxis from the airport to the hotel zones cost about R$35 (US$18/£9.50). Regular city buses aren't worth the trouble. They will take you only to the main bus station, leaving you a painfully long walk (or a taxi ride) from the hotels. *Note:* Brasilia's layout is so striking when viewed from the air that it's worth getting a window seat on the flight in.

BY BUS Long-distance buses arrive at the **Rodoferroviario** (© 061/3363-2281), located at the far western point of the Eixo Monumental. Keep in mind that Brasilia really *is* in the middle of nowhere: 1,000km (620 miles) from Salvador, 930km (577 miles) from Rio, and 870km (539 miles) from São Paulo.

VISITOR INFORMATION

The official government tourist agency **Setur** has information booths at the airport (© 061/3033-9488; daily 7:30am–10:30pm) and in the Conjunto Nacional shopping mall (© 061/3326-7387; daily 10am–10pm). The infoBrasilia site www.info brasilia.com.br has short biographies of the city's founders, and some great photos.

CITY LAYOUT ✪✪✪

What makes Brasilia unique—besides its amazing architecture—is the city's layout. Two main traffic arteries divide the city. **Eixo Monumental** runs dead straight east/west; **Eixo Rodoviario** runs north/south, curving as it goes. Seen from above, the city resembles an airplane or an arrow notched into a partially bent bow. Where these two axes intersect is the city's central bus station, the **Rodoviaria** (not the same as the long-distance bus station; see "Getting Around," below).

The other main distinguishing feature of the city plan is the strict separation of uses by zoning. All of the city's important government buildings are located at the "point" of the arrow—that is, on the eastern end of the Eixo Monumental. All of the city's hotels can be found in two hotel districts near the Rodoviaria. Similarly, the city's offices, shopping malls, theaters, and hospitals are in their individually designated clumps, usually close to where the "bow" meets the "arrow."

Because the plan is so simple, people mistakenly believe it's easy to find their way around. Figuring out how to navigate Brasilia requires delving back into the city structure in a bit more detail.

The Eixo Monumental (the east-west avenue with all the monuments and government buildings) divides the city into two perfectly symmetric wings, the **Asa Norte,** or N (north wing), and **Asa Sul,** or S (south wing). (Always check whether an address is in the south or north wing; otherwise, you could find yourself in the complete opposite part of town.) The various single-use zones (one in each wing) are designated on maps by letter codes. SHS for Setor Hoteleiro Sul (hotels), SBN for Setor Bancario Norte (banks), or SCS for Setor Comercial Sul (commercial business).

Address Decoding: Addresses in Brasilia read like a futuristic code: "SQN 303, Bl. C, 101" or "SCS, Q. 7, Bl. A, loja 43" or "SHN, Q. 5, Bl. C." Here's how to do the decoding. The first three letters are the sector code (for example, SHS for Setor Hoteleiro Sul—hotels). Within each sector, a group of about 10 or so buildings is called a *Quadra*. Sometimes you can tell the buildings of a Quadra belong together either by appearance or spacing. Within each Quadra individual buildings are identified as *Conjunto* (conj.) or *Bloco* (B or Bl.). An individual store or office can be identified by *loja* or *lote*. So an address that reads "SCS Q. 7, Bl. A, loja 43" means that the office is located in the Setor Commercial Sul (the commercial zone in the south wing), Quadra 7 and building A, and the shop number is 43. "SHN, Q. 5, Bl. C" would be Setor Hoteleiro Norte (the hotel zone in the north wing), Quadra 5, building C.

Residential addresses are given a three-letter prefix—SQN (Super Quadra Norte) or SQS (Super Quadra Sul). Within each wing, each Super Quadra is given a three-digit number (for example, 203, 404, or 508). Each Super Quadra then consists of 16 buildings or *Blocos* (Bl. or B) that are identified by a letter. Within each Bloco there are apartment numbers. So SQN 303, Bl. C, 101 refers to Super Quadra 303 in the north wing. Within that Super Quadra you look for building C and apartment 101.

Not that the information above isn't already confusing, but especially when looking for restaurants or bars, it's important to note the following distinction. SCLN (or CLN) means Setor Commercial Local Norte and refers to the *local* block of retail and commerce that is found within each Super Quadra; CLN404 is the 1 block of small shops and restaurants found within the Super Quadra 404 in the north wing. Do not confuse this with SCN, Setor Commercial Norte, which is the large mall sector adjacent to the Eixo Monumental.

GETTING AROUND

The bus hub in the center of town, where the Eixo Monumental and Eixo Rodoviario intersect, is called the **Rodoviaria.** All city buses go through the Rodoviaria. It's where you transfer from an east-west to a north-south bus. Most of the city's malls and hotels are within walking distance of the Rodoviaria.

As long as you're on the Eixo Monumental looking at monuments or shopping, Brasilia is very easy to understand. Stray into the residential sections, and confusion ensues. One of the drawbacks of Costa's mass-production mentality is that every single superquadra in Brasilia looks identical. There are no landmarks whatsoever, so pay *close* attention to the street addresses. Confuse north with south, or get even one digit wrong, and you'll never find your destination. For visitors, it's often wiser to save yourself the hassle and just take taxis.

BY BUS   Buses run from the tip of the south wing to the tip of the north wing, along W1 and W3 on the west side of the Eixo Rodoviario (the bow) and on L1 and L3 on the east side of the Eixo Rodoviario. To travel across town all you need to do is catch a bus traveling to the opposite part of the city: from Asa Sul catch a bus that says ASA NORTE, or vice versa.

On the Eixo Monumental you can catch buses labeled PLANO PILOTO CIRCULAR that just circle up and down this main boulevard. Many buses will go via the Rodoviaria,

Brasilia Accommodations, Dining & Attractions

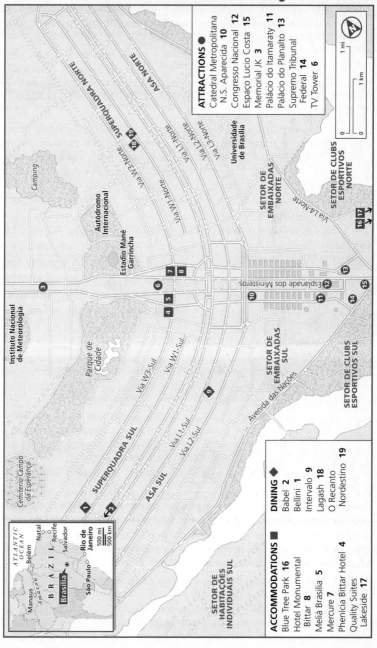

ATTRACTIONS ●
Catedral Metropolitana
N.S. Aparecida **10**
Congresso Nacional **12**
Espaço Lucio Costa **15**
Memorial JK **3**
Palácio do Itamaraty **11**
Palácio do Planalto **13**
Supremo Tribunal
Federal **14**
TV Tower **6**

ACCOMMODATIONS ■
Blue Tree Park **16**
Hotel Monumental
Bittar **8**
Meliá Brasilia **5**
Mercure **7**
Phenicia Bittar Hotel **4**
Quality Suites
Lakeside **17**

DINING ◆
Babel **2**
Bellini **1**
Intervalo **9**
Lagash **18**
O Recanto
Nordestino **19**

which is right in the center of town. These will get you pretty close to the main monuments, hotels, and malls along the Eixo Monumental. Bus tickets are R$1.80 (US90¢/£.50).

BY TAXI Taxis are plentiful and my preferred transportation method, especially if I can't easily figure out where it is I'm going. Just hand the address to the driver and he'll figure it out. From the center of town to the tip of the Asa Sul costs approximately R$25 (US$13/£7). To contact a taxi call **Brasilia** (© **061/3344-1000**) or **Rádio Táxi** (© **061/3325-3030**).

BY CAR Brasilia was designed specifically for cars. One of the big selling points of the original plan was that it made streetlights unnecessary. All intersections were originally designed to be roundabouts (there are now traffic lights, but not that many). The rule for roundabouts: The car that's already in the roundabout (for example, going around on a curve) has the right of way. Traffic is relatively calm in Brasilia; residents are fairly courteous drivers (they stop religiously for pedestrians), but they're fierce if you break the roundabout rule.

FAST FACTS: Brasilia

Banks & Currency Exchange **Air Brazil Turismo,** SHS, Q. 1, Bl. A, loja 33/4—in the National Hotel (© **061/3321-2304**). The **Banco de Brasil** (© **061/3424-3000**) on the second floor of the Conjunto Nacional and in Brasilia Airport (© **061/ 3365-1183**) both have 24-hour ATMs.

Car Rental **Avis** (© **061/3365-2344**); **Localiza** (© **061/3365-1288**); and **Unidas** (© **061/3364-2955**).

Dentist For dental emergencies contact **Instituto Brasiliense de Odontologia,** SCLS406, Bl. A, loja 35, Asa Sul (© **061/3244-5095**).

Embassies *Australia,* SES, Q. 801, conj. K, lote 7 (© **061/3226-3111**; www.brazil. embassy.gov.au). *Canada,* SES Av. das Nações, Q. 803, lote 16 (© **061/3424-5400**; www.canada.org.br). *United States,* SES Av. das Nações, Q. 801, lote 3 (© **061/3312-7000**; www.embaixada-americana.org.br). *Great Britain,* SES Av. das Nações, Q. 801, lote 8 (© **061/3229-2300**; www.uk.org.br).

Emergencies For police and emergencies dial © **190**; for fire brigade and ambulance dial © **193**.

Hospitals All hospitals are in the Hospital section (SHLS and SHLN). **Hospital Santa Lucia,** SHLS, Q. 76, conj. C (© **061/3445-0000**; www.santalucia.com.br).

Internet Access **Cyber Point,** bottom floor of the Conjunto Nacional mall (© **061/3036-14955**; R$6 (US$3/£1.60) per hour. Open Monday through Saturday from 8am to 10pm; Sunday noon to 6pm.

Pharmacies Try **Drogaria Distrital,** Shopping Conjunto Nacional, ground floor (© **061/3328-0405**).

Weather Brasilia is hot. Oddly enough, it is hotter in the winter than in the summer. In the summer (Dec–Mar), cooling rains fall almost daily. In the winter, it can be dry as a bone for several weeks while temperatures climb to 95°F (35°C) or higher.

2 Where to Stay

With few exceptions (see below) the vast majority of hotels in Brasilia are located in one of the two hotel sectors: SHN (Setor Hoteleiro Norte, north hotel section) or the SHS (Setor Hoteleiro Sul, south hotel sector). The areas are within a 10-minute walk of each other, and of the city's two shopping sectors. The only variety is the level of luxury and size of the building.

The majority of hotel guests in Brasilia are politicians and businesspeople. As a result, demand for hotel rooms is huge on weekdays and almost nonexistent on weekends. It pays to schedule your visit to Brasilia on the weekend. (Most monuments are open Sat and Sun and closed Mon). Hotels often offer 2 nights for the price of 1, with dinner and drinks thrown in. For the same reason, low season in Brasilia is during statutory holidays, January and February, and Carnaval. If you must visit Brasilia midweek, book well ahead of time (at least a month).

Hotels are concentrated in their own area with few services around, so amenities tend to be plentiful; many hotels offer fine dining, shopping, salons, car rental, and business centers. Even when not staying at a top luxury hotel, you can utilize the facilities in adjacent hotels.

LAKESIDE

The exception to the hotel sector rule are the hotels situated on the shores of the lovely man-made lake surrounding the city. Staying here means a minimum R$15 (US$7.50/£4) cab ride whenever you want to visit any sites or shopping or restaurants. But then staying at the regular hotel sectors will still involve a cab for restaurants and nightlife. And the lake is lovely. It's a trade-off.

EXPENSIVE

Blue Tree Park ★★★   The Blue Tree Park sits at the edge of the artificial lake created to surround the city. You're a 15-minute taxi ride from the sights and the ministry buildings, which can make it a bit inconvenient if you have meetings to attend, but the pool deck and lake views make it worthwhile if you have leisure time to spend. Rooms feature a sophisticated modern decor, with firm queen-size beds and top-quality linen, plus a good-size work desk with an adjustable/reclinable desk chair. Even better are the amenities—the pool deck overlooking the lake, the tennis courts, spa, sauna, and exercise room. The hotel restaurant, Herbs, features funky "Jetsons" furnishings and innovative cuisine.

Setor de Hoteis e Turismo Norte, Trecho 1, lt. 1-B, bl. C (Lago Norte), Brasilia, 70800-200 DF. ℂ **0800/150-500** or 061/3424-7000. Fax 061/3424-7001. www.bluetree.com.br. 394 units. Standard double R$320 (US$160/£86); superior double R$375 (US$188/£101). Off season rates 40% discount. AE, DC, MC, V. Free parking. **Amenities:** Restaurant; bar; outdoor pool; gym; spa; sauna; concierge; tour desk; car rental; business center; salon; room service; massage; laundry service; nonsmoking rooms. *In room:* A/C, TV, dataport, minibar, fridge, hair dryer, safe.

MODERATE

Quality Suites Lakeside ★★ *Value*   Of Brasilia's two lakeside hotels, the Quality is undoubtedly the better value. Like the Blue Tree, the Quality nestles by the shores of a man-made lake, but the Quality makes even better use of its location, including not just a lakeside pool deck, but also a marina where you can rent boats and jet skis. It also has tennis courts, a soccer field, and a good-quality gym. Rooms are comfortable but not luxurious, featuring a firm queen-size bed plus good-size desk, and clean and functional bathrooms. Unfortunately, none of the rooms offer much in the way of a view. On the other hand, on any given night the Quality comes in at least R$100 (US$50/£27) cheaper than the Blue Tree, a large savings considering the minor differences.

Setor de Hoteis e Turismo Norte, Trecho 1, lt. 1-B, bl. C (Lago Norte), Brasilia, 70800-200 DF. © 061/3035-1100. Fax 0613035-2144. www.atlanticahotels.com.br. 177 units. Standard double R$185 (US$93/£50); superior double R$230 (US$115/£62). Off season 20% discount. AE, DC, MC, V. Free parking. **Amenities:** 2 restaurants; bar; outdoor pool; gym; spa; sauna; marina w/boat and jet ski rental; concierge; tour desk; car rental; business center; salon; room service; massage; laundry service; nonsmoking rooms. *In room:* A/C, TV, dataport, safe, minibar, fridge, hair dryer.

SETOR HOTELEIRO SUL
EXPENSIVE

Mercure Brasilia Eixo ♣♣♣ This 5-year-old hotel offers comfortable and pleasant accommodations in the heart of the hotel sector. The decorations are modern and bright and the spacious rooms feature a king-size bed, kitchen, 29-inch TV, and views of the city. The hotel also offers a swimming pool and sauna. Time your visit during the weekend and the rate drops by more than 50% and includes breakfast. On weekdays, there is an additional charge of R$18 (US$9/£5) per person for breakfast.

SHN, Q. 5, Bl. G, Brasilia, 70710-300 DF. © 061/3424-2000. Fax 061/3424-2001. www.mercure.com.br. 358 units. Superior double R$380 (US$190/£103); Deluxe double R$400 (US$200/£108). Weekends and off season Superior double R$130 (US$65/£35); Deluxe double R$170 (US$85/£46). AE, DC, MC, V. Free parking. **Amenities:** 2 restaurants; bar; pool; sauna; concierge; tour desk; business center; limited room service; laundry service; dry cleaning; nonsmoking rooms. *In room:* A/C, TV, dataport, kitchen, minibar, fridge, hair dryer.

Meliá Brasilia ♣♣ One of the newer luxury hotels in town (built in 2003), the Meliá offers top-quality accommodations and the little extras business travelers need. Rooms are spacious, with king-size beds with good linen, nice lighting, and modern decor. Desk space is more than adequate; amenities are excellent and include the use of a heated outdoor pool and full business center.

SHS, Q. 6, Bl. D, Brasilia, 70316-000 DF. © 061/3218-4700. Fax 061/3218-4705. www.solmelia.com. 270 units. Standard double R$255 (US$128/£69); Superior double R$295 (US$148/£80); deluxe double R$355 (US$178/£96). Weekends and off season Standard double R$145 (US$72/£39); Superior double R$185 (US$92/£50); deluxe double R$225 (US$112/£61). AE, DC, MC, V. Free parking. **Amenities:** Restaurant; bar; outdoor pool; gym; sauna; concierge; tour desk; car rental; business center; salon; room service; laundry service; dry cleaning; nonsmoking rooms. *In room:* A/C, TV, dataport, minibar, fridge, hair dryer, safe.

MODERATE

Hotel Phenicia Bittar ♣ One of the smaller hotels in the Setor Sul, the Phenicia recently renovated its floors and rooms as part of a transformation into a boutique hotel. The renovated rooms have either lovely hardwood floors or new carpets, double or twin beds, light-wood furniture, a sitting area, and brand-new beds. The renovated suites are particularly nice. They feature a living room with a dining table, large desk, and a spacious bedroom with a second desk, furnished with stylish furniture. A third bed can easily be added for those with children.

SHS, Q. 5, Bl. J, Brasilia, DF 70322-810. © 0800/707-5858 or 061/3321-4342. Fax 061/3225-1406. www.hoteisbittar.com.br. 130 units (showers only). R$165 (US$83/£45) double. Discount 30% on weekends and low season. AE, DC, MC, V. Free parking. **Amenities:** Restaurant; tour desk; car rental; business center; salon; room service; laundry service. *In room:* A/C, TV, dataport, minibar, fridge.

SETOR HOTELEIRO NORTE

Hotel Monumental Bittar ♣ The low-rise Monumental looks unassuming but it's actually a pleasant, moderately priced hotel. A recent spruce-up by the Bittar chain has meant new bedding and drapery. Rooms have either wall-to-wall carpeting or wood floors. The latter is far more comfortable. Rooms with double beds are better than those with two twins; they have larger desks and closets and are larger overall. Avoid the east-facing ones, which face the main street. A few rooms are adapted for travelers with disabilities.

SHN, Q. 3, Bl. B, Brasilia, 70710-300 DF. ℭ 0800/707-5858 or 061/3328-4144. www.hoteisbittar.com.br. 111 units (showers only). R$140 (US$70/£38) double. R$30 (US$15/£8) extra person. R$100 (US$50/£27) on weekends and low season. AE, DC, MC, V. Free parking. **Amenities:** Restaurant; bar; tour desk; car rental; business center; salon; room service; laundry service; dry cleaning; nonsmoking rooms. *In room:* A/C, TV, dataport, minibar, fridge.

3 Where to Dine

Brasilia has some outstanding restaurants; politicians and businesspeople prefer to eat well. The restaurants at the mall food courts can be excellent for lunches and light meals. In the **Park Shopping, Marietta N.Y. Coffee** (ℭ 061/3233-5460; www.marietta. com.br) has excellent sandwiches as well as wraps, salads, good coffees, baguettes, croissants, and pasta.

For almost anything else, you're looking at a bus or taxi ride. The **Porcão** chain has another of its incredible all-you-can-stuff-yourself-with steakhouses in Brasilia, this one in a privileged position on the lakeshore by the Pres. Costa e Silva bridge. **Porcão** (SCS Sul, Tr. 2, CJ 35; ℭ 061/3223-2002; www.porcao.com.br). Open daily 11:30am to midnight.

The city's fine-dining establishments are scattered throughout the residential wings, the Asa Sul (south wing) and Asa Norte (north wing), or off in the Club Sectors. At night they can be difficult to find; taking a taxi is recommended.

ASA SUL

Babel ℛ ITALIAN   Fusion has finally found its way to Brasilia. Babel mixes ingredients from eastern and western schools of cooking to intriguing and delicious effect. Think duck filet with shitake couscous, or lightly breaded shrimp in tamarind sauce with red-pepper risotto. Wine list from Argentina, Australia, and California.

SCLS 215, Bl. A, loja 37. ℭ 061/3345-6042. Main courses R$25–R$60 (US$13–US$30/£7–£16). MC, V. Mon–Sat 7–11:30pm. Bus: W3 Asa Sul.

Belini ℛ ITALIAN *Finds*   This gourmet complex encompasses a deli, food store, restaurant, cafe, and cooking school. It's a great place to grab an espresso and some sweets, or buy some fresh bread and cold cuts for an impromptu picnic. The casual outdoor patio serves sandwiches (the pastrami, mortadella, and brie is good) for R$6 to R$10 (US$3–US$5/£1.50–£2.50). For a more formal occasion, the restaurant upstairs serves fine Italian dishes such as lamb filet with mint sauce and risotto, or large prawns in an apple-and-ginger sauce. The restaurant also serves breakfast and afternoon tea.

SCLS 113, Bl. D, loja 36. ℭ 061/3345-0777. www.belini-gastronomia.com.br. Main courses R$9–R$40 (US$4.50–US$20/£2.50–£11). MC, V. Restaurant Tues–Sat noon–3pm and 7pm–midnight; Sun noon–4pm. Bakery daily 7am–11pm. Bus: W3 Asa Sul.

Intervalo ℛ BRAZILIAN   Customers return week after week to savor the specials at this small, elegant restaurant. On Sunday the star attraction is *lombo Vila Rica,* a hearty dish of grilled pork tenderloin, accompanied by the traditional *feijão tropeiro* bean dish from Minas Gerais. The Tuesday special is *Assado d'el Rey,* a delicious roast beef marinated in red wine and garlic for up to 40 hours before it is slowly cooked. The menu also offers a range of other choices, such as grilled fish with almonds and butter sauce or trout in a green-grape sauce. Whatever the day of the week, consider the special; it never disappoints!

SCLS 404, Bl. A, loja 27. © **061/3223-5274**. R$21–R$45 (US$11–US$23/£6–£12). AE, V. Mon–Sat 11:30am–midnight; Sun 11:30am–5pm. Bus: L1 Asa Sul.

ASA NORTE

Lagash ★★ MIDDLE EASTERN   The best Middle Eastern food in Brasilia. (Okay, there's not a lot of competition, but the quality here is excellent.) Appetizers include baba ghanouj, made with eggplant and tahini; hummus; and roasted *merguez* (lamb sausage). The most popular entree is the Moroccan lamb—tender pieces of boneless lamb cooked with nuts, scallions, onions, and rice. The wine list is heavy on the Italian and French reds to accompany the hearty and spicy dishes.

SCLN 308, Bl. B, loja 11. © **061/3273-0098**. R$20–R$60 (US$10–US$30/£5.40–£16). AE, DC, MC, V. Mon–Sat noon–4pm and 7pm–midnight; Sun noon–6pm. Bus: W3 Asa Norte.

O Recanto Nordestino BRAZILIAN   Recanto Nordestino serves up a wide variety of traditional, hearty, simple Nordestino dishes. The best known is the *carne de sol Nordeste* (a kind of sun-dried meat) served with rice, beans, cassava root, and vinaigrette. Other dishes include *linguiça* sausage (made with pork, chicken, or lamb) and roasted goat. A meeting place for homesick Nordestinos, the restaurant gets quite lively on the weekends.

SCLN 308, Bl. D, loja 29. © **061/3340-8988**. Main courses R$12–R$32 (US$6–US$16/£3.25-£8.50). No credit cards. Mon–Sat 8am–midnight; Sun 8am–5pm. Bus: W3 Asa Norte.

ELSEWHERE

Alice ★★★ FRENCH   Alice serves her meals in a lovely large room bedecked with mirrors with a view out into the garden of this private home in Brasilia's swank mansion district. Chefs in the open kitchen prepare regional French cuisine, with dishes such as boar with red-wine sauce, or free-range chicken with spices and couscous. The wine list features some fine French vintages, as well as the usual suspects from Argentina and Chile. Note that there is no sign outside. In the Setor de Habitacoes Individuas Norte (individual house sector) where Alice lives, signs aren't allowed; make sure your taxi driver knows where he is going before you set out.

SHI Norte Ql.11, Cj. 9 casa 17 (lago norte). © **061/3368-1099**. Reservations required. Main courses R$25–R$60 (US$13–US$30/£6.75–£16). AE, DC, MC, V. Fri–Sat 8pm–2am. No public transit.

Patu Anu ★★★ BRAZILIAN   The ultimate Brazilian dining experience. Located opposite the presidential palace (Palácio de Alvarado) but on the far side of the lake, the restaurant features an outdoor deck with stunning views and a sumptuous indoor dining room. Chefs here take traditional local ingredients and traditional Brazilian recipes, and tweak them slightly to bring them up to the level of haute cuisine. Appetizers include delicacies such as skewers of capybara, boar, lamb, and baby buffalo with a spicy chocolate sauce, while mains include fresh sole roasted in banana leaf with mango chutney and coconut milk rice, or prawns flambéed in ginger liqueur with fresh fruit risotto. Wines are perhaps the only disappointment. Patu Anu's wine list, while of respectable length and quality, is noticeably lacking in Brazilian vintages. Still, a dining experience not to be found anywhere else on earth.

Setor de Mansões de Lago Norte, trecho 12, cj.1 casa 7 (Lago Sul). © **061/3369-2788**. www.patuanu.com.br. Reservations required. Main courses R$38–R$65 (US$19–US$33/£10–£18). DC, MC, V. Tues–Sat 8:30pm–2am; Sun 1:30–6pm. No public transit.

4 Exploring Brasilia

A day is enough to see all that Brasilia has to offer. The heat of Brasilia's sun makes it a good idea to get an early start. The eastern half of the Eixo Monumental is where you'll find some of the best modern architecture in the world. Time your visit to the TV Tower around sunset. The ride is free, and from the 72m-high (240-ft.) platform you have a 360-degree view of the city.

Some other advice: If it's sunny, bring a hat. There is little shade, and it gets *hot;* also bring a water bottle, because you won't find as many street vendors as elsewhere in Brazil. If you plan on visiting the cathedral, any monuments, or government buildings, do not wear shorts or a tank top. And perhaps most importantly, *be careful crossing the Eixo Monumental.* Cars go fast here and you must cross a lot of lanes.

THE TOP ATTRACTIONS

Catedral Metropolitana Nossa Senhora Aparecida ★★★   The cathedral is surprisingly small from the outside, but once you descend through the walkway, you emerge in the brightest and most spacious church you have ever seen. The floors and walls are made of white marble, with an expanse of glass overhead. The altar is surprisingly sparse, all white marble decorated with a plain image of Christ on the cross. Sculptor Alfredo Ceschiatti designed the statues of the four apostles in front of the cathedral, as well as the angels suspended from the ceiling inside. You'll spot his name on other sculptures around Brasilia, such as the figure of Justice in front of the Federal Supreme Court.

Esplanada dos Ministerios. © **061/3224-4073.** Daily 8am–5pm. Mass Mon–Fri 6:15pm; Tues–Fri 12:15pm; Sat 5pm; Sun 8:30am, 10:30am, and 6pm. No touring of the cathedral during Mass. No shorts or Bermudas. Bus: Rodoviaria (short walk to the cathedral) or the Plano Piloto Circular.

Congresso Nacional   One of Brasilia's best-known images is the shot of the two towers on the Planalto Central, flanked by the two "bowls," one faceup and one facedown. It is quite beautiful in an abstract way, contrasting with the red dirt and blue sky. The inside is open to the public for English-language tours (including a visit to the Chamber of Deputies when in session), though it's really of only moderate interest to non-Brazilians. No shorts or tank tops allowed. If you don't take the tour, you're only allowed in the museum and the lobby.

Esplanada dos Ministerios. © **061/3216-1771.** Free admission. Mon–Fri 9am–5pm. Free tours leave Mon–Fri at 9:30am, 10:30am, 11:30am, 2:15pm, 3pm, and 3:45pm. Bus: Plano Piloto Circular.

Espaço Lucio Costa ★   Brasilia owes its shape and design to urban planner and architect Lucio Costa. This space, sunken beneath the surface of the square, contains a full-scale model of the city. Shy of a visit to the TV Tower it's the best way to get a bird's-eye view of his plan. Disappointingly, the Espaço has little information on Costa's life and career. On the back wall there are some photos of the city's constructions and, best of all, reproduced and enlarged copies of Costa's original submission, the one that won him the competition.

Praça des Tres Poderes. © **061/3325-6163.** Free admission. Tues–Sun 9am–6pm. Bus: Plano Piloto Circular.

Memorial dos Povos Indigenas   Architect Oscar Niemeyer modeled the Monument to the Indigenous Peoples on the houses of the Bororó Indians. Just before the memorial was completed it was redesignated as an arts museum, until the uproar caused it to be re-redesignated. So far, however, it seems underutilized. Varying exhibits highlight the art and daily life of Brazilian Indians. Headdresses of colorful feathers, pottery, baskets, hammocks, nets, spears, and paddles are on display. Unfortunately, there isn't any signage at all to indicate the origin or usage of the items. Museum staff come in varying degrees of helpfulness.

Praça do Buriti, Eixo Monumental Oeste. ✆ 061/3226-5206. Free admission. Tues–Fri 9am–5pm; Sat–Sun 10am–5pm. Bus: Plano Piloto Circular.

Memorial JK ✮ This remarkably shaped monument was built in 1980 by Niemeyer to honor the founder of Brasilia, Juscelino Kubitschek. Inside on the second floor, the former president's remains rest beneath a skylight in a granite tomb, his only epitaph an inscription on the coffin reading O FUNDADOR. Aside from this slightly spooky scene, the memorial contains a lot of JK's junk that no one could ever care about (JK's ribbons and medals, JK's suits and tie clips) and, upstairs, some fairly interesting stuff about Brasilia, including photographs of the city under construction and copies of the designs that didn't get chosen.

Eixo Monumental Oeste. ✆ 061/3225-9451. Admission R$4 (US$2/£1). Tues–Sun 9am–6pm. Bus: Plano Piloto Circular.

Palácio do Itamaraty ✮✮✮ One of the most beautiful modernist structures ever created (designed by Niemeyer with landscaping by Burle Marx and detailing by Milton Ramos), the Palácio do Itamaraty now serves as a ceremonial reception hall for the Department of Foreign Affairs. The interior is a match for the outside, so it's worth taking the tour. The ultra-modern structure—mostly open space inside—is decorated with rich antique furnishings of Persian carpets, hand-carved jacaranda-wood furniture, and 18th- and 19th-century paintings. Somehow it really works. Guided tours only. Hours are limited.

Esplanada dos Ministerios. ✆ 061/3411-8051. Free admission. Mon–Fri 2–4:30pm; Sat–Sun 10am–3:30pm. Guided tours only, call to confirm; no shorts or tank tops allowed. Bus: Plano Piloto Circular.

TV Tower ✮✮✮ (Value) The best view in town is free! Just take the elevator up to the 72m-high (240-ft.) lookout, and Brasilia is laid out at your feet. You'll get the best perspective of the Eixo Monumental with the ministry buildings lining the boulevard like dominos waiting to be knocked over. If you get one of those fiery red Brasilia sunsets, it's worth heading back to the tower to take in the view. You can skip the gem museum without qualms.

Eixo Monumental (close to the bus station and malls). ✆ 061/3321-7944. Free admission. Tues–Sun 9am–6pm; Mon 2–6pm. Bus: Rodoviaria.

ARCHITECTURAL HIGHLIGHTS

The important buildings in Brasilia were all designed by architect **Oscar Niemeyer.** The strength of this Brazilian über-modernist has always been with form; his structures are often brilliant. His weakness has always been detailing, materials, and landscaping. These bore Niemeyer, who prefers to work purely with bare concrete. Left to his own devices, Niemeyer creates austere, even boring, collections of pure geometry, like the Monument to Latin America in São Paulo. Fortunately, in Brasilia Niemeyer was teamed up with Brazil's best landscape designer, **Roberto Burle Marx,** and detailing- and materials-focused architects like **Milton Ramos,** and talented sculptors and artists like **Alfredo Ceschiatti.** Every building also had to conform to the overall plan of **Lucio Costa.** The result is a collection of buildings that has rightly been called the highest expression of architectural modernism on earth. Niemeyer's work is scattered far and wide throughout the city, but the best of the best is on the eastern portion of the Eixo Monumental, from the Rodoviario to the Praça dos Tres Poderes on the far side of the Congresso Nacional.

Several of these buildings are covered under "The Top Attractions" section above: the **Congresso Nacional,** the **Catedral Metropolitana,** and the **Palácio do Itamaraty.** Also worth mentioning is a structure that no one would ever put in a top attraction, the standard ministry buildings, 17 of which flank the **Esplanada dos Ministerios** like big glass-and-concrete dominos. The idea with these boring, repetitive buildings is that they be boring and repetitive. Costa and Niemeyer had notions that this rigidly enforced equality would cut back on bureaucratic infighting (as if) and, more importantly, provide an urban fabric against which the monumental buildings would stand out. That, at least, succeeded brilliantly.

Behind the Congresso Nacional stands the wide, austere Praça dos Tres Poderes (see "Outdoor Plazas," below). On the north side of the square, the **Palácio do Planalto** is well worth a look. Visitors aren't allowed into this building, but can watch the not-very-exciting changing of the guard every 2 hours. Similar in form is the **Supremo Tribunal Federal,** the office of the Brazilian Supreme Court located on the other side of Three Power Plaza. The tribunal is open for guided visits, but only on weekends and holidays between 10am and 2pm.

PLAZAS & PARKS

OUTDOOR PLAZAS   Behind the Congress building, the **Praça dos Tres Poderes (Plaza of the Three Powers)** is immediately identifiable by the huge Brazilian flag flapping 99m (330 ft.) above the hot, wide-open space below. The plaza is named for the three branches of government that surround it: the legislative branch in the **Congresso Nacional** (see "The Top Attractions," above), the judiciary in the **Supremo Tribunal Federal,** and the executive in the presidential **Palácio do Planalto** (see "Architectural Highlights," above). The praça itself is unrelieved Niemeyer, a vast expanse of pure white stone, with nowhere to hide from the blazing Brasilia sun. Don't visit on a hot afternoon, or you'll fry. Near the front of the square there's a long white marble box about the size and shape of a truck semi-trailer, but cantilevered one floor off the ground. This is the **Museu de Cidade** (Tues–Sun 9am–6pm; free admission). Inside it's a bare marble room with eight inscriptions on each long wall telling the story of Brasilia. No maps, no photos, just words. Next to it, below the square, is the **Espaço Lucio Costa** (see "The Top Attractions," above). Toward the southern side of the square there's the awkward-looking **Panteão da Patria Tancredo Neves** (Tues–Sun 9am–6pm; free admission). The building's two interlocking rhomboids are supposed to suggest a dove, but it's hard to see. Inside the Homeland Pantheon it's dark as the tomb, with lighting only on a mural depicting the life and gruesome death of 18th-century rebel Tiradentes, and a book with brass pages, each inscribed with the name of a Congressionally approved Brazilian hero. It's short reading so far—just four pages.

PARKS & GARDENS   Brasilia's prime leisure space, the **Parque da Cidade,** was landscaped by Burle Marx. The park is mostly grass fields intersected by jogging and cycle paths (best inline-skating terrain I have ever seen!). You'll also find playgrounds and a small fair.

ORGANIZED TOURS

AIR TOURS For a bird's-eye view of Brasilia, take a 10-minute helicopter tour. Helicopters take off from next to the TV Tower Tuesday through Sunday from 9am to 7pm and fly over the Eixo Monumental at an altitude of 135m (450 ft.). Contact **Esat Taxi Aéreo** (© **061/3323-8777;** www.esataerotaxi.com.br). Cost is R$480 (US$240/£130) for four people.

BOAT TOURS ⚓ Tours take place on the lake, Lago Paranoá. Leaving from ASBAC (yacht club in the Asa Sul, close to Setor de Embaixadas Sul), the 2-hour tour passes the Palácio da Alvorada, the official residence of the Brazilian president (not open to the public) and continues around the lake. It's a great way to see the city from the water. Contact **Tôa Tôa** (© **061/9982-1161).** Departures are at 10am and 2pm and the cost is R$20 (US$10/£5.40) per person.

SPECIALTY TOURS To take a specialized half-day **architectural tour** of the city, contact **Prestheza Turismo,** Patio Brasil Shopping, Sala 917 (© **061/3226-6224;** www.prestheza.com.br). The company also offers a variety of other tours, such as a visit to the Vale do Amanhecer (Valley of the Dawn) spiritual community or to one of the national or regional parks in the area. Half-day tours start at R$80 (US$40/£22) per person.

5 Shopping

Shopping in Brasilia means malls. The granddaddy of Brasilia malls is the **Conjunto Nacional** (see below). Other shopping malls close to the hotel districts include the **Patio Brasil** (SCS Q.7 Bl. A; © **061/2107-7400;** www.patiobrasil.com.br), located in the South Wing not far from the Meliá hotel. Near the hotel sector in the north wing, the **Brasilia Shopping** (SCN, Q.5, lote 2; © **061/3328-5259;** www.brasilia shopping.com.br) has a number of movie theaters and an excellent food court, as well as a very popular bar, **Frei Caneca Draft** (see "Brasilia After Dark," below). Malls are open Monday through Saturday 10am to 10pm, Sunday 2 to 8pm.

For non-mall shopping there is the **Feira de Artesanato da Torre de Televisão,** a large crafts fair that takes place every weekend underneath the TV Tower on Eixo Monumental, with crafts from the Northeast. It's open from 8am to 6pm.

Conjunto Nacional Built in 1971, the Conjunto Nacional was the first mall in Brasilia. Stores include two large drugstores, the Pão de Açúcar supermarket, and a post office (Mon–Sat 9am–10pm). Philip Martin, a Brazilian chain of fun casual clothes, has excellent sales. The large Siciliano bookstore has a CD department, English books, and a good variety of English magazines. Asa Norte, SCN. © **061/3316-9733.** www.cnbshopping.com.br. Bus: Rodoviaria.

6 Brasilia After Dark

There's a fair bit of stuff to do in Brasilia after dark, but there is no "scene" as such. Bars and cafes have sprung up in discrete, widely separate spots throughout the small commercial zones in the two residential wings. Best to decide what you're in the mood for, then choose your spot and stick with it.

THE PERFORMING ARTS

Teatro Nacional Most classical concerts and dance and theater performances in Brasilia take place in one of the three concert halls here. For program information, phone the events calendar hot line at ℂ **061/3325-6239.** The box office (in the main lobby area) is open daily noon to 8pm. Setor Cultural Norte. ℂ **061/325-6240.**

BARS & DANCE CLUBS

Armazém do Brás *Finds*   The Armazém resembles a São Paulo–style Italian cantina. The buffet (available Sat–Wed only) allows you to load up on olives, sun-dried tomatoes, marinated eggplant, and other goodies (R$36/US$18/£10 per kilo), great for sharing and nibbling with a glass of wine or imported beer. Hours are Monday through Saturday 9am to 2am, Sunday and holidays 6pm to 2am. CLN 107, Bl. B, loja 49, Asa Norte. ℂ **061/3340-7317.** R$9–R$27 (US$4.50–US$11/£2.40–£7). No credit cards.

Bar Brasilia   In the mood for a nice cold beer and a lively crowd? Head to Bar Brasilia. Located in the South wing, the bar is inspired by the classic Rio botequim. The lovely antique wooden furnishings, such as the bar shelves that were rescued from an old pharmacy, predate most of the buildings that surround this bar. Make sure you try some of the *kibes* (savory snack made with ground beef) or the *bolinhos de bacalhau* (deep-fried codfish dumplings). Open daily 4pm to 2am. 506 S, Bl. A, loja 15. ℂ **061/ 3443-4323.**

Frei Caneca Draft   A popular hangout for the late-20- to 40-year-old crowd, the club has a large covered patio as well as a dance floor and bar. DJ'ed music varies from big band to forró to MPB *(música popular brasileira).* Cover charges are steep, but early birds can get away with just a minimum consumption of R$15 (US$7.50/£4) per person before 8pm Monday to Wednesday. Brasilia Shopping, SCN. ℂ **061/3327-9467.** Cover R$15 (US$7.50/£4) women, R$22 (US$11/£6) men.

Gate's Pub   It looks like a British pub on the outside, but that's where the authenticity stops: The beer is cold, the crowd is beautiful, and the music hip. On Thursday night this is the place to come for forró. Open Monday 8pm to 2am, Tuesday through Sunday 9pm to 4am. SCLS 403, Bl. B, loja 34. ℂ **061/3225-4576.** www.gatespub.com.br. Cover R$5–R$15 (US$2.50–US$7.50/£1.30–£4).

Othello Piano Bar   For a mellow night out away from the teenage crowds, check out Othello Piano Bar. The owner is a transplanted Carioca who can't forget his favorite music from the Rio botequins. Come here for MPB, samba, or *choro.* Open Tuesday through Sunday 6pm to 2am. CLN 107, Bl. D, loja 25. ℂ **061/3272-2066.** Cover R$5–R$15 (US$2.50–US$7.50/£1.30–£4).

16

Iguaçu & the Falls

There are but three great waterfalls in the world, and curiously they seem to all fall on borders: Niagara Falls, on the border between the United States and Canada; Victoria Falls, between Zimbabwe and Zambia; and Iguaçu Falls, which form the border between Brazil and Argentina.

I've seen them all. Iguaçu is without doubt the most beautiful of the three. Niagara is impressive, but marred by 2 centuries of industry and kitsch. Victoria Falls in Africa is higher, but also narrower, and the mist thrown up by all that water funneling into such a tiny gorge greatly obscures the view.

In Iguaçu, the water pours down over not one but some 275 different cataracts, spread over a precipice some 5km (3 miles) wide and 81m (266 ft.) high.

The fine mist tossed up by all that falling water precipitates down and creates a pocket microclimate of lush rainforest, filled with tropical birds and an abundant population of glorious tropical butterflies.

Iguaçu has been attracting visitors since the first European explorer stumbled across the area in the 1540s. In the 1930s more than 1 million acres on the Brazilian side was made into a national park, and in 1985 the falls were designated an UNESCO World Heritage Site.

Iguaçu Falls never quite achieved the same iconic status as Niagara. The Iguaçu Falls did get one good breakout role, though, when they were cast almost as a supporting actor in the Robert DeNiro film, *The Mission* (worth renting for its story of the expulsion of the Jesuits, in addition to the great film footage of the falls).

Debate is endless as to whether the view from the Brazilian or Argentine side is better. You should really visit both sides to see for yourself.

Aside from the falls, there's not a lot to see in Iguaçu. Beyond the immediate zone of the falls, the national park is closed to visitors. The zodiac trips upstream toward the falls are highly recommended. There are also rubber raft trips through the rapids downstream, as well as an extraordinary 50m (164-ft.) rappel from the top of the gorge all the way down to the edge of the Iguaçu River.

The falls are remote enough that a 1-day trip is, well, insane. With a Brazilian air pass, Iguaçu makes a perfect 2-day stopover. Those with limited time, or money, should consider whether the falls—glorious though they certainly are—are worth the 1,000km (620-mile) trip from Rio or São Paulo.

1 Iguaçu Essentials

BY PLANE Both **Gol** (© 0300/115-2121) and **TAM** (© 045/4002-5700) have daily flights, connecting through São Paulo or Curitiba. Book ahead in peak season; flights fill up quickly.

Foz do Iguaçu

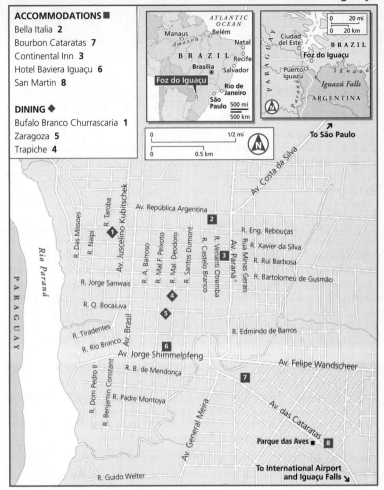

ACCOMMODATIONS ■

Bella Italia **2**

Bourbon Cataratas **7**

Continental Inn **3**

Hotel Baviera Iguaçu **6**

San Martin **8**

DINING ◆

Bufalo Branco Churrascaria **1**

Zaragoza **5**

Trapiche **4**

The **Aeroporto Internacional Foz do Iguaçu** (© **045/3521-4200**) is on BR-469 halfway between downtown and the national park. The 13km (8-mile) taxi ride to downtown Iguaçu costs about R$30 to R$40 (US$15–US$20/£8–£11). Many of Iguaçu's hotels are on the highway into town, making taxi fare considerably less. A bus connecting the airport to downtown takes 45 minutes; the fare is R$1.50 (US75¢/£.40). The airport's tourist information desk is open daily from 9am to midnight.

BY BUS   Long-distance buses arrive at the **Terminal Rodoviario,** Av. Costa e Silva s/n (© **045/3522-3633**). The station is 4km (2½ miles) northeast of downtown. The bus station has a tourist information office, open daily from 9am to 6pm. For buses to Rio de Janeiro, São Paulo, Curitiba, or Florianópolis, as well as long-distance buses to Argentina (Buenos Aires) and Paraguay (Asunción), contact **Pluma** bus company (✆ **045/3522-2515**). For buses across to Puerto Iguazú, see "Getting Around," below.

BY CAR   Foz do Iguaçu is 1,200km (744 miles) from São Paulo and 620km (384 miles) from Curitiba on BR-277.

VISITOR INFORMATION

Iguaçu's tourist bureau employs excellent English-speaking attendants who have up-to-date and accurate information at their fingertips. They also give out free maps of the city. The main **tourist information center** is at Praça Getulio Vargas (Av. JK and Rua Rio Branco) (✆ **045/3521-1455;** www.fozdoiguacu.pr.gov.br; Mon–Fri 9am–5pm). There are also tourist information booths at the airport and bus station (see "By Plane" or "By Bus," above), or you can call the Iguaçu tourist information service **Teletur** (✆ **0800/ 451-516** toll-free within Brazil). The service operates daily from 7am to 11pm.

CITY LAYOUT

A small, modern city of 250,000 people, Foz do Iguaçu (normally just called Iguaçu) is effectively located on a peninsula. West of the city is the **Rio Paraná** and, beyond that, Paraguay. North of the city lies **Lago de Itaipu,** a great man-made lake created by putting up the world's largest hydroelectric dam across the Rio Paraná; the dam is well worth a visit. To the south of the city lies **Rio Iguaçu** and, beyond it, Argentina. The **falls** are upstream on this river, a 28km (18-mile) drive southeast from downtown. The city's downtown is small and easy to navigate, but offers few attractions. Just north of downtown, **BR-277** comes in from Curitiba and São Paulo and crosses the **Ponte da Amizade (Friendship Bridge)** into Paraguay. At the southern end of downtown, **Avenida das Cataratas** (BR-469) tracks southeast toward **Iguaçu National Park** and the falls. There are quite a few good hotels, some other attractions, and restaurants along this road. About 7km (4¼ miles) from downtown, there's a turnoff for the **Ponte Tancredo Neves,** which crosses into Argentina. Public buses take this route, and border formalities are minimal. The road to the falls, now called **Rodovia das Cataratas,** continues past the airport turnoff until, at 17km (11 miles) from the city, it reaches the gates of **Iguaçu National Park.**

GETTING AROUND

BY BUS   City buses begin and end their routes at the **Terminal Urbana** on Avenida Juscelino Kubitschek (also called Av. J.K.–pronounced "zhota ka") at the corner of Avenida República Argentina. Buses for the airport and the falls run along Avenida JK and Avenida Jorge Schimmelpfeng to the Avenida das Cataratas. Falls buses are marked CATARATAS (fare is R$2/US$1/£.50) or PARQUE NACIONAL (fare is R$1/US50¢/£.25). They run every 20 minutes until 6:40pm. The trip to the park gate and visitor center takes 45 minutes. From the park gate, a free shuttle (departing every 20 min.) will take you the rest of the way to the falls. Getting to the Argentine Falls by bus is cheap but time-consuming. The one-way trip takes about 90 minutes (see the review for Parque Nacional Iguazú [Argentine Falls] below for details).

BY TAXI   There are taxi *pontos* (stands) throughout the city or you can flag a taxi on the street. A trip across town costs around R$15 (US$7.50/£4). A trip from the city center to a hotel on the Avenida das Cataratas costs between R$20 (US$10/£5.40) and R$35 (US$18/£9.50). A taxi from the center of town to the park gates costs R$40 (US$20/£11). Hiring a taxi to take you to the Argentine Falls and wait while you see

them then bring you back costs about R$180 (US$90/£49). **Coopertaxi** (© **0800/
524-6464** or 045/3529-8821) has cabs available 24/7.

BY CAR   Renting a small car to travel to the Argentine Falls is a reasonable option.
The cost is about the same as a tour, and rental and border hassles are minimal. You'll
need a credit card, a valid state or provincial driver's license, and some other piece of
ID (for example, a passport). Prices at **Avis** (© **045/3529-6160**) and **Yes** (© **045/
3522-2956**) are similar: about R$110 (US$55/£30) for a subcompact with air-condi-
tioning for a 24-hour day with unlimited mileage, plus R$15 to R$30 (US$7.50–
US$15/£4–£8) for optional insurance. Gasoline is extra. Expect to spend about R$25
(US$13/£6.75) for a trip to the Argentine Falls. Both companies provide free hotel
pickup and drop-off. With Avis, airport drop-off is free; Yes charges R$10
(US$5/£2.70).

FAST FACTS: Foz do Iguaçu

Banks & Currency Exchange **Banco do Brasil,** Av. Brasil 1377 (© **045/3521-
2525**), has a 24-hour ATM. The HSBC branch is nearby at Av. Brasil 1151 (© **45/
3523-1166**).

Consulates Paraguay, Rua Bartolomeu de Gusmão 738 (© **045/3523-2898**);
Argentina, Travessa Vice-consul E. R Bianchi 26 (© **045/3574-2969**).

Dentist **Clinica Odontologica** (© 045/3523-5965). On call 24 hr.

Hospital **Hospital Internacional,** Av. Brasil 1637 (© 045/3523-1404).

Pharmacies **Farmarede,** Av. Brasil 46, Centro (© **045/3572-1363**), is open 24
hours and will deliver to your hotel.

Weather In the summer Iguaçu is warm and muggy, but in the winter there's a
very un-Brazilian chill. From April to September daytime temperatures drop to
50°F to 68°F (10°C–20°C). The falls are best seen in the summer from January to
March when there is plenty of water.

---

2 Where to Stay in Iguaçu

Iguaçu has a wide variety of accommodations, with the more affordable options in
town and the luxury accommodations found on the Avenida das Cataratas. High season is from December to February and in July; outside of these months you can usually negotiate a discount of 20% to 40%.

CENTRO
EXPENSIVE
Continental Inn *Finds*   Located in town, the Continental Inn is a real gem. The
comfortable regular rooms feature firm twin or double beds, modern Art Deco–ish
decor, good desk space, and showers with lots of high-pressure hot water. The suites are
outstanding; regular suites feature a separate sitting area, firm queen-size bed, and a large
round bathtub. The top-quality master suites have hardwood floors, king-size bed, fancy
linens, a large desk, separate sitting area, walk-in closet, and a bathroom with Jacuzzi tub
and a view over the city. Rooms for travelers with disabilities are available. *Note:* Make
sure when reserving your room that you insist on staying at the Continental Inn. The

hotel has another property, Recanto Park, which is not as nice and is often used in case the Continental is overbooked, even when the reservation was originally confirmed for the Continental Inn.

Av. Paranà 1089, Foz do Iguaçu, 85852-000 PR. ℂ 0800/707-2400 or 045/3523-5000. www.continentalinn.com.br. 113 units (102 with showers only). R$200 (US$100/£54) double; R$250–R$285 (US$125–US$143/£68–£77) suite; R$350 (US$175/£95) master suite. In low season 20% discount. Children under 5 stay free in parent's room, 5 and over R$30 (US$15/£8) extra. AE, DC, MC, V. Free parking. **Amenities:** Restaurant; large pool; exercise room; sauna; game room w/video arcade; business center; room service; laundry. *In room:* A/C, TV, dataport, minibar, fridge, hair dryer, safe.

MODERATE

Bella Italia *(Value)*   Rooms at this mid-priced hotel are pleasant enough—queen-size bed, writing desk, tub/shower combo in the bathroom, and a small balcony with a downtown view—but what makes the *Italia* so *bella* in terms of value is its packages. The Iguassu Passport package costs R$240 (US$120/£65) per person (based on double occupancy), and includes 1 night's accommodations with breakfast, plus the Macuco Safari boat ride, entrance to the Bird Park, lunch at Porto Canoas restaurant by the falls, and dinner at the hotel. Park entrance fees and transfers are not included. Still, given that the cost of just the Macuco Safari and Bird Park entrance is R$170 (US$85/£46), that works out to R$70 (US$35/£19) per person (or R$140/US$70/£38 per couple) for a good-quality room plus breakfast, lunch, and dinner. Other packages include canyoning and rafting activities (see www.iguazufallshotels.com/iguazufallshotels/passaportes for details). The only real drawback to the hotel is the traffic noise. The best rooms and suites face downtown, and though the glass provides good sound insulation, there is still some traffic murmur, especially during rush hour. However, for those who are up early and out sightseeing all day, this shouldn't be an issue.

Av. República Argentina 1700 (corner of Rua Venanti Otremba), Foz do Iguaçu, 85852-090 PR. ℂ 045/3521-5000. Fax 045/3521-5005. www.iguazufallshotels.com. 135 units. R$250 (US$125/£68) double; R$325 (US$163/£88) suite. 20% discount for business travelers or in off season. Extra person add 30%. Children 7 and under stay free in parent's room, 8–12 R$30 (US$15/£8) extra. AE, DC, MC, V. Parking R$6 (US$3/£1.50) daily. **Amenities:** Restaurant; bar; small pool and children's pool; small weight room; business center; Wi-Fi; 24-hr. room service; laundry; nonsmoking floors. *In room:* A/C, TV, Internet, minibar, hair dryer, safe.

INEXPENSIVE

Hotel Baviera Iguaçu *(Value)*   The Hotel Baviera provides a great low-budget option in town. Five of the rooms are suites with two bedrooms and a large closet area. These will easily accommodate four people and sometimes six. Other rooms are doubles, sometimes with a third twin bed. The German owners take pride in running a spotless establishment and serving up an excellent breakfast spread; the freshly baked goods, excellent breads, cheeses and cold cuts, and fresh fruit should keep you going well into lunchtime.

Av. Jorge Schimmelpfeng 697, Foz do Iguaçu, 85851-110 PR. ℂ 045/3523-5995. www.hotelbavieraiguassu.com.br. 23 units (showers only). R$106 (US$58/£29) double. Children 6 and under stay free in parent's room, over 6 R$20 (US$10/£5.40) extra. AE, DC, MC, V. Free parking. **Amenities:** Laundry. *In room:* A/C, TV, dataport, minibar, fridge.

ON THE PARK ROAD

Hotel das Cataratas ✸✸✸   Iguaçu's most famous hotel, and the only hotel located inside the national park, was bought late in 2007 by the Orient Express group. The new owners have kept the traditional look and feel, but put a new emphasis on outdoor activities, including rafting the river below the falls, abseiling and rappelling down the Iguaçu gorge, and rock and tree climbing, along with more sedate adventures such as walking, hiking, golf, tennis, archery, and simply relaxing by the pool.

The hotel offers a variety of packages combining a 2-day stay with adventure sports or nature walks. Rooms have remained largely unchanged under the new regime (they had been recently renovated in any case). Standard rooms are not overly large, but have nice hardwood floors and firm twin or double beds; bathrooms have large granite countertops and modern tub/shower combos. (Some rooms have carpet instead of hardwood floors; state your preference when you reserve.) The superior rooms are slightly larger, but offer views of the forest or gardens. The deluxe rooms all have beautiful hardwood floors, dark-wood furniture, and bathrooms with large bathtubs; a few have balconies. Rooms are spread out over a number of wings, connected by spacious corridors. Guests also have use of a large pool complex and a forested area behind the hotel with nature walks and trails to explore. Perhaps the only drawback to staying here is that it's 25km (16 miles) from town. For many, this rather limited sacrifice is more than made up for by the magic of staying so close to the falls.

Parque Nacional do Iguaçu, Foz do Iguaçu, 85863-000 PR. © 800-837-9051 (toll-free in the U.S.) or 45/2102-7000. www.hoteldascataratas.com. 200 units. Check the website for Internet deals. Rack rates R$520 (US$260/£140) standard double; R$600 (US$300/£162) superior double, R$680 (US$340/£184) deluxe double. Children under 10 stay free in parent's room. AE, DC, MC, V. Free parking. Take the road to Iguaçu Falls, go straight toward the gate, do not turn left into the visitor's area. Reservations recommended. **Amenities:** 2 restaurants; bar; large outdoor pool; tennis court; children's programs; game room; concierge; tour desk; business center (24-hr. Internet access); shopping arcade; salon; 24-hr. room service; laundry service. *In room:* A/C, TV, minibar, fridge, hair dryer, safe.

EXPENSIVE

Bourbon Cataratas ★★★ *(Kids)*   The real draw of the Bourbon is its leisure space. True, all the rooms are beautifully appointed. In the original wing, the standard rooms look out over the front of the hotel, whereas the superior rooms have a veranda and look over the pool. The new wing houses the master suites—really just a room, but with newer furnishings and huge windows providing lovely views. Out back, there's a 2km (1.25-mile) trail through orchards and lovely gardens; keep an eye out for toucans, parakeets, and colorful butterflies in the aviary. The vast pool complex includes three large pools, one especially for children. In high season, activity leaders organize all-day children's activities. But wait, there's more: a top-notch gym and indoor pool, a climbing wall and tennis courts, a soccer field, and a beach volleyball court.

Rodovia das Cataratas, Km 2.5, Foz do Iguaçu, 85853-000 PR. © 0800/451-010 or 045/3521-3900. www.bourbon. com.br. 311 units. R$415–R$540 (US$208–US$270/£112–£146) double superior or master. Extra person R$140 (US$70/£38). AE, DC, MC, V. Free parking. Bus: Parque Nacional or Cataratas. **Amenities:** 3 restaurants; huge pool complex (2 outdoor pools, 1 small indoor pool); outdoor lighted tennis courts; sauna (dry and steam); children's programs; game room; concierge; tour desk; car rental; business center; shopping arcade; salon; room service; massage; laundry service; nonsmoking rooms. *In room:* A/C, TV, dataport, minibar, fridge, hair dryer, safe.

MODERATE

San Martin ★ *(Kids)*   Also located on the park road, the San Martin is near the park entrance, close to the bird park. Although the accommodations are slightly dated, the rooms are clean and pleasantly furnished and the rates are very affordable. Most of the superior rooms have been renovated and now feature hardwood floors and elegant, modern furnishings, quite an improvement from the '70s brown that still reigns in the standard rooms. The nicest rooms are the superior class rooms. These feature king-size beds and are much bigger than the standard rooms. Families will appreciate the two-bedroom suits that come with two double and two single beds. Also great for kids are the hotel's parklike grounds with several play areas, a soccer field, a swimming pool, and gardens.

Rodovia das Cataratas, Km 17, Foz do Iguaçu, 85853-000 PR. © **0800/645-0045** or 045/3521-8088. www.hotel sanmartin.com.br. 135 units. R$165 (US$85/£46) double standard; R$200 (US$100/£54) double superior; R$325 (US$162/£88) family superior, sleeps 4–6 people. Extra person R$60 (US$30/£16). AE, DC, MC, V. Free parking. Bus: Parque Nacional or Cataratas. **Amenities:** restaurant; swimming pool; tennis court; sauna; children play area; game room; tour desk; business center; 24-hr. room service; laundry service; nonsmoking rooms. *In room:* A/C, TV, minibar, safe.

3 Where to Dine in Iguaçu

Don't come to Iguaçu for the culinary experience. Menus are rarely adventurous, but expect excellent Brazilian beef and fresh-caught fish from the Iguaçu or Paraná rivers. In addition to the restaurants below, most hotels outside of downtown also offer good dining options.

EXPENSIVE

Zaragoza SPANISH   For those who are tired of eating steak, Zaragoza offers a wonderful alternative: international cuisine with a strong Spanish flavor. The menu is particularly strong on seafood such as prawns, lobster, and local fish served grilled or broiled. On Saturday, there's a traditional Brazilian *feijoada,* and on Sunday people come from far and wide to savor the paella for lunch. The wine list includes national and imported wines with the emphasis on Spanish, Argentine, and Portuguese vintages.

Rua Quintino Bocaiúva 882, Foz do Iguaçu. © 045/3574-3084. www.restaurantezaragoza.com.br. Main courses R$28–R$58 (US$14–US$29/£7.50–£16). AE, V. Daily 11:30am–3pm and 7pm–midnight.

MODERATE

Bufalo Branco Churrascaria CHURRASCO   Likely the best place in the city for *churrasco* (grilled meat). Appetizers from the grill include sausage, turkey breast with bacon, and chicken hearts. For the main course, waiters offer a range of popular cuts such as *picanha* (rump steak), *alcatra* (top sirloin), filet mignon, *maminha* (a fattier rump steak), and *contra filet* (entrecôte). *Surubim* (grilled fish) is also available, as are cold dishes, salads, and desserts.

Rua Engenheiro Rebouças 530, Foz do Iguaçu. © 045/3523-9744. www.bufalobranco.com.br. R$30 (US$13/£8) per person, children under 5 eat free, ages 5–10 R$15 (US$6.25/£4). AE, DC, MC, V. Daily 11am–11pm.

Trapiche ⊕ SEAFOOD   For some excellent seafood try the Trapiche. The large menu includes everything from grilled fish such as tilapia, salmon, and trout to Bahian seafood stews such as moqueca, bobó and *caldeirada* (with crab, shrimp, and octopus). The kitchen also takes pride in serving up high-end seafood such as lobster and oysters.

Rua Marechal Deodoro 1087, Centro. © 045/3527-3951. Main courses R$30–R$60 (US$15–US$30/£8–£16). The more expensive dishes serve 2 people. AE, MC, V. Mon–Thurs 5pm–midnight; Fri–Sun 11am–midnight.

4 Exploring Iguaçu Falls

Your first priority should be to visit the Brazilian Falls. The walk along the gorge starting from just below the soft-pink **Tropical Hotel** ⊕⊕⊕ is spectacular. Keep an eye out for the hundreds of colorful butterflies. Make the time to get up close and personal with the falls on a zodiac ride. (*Note:* In the zodiac, a motorized inflatable rubber boat, you *will* get drenched.) Time permitting, pay a visit to the Parque das Aves for a close-up of the many bird species that inhabit the park. Also worth a look is Itaipu Dam, the world's largest hydroelectric project.

THE FALLS THEMSELVES

Parque Nacional do Iguaçu (Brazilian Falls) ✮✮✮ The Brazilian Falls now boast a newly renovated visitor center and a new restaurant—Canoas—above the falls. A new observation deck is also complete. The elevator is a work in progress. The **visitor center** is where you park your car or get off the bus and buy your entry tickets. The building has a gift shop and a small display area with some park history. From here, you board a shuttle bus and set off down the parkway for the falls. The bus will stop at the **Macuco Safari center** (from where rafting and zodiac trips depart, but do that after you've seen the falls), the pink **Tropical Hotel,** and then at **Canoas** restaurant before heading back to the visitor center. The Tropical is the place to get off. A small viewpoint at the foot of the hotel lawn is where you get your first magical view of the falls. From here, the pathway zigzags down the side of the gorge and trundles along the cliff face, providing views across the narrow gorge at water cascading down in a hundred different places. There are 275 separate waterfalls, with an average drop of 60m (197 ft.). While you walk, you'll see colorful butterflies fluttering about the trail and grumbling coati (a larger relative of the raccoon) begging for food. At the end of the trail an elevator will lift you up to the restaurant by the edge of the falls. Before going up, take the elevated walkway leading out *in front* of one of the falls. The wind and spray coming off the falls are exhilarating and guaranteed to have you soaked in seconds. (You can buy a plastic coat from the souvenir stand for R$5/US$2.50/ £1.35.) Allow at least a half-day.

Rodovia dos Cataratas, Km 18. ✆ 045/3572-2261. www.cataratasdoiguacu.com.br. Admission R$20 (US$10/£5.40) adults, R$5 (US$2.50/£1.35) children 2–6, includes transportation inside the park. Parking R$8 (US$4/£2.15). Daily 9am–5pm (summer until 6pm). Bus: Cataratas or Parque Nacional.

Parque Nacional Iguazú (Argentine Falls) ✮✮✮ Visitors to the Argentine Falls arrive at a brand-new complex, which consists mostly of restaurants and gift shops. A small visitor center does have displays on the history and ecology of the falls, but text is exclusively Spanish (*No!* They do not, will not, cannot provide an English-language pamphlet.) Leave them then to their lonely pride, because the chief attraction of the new and improved Argentine park is the **Devil's Throat walkway** ✮✮✮. To reach it, you take a free small-gauge railway, which departs every 30 minutes from 8am to 4pm, either from the visitor center station or from a second station located 600m (1,968 ft.) down a paved walking trail. The train takes about 20 minutes to trundle the 3km (2 miles) up to the Devil's Throat station, where waiting videographers will film your every move and later try to sell you a souvenir videotape. From here it's about a 1km (.5-mile) walk along the steel catwalk to the falls, where you will once again find yourself accosted by photographers, this time offering R$15 (US$7.50/£4) large-format shots of you with the falls in the background. Thankfully, all this crass commercialism fades in importance once you reach this viewpoint. There is something both magical and awesome in that much water falling in one place; nothing people do seems to mar it. The return train leaves on the half-hour, with the last departure at 5:30pm.

There are several other trails in the park. The **Circuito Superior (Upper Trail)** loops around the top of the falls. The steep **Circuito Inferior (Lower Trail)** ✮✮ has been much improved, to the point that much of it is wheelchair accessible. It leads down to the edge of the Iguazú River, offering some excellent views up toward the falls. It's the only way to reach **Isla San Martin** ✮, an island that's surrounded on all sides by falling water—well worth the short boat ride (currently free of charge). The last boat back leaves at 5pm. Expect to spend at least 4 hours in the park, more if you take a boat excursion (see below).

Boat tours   Iguazu Jungle Explorer (© **03757/421696**) operates a number of fast zodiac excursions. The *Adventura Nautica* (R$35/US$17/£9.50) leaves from the bottom of the Circuito Inferior and blasts up as close as driver and passengers dare to one of the big falls on the Argentine side. The *Gran Aventura* (R$70/US$35/£19) does much the same but starts 5km (3 miles) farther down the river, giving you a truck trip through the forest and a bit more time on the river; the *Aventura Nautica* is better value. The *Ecological Tour* (R$20/US$10/£5.40) begins at the Devil's Throat boardwalk above the falls. Passengers hop into rubber rafts and drift 2km (1¼ miles) downstream through the forest, then disembark and get trucked back to the visitor center. Please note that rates are approximate as they are calculated from the Argentine peso.

Av. Victoria Aguirre 66, Puerto Iguazú, 3370 Misiones, Argentina. © 03757/420-722. www.iguazuargentina.com. Admission R$40 (US$20/£11) adults, R$20 (US$10/£5.40) children ages 6–11, free for under 6. Oct 1–Mar 31 daily 7:30am–6:30pm; April 1–Sept 30 daily 8am–6pm. *Getting There:* From Foz do Iguaçu take the PORTO IGUAZÚ bus from downtown. Customs formalities at the border are minimal. Stay on the bus, tell the Customs officer who boards that you're going to the Parque Nacional and—for citizens of the U.S., U.K., Canada, and Australia—you'll be waved through without even a stamp in your passport. The bus then goes to the main bus station in Puerto Iguazú. Go to stall no. 5, where a bus departs every hour 7:40am–7:40pm for the 20-min. trip to the park. Including connections, total trip time from Brazil will be at least an hour. The bus from Brazil to Argentina costs R$3 (US$1.50/£.80), and the 1 from Puerto Iguazú to the falls costs R$5 (US$2.10/£1.05). A taxi to or from the Argentine side costs about R$80 (US$40/£22) each way. *Getting Back:* The bus from Parque Nacional to the Puerto Iguazú bus station departs hourly 8am–8pm. Once back at the bus station, go to stall no. 1 and catch the bus marked FOZ DO IGUAÇU back to Brazil.

OTHER TOP ATTRACTIONS

Canion Iguaçu (Rappel and Climbing Park) ★★   This company has converted a part of the park into a delightful adult playground. Very popular is the *arvorismo* (tree-climbing) trail, an obstacle course made out of ropes, wires, and platforms attached to the trees. The lower portion of the course starts out at just 3 feet above the forest floor; this lower section is appropriate for younger children 5 to 10 years of age. The more challenging higher obstacles will take you at least 25 feet up into the trees. If that doesn't make your stomach flip there's the 120 feet of rappel off a platform overlooking the falls. Maybe your thing is going up instead of down? The park offers a variety of climbing options. Beginners can try the artificial wall while more experienced climbers can explore over 33 different routes on the basalt rock face. And, last but not least, the company runs daily rafting trips over a 4km (2½-mile) stretch of the river. The run covers about 2km (1¼ miles) of rapids with a three-plus rating; the rest is calmer water that gives you a chance to observe the forest and the river. If you're traveling with children, be sure to check on minimum age and height requirements for certain activities.

Parque Nacional do Iguaçu. © 045/3529-6040. www.campodedesafios.com.br. Rappel R$70 (US$35/£19). Rafting R$80 (US$40/£22). Tree climbing R$80 (US$40/£22) for higher part, R$40 (US$20/£11) for lower part only. Climbing R$50 (US$25/£14). Daily 9am–5:30pm. Bus: Parque Nacional or Cataratas.

Itaipu Dam ★★   The world's largest hydroelectric project stands 10km (6¼ miles) upriver from Foz do Iguaçu on the Rio Paraná. The project produces over 90 billion kilowatt hours per year, nearly 25% of Brazil's supply. Visitors are shown a 30-minute video on the dam's construction, featuring endless shots of frolicking children and nothing on the dam's environmental impact. Then you board a bus that crosses to an observation platform in the midpoint of the dam. For a much more in-depth look at the dam, which includes a visit to the Production Building and the Central Command Post, book the Special Tour. There is a fee for this tour (see below) and sandals and shorts are not allowed. The Technical Tour (where you go inside the dam to see the turbines) is available only by prior arrangement. Contact the visitor center at least a week in advance. It is mostly of interest to engineers and people with a technical background who want to see the ins and outs of the dam.

Av. Tancredo Neves 6702. (✆) **045/3520-6999** or 045/3520-6405. www.itaipu.gov.br. Free admission on regular 11/2-hr. guided tours Mon–Sat at 8am, 9am, 10am, 2pm, 3pm, and 3:30pm. Special 2-hr. tours R$30 (US$15/£8) Mon–Sat 8:30am, 9:30am, 10am, 2pm, 2:30pm and 3:3-pm. Bus: 110 or 120.

Macuco Boat Safari ✿✿✿   Niagara Falls has the *Maid of the Mist.* Iguaçu has *Macuco.* I know which one I'd choose. *Macuco* participants pile aboard 25-foot zodiacs, the guide fires up twin 225-horsepower outboards, and you're off up the river, bouncing over wave trains, breaking eddy lines, powering your way up the surging current until the boat's in the gorge, advancing slowly toward one of the (smaller) falls. As the boat nears, the mist gets thicker, the roar louder, the passengers wetter and more and more thrilled (or terrified), until the zodiac peels away, slides downstream, and hides in an eddy until everyone's caught his or her breath. Then you do it all again. Allow 1 hour for the entire trip.

Parque Nacional do Iguaçu. (✆) **045/3523-6475.** www.macucosafari.com.br. R$150 (US$75/£41) per person, children 7–12 half price. Mon 1–5:30pm; Tues–Sun and holidays 8am–5:30pm. Bus: Parque Nacional or Cataratas.

Parque das Aves ✿✿   Set in 4.8 hectares (12 acres) of lush subtropical rainforest, the Bird Park offers the best bird-watching in Iguaçu. A large number of birds are in huge walk-through aviaries, some 24m (80 ft.) tall and at least 60m (200 ft.) long, allowing visitors to watch the birds interact as they go about their daily routines. Highlights include the toucans and multicolored tanagers as well as a Pantanal aviary with roseate spoonbills, herons, and egrets. Signage is in English. The best time to visit is early in the day when the birds are most active. Allow 2 hours.

Rodovia das Cataratas, Km 17, 300m (984 ft.) before the national park entrance. (✆) **045/3529-8282.** www.parque dasaves.com.br. R$20 (US$10/£5.40), free for children under 9. Daily 8:30am–5:30pm. Bus: Parque Nacional or Cataratas.

SPECTACULAR VIEWS

The confluence of the Rio Iguaçu and the Rio Paraná, about 7.5km (4½ miles) south of the town of Foz do Iguaçu on Avenida General Meira, is also the spot where Brazil, Paraguay, and Argentina all meet. Called the **Marco das Três Fronteiras,** it features a public viewing platform with good views up and down the Iguaçu and Paraná rivers.

ORGANIZED TOURS

BOAT TOURS   The **Iguaçu Explorer,** operated by Macuco Safari, offers a boat tour along the Iguaçu and Paraná rivers. Although there are no views of the falls, this leisurely tour is a great way to see the region from the water. Highlights include a view of the Tancredo Neves bridge that connects Brazil and Argentina, the tri-border marker, and a visit to a small regional museum on the Paraguay side. The vegetation along the way is quite nice but if you're going to the Pantanal or the Amazon I would skip this excursion. If not it's a good way to get a small taste of the country's natural wonders. Tours cost R$90 (US$45/£24), lunch included. Departure times vary. Details at (✆) **045/3523-6475** or www.macucosafari.com.br.

GUIDED TOURS & TRANSFERS A number of tour operators organize transportation and guides for visits to the falls. Trips can be customized to include visits to other attractions such as the bird park, Macuco Safari, or the Itaipu Dam. The most popular service is the 1-day visit to the Argentine Falls, which at most agencies costs around R$60 (US$25/£13) per person plus R$28 (US$12/£6) per car in tolls. Reputable companies include **Conveniotur,** Rua Rui Barbosa 820 (✆ 045/3523-3500; www.conveniotur.com.br) and **Central Tours** (✆ 045/3526-4434; www.centraltours. com.br) and **Loumar Tourismo** (✆ 045/3572-5005; www.loumarturismo.com.br). Loumar also offers a 1-day excursion to the shopper's paradise of Paraguay.

A HELICOPTER TOUR
Helisul–Helicopter Tours Taking the helicopter tour in the park involves a small moral dilemma. The noise from the helicopters does scare the wildlife. Park naturalists say that toucans appear only when it's rainy, windy, or fogged in—days that the copters are grounded. The helicopters are one of two issues over which UNESCO threatened to pull Iguaçu's World Heritage designation (the other was a plan to reopen highway BR-373, cutting the park in half). On the other hand the company has invested in the newest, quietest helicopters. And the view of the falls and canyon from the air truly is spectacular.

Av. das Cataratas, Km 16.5, Foz do Iguaçu. ✆ 045/3529-7474. www.helisul.com. 10-min. flight over the falls and park R$150 (US$75/£41) per person, 3-person minimum. Children are free if they don't occupy a seat. 35-min. flight over the falls and park, Itaipu Dam, and Three Borders monument, R$1,400 (US$700/£378) total; can be divided by up to 4 passengers. Daily 9am–6pm: Parque Nacional or Cataratas.

OUTDOOR ACTIVITIES
Just outside of Iguaçu Park is **Iguaçu Golf Club,** Av. das Cataratas 6845 (✆ 045/ 3529-9999), an 18-hole, par-72 golf course. In addition to the course, the club also has a 300-yard driving range and putting green, golf-club rental, a gift shop, and a large leisure area with a restaurant, lounge, sauna, and swimming pool. It's open daily year-round from 7am to sunset. Fees for visitors are R$150 (US$75/£41) for 18 holes, R$75 (US$37/£20) for 9 holes. Cart rental is R$120 (US$60/£32) for 18 holes and R$75 (US$37/£20) for 9 holes. To get there, take the PARQUE NACIONAL or CATARATAS bus.

5 Shopping in Foz do Iguaçu
SHOPPING AREAS
Foz do Iguaçu's *centro* is a popular shopping district. Most shops are concentrated around **Avenida Brasil, Rua Barbosa, Rua Almirante Barroso,** and **Quintino Bocaiuva.** You'll find many clothing and shoe stores, as well as excellent leather goods such as jackets and purses.

A Rendeira This shop next to the Bourbon hotel sells some of the finest linen and lace: tablecloths, napkins, blouses, beautiful baby dresses, and much more. Rodovia das Cataratas, Km 2.5. ✆ 045/3529-8989.

Tres Fronteiras *(Finds)* You can find anything here, from all regions of Brazil: T-shirts, carvings, carpets, hats, hides, semiprecious stones, precious stones, you name it; anything you ever considered picking up and didn't, it's here at reasonable prices. BR 469 Rodovia das Cataratas, Km 11 (just before the turnoff for Argentina). ✆ 045/3523-6565. www.tresfronteiras.com.br.

6 Iguaçu After Dark

The corner of Avenida JK and Avenida Jorge Schimmelpfeng is Iguaçu's prime nightlife area, home to a number of restaurant/pubs, most with large patios. Two of the favorites are **Bar do Capitão** (Av. Jorge Schimmelpfeng 288; ℂ 045/3572-1512) and **Tass Bier and Club** (Av. Jorge Schimmelpfeng 450; ℂ 045/3523-5373). Both are open daily from 6pm to 1am, and Friday and Saturday until the last customer. In addition to cachaças and great cocktails, the **Cachaçaria Água Doce** (Rua Benjamin Constant 63; ℂ 045/3523-7715) features live music on Friday and Saturday.

17

The Pantanal

It's a secret that, until recently, was known only to film crews: The best place in South America to see wildlife is not the Amazon but the Pantanal, a Florida-size wetland on the far western edge of Brazil that bursts with animals—capybaras, caimans, jaguars, anacondas, giant otters, colorful hyacinth macaws, kites, hawks, and flocks of storks and herons hundreds strong. In fact, many species that live in the Amazon and are next to impossible to see there can be viewed here in abundance. The Pantanal is home to over 700 species of birds, 100 mammal species, more than 250 fish species, and 80 reptile species.

The largest flood plain in the world, the Pantanal has a rhythm governed by its rivers. In the wet season (Nov–Apr), rivers swell and spill over to cover a vast alluvial plain for months. Millions of birds are attracted by this aquatic paradise, as mammals take refuge on the remaining few mounds of dry land. As the water drains (from May onward), the land dries up and the situation slowly reverses: Animals congregate around the few remaining water pools. Fish get trapped in these pools, and birds and mammals alike gather for water and food as they wait for the rains to start.

Most farmers use the land for cattle grazing in the dry season only, moving the cattle when the fields flood. Few roads of any kind exist in the Pantanal; the best way to explore the area is to make like the locals and head out on horseback. Many of the area's *fazendas* (cattle ranches) have slowly converted to tourism. Staying at one of these lodges is the best way to get a feel for the region.

A stay in a Pantanal lodge normally involves a number of activities—a boat trip to spot birds and caiman, a horseback trip through the fields, bird spotting by foot or in an open vehicle, and often

Gateways to the Pantanal

There are three gateway cities to the Pantanal: **Cuiabá,** which connects to the Transpantaneira Highway and gives access to the South Pantanal; **Campo Grande,** which leads in to the South Pantanal; and most isolated of all, **Corumbá,** which stands on a cliff top looking over the Pantanal itself, and provides access to lodges in the southwest of the ecosystem. None of these cities is really worth visiting in itself. Most lodges will pick you up at the airport and whisk you out into the swamp with nary a second glance at the city. Should you get caught in the city of Cuiabá, you're only an hour and a half from the Transpantaneira Highway (see "Driving The Transpantaneira," below). A number of small lodges will take you out to see the birds and wildlife; depending on the time of year you'll either head out in a four-wheel-drive, canoe, boat, on foot, on horseback, or a combination of these.

a nighttime excursion to see nocturnal animals. Some lodges offer additional activities such as canoe trips, fishing expeditions, or specialized bird-watching outings. If you have a specific interest, it's a good idea to make contact ahead of time.

1 Tour Operators in the Pantanal

Whether you decide to go to the North Pantanal or the South, whichever lodge you decide to visit, you may find it easier and quite possibly even cheaper to arrange your visit through a tour operator, who can arrange not only your stay but your transfers to and from the lodge, and even help out with flights to the gateway cities. Sometimes there is a premium on top of the lodge costs for this service. Sometimes the operator can make up his costs through the discount he gets from the lodge, in effect passing this savings on to you. In any case, it's worth checking out what they have to offer. You can always book directly with a lodge afterward if you decide the service being offered isn't worth the money or effort.

There are two particularly good operators that offer expeditions to lodges in either the North or the South Pantanal. Located in the U.S., **Brazil Nuts** (© 800/553-9959; www.brazilnuts.com) offers packages to a number of lodges, including the two pioneers of Pantanal eco-tourism, **Araras Eco Lodge** ✸✸✸ in the North, and **Caiman Ecological Reserve** ✸✸ in the South.

Located in Campo Grande, **Open Door** (© 067/3321-8303; www.opendoortur.com.br) has some excellent packages for the Pantanal, for Bonito, and for combinations of the two. Open Door works with a wide variety of lodges in both the North and South Pantanal, including difficult-to-reach reserves such as **Fazenda Barranco Alto** ✸✸✸ and **Fazenda Rio Negro** ✸✸.

In the individual sections on the North and South Pantanal below, we list a number of very good, but more regionally focused, tour agencies.

2 Cuiabá & the North Pantanal

The capital of Mato Grosso state, Cuiabá is a modern, pleasant town of 430,000 that sits in the middle of Brazilian cattle country. It's a great place to stock up on boots, saddles, and other Western gear. The city serves as the main gateway to the northern part of the Pantanal—the Transpantaneira Highway starts just 98km (61 miles) away—and as the jumping-off point to the Chapada dos Guimarães.

ESSENTIALS
ARRIVING
BY PLANE   TAM (© 0800/570-5700 or 065/4002-5700; www.tam.com.br), **Gol** (© 0300/115-2121; www.voegol.com.br), and **Varig** (© 092/4003-7000; www.varig.com.br) fly into Cuiabá from either Rio de Janeiro or São Paulo, or both. Cuiabá's airport, **Aeroporto Marechal Rondon** (© 065/3614-2510), is located 7km (4¼ miles) south of the city center, in the adjacent municipality of Varzea Grande. A taxi to downtown will cost about R$25 (US$13/£7). Tours to a Pantanal lodge normally include transfers, but it's worthwhile to double-check.

BY BUS   Cuiabá's efficient bus terminal, **Engenheiro de Sá** (© 065/3621-1040), is on Av. Marechal Deodoro s/n in Alvorada, just north of the city center. Buses to Campo Grande, gateway to the South Pantanal, depart daily at 7am, 8pm, and 9:30pm and take approximately 10 hours. The overnight buses have comfortable reclining chairs. Contact **Motta** (© **065/3621-2514;** www.motta.com.br). The fare is R$60 (US$30/£16).

VISITOR INFORMATION

The state tourist office, **Secretaria de Turismo** (© **065/3613-9300;** www.sedtur. mt.gov.br), is located too far from downtown to be of any use.

FAST FACTS: Cuiabá

Car Rental **Unidas,** Av. Gov. João Ponce Arruda 920 (© **065/3682-4052**), and **Localiza,** Rua Mal Rondon, s/n (airport) (© **0800/979-2000** or 065/3682-7900).

Currency Exchange & Banks **Banco do Brasil,** Av Pres Getúlio Vargas 553 (© **065/ 3624-1944**), has a 24-hour ATM.

Hospital **Hospital Santa Casa de Misericórdia,** Praça do Seminário 141 (© **065/ 3321-0166**).

Internet Access Digitus Informática Av Ten Cel Duarte, 595 (© **065/3321-0166**) R$4/hour (US$2/£1).

Weather The state of Mato Grosso is hot and muggy in the summer; temperatures can rise to 95°F to 104°F (35°C–40°C). Most rain falls from December to March. In the winter (June–Sept) it can cool off significantly, with temperatures as low as 59°F (15°C).

WHERE TO STAY IN CUIABÁ

Most lodges will pick you up at the airport, sparing you the need to stay in Cuiabá. If you do find yourself stuck, the following places will get you through the night.

EXPENSIVE

Hotel Amazon Plaza ⟨⋆⟩   Closed, gutted, and renovated in 2003, the Amazon has the feel of a brand-new hotel. Rooms are clean and comfortable, if a bit spare. Downstairs there's a pleasant outdoor pool, and a lovely poolside bar. The location halfway down Getulio Vargas is convenient to the old downtown and the restaurants of Goiaberas.

Av. Presidente Getulio Vargas 600, Cuiabá, 78045-300 MT. © 065/2121-2000. Fax 065/2121-2001. www.hotel amazon.com.br. 120 units. Standard R$150 (US$75/£41); deluxe R$220 (US$110/£59). Extra person add R$25 (US$12/£7). Children 5 and under stay free in parent's room. AE, DC, MC, V. Free parking. **Amenities:** Restaurant; bar; business center; room service; laundry. *In room:* A/C, TV, high-speed Internet, minibar, fridge.

Intercity Cuiabá ⟨⋆⟩⟨⋆⟩   Brand spanking new, the Intercity offers tastefully decorated rooms with queen-size beds and an elegant modern workspace, a large pool, and good weight room, plus free Wi-Fi and free high-speed Internet, and a location near the city's better restaurants. Perfect for the business traveler, or overnighting tourist.

Rua Presidente Artur Bernardes 64, Goiaberas, Cuiabá 78043-365 MT. © 0800/600-7700 or 065/3025-9900. Fax 065/3035-9907. www.intercityhoteis.com.br. 80 units. R$325 (US$163/£88) double. Children 10 and under stay free in parent's room. AE, DC, MC, V. Free parking. **Amenities:** Restaurant; bar; large outdoor pool; weight room; business center; free Wi-Fi; room service; laundry. *In room:* A/C, TV, free high-speed Internet, minibar, fridge, hair dryer, safe.

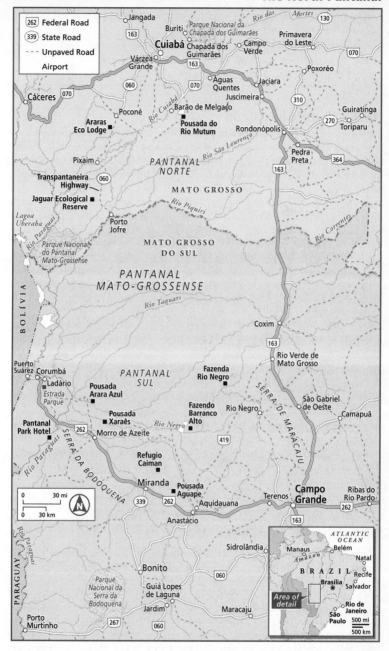

> (*Tips* **A Health Warning: Yellow Fever**
>
> In this region of Brazil, yellow fever is endemic, and you should get a shot at least 10 days before you travel to the Pantanal. Health authorities may ask for proof of vaccination, so carry your vaccine certificate.

WHERE TO DINE IN CUIABÁ

Most of Cuiabá's better restaurants are located in the Goiabeiras neighborhood, conveniently located close to the city's hotels. Cuiabá's a bit far from the sea, so **Peixaria Popular** ⚬ (Av. S. Sebastião 2324, Goiabeiras; ℓ 065/3322-5471) offers fish from the great inland fishery of the Pantanal. *Pintado, dourado, paçu*, and *piraputanga* are served up grilled, fried, or in filets. **Getulio Grill** ⚬ (Av. Getulio Vargas 1147, across from Praça Santos Dumont; ℓ 067/3624-9992) offers steak and excellent local fish dishes. *Piraputanga* is a less-known local fish, served stuffed with palm hearts. At night, it's also a popular local tavern. **Mercearia da Pizza** (Av. Filinto Muller 840; ℓ 065/3623-0800) is the best pizza place in town, while **Taberna Portuguesa** (Av. Ipiranga 560; ℓ 065/3321-3661) specializes in hearty Portuguese fare. Think codfish and potatoes.

SHOPPING IN CUIABÁ

In the main commercial district around the Praça da República, you'll find stores selling clothing and shoes, as well as stationery, toiletries, film, batteries, and food.

NATIVE & REGIONAL ARTS AND CRAFTS   Funai, the Brazilian federal Indian department, runs the **Artindia** store to promote indigenous arts and crafts. Located at Rua Pedro Celestino 301, Centro (ℓ 065/3623-1675), open Monday through Friday from 8 to 11:30am and 1:30 to 5pm. **Casa do Artesão,** Rua 13 de Junho 315 (ℓ 065/3316-3151), located near the river, is open daily from 8am to 6pm. Located in a lovely colonial building, the Casa's collection is very large.

COWBOY EQUIPMENT & CLOTHES   Cuiabá is the place to pick up everything you need for that real Pantaneiro cowboy look. If you need a hat, boots, or jeans, stop by **Texas Country,** Av. Getulio Vargas 1021, Centro (ℓ 065/3624-0721). **Selaria e Sapataria Centro Oeste,** Av. Ten. Cel. Duarte 318 (ℓ 065/3622-1584), is another great store to get properly outfitted. The store sells quality clothing and gear for real cowboys—boots, hats, good jeans, gloves, spurs, and chaps; if you're going riding, your various body parts will thank you for any purchases made here.

EXPLORING THE NORTH PANTANAL

Three days is the minimum reasonable itinerary for the Pantanal. With wildlife viewing, the longer you spend in an area, the better your chances of seeing animals. Spend the minimum possible time in Cuiabá then a take a slow wildlife-spotting drive out along the Transpantaneira to a lodge (see "Lodges in the North Pantanal," below). Take a guided hike, and after sunset, go for a spotlight drive on the Transpantaneira to see the night creatures: capybaras, tarantulas, and (with the most incredible of luck) jaguars. I also strongly recommend that you take the time to explore the Pantanal as it was meant to be seen, on the back of a horse. Canoeing one of the North Pantanal's small rivers is a great way to spot monkeys and giant river otters.

After exploring the Pantanal, consider a 1-day or overnight trip to the Chapada dos Guimarães, the highlands to the north of Cuiabá (see "A Side Trip from Cuiabá: Chapada dos Guimarães," below). The beautiful red-rock formations, plateaus, and canyons offer excellent hiking and fabulous views, great waterfalls and swimming holes, and some excellent birdlife, including red macaws.

TOUR OPERATORS IN THE NORTH PANTANAL

All tour operators work with one or more Pantanal lodges. These operators provide a package itinerary—usually quite flexible—that includes transportation to a lodge, plus nature tours and guide services.

One of the best tour operators is **Pantanal Explorer,** Av. Governador Ponce de Arruda 670, Varzea Grande (© 065/3682-2800; fax 065/3682-1260; www.pantanal explorer.com.br). Stays in the Pantanal are at the excellent Araras Eco Lodge. In addition, the company offers trips to the Chapada dos Guimarães and boat trips in the Pantanal, as well as eco-tours to the Mato Grosso part of the Amazon rainforest, excellent if you do not have an opportunity to head up to the Amazon. All of these trips can be combined with a Pantanal stay.

Another good tour operator is **Anaconda Turismo,** Av. Isaac Povoas 606, Centro, Cuiabá, (© 065/3028-5990; www.anacondapantanal.com.br). This operator works with a large number of fazendas and pousadas and can customize a package according to your interests. It also operates in the Chapada dos Guimarães (see below) and can organize fishing expeditions.

DRIVING THE TRANSPANTANEIRA

There are a couple of ironies about the Transpantaneira. Though the name implies that the road traverses the entire flood plain, the highway stops in Porto Jofre, 144km (89 miles) from where it began, and at least that far from the opposite edge of the Pantanal. The other irony is that the project, which if completed would likely have destroyed the Pantanal (by skewing the ecosystem's drainage pattern), has instead, in its unfinished state, become one of the great wildlife-viewing areas of the world. Ditches on either side of the roadbed have become favorite feeding grounds for kingfishers, capybara, egrets, jabiru storks, giant river otters, and caiman by the dozen. Spend but a day on the Transpantaneira, and you'll see more wildlife than you'd see in a week in the Amazon.

LODGES IN THE NORTH PANTANAL

Araras Eco Lodge 𝒦𝒦𝒦   Araras Lodge is the best spot for exploring the North Pantanal. The location by the Transpantaneira is excellent, and lodge owner Andre Thuronyi has done extensive work to improve the local wildlife habitat. With only 19 rooms, the lodge is pleasantly small and rustic. No fancy rooms or amenities; each guest room comes with a private bathroom and a hammock on the veranda. The guides are usually knowledgeable. Activities include hikes along a rustic boardwalk through the flooded fields to the lodge's lookout tower. One afternoon as we watched the sun set over the Pantanal, a group of five hyacinth macaws flew right over us, attracted by our guide who sounded a credible macaw call. Other excursions include boat or canoe trips on a small local river known for large hawks and giant river otters (we saw both). On drives along the Transpantaneira, even in a 3-hour time span, you'll lose track of the number of birds you'll see. Fortunately the guide always seems to remember their names. Horse lovers will be in heaven riding through the flooded fields. If you know how to ride, the guides are happy to let you have some fun and gallop through the fields, startling caiman and snakes underfoot. The food is delicious and plentiful, often including excellent local fish. Araras Eco Lodge offers a package deal with a 3-night stay at the lodge and a 1-night stay in the Chapada dos Guimarães for some good hiking and swimming.

Transpantaneira Hwy. Reservation office: Av. Governador Ponce de Arruda 670, Varzea Grande, MT. © 065/3682-2800. Fax 065/3682-1260. www.araraslodge.com.br. 19 units (showers only). R$980 (US$490/£265) per person for a 3-day, 2-night package, 6-day package (including the Chapada Guimarães) R$2,484 (US$1,242/£671), including airport pickup and drop-off plus all meals and guided activities. Extra person add about 25%. Children 10 and under stay free in parent's room. AE, DC, MC, V. Free parking. **Amenities:** Restaurant; bar; outdoor pool; laundry. *In room:* A/C, no phone.

Jaguar Ecological Reserve 𝒢𝒢★   Wildlife viewing is always a matter of luck and patience, particularly when it comes to large predators like jaguars. But one of the best ways of improving your odds is to visit this lodge—the centerpiece of a private ecological reserve—where an astonishing one in four guests sees one of these huge South American cats. It's a very long way (110km/68 miles) down the bumpy Transpantaneira, and the accommodations are expensive and only basic, but for a view of that big cat it may be worth it. For the 75% of guests who do not see jaguars, there is still the usual vast array of caiman and colorful birds, so rare in the rest of the world, so common in the Pantanal. Note that it's probably best to book your stay here through **Open Door Tours** (© **067/3321-8303;** www.opendoortur.com.br). The JER has been in operation for a number of years, and while operations in the field run smoothly, their booking operations have been a little on the amateur side. Better to deal with professionals.

Transpantaneira Km 110, Poconé, MT. © **065/3646-8557** (office) or 067/9919-5518 (lodge). www.jaguarreserve.com. 9 units (showers only). 4-day 3-night package R$1,290 (US$645/£348) per person, meals and transfers included. Free parking. **Amenities:** Wildlife viewing. *In room:* No phone.

Pousada do Rio Mutum   This pousada is highly recommended for those who enjoy fishing. The *pintado* catfish is a particularly prized catch, but anglers can also expect to hook *dourado, paçu,* or *piraputanga.* (The best months for fishing are Feb–Oct; there is no fishing Nov–Jan during spawning season.) For nonfishers there

---

⌒Moments A Birding Convert

I have to admit, I always thought birding was boring: get up at dawn, sit in a blind, wear camouflage, and just be really quiet. But my first visit to the Pantanal opened my eyes. Just driving along the Transpantaneira for an hour I spotted parakeets, tanagers, hawks, egrets, and the amazing 5-foot-tall jabiru stork. In less than 2 hours I counted at least 20 different species. That evening as I stood on a viewing platform to see the sun set over the flooded fields, I heard the unmistakable shrieks of a macaw. As my eyes adjusted to the low light I was able to spot three hyacinth macaws flying within a few feet of the platform. On a horseback ride the next day, splashing loudly through the wet fields, I still managed to log at least 15 species, including roseate spoonbills, toucans, egrets, herons, and cormorants. Not just one or two of each—great big flocks. Now there's a sport I can get in to!

are tours of the Pantanal ecosystem by boat, foot, and canoe. The lodge also offers special bird-watcher packages, which do many of the same activities but are accompanied by a bird expert. Accommodations are in simply furnished rooms that come with private bathrooms and a veranda. All meals and activities are included. This region is a bit east of Poconé, and access is through the town of Barão de Melgaço.

Av. Isaac Póvoas 1177, Cuiabá, 78045-640 MT. © 065/3052-7022. www.pousadamutum.com.br. 22 units (showers only). 3-day, 2-night packages from R$825 (US$413/£222) per person, including meals and pickup/drop-off at airport. MC, V. **Amenities:** Restaurant; bar; pool. *In room:* A/C, no phone.

3 A Side Trip from Cuiabá: Chapada dos Guimarães

In appearance, the Chapada dos Guimarães has much in common with the desert buttes of Arizona or Utah—weird, wonderful formations of bright red rock, and long beautiful canyons. Vegetation is dry and scrubby, except where the many river channels flow; then you get waterfalls streaming down into basins lush with tropical vegetation. Officially, more than 32,000 hectares (80,000 acres) of this vast highland were set aside in 1989 as a national park—the Parque Nacional da Chapada dos Guimarães. Only about half of the total area has been expropriated; much of the rest still lies in private hands, including the small town—also called Chapada dos Guimarães—within the park boundaries. It's a quiet, laid-back place with a slight counterculture feel, and the most convenient base from which to set off exploring. Hiking nearby is excellent; trails are clear even if—as ever in Brazil—they're completely without markers or signage. Most trails end at a viewpoint, a waterfall, or a natural pool (sometimes all three!). Wildlife is not up to the standard set by the Pantanal, but in the Chapada you do have the opportunity of seeing the gorgeous red macaw, often playing in the thermals by a cliff side.

GETTING THERE

BY CAR   The Chapada is 74km (46 miles) north of Cuiabá. The best way to get there is by rental car (see "Fast Facts: Cuiabá," earlier in the chapter). Roads are excellent. Follow the MT-251 to the park and the town of Chapada dos Guimarães.

BY BUS   Direct buses operated by **Viação Rubi** (© 065/3624-9044) leave from Cuiabá's rodoviaria and take about 1 hour. Cost is R$8 (US$4/£2) and departures are daily at 9am, 10:30am, 2pm, and 6:30pm.

VISITOR INFORMATION

The **tourist office** is at Rua Quinco Caldas s/n (© 065/3301-2045). The park visitor center (© 065/3301-1133) is located on highway MT-251 about 8km (5 miles) past the park entrance, and about 15km (9 miles) before the town of Chapada dos Guimarães. An excellent local tour operator, **Ecoturismo Cultural,** Praça Dom Wunibaldo 464 (© 065/3301-1693; www.chapadadosguimaraes.com.br), arranges day trips with guides and transportation and can assist with accommodations.

All tour operators listed under "Tour Operators in the North Pantanal," above, can provide day trips or overnight packages to the Chapada, in combination with a visit to the Pantanal or as a separate trip.

EXPLORING THE PARK

Two days are plenty to explore the Chapada. Even if you only have a day, you can still see the "best of the Chapada"—take in the magnificent views, frolic in a few waterfalls, and get some hiking in, all before sunset.

RECOMMENDED HIKES

All times are one-way for the hikes listed below. Trail heads have sizable parking lots, but on weekends the sights closest to town can get crowded. There is no public transportation in the park or surrounding area.

CACHOEIRA VEU DE NOIVA   The tallest waterfall in the park is the gorgeous **Véu de Noiva.** The trail head is at the park visitor center, about 15km (9 miles) from the town of Chapada dos Guimarães. From the visitor center it is a short and obvious walk to the lookout.

MIRANTE DA GEODESIA   This lookout marks the geodesic center of Brazil. The spot also happens to mark a fabulous lookout over the lowlands below the Chapada, with Cuiabá in the distance. Short trails below the lookout take you down some of the cliffs with more views. The parking lot lies 8km (5 miles) east of the town of Chapada dos Guimarães.

CIDADE DE PEDRA   The City of Stone is named after the beautiful eroded rock formations that look like the ruins of buildings. A short hike takes you through these rocks to the edge of a canyon, where the sheer cliffs drop 350m (1,148 ft.) straight down. To reach the trail head, go west from town on MT-251 for about 2km (1¼ miles), turn right (there's a small sign), and follow the smaller, rougher blacktop road straight on for 13km (8 miles).

PAREDÃO DO ECO   A 20-minute hike takes you to the edge of a mini–Grand Canyon. Steep cliff walls and eroded rocks in various shapes form an amazing pattern, and on the far side where the walls are the steepest and sheerest you can often spot scarlet red *araras* (macaws). At sunrise and sunset the light bathes the rocks in a warm red glow. To reach the trail head, follow the same directions for Cidade de Pedra, above. About 12km (7½ miles) along the blacktop road, take the left turn on a dirt road and follow it for 3km (2 miles).

MORRO SÃO JERÔNIMO   The highest point in the Chapada, this tabletop mountain can be reached by a 4-hour hike. Bring water and sunscreen. The trail for the Morro begins at the visitor center parking lot. The peak is almost due south, but trails are poorly marked. Follow the signs to Cachoeira Véu de Noiva, then to Casa de Pedra, and then to Morro São Jenônimo.

WHERE TO STAY

Pousada Penhasco ⭐ *(Kids)*   The Penhasco has a great location, on the edge of a cliff with a view out over the flatland below, all the way to Cuiabá. Rooms are in small cabins spread out over the property. The cabins are simple, but spacious and pleasant, with tile floors, queen-size or single beds, and functional clean bathrooms. The best cabins are the ones closest to the cliff edge—try to reserve one of these if you can. The inn boasts extensive amenities, including a beautifully landscaped outdoor pool area.

⟨Tips⟩ Hiking Tips

Wear high-top shoes or boots—not sandals—as the rocks and sand are perfect spots for snakes (some may be poisonous). Be careful when sitting down and putting your hands on the rocks.

> ⌒*Tips* **Where to Find Local Art**
>
> For local art and crafts, visit **Artes da Chapada Artesanatos,** Rua Cipriano Curvo 464, Centro (© **065/3301-2739**). Open Monday through Saturday from 10am to 7pm. On the Chapada's central square there is a daily fair of indigenous art, with baskets and necklaces made by tribes from the Mato Grosso interior.

Rodovia Penhasco (2.5km/1½ miles from the center of town), Boa Clima, Chapada dos Guimarães, MT 78065-010. © **065/3301-1555** or 065/3624-1000. www.penhasco.com.br. 40 units (showers only). R$219 (US$110/£59) double. Seasonal discounts available. Extra person add R$65 (US$33/£18). Children 5 and under stay free in parent's room. AE, DC, MC, V. Free parking. **Amenities:** Restaurant; bar; 2 large outdoor pools; tennis courts; sauna; game room; laundry. *In room:* A/C, TV, minibar, fridge, no phone.

Solar do Inglês ♣ This small but charming pousada with a lovely English garden (plus a very un-English pool) is the perfect adult's getaway, an excellent spot for an escaping couple. Rooms are lovingly decorated in antiques and bric-a-brac. In addition to a hearty breakfast, the pousada serves a proper afternoon tea, at 5pm on the dot.

Rua Cipriano Curvo 142, Centro, Chapada dos Guimarães, MT 78195-000. © **065/3301-1639**. www.chapadado sguimaraes.com.br/solardoingles. 8 units (showers only). R$190 (US$95/£51) double. Extra person add 25%. Children under 14 not accepted. AE, V. Free parking. **Amenities:** Bar; pool; sauna; laundry. *In room:* A/C (in 7 rooms), fan only (1 room), TV, minibar, hair dryer.

WHERE TO DINE

Morro dos Ventos ♣♣ *(Finds)* BRAZILIAN Perched on the edge of a cliff, the restaurant offers fabulous views of the plains below the Chapada. With luck you'll spot red *araras;* if not, you'll likely hear their shrieks echoing off the cliffs. The menu offers regional home cooking. Dishes serve at least three people. A good choice is the chicken stew with okra served in a heavy cast-iron pot with generous side dishes of beans, salad, *farofa,* and rice. Other options include the *pintado* or *paçu;* on weekends there's an outstanding *feijoada.*

Chacara Morro dos Ventos, via Estrada do Mirante Km 1. © 065/3301-1030. www.morrodosventos.com.br. Main courses R$21–R$35 (US$11–US$18/£5.50–£9.50) for 2. V. Daily 9am–6pm.

4 Campo Grande & the South Pantanal

Campo Grande is a fairly new town and an important transportation hub for the region. When Mato Grosso state was split in two in the '70s, Campo Grande became the capital of Mato Grosso do Sul. As with Cuiabá, there's nothing about Campo Grande that merits a visit, and most lodge packages will whisk you out of town and get you out into the field right away. The Pantanal in Mato Grosso do Sul is less wild, more given over to cattle ranching, and significantly harder to access than in the north. That said, the avian life is still remarkable, and the lodges are larger, more established, and more luxurious by far.

As in the north, a stay in a Pantanal lodge normally involves a number of activities—a boat trip to spot birds and caiman, a horseback trip through the fields, bird spotting by foot or in an open vehicle, and often a nighttime excursion to see nocturnal animals. Some lodges offer additional activities such as canoe trips, fishing expeditions, or specialized bird-watching outings. If you have a specialized interest, it's a good idea to make contact ahead of time.

The only roads around the Pantanal skirt the edges of the flood plain. From Campo Grande to Corumbá the BR-262 follows the southern border of the Pantanal, affording small inroads here and there, particularly around Miranda, Aquidauana, and toward Corumbá. However, with many of the more isolated lodges, such as the Fazenda Rio Negro and the Fazenda Alto Barranco, the only way in during many of the wetter months is by airplane. A three-passenger plane from Aquidauana will charge about R$1,200 (US$600/£324) to make the 30-minute flight (the pilot charges for an hour of flying time, because he has to return empty). The round-trip flight cost is thus around R$2,400 (US$1,200/£648) for three people. This extra cost should be factored in.

ESSENTIALS

GETTING THERE

BY PLANE   TAM ✆ **0800/570-5700** or 065/4002-5700; www.tam.com.br), **Gol** (✆ **0300/115-2121;** www.voegol.com.br), and **Varig** (✆ **092/4003-7000;** www.varig.com.br) service Campo Grande from Rio and São Paulo. Campo Grande's airport (✆ **067/3368-6093**) is 7km (4¼ miles) west of downtown. A taxi to downtown (the best option) costs about R$25 (US$13/£7).

BY BUS   The bus station in Campo Grande is at Rua Dom Aquino and Rua Joaquim Nabuco (✆ **067/3321-8797**). Buses connect Campo Grande to Cuiabá (approximately 10 hr.), Bonito (5 hr.), and Corumbá (7 hr.).

VISITOR INFORMATION

There is a **tourist information booth** at the **airport** (✆ **0800/647-6050** or 067/3363-3116) and the **main bus terminal** (✆ **067/3382-2350**). Both are open 9am to 6pm Monday through Saturday, but neither offer English-speaking staff. However, they can offer a few maps of the city, and some information on the Pantanal, Bonito, and other sights of interest.

FAST FACTS: Campo Grande

Car Rental Try either **Localiza** (✆ **0800/979-2000** or 067/3363-4598) or **Avis** (✆ **067/3325-0036**), both at Campo Grande airport.

Consulates *Bolivian* consulate, Rua 13 Maio, 2500, Centro (✆ **067/3025-4453**); *Paraguayan* consulate, Rua 26 de Agosto 384, Centro (✆ **067/3784-6610**).

Currency Exchange & Banks **Banco do Brasil**, Av. Afonso Pena 2202 (✆ **067/ 3326-1064**) Open 11am to 4pm Monday to Saturday, 24-hour ATM.

Hospital **Hospital Santa Casa**, Rua Eduardo Santos Pereira 88 (✆ **067/ 3322-4000**).

Internet Access Virtual Cafe, Rua 14 Julho 1647 (✆ **067/3384-0092**). Daily 8am to 8pm; cost is R$6 (US$3/£1.60) per hour.

TOUR OPERATORS IN THE SOUTH PANTANAL (CAMPO GRANDE)

It's worth contacting both the lodge and a tour operator and comparing prices. Often (though not always) the tour operator can offer a lodge package with airport pickup and transfers for the same or less than you might get booking directly with the lodge.

Located in Campo Grande, **Open Door** has some excellent packages for the Pantanal, for Bonito, and for combinations of the two. If you're just interested in the **Pantanal,** a **4-day/3-night** package tour at a Pantanal lodge including all meals and activities, with transfer from and to Campo Grande airport, starts at R$1,398 (US$699/£378). Trips to **Bonito** include admission to a few of the most popular activities, such as a visit to the blue lake cave and snorkeling on the Rio Sucuri. A **2-night/3-day Bonito** trip starts at R$812 (US$341/£170), including accommodations and transfers from and to Campo Grande. **Six-day, 5-night combo tours,** with a 3-night stay in the Pantanal and a 2-night stay in Bonito, including all transfers, start at R$2,460 (US$1,230/£664) per person. Contact Open Door at Rua Barão do Rio Branco, Campo Grande 314 ((C) **067/3321-8303;** www.opendoortur.com.br). The agency is quick in responding to e-mail.

N & T Japantour, Av. Afonso Pena 2081, room 20, Campo Grande ((C) **067/3382-9425;** www.japantour.com.br) also provides packages to several Pantanal lodges at comparable prices.

Mostly geared toward backpackers, **Pantanal Trekking Tour,** Rua Jaoquim Nabuco 185, Campo Grande ((C) **067/3042-0508;** www.pantanaltrekking.com), offers more rustic 3- to 5-day overland trips through the Pantanal—mostly along the Estrada Parque, a dirt road through the South Pantanal—between Campo Grande and Corumbá. Trips include guides and activities such as horseback riding. Price depends on itinerary and number in group, but starts at about R$200 (US$100/£54) per day per person.

EXPLORING CAMPO GRANDE & THE SOUTH PANTANAL

There's not much to keep you dawdling in Campo Grande. Those who are booked on package tours to Bonito or the Pantanal can time their arrivals to connect with their transfers onward, eliminating the need to stay in Campo Grande for a night.

Because of the distance and the difficulty of access, there is no 1-day option for the South Pantanal. Either commit to 3 days, or don't bother to come. The Caiman Lodge is one of the best ranches in the South Pantanal and a wonderful, cushy way to explore the ranch land and see some amazing wildlife. If you have a few extra days in this region, consider a 2-day side trip to Bonito to swim in the crystal-clear waters of the Rio Prata or Sucuri, and maybe try some rappelling or caving (see "A Side Trip to Bonito," below).

WHERE TO STAY IN CAMPO GRANDE
MODERATE
Bristol Exceler Plaza Hotel   The Exceler offers amenities that are hard to find in town, including tennis courts, a swimming pool, and a sauna. The rooms are spacious and comfortably furnished, with tile floors, firm queen-size beds, and a small desk area. Ask for a room specifically on the 9th or 10th floor facing east, and you'll get city views. The suites offer jetted tubs, a queen-size bed, and a small anteroom with couch.

Av. Afonso Pena 444, Campo Grande, 79005-001 MS. (C) **067/3312-2800.** Fax 067/3321-5666. www.bristolhoteis.com.br. 80 units (showers only). R$165–R$225 (US$83–US$113/£44–£61) double; R$230–R$275 (US$115–US$138/£62–£74) suite. Extra person add R$35 (US$18/£9.50). Children 7 and under stay free in parent's room. AE, DC, MC, V. Free parking. **Amenities:** Restaurant; bar; outdoor pool; tennis court; sauna; tour desk; business center; 24-hr. room service; laundry. *In room:* A/C, TV, high-speed Internet, minibar, fridge.

INEXPENSIVE
Indaiá Park Hotel   *(Kids)*   The Indaiá is an all-around pleasant hotel just a few blocks from downtown. Rooms come in doubles, triples, or quads, easily accommodating a family. All rooms are good-size and come with large desks and an armchair,

and beds are big and firm with goose-down pillows. For a bit more space it's worth spending the extra R$35 (US$18/£9.50) to get a suite. Although the furniture is slightly dated, you upgrade to a bathroom with jetted tub, a king-size bed, and a sitting area with armchairs in your larger bedroom.

Av. Afonso Pena 354, Campo Grande, 79005-001 MS. ℂ **067/2106-1000.** Fax 067/321-0359. www.indaia-hotel.com.br. 128 units (showers only). R$115 (US$58/£31) double; R$150 (US$75/£41) suite. Extra person add R$35 (US$18/£9.50). Children 6 and under stay free in parent's room. AE, DC, MC, V. Free parking. **Amenities:** Restaurant; bar; outdoor pool; tour desk; business center; room service; laundry. *In room:* A/C, TV, free Internet, minibar, fridge.

WHERE TO DINE IN CAMPO GRANDE

Dining options include **Casa Colonial,** Av. Afonso Pena 3997 (ℂ **067/3383-3207**). The house special here is grilled chicken (delicious!), picanha beef, or roasted pork. At the popular Portuguese restaurant **Acepipe,** Rua Eduardo Santos Pereira 645 (ℂ **067/3383-4287**), the house specialty is *bacalhau* (cod), served grilled or with egg and onion. Surprisingly enough, Campo Grande is also a good city for Japanese food, a legacy of the Japanese laborers who worked building the railroad through the state in the 19th century. For a big bowl of soba noodles, try **Soba Shimada,** Av. Mato Grosso 621 (ℂ **067/3321-5475;** daily 6–11pm), or for something more simple, any of a half-dozen kiosks at the Feira Central, located next to the train station. For a full-menu Japanese restaurant, try **Kendô,** Av. Alfonso Pena 4150 (ℂ **067/3382-9000**). Open Tuesday to Sunday 7pm to midnight.

Fogo Caipira 🌟🌟 BRAZILIAN   Go hungry and with friends if you can—the portions here are huge! One of the best restaurants in Campo Grande, Fogo Caipira serves up hearty regional fare such as *pintado* fish, served in a large casserole dish, stewed with tomatoes, banana, and cilantro. For meat eaters, there's *carne seca na moranga,* dried beef stewed with pumpkin and creamy cheese, served in a pumpkin. Desserts are on the house and include a selection of candied fruits that go well with a strong espresso.

Av. Rua José Antonio 145, Centro. ℂ **067/3324-1641.** Main courses R$18–R$30 (US$9–US$15/£5–£8) for 2. AE, DC, MC, V. Mon–Fri 5–11pm; Sat 11am–midnight; Sun 11am–4pm. Bus: via Shopping Campo Grande.

LODGES IN THE SOUTH PANTANAL (CAMPO GRANDE)

Fazenda Barranco Alto 🌟🌟   This South Pantanal farm lies on the Rio Negro, in a region known for its landscape of small salt lakes (called *salinas*) and freshwater ponds, as well as its large populations of animals and birds. The owner has counted 407 bird species so far; hyacinth macaws are common, as are trogons, jacamars, toucans, raptors, and many other species. There are also several mammal species; the property spreads along 15km (9 miles) of the Rio Negro, and so provides an excellent habitat for capybara and giant river otters. Jaguars are spotted now and then by the river (but no guarantees). The best time to visit is from March to October. For migrant birds the best months are July to October. All tours are accompanied by either the owner, Lucas Leuzinger (who has a master's in biology), or his wife Marina (who has a master's in agronomy), together with local Pantanal guides. Tours include horseback riding to spot animals, or watching the daily work of the cowboys on the farm, or trips by jeep in search of tapirs, anteaters, marsh deer, giant otters, and others. There is also swimming, fishing, and canoeing on the Rio Negro. Bird-watching is also popular. The farm guesthouse has a triple and three double rooms, all simply but comfortably furnished with firm double or single beds. All rooms have a private veranda. There are never more than nine guests on the farm. The best way to reach the fazenda is by private plane from Campo Grande. The pilot charges R$1,500

(US$750/£405), which covers the flight in *and* out. The plane can fit three passengers, provided they bring limited luggage. In the dry season (Mar–Oct) you can also come in by 4×4. The 6-hour drive costs R$900 (US$450/£243) (again, in and out) with room for four to five people.

Caixa postal 109, Aquidauana, 79200-000 MS. © 067/9986-0373. www.fazendabarrancoalto.com.br. 4 units (showers only). R$340 (US$170/£92) per person per night, including all meals, drinks (including beer), guides, and activities. Owner recommends staying 4 days, but there is no minimum. Children up to 5 stay free in parent's room, 6–13 50% adult rate. AE, MC, V. **Amenities:** Internet; laundry. *In room:* A/C, hammock, no phone.

Fazenda Rio Negro 🦋🦋   This fazenda is part of a 7,700-hectare (19,000-acre) private nature reserve owned by the Washington, D.C.–based NGO Conservation International (www.conservationinternational.org). There are scientific researchers at the lodge, and guests are occasionally allowed to tag along with their activities, but the main attraction here remains the incredibly rich Pantanal wildlife. The range of activities includes hiking, horseback riding, and canoeing in the Rio Negro, as well as jeep and wildlife watching trips. The lodge is in a classic old Pantanal-style ranch house, with vast dining rooms and spacious verandas. The main house itself has two VIP suites and two other rooms. The standard rooms are in a second guesthouse about 100m (328 feet) away. All are comfortable but nothing fancy. Guests usually stay for 3 days. The program of activities normally evolves as follows: Day 1: hiking and boat trip; Day 2: jeep safari and horseback riding; Day 3: canoeing and a night safari. However, the schedule is flexible. The only way into the ranch is by plane. The lodge quotes the following rates, but guests are welcome to shop around. Better rates may well be available. Van to/from Aquidauana, then three-passenger plane to/from the lodge: R$3,100 (US$1,550/£837).

Rua Parana 32, Campo Grande, 79021-220 MS. © 067/3326-0002. www.fazendarionegro.com.br. 13 units (showers only). R$350 (US$175/£95) per person standard room; R$450 (US$225/£122) per person VIP suite, including all meals, guides, and activities. Children 4 and under stay free in parent's room, 5–11 R$200 (US$100/£54) per day. AE, MC, V. **Amenities:** Bar; horses; canoes; laundry. *In room:* A/C, no phone.

Pousada Aguapé 🦋   Though still a working ranch, the Aguapé has largely transformed into a tourism and fishing lodge. It's located on 60km (37 miles) of dirt road from Aquidauana, itself 130km (81 miles) of paved highway from Campo Grande. Accommodations are in comfortable but simple rooms. Activities include horseback riding, trail walking, fishing for piranhas, a boat tour on the Aquidauana River, a nighttime search for caiman, and some time helping out with the cattle. The grounds are well equipped for downtime, with pool, volleyball court, and soccer pitch. Avid fishermen can skip the eco-tourism activities and make use of the boats and drivers to fish the Aquidauana.

Rua Marechal Mallet 588, Aquidauana. © 067/3258-1146 or 067/9986-0351 (cellphone). www.aguape.com.br. 15 units (showers only). R$280 (US$140/£76) per person. Children 3 and under stay free in parent's room, 4–5 R$75 (US$38/£20), 6–10 R$150 (US$75/£40). AE, DC, MC, V. Free parking. **Amenities:** Restaurant; bar; pool; soccer field; horse riding; fishing. *In room:* A/C, no phone.

Refugio Caiman 🦋🦋 *Kids*   The most luxurious lodge in the Pantanal, the Refugio Caiman is set on a huge cattle ranch outside the town of Miranda, about 250km (155 miles) from Campo Grande. The land is not as rugged as in the North Pantanal; years of ranching, draining, and road building have left their mark. However, the Refugio is still every bit the working cattle ranch. Every morning ranch hands head out to look after the cattle. In late afternoon they practice rodeo moves in the corral. Soft-adventure activities here are very safe—perfect for families with young children. Avid horseback riders should avoid this place; there is no trotting or galloping allowed (ever!), no matter how good your riding skills. Excursions are geared to those who lack the fitness level for longer hikes or expeditions. Fortunately, even with the somewhat stronger human imprint, the population of wildlife is still quite stunning. Huge jabiru storks, flocks of roseate spoonbills, egrets of all shapes and sizes, caiman, and capybaras can all be seen within steps of the lodge. Hyacinth macaws are frequently spotted. The food is outstanding and the accommodations, in an old hacienda with a new central pool, positively luxurious. Listed below are the rack rates. Contact tour operators for less expensive packages. Transportation from Cuiabá is not included. The lodge can arrange this for R$140 (US$70/£38) per person, one-way. When booking a package the transfers can be included.

Reservations: Av. Brigadeiro Faria Lima 3015, cj. 161,Itaim Bibi São Paulo. ℭ 011/3706-1800. Lodge ℭ 067/ 3242-1450. www.caiman.com.br. 25 units (showers only). R$395 (US$197/£100) per person per night, including all meals, guides, activities, and insurance. Children 2 and under stay free in parent's room; children 3–10 pay 50% adult rate; children over 10 pay full adult rate. AE, DC, MC, V. Free parking. **Amenities:** Restaurant; bar; outdoor pool; game room; laundry. *In room:* A/C, no phone.

5 A Side Trip to Bonito

You have to admire Bonito. Though located in the middle of nowhere—it's 300km (186 miles) from Campo Grande, and Campo Grande is *already* the end of the earth for most Brazilians—this small town has turned itself into a prime eco-tourism destination for Brazilians and foreigners who come to snorkel, raft, and rappel. To accommodate these eco-tourists, Bonito's tourism industry has created the kind of collusion that would make oil companies envious. All excursions cost the same, no matter where and how you book them. All trips are guided, numbers are capped each day, and transportation is not provided. Only taxis offer transportation and—you guessed it—they all charge the exact same fare. Brazilians first arrived after the town was featured in a nightly soap opera (if the moon had been featured in one of those *novelas*, the Brazilians would have been the first ones to land there), and more and more international travelers are drawn to Bonito as well.

The attraction is not the town. What people come for are the rivers; the numerous streams that bubble up from the substrate of limestone rock are so free of impurities that you get the kind of crystal-clear visibility normally found only in tropical oceans. You can see 21 to 30m (70–100 ft.) in these fast-flowing rivers, and they're full of freshwater *dourado* and *pintado*, not to mention the occasional anaconda. The area also has numerous caves and waterfalls. However, all of the prime terrain is on private land and you're only allowed on as part of an excursion.

Is the trip worth it? It's a long way to go, but the rivers are fun and fascinating. It's also instructive to see this little town in action, gouging tourists who fork over the bucks as a matter of course. A package tour with transportation and admission (such as the ones offered by Open Door in Campo Grande) is recommended; you will get no better prices once you get there, and at least it'll save the frustration of opening your wallet every time you want to do something.

ESSENTIALS
GETTING THERE
BY CAR To reach Bonito take the BR-060 from Campo Grande to Guia Lopes da Laguna and then the MS-382 to Bonito. Count on a 4-hour drive. The road is now completely paved.

BY BUS   From Campo Grande, take **Viação Cruzeiro do Sul** (© **067/3312-9710;** www.cruzeirodosulms.com.br/canais/passageiros/linhas). Tickets cost R$39 (US$20/ £11), and the bus ride takes about 5 hours. Daily departures at 7am, 9am, 11am, 4pm, 7pm, and 11pm.

VISITOR INFORMATION
The official **tourist office** is at Rua Cel. Pilad Rebuá1780 (© **067/3255-1850**); it's open daily from 9am to 5pm. The Bonito tourist information site is www.portal bonito.com.br.

GETTING AROUND
Getting around Bonito without a car means getting gouged by taxis. Tour operators don't provide transportation; taxi companies all charge the same high rates. If you haven't come with a package tour, think seriously about renting a car. The only car-rental agency is **Yes** (© **067/3255-1702**).

FAST FACTS: Bonito   Bank Banco do Brasil, Rua Luiz Costa Leite 132 (& 067/3255-1121).
Internet Access Rhema Cópias Lanhouse, Rua Pilad Rebua, 1626 (© 067/ 3255-4271). Open daily from 8:30am to 10pm; R$8 (US$4/£2) per hour.

EXPLORING THE AREA
All of the activities listed below (plus quite a few others) are sold through tour operators in Bonito. One operator with a good English website is **Ygarapé Tour,** Rua Pilad Rebuá 1823 (© **067/3255-1733;** www.ygarape.com.br). Every tour operator offers the same packages at the same price, so don't waste time shopping around. Numbers are limited, so it's key to book your excursions as early as possible. Avoid long weekends and high season in January, February, and July if you can; the popular trips fill up quickly.

All activities are guided. If you are a real outdoors do-it-yourselfer, Bonito will drive you insane. On the other hand, if you are a novice adventurer or are traveling with young children or older people, this is the perfect environment to try some rafting, snorkeling, or hiking. If you are driving, ask for detailed directions; some of these attractions can be tricky to find. The prices listed below are for the peak season. Some of the tours offer a small discount (up to 20%) in the low season.

Aquario Natural ⚐   The best known of the springs and rivers that people swim in is the Aquario Natural. Starting at the wellspring of the Rio Baia Bonita, you snorkel a .5km (½-mile) stretch of crystal-clear river with amazing underwater views of fish. The downside is that this is also the busiest excursion, and your time on the river (an hour or so) is shorter than some of the others.
Road to Jardim, Km 7. R$145 (US$73/£39).

Cachoeira do Rio do Peixe   For a more mellow activity, take a visit to the water-fall of Rio do Peixe. Over 10m (30 ft.) tall with crystal-clear pools and caves to swim in, it's a great spot to spend a hot afternoon.
Road to Bodoquena, Km 35. R$75 (US$38/£20) with lunch.

Floating the Sucuri ★★ First you walk through the forest to see where the Sucuri River gurgles up through limestone fissures. A bit farther down, once the river has gained some depth and momentum, you get in the water for your 2km (1¼-mile) snorkel trip. It's like floating in an aquarium with an amazing number of fish to look at. Drift and enjoy the view.

Road to São Geraldo, Km 20. R$115 (US$57/£31), includes lunch.

Gruta do Lago Azul Tour operators promote this tour as a must-see, which is likely why it's always packed. Every 15 minutes a group sets off on the 351m (1,170-ft.) trail into the 69m-deep (230-ft.) cave. The calcium formations are certainly cool—amazing stalactites, stalagmites, stone flowers, and dish-shaped travertines. The lake at the bottom is an eerie clear blue; it's also fenced off to prevent people from sticking in their little fingers or toes. While you make your way back up, the next two groups will already be on their way down. From mid-December to mid-January, from 8:30 to 9:30am, the sun hits the lake directly—an impressive sight.

Road to Campo dos Indios (Fazenda Jaraguá). R$25 (US$13/£7).

Rafting on the Rio Formosa The rapids are nothing to write home about, but it is a peaceful float. This 7km (4¼-mile) trip takes you over some small rapids, and you'll stop along the way for a swim in some of the waterfalls. Keep your eyes peeled for birds, monkeys, and butterflies.

Road to Ilha do Padre, Km 12. R$50 (US$25/£14).

Rappelling and Snorkeling in Anhumas Abyss ★★★ Book ahead for this most popular adventure, especially during weekends or holidays. If you have never rappelled before, you will learn how and be provided with all the gear for the grand descent of 72m (236 ft.) into an abyss packed with stalactites and stalagmites. At the bottom you can snorkel in the crystal-clear water.

Road to Campo dos Indios (Fazenda Jaraguá). R$350 (US$175/£95) for snorkel and rappel.

Rio da Prata ★★ The tour starts with a 50-minute walk through the forest. The subsequent 2.5km (1½-mile) float in the Rio da Prata among the *paçu, dourado, piraputangas,* and *pintados* is one of the longest.

Fazenda Cabeceira do Prata BR-267 to Jardim, Km 55. R$117 (US$59/£32).

WHERE TO STAY

Águas de Bonito ★ The Águas is more like a small resort, with an outdoor pool and whirlpool, lighted tennis courts, and meals included. The rooms are tile-floored and spotless, featuring a double or two single beds, plus a clean, functional bathroom. Each room comes with a small veranda and hammock. The best ones are on the second floor of the two-story chalets.

Rua 29 de Maio 1679, Bonito, MS 79290-000. ℭ 067/3255-2330. www.aguasdebonito.com.br. 30 units (showers only). High season (Dec–Feb and July) R$220–R$280 (US$110–US$140/£59–£76) double; low season R$130–R$180 (US$65–US$90/£35–£49) double. Extra person add 25%. Children 4 and under stay free in parent's room. MC, V. Free parking. **Amenities:** Restaurant; bar; outdoor pool; lighted tennis courts; Jacuzzi. *In room:* A/C, TV, minibar, fridge, safe.

Santa Esmeralda ★★ Perhaps the nicest place in all Bonito, Santa Esperalda is located in a green piece of parkland on the banks of the Rio Formosa. Accommodations are in pretty, self-contained bungalows, each with a hammock and a broad front veranda. Guests can swim in the river, or lounge in the natural pools and small waterfalls, or go for a paddle in the complimentary kayaks. There's a pleasant outdoor restaurant, where both breakfast and dinner (included) are served. The only potential drawback is the location, a 17km drive out of town.

Rodovia Guia Lopes Km 17, Bonito, MS 79290-000. (✆ 067/3255-2683. www.hotelsantaesmeralda.com.br. 16 units (unheated showers only). High season Dec–Mar R$275 (US$142/£70) double; Apr–Nov R$185 (US$93/£47) double. Extra person add R$30 (US$15/£8). Children 10 and under stay free in parent's room. AE, DC, MC, V. Free parking. **Amenities:** Free kayaks; river swimming; waterfalls; dinner included. *In room:* A/C, TV, fridge, no phone.

Wetiga 🦆🦆   This beautiful modern hotel with an innovative design features extensive use of aroeira tree trunks in its structure. The hotel is built in a U around a central reflecting pool, so most units have pleasant balconies overlooking the pool. Rooms are new and modern, with tile floors and queen-size beds with nice linen. The restaurant (dinner is included) serves innovative cuisine using local ingredients, with the option of outdoor dining by the pool.

Rua Coronel Pilad Rebuá 679, Bonito, MS 79290-000. (✆ 067/3255-1699. www.wetigahotel.com.br. 67 units (showers only). High season (Dec–Feb and July) R$360–R$400 (US$180–US$200/£97–£108) double; low season R$280–R$360 (US$140–US$180/£76–£97) double. Extra person add 25%. Children 4 and under stay free in parent's room. MC, V. Free parking. **Amenities:** Restaurant (dinner included); bar; outdoor pool; Jacuzzi. *In room:* A/C, TV, minibar, fridge, safe.

WHERE TO DINE

Aquária Restaurante SEAFOOD   Dine on the main-street patio—you'll see all of Bonito file by. The food is simple home cooking, with lots of local fish such as grilled *pintado* or *dourado* served with a mushroom caper sauce. All dishes are served with rice, fries, and salads and are plenty for two. There are also individual *churrasco* plates such as the *picanha* with fries and salad for R$10 (US$5/£2.70).

Rua Pilad Rebuá 1883. (✆ 067/3255-1893. Main courses R$22–R$30 (US$11–US$15/£5.50–£7.50) for 2. No credit cards. Daily 10am–4pm and 6–11pm.

Cantinho do Peixe BRAZILIAN   The best fish place is town serves up locally caught pintado and dourado, simply grilled and served with lots of farofa and fries on the side. The menu includes chicken and various grilled beef dishes, such as *picanha* and *alcatra*.

Rua 31 de Março 1918. (✆ 067/3255-3381. Main courses R$18–R$28 (US$9–US$14/£5–£7.50). No credit cards. Daily 11am–3:30pm and 6:30pm–midnight.

Taboa Bar BRAZILIAN   Taboa is the nighttime gathering place. Sidewalk tables pack the street, and inside locals and visitors quickly fill up the tables. The drink of choice is *cachaça;* the house special is served with honey, cinnamon, and *guarana* powder. For food there are starters such as the *caldinho de feijão,* a tasty bean soup, as well as small plates with grilled fish, chicken, or beef.

Rua Pilaud 1837. (✆ 067/3255-1862. www.taboa.com.br. Everything under R$22 (US$11/£6). No credit cards. Daily 5pm–2am.

6 Corumbá & the South Pantanal

> *Corumbá looks like a city from a Jules Verne novel.*
> —*Tristes Tropiques,* Claude Levi-Strauss

I'm not entirely sure what the great French anthropologist had in mind when he set down that thought about Corumbá back in 1933. My guess is that it was a comment on the city's otherworldly setting. Corumbá clings to a low cliff top, at the bottom of which, beyond the docks and riverboats, there begins a vast brown and green prairie of water that swirls and broods its way over the horizon, constrained finally by a distant smudge of low gray hills. Looking up from the river, or out from the city, Corumbá appears as the sole outpost of civilization in an otherworldly landscape of water.

It's a difficult place to reach. For hundreds of years the only travel route to Corumbá was by water, either across the Pantanal by canoe or up the Paraguay River by boat, through sometimes hostile Argentina and Paraguay. A railway linking Corumbá to Campo Grande wasn't built until the early 20th century. A road wasn't built until the 1970s.

The isolation has left the Pantanal close to Corumbá more pristine than in more settled places farther east. But the difficulty of access has been a challenge to the city's eco-tourism operators. Though Corumbá is more truly a Pantanal city than either Cuiabá in the north or Campo Grande in the east, both of the latter get more Pantanal-bound visitors. Lodges located closer to Corumbá keep their offices in Campo Grande, where they also pick up and drop off most of their paying visitors.

Corumbá's one true forte is sport fishing. The Paraguay River offers larger, more varied sport fish than anywhere else in Brazil, as well as better fishing infrastructure. There are lodges, camps, and even floating lodges that cruise up the river, allowing guests to fish away the day and relax with a cold beer in the evening. Eco-tourism also exists. Many of the lodges have fishing and eco-tourism options, allowing visitors to combine the two.

Is it necessary to visit Corumbá? No. Even if you're visiting a local lodge, it's possible to land and leave the same morning. What is worth doing, if time allows, is a visit to the cliff top Avenida Rondon, where you can look out over the Pantanal and wonder if even Jules Verne would ever have thought of a city in a landscape so strange.

ESSENTIALS
GETTING THERE
BY PLANE   TAM (© **0800/570-5700** or 067/4002-5700; www.tam.com.br) is the only national carrier that offers regular flights to Corumbá. Corumbá's airport is 5km (3 miles) north of downtown on Rua Santos Dumont (© **067/231-3322**). A taxi to downtown (the best option) costs about R$25 (US$13/£7).

BY BUS   The bus station is on Rua Porto Carrero (© **067/3231-2033**) about 3km (2 miles) west of downtown. **Andorinha** (© **067/3231-2033** or 0300/210-3900; www.andorinha.com) has nine buses per day to Campo Grande (approximately 6 hr.). It costs R$72 (US$36/£20).

VISITOR INFORMATION
The tourist information office, **Setur,** is on Rua Manuel Cavassa 275 on the waterfront (© **067/3232-5221;** www.corumba.com.br). It's open Monday through Friday noon to 6pm.

TOUR OPERATORS IN THE CORUMBÁ PANTANAL
As with other parts of the Pantanal, local tour operators can set up all the logistics of your journey, sometimes cheaper than you can do by contacting the lodge directly. It's worthwhile making contact, if only to compare prices. Operators in Corumbá have, in recent years, been eager enough for business to offer serous discounts (Pantur has

been offering a two-for-one deal on airfare). **Pantur** (© 067/3231-2000; www.
pantur.com.br) offers day tours along the Estrada Parque into the Pantanal, and fishing
expeditions along the Paraguay. **Perola do Pantanal** (© 067/3231-1470; www.perola
dopantanal.com.br) specializes in multiday fishing expeditions along the Paraguay,
but also offers photo safaris along the Estrada Parque. **Canaã Viagens e Turismo**
(© 067/3231-3667; www.corumba.com.br/canaa) also specializes in fishing expeditions, but offers a few eco-tourism options as well. Generally speaking, a 5-day, 4-night
eco-tourism adventure includes accommodations at a Pantanal fazenda, horseback-
riding trips, and wildlife watching, and starts at about R$1,200 (US$600/£324) per
person.

CITY LAYOUT

Corumbá is a small and pretty city, laid out in a perfect grid on a cliff top, overlooking the Pantanal toward the west. The center of the city is a green city square called
Praça da Independencia. Bordering the square to the north and south are two of
Corumbá's principal streets, the **Rua 15 de Novembro** and the **Rua Frei Mariano.**
To the west of Praça Independencia, the 2 blocks of Rua Frei Mariano between **Rua
13 de Junho** and **Avenida Rondon** is Corumbá's principal shopping district. North
1 block along Rua 13 de Junho is another, slightly seedy square called the **Praça da
República.** On the east side of that square is the **Museu do Pantanal.** Avenida Rondon itself is a wide boulevard running along the edge of the cliff overlooking the
Paraguay River and Pantanal. It's a pretty street lined with tall Imperial palms, where
Corumbáianos like to stroll in the evening. At the intersection of Rua Frei Mariano
and Avenida Rondon, a small street—**Ladeira Jose Bonifacio**—runs steeply downhill
to the marina and port area, the **Porto Geral.** The port is currently about half-reno-
vated; there are a number of outdoor cafes and a few restaurants on the waterfront. It's
also the place to find the tourism office, and fishing and tour operators.

GETTING AROUND

BY BUS   Corumbá is so compact you can walk pretty much everywhere in the center of town.

BY TAXI   There are taxi stands all over town. Taxis can also be hailed on the street,
or by calling **Taxi Ponto One** (© 067/3231-4043). Taxis are relatively more expensive than elsewhere in Brazil. A trip from the bus station into downtown will set you
back about R$25 (US$13/£7).

FAST FACTS: Corumbá

Car Rental **Localiza,** Rua Cabral 22064, Centro (© 067/3231-6000).

Consulates **Bolivian** consulate, Rua Cabral 1607 (© 067/3231-5605).

Currency Exchange & Banks **Banco do Brasil,** Rua 13 de Junho 914 (© 067/
3231-2686). **HSBC,** Rua Delamare 1068, has an ATM (© 067/3231-5455).

Hospital **Clinica Prontomed,** Rua Major Gama 782 (© 067/3231-1301).

Internet Access **Cyber Point,** Rua Major Gama 1387 (© 067/3232-4381). Open
Monday to Saturday 9am to 11pm; cost is R$8 (US$4/£2) per hour.

EXPLORING CORUMBÁ & THE SOUTH PANTANAL

Though Corumbá is a charming, almost–Norman Rockwell kind of city, the real attraction here is the Pantanal. The area around Corumbá offers wildlife viewing, akin in quality to that found in the North Pantanal, and better than that found in areas closer to Campo Grande. Corumbá is also the best place in all of Brazil for sport fishing.

ATTRACTIONS

Though truly impressive, **Forte Coimbra** (no phone) is also 3 hours downriver from Corumbá. The fort was built in 1775 to protect Brazil's western frontier, and was occupied for several years during Brazil's 19th-century war with Paraguay. Access is by boat.

WHERE TO STAY IN CORUMBÁ
MODERATE

Hotel Gold Fish ⚑⚑   This is the nicest place to stay in Corumba, located 8km (5 miles) outside of the old downtown, on the banks of the River Paraguay. Rooms are pleasant, clean, and simple, but it's the amenities that make this Fish worthwhile. There's a large outdoor pool and deck overlooking the river, plus a children's play area and outdoor bar and sitting area. Down the stairs on the river itself there's a separately run sport-fishing operation. The hotel caters largely to sport fishermen who can spend the day out on the water while leaving their wives and children to relax by the pool.

Av. Rio Branco 2799 (on the road to Ladario) Corumbá, 79005-001 MS. ☎ 067/3231-5106. Fax 067/3231-5108. 87 units (showers only). R$100–R$160 (US$50–US$80/£27–£43) double. Extra person add R$30 (US$15/£8). Children 6 and under stay free in parent's room. DC, MC, V. Free parking. **Amenities:** Restaurant; bar; outdoor pool; children's play area, barbecue; laundry. *In room:* A/C, TV, minibar, fridge.

Hotel Nacional Palace ⚑   Corumbá's top hotel is a pleasant mid-level establishment about a 10-minute walk from the center of town. Rooms are clean and comfortable, with tile floors, firm single or double beds, and bathrooms with hot showers. The large outdoor swimming pool and game room with pool table will fill your leisure time.

Rua América 936, Corumbá, 79005-001 MS. ☎ 067/3234-6000. Fax 067/3234-6002. www.hnacional.com.br. 100 units (showers only). R$130 (US$65/£35) double. Extra person add R$25 (US$13/£7). Children 7 and under stay free in parent's room. AE, DC, MC, V. Free parking. **Amenities:** Bar; outdoor pool. *In room:* A/C, TV, minibar, fridge.

WHERE TO DINE IN CORUMBÁ

Fine dining is not the reason to come to Corumbá, but there are some good restaurants serving local Pantanal fish in traditional ways. The specialty at **Ceará,** Rua Albuquerque 516 (☎ **067/231-1930**), is *pintado à urucum* (baked with dendê oil and coconut milk and covered with mozzarella cheese) or *à pantaneira* (fried with banana and manioc). Open Tuesday through Sunday 11am to 2:30pm and 6pm to midnight. For steak and simple meat dishes, there's **Avalom,** Rua Frei Mariano 499 (☎ **067/ 3231-4430**), open Monday to Saturday 11am to 3pm and 5:30 to 11pm.

LODGES IN THE SOUTH PANTANAL (CORUMBÁ)

Note: The lodges listed below also regularly arrange transfers from Campo Grande. They also offer both eco-tourism trips and sport-fishing packages. Both lodges are located off the **Estrada Parque (Park Road)** a little-traveled dirt and gravel road crisscrossed by innumerable small water courses that—much like the Transpantaneira in the North—offer tremendous wildlife-viewing opportunities.

Fazenda Xaraés ⚑   Located by the banks of the Rio Abobral, the Xaraés is very much a *fazenda* (ranch) experience, with visits to the corrals, rides in bullock carts, and outings to herd the cattle. In addition to horseback riding, guests can take advantage of the river to set out for self-guided paddles, as well as motorized bird-watching, night hunts for caiman and 4×4 photo safari expeditions. Accommodations are in rustic but comfortable quarters by the riverbank. There's also a pleasant ranch-style main house, with bar and snooker table and small library. Access to the Fazenda is over a rough 13km (8-mile) track, in a 4×4 provided by the hotel. Meals included.

Estrada Parque Km 17, Abobral, Corumbá. (℃ 067/9906-9272. Fax 018/9906-9282. www.xaraes.com.br. 17 units (showers only). 3-day package R$825 (US$437/£223) per person. Children 6–12 50% of adult rate. Under 5 stay free in parents room. V. Free parking. Access by 4×4 from Miranda. **Amenities:** Restaurant; bar; outdoor pool; soccer pitch; canoes. *In room:* A/C, TV, fridge.

Pantanal Park Hotel ⒢   Located on the shores of the Paraguay River, the lodge specializes in fishing trips; *paçu, barbado, pintado,* and more are abundant. Eco-tourists have the option of horseback riding, bird spotting, piranha fishing, and nighttime caiman-spotting trips. Accommodations are in smaller chalet buildings, with four apartments per building. These vary in quality. The most basic ones—on the ground floor of the buildings—are clean and comfortable, with firm single beds and functional bathrooms. The more luxurious upstairs rooms have a screened-in sitting area with TV and couches and chairs. Common lodge areas include a large outdoor pool and main building with restaurant and bar with nightly karaoke. All meals are included.

Reservations: (℃ 018/3908-5332. Fax 018/3908-1333. Lodge 067/9987-3267. www.pantanalpark.com.br. 41 units (showers only). 3-day package R$535 (US$267/£144) per person. Children 5–10 years old R$400 (US$200/£108). Under 5 stay free in parent's room. AE, DC, MC, V. Free parking. Access by boat from the Paraguay River bridge in Porto Morrinho. **Amenities:** Restaurant; bar; large outdoor pool; soccer pitch; game room; laundry. *In room:* A/C, TV, fridge, no phone.

Pousada Arara Azul ⒢   Located in the Nhecolandia region of the Pantanal, about 40km (25 miles) up an unpaved road, the Arara Azul lives up to its name—it's thick with blue (hyacinth) macaws. The pousada is nestled in between two large ponds. In addition to the macaws, lots of wading birds and plenty of caiman live here. Rooms are small, rustically furnished, but clean and pleasant. The pousada eco-tourism activities include horseback riding, nature walks, evening trips to seek out caiman, and photo safaris on a cart pulled by a tractor. Between wildlife viewing, a pleasant outdoor pool will entertain you. Meals are excellent.

Estrada Parque, Km 35, Corumbá. (℃ 067/9987-1530 or (reservations) 011/3865-5131. www.fazendaararaazul. com.br. 40 units (showers only). R$300 (US$150/£75) per person, per day. No credit cards. For packages contact directly via website. **Amenities:** Restaurant; bar; pool; laundry. *In room:* A/C, fridge, no phone.

FISHING OPTIONS IN THE CORUMBÁ PANTANAL

For serious fishermen and women, it's possible to head out on a sport-fishing boat-hotel. Boats vary in size and level of luxury, from small and simple to larger and luxurious. Nearly all offer packages that include meals and accommodations in small cabins, plus a guide and a small aluminum boat with an outboard motor from which you fish during the day. Drinks are always available and always cost extra. Guests normally bring their own fishing gear.

The *Almirante* (℃ **017/3231-9922;** www.barcoalmirante.com.br) is a well-kept modern boat that can accommodate 18 people in six air-conditioned cabins. A 6-day fishing package on the *Almirante* starts at about R$1,800 (US$900/£486) per person. The *Cabexy II* (℃ **067/3231-4683;** www.pantanaltours.tur.br) has a smaller, four-cabin boat with space for eight people and four fishing boats. Trips on the *Cabexy II* last 5 days and start at R$1,500 (US$750/£405) per person. The very large **Kalypso** (℃ **067/3231-1460;** www.peroladopantanal.com.br) has 28 cabins, about half of which are individual units, plus a deck-top pool and Jacuzzi. Six-day packages start at R$1,800 (US$900/£486).

18

Fernando de Noronha

Fernando de Noronha may be the desert island upon which people dream of being marooned. On Noronha, verdant mountains descend to sheer cliffs, which in turn fall onto wide sandy beaches that have known neither condo nor cabana. Beneath the waves live coral and colorful fish, manta rays, and lemon sharks. Sea turtles lay eggs by the thousands on the beaches facing out toward the Atlantic. And then there are the spinner dolphins. Early in the morning, in a bay named, appropriately, Baía dos Golfinhos (Bay of Dolphins), spinner dolphins gather in pods of more than 1,000 to frolic and spin in the morning sunshine. Come afternoon, they set off on a daily circuit around the main island. It's an island ecosystem in all its tropical glory.

Noronha was Brazil's first national marine park. All of the water and 70% of the land on and around Ilha de Fernando de Noronha is national park, administered by the Brazilian environment agency IBAMA. Development is strictly controlled, and visitors must pay a daily tax that supports environmental preservation.

Even with the rules, there is plenty to do on Noronha. The archipelago is the best dive spot in Brazil, and one of the better ones in the world. It's also known as a surfing hot spot. Visitors can rent dune buggies and explore the island's pristine beaches.

For most of its history, of course, people have tried to escape from Noronha. From the 17th until the 20th century, Fernando de Noronha served an as an inescapable political prison. This 21-island archipelago sits way out in the Atlantic, 360km (223 miles) from Natal, 545km (337 miles) from Recife, and 2,600km (1,612 miles) from the African coast. From the 1940s to the 1980s the island was under the direct rule of Brazil's armed forces, which used it as both a base and prison. (For a time in the 1960s the island also served as a satellite tracking station for the U.S. armed forces.) Not until 1988, when much of the island was incorporated in the new marine park, did Fernando de Noronha meet its destiny as a sought-after tropical paradise.

Unfortunately, now that everyone wants to get to Noronha—particularly after the discovery of the island by Brazil's movie-star glitterati—prices for accommodations on the island have zoomed to ridiculous heights. Modest little pousadas offering little more than a room in the family home now charge upwards of R$250 (US$125/£68) a night—as much as some luxury hotels in other parts of Brazil. Prices for meals and tours haven't yet followed suit, though it may be just a matter of time. The islands do remain a special, even magical place. If you can accept being gouged with equanimity, by all means come and experience the magic. If coughing up such large amounts seems likely to stick in your craw, it may be best to steer clear of Noronha until the natives there come to their senses.

1 Fernando de Noronha Essentials

GETTING THERE

Trip (© **081/3619-1148** or 0300/789-8747; www.voetrip.com.br) has flights from Natal and Recife. **Varig (Nordeste)** (© **081/3619-1144** or 081/4003-7000) has daily flights from Recife, Rio de Janeiro, and São Paulo. The **Aeroporto Fernando de Noronha** (© **081/3619-1311**) is in the middle of the island, a R$20 (US$10/£7.50) taxi ride from anywhere.

VISITOR INFORMATION

The official government website, **www.noronha.pe.gov.br**, has an English-language version with much useful information. Free maps of the island (with English text) are available in pamphlet racks at the airport. There is an intermittently staffed and not very useful **tourist information office** on the lower floor of the Palácio São Miguel (city hall) in the island's largest town, **Vila Remédios** (© **081/3619-1352**). There's good information on the island's natural history at the **Projeto Tamar** office at Av. do Boldró s/n (© **081/3619-1171**; www.tamar.org.br). High season in Fernando de Noronha is in July, and December through March, especially the time between Reveillon (New Year's Eve) and Carnaval. Pousadas fill up, and prices for everything rise. In low season (all other times) prices are slightly more reasonable and bargaining is possible—though Fernando de Noronha is still pricier than the rest of Brazil.

ISLAND LAYOUT

The main island, Ilha de Fernando de Noronha, has two distinct sides, a gentle one facing the Brazilian coast and a rockier, rougher one facing the Atlantic. The inshore coast is the place for surfing and lazing on the beach. The offshore beach is for watching the waves crash in.

One paved road, **BR-363,** runs from Baía do Sueste at one end of the island to the port in Baía Santo Antonio at the other. The most settled area on Noronha is **Vila dos Remédios.** This is where you'll find the city hall, the church, the old fort, the only bar/disco, the post office, and the offices of **Atlantis Divers.** Up a small hill about 1km (½ mile) away is **Vila do Trinta.** This area has a couple of restaurants, the police, pharmacy, and main grocery store all together inside the walls of the old armory. **Porto Santo Antonio** has several watersports operators and a few restaurants and pubs. The hospital, school, and other services for locals are located on BR-363 in the

---

Renting a Dune Buggy 🐞🐞

Tooling around back roads to various beaches is one of the most fun things to do on the island. Buggies can be rented just about anywhere—ask at your pousada. **LocBuggy** (© **081/3619-1490**; www.locbuggy.com.br) provides 24-hour service, and also rents motorcycles and 4×4s. Other agencies include **Locadora Morro do Farol** (© **081/3619-1392**) in Al. Boldro, and Locadora Marlin in Remédios (© **081/ 3619-1223**). A driver's license is not required. The price is currently R$125 (US$63/£34) per day, though if you rent for several days you can often get a 10% to 20% discount. The cost is the same with or without driver. Gas costs about R$4.50 (US$2.25/£1.20) per liter (about US$7.25 per gallon). A day of exploring around the island will eat up about half a tank, currently about R$65 (US$33/£18).

middle of the island. The old American army base at **Alameda do Boldró** has boring necessary stuff like the power station and the water plant, but it also has the **Tamar Visitor Center,** which features a small museum where they hold nightly nature talks.

GETTING AROUND

BY BUS   A public bus runs along the main highway (BR-363) from Baía Sueste to Porto Santo Antonio with stops along the way. The bus runs from 5am to 10pm. Cost is R$2.50 (US$1.25/£.65).

BY TAXI   Chances are, wherever you go on the island there'll be a taxi *ponto* with a buggy driver waiting for your business. Should you find yourself unaccountably taxiless, **NorTax** (✆ **081/3619-1314**) will dispatch a buggy from its fleet. Prices for all drivers are fixed according to a table, which the driver will be happy to flash in your face should you utter so much as a peep about the cost. The fare from Vila dos Remédios to Baía do Sueste on the far end of the island costs about R$32 (US$16/£8.50); from Vila Remédios to the Tamar Visitor Center is R$15 (US$7.50/£4); from Vila Remédios to the port, R$12 (US$6/£3.25).

FAST FACTS: Fernando de Noronha

Note: For all its charm, Fernando de Noronha is essentially a small town, as lacking in services as the next village on a desert island in the middle of the ocean. If a service or resource isn't listed below, it means Fernando de Noronha doesn't have it.

Currency Exchange & Banks   Bring *lots* of cash to the island. The only bank on the island provides absolutely no services to visitors. Dive operators and most pousadas take credit cards; so, increasingly, do many tour operators and restaurants. However, taxis and buggy rentals most often do not. In a pinch, you may be able to cash a traveler's check at Atlantis Divers (see "Diving," later in this chapter)—but don't count on it.

Hospitals   Hospital São Lucas, BR-363 s/n, in Vila da Floresta (✆ **081/3619-1377**).

Internet Access   Cia da Lua (✆ **081/3619-1631**) in Vila dos Remédios. R$12 (US$6/£3.25) per hour.

Pharmacies   Lojinha de Mãezinha, Vila Remédios (✆ **081/3619-1104**), open Monday through Saturday from 8am to 6pm. Selection is quite limited.

Police   Policia Civil (✆ **081/3619-1179**).

Post Office   The main post office, opposite the town hall (Palácio São Miguel) in Vila Remédios (✆ **081/3619-1135**), is open Monday through Friday from 8am to 12:30pm.

Taxes   There is a special environmental tax—currently R$33 (US$17/£9) per day, R$205 (US$103/£56) per week—payable (cash only) at the airport when you arrive, or in advance using the Internet. Go to www.noronha.pe.gov.br/ctudo-taxa.asp, then fill in and print out the form. Pay the fee at any Banco do Brasil or Loterica (lottery selling booth). Make sure they stamp your form. If you decide to stay longer than anticipated, go to the airport and pay the extra days *before* your time expires. If you overstay and try to pay up at the airport upon

Fernando de Noronha

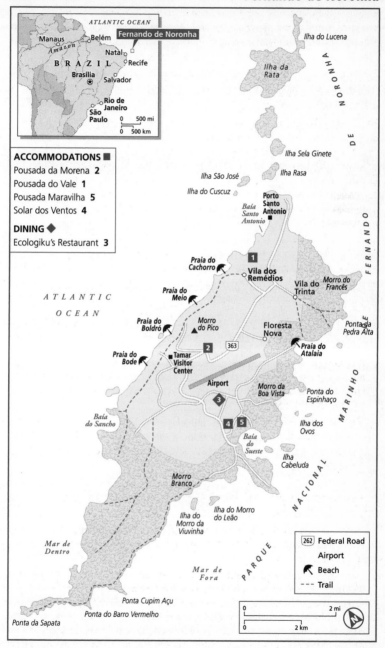

ATLANTIC OCEAN

Fernando de Noronha

Manaus • Belém

Amazon

B R A Z I L

Natal

Recife

Brasília ⊛

Salvador

Rio de Janeiro

São Paulo

0   500 mi

0   500 km

ACCOMMODATIONS ■

Pousada da Morena **2**

Pousada do Vale **1**

Pousada Maravilha **5**

Solar dos Ventos **4**

DINING ◆

Ecologiku's Restaurant **3**

Ilha do Lucena

Ilha da Rata

N O R O N H A

Ilha Sela Ginete

Ilha São José

Ilha Rasa

Ilha do Cuscuz

Porto Santo Antonio

D E

Baía Santo Antonio

F E R N A N D O

ATLANTIC

OCEAN

Praia do Cachorro

Vila dos Remédios **1**

Vila do Trinta

Morro do Francês

Praia do Meio

Morro do Pico

Floresta Nova

Ponta da Pedra Alta

Praia do Boldró

2 363

Tamar Visitor Center

Praia do Atalaia

Praia do Bode

Airport **3**

Morro da Boa Vista

Ponta do Espinhaço

M A R I N H O

4 **5**

Ilha dos Ovos

Baía do Sancho

Baía do Sueste

Ilha Cabeluda

Morro Branco

N A C I O N A L

Ilha do Morro da Viuvinha

Ilha do Morro do Leão

Mar de Dentro

P A R Q U E

262 Federal Road

Airport

Mar de Fora

Beach

Ponta Cupim Açu

Trail

Ponta do Barro Vermelho

Ponta da Sapata

0   2 mi

0   2 km

465

leaving, you'll be charged twice the regular rate for your extension. Divers and boaters who enter the marine park are charged a day tax of R$15 (US$7.50/£4). As in the rest of Brazil, hotels normally add 10% to the bill.

Weather The weather is hot year-round, with an average daily temperature of 86°F (30°C). Ocean temperature is 82°F (28°C) year-round. The rainy season is February to July, the dry season from August to January. Surfing season is December to March.

2 Where to Stay

Pousadas in Noronha used to be simple, even makeshift affairs, but at some point in the last few years Brazil's movie-star glitterati and their attendant national media discovered the island. Supply and demand have gone seriously out of whack, and prices everywhere have zoomed up into the red-line zone that economists label "just-plain-stupid." Many pousadas tripled and quadrupled their rates, while making no improvements in quality. Others, more justifiably, invested in major upgrades, and so can at least offer a quality commensurate with the price tag. There is no longer anywhere inexpensive place to stay on Noronha, but on a desert island in the middle of the Atlantic, there's not much you can do about it.

The pousadas listed below, while not inexpensive, at least offer something different or special. Given demand on the island they may well be booked. If so, try the **Dolphin Hotel** (© 085/3619-1100; www.dolphinhotel.tur.br), which offers small clean rooms and a pool for R$555 (US$277/£138) a night, or **Pousada Sueste** (© 085/3619-1164; www.pousadasueste.com.br), which has a small pool and a view down to Sueste Bay, plus small clean rooms with smaller bathrooms for R$335 (US$168/£91) a night.

The prices listed are for the high season—January through February and July through September, plus all holidays. In low season—March through June and October through December—most pousadas lower their prices by about 20% to 25%.

VERY EXPENSIVE

Pousada Maravilha ★★★   Everything in this pousada is brand spanking new and built with exquisite taste in a Japanese-inspired style. Guests can stay either in self-contained bungalows or in the main pousada building. Outside, the bungalows feature a spacious veranda with hammock, cushioned deck chairs, and breakfast table. Inside bungalows have tile floors, a vaulted ceiling and king-size four-poster bed with firm mattress and lovely white linens. Bathrooms in both are large and lovely, with his-and-her sinks and mirrors, acres of counter space, and large hot showers. Rooms in the main building are slightly less luxurious, but still feature tasteful decor, king-size futon-style beds, and lovely bathrooms. All guests have use of the small "infinite-horizon" pool and pool deck with gorgeous views down to Baía Sueste. The pousada is a favorite with the stars of Brazil's insanely popular nighttime soap operas.

BR-363 s/n, Sueste, Fernando de Noronha, 53990-000 PE. ©/fax 081/3619-0028. www.pousadamaravilha.com.br. 8 units. R$1,450 (US$725/£392) bungalow; R$1,350 (US$675/£365) deluxe room. Children 6 and under stay free in parent's room. DC, MC, V. Free parking. **Amenities:** Restaurant; pool; bar; sauna. *In room:* A/C, flatscreen TV, DVD, minibar.

EXPENSIVE

Pousada da Morena ⭐ Pleasant and clean accommodations, at a price that's considered reasonable by Noronha standards. Both rooms and bungalows have tile floors, comfortable double beds, and solar-heated showers. Out front each has a small veranda with hammock. Two of the bungalows have a partial view of the sea and Mount Pico. The pousada is located adjacent to the one of the island's better restaurants, the **Trattoria do Morena.**

Rua Nice Cordeiro 2600, Floresta Velha, Fernando de Noronha, 53990-000 PE. ℂ 081/3619-1142. 2 rooms, 3 bungalows. R$418 (US$209/£113) double; $484 (US$242/£131) bungalow. Children 10 and under pay 50% adult rate. MC. Free parking. **Amenities:** Restaurant; free Internet. *In room:* A/C, TV, fridge.

Pousada do Vale ⭐ Located in a lovely garden area just a short walk from Vila Remédios, the Pousada do Vale offers the best compromise between quiet isolation and close proximity to town. Rooms are bright and reasonably sized, featuring comfortable queen-size beds with good linens and clean and functional bathrooms. The best two rooms are the Marlim, which is somewhat larger and has a sizeable balcony with a hammock, and the Golfinho room. The Golfinho is a tail-fin smaller, but it also features a balcony and hammock. The two-story "bungalows" are tall and narrow, but bright and airy inside, with hammock-equipped verandas front and back, plus king-size beds and saunas. The beach is but a 250m (820-ft.) stroll away, and the pousada has beach chairs, umbrellas, and towels for its guests. Room rates include breakfast and a light afternoon tea.

Rua Pescador Sérgio Lino 18, Jardim Elizabeth (down the cobblestone street from Vila Remédios), Fernando de Noronha 53990-000 PE. ℂ/fax 081/3619-1293. www.pousadadovale.com. 5 rooms, 2 bungalows. R$594–R$684 (US$297–US$342/£160–£185) double; R$846 (US$423/£228) bungalow. Children 3 and under stay free in parent's room. AE, MC, V. Transfer to and from airport included. **Amenities:** Restaurant; beach service; laundry; Internet (1 hr. per day free); free Wi-Fi. *In room:* A/C, TV, Internet (bring your own laptop), minibar, fridge, safe.

Solar dos Ventos ⭐⭐ The Solar features comfortable self-contained bungalows on a green piece of land with a view down to Baía do Sueste. Each unit features a double and two single beds, a couch, a breakfast table, and a balcony with a hammock. The grounds are nicely landscaped, and each cottage is given a nice bit of space. The only drawback is the location at the far end of the island, a R$22 (US$11/£6) taxi ride from the restaurants and services in Vila Remédios and the port. But if you have a buggy, it doesn't matter.

Estrada do Sueste s/n, Fernando de Noronha, 53990-000 PE. ℂ 081/3619-1347. Fax 081/3619-1253. www.solarnoronha.hpg.ig.com.br. 8 bungalows. R$480 (US$240/£130) double. Children 11 and under pay 50% adult rate. DC, MC, V. Free parking. *In room:* A/C, flatscreen TV, minibar.

3 Where to Dine

There is one truly excellent restaurant in Noronha (see review for Ecologiku's below), and then there are the others. In the port there's **Visual do Porto** (ℂ **081/3619-1129;** Mon–Sat 11am–10pm), which serves standard Brazilian fare. For seafood, there's **Varandão do Ilha** in Vila do Trinta (ℂ **081/3619-1546;** Tues–Sun noon–11pm). On the road to the beach at Praia do Boldró there's **Tartarugão** (ℂ **081/3619-1331;** Wed–Sun noon–3pm and 6–11pm), which serves seafood snacks and Brazilian fare from a lovely beachside spot. **Trattoria do Morena,** Rua Nice Cordeiro 2600, above BR-363 near the school (ℂ **081/3619-1142;** Mon–Sat 7–10:30pm), serves good pasta in generous portions. For expensive fine dining, there's the restaurant at the **Pousada Maravilha** (© **081/3619-1290;** daily noon–3pm and 8–11pm). The menu leans toward Italian-inflected seafood dishes. For coffee and lighter fare, there's **Cacimba Bistrô,** on Praça Eurico Dutra in Vila Remédios (© **081/3619-1200;** daily 9:30am–10:30pm).

Ecologiku's Restaurante 🏵🏵 SEAFOOD   Not only is this the best restaurant on the island, but it also would rank up there with many on the mainland. Six plastic tables with checkered tablecloths sit on a patio in a garden at the far end of the island. The kitchen specializes in seafood caught and cooked that day—simple but delicious. Lobsters are brought to your table, weighed, then taken back to be boiled, and served slathered in butter. The house special is the Sinfonia Ecologiku, a spiced and tasty hot pot of fish, octopus, shrimp, and sweet lobster, all in a rich seafood broth.

Estrada do Sueste, Sueste, PE 53990-031. © **081/3619-1807.** Main courses R$24–R$44 (US$12–US$22/ £6.50–£12). MC. Daily 7–10:30pm. (Closes every other Sat.)

4 Exploring Fernando de Noronha

Check with the **Projeto Tamar** office as soon as you arrive to see if any sea turtle nests will be hatching soon. If a turtle hatching is in the offing, rearrange your plans to see it—you won't be disappointed.

If your time is limited, find your pousada and then head out on a boat tour to see the island from the water. Go for an afternoon cruise to see the spinner dolphins or just to snorkel. If you have a bit more time, go diving or snorkeling around Baía do Sancho (see "Outdoor Activities & Watersports," below), saving time for a leisurely walk on the beach. Another great way to see the island is to rent a buggy and explore at will (see "Getting Around," above).

HITTING THE BEACHES

Baía do Sueste 🏵 is a pretty crescent beach with some good snorkeling. It's perfect for children, thanks to its large shallow areas and complete absence of waves. The beach has a snack stand and bathrooms.

Baía do Sancho 🏵🏵 is one of the prettiest beaches in all of Brazil. Access is via a series of precarious-looking iron ladders bolted into crevasses that somehow make it down through 30m (100-ft.) sheer red cliffs (clearly, don't try this if you're afraid of heights). The beach features lovely red-tinged sand, cliffs with nesting seabirds, and crystal-clear blue water with lots of fish and places to snorkel.

Praia do Atalaia 🏵🏵 is a unique beach on the outer shore of Noronha. A thick shelf of volcanic rock extends halfway through the surf line, providing a bulwark for some quiet natural pools where lots of tropical fish get trapped at low tide. Only 30 people are allowed in per day, and no suntan lotion can be worn when you swim in the pools. Access is through checkpoints monitored by IBAMA (Brazil's environmental agency), or via a trail from Vila do Trinta or a road from Baía do Sueste. If you don't know any better, you can also come in (as I did) on the uncontrolled trail from Enseada da Caieira. Arrive when the tide's coming in, and you can stand immersed to your waist by the outer edge of the rock shelf as huge waves come rolling in, only to smash themselves to harmlessness on the thick volcanic rock. It's reckless but a lot of fun.

The **surf beaches** are all on the inshore side of the island, facing back toward the Brazilian mainland. From west to east they are **Cacimba do Padre, Praia do Bode, Praia do Boldró, Praia da Conceição, Praia do Meio,** and **Praia do Cachorro.**

Most have one or two small *barracas* (beach kiosks). They're good places to hang out for a morning or afternoon. Be careful swimming, and keep an eye on the shore. These beaches have currents that sweep parallel to the shoreline; it's easy to get carried along.

OUTDOOR ACTIVITIES & WATERSPORTS

DIVING 𝒢𝒢𝒢   Walk into any dive shop throughout Brazil, and I guarantee they'll have a poster of Fernando de Noronha. Not only is it the best place for diving in Brazil, it's also one of the better spots in the world. Water temperature is a constant 82°F (28°C), and especially in the dry season, underwater visibility approaches almost 30m (100 ft.). Underwater there's a wide variety of stunning sea life: rays of all types (mantas are not uncommon); sea turtles; lemon sharks and reef sharks; clownfish; and large schools of anthias, surgeonfish, parrotfish, and sweetlips. The coral formations are only average, but thanks to the island's volcanic heritage you'll come across numerous caves, including a number of terrific swim-throughs.

The only drawback to diving on Noronha is the tight control. You are not allowed to dive except with one of the island's three dive companies. All three companies have implemented a system in which four divers are shepherded underwater by a dive instructor. Exploring on your own is not possible.

Far and away the best diving outfit on the island is **Atlantis Divers,** Caixa Postal 20, in Vila Remédios (℗ **081/3619-1371,** or in Natal 084/3206-8840; www.atlantis noronha.com.br); a distant second best is **Águas Claras,** Alameda do Boldró s/n (℗ **081/3619-1225;** www.aguasclaras-fn.com.br).

Atlantis has a fleet of three custom-built catamarans—one 11m (35 ft.) and the other two 13m (44 ft.) long—plus a 9.6m (32-ft.) launch—all brand-new and specially built for diving. They're a pleasure to use. Atlantis also recently inaugurated a live-aboard catamaran—the *Atlantis Voyager,* which cruises the best reefs, islands, and wrecks off the Brazilian coast. For information, see the website. Águas Claras uses 12-man open zodiacs or a converted fishing boat.

Atlantis charges R$200 (US$100/£54) for two dives, plus R$68 (US$34/£18) to rent a wet suit, BCD (buoyancy control device), and regulator. With the mandatory R$10 (US$5/£2.70) IBAMA tax, the total for two dives comes to R$278 (US$102/£51). Prices at Aguas Claras are comparable. Morning, afternoon, and night dives are offered. If you've never dived, both companies offer one-on-one escorted baptism dives for about R$225 (US$113/£61) plus IBAMA tax. You can also take a 5-day course to get your PADI diving certificate, for about R$1,000 (US$500/£270). Atlantis also offers nitrox courses and scooter courses, and for experienced divers, the Atlantis launch is available for custom excursions.

DOLPHIN-WATCHING 𝒢𝒢   Spinner dolphins congregate on Noronha in numbers virtually unmatched anywhere else. The best (and least obtrusive) way to see them is from the **cliff-top lookout** above Baía dos Golfinhos (Dolphin Bay). Monday to Saturday from 5:30am until sunset a researcher from the nonprofit **Projeto Golfinho Rotador** (℗ **081/3619-1846;** www.golfinhorotador.org.br) is on hand to answer questions and pass out binoculars between regular 15-minute counts of dolphin activity. Note that from 5:30 to 7am, the Projeto's binoculars are reserved for those who have come on the paid "Mirante de Golfinhos" tour offered by **Atalaia Turismo** (℗ **081/3619-1328;** www.atalaia-noronha.com.br). Cost is R$30 (US$15/£8). The dolphins usually arrive around 6am and depart between 3 and 5pm on their nightly feeding trip around the island. They're most active in the morning, when they're just coming off an evening's feeding, so I recommend showing up at sunrise. In dry season the bay will have between 500 and 1,200 dolphins jumping and spinning about. In the wet season the bay will have between 5 and 300 dolphins. The bay itself is off-limits to all but accredited scientists.

Boat tours (see "Boat Tours & Operators," below) now cruise past the edge of Dolphin Bay, hoping to be surrounded by a spinner school coming out for the day. The afternoon tours offer the best odds of spotting dolphins.

HIKING   Note that on trails within the national park you may be required to register with IBAMA and bring along a local guide. This has long been park policy; it's just never been enforced. Recently, however, the park has mooted plans to outsource the guiding and enforcing to tourism operators (mostly as a way of generating more revenue). If you want a guide, contact **ACITUR,** the Ecotourism Guides Association of Fernando de Noronha, located at the TAMAR offices on Avenida Boldró (© 081/3619-1399), or book one of the tours through LocBuggy (© 081/3619-1490). If you don't, your best bet is to simply show up at the trail head. Odds are no one will complain.

The **Trilha do Capim-açu,** which starts near the Dolphin Bay lookout and runs 7km (4.25 miles) as far as the lighthouse on Ponta da Sapata, is really not worth taking. The trail runs through dense forest from beginning to end, with only one small viewpoint on the very first ridge. A much better plan is to hike along or above **Praia do Leão.** The territory is open so you can always see where you're going. More importantly, the beach is wild and beautiful, and the views amazing. If you're happy jumping between rocks, you can also reach the lighthouse on Ponta de Sapata on this route. One other good but tricky trail runs from **Enseada da Caieira** near the port along the outer coast over a couple of tall rocky headlands to **Praia de Atalaia.** For an easier hike with worthwhile views, try the 2.5km (1.5-mile) walk from the **Dolphin Bay Lookout** along the cliff top to **Baía do Sancho.** Another nice walk—best done at low tide—goes from **Praia do Boldró** along the beach east to **Praia do Cachorro** below Vila Remédios. This 2.5km (1.5-mile) walk features nature signs posted by IBAMA, but whatever was on them has long since been erased by the sea.

HORSEBACK RIDING   There aren't any huge long beaches upon which to gallop on Noronha, but there are some good trails, back roads, and shorter beaches to explore. Three people offer horseback riding on the island: **Samuel** (© 081/3619-1141), **Ronaldo** (© 081/3619-1250), and **Valter** (© 081/3619-1764). Going with them is a matter of calling, saying what you're interested in, and seeing what's possible. Cost is around R$35 (US$18/£9.50) per hour per person

MOUNTAIN BIKING   In Vila Remédios, **Pousada Solimar** (© 081/3619-1965) rents mountain bikes for R$30 (US$15/£8) per day.

PROJETO TAMAR ✦✦✦   The Brazilian sea turtle conservation organization, Tamar, has a site on Noronha with a shop, small lecture theater, and cafe; the address is Av. do Boldró s/n (© 081/3619-1171). It's worth checking in every day or so to see if any turtle nests are likely to hatch soon. Watching hundreds of newly hatched turtles scramble into the surf is an experience not to be missed. The shop is open Monday through Friday from 9am to 11pm, Saturday and Sunday from 9am to 1pm and 3 to 11pm. There are nature talks (in Portuguese only) and videos nightly starting at 8:30pm.

SEA KAYAKING 🔹 Tours depart Porto Santo Antonio at 9am and 3pm for a 3-hour paddle along the island's sheltered coast, with a stop to snorkel at Praia de Conceição. A small motorboat tags along with water and snacks. Cost is R$75 (US$38/£20). Call **Edlene** at **Remos da Ilha** (✆ 081/3619-1914).

SNORKELING 🔹 A number of operators offer organized snorkeling tours (see "Boat Tours & Operators," below). For do-it-yourselfers, **Santuário** (✆ **081/3619-1247**), in the port of Santo Antonio, rents masks and snorkels for R$18 (US$9/£5) per day for a mask, snorkel, and fins. Baía do Sancho and Baía do Sueste both offer good snorkeling.

SURFING 🔹 The surf season in Noronha runs from **December to March,** the opposite of that in the rest of Brazil. (Outside of this time there are *no surfable waves.*) Surfing takes place not on the outer shore beaches, which are steep and rocky, but on the sandier beaches facing Brazil's Atlantic coast. The best surf beaches are **Cachorro, Cacimba do Padre, Bode, Boldró, Conceição,** and **Meio.** Waves average 2m (6½ ft.), but sometimes reach as high as 5m (17 ft.). Bring your board and the gear you need. There are no surf shops on the island. For further information, contact Roberto Flor at the **Fernando de Noronha Surf Association** (✆ 081/3619-1324).

ISLAND TOURS

TOUR OPERATORS Formerly just a buggy rental company, **LocBuggy** (✆ 081/3619-1490; www.locbuggy.com.br) is evolving into a full-service tour agency, currently offering a variety of tours including a dawn trip to see the spinner dolphins, a historic walk, an island tour, several hikes, trips to Atalaia beach, and planasubbing. Reservations can be made in advance via the company website. A similar range of tours is offered by **Alquimista Tour** (✆ 081/3619-1283; www.alquimistanoronha.com.br).

BOAT TOURS & OPERATORS There are a couple of different options for getting out on the water. You can go on a 3- to 4-hour **dolphin/snorkeling cruise.** Tours depart Porto Santo Antonio and run along the inside shore of Noronha, looking at the steep cliffs and seabird rookeries on Ilha do Meio and Ilha do Rata, before heading down to cruise the edge of Dolphin Bay, hoping to be surrounded by a spinner school coming out for the day. The 3-hour tours go as far as Ponta da Sapata and include a stop for snorkeling in Baía do Sancho. Afternoon tours have better luck with dolphins. Morning tours focus on snorkeling. The other alternative is a **planasub tour.** Planasub (also called aquanaut) is a strange but fun activity in which you get towed at a fast speed behind a boat holding on to a board or piece of shaped plastic. By tilting your board up or down you can dive way down and then shoot back up when your breath runs out. You're wearing a mask and snorkel, and in the clear water it's a bit like gliding through a science fiction film (*Fantastic Voyage,* for example).

   Abatur, in the building across the street from the port (✆ 081/3619-1360), uses converted 7.5m (25-ft.) wooden fishing boats. They offer a dolphin-spotting and snorkeling cruise for R$70 (US$35/£19) per person, with departures daily at 8:30am and 1pm. Abatur's 2-hour planasub trips cost R$70 (US$35/£19) and depart daily at 9am and 1:30pm. They take six people, and each person is guaranteed 30 minutes of planasubbing. All prices include transfer to and from the port (cash only). Abatur also has moonlight cruises and tours to the offshore island, but these depend on weather and demand.

Santuário, on the dock at Porto de Santo Antonio (© **081/3619-1247**), offers plana-subbing, snorkeling, and dolphin spotting on a modern speedboat. Planasub tours are 2 hours long, depart at 9am and 2pm, and cost R$75 (US$38/£20) per person. Snorkeling tours leave in the morning and afternoon on demand. Cost is R$75 (US$38/£20) per person. Dolphin tours leave in the afternoon. Cost is R$70 (US$35/£19) per person. Cost includes transfer to and from the port.

OTHER THINGS TO SEE & DO

The only historic buildings of note are found in Vila Remédios. The most impressive structure is the **Forte dos Remédios,** built by the Portuguese in 1737. It's a wonderful crumbling structure, with old cannons half-buried in the dirt and ramparts on the edge of collapse. Extending from the fort there are a number of old stone roads, many built by convict labor. One leads back to the Vila Remédios plaza, a steep cobblestone square with a pretty yellow-and-white baroque church at the top. This is the **Igreja Nossa Senhora dos Remédios,** built in 1772. Farther uphill is an attractive bright red colonial building known as the **Palácio São Miguel.** It now serves as the administrative headquarters of the island. A small history museum, the **Memorial Noronhense** (open daily 8am–4pm) is located at the bottom of the hill below the church. The museum does a good job showing the history of the island, from its discovery in 1503 by Amerigo Vespucci, through the years when the Dutch, Portuguese, and French all fought for possession, to its years as a political prison and then American army base from the '40s to the '60s.

19

Florianópolis

The Ilha de Santa Catarina, aka Florianópolis, is known throughout Brazil for its miles and miles of gorgeous beaches, excellent seafood, and traditional Azorean fishing villages. Figuring out the names may be the only complicated part of a visit to this most laid-back of Brazilian beach destinations. Florianópolis, the city, is the capital of the *state* of Santa Catarina. Florianópolis is also located on the *island* of Santa Catarina. Island and city together are usually just referred to as Florianópolis, which people often then shorten to Floripa. Confused? Don't worry, it's the beaches that matter.

The *city* of Florianópolis is small and pleasant but of no real interest except as a jumping-off point to the island's countless beaches. Brazilians are infatuated with Floripa and flock here en masse in summer. Perhaps Brazilians see in Floripa a model of what their country could be, or perhaps in a land with so much tropical exuberance, the opposite becomes exotic. In any case, when Brazilians rave about Florianópolis, they mention the fair-skinned, green-eyed residents, the affluent communities, the quaint Portuguese fishing villages, the pristine and unpolluted beaches, and the calm traffic.

That said, there is more than enough variety on the island to customize a visit according to your interests. The northeastern part of the island of Florianópolis (which is, officially, the Ilha de Santa Catarina, except nobody calls it that) is an urbanized, heavily visited beach scene, particularly in the high summer months of December, January, and February. Farther south in the center of the island there's the Lagoa da Conceição, a large lagoon partially surrounded by tall sand dunes. Nearby, the small quiet community of Lagoa da Conceição boasts some of the best restaurants in the region. Just to the east are the beaches of Galheta, Mole, and Joaquina—beautiful, wide, sandy beaches surrounded by lush green hills and blessed with large, surfable waves. Farther south toward Campeche, the beaches become more rugged and almost deserted. Even in the summer you won't find large crowds here. Finally, over to the west side of the island facing the mainland, you will find the quaint Azorean fishing village of Riberão da Ilha, accessible only via a gorgeous, narrow, winding, seaside road offering views of the Baia Sul and the lush hills of the mainland across the bay.

1 Florianópolis Essentials
ARRIVING
BY PLANE   TAM (© 048/4002-5700), **Varig** (© 048/4003-7000), and **Gol** (© 0300/115-2121) all fly to Florianópolis. There are daily flights to/from all major cities in Brazil; it's about a 2-hour flight from Rio de Janeiro and a 1-hour flight from São Paulo. All flights arrive at **Aeroporto Hercílio Luz** (© 048/3331-4000). Taxis from the airport to the northern beaches (Praia dos Ingleses) cost R$60 to R$70

(US$30–US$35/£16–£19); to the southern part of the island (Campeche), R$30 (US$15/£8); and to downtown, R$25 (US$13/£7).

BY BUS   Long-distance buses arrive at the **Rodoviaria Rita Maria,** Av. Paulo Fontes s/n (© **048/3224-2777**). **Auto Viação 1001** (© **048/3223-7766**) offers daily departures to São Paulo for R$90 to R$160 (US$45–US$80/£24–£43); the trip takes approximately 10 hours.

VISITOR INFORMATION

Florianópolis's **airport** has a tourist information center (© **048/3331-4101**) in the arrivals hall, open daily 8am to 8pm. The **main tourist information center** is in downtown Florianópolis, Praça XV de Novembro s/n, Centro (© **048/3222-4906**), open daily 8am to 6pm.

CITY/ISLAND LAYOUT

The city of Florianópolis straddles the narrow part of the straight about halfway down the island, and is connected to the mainland by two bridges. The oft-photographed, scenic **Hercílio Luz suspension bridge** is currently closed for renovations. The city itself serves mostly as a transfer point for those arriving or departing by bus. The historic downtown sits just a hop and a skip from the small but efficient Rita Maria bus station, the departure and arrival point for all long-distance buses. If you want to do a bit of shopping, just follow the elevated walkway across the main road for a short walk to the Praça XV, one of the city's main squares. The **Rua Felipe Schmit** and the **Rua Cons. Mafra** and its cross streets around the Praça XV are closed to traffic and packed with stores; specialty items include shoes and leather goods such as belts and wallets. Thanks to the cooler climate, the stores stock excellent boots and sweaters that will hold up to Northern Hemisphere falls and winters. A bustling indoor market is located at **Av. Paulo Fontees s/n,** almost on the corner of the **Praça Fernando Machado.**

The island itself is long and thin (approximately 70km/43 miles from north to south) and features a number of distinct regions. The most urbanized beaches are those near the northern tip of the island; **Praia dos Ingleses, Canasvieiras,** and **Jurerê** are popular destinations in the summer. Farther south, facing the open Atlantic on the east side of the island, are the much less developed beaches of **Praia Mole** and **Joaquina.** Both are popular with locals on the weekends. Close to the northern end of **Praia Mole** (toward the dunes where a trail connects to the nearby clothing-optional **Galheta** beach), you'll find a large concentration of gay visitors. However, the beach is family-friendly and also popular with surfers. The **Lagoa da Conceição** forms the center of the island. This large lagoon is the year-round nightlife and dining hub, attracting both locals and visitors. The southern part of the island is divided into two regions, the beaches (on the east side, facing the ocean) and **Riberão da Ilha** (on the west side, opposite the mainland). The ocean-facing beaches such as **Campeche** and **Armação** are mostly undeveloped, and even in the peak of the tourist season (Dec–Feb) it's easy to find a near-deserted stretch of sand. Farther south toward the tip of the island, the beaches of **Lagoinha do Leste** and **Naufragados** are only accessible by a short hike. Facing toward the mainland, **Riberão da Ilha** features Portuguese (actually Açorean [fishermen from the Azores]) settlements that have been beautifully preserved.

Access to the various parts is by well-paved state highways. From downtown Florianópolis there are three main roads: the **SC-401** goes north to the beaches of **Ingleses**

Florianópolis

ACCOMMODATIONS ■
Ingleses Praia Hotel **2**
Pousada da Vigia **1**
Pousada das Palmeiras **6**
Pousada Panareia **12**
Pousada Vila Tamarindo **10**
Praia Mole Park Hotel **4**

DINING ◆
Bistrô D'Acampora **3**
Bistro Isadora Duncan **9**
Mar Massas **8**
Ostradamus **11**
Pizzeria Basilico **5**
Villa Magionne **7**

Praia Lagoinha
Praia Ponta das Canas
Praia Brava
Praia Cachoeira do Bom Jesus
Praia Canasvieiras
Praia do Forte
Praia Jurerê
Praia Ingleses
Praia Daniela
Praia Moçambique
Praia Sambaqui
Praia Sto. Antônio de Lisboa
Praia Cacupé
Praia Barra da Lagoa
BARRA DA LAGOA
Baía Norte
FLORIANÓPOLIS
SÃO JOSÉ
Praia Mole
CANTO DA LAGOA
Praia Joaquina
ATLANTIC OCEAN
Baía Sul
Aeroporto Hercílio Luz
Praia Campeche
Ilha do Campeche
Praia Ribeirão da Ilha
Praia Morro das Pedras
Praia Armação
Praia Matadeiro
Lagoa do Peri
Praia Lagoinha do Leste
Praia Tapera
Praia Pântano do Sul
Praia Solidão
Praia Caieira da Barra do Sul
Praia Saquinho
Praia Naufragados

SANTA CATARINA
ILHA DE SANTA
Lagoa da Conceição

Beach
262 **Federal Road**
339 **State Road**

0 — 3 mi
0 — 3 km

ATLANTIC OCEAN
Manaus
Belém
Natal
Amazon
BRAZIL
Recife
Brasília
Salvador
São Paulo
Rio de Janeiro
Florianópolis
500 mi
500 km

and **Canasvieiras.** The **SC-404** cuts across the center of the island to the restaurant and nightlife area of Lagoa. The **SC-405** dips south toward **Ribeirão da Ilha.** A fourth highway, the **SC-406,** runs along the eastern side of the island, connecting to the SC-405 in the south and the SC-401 near the northern beaches.

GETTING AROUND

BY BUS   Local bus service on the island is slow and infrequent. In Florianópolis a vehicle is strongly recommended (see "By Car," below).

BY TAXI   Taxis are easily found in the city or at the airport, and hard to find elsewhere. To call a cab from anywhere on the island dial © **197** or call © **048/3240-6009.** Taxi fares add up; a one-way ride from Campeche to the bus station costs R$30 (US$15/£8). After two or three rides it's better to rent a car.

BY CAR   In Florianópolis, a car is almost a must. You will get a lot more out of your visit with your own transportation, allowing you to explore as you please. Traffic is relaxed; speed limits and regulations are strictly obeyed. Florianópolis is also extremely safe. You can safely park anywhere (though you should remove valuables from the car). At the airport there's a **Localiza** rental office (© **048/3236-1244**) as well as a **Hertz** office (© **048/3236-9955**). **Lemans Rental Car** (© **048/3222-9999** or 048/3348-0300) is known for reliable service. They deliver and pick up from anywhere, including the airport and bus station.

FAST FACTS: **Florianópolis**

Banks   **Banco do Brasil,** Praça XV de Novembro 321 (© **048/3221-1677**) is open Monday through Friday 10am to 4pm and has a 24-hour ATM. The **HSBC** is located on Rua Felipe Schmidt 376, Centro (© **048/3221-9000**).

Car Rental   Rental charges with unlimited mileage start at R$90 (US$45/£24) for a Fiat Palio (the smallest two-door Fiat) without air-conditioning. Insurance costs R$30 (US$15/£8) per day, or check if your credit card already covers car insurance. Try **Lemans** (© **048/3222-9999**) or **Hertz** (© **048/3236-9955**, airport).

Hospitals   **Hospital Governador Celso Ramos,** Rua Irmã Benvarda s/n, Centro (© **048/3251-7000**).

Weather   Florianópolis has a temperate climate; summers (Nov–Mar) are hot and sunny but fall and winter (May–Sept) can be downright chilly, with temperatures falling below 50°F (10°C).

---

2 Where to Stay in Florianópolis

The island offers great variety, everything from small pousadas to five-star resorts and high-rise hotels. The northern part of the island is worth it only during the summer months. Out of season, restaurants and shops close and the area feels dreary. Halfway down the east coast of the island, Praia Mole offers excellent accommodations in one of the nicest beach areas, only a short drive from Lagoa's restaurants and nightlife options. In the south, Campeche offers quiet accommodations on a beach that is often deserted and great for long walks. Note that accommodations rates do not cover holidays such as New Year's, Carnaval, and Easter, when hotels and pousadas sell packages, normally at inflated prices, and usually with a minimum stay of 3 nights.

NORTH ISLAND

Ingleses Praia Hotel ⓡ *(Kids*   Right on the beach, the Ingleses Praia Hotel offers a large outdoor pool and playground, making it perfect for kids. Deluxe rooms feature at least a partial ocean view, while the super-deluxe rooms and suites offer a full ocean view. The super-deluxe units are the best value: for little extra (R$12–R$24/US$6–US$12/£3.25–£6.50) you get a flat with full kitchen and small den that can accommodate four people comfortably. For luxury, book an oceanfront suite. These offer room for eight, with two bedrooms and two bathrooms as well as a sitting room and kitchen. The hotel is within walking distance of restaurants and shops in Praia dos Ingleses. Check the website for packages in the low season: a 3-night stay can cost R$85 (US$35/£17) per night.

Rua Dom João Becker 447, Praia dos Ingleses, Florianópolis, 88058-600 SC. ⓒ/fax 048/3261-3300. www.ingleses praia.com.br. 110 units. Apr–Nov R$175 (US$88/£47) double deluxe or super deluxe, R$500 (US$250/£135) suite; Dec–Mar R$377 (US$189/£102) deluxe or super deluxe, R$1,031 (US$516/£278) suite. Extra person R$75 (US$20/£10). Children 5 and under stay free in parent's room. AE, DC, MC, V. Free parking. **Amenities:** Restaurant; bar; indoor heated pool; large outdoor pool; exercise room; Jacuzzi; limited room service; laundry. *In room:* A/C, TV, dataport, minibar, safe.

Pousada da Vigia ⓡⓡ   Located literally on the northern tip of the island, this lovely pousada has one of the finest beach views around. All but one of the rooms feature an ocean view and all but one of the nine oceanview rooms come with a lovely private veranda. The rooms are beautifully appointed (though a tad on the small side) and the pousada offers top-notch amenities such as a heated indoor pool, beach service, sitting room with home theater, and spa treatments. The two best rooms are suites 9 and 10. These feature a master bedroom with king-size bed, a deluxe bathroom with jetted tub for two, a living room with home theater and DVD, and a spacious deck with sauna, barbecue, and outdoor Jacuzzi. The pousada is located between Ponta das Canas and Praia Brava in Lagoinha. Driving from the airport, take the SC-401 to Canasvieiras. From there you will see signs to Lagoinha. The pousada also offers a transfer service if contacted ahead of time.

Rua Con. Walmor Castro 291, Lagoinha, Florianópolis, 88056-770 SC. ⓒ 048/3284-1789. Fax 048/3284-1108. www. pousadavigia.com.br. 10 units. Mar–Nov R$215–R$305 (US$108–US$162/£58–£82) double, R$470 (US$235/£127) master deluxe; Nov–Feb R$320–R$480 (US$160–US$240/£86–£130) double, R$720 (US$360/£195) master deluxe. Children 2 and under stay free in parent's room. AE, DC, MC, V. Free parking. **Amenities:** Restaurant; bar; small indoor heated pool; exercise room; Jacuzzi; limited room service; laundry. *In room:* A/C, TV, dataport, minibar, safe.

MID-ISLAND

Pousada das Palmeiras ⓡ   More Bali than Florianópolis, Pousada das Palmeiras offers high-end accommodations in a lush tropical setting. The four units are all beautiful split-level cabanas with verandas set in a lovely garden. All come with fully equipped kitchens, high ceilings, king-size beds, DVD and CD players, and views of the lagoon and gardens. All are charmingly furnished with lots of wood and bamboo, bright colors, and interesting artwork. The units *Ar, Bambu,* and *Lagoa* feature a Jacuzzi tub for two. The two-story *Bungalow Mar* is the largest unit and features a full kitchen, sitting room and Jacuzzi tub for two with fabulous views. Situated just a few minutes from the main village, the location is ideal for those who like to go out at night.

Rua Laurindo da Silveira 2720, Canto da Lagoa, Florianópolis, 88056-770 SC. ⓒ 048/3232-6267 or 048/9962-2900. www.pousadadaspalmeiras.com.br. 6 units. Mar–Nov R$200–R$280 (US$100–US$140/£54–£76) double); Dec–Feb

R$250–R$370 (US$125–US$170/£68–£100) double. Extra person add R$50–R$90 (US$25–U$45/£14–£24) in low season and R$80–R$130 (US$40–US$65/£22–£35) in high season. Children 2 and under stay free in parent's room. AE, DC, MC, V. Free parking. **Amenities:** Laundry. *In room:* A/C, fan, TV/DVD, dataport, kitchen, safe, no phone.

Praia Mole Eco Village ★★ *(Kids)* Set astride a piece of land between Praia Mole and the lagoon, this large hotel features beautiful large trees and lush gardens with tennis courts, a soccer field, and orchid park. Rooms are spread out over several buildings. The smallest building, overlooking the beach, has the feel of a small European seaside hotel. When reserving a room, make sure to request a *frente mar* and not a *vista mar;* the latter one has only a partial ocean view. The central building sits in the middle of the property, close to the swimming pool and leisure area. Request a *superior* apartment as it features a veranda overlooking the garden. The third large building, the Solar, sits closer toward the lagoon and rooms have either lagoon or garden views; in this building all rooms feature a veranda. Finally, for those who want a bit more privacy and space, there are 18 bungalows, with one or two bedrooms. These all have large balconies with views of the garden and lagoon.

Estrada Geral da Barra da Lagoa 2001, Florianópolis, 88062-970 SC. © **048/3239-7500.** Fax 048/3232-5482. www.praiamole.com.br. 98 units. May–Nov R$145–R$190 (US$73–US$95/£39–£51) standard or lagoon view double, R$240–R$310 (US$120–US$155/£65–£84) oceanview or bungalow double; Dec–Apr R$290–R$365 (US$145–US$183/£78–£99) standard or lagoon view double, R$400–R$460 (US$200–US$230/£108–£124) oceanview or bungalow double. Extra person add R$60–R$90 (US$30–US$45/£16–£24). Children 5 and under stay free in parent's room. AE, DC, MC, V. Free parking. **Amenities:** Restaurant; bar; large indoor heated pool; tennis courts; exercise room; Jacuzzi; watersports rental; limited room service; laundry. *In room:* A/C, TV, dataport, minibar, hair dryer.

SOUTH ISLAND

Pousada Penareia ★★ Overlooking Armação Beach, this pousada is a labor of love by a dentist and an architect who simply fell in love with this part of the island. This 12-room pousada is perfect for more active travelers. The owners will happily lend you an inflatable kayak, a set of *frescobol* (a type of racquetball played on the beach), soccer balls, bikes, or provide you with hiking tips. The pousada itself is very pleasant. All rooms are very bright and spacious; the beds are very comfortable (new mattresses and box springs) and even the standard rooms feature a private veranda with a hammock (but no air-conditioning). The special rooms are a bit bigger and do have air-conditioning. The best rooms are the deluxe ones that come with a Jacuzzi tub, a TV/DVD- and CD-player and a large veranda with barbecue set. A few steps down from the pousada there is a wonderful deck overlooking the beach, the perfect sunrise spot!

Rua Hermes Guedes da Fonseca 207, Praia da Armação, Florianópolis, 88063-000 SC. © **048/3338-1616.** www.pousadapenareia.com.br. 12 units. Mar–Nov R$120–R$150 (US$60–US$75/£32–£41) standard or special double, R$180 (US$90/£49) deluxe double; Nov–Feb R$180 (US$90/£49) standard or special double, R$250 (US$113/£68) deluxe double. Extra person add R$40 (US$20/£11). No children under the age of 12. AE, DC, MC, V. Free parking. **Amenities:** Game room; massage; laundry. *In room:* A/C or fan, TV, fridge, safe.

Pousada Vila Tamarindo ★★ This lovely small pousada is located just behind Praia do Campeche, one of the nicest beaches of the southern part of the island. The beach itself is protected (no construction is allowed on its waterfront), so even in high season it's not too busy here. The 13 apartments are pleasantly furnished in bright colors and decorated with local artwork. All have ocean-facing verandas; if you leave your door open you can fall asleep to the sounds of the surf. The ground-floor suites have a fan but no air-conditioning and are considered standard rooms. The deluxe rooms on the first floor feature air-conditioning and better ocean views. For families or couples traveling together there are two two-bedroom apartments. The pousada also has two master suites that offer a bit more luxury and are perfect for a romantic vacation. The suites feature a spacious sitting room, larger veranda, Jacuzzi tub, and one of them even comes with a fireplace. *Note:* The region around Campeche is very quiet and a car is required to get around to restaurants and attractions.

Av. Campeche 1836, Praia do Campeche, Florianópolis, 88063-000 SC. © 048/3237-3464. Fax 048/3338-2185. www.tamarindo.com.br. 15 units. Mar–Nov R$120–R$150 (US$60–US$75/£32–£41) standard double, R$150–R$185 (US$75–US$93/£41–£50) deluxe double, R$250–R$350 (US$125–US$175/£68–£95) master suite double; Nov–Feb R$180 (US$90/£49) standard double, R$220–R$240 (US$110–US$120/£60–£65) deluxe double, R$340–R$400 (US$170–US$200/£92–£108) master or bungalow double. Extra person add R$40–R$70 (US$20–US$35/£11–£19). Children 8 and under stay free in parent's room. AE, DC, MC, V. Free parking. **Amenities:** Outdoor pool; game room; massage; tour desk; car rental; laundry. *In room:* A/C or fan, TV, minibar, no phone.

3 Where to Dine in Florianópolis

There are two seafood specialties for which Florianópolis is especially well known. The first is *sequencia de camarão* (shrimp in sequence), which consists of a number of shrimp dishes served one after another. Normally, there's *casquinha de siri* (baked crab-meat), followed by steamed shrimp, breaded shrimp, garlic shrimp, and then a fish filet with shrimp sauce. The other Floripa specialty is the oyster. Most oysters served in Brazil come from the area around Riberão da Ilha. Here at the source they're fresher and cheaper (R$12/US$5/£2.50 a dozen). Always call ahead for opening hours during the low season, as many restaurants adjust their times during the quiet period

NORTH ISLAND

Bistrô d'Acampora ✦✦✦ FRENCH/ITALIAN   If you are in the mood for dining in an intimate setting, try this cozy restaurant located inside the home of the d'Acamporas. At this dining room cum art gallery, chef Zeca and his wife will welcome you for an extraordinary "home-cooked" meal. The talented and experienced chef takes his classic French and Italian training and uses fresh local ingredients to serve up his favorite dishes. There is no set menu but there is always a selection of salads, such as the mango salad with greens and fresh crabmeat. Main courses can be *trés* French, such as the confit de canard or a dish made with fresh local seafood, like the catch of the day and some local oysters or prawns in a bisque sauce served on a bed of Moroccan couscous. Of course no good meal is complete without a dessert; you better hope that on the day you go, Zeca is serving his scrumptious chocolate tort with pecans and crème anglaise. The restaurant also has a fantastic wine list with over 400 labels, including everything from an outrageous R$1000 (US$500/£250) bottle of Barolo Riserva Villero 1997 to many affordable options in the R$60–R$100 (US$30–US$50/£15–£25) range.

SC 401 to Canasvieiras, Km 10 (Santo Antônio e Lisboa), on the northwest side of the island. Florianópolis. © 048/ 3235-1073. Reservations required. 3-course meal (without wine) approximately R$70–R$90 (US$35–US$45/£19–£24). DC, MC, V. Tues–Sat 8pm–midnight.

LAGOA

Bistro Isadora Duncan ✦✦ BRAZILIAN/SEAFOOD   There's no better place than Bistro Isadora Duncan for a romantic dinner. The lovely antiques-furnished house offers only a handful of tables in the dining room by the fireplace or on the veranda overlooking the lake. The tagline for the kitchen is "cozinha artesanal," which means craftlike cooking. The staff takes pride in making dishes from scratch using only the freshest ingredients. The menu is kept fairly small with a handful of seafood and meat dishes. In the land of the prawn you can't go wrong with the *camarões abençoados* (blessed prawns), served in a creamy Gorgonzola sauce with sautéed potatoes, or the *camarões encantados* (enchanted prawns), prawns flambéed in orange juice, served with wild rice. And if it is a romantic dinner, why not start off with a plate of local oysters au gratin? The restaurant normally doesn't open afternoons but in high season it's worth calling—the location makes for a wonderful lunch spot.

Rod. Jornalista Manuel de Menezes 2658, Fortaleza da Barra Florianópolis. ⓒ 048/3232-7210. www.bistroisadora duncan.com.br. Reservations recommended on weekends and in high season. Main courses R$35–R$48 (US$18–US$24/£9.50–£13). MC, V. Mon–Sat 7pm–midnight.

Mar Massas 𝑅𝑅 ITALIAN   This cozy Italian cantina has a privileged spot, perched on the hillside overlooking the southern end of the lagoon. The atmosphere is casual with paper place mats, checkered tablecloths, and chianti bottles for decorations. The menu offers a wonderful range of seafood pastas such as the *tagliatelle a Don Edson* with prawns, mushrooms, and a mustard-cream sauce, or the *tortelli Alleluia,* stuffed with sweet pumpkin and served with a generous helping of grilled prawns in pesto. Even the *piccolo* (small-) size plates are generous enough to serve two small appetites, especially if you are having an appetizer and dessert.

Rua Laurindo Januário da Silveira 3843, Morro do Badejo, Lagoa, Florianópolis. ⓒ 048/3232-6109. Main courses R$33–R$48 (US$16–US$24/£9–£13). DC, MC. Tues–Fri 6pm–midnight; Sat–Sun noon–11:30pm; Jan–Apr also Mon 6pm–midnight.

Pizzaria Basilico 𝑅𝑅 PIZZA   The best place on the island for pizza, Basilico serves them plain and simple, thin-crusted, in 30 varieties. If you order a large you can choose three different flavors. The options include the Portuguesa, with ham, slices of boiled egg, and olives; the ricotta, with mozzarella, tomato sauce, fresh ricotta, and slices of tomato; or the spicy Maçarico, with tomato sauce, sausage, hot peppers, and onions. The patio sprawls out in several directions and a roaring fireplace adds much-needed warmth on chilly evenings.

Rua Laurindo Januário da Silveira 647, Lagoa, Florianópolis. ⓒ 048/3232-1129. Main courses R$30–R$50 (US$15–US$25/£8–£14). MC. Daily 7pm–midnight.

Villa Magionne 𝑅𝑅𝑅 MEDITERRANEAN   One of the best restaurants in Florianópolis, Villa Mangionne is located in a lovely small house overlooking a garden by the lagoon; you literally dine in the owner's living room. The menu includes salads, pastas, steak, and risottos. Make sure you start with one of the salads; the Moroccan salad is a delicious heap of crunchy lettuce hearts topped with toasted almonds, orange slices, and an orange vinaigrette. For a main course, stick with pasta. All are made from scratch with the freshest ingredients. Our favorite is the *ravioli de anatra,* a freshly made ravioli stuffed with tender duck served in a duck broth seasoned with mushrooms and cream. Also good is the *tonnarielli al filetto,* pasta served with a generous portion of filet mignon strips flambéed in bourbon. Desserts are equally scrumptious and made in-house. We recommend the *torta romeo ande giulietta,* a guava compote twist on the traditional cheesecake.

Rua da Amizade 273, Lagoa, Florianópolis. ⓒ 048/3232-6859. www.restaurantevillamagionni.com.br. Reservations required. Main courses R$40–R$68 (US$20–US$34/£11–£18). DC, MC. Mon–Fri 7pm–midnight; Sat noon–5pm and 7pm–midnight; Sun noon–5pm. In low season closed Mon–Tues.

SOUTH ISLAND

The southern part of the island, especially around Riberão da Ilha, is where the oyster farms are located. Looking out over the water you'll note the white floats that mark the locations of the baskets that contain the various-size oysters. These are placed just far enough from the shore to get the most of the tides and the current. Numerous restaurants in this part of the island serve up fresh oysters.

Ostradamus ★★ SEAFOOD   Ostradamus is one of the more upscale oyster restaurants on this part of the island. This large waterfront restaurant serves up bivalves in a variety of delicious ways: plain, steamed, grilled and topped with a béchamel sauce, smoked, or served with garlic and olive oil. All are freshly harvested from the farms just outside the restaurant's door. The menu also offers prawns, squid, clams, and grilled fish. On Thursday night, the kitchen serves up oysters prepared in over 30 different ways—a feast for oyster lovers.

Rodoviaria Baldicero Filomeno 7640, Freguesia do Riberão, Florianópolis. ℂ 048/3337-5711. www.ostradamus. com.br. Reservations recommended. Main courses R$36–R$45 (US$18–US$23/£10–£12) for 2. V. Mon–Sat noon–11pm; Sun noon–6pm. In low season closed on Mon.

4 Exploring Florianópolis

BEACHES

Florianópolis's main attraction is the more than 100 beaches scattered across the island. Each has its own character. Starting clockwise from the northern part of the island, the most visited beaches are **Canasvieiras, Jururê,** and **Praia dos Ingleses.** Canasvieiras and Jururê lie on the bay side of the island and have pleasant calm waters with almost no waves. Praia dos Ingleses faces the open ocean and often has rougher surf. All three are very urbanized and packed in the summer months when tourists flock here from all over Brazil. Jururê is popular with Brazilian celebrities, many of whom own houses or condos in the exclusive subdivisions. At the northern tip of the peninsula in between Praia dos Ingleses and Canasvieiras sits **Lagoinha,** a lovely small beach backed by a small fishing village. This is one of the best sunset spots on the island. Moving clockwise along the eastern coast of the island you come to **Praia do Moçambique,** at 19km (12 miles) the longest stretch of strand on the island. An ecological reserve runs alongside for the beach's entire length, forming a construction-free buffer zone of thick vegetation between beach and road.

Heading south from Praia do Moçambique, you'll come to **Praia Mole,** the hotshot surf beach at the moment. Largely unspoiled, the beach is framed by green hills and rocky outcrops, and the sand is white and very soft. Only accessible on foot from Praia Mole, **Praia da Galheta** is the island's clothing-optional beach and a popular gay cruising area. Just south of Praia Mole is **Praia da Joaquina.** To reach this beach you drive past the shifting sand dunes east of the Lagoa. It was once one of the island's more popular beaches, particularly with surfers, but these days Praia Mole seems to get most of the action.

Campeche is far enough south that even in high season it's not hard to find a quiet spot here. The beach is very wide, but large waves can make it dangerous for swimming. Another favorite surf destination (and a spot where one can often see dolphins) is **Praia da Armação,** just south of Campeche. For even more isolated bliss check out **Lagoinha de Leste.** Sandwiched between **Armação** and **Pântano do Sul,** this environmentally protected headland is only accessible by foot along a 4km (2.5-mile) trail. The beach sits nestled at the bottom of a large hill and is cut in half by a small river that flows into the ocean.

Following the SC-406 all the way to the end will lead you to **Pântano do Sul,** located on the eastern side of the skinny southern tip of the island. It's one of the main

---

Tips **Getting Around in Florianópolis: Rent a Car**

To make the most of your visit to Floripa you really need a car. This will allow you to explore the more remote beaches and towns at your own pace. The good news is that the roads are in great shape, the island is easy to navigate and traffic is calm, and you can safely stop and park almost anywhere without any extra safety precautions. Of course, you want to remove all valuables from the vehicle when parking. See car-rental information in "Fast Facts: Florianópolis," earlier in this chapter.

---

fishing communities on the island and has a busy, bustling atmosphere. However, the boat traffic (and dirty gray sand) make it less than ideal for swimming. From Pântano do Sul, the only access to the western side of the island is on foot. Drivers will have to backtrack all the way to the junction at Praia da Armação before heading west.

The **Lagoa da Conceição** sits almost at the center of the island, to the east of the city of Florianópolis and west of Praia Mole. The lagoon is about 30% fresh water. The water temperature is balmy—in the summer it can reach 80°F (26°C). Watersports are allowed on the lagoon, but jet skis have been banned.

SIGHTSEEING

In the southern part of the island, the western shore facing the mainland lacks beaches entirely, but in compensation offers some fabulous driving and sightseeing. South of the airport, heading down the SC-405 toward **Riberão da Ilha** leads to a small windy road that hugs the coastline virtually all the way to the southern tip of the island. Don't miss a visit to this part of the island! It's a region of small villages with colorful Portuguese-style houses, settled by fishermen from the Azores. Their descendants still live in this region and make a living fishing or raising oysters. Note that although Riberão da Ilha looks like it's just a short drive away, the road is windy and there are viewpoints and picturesque villages to distract you along the way. Plan to spend at least half a day, or more with lunch or dinner at a seafood restaurant in Riberão da Ilha.

BOAT TOURS

The traditional excursion is the schooner trip around the western side of the island. **Scunasul Tours** (© **048/3225-1806;** www.scunasul.com.br) leaves from downtown Florianópolis, heading underneath the Hercílio Luz suspension bridge to the north bay. The tour visits two beautifully preserved fortresses on small islands. A lunch stop and time for a swim are included in this leisurely day on the water. Another great boat trip is a visit to the **Ilha do Campeche,** located off Praia do Campeche, on the eastern side of the island. The boat leaves from downtown and cruises south. Once at the island you will have time to hike, swim, or snorkel (additional cost is R$3/US$1.50/£.80 for a guide, R$15/US$7.50/£4 for snorkel equipment). Tours cost R$30 (US$15/£8) per person, free for children under 5; 5- to 12-year-olds pay half price.

SCUBA DIVING

Florianópolis is not a diver's paradise, but if you want to check out the waters, **Parcel** (© **048/3284-5564;** www.parcel.com.br) offers a number of dive tours depending on the weather and group size. One regular trip heads out to the biological reserve of Arvoredo. A 4-hour tour, including two dives and equipment, costs R$120 (US$60/£32).

HIKING

The island has several excellent hiking trails. **Recrearte** (© **048/3246-2821;** www. guiafloripa.com.br/recrearte) and **Triptur** (© **048/3269-3929;** www.triptur.com.br) run daily hikes to **Lagoinha do Leste,** the **lighthouse at Naufragados, Santinho, Moçambique,** and **Morro dos Ingleses.** The less-developed southern part of the island is best for hiking as it has several preserved beaches and parks. Even in the peak season you can find some secluded spots. Excursions start at R$50 to R$65 (US$25–US$33/£14–£18) per person, based on two people.

WINDSURFING

The prime windsurf spot in Florianópolis is the Lagoa da Conceição. If you know how to windsurf you can rent a board from **Open Winds** (© **048/3232-5004;** www.open winds.com.br). Beginner boards cost R$35 (US$17/£9.50) for the day; advanced surfers can rent better equipment for R$45 (US$23/£12) for the day. For those needing lessons, Open Winds has an 8-hour beginner's program for R$680 (US$340/£183) that you can take over a couple of days. Private lessons are R$150 (US$75/£40) per hour.

5 Florianópolis After Dark

CLUBS & BARS

Every summer, bars and clubs come and go in the northern part of the island around **Praia dos Ingleses.** Most of the year-round nightlife options can be found around the **Lagoa da Conceição,** where locals and tourists mingle. To start the evening off with a fabulous view, head up to the Morro da Lagoa da Conceição, just west of the village. Follow the Rodovia Admar Gonzaga up the hill; the road will switch back until you get to the lookout. Just across from the lookout is where you find **Mandalla,** Rod. Admar Gonzaga 4720 (© **048/3234-8714**). This bar sits perched high above the road and offers spectacular views of the lagoon and the village below. On most nights, Mandalla has live bands starting at 10pm (closed Mon). Back down in the village there are a couple of nightlife options within an easy stroll of one another. **Drakkar,** Av. Afonso Delambert Neto 607, Lagoa (© **048/3232-8848;** www.bardrakkar.com.br), is a happening live-music venue with a varied program. Open as early as 6pm, it's perfect for an early-evening cocktail. The live music usually doesn't get started until 10pm. To dance the night away and listen to some great local bands, head out to Praia Mole's **Latitude 27,** Estrada Geral da Barra da Lagoa 565 (between Lagoa and Praia Mole; © **048/3234-2420**). Local bands present themselves on the stage, and a large dance floor provides plenty of space to dance Thursday through Saturday. Downtown is where you'll find popular local bar **Skuna,** Avenida Beira Mar (underneath the bridge; © **048/3225-3138**). It opens only on Tuesday, Friday, and Saturday at 10pm. The best features of the Scuna are the two large patios overlooking the city's waterfront.

Appendix:
Brazil in Depth

Brazil is a peculiar combination, simultaneously old and young. "Old" in the sense that, though charted and colonized by Europeans at roughly the same time as North America, European civilization took root faster and flowered far earlier here. While Virginia Company adventurers starved to death on the James River and Massachusetts Bay colonists subsisted in rude huts clustered around a single narrow church, Brazilian cities like Salvador and Olinda boasted paved streets, walls and houses of stone, and high cathedrals gilt with gold. "Young" because Brazil as a country did not achieve independence until 1822, and didn't throw off the monarchy and proclaim itself a republic until 1888. In today's Brazil elements of old and new coexist in every aspect of society: architecture, technology, culture, festivals, food, business attitudes—all mix the most modern with the most tradition-bound.

1 A Look at the Past

IN THE BEGINNING
No one is quite sure when or how Brazil's first inhabitants arrived. The long-favored theory—that Native Americans arrived about 10,000 years ago, most likely from Asia via a land bridge over the Bering Sea—is now under serious attack. Some archaeologists claim canoe-based cultures might have paddled their way down the coasts; others suggest seafaring peoples could have made the journey from Africa. The date of first arrival now varies from 10,000 to as far back as 30,000 years ago.

However and whenever they first arrived, by the year A.D. 1500 between one and eight million aboriginals lived in Brazil, speaking nearly 170 different languages. Unlike in the Inca territory across the Andes, Brazil's indigenous civilization was largely tribal: small groups living in villages making a subsistence living from the local environment.

THE PORTUGUESE ARRIVE
In 1500 the first Europeans arrived: 13 ships under the command of **Pedro Alvares Cabral,** a Portuguese explorer sent to find a Western trade route to India. Cabral tarried only briefly on the coast, but the reports he sent back were encouraging enough for other captains to set out. In particular, what the Europeans were after was **pau-brasil,** a type of wood that could be processed to yield a rich red dye. Coastal Indians were induced to cut and sell timber in return for metal implements such as axes. It was an efficient system, so much so that within a little over a generation the trees—which by then had given their name to the country—were all but nonexistent.

What worried Portuguese **King João III,** however, was the number of French and Spanish ships taking part in the trade. In an attempt to establish Portuguese authority (while saving the cost of a formal colony) the king divided the Brazilian coast into 15 parcels or **"captaincies,"** each of which was given to a Portuguese noble as his hereditary property, on the understanding he'd show the flag, build up a colony at his own expense, and maybe generate some tax revenue for the royal treasury.

A few of the newly arriving captains managed to establish themselves by forging alliances with local Indian tribes. Mostly, however, the Portuguese arrivals generated hostility. Many of the new settlements were burned out and destroyed, the would-be settlers killed. Establishing colonies in Brazil was going to require the sort of armed force only a king could provide.

In 1549 King João revoked the captaincies and sent out a force of 1,500 men—soldiers, priests, artisans, and administrators—under the command of Brazil's first governor-general, **Tomé de Sousa.** Landing at **Salvador** in what is now the state of **Bahia,** de Sousa's force was large enough to turn the tide. Warfare with Brazil's native inhabitants would continue for another 200 years or so, but for the most part the Portuguese would have the upper hand.

SUGAR CANE & SLAVERY

What made the expense worthwhile—in the eyes of the crown—was **sugar.** The cash crop of the 16th century, it grew well in the tropical climate of northeast Brazil. **Salvador,** the new capital, was soon surrounded by rapidly expanding plantations of sugar cane.

Turning that cane into sugar, however, was backbreaking work, and the Portuguese were critically devoid of labor. Short of enslavement (also attempted), local Indians were uninterested in the repetitive drudgery of cutting cane. In any case, disease had ripped through indigenous peoples, sending their population on a downward spiral. (One that didn't end, in fact, until the 1960s, at which time Brazilian Indians numbered just a few hundred thousand.)

So the Portuguese began to import **slaves,** captured or bought in West Africa. Brazil was soon one leg on a lucrative maritime trade triangle: guns and supplies from Portugal to Africa, slaves from Africa to Brazil, sugar from Brazil back to Europe. Within a few decades, colonial cities such as Salvador and **Olinda** were fabulously rich.

A DUTCH THREAT & THE RISE OF RIO

Other European powers took note. In 1624 a **Dutch expedition** conquered and briefly occupied the Brazilian capital of Salvador, leaving a year later after a Portuguese fleet counterattacked. The next year the Dutch were back, burning Olinda to the ground, taking control of **Pernambuco** and establishing their own capital city of **Recife.** Under the leadership of **Maurits van Nassau,** Dutch Brazil was soon a thriving colony, exporting ever-larger quantities of sugar. When internal politicking forced Nassau out of the colony in 1644, however, Dutch fortunes began to wane. A rebellion of the local Portuguese planters, followed by renewed attacks from Portugal, finally forced the surrender of Dutch forces in 1654. Never again would another European power successfully challenge Portuguese control of the country.

Free of external threat, the settlers turned their attention inland. Small expeditions of Brazilian adventures—called *bandeirantes* because they often carried the royal flag—began exploring westward seeking gold, minerals, or other treasure. **Gold** and diamonds were soon uncovered in what would later be the state of **Minas Gerais,** followed by further gold strikes farther west in Mato Grosso. The resulting flood of miners and other settlers gave effective control of the interior to Portugal—a fact recognized by the **1750 Treaty of Madrid,** which gave the entire Amazon basin and those lands east of the Rio Prata to Brazil.

In addition to the miners, the other main beneficiary of the Minas gold rush was **Rio de Janeiro,** the major transshipment point for gold and supplies. In recognition of this, in **1762** the **colonial capital** was officially transferred to Rio.

Stunning as its physical setting was, Rio was hardly then the cidade maravilhosa it would become. Indeed, it would likely have remained little more than a backwater colonial capital had it not been for **Napoleon.** In **1807,** having overrun most of western Europe, the little French emperor set his sights on Portugal. Faced with the imminent conquest of Lisbon, Portuguese **Prince Regent João** (later **King João VI**) fled to his ships, opting to relocate himself and his entire court to Brazil. And so it was that in **March 1808** the king and 15,000 of his nobles, knights, and courtiers arrived in the rather raw town of Rio.

INDEPENDENCE ARRIVES

The changes wrought by the royal presence were enormous: palaces, parks, and gardens were built all over the city. A new administrative class was formed. Indeed, the denizens of Rio got so used to being at the center of things that the king's return to Portugal in 1821 created no small outrage. Used to being at the heart of the empire, Brazilians—among them the king's 23-year-old son Pedro—were outraged at the prospect of being returned to the status of mere colony. In January 1822 Pedro announced he was remaining in Brazil. Initially, he planned on ruling as prince regent, but as the year wore on it became clear that Lisbon was not interested in compromise, so on **September 7, 1822,** Pedro declared **Brazil independent,** and himself · **Emperor Pedro I.**

His reign lasted only 9 years. In acceding to the throne Dom Pedro had agreed to rule as a constitutional monarch, but in practice sharing power with a parliament of meddling politicians went against his aristocratic nature. A costly war with **Argentina**—which led to the creation of **Uruguay** in 1828—only lessened his popularity. Finally in April 1832, Dom Pedro was presented with an ultimatum demanding he appoint a reformist cabinet. He chose instead to **abdicate.** His 5-year-old son became Emperor Pedro II.

Brazil in this period was a deeply conservative country, with a few very wealthy plantation owners, a tiny professional class, and a great mass of slaves indentured into cultivating either sugar or Brazil's new cash crop, **coffee.** Though the antislavery movement was growing powerful across the globe, Brazil's conservative landowning class was determined to hold on to slavery at all costs.

Taking power in 1840 at the tender age of 14, **Dom Pedro II** found himself in a political bind. Though he personally favored abolishing slavery, the conservative slave owners were also the chief supporters of the monarchy. The liberal abolitionists in the parliament were republicans to a man. Faced with this intractable situation, Dom Pedro opted to ally himself with the conservatives. He would move forward on the slavery issue, but at a glacial pace.

In the 1850s, under heavy pressure from Britain, Brazil finally moved to halt the **importation** of slaves from Africa. Slavery was still legal within the country, but its days were clearly numbered. Seeking a new source of labor, in 1857 Brazil opened itself up to **immigration.** Thousands poured in, mostly **Germans** and **Italians,** settling themselves in the hilly, temperate lands in the south of Brazil. Not only did they provide alternate labor on coffee plantations, but these newcomers also established their own small farms and vineyards, or else moved into Brazil's growing cities, giving the southern part of Brazil a very European flavor.

Through the 1860s and 1870s, the government showed little interest in confronting the slavery issue. A law passed in 1871 envisioned the legal end of slavery—but not until 1896. Another passed in 1885 promised to free only those slaves over the age of 65. As immigration continued, the plantation class became an increasingly tiny fraction of the populace, albeit one that maintained a stranglehold on Brazilian politics. Dom Pedro himself seemed to have lost interest in governing, spending much of his time on extended trips abroad. Finally in **1888,** his daughter the **Princess Regent Isabel** passed the **Lei Aurea,** which set Brazil's slaves free. There were celebrations in the streets, but by this time the monarchy was so thoroughly associated with the plantation owners, it had little popular support. When reformist army officers and other liberals staged a coup in 1889, Pedro II's 57-year rule came to an end.

The **republic** that took its place had many of the same ills of the old regime. In a country with an increasingly large working class, the government remained in the hands of the coffee-growing elite. Corruption was endemic, rebellions a regular occurrence. Finally in 1930 reformist army officers staged a **bloody coup.** After several days' fighting, a military-backed regime took charge, putting an **end to the Old Republic** and ushering in the 15-year reign of the fascinating, maddening figure of **Getulio Vargas.**

THE AGE OF VARGAS & A NEW CAPITAL IS BORN

A pol to his fingertips, Vargas managed to ride each new political wave as it swept in. He began his time in office as a **populist,** legalizing unions and investing in hundreds of projects designed to foster Brazil's industrial development. When the workers nevertheless looked set to reject him in renewed elections, Vargas tore up the constitution and instituted a **quasi-fascist dictatorship,** complete with a **propaganda ministry** that celebrated every action of the glorious leader Getulio. In the early 1940s when the **United States** made it clear Brazil had better cease its flirtation with Germany, Vargas dumped his fascist posturing,

declared war on the Axis powers, and sent 20,000 Brazilian troops to take part in the **invasion of Italy.** When the troops came home at war's end, the contradiction between the fight for freedom abroad and the dictatorship at home proved too much even for Vargas' political skills. In 1945 in a very **quiet coup,** the army removed Getulio from power.

In 1950 **Vargas returned,** this time as the democratically elected president. His reign was a disaster. By 1954 there were riots in the streets, the army was on the verge of mutiny, and even his own vice president was calling for his resignation. Vargas, instead, retired to his office in the Catete Palace in Rio, and on the night of August 4, 1954, put a bullet through his heart.

In 1956, **Juscelino Kubitschek** (known as JK) took office, largely on the strength of a single bold promise: Within 4 years, he would **transfer the capital** from Rio de Janeiro to an entirely new city located somewhere in Brazil's vast interior. Few thought he could do it.

The site chosen in Brazil's high interior plateau—the *sertão*—was hundreds of miles from the nearest paved road, not to mention the nearest airport. Undaunted, JK assembled a team of Brazil's top **modernist architects**—among the best in the world at the time—and an astounding 4 years later, the new capital of **Brasilia** was complete.

DICTATORSHIP & AGAIN, DEMOCRACY

Democracy, unfortunately, did not fare well in the arid soil of the *sertão*. In 1964 the army took power in a coup, ushering in an ever more repressive **military dictatorship** that would last for another 20 years.

For a time, no one much complained. Thanks to massive government investment, the economy boomed. São Paulo, which had been little more than a market town in the 1920s, exploded in size and population, surpassing Rio to become the heart of Brazil's new manufacturing economy. These were the days of the Brazilian "economic miracle."

On the soccer field Brazil ruled. True, in the 1950 World Cup—held in the specially built Maracanã stadium in Rio—Brazil lost in a 2-to-1 final to underdog Uruguay. (The shame of that defeat haunts Brazil to this day.) Brazil came back strong, however, taking the World Cup championships in 1958, 1962, and 1970, making Brazil the first three-time champion in World Cup history. (They won a fourth championship in 1994 and a fifth in 2002.)

In the early '70s, however, it became clear that much of the economic "miracle" had been financed on easy international loans, much of that invested in dubious development projects (roads that disappeared back into the forest, nuclear power plants that never functioned) or channeled directly into the pockets of various well-connected generals. The international banks now wanted their money back, with interest. As discontent with the regime spread, the military reacted with ever-stronger repression.

The 1980s were perhaps Brazil's worst decade. Inflation ran rampant, while growth was next to nonexistent. Austerity measures imposed by the International Monetary Fund left governments with little money for basic infrastructure—much less social services—and in big cities such as Rio and São Paulo, favelas (shantytowns) spread while crime spiraled out of control.

In the midst of this mess, the army began a transition to democracy. In 1988, in the first direct presidential election in over 2 decades, Brazilians elected a good-looking millionaire named Fernando Collor de Mello. It proved to be a bad move, for Collor was soon found lining his pockets with government cash. The civilian government did prove capable of

legally forcing him from office, however, paving the way in 1992 for the election of Fernando Henrique Cardoso.

Though an academic Marxist for much of his career, once in office FHC proved to be a cautious centrist. In his 8 years in office he managed to reign in inflation, bring some stability to the Brazilian currency, and begin a modest extension of social services to Brazil's many poor.

The main opposition throughout this period was the Workers Party (PT), lead by Luiz Inácio Lula da Silva, a charismatic trade unionist with a personal rags-to-riches story. Born into poverty in the Northeast, Lula, as he is usually known, left school to work as a shoeshine boy, got a job in a São Paulo factory, joined the metal workers' union, and began to get involved in politics. During the waning days of Brazil's dictatorship he and others formed the Workers Party, and only just lost Brazil's first democratic election in 1988, thanks in large part to some blatant scare-mongering by the Globo print and television conglomerate. Lula persevered, however, contesting the following two elections against FHC, while refining and moderating policies to bring them into a form more acceptable to the Brazilian electorate. Finally in 2002, in his fourth attempt, Lula was elected Brazilian president, the first democratically elected leftist ever to hold power in Brazil.

Hopes for Lula's first term in office were enormous. Confounding expectations of financial markets and right-wing critics, Lula in office proved to be an economic moderate, continuing the tight-money policy of his predecessor. But to the disappointment of his supporters on the left, Lula also proved to be a poor and often absent administrator. Many of the hoped-for reforms—from the distribution of land, to access to education and healthcare, to environmental policy—were never enacted. Worse, his government, which had pledged to clean up Brazilian politics, has been plagued by corruption scandals as bad as or worse than any of his predecessors. In his run for reelection in 2006, Lula lost the support of the reformist middle class, but his popularity among Brazil's more numerous poor was enough to win him a second term in office.

In the cities, things have certainly improved since the 1980s. The **1992 Environment Conference** in Rio was a watershed for Brazil. Politicians woke up to the fact that the country was developing a reputation for crime and lawlessness. Governments, having paid off the worst of the '80s debts, now had funds available, which they proceeded to spend on increased policing, better street lighting, and on extending services such as sewers, water, and schooling to urban slum dwellers. In the shantytowns of Rio and São Paulo, gangs remain stubbornly entrenched, but the major cities of Brazil are nonetheless cleaner and safer than they've been in a generation. Though they're a few years yet from matching the new improved Manhattan for safety, Brazil's cities are far and away superior when it comes to sheer *joie de vivre*.

BRAZIL TODAY

Brazil is a land of incredible diversity, a place where native hunters, Pantanal cowboys, priests of West African gods, and city slickers with roots in Italy, Syria, Portugal, and Japan all happily call themselves Brazilian. An extraordinary ability to enjoy life may be the one and only thing they have in common. Making that first million by age 30, scaling a mountaintop because it's there—these aren't the things that animate Brazilians. Friends, and especially family, are what matter, plus beer and a beach, bar, or soccer stadium in which to enjoy it all. Whether this general disinterest in things political is the result or the cause of Brazil's rather painful 20th-century history is a chicken-and-egg question. What is certain is that having experienced both the giddy expansion of the "economic miracle" of the 1960s and the debt, recession, and inflation crises that followed, Brazil has now settled into something approaching normality. Inflation is manageable, crime is decreasing, and the army is safely back in the barracks where it belongs.

Challenges in the future include getting a grip on corruption (not the petty kind that bothers tourists, but the lose-a-billion-dollars-in-a-Swiss-bank-account kind that bothers taxpayers); coping with growth as Brazil's already huge cities continue to expand; and finding a way to balance environmental preservation—particularly in the Amazon—with the demand for economic development. If Brazilians have learned the hard way that they can't solve these problems at the drop of a hat, they can at least behave like the rest of the democratic world and somehow muddle through—having fun even as they muddle.

Index

I don't speak sign language.

A hotel can close for all kinds of reasons.

Our Guarantee ensures that if your hotel's undergoing construction, we'll let you know in advance. In fact, we cover your entire travel experience. See www.travelocity.com/guarantee for details.

** travelocity·
You'll never roam alone.

There's a parking lot where my ocean view should be.

 À la place de la vue sur l'océan, me voilà avec une vue sur un parking.

 Anstatt Meerblick habe ich Sicht auf einen Parkplatz.

 Al posto della vista sull'oceano c'è un parcheggio.

 No tengo vista al mar porque hay un parque de estacionamiento.

 Há um parque de estacionamento onde deveria estar a minha vista do oceano

 Ett parkeringsområde har byggts på den plats där min utsikt över oceanen borde vara.

 Er ligt een parkeerterrein waar mijn zee-uitzicht zou moeten zijn.

 هنالك موقف للسيارات مكان ما وجب ان يكون المنظر الخلاب المطل على المحيط .

 眼前に広がる紺碧の海・・・じゃない。窓の外は駐車場！

 停车场的位置应该是我的海景所在。

— I'm fluent in pig latin.

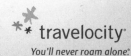